CANADIAN CRIMINAL JUSTICE

CANADIAN CRIMINAL JUSTICE

SECOND EDITION

CURT T. GRIFFITHS
SIMON N. VERDUN-JONES

 Harcourt Brace & Company, Canada

Toronto Montreal Orlando Fort Worth San Diego Philadelphia
London Sydney Tokyo

Canadian Cataloguing in Publication Data

Griffiths, Curt T. (Curt Taylor), 1948-
    Canadian criminal justice
2nd ed.
Includes bibliographical references and index.
ISBN 0-7747-3403-5

1. Criminal justice, Administration of — Canada.
I. Verdun-Jones, Simon N. (Simon Nicholas), 1947-
II. Title.
KE8813.G47 1993 354.71'05   C93-094862-9
KF9223.G74 1993

Publisher: Heather McWhinney
Editorial and Marketing Manager: Dan Brooks
Developmental Editor: Lynne Missen, The Editorial Centre
Copy Editor: Tracy Bordian, The Editorial Centre
Cover Design and Interior Illustrations: Falcom Design
Cover Art: Sorel Etrog, *Study After El Greco's Laocoön*. Oil on masonite.
    213.3 x 365.7 cm (total of three panels). Art Gallery of Hamilton,
    Anonymous gift, 1981.
Interior Design: Tracy Bordian, The Editorial Centre
Printing and Binding: Data Reproductions Corporation

Printed and bound in the United States of America

1 2 3 4 5   98 97 96 95 94

For Kelly

Curt Taylor Griffiths

For Carmen and Maritza

Simon N. Verdun-Jones

ABOUT THE AUTHORS

CURT T. GRIFFITHS is a Professor in the School of Criminology and Director of the Northern Justice Society Resource Centre at Simon Fraser University. Outside of his extensive writing in the Canadian criminal justice area, Professor Griffiths's interests include policing, corrections, Aboriginal peoples and the criminal justice system, and comparative criminal justice systems. He has co-authored with John W. Ekstedt *Corrections in Canada: Policy and Perspectives*, and is co-editor, along with Margaret A. Jackson, of *Canadian Criminology: Perspectives on Crime and Criminology.*

SIMON N. VERDUN-JONES is a Professor of Criminology and former Director of the School of Criminology at Simon Fraser University, Editor-in-Chief of the International Bulletin of Law and Mental Health, and Special Editorial Consultant to the *Canadian Journal of Criminology*. In addition to his publications in Canadian criminal justice and criminal law, Professor Verdun-Jones's major interests are in the area of Canadian and international mental health law, comparative criminal justice, family violence and the law, and adult guardianship. Simon N. Verdun-Jones is the author of *Criminal Law in Canada: Cases, Questions and the Code.*

PREFACE

It seems only yesterday that the first edition of *Canadian Criminal Justice* appeared, although in fact it has been four years. During that time, we have been gratified by the acceptance this book has received from educators across the country. In preparing the second edition of the text, we were confronted by a number of challenges, including the exponential growth in research on the criminal justice process, the changes in legislation and in federal and provincial/territorial criminal justice policy and the growing number of court decisions that are serving to further define life under the *Canadian Charter of Rights and Freedoms.*

This edition of the text has involved updating descriptive materials on the criminal justice system, integrating recent research, and rewriting several chapters. Every attempt has been made to distill the vast amount of materials on the justice system and to present them in such a way so as to stimulate thought and discussion. The overall objective of the text remains the same: to present not only a description of the various components of the criminal justice process, but also, through the use of as much Canadian research as possible, to present a critical analysis of the justice system. As with the first edition, an instructors' manual has been provided to enhance the materials presented in the text.

The production of this edition has been aided immensely by the research assistance of Dana Christensen and Roland Vogel, and by the team at The Editorial Centre, including Lynne Missen, Greg Ioannou, and Tracy Bordian. We owe a debt of gratitude to Lisa Charters at Butterworths, who was always there to provide the "persuasive push" we needed to get the job done. We are particularly appreciative of the support and enthusiasm of Dan Brooks at Harcourt Brace, our new editor. We would also like to acknowledge the many students and instructors who have offered their views on how the book could be improved, and we have made every effort to use their suggestions. As with the first edition, we welcome all opinions and criticisms (and, of course, praise) about the book. Be assured that this input will be used in the preparation of the next edition of *Canadian Criminal Justice.*

Curt Taylor Griffiths and Simon N. Verdun-Jones
Burnaby, British Columbia
June, 1993

A Note from the Publisher

Thank you for selecting *Canadian Criminal Justice, Second Edition,* by Curt T. Griffiths and Simon N. Verdun-Jones. The author and publisher have devoted considerable time to the careful development of the book. We appreciate your recognition of this effort and accomplishment.

We want to hear what you think about *Canadian Criminal Justice.* Please take a few minutes to fill in the stamped reply card at the back of the book. Your comments and suggestions will be valuable to us as we prepare new editions and other books.

CONTENTS

LEGISLATION

Act for the Prevention of Cruelty to, and Better Protection of, Children
    S.O. 1893, 56 Vict., c. 45.
Act for the Protection and Reformation of Neglected Children, S.C. 1888,
    51 Vict., c. 40.
Act of 23 May 1877.
Act to Amend the Criminal Code (Victims of Crime), S.C. 1988, c. 30.
Act to Amend the Juvenile Delinquents Act, 1908, S.C. 1924, 14 & 15
    Geo. V, c. 53.
Act to Provide for the Conditional Liberation of Penitentiary Convicts,
    S.C. 1899, 63-64 Vict., c. 49.
An Act for Establishing Prisons for Young Offenders, S.C. 1857, 20 Vict.,
    c. 28.
Act for Respecting the Trial and Punishment of Juvenile Offenders, Cons.
    S.C. 1859, c. 106.

1 CANADIAN CRIMINAL JUSTICE: AN INTRODUCTION

The Canadian criminal justice system includes a series of key stages, ranging from the decisions of citizens to telephone the police through to the supervision of offenders released from correctional institutions (see Figures 1.1 and 1.2). However, the justice process is much more than criminal statutes, organizational structures, and formally stated objectives. It is a human process — one characterized by discretion and inconsistency rather than machine-like precision and predictability. The processing of criminal cases takes place within the social, economic, and political backdrop of Canadian society, which may significantly influence the operation of the criminal justice process, as well as the outcome of individual cases.

THE LEGISLATIVE AND POLITICAL BASES OF CRIMINAL JUSTICE

Several pieces of legislation provide the foundation and general framework within which the criminal justice system operates. Under the *Constitution Act, 1867,* the federal Parliament is given exclusive authority to enact criminal laws and the procedures to be followed in criminal matters. Jurisdiction over the administration of justice is given to the provinces, as is responsibility for establishing and maintaining a system of provincial courts. However, the federal government is also involved in the provision of justice services, the most notable example being the Royal Canadian Mounted Police (RCMP), which acts as a federal, provincial, and municipal police force in many areas of the country.

The criminal law in Canada is primarily set forth in the *Criminal Code,* which was first enacted by Parliament in 1892 and has been continually revised. There are over 800 sections in the *Criminal Code,* covering substantive offences and the procedures to be followed in the administration of justice. There are other federal statutes that create criminal offences. Among the more significant of such statutes are the *Food and Drugs Act* and the *Narcotic Control Act.* The *Young Offenders Act* provides the legislative framework for the administration of youth justice in Canada and represents a philosophical shift in the response to youth in conflict with the law from the *Juvenile Delinquents Act,* which it replaced. One of the newest

FIGURE 1.1
THE CANADIAN CRIMINAL JUSTICE SYSTEM
Jurisdictions and Responsibilities*

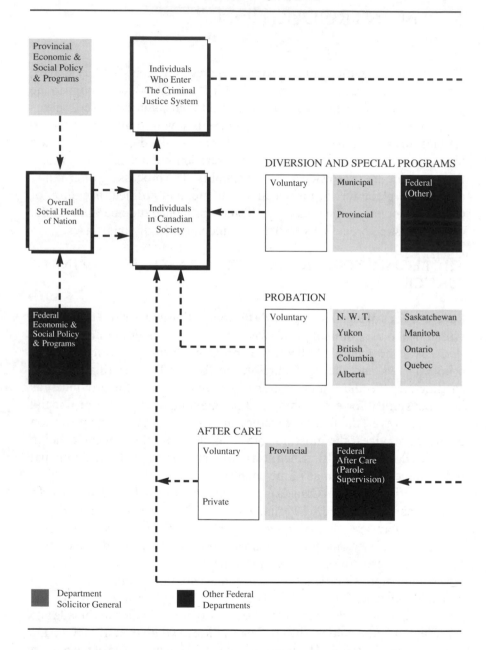

FIGURE 1.1
THE CANADIAN CRIMINAL JUSTICE SYSTEM
Jurisdictions and Responsibilities*

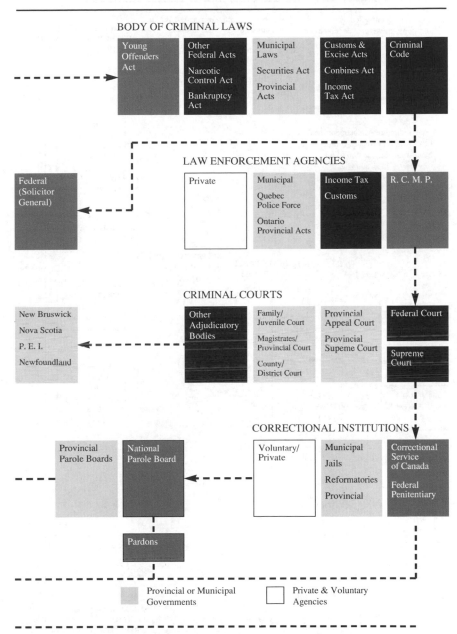

BODY OF CRIMINAL LAWS

| Young Offenders Act | Other Federal Acts / Narcotic Control Act / Bankruptcy Act | Municipal Laws / Securities Act / Provincial Acts | Customs & Excise Acts / Conbines Act / Income Tax Act | Criminal Code |

LAW ENFORCEMENT AGENCIES

| Federal (Solicitor General) | Private | Municipal / Quebec Police Force / Ontario Provincial Acts | Income Tax / Customs | R. C. M. P. |

CRIMINAL COURTS

| New Bruswick / Nova Scotia / P. E. I. / Newfoundland | Other Adjudicatory Bodies | Family/ Juvenile Court / Magistrates/ Provincial Court / County/ District Court | Provincial Appeal Court / Provincial Supeme Court | Federal Court / Supreme Court |

CORRECTIONAL INSTITUTIONS

| Provincial Parole Boards | National Parole Board | Voluntary/ Private | Municipal Jails / Reformatories / Provincial | Corrcctional Service of Canada / Federal Penitentiary |

Pardons

Provincial or Municipal Governments

Private & Voluntary Agencies

* Since this chart was published responsibility for the *Young Offenders Act* has been shifted to the Department of Justice.

Source: *Beyond the Walls* (Ottawa: Communications Branch of Correctional Service of Canada, Ministry of the Solicitor General of Canada, 1983), pp. 4 & 5. Reproduced with permission of the Minister of Supply and Services Canada, 1993.

FIGURE 1.2
FLOW OF CASES THROUGH THE CANADIAN
CRIMINAL JUSTICE SYSTEM

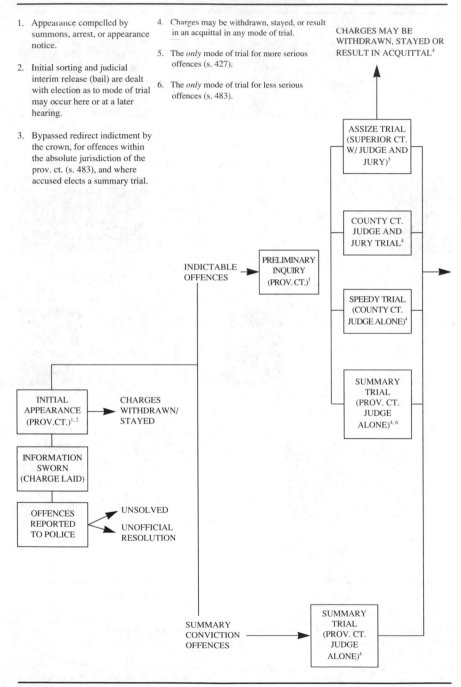

1. Appearance compelled by summons, arrest, or appearance notice.

2. Initial sorting and judicial interim release (bail) are dealt with election as to mode of trial may occur here or at a later hearing.

3. Bypassed redirect indictment by the crown, for offences within the absolute jurisdiction of the prov. ct. (s. 483), and where accused elects a summary trial.

4. Charges may be withdrawn, stayed, or result in an acquittal in any mode of trial.

5. The *only* mode of trial for more serious offences (s. 427).

6. The *only* mode of trial for less serious offences (s. 483).

CHARGES MAY BE WITHDRAWN, STAYED OR RESULT IN ACQUITTAL[4]

ASSIZE TRIAL (SUPERIOR CT. W/ JUDGE AND JURY)[5]

COUNTY CT. JUDGE AND JURY TRIAL[4]

PRELIMINARY INQUIRY (PROV. CT.)[3]

INDICTABLE OFFENCES

SPEEDY TRIAL (COUNTY CT. JUDGE ALONE)[4]

SUMMARY TRIAL (PROV. CT. JUDGE ALONE)[4, 6]

INITIAL APPEARANCE (PROV.CT.)[1, 2]

CHARGES WITHDRAWN/ STAYED

INFORMATION SWORN (CHARGE LAID)

OFFENCES REPORTED TO POLICE

UNSOLVED

UNOFFICIAL RESOLUTION

SUMMARY CONVICTION OFFENCES

SUMMARY TRIAL (PROV. CT. JUDGE ALONE)[4]

FIGURE 1.2
FLOW OF CASES THROUGH THE CANADIAN CRIMINAL JUSTICE SYSTEM

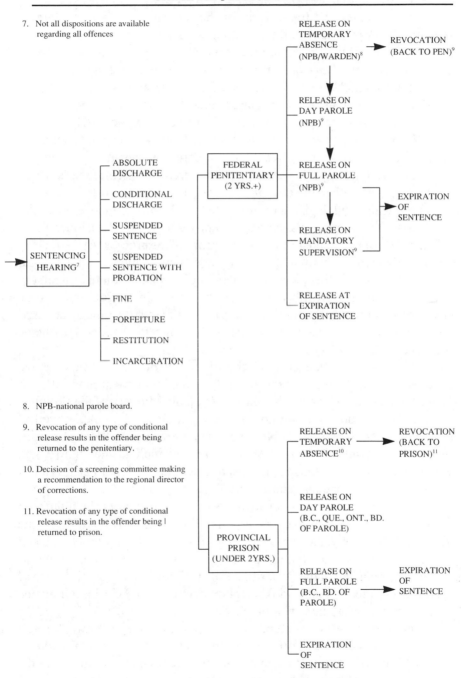

7. Not all dispositions are available regarding all offences

RELEASE ON TEMPORARY ABSENCE (NPB/WARDEN)[8] → REVOCATION (BACK TO PEN)[9]

RELEASE ON DAY PAROLE (NPB)[9]

ABSOLUTE DISCHARGE

FEDERAL PENITENTIARY (2 YRS.+)

RELEASE ON FULL PAROLE (NPB)[9] → EXPIRATION OF SENTENCE

CONDITIONAL DISCHARGE

SUSPENDED SENTENCE

RELEASE ON MANDATORY SUPERVISION[9]

SENTENCING HEARING[7]

SUSPENDED SENTENCE WITH PROBATION

FINE

RELEASE AT EXPIRATION OF SENTENCE

FORFEITURE

RESTITUTION

INCARCERATION

8. NPB-national parole board.

9. Revocation of any type of conditional release results in the offender being returned to the penitentiary.

RELEASE ON TEMPORARY ABSENCE[10] → REVOCATION (BACK TO PRISON)[11]

10. Decision of a screening committee making a recommendation to the regional director of corrections.

RELEASE ON DAY PAROLE (B.C., QUE., ONT., BD. OF PAROLE)

11. Revocation of any type of conditional release results in the offender being l returned to prison.

PROVINCIAL PRISON (UNDER 2YRS.)

RELEASE ON FULL PAROLE (B.C., BD. OF PAROLE) → EXPIRATION OF SENTENCE

EXPIRATION OF SENTENCE

pieces of legislation, the *Corrections and Conditional Release Act* (1992), provides the legislative framework for the federal corrections system. It replaces the *Parole Act* and the *Penitentiary Act*.

Note that all legislation, both at the federal and provincial levels, is subject to the *Canadian Charter of Rights and Freedoms,* enacted in 1982. As the fundamental law of the land, the *Charter* guarantees basic rights and freedoms that may, in certain circumstances, be enforced by the courts in the face of legislative provisions that infringe upon them. The courts' recently acquired power to strike down legislation as unconstitutional, in light of the *Charter,* has affected a dramatic change in the Canadian constitutional landscape. For example, the Supreme Court of Canada struck down the provisions in the *Criminal Code* relating to abortion.[1]

Politicians and legislatures exert considerable influence over the operation of the criminal justice system, and through their decision making affect both the policy and line-level operations of the process. At the federal level, Parliament is involved in making additions or modifications to the *Criminal Code* and other pieces of federal legislation. Through its decision making, Parliament not only determines the types of behaviour that will be considered criminal, but also the provisions for responding to accused persons. Federal legislators also control the budgets of federal agencies involved in the delivery of justice services.

The political influence over the operation of the criminal justice process extends to the federal and provincial ministries charged with justice-related functions. At the federal level, the Ministry of the Solicitor General has responsibility for policing, corrections, and parole, as well as specialized activities such as National Crime Prevention Week. Components of the Ministry of the Solicitor General include the RCMP, the Correctional Service of Canada, a Secretariat, the National Parole Board (NPB), and the Canadian Security Intelligence Service.

The federal Department of Justice assumes a primary role in the area of criminal justice policy and has responsibility for the *Criminal Code*, the *Young Offenders Act*, the administration of justice at the federal level, and for criminal prosecution not assigned by statute to the provincial governments. The mandate of the Department of Justice also includes the areas of victims of crime, women and Aboriginal peoples and the criminal justice system, and international criminal justice.

The provincial legislatures are responsible for creating "quasi-criminal" law, which is a form of criminal law set out in the *Constitution Act, 1867*. Briefly, the *Act* provides that a number of matters fall within the exclusive jurisdiction of the provinces, including municipal institutions, health, education, highways, and liquor control. The province may enforce this legislation by fines, imprisonment, or other penalties.

The offences that may be created by provincial legislatures are generally far less serious than the offences contained in the *Criminal Code* or other federal legislation such as the *Narcotic Control Act*. While the maximum penalties that may be imposed for violation of provincial statutes are generally no more than a fine or a maximum term of six months' imprisonment, or both, the penalties under the *Criminal Code* and the *Narcotic Control Act* may be as severe as life imprisonment.

THE "SYSTEM" OF CRIMINAL JUSTICE

Among criminal justice scholars seeking to understand and explain the criminal justice process, there has been an ongoing debate about whether the various agencies and departments involved in the administration of justice constitute a unified "system." While this text makes no attempt to resolve this (perhaps irresolvable) dispute, it is important to consider each perspective of the system/non-system debate. Although some attributes of the Canadian criminal justice process seem to qualify it as a system, others operate to lessen the unity of action of the various agencies involved in the administration of justice.

All criminal justice agencies in Canada operate under the *Constitution Act, 1867*, and process offenders under the provisions of the *Criminal Code* and in accordance with established rules of procedure and evidence and the tenets of the *Canadian Charter of Rights and Freedoms.* Further, there is an interdependence among criminal justice agencies such that the activities of one component are likely to have an impact upon the others. The selective enforcement practices of the police, for example, may significantly affect the number and types of cases presented to Crown counsel for prosecution, while the sentencing patterns of the courts will have a direct impact on the population of correctional institutions and on the use of non-institutional programs and services.

These interdependencies are even greater in rural and remote areas of the country, where justice services are delivered by small RCMP detachments and via circuit courts. The demography of Canada, then, including its large land areas and sparse population, may serve to increase the interdependency of the criminal justice system. As we shall see, however, this also results in a wide variety of settings in which the administration of justice occurs, from the southern, urban centres such as Montreal, Calgary, and Vancouver, to remote communities in the northern portions of the provinces and in the communities of the Yukon and Northwest Territories. These environments present different challenges to the justice system and its personnel, who must adapt the requirements of legislation to the needs of victims, communities, and offenders.

The legislative and jurisdictional arrangements for the criminal justice process in Canada also serve to provide some degree of uniformity across the country. First, all criminal justice agencies and organizations operate under the national *Criminal Code*. This is in contrast to the United States and Australia, where each state government is responsible for enacting criminal statutes and establishing a system of criminal justice. Federal criminal statutes in the United States and Australia cover only a narrow range of offences.

The involvement of the RCMP in policing at the municipal, provincial, and federal levels in Canada makes it a truly national police force. There is no counterpart in the United States, where policing is organized primarily at the municipal and county levels, or in Australia, where each of its six states has its own police force. In the United States, the activities of the state police (or state patrol) are confined to the control of highway traffic, and federal forces such as the FBI and the Secret Service are involved in enforcing federal statutes.

In Canada, correctional services are divided between the provincial and federal governments on the basis of the length of sentence received by the offender. This has resulted in the creation of an extensive system of custodial and non-custodial facilities and programs operated by the federal Correctional Service of Canada for offenders who receive a sentence or sentences totalling more than two years. In the United States and Australia, on the other hand, state governments are responsible for operating correctional systems for offenders convicted of violating state criminal statutes, and only those offenders convicted of federal statutes are sent to the federal correctional system.

A unique attribute of the U.S. system of criminal justice is the election of criminal justice officials, including county sheriffs, county prosecutors, and district and state judges. No such provision for the election of criminal justice personnel exists in Canada. The prosecution function in Canada is performed by Crown counsel, who are appointed by provincial and federal governments, as are criminal court judges.

The structure of Canadian criminal justice may, then, serve to increase its functioning as a system, although there are forces at work to counter the ability of criminal justice agencies and personnel to act in concert.

First, each of the major components of the criminal justice system — the police, courts, and corrections — has a different mandate. The courts, for example, are supposed to serve as a check and balance against the potential excesses of the other components.

Second, the activities and decision making of criminal justice personnel in all components of the system are characterized by considerable diversity and by variability rather than uniformity. This variability exists not only between jurisdictions, but also within individual agencies in the same jurisdiction. Among judges in the Provincial Court, for example, there may be a wide range of individual philosophies and "styles," resulting in disparity in sentencing practices. Similar disparities exist among police officers and other decision makers in the criminal justice system who are given considerable professional autonomy and discretion to do their jobs.

Third, despite the extensive involvement of the federal government in formulating criminal legislation and in the policing and corrections areas, there is no single coordinating agency or authority with the mandate to establish uniform operating guidelines and procedures for criminal justice agencies and personnel. Even where guidelines do exist, such as the criteria listed in the *Corrections and Conditional Release Act* relating to a grant of parole by members of the NPB, they do not, in practice, operate to control or confine the discretion exercised by members in their decision making.

This diversity in objectives and mandates, and the broad discretionary powers exercised by criminal justice personnel, have led many observers to characterize the justice system as a network of interrelated, yet independent, individuals and agencies, rather than as a system, *per se*. While cases in the Canadian criminal justice system flow through an established structure, the actual dynamics of the criminal justice process are varied and cannot be understood solely through an examination of a case-flow chart. Agencies and personnel throughout the Canadian criminal justice system often pursue conflicting goals, are influenced by external agencies and publics, and have broad discretionary powers in carrying out their tasks.

THE APPLICATION OF THE CRIMINAL LAW

A significant contribution to understanding the operation of the criminal justice process was made by the late Herbert Packer (1968), who identified two competing value systems underlying the administration of criminal justice: the *crime control model* and the *due process model*.

The crime control model views the primary purpose of the criminal justice system as the protection of the public through the deterrence and incapacitation of offenders. Criminal offenders are responsible for their actions, and the administration of justice should be swift, sure, and efficient. There is a strong presumption of guilt and confidence that an efficient justice system will screen out innocent persons at the police or prosecutorial stages. There is also an emphasis on compensation for victims of crime.

The due process model, on the other hand, emphasizes procedural fairness and a presumption of innocence. The onus is on the criminal justice process to prove guilt, and there is a requirement that agencies and decision makers follow proper procedures in making such a determination. The possibility exists that an accused person may be factually guilty, but legally innocent, if the proper procedures and rights of the accused have been violated. The due process model evidences a concern with structuring and confining the discretionary power of criminal justice decision makers.

Because of their location in the process, different components of the criminal justice system may tend toward one perspective or the other. The police, for example, have long been identified with the crime control perspective, while the courts have traditionally been viewed as operating within a due process approach. In fact, different components of the criminal justice system may be operating under different models, or be in pursuit of different, often conflicting, goals, decreasing the unity of the system and raising the spectre of organizational conflict between the components.

Several observers, however, have noted that there is often a degree of organizational cooperation between criminal justice agencies that undermines the adversarial nature of the criminal justice system and increases its interdependency. The term "courtroom workgroup," for example, has been used to depict the extent of cooperation in case processing between judges, defence lawyers, and prosecution lawyers, a process in which the defendant is an outsider (see Eisenstein and Jacob, 1977; Ericson and Baranek, 1982).

A CRITICAL PERSPECTIVE OF CANADIAN CRIMINAL JUSTICE

Two explanations of the formulation and implementation of criminal law must also be considered in any study of the criminal justice system: the *value consensus model* and the *conflict model*. The value consensus perspective views legislation as reflecting the needs and values of society and the application of the law as serving to reaffirm consensual interests. This view has been challenged by the emergence of a critical perspective, which considers legislation a consequence of specific group interests and the criminal justice system as a means of social control. While advocates of the consensus model view the criminal law as an expression of the values held by the majority of society, proponents of the conflict model contend that law is an instrument of social control used by the powerful to protect their vested interests.

From the critical perspective, discussions about whether the criminal justice process meets the criteria for an integrated system are less important than discussions about the role played by the criminal justice system as a key element of social control in the maintenance of the dominant economic and social order (Ratner and McMullan, 1987). There is little doubt that the critical perspective can provide us with key insights into the operation of the criminal justice system both historically and during contemporary times.

As the discussions in the following chapters will reveal, all segments of the criminal justice system have, at one time or another, been the subject of controversy. While the exploits of the RCMP have been the subject of considerable "mythmaking," less well known are the difficulties that the force has faced over the years. The early RCMP, for example, experienced numerous internal problems. In the criminal courts, plea bargaining (while not recognized or sanctioned under the *Criminal Code*) plays a key role in the processing of cases. As well, Canadian judges exhibit considerable disparity in their patterns of sentencing.

Canadian correctional institutions have been the scene of brutality and violence. Prisons are populated largely by young, uneducated offenders from the lower socioeconomic levels of society. The negative consequences of unchecked discretion surrounding the decision making of parole boards and the supervision of offenders in the community have been documented. In recent years, many previously "invisible" problems have been brought to the fore. Chief among these is the "Third World" status of many Aboriginal peoples in Canada and the impact that their marginalized position in society has on their victimization, criminal behaviour, and involvement in the criminal justice system. Another is the violence against women in all segments of society.

The intent of this volume is to provide both a description and analysis of the operation of the Canadian criminal justice system, from policing to corrections. We will examine much of the folk-wisdom that has surrounded discussions of the criminal justice process and attempt to present a balanced assessment of each segment of the system. The materials presented in this volume are designed to provide the foundation for further study and research on the Canadian criminal justice system.

CRIMINAL JUSTICE THEMES

The enormous complexity of the criminal justice system in Canada precludes definitive discussions in the space of one volume. There are, however, several themes that will emerge throughout the following chapters, and we hope they will provide readers with a more thorough understanding of the criminal justice process, as well as of the forces that shape its day-to-day operation.

First, an effort has been made to construct the historical basis of the criminal justice process, noting the key events, and in some instances, personalities, that shaped the development of the Canadian criminal justice system. Second, the operation of each component of the criminal justice system is tied to the larger Canadian context, and the influences from the social, cultural, political, and economic spheres are noted. Third, the role of the public as a key component of the criminal justice process, from the stage of victimization, to calling the police, to participation in the courts, and to involvement in the criminal justice process is discussed. Fourth, the findings of research on the criminal justice process are used to construct a composite picture of the operations of the system. Finally, the human dimension of the criminal justice process, and all it entails, is illustrated.

Readers should be forewarned, however, that the Canadian criminal justice system is encountering serious difficulties in carrying out its mandate, and concerns are increasingly being voiced not only about the costs of the enterprise, but also its effectiveness. Historically, the development and expansion of criminal justice agencies have been accompanied by a shift of responsibility for addressing problems in the community from the public to these agencies and by increasing community demands on criminal justice organizations. As the twentieth century draws to a close, the search for alternative mechanisms for the prevention and control of criminal behaviour that are not only less expensive, but more effective and more closely aligned with the community, is underway. The final destination of this search is still unclear.

NOTES

[1]*Morgentaler, Smoling, and Scott v. The Queen* (1988), 37 C.C.C. (3d) 449 (S.C.C.).

REFERENCES

Eisenstein, J., and J. Jacob. 1977. *Felony Justice*. Boston: Little, Brown.

Ericson, R.V., and P.M. Baranek. 1982. *The Ordering of Justice: A Study of Accused Persons as Dependants in the Criminal Process.* Toronto: University of Toronto Press.

Packer, H.L. 1968. *The Limits of the Criminal Sanction*. Stanford: Stanford University Press.

Ratner, R.S., and J.L. McMullan. 1987. *State Control: Criminal Justice Politics in Canada*. Vancouver: University of British Columbia.

2 Crime, Criminal Justice, and the Canadian Public

As a backdrop for our discussion of the Canadian criminal justice system, it is important to consider the nature and extent of crime in Canada as reflected in official crime rates, public perceptions of crime, the extent to which members of the public are "at risk" from crime, and how the criminal justice system attempts to address the needs of crime victims.

CONSIDERING CRIME PATTERNS: SOME CAUTIONARY NOTES

Discussions of crime patterns in Canada are generally premised on official statistics and, because of this, several caveats are in order.

First, official crime statistics, which provide the basis for calculating crime rates in Canada, have many limitations and should be used only as *general indicators* of criminal activity. Surveys of victims of crime indicate that, for most offence categories, there is a "dark figure" of crime that remains unreported and does not show up in police reports or in the statistics compiled by other criminal justice agencies.

Differences in official crime statistics that emerge between jurisdictions and regions in Canada may be a function of many factors, including: (1) demographic attributes, such as the size and composition of the population; (2) characteristics of the individual community, such as the socioeconomic status of its residents, their involvement in crime prevention initiatives, and their willingness to call the police and to report crimes; (3) characteristics of the police force in the community, such as the manner in which the department deploys officers and allocates resources, and the methods it uses in collecting and recording criminal offences; and (4) the activities of other criminal justice agencies in the community, including the case screening and charging practices of the Crown counsel and the extent to which plea negotiation takes place (see Hackler and Cossins, 1989).

Second, any discussion of the amount and types of criminal activity is limited by the particular period of time chosen for study, and in this chapter we are able to provide only a "snapshot" of the nature and extent of criminal activity in Canada. Readers are encouraged to become familiar with the patterns of crime in their province/territory and to consider the variations in crime patterns between rural and urban areas.

Third, our discussion is hindered by the fact that there have been few inquiries into the patterns of crime at the provincial/territorial and municipal levels or into how the patterns of criminality in the various jurisdictions have fluctuated over time. Observers have noted that, historically, crime rates in Canada have shown a steady increase from the early 1800s to the mid-1970s and are more similar to those in France than the rates in England or the United States (see Brantingham and Brantingham, 1984).[1]

Finally, official statistics tend to be gathered on the more "traditional" types of offences, for example, robbery, homicide, and break and enter. While it is important to have information on these types of crimes, less attention has been given to the collection of statistical information on "white collar" offences, including crimes against the environment, stock market fraud and manipulation, and offences committed by people in positions of trust, for example, lawyers and corporate executives.

CANADIAN CRIME RATES

In Canada, the primary method by which statistics on crime rates are gathered is through the Uniform Crime Reporting system, which was established in 1962. Information is gathered and reported on those crimes that come to the attention of the police either through citizen reporting or through proactive police activities. Policing agencies participating in the Uniform Crime Reporting system include municipal police forces, the Quebec and Ontario provincial police, the RCMP, the Canadian National and Canadian Pacific Railways police, Ports Canada police, and the Royal Newfoundland Constabulary. The Uniform Crime Reports are comprised of "actual offences — those reported or detected offences that have been found, upon preliminary investigation, to have actually occurred, as opposed to being 'unfounded.'" [2]

Other sources of information about crime patterns are victimization studies, which are designed to provide insights into the more "hidden" dimensions of criminal activity. Samples of the general public are asked questions that might include their fear of crime, their perceptions of the nature and extent of criminal activity in their neighbourhood, whether they have been the victim of a crime, and whether or not they reported this crime to the police. In addition, some victimization surveys include questions relating to attitudes toward the police and other components of the criminal justice system. The findings of these surveys, in conjunction with official statistics, assist in constructing a more accurate picture of crime in Canada.

Figure 2.1, comprised of statistics from the Uniform Crime Reporting system (Canadian Centre for Justice Statistics, 1992a), illustrates that in 1991, over 3.4 million offences (excluding traffic offences) were reported to the police. These offences were distributed as follows: *Criminal Code* offences (84%), federal statute offences (2.7%), provincial statute offences (10%), and municipal by-laws (3.3%). Narcotic and drug offences accounted for nearly two-thirds of all federal statute offences in 1990, and *Liquor Act* offences accounted for almost 60% of the total provincial statute offences.

The trend line in Figure 2.1 indicates that, with the exception of yearly decreases during the period 1981-1984 and a slight dip in 1988, the total number of offences committed has steadily increased.

Observers have noted that, while the involvement of males in criminality has not changed significantly over the past several decades, there has been an increase in female criminality. Women tend to commit and be convicted of property-related offences, and a large percentage of these involve fraud and theft (see Axon, 1989; Canadian Centre for Justice Statistics, 1990b; Chunn and Gavigan, 1991; Hatch and Faith, 1989-90; Johnson, 1986; 1987; Silverman and Kennedy, 1987). Increased attention has also been given to the involvement of the elderly in criminal activity (Fattah and Sacco, 1989).

There are several possible explanations for the increase in Canadian crime rates. Police agencies may have altered their enforcement strategies and increased their "catch" rate. Some evidence suggests that there has been an increased level of citizens' reporting of crime, particularly for certain types of offences such as sexual assaults. There has also been an increase in the number of people in Canada who fall within the "high crime risk" age group of 18-25 year olds. Note that a rise in official crime rates may be due to a number of factors other than an absolute increase in the amount of criminal activity.

Figure 2.2 presents official data on the rates of *Criminal Code* offences per 100,000 for the decade 1981-1991. Following decreases during the period 1981-1985, and a brief decrease during 1988, the crime rate continued to climb. Figure 2.3 presents the rates per 100,000 for specific categories of crime. It indicates property crimes comprise the vast

FIGURE 2.1
TOTAL OFFENCES 1981-1991 AND PERCENTAGE DISTRIBUTION OF 1991 DATA, CANADA

Total of all offences

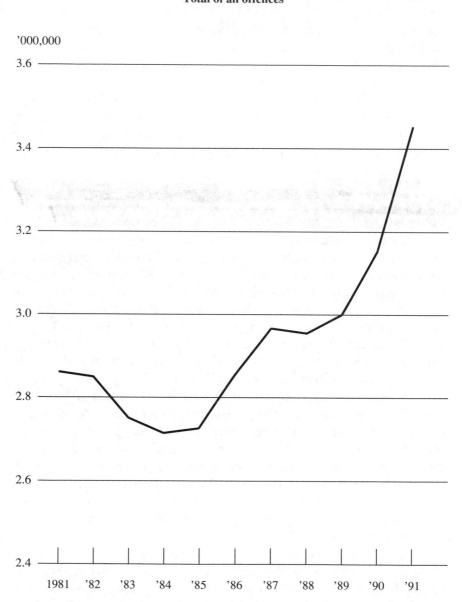

Source: Adapted from Canadian Centre for Justice Statistics. Canadian Crime Statistics, 1991 (Ottawa: Statistics Canada, 1992a), p. 27. Catalogue no. 85-205. Reproduced with permission of the Ministry of Industry, Science, and Technology, 1993.

FIGURE 2.2
RATE PER 100,000 POPULATION OF TOTAL OFFENCES,
CANADA, 1981-1991

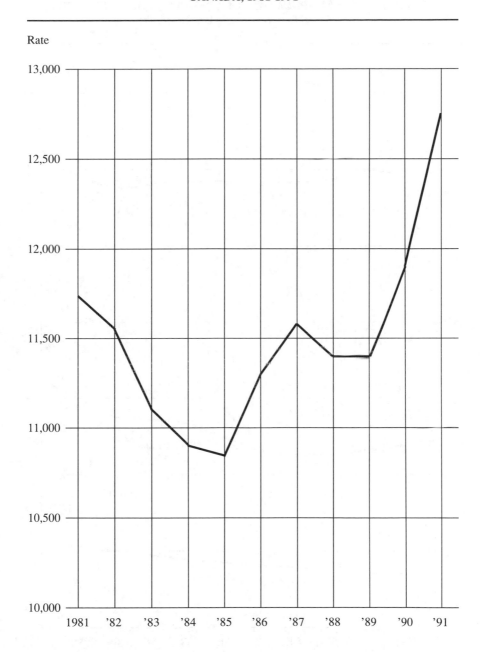

Source: Adapted from Canadian Centre for Justice Statistics. *Canadian Crime Statistics, 1991* (Ottawa: Statistics Canada, 1992a), p. 28. Catalogue no. 85-205. Reproduced with permission of the Ministry of Industry, Science, and Technology, 1993.

FIGURE 2.3
RATE PER 100,000 POPULATION OF CRIMINAL CODE OFFENCES,
BY CATEGORY, CANADA, 1981-1991

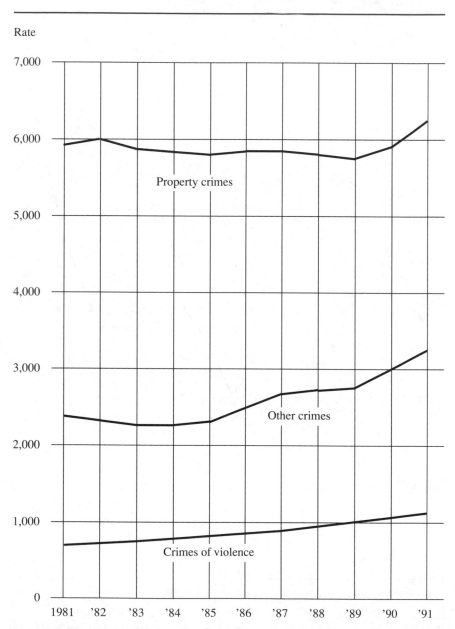

Source: Adapted from Canadian Centre for Justice Statistics. *Canadian Crime Statistics, 1991* (Ottawa: Statistics Canada, 1992a), p. 29. Catalogue no. 85-205. Reproduced with permission of the Ministry of Industry, Science, and Technology, 1993.

majority of offences committed in Canada and that the actual rate of violent crime is quite low when compared with property crime and other *Criminal Code* offences. However, in 1991, there were increases in the rates of violent crime (8%), property crimes (9%), and other crimes (7%) over 1990. Although these increases were the largest for any year during the ten-year period 1981-1991, it is difficult to predict whether the upward trend for each of these major categories of crime will continue during the 1990s.

In Figures 2.4, 2.5, and 2.6, the rates of *Criminal Code* offences per 100,000 population are presented for Canadian provinces and territories in a "crime map" format. While such depictions provide a general overview of the official crime rates across Canada, they are premised on official statistics that have definite limitations. Crime maps also obscure the variations in crime rates between communities and regions in the provinces and territories. Also, they are of little assistance in understanding the incidence of more "hidden" criminal offences, such as domestic assault and sexual assault, which typically have had low report rates.

The crime maps reveal the following key patterns.

▸   *All jurisdictions, with the exception of the Yukon, have experienced increases in* Criminal Code *offences over the past decade.*

The highest percentage increases during this period were in the Northwest Territories (67%), Prince Edward Island (45%), Nova Scotia (36%), Alberta (32%), Saskatchewan (28%), and British Columbia (26%). Small increases during this period were recorded in the other provinces.

▸   *There is considerable regional variation in Canadian crime patterns.*

The rates of *Criminal Code* offences increase as one moves from east to west. In 1991, for example, the homicide rate in British Columbia was 3.9 per 100,000 population, while in Prince Edward Island, it was only 1.5 per 100,000 population (Canadian Centre for Justice Statistics, 1992b). There are, however, some notable exceptions to this east-west pattern. The armed robbery rate in Quebec is three times that of Vancouver, four times that of Calgary and Edmonton, and eight times that of Toronto (Gabor and Normandeau, 1987). In fact, the rates of robbery in Quebec are similar to those reported in the United States (Gabor and Normandeau, 1989).[3]

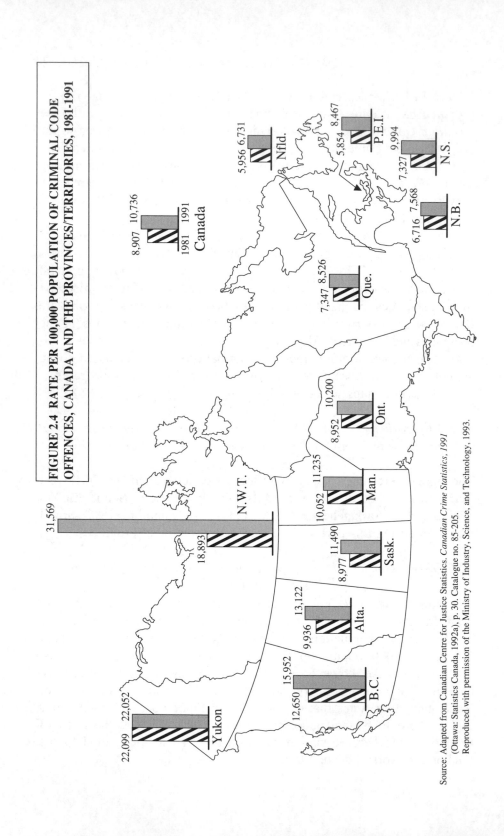

FIGURE 2.4 RATE PER 100,000 POPULATION OF CRIMINAL CODE OFFENCES, CANADA AND THE PROVINCES/TERRITORIES, 1981-1991

Canada
8,907 10,736
1981 1991

Nfld.
5,956 6,731

P.E.I.
5,854 8,467

N.S.
7,327 9,994

N.B.
6,716 7,568

Que.
7,347 8,526

Ont.
8,952 10,200

Man.
10,052 11,235

Sask.
8,977 11,490

Alta.
9,936 13,122

B.C.
12,650 15,952

Yukon
22,099 22,052

N.W.T.
18,893 31,569

Source: Adapted from Canadian Centre for Justice Statistics. *Canadian Crime Statistics, 1991* (Ottawa: Statistics Canada, 1992a), p. 30. Catalogue no. 85-205.
Reproduced with permission of the Ministry of Industry, Science, and Technology, 1993.

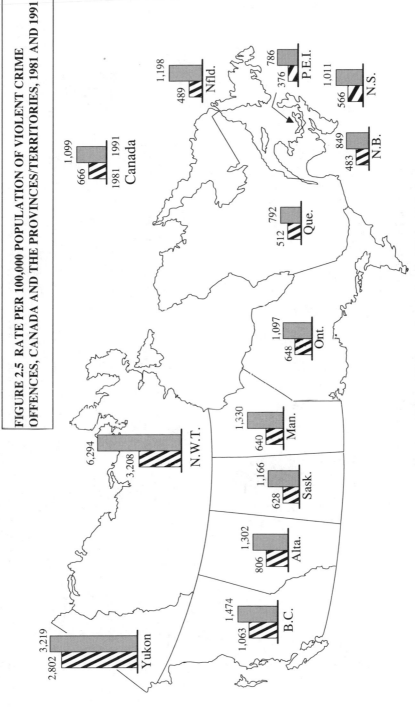

FIGURE 2.5 RATE PER 100,000 POPULATION OF VIOLENT CRIME OFFENCES, CANADA AND THE PROVINCES/TERRITORIES, 1981 AND 1991

Canada
666 (1981) 1,099 (1991)

Nfld.
489 1,198

P.E.I.
376 786

N.S.
566 1,011

N.B.
483 849

Que.
512 792

Ont.
648 1,097

Man.
640 1,330

Sask.
628 1,166

Alta.
806 1,302

B.C.
1,063 1,474

N.W.T.
3,208 6,294

Yukon
2,802 3,219

Source: Adapted from Canadian Centre for Justice Statistics. *Canadian Crime Statistics, 1991* (Ottawa: Statistics Canada, 1992a), p. 33. Catalogue no. 85-205.

Reproduced with permission of the Ministry of Industry, Science, and Technology, 1993.

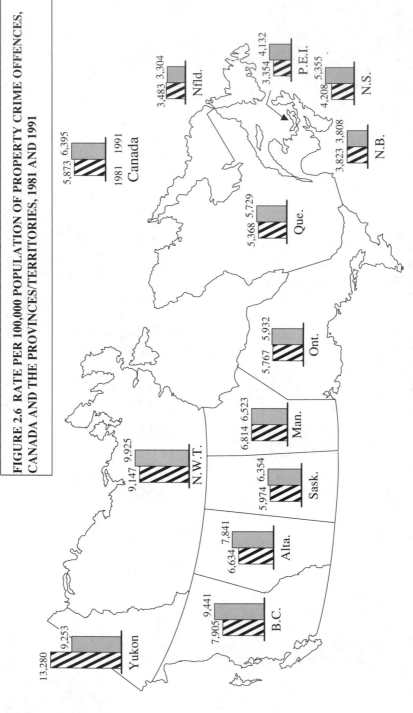

FIGURE 2.6 RATE PER 100,000 POPULATION OF PROPERTY CRIME OFFENCES, CANADA AND THE PROVINCES/TERRITORIES, 1981 AND 1991

Canada
1981 1991
5,873 6,395

Nfld.
3,483 3,304

P.E.I.
3,354 4,132

N.S.
4,208 5,355

N.B.
3,823 3,808

Que.
5,368 5,729

Ont.
5,767 5,932

Man.
6,814 6,523

Sask.
5,974 6,354

Alta.
6,634 7,841

B.C.
7,905 9,441

N.W.T.
9,147 9,925

Yukon
13,280 9,253

Source: Canadian Centre for Justice Statistics. *Canadian Crime Statistics, 1991* (Ottawa: Statistics Canada, 1992a), p. 41. Catalogue no. 85-205. Reproduced with permission of the Ministry of Industry, Science, and Technology, 1993.

Several studies have attempted to explain regional variations in crime rates. Kennedy, Silverman, and Forde (1988), for example, examined the impact of economic and cultural factors on homicide rates across the country, but found little evidence that there were regional "cultures of violence" that might explain the increases in homicide rates as one moves from east to west.

McMullan and Swan (1989) examined arson in Nova Scotia and found that the high rates of arson were associated with the unique socioeconomic and sociopolitical attributes of the province. Felt (1987) has examined interpersonal violence in rural Newfoundland and found that the culture and tradition of communities functioned to keep the rates of violence much lower than in other regions of Canada.

From a study of crime patterns in Ontario, Rattner and McKie (1990) reported that the numbers of Aboriginal peoples in an area and the level of unemployment were both related to the rates of violent crime. The property crime rate was closely related to demographic attributes of the communities, including the number of young males in the community (see also Forde, Kennedy, and Silverman, 1990). A considerable amount of research needs to be done to gain a more accurate indication of the true nature and extent of crime in Canada and the factors associated with specific offence patterns in specific regions of the country.

▸   *The highest rates of property offences and violent crimes in Canada occur in the Yukon and in the Northwest Territories.*

While often "invisible" to the majority of Canadians who reside in urban areas near the U.S. border, many remote and rural areas of the country experience exceedingly high rates of crime. This is due in some measure to the conflict with the law experienced in many Canadian Aboriginal communities, which will be addressed in detail in Chapter 15.

▸   *While Canadian crime rates are generally lower than those in the United States, the differences aren't as straightforward as one might assume.*

A commonly asked question is "How do Canadian crime rates compare with those in the United States?" Brantingham presents comparative crime data indicating that while Canada has lower aggregate crime rates than the States, the patterns are complex and bear close examination: "Some

Canadian jurisdictions have very high rates for some types of crime and rank with the worst of American states. Some American states have very low rates for some types of crime and rank with the very best of the Canadian provinces" (1991:387).

Among Brantingham's (1991:387-389) more specific findings:

> ▸ overall, Canada has less violent crime than the United States, although the rates of violent crime in the Yukon and in the Northwest Territories are some of the highest in North America;
>
> ▸ in Canada, the highest crime rates occur in smaller cities in the western portion of the country, rather than in highly populated urban areas;
>
> ▸ during the 1980s, Canada had higher rates of break and enter than the United States; and
>
> ▸ the differences in violent crimes, such as homicide, between the two countries may be due in large measure to strict Canadian gun control laws.[4]

PUBLIC PERCEPTIONS OF CRIME, FEAR OF CRIME, AND THE RISKS OF VICTIMIZATION

In recent years, Canadian researchers have given increasing attention to assessing public perceptions of crime and the extent to which citizens fear being the victims of criminal activity. These are then contrasted with the actual risks of victimization for various groups of Canadian citizens.

The *Canadian Urban Victimization Survey* (Solicitor General of Canada, 1984; 1985a; 1985b), conducted by the federal government in the early 1980s, provided the first insights into public perceptions of crime and the criminal justice system, the fear of victimization, and the actual risk of victimization. More recent studies by Statistics Canada (Sacco and Johnson, 1990) and a number of university-based researchers have contributed to our growing knowledge of this important area of study.[5]

Again, bear in mind some cautionary notes about research surveys. Critical events, such as a series of particularly heinous crimes, can rapidly alter the views of citizens in a community. Many factors may contribute to the perceptions that citizens have of crime, including their socioeconomic status, ethnicity, and the region of the country in which they live. Further, it is likely that members of various ethnic groups who may have only limited skills in English as well as Aboriginal peoples living in remote and rural areas are not included in the surveys, many of which are obtained via telephone interviews. Therefore, the surveys may not represent a fair cross-section of Canadian society.[6] Researchers have only recently begun to explore these issues (see Goff, 1989). Some of the more significant research findings to date are the following.

▸ *Canadians are becoming increasingly fearful of crime, particularly violent crime, and of being the victim of a crime.*

Canadians are particularly concerned about being victimized by violent crimes. However, while the rates of violent crime have increased over the past decade, police statistics indicate that violent crimes represent only about 6% of the total crimes reported. Residents of urban areas and victims of crime are most likely to perceive an increase in crime, and Sacco and Johnson (1990:45) found that women, the elderly, and urban dwellers expressed the greatest concern about personal safety. In a survey of residents in rural Nova Scotia, Murphy and Clairmont (1990:25) found that women had significantly higher rates of crime fear than men, as did those residents from lower income levels. Thus, those residents who felt the most vulnerable evidenced the highest fear levels. Significantly, however, rural Nova Scotians in their sample indicated that they felt safer during the day and night than their urban counterparts in Halifax. In fact, Murphy and Clairmont found that the actual rates of crime in the rural areas were lower.

Many citizens, particularly women and the elderly, have altered their activities because of fear of crime. Of those surveyed by Sacco and Johnson (1990), 25% felt unsafe walking alone at night in their neighbourhood, with the highest fear responses reported in Quebec (36%) and the lowest in the Atlantic provinces (18%). These researchers also found that women were more likely to engage in "defensive" behaviour than men, as were those citizens who had been crime victims. Brillon, Louis-Guerin, and Lamrache (1984) found that 41% of their respondents made adjustments to their daily life due to the fear of victimization, with the chief pattern of avoidance being that of not going out at night.

▸ *The fear of crime is strongly related to perceived vulnerability, although neither are related to the actual risks of victimization.*

The greatest fear of being victimized is expressed by women and the elderly, residents of lower socioeconomic status, and those who have been previously victimized. A study conducted by Environics (Adams, 1990) showed that of those surveyed, 29% expressed a fear of walking at night in their neighbourhood, but only 9% reported that they had actually been victimized. A CBC-*Globe and Mail* news poll conducted in 1991 found that 59% of the women surveyed were concerned about being a victim of a crime when they are out after dark (*Globe and Mail*, November 5).

Although women and the elderly express the highest levels of fear of crime, the actual patterns of victimization are quite different. There is an inverse relationship between age and victimization: as age increases, the risks of victimization decrease. Ironically, those persons under the age of 25, who express the least concern with crime, are most likely to be the victims of personal offences. In addition, there are higher rates of personal victimization among single males who reside in urban areas and who are either students or are unemployed. However, while the elderly are less likely to be victimized, the physical, emotional, and economic consequences of victimization may be much more severe than for younger persons. For the elderly, the fear of crime may be as significant as the consequences of actual victimization (see Brillon, 1987).

There is some validity to urban residents feeling more vulnerable to crime in the rates of property victimization, however. Sacco and Johnson (1990) report that the rate of victimization of urban households is 70% higher than in rural areas. Similar to the official rates of crime discussed earlier, the rates of personal and residence victimizations increase as one moves from the east to the west across Canada.

▸   *Canadians are safer on the street than in their homes and are less likely to be harmed by strangers than by someone they know.*

Among the findings reported by Sacco and Johnson (1990) was that the majority of violent crimes occurred in or around the household of the victim and that in most instances, the victim was familiar with the offender. The vast majority of physical and sexual assaults against women occur in their homes and are committed by a person known to the victim.

▸   *Women in Canada are more likely than men to be the victims of sexual assault and may experience much higher rates of personal victimization than men.*

Actual rates of victimization of women in Canada are difficult to determine. It can be anticipated that in both official statistics and self-report measures in victimization studies, the amount and seriousness of violence against women is severely underreported. There appears to be massive underreporting of such crimes as spousal assault and sexual assault against children in the home. Recently, Canadian researchers have given increasing attention to the "risk factors" for various offences, including violence against women (see Kennedy and Dutton, 1989; Smith, 1990).

In sum, it is clear that compared to the actual risks of victimization, the perceptions and fears Canadians have about crime and victimization are often exaggerated. Some evidence suggests that the mass media plays a significant role in creating the perceptions (and misconceptions) that Canadians have of crime (Ericson, Baranek, and Chan, 1987; Gebotys, Roberts, and DasGupta, 1988). This is not surprising, given that the media, particularly television, is the primary information source for most citizens. The images that citizens hold of crime are often similar to those portrayed in novels and in televised police dramas. However, Gommes's (1986) finding that there was no relationship between exposure to media and fear of crime suggests that the role of the media in creating public perceptions of crime is complex and remains to be explored.

While it might be assumed that citizens' fear of crime and perceptions of vulnerability would lead to increased participation in police-sponsored crime prevention programs, the results of the Canadian Urban Victimization Survey (Solicitor General of Canada, 1984:8) reveal that Canadians are not likely to take advantage of the opportunity to participate in programs that are designed to reduce their chances of being victimized. The difficulties in mobilizing and sustaining community support for and participation in crime prevention initiatives will be considered further in Chapter 5.

THE VICTIMS AND WITNESSES OF CRIME

Since the mid-1970s in Canada, there has been an increasing concern with victims and witnesses of crime and the impact of victimization on both individuals and communities (see Fattah, 1991). The increased focus on the victims of crime by the federal and provincial/territorial levels of government in the early 1980s was reflected in the creation of the Federal-Provincial Task Force on Justice for the Victims of Crime (Canada, 1983).

Included in the mandate of the task force was an examination of victim needs, as well as of the requirements for effective victim services. In its final report, the task force (Canada, 1983:155-167) made 79 recommendations, including several proposed amendments to the *Criminal Code* that would facilitate the return of property to victims, increase the use of restitution, insure criminal injuries compensation, and provide for the participation of victims at the sentencing stage of the Criminal Court.

The *Corrections and Conditional Release Act* (Bill C-36), passed in 1992, contains several provisions under which the victims of crime may be provided with information about the offender. Upon request of the victim, the federal corrections service will disclose the offender's name, offence, date of sentence, and the eligibility and review dates for temporary absence permits and parole. Additional information that may be provided at the discretion of the commissioner of corrections are the offender's age, residence, release date, and conditions of release, including the offender's destination upon release. These provisions of Bill C-36 will increase the information available to the victims of crime.

Part of the impetus for these developments has come from the view that the criminal justice system has traditionally given more attention to the perpetrators of crime than to victims. There is also the recognition that the psychological harm inflicted by criminal offenders on their victims and on communities in the past have not been adequately addressed by the criminal justice system. In many areas of the country, citizen-initiated groups have been formed that lobby for legislation and programs for crime victims. These include groups such as Victims of Violence in Vancouver, formed by the mother of a child killed by serial killer Clifford Olson in British Columbia during the early 1980s. In 1993, the federal government opened the Canadian Resource Centre for Victims of Crime, which serves as a clearinghouse for materials on issues affecting victims of crime. The centre also provides assistance to victims and their families.

Crime victims and the witnesses to crime require specialized attention to address the physical and emotional consequences of crime. Tables 2.1 and 2.2 present the results of research studies that have documented the psychological impact of sexual assault against women and children (Hanson, 1990). Victims may also have little information on how the case of the alleged offender will proceed through the various stages of the criminal justice system (Stuebing, 1984). Increased attention is being given to ensure the active involvement of victims in the

TABLE 2.1
THE SEVERITY OF TRAUMA ASSOCIATED WITH
ADULT SEXUAL VICTIMIZATION

Time since attack	Severity of trauma
less than two days	75% unable to do ordinary daily tasks. 40-50% severe psychological disturbance. 5-10% no clinically significant symptoms. Overall levels similar to hospitalized psychiatric patients.
two weeks	Most are able to do ordinary daily tasks. 50% moderate to severe symptoms. 20-40% clinically depressed. 25% severe, generalized anxiety. Overall levels similar to psychiatric out-patients.
4 months to 1 year	Gradual return to near-normal levels on most indices of mental health.
greater than 1 year	25% report continuing negative effects. Increased vulnerability to other mental health problems.

Source: R. Carl Hanson. 1990. *The Psychological Impact of Crime*. Ottawa. Solicitor General of Canada. p. 68.

TABLE 2.2
THE SEVERITY OF TRAUMA ASSOCIATED WITH
CHILD SEXUAL VICTIMIZATION

Time since attack	Severity of trauma
immediate (prior to disclosure)	Distressing, but the severity of the immediate trauma is not known.
1 to 12 months (after disclosure)	50-70% significant psychological symptoms.
greater than 1 year	Persisting negative effects noted in initial studies.
greater than 10 years (sexually abused children as adults)	50% report some lasting negative effects. Increased risk (double) for depressions, substance abuse, anxiety disorders and dissociation. Increased risk (3-4 times) for physical and/or sexual abuse as adults.

Source: R. Carl Hanson. 1990. *The Psychological Impact of Crime*. Ottawa: Solicitor General of Canada. p. 73.
Reproduced with permission of the Minister of Supply and Services Canada, 1993

prosecution of alleged offenders (Department of Justice, 1986a; 1986b; Daubney, 1988).

An additional problem confronting the criminal justice system is making victims aware of the services and programs that are available. Some evidence suggests that many crime victims do not make use of the resources that have been developed. In their victimization survey, for example, Sacco and Johnson (1990:105, 107) found that in only 5% of the victimization incidents did the victims of crime contact a victim support agency for advice or assistance. When questioned further as to why such services were not used, only one-third stated that they knew about the services. Knowledge of services was highest among the more educated victims in the sample who resided in urban areas.

Among those who knew of such services but did not use them, the most common reasons given were that it was "not necessary" or "not worth the trouble." In fact, Sacco and Johnson (1990:97) found that, even where the victimization had resulted in injury, few sought medical assistance. This suggests that the police and other agencies and organizations that operate victim services must be proactive in disseminating information to the general public and in contacting crime victims and making the services available. In Chapter 3, we will see that, for a variety of reasons, many crime victims do not telephone the police for assistance in the first place.

In 1987, Manitoba was the first jurisdiction to enact legislation specifically designed to provide justice for crime victims. The *Victims of Crime Act* includes sections on victim assistance, the treatment of victims, the provision of information to the victims of crime, and consideration of victims' needs during the criminal justice process.

The services for the victims of crime in Canada can be divided into five broad categories:

> ▸ crisis intervention services operated by community-based agencies, the police, and for specific types of victims such as the elderly, children, and women;
> ▸ programs designed to protect the rights of victims and witnesses and ensure their participation in the criminal justice process by providing information on the status of the case and on criminal court procedures;
> ▸ criminal injuries compensation programs that provide financial remuneration to the victims of crime;

> ▸ restitution and victim-offender reconciliation programs; and
> ▸ information and referral services for victims and witnesses
> of crime (Norquay and Weiler, 1981).

Across Canada, there are a wide range of services for the victims of crime operated by government and private, non-profit agencies, a large number of which rely heavily on voluntary support for their operation. Many police departments operate victim service programs as part of their agencies, while others have entered into collaborative arrangements with community agencies and organizations (see Moylan, 1990).

The victim assistance program operated by the Winnipeg Police Department is illustrative of the programs developed by many municipal, provincial, and RCMP detachments. The program provides information to victims on the progress of case investigations, facilitates the return of property to victims, and refers victims to other services in the community. The victim assistance program also sponsors training sessions for officers to sensitize them to the needs of victims and inform them of the various resources available in the community (see Brickey and Guest, 1984).[7]

The Victim Services Unit in the Edmonton Police Department provides similar services to crime victims. An evaluation of the program by Pullyblank (1986) indicated that the program was successful in meeting victim needs. In Ottawa, the Salvation Army operates a victim assistance program in collaboration with the Ottawa Police Department, and in Montreal, the Integrated Victim Assistance Program is run by the University of Montreal in close cooperation with the Montreal Urban Community Police (see also Canyltec Social Research, 1987; Meredith, 1984a; 1984b).

In addition, many police agencies have developed specialized victim services. A robbery trauma program is operated by police services in Edmonton and Calgary to assist the victims of robberies. The Edmonton police have established a death notification program in which volunteers provide assistance to families after the initial notification of death has been made by police officers. The Metropolitan Toronto Police Victim/Witnesses Assistance Program provides interpreters who speak a variety of languages to assist victims of crime.

It has also been recognized that the witnesses to crime may have special needs that require attention. This has led to the creation of programs such as the Ottawa Witness Coordinator Project, which operates within the Crown Attorney's office in Ottawa. Similar witness assistance programs have been established across the country from St. John and Campbellton, New Brunswick, to Victoria, British Columbia. These programs are most often affiliated with Crown Prosecutor's offices, use both paid staff and volunteers, and provide information to witnesses on court procedures and case details (see Abt Associates, 1985).

There has also been an exponential growth in services for specific groups of victims, including battered and sexually abused women and children, the elderly, and indigenous peoples. This has included the establishment of "safe" houses, sexual assault centres, various crisis intervention services (including 24-hour "hotlines"), counselling, and information on shelters (see McLeod, 1987).[8]

Criminal Injuries Compensation

One method by which the needs of crime victims are met is through criminal injuries compensation. The first criminal injuries compensation plan was created in Saskatchewan in 1967, and since that time all provinces and territories, with the exception of Prince Edward Island, have enacted legislation that provides financial compensation for injuries or death incurred from a crime committed by another person or from efforts to prevent a crime or arrest an offender, with or without the assistance of a police officer.[9] Compensation may also be provided for the surviving dependants of a victim of crime and to those responsible for maintenance of the victim. Compensation is generally limited to instances of violent crime, with insurance companies providing recompense for the victims of property offences. Crime victims may also seek compensation through civil suits. In a recent case in British Columbia, the court awarded a victim $50,000 in damages for trauma inflicted by the defendant who was convicted of sexual assault (Van Ginkel, 1990). In 1991, an Ontario court ordered a convicted child abuser to pay $31,000 in damages to the family of the abused child (Fine, 1991). In a subsequent decision in 1992, an Ontario court ordered a man to pay $280,000 in damages to his daughter (now 23), whom he had sexually abused from the time she was five years old (Claridge, 1992).

In some jurisdictions, applications for compensation are made to the Workers' Compensation Board, while in others an administrative tribunal known as the Criminal Injuries Compensation Board receives and adjudicates requests for compensation. In the Northwest Territories, applications are filed with the Department of Justice and Public Services.

These compensation programs are operated on a cost-sharing basis between the provincial/territorial and federal governments. Monies awarded to applicants may be made in a lump sum or in periodic payments. In 1985-86, the last year for which published figures are available, $22.9 million was paid out in compensation to victims, an increase of 76.6% from 1980, when awards totalled $13 million (Canadian Centre for Justice Statistics, 1986).[10]

There is some concern that crime victims are reluctant to seek compensation, whether through the courts or from insurance companies. In their victimization study, Sacco and Johnson (1990:106) found that only 1% of the victims had sought compensation through the courts and 16% through insurance companies. Those victims with higher household incomes were more likely to seek compensation than lower-income victims of crime. These findings again suggest that the crime victims are either not aware of their options to seek redress or that organizations and agencies must encourage victims to seek compensation, particularly those victims from lower income levels who may have a higher likelihood of becoming crime victims.

An evaluation of the *Service d'indemnisation des victimes d'actes criminels du Quebec* (Quebec crime prevention scheme, or IVAC) (Baril *et al.* 1984a) provides some insights into the operation of criminal compensation programs, as well as the limitations of such programs. Among the findings of this evaluation was that while victims were generally satisfied with the IVAC in terms of its provision of financial compensation, there was less enthusiasm among those who had expectations that IVAC could assist them in dealing with the psychological effects caused by the victimization experience. The psychological and support needs of the victims were viewed as paramount to financial compensation, a situation that often resulted in conflict between the IVAC program and its clients.

Victim Involvement in the Criminal Justice System

Ways to increase victim participation in the criminal justice process, from reporting crimes to appearing in court as witnesses, to presenting victim impact statements at the sentencing stage and during parole board hearings, have been the subject of debate throughout North America.

In 1988, the *Criminal Code* was amended to alter the manner in which the courts handle crime victims. Bill C-89 requires convicted offenders to pay restitution to their victims and mandates that offenders convicted of *Criminal Code* or narcotic offences contribute up to 15% of any fine to a fund to be used by the provincial victim compensation programs. The legislation also allows criminal courts to accept victim impact statements, both in written form and, in certain circumstances, in person from the victim in the courtroom. The *Corrections and Conditional Release Act* (Bill C-36), enacted in 1992, provides for individual citizens, upon approval by the parole board of a written application, to observe parole hearings in person. This would seem to raise the possibility that crime victims could attend parole hearings, although among the guidelines for approving citizen requests to attend is that the presence of the observer will not disrupt the hearing nor impair the integrity of the hearing nor the interests of the parole board or of the inmate.

In the United States, several states have enacted legislation requiring input from the victim at various stages of the criminal justice system. Since 1982 in California, for example, victims or their next of kin have had the right to present their views on crime and its impact during sentencing hearings and to appear before the state board of parole when the offender is being considered for release (see Ranish and Shichor, 1985). The State of Utah has enacted legislation providing victims of crime and their families with the opportunity to appear before the parole board to testify against the offender (May, 1989).

One U.S. observer, Karen Kennard (1989), argues that reforms designed to increase victim participation in the sentencing process have been less than successful because a great majority of cases are disposed of through plea negotiations prior to trial. Victims are generally excluded from such negotiations between the prosecutor and defence lawyer. To increase victim participation in the criminal justice process, Kennard (1989) and Welling (1987) have proposed that victims participate in the plea negotiation process and have the right to veto plea bargains that they find either too harsh or too lenient. Others (see Spencer, 1987; Young, 1987) have argued for an amendment to the U.S. Constitution that would provide for victim participation in the criminal justice system.

There appears to be widespread public support for increasing the involvement of victims in the criminal justice process. Numerous concerns have been raised by legal scholars and researchers (primarily in the United States where the practice is widespread), focusing on issues of justice and fairness and the extent to which victim participation might compromise the administration of justice and the rights of offenders (see

Henderson, 1985; Kelly, 1987). Rubel (1986:24) has argued, for example, that efforts to address the concerns of victims should not be "foisted upon the courts," which, he contends, already consider the public interest in their procedures and decision making.

In support of his position, Rubel (1986:239) cites a study by John Hagan (1982), who found few differences between victims who attended court and those who did not in terms of demands for severity of sentence. Hagan also found that contacts between the victim and defence counsel, prosecutors, and the police served only to aggravate tensions between the victim and the accused (see also Davis, Kunreuther, and Connick, 1984).

In contrast to these assertions, it might be argued that traditionally the criminal court process has been far removed from the victim and the community and that the arena in which the adversarial proceedings take place often obscures the original causes of the conflict and the psychological impact on the victim. Certainly the legislative changes that have occurred at the federal and provincial levels indicates that there is widespread support for increasing the role of crime victims in the criminal justice process.

In a recent in-depth review of research on the impact of victim involvement in the sentencing process in the United States, Erez (1990) reported the following findings.

- ▶ Victims do not appear to be more punitive in their views than the general public and usually do not request the maximum penalty available.
- ▶ Involving victims in the criminal justice process increases their satisfaction with the system.
- ▶ Including victims in the criminal justice process does not result in increased sentence severity.
- ▶ Victim impact statements play only a small role in the selection of a disposition by the criminal court judge.
- ▶ Including victims in the criminal court process has a high symbolic value and contributes to the victims' perception that "justice" has been done.

It is not possible to determine whether these findings can be applied to victim involvement in the sentencing process. One Canadian study (Roberts, 1992) involved an examination of the Victim Impact Statement Program in British Columbia, and it produced several interesting findings.

- In the four cities studied, victim impact statements were requested in only a small percentage (2% to 6%) of the cases in which charges were approved by Crown counsel.
- An even smaller percentage (1% to 2%) of victim impact statements were actually filed in court in cases where charges were approved by Crown counsel.
- There was considerable variation in the use of victim impact statements by Crown counsel offices in the four cities studied.
- Those victims who are not "targeted" by the Crown counsel office for a victim impact statement were generally not informed that they have a right to submit one.
- Defence counsel tended to feel that victim impact statements had a negative impact on their client's case.
- While most of the judges surveyed had little experience with victim impact statements in their courtrooms, most felt that it was a positive development and several stated that they routinely requested such information if it was not available.

Victim-Offender Reconciliation

In an attempt to address the needs of crime victims while insuring that criminal offenders are held responsible for their offences, several provinces have developed victim-offender reconciliation programs (VORPs). These programs, which are operated both by provincial agencies and private non-profit organizations, are generally restricted to cases involving minor offences. The technique of mediation is often used as the basis of VORPs, which operate at the post-change, pre-trial stage and involve the voluntary participation of the victim and the offender.

The first VORP was established in Kitchener/Waterloo, Ontario, in 1974. Since that time, the programs have spread across the country. These programs were developed during the search for alternative ways to respond to criminal offences.

The general objectives of VORPs are exemplified by those of the Langley, British Columbia program:

VORP seeks to:
- effect reconciliation and understanding between victim and offender;

- ‣ facilitate the reaching of an agreement between victim and offender regarding restitution;
- ‣ assist offenders in directing payment of their "debt to society" to the ones in that society to whom that debt is due: to their victims!;
- ‣ involve community people in work with problems that normally lead into the criminal justice process; and
- ‣ identify crime that can be successfully dealt with in the community (Langely, British Columbia Victim-Offender Reconciliation Program, 1988).

In VORPs, a mediator assists the offender and the victim in arriving at a settlement. Participation on the part of both the offender and the victim is voluntary. Referrals to VORPs generally come from the police, the courts, and probation offices.

VORPs have been operating in Ontario for over a decade and involve programs for both adult and young offenders at the pre-sentence and post-plea stages. The conciliation agreement that is mediated between the offender and the victim is reached prior to the passing of sentence in court and is included in the probation order. One of the better-known programs is operated in Kitchener by the Mennonite Central Committee. In the Yukon, the focus of the VORP is on family mediation, particularly the resolution of issues surrounding child custody and support.

Evaluations of VORPs suggest that they may be a viable alternative to the formal criminal justice process and that they increase the participation of the victim and the offender in the resolution of conflicts. Stephen Brickey (1986) argues that VORPs provide an opportunity for the victim and the offender, both of whom have traditionally been "marginalized" and generally excluded from the criminal justice process, to assume a more active involvement in the resolution of disputes.

There are, however, many unanswered questions about the use and effectiveness of VORPs. In an evaluation of two Canadian VORPs, Dittenhoffer and Ericson (1983) found that judges and prosecutors were less than enthusiastic about using VORPs as alternative dispositions in the Criminal Court, thus undermining their potential effectiveness.[11] Also, Sacco and Johnson (1990:70) found that only 31% of the crime victims surveyed were familiar with VORPs. As with victim assistance programs, the level of awareness was greatest among crime victims with higher levels of education who lived in urban areas.

We can assume that there is considerable variability in the views toward and use of VORPs across the country. Among the areas requiring further research are the issues surrounding the operation of VORPs, the attitudes of criminal justice personnel toward these programs, and the extent to which crime victims are aware of and use the service.

As seen in Chapter 1, the criminal justice system has not always been successful in resolving conflicts. VORPs are one mechanism for conflict resolution outside of the traditional adversarial process of the criminal courts. Among the issues requiring further research are the extent criminal courts use VORPs as alternatives for dispute resolution, the cost of VORPs as compared to processing cases through the criminal courts, and the potential for expanding the use of VORPs (see Coates, 1990).

CANADIAN ATTITUDES TOWARD THE LAW AND THE CRIMINAL JUSTICE SYSTEM

Any initiatives that are designed to increase public participation in the criminal justice system, from reporting crime, to appearing as witnesses, or participating in crime prevention activities, must address the attitudes that Canadians hold toward the law and the criminal justice system.

It has been noted that Canadians, particularly the victims of crime, often feel alienated from the criminal justice system. Further, many members of the general public have a distorted view of the nature and extent of crime, of their actual risks of being victimized, and of how the criminal justice system responds to crime. These attitudes are aptly summarized by a recent report of the federal government:

> Canadians overestimate our rate of violent crime, underestimate the sentences prescribed and imposed for specific offences, underestimate the severity of prison, overestimate the ease with which parole is granted, underestimate the length of time served by most offenders before parole is given, and overestimate the number of offenders on parole who commit new crimes (Solicitor General of Canada and Department of Justice, 1990:2).

In discussing the patterns of crime in Canada, we noted that there were limitations of official statistics that required us to exercise caution in making generalized statements. This is also the case when discussing what Canadians think about crime and the criminal justice system. While researchers have urged that extreme caution be used in generalizing from the findings of specific attitude surveys and studies (see Zamble, 1990; Himelfarb, 1990), opinion research can be useful in identifying potential "trouble" areas in the relationship between the criminal justice system and the general public. This, in turn, alerts criminal justice agencies and policymakers to issues that require their attention.[12]

Generally, it appears that the majority of Canadians have a limited knowledge of the criminal justice system, its mandate, and its operation (Adams, 1990; Roberts and Doob, 1989). For many citizens, actual contact with the criminal justice system may be limited to a traffic stop by police. As in the case of crime, the media may assist in creating among citizens inaccurate perceptions of the criminal justice system. In a study of the media and sentencing for the Canadian Sentencing Commission (1987), Roberts (1988) found that the media present a distorted image of sentencing to the general public. More specially, newspaper stories on sentencing were brief, provided little information on the case or on the sentencing provisions under the *Criminal Code*, and the majority of stories focused on crimes against the person and cases in which incarceration was the disposition.

Researchers have given increased attention to assessing the views that Canadians hold toward the criminal law and the criminal justice system. Adams (1990:13) concluded from a review of survey findings that "most people believe the criminal justice system is good in theory but flawed in practice." Among the findings of the research conducted to date are the following.

▶ *Canadians view the criminal courts as treating criminal offenders too leniently.*

A large number of Canadians view the criminal courts as being too lenient with offenders at the sentencing stage and as placing too much emphasis on the rights of offenders. However, there appears to be little support for reducing the discretion that judges exercise in disposing of criminal cases (Adams, 1990).

Roberts and Doob (1989) have challenged the oft-reported finding that the public is more punitive in sentencing than criminal court judges. They argue that the public is generally ignorant of actual sentencing practices in the court, underestimate the severity of *Criminal Code* penalties, have only a limited knowledge of actual crime patterns, and are misinformed by media reporting (see Roberts and White, 1986).

In a survey of sentencing and public opinion for the Canadian Sentencing Commission, Roberts and Doob (1989) found that the sample of Canadians questioned were, in fact, *less* punitive in their use of imprisonment than criminal court judges. In their study, there were no significant differences between the actual sentencing practices of the courts and the opinions of the sample surveyed.

A recent study by Ouimet and Coyle (1991) in Montreal found that the level of fear of crime expressed by the respondents in the sample was not related to their demands for punitive sanctions by the court, a finding that challenges the oft-cited reason by criminal court judges for imposing severe sentences on offenders: public fear of crime.

▸   *Many Canadians feel that the criminal law is applied in a manner that favours certain groups over others.*

Many of the respondents interviewed by Moore (1985), and nearly seven in ten of those surveyed in the study reported by Adams (1990), felt that the law and the criminal courts tended to favour the wealthy, while those with low incomes, crime victims, and female victims of sex crimes were felt to be treated in a discriminatory fashion.

▸   *There is widespread support for the reinstatement of capital punishment, for tightening up parole requirements and supervision, and for including rehabilitation as one, but not the primary, objective of corrections.*

While capital punishment was abolished by Parliament in 1976 and a motion to introduce the death penalty was defeated in a "free" vote by members of Parliament in 1987, public opinion polls reveal that the majority of Canadians favour the use of the death penalty in certain cases. With respect to corrections, Moore (1985:55) reported that respondents tended to view prisons as doing only a "fair to good" job of protecting society and punishing offenders.

It appears that many Canadians have little knowledge of how the correctional system actually works. Many respondents in Adams's survey (1990:12) suggested that there should be different security levels through which offenders would pass as they progressed toward eventual release. This is a key attribute of federal and provincial correctional systems, suggesting that a major information gap needs to be addressed.

► *Canadians who have had actual experiences with the criminal justice system tend to hold less favourable attitudes toward it.*

An emerging body of research evidence suggests that persons who have been victimized or had some other type of contact with the criminal justice system are less positive in their perceptions of the systems and its personnel. Sacco and Johnson (1990:11) found, for example, that individuals who had been involved with the criminal courts in the preceding year were more likely to view the courts as doing a poor job in terms of providing justice quickly than those persons who had not had such contact. Similarly, these authors (1990:10) reported that those persons who had been victims of crime were less likely to state that the police were doing a good job. We must, therefore, be concerned not only with the perceptions that the general public holds toward the justice system, but the views of those who have actually had to make use of it.

► *There may be considerable variability across the country, between and within communities in the perceptions of the law and the criminal justice system.*

It can be expected that public attitudes toward the criminal justice system and its agents may change over time, may vary between communities, or even, as we shall see in our consideration of public attitudes toward the police, within the same neighbourhood. Moore (1985), for example, found considerable variability between respondents in the three cities studied in their perceptions of the law and the legal system. Respondents in Montreal — as opposed to their counterparts in Toronto and Winnipeg — were more likely to be strongly oriented toward law enforcement in responding to crime, to feel that the legal system was inefficient, and to perceive that laws were enacted to benefit certain groups of people.

► *There are jurisdictions where relations between the criminal justice system and cultural and ethnic minorities are strained.*

There may also be tensions and conflict between the criminal justice system and certain groups in Canadian society, for example, indigenous peoples, religious minorities such as the Doukhobors, and ethnic and immigrant groups. In Chapter 15, we'll explore in greater detail the issues surrounding Aboriginal peoples and the law.

These findings suggest a pressing need not only to develop mechanisms for educating the public about the criminal justice system and its operation, but also to consider how the community can become more involved, in a significant way, in both preventing and responding to crime. As we will see in Chapter 5, police agencies have taken a number of initiatives to secure the active participation in the crime prevention and crime control effort. However, few such initiatives have been undertaken by the judiciary or corrections. At present, the majority of Canadians are "outsiders" to their own criminal justice system (see Canadian Centre for Justice Statistics, 1991a).

THE COSTS OF THE CRIMINAL JUSTICE SYSTEM

As previously noted, a major attribute of the Canadian criminal justice system is its high cost. In 1989-90, justice services, including policing, adult corrections, courts, and legal aid, cost $7.7 billion, and there were over 100,000 people employed in the system (Canadian Centre for Justice Statistics, 1991b:1). Overall, criminal justice expenditures accounted for 2.6% of total government spending. Throughout the text, we will note the expenditures for the various components of the criminal justice system. At this juncture, it is sufficient to note that policing services consume the largest portion of the criminal justice dollar ($4.68 billion or $179 for every Canadian), followed by expenditures for adult corrections ($1.65 billion or $65 per Canadian), and a much smaller percentage for the operation of the courts ($640 million or $25 per Canadian). The overall rate of criminal justice spending has slowed in recent years, although in areas such as corrections, there have been sharp increases in expenditures, particularly in relation to the operation of correctional facilities.

NOTES

[1]A consideration of the historical context of crime in Canada is beyond the scope of the text. However, readers are encouraged to examine the rapidly expanding literature in this area. See Carrigan (1991), Hatch (1991), and MacLeod (1988) for a historical overview of crime and justice in Canada, and Lachance (1981), Weaver (1986), and McGahan (1988) for specific case studies from the historical record.

[2]For a more detailed discussion of the various operational attributes of the

Uniform Crime Reporting (UCR) system, as well as the limitations of using data collected by this system, see the annual report *Canadian Crime Statistics*, produced by the Canadian Centre for Justice Statistics, a division of Statistics Canada. Hackler and Don (1990) remind us that differences in recorded and reported crime rates among different jurisdictions across Canada are due in part to how the criminal justice agencies in those areas operate, rather than solely to variations in the amount of criminal activity. A recent debate surrounding the UCR system has centred on whether data on the "racial origin" or ethnicity of offenders should be included in the data-gathering process (Doob, 1991).

[3]For statistical summaries of general crime patterns in Canada, as well as for specific types of offences, for example, homicide, see the Juristat Service Bulletins and the annual reports, *Canadian Crime Statistics* and *Homicide in Canada*, published by the Canadian Centre for Justice Statistics, a division of Statistics Canada.

[4]Many observers have argued that there are key value differences between U.S. and Canadian society that have a significant impact on a broad range of issues, including crime patterns (see Baer, Grabb and Johnston, 1990; Grabb and Curtis, 1988). Research by Sproule and Kennett (1989) and Sloan *et al.* (1988), for example, suggests that the lower Canadian violent crime rate is due in large measure to strict gun control laws, although this has been disputed by another Canadian observer (see Mundt, 1990).

[5]See Adams, 1990; Brantigham, Brantingham *et al.*, 1986; Brillon, Louis-Guerin, and Lamrache, 1984; Brillon, 1987; Gomme, 1986; Keane, 1992; Kennedy and Forde, 1990; Kahn and Kennedy, 1985; Murphy and Clairmont, 1990; Sacco, 1988.

[6]Murphy and Clairmont (1990) point out that most of the victimization studies that have been carried out in Canada have been conducted in urban settings, and thus we have little knowledge of the rates and types of victimization in rural areas. In perhaps the most extensive study of victimization in a rural area in Canada conducted to date, Murphy and Clairmont surveyed a sample of residents in Kings County, Nova Scotia. Among the findings of the study (1990:17-18) were that a large number of crimes/victimization were not reported to the police, that the rural rates of victimization were lower than those reported in the urban surveys, and that gender, income, and location of residence did not affect the likelihood of victimization.

[7]For a current overview of police agencies and victim services across Canada, see Moylan (1990).

[8]For an insightful examination of the dynamics surrounding the formulation of federal government policy for crime victims, see Rock (1986; 1988).

[9]For a comprehensive analysis of the Criminal Injuries Board of Ontario, as well as an extensive discussion of the history and development of criminal injuries compensation boards across the country, see Bailey (1989).

[10]For a detailed report on the structure and operation of criminal injuries compensation programs across Canada, see the report *Criminal Injuries Compensation in Canada, 1986* (Canadian Centre for Justice Statistics, 1988). See also Hastings (1983) for an in-depth examination of the rationale, structure and operation, and evaluation of criminal injuries compensation programs operating in Canada.

[11]For a U.S. survey of VORPs involving the use of mediation, see Hughes and Schneider (1989).

[12]Zamble (1990) cautions us that the polling techniques that have been used by many studies to ascertain public views of the law and the criminal justice system are not sufficient to measure the complexity of citizens attitudes. He reminds us that how questions are asked of the general public may play a significant role in the responses that are forthcoming and that we must be careful in considering the findings of public opinion research.

REFERENCES

Abt Associates. 1985. *Access to Justice — Review of Court-Based Victim/Witness Projects*. Ottawa: Supply and Services Canada.

Adams, Michael. 1990. "Canadian Attitudes Toward Crime and Justice." 2 *FORUM on Corrections Research*. 10-13.

Axon, L. 1989. *Criminal Justice and Women: An International Survey*. Ottawa: Solicitor General of Canada.

Baer, D., E.G. Grabb, and W.A. Johnston. 1990. "The Values of Canadians and Americans: A Critical Analysis and Reassessment." 68 *Social Forces*. 693-713.

Bailey, S. 1989. "Pennies from Heaven: The Ontario Criminal Injuries Compensation Board." 5 *Journal of Law and Social Policy*. 112-64.

Baril, M., S. LaFalmme-Cusson, and S. Beauchemin. 1984a. *Crime Victims. Working Paper No. 12. Crime Victims Compensation: An Assessment of the Quebec IVAC Program*. Ottawa: Policy Planning and Development Branch, Department of Justice.

Baril, M., S. Durand, M.-M. Cousineau, and S. Gravel. 1984b. *Victimes d'Actes Criminels. Document de travail no. 10. Mais Nous, Les Temoins...:Une étude exploratorie des besoins des temoins au Palais de Justice de Montreal*. Ottawa: Direction de la planification et de l'elaboration de la politique, Ministere de la Justice.

Brantingham, P.B. 1991. "Patterns in Canadian Crime." In M.A. Jackson and C.T. Griffiths, eds. *Canadian Criminology: Perspectives on Crime and Society*. Toronto: HBJ-Holt. 372-402.

Brantingham, P.J., and P.L. Brantingham. 1984. *Patterns in Crime*. New York:

Macmillan.

Brantingham, P.J., P.L. Brantingham, and D. Butcher. 1986. "Perceived and Actual Crime Risks." In R.N. Figlio, S. Hakin, and G.F. Renget, eds. *Metropolitan Crime Patterns*. Monsey, New York: Criminal Justice Press.

Brickey, S. 1986. "The Marginalization of Victims and Offenders." In S. Brickey and E. Cormack, eds. *The Social Basis of Law: Critical Readings in the Sociology of Law*. Toronto: Garamond Press. 243-51.

Brickey, S. and A. Guest. 1984. *Crime Victims. Working Paper No. 8. The Evaluation of the Winnipeg Victim/Witness Assistance Program*. Ottawa: Policy Planning and Development Branch, Department of Justice.

Brillon, Y. 1987. *Victimization and Fear of Crime Among the Elderly*. Toronto: Butterworths.

Brillon, Y., C. Louis-Guerin, and M.-C. Lamarche. 1984. *Attitudes of the Canadian Public Toward Crime Policies*. Montreal: International Centre for Comparative Criminology, University of Montreal.

Canada. Federal-Provincial Task Force on Justice for the Victims of Crime. 1983. *Report*. Ottawa: Supply and Services Canada.

Canadian Centre for Justice Statistics. 1986. *Criminal Injuries Compensation*. Ottawa: Supply and Services Canada.

_____. 1987. *Sentencing Reform: A Canadian Approach*. Ottawa: Supply and Services Canada.

_____. 1990a. *Canadian Crime Statistics, 1989*. Ottawa: Supply and Services Canada.

_____. 1990b. *Women and Crime*. 10 Juristat Service Bulletin. Ottawa: Statistics Canada.

_____. 1991a. *Public Perceptions of Crime and the Criminal Justice System*. 11 Juristat Service Bulletin. Ottawa: Statistics Canada.

_____. 1991b. *Government Spending on Justice Services*. 11 Juristat Service Bulletin. Ottawa: Statistics Canada.

_____. 1992a. *Canadian Crime Statistics, 1991*. Ottawa: Minister of Industry, Science and Technology.

_____. 1992b. *Homicide in Canada, 1991*. 12 Juristat Service Bulletin. Ottawa: Statistics Canada.

Canyltec Social Research Corporation. 1987. *An Evaluation of Two Approaches to Delivery of Police-Based Victim Assistance: Neighbourhood-Focused vs. Headquarters-Based*. Ottawa: Solicitor General of Canada.

Carrigan, D.O. 1991. *Crime and Punishment in Canada: A History*. Toronto: McClelland and Stewart.

Chunn, D.D.E., and S.A.M. Gavigan. 1991. "Women and Crime in Canada." In M.A. Jackson and C.T. Griffiths, eds. *Canadian Criminology: Perspectives on Crime and Society*. Toronto: HBJ-Holt. 275-314.

Claridge, T. 1992. "$280,000.00 Awarded to Incest Victim." Toronto *Globe and*

Mail (October 12):A-1.

Coates, R.B. 1990. "Victim-Offender Reconciliation Programs in North America: An Assessment." In B. Galaway and J. Hudson, eds. *Criminal Justice, Restitution, and Reconciliation.* Monsey, New York: Criminal Justice Press. 125-34.

Daubney, D. (Chair). 1988. *Taking Responsibility. Report of the Standing Committee on Justice and Solicitor General on Its Review of Sentencing, Conditional Release and Related Aspects of Corrections.* Ottawa: Supply and Services Canada.

Davis, R.C., F. Kunreuther, and E. Connick. 1984. "Expanding the Victim's Role in the Criminal Court Dispositional Process: The Results of an Experiment." 75 *Journal of Criminal Law and Criminology.* 491-505.

Department of Justice. 1986a. *Access to Justice — Review of Court-Based Victim/Witness Projects.* Ottawa: Supply and Services Canada.

_____. 1986b. *Access to Justice — Survey of Victims' Legal Information Needs.*Ottawa: Supply and Services Canada.

Dittenhoffer, T., and R.V. Ericson. 1983. "The Victim-Offender Reconciliation Program: A Message to Correctional Reformers." 33 *University of Toronto Law Journal.* 315-47.

Donelson, A.C. 1985. *Impaired Driving. Report No. 4. Alcohol and Road Accidents in Canada: Issues Related to Future Strategies and Priorities.* Ottawa: Department of Justice.

Donelson, A.C., and D.J. Bierness. 1985. *Impaired Driving. Report No. 2. Legislative Issues Related to Drinking and Driving.* Ottawa: Department of Justice.

Doob, A.N. 1991. *Workshop on Collecting Race and Ethnicity Statistics in the Criminal Justice System — A Report.* Ottawa: Solicitor General of Canada.

Erez, E. 1990. "Victim Participation in Sentencing: Rhetoric and Reality." 18 *Journal of Criminal Justice.* 19-31.

Ericson, R.V., P.M. Baranek, and J.B.L. Chan. 1987. *Visualizing Deviance: A Study of News Organization.* Toronto: University of Toronto Press.

Fattah, E.A. 1991. *Understanding Crime Victimization.* Scarborough, Ontario: Prentice-Hall.

Fattah, E.A., and V. Sacco. 1989. *Crime and Victimization of the Elderly.* New York: Springer-Verlag.

Felt, L.F. 1987. *"Take the 'Bloods of Bitches' to the Gallows": Cultural and Structural Constraint Upon Interpersonal Violence in Rural Newfoundland.* St. John's, Newfoundland: Institute of Social and Economic Research, Memorial University of Newfoundland.

Fine, S. 1991. "Family Wins $31,000.00 in Damages After Suing Molester of Child." Toronto *Globe and Mail* (November 27):A1-A2.

Forde, D.R., L.W. Kennedy, and R.A. Silverman. 1990. *Age and Homicide in*

Canada: A Multi-Level Analysis. Edmonton: Centre for Criminological Research, University of Alberta.

Gabor, T., and A. Normandeau. 1987. *Armed Robbery: Cops, Robbers, and Victims*. Springfield, Illinois: Charles C. Thomas Publishers.

———. 1989. "Armed Robbery: Highlights of a Canadian Study." 13 *Canadian Police College Journal*. 273-82.

Gebotys, R.J., J.V. Roberts, and B. DasGupta. 1988. "News Media Use and Public Perceptions of Crime Seriousness." 30 *Canadian Journal of Criminology*. 3-16.

Goff, C. 1989. "The Seriousness of Crime in Fredericton, New Brunswick: Perceptions Toward White-Collar Crime." 31 *Canadian Journal of Criminology*. 19-34.

Gomme, I.M. 1986. "Fear of Crime Among Canadians: A Multi-Variate Analysis." 14 *Journal of Criminal Justice*. 249-58.

Grabb, E.G., and J. Curtis. 1988. "English Canadian-American Differences in Orientation Toward Social Control and Individual Rights." 21 *Sociological Focus*. 127-41.

Griffiths, C.T., and J.C. Yerbury. 1991. "Minorities and Crime." In M.A. Jackson and C.T. Griffiths, eds. *Canadian Criminology: Perspectives on Crime and Society*. Toronto: HBJ-Holt. 315-46.

Hackler, J., and D. Cossins. 1989. *Police Screening Patterns in Five Western Canadian Cities: Looking at the Data a Different Way*. Edmonton: Centre for Criminological Research, University of Alberta.

Hackler, J., and K. Don. 1990. "Estimating System Biases: Crime Indices that Permit Comparison across Provinces." 32 *Canadian Journal of Criminology*. 243-63.

Hagan, J. 1982. "Victims Before the Law: A Study of Victim Involvement in the Criminal Justice Process." 73 *Journal of Criminal Law and Criminology*. 317-30.

Hanson, R.K. 1990. *The Psychological Impact of Crime: A Review*. Ottawa: Solicitor General of Canada.

Hastings, R. 1983. *Crime Victims. Working Paper No. 6. A Theoretical Assessment of Criminal Injuries Compensation in Canada: Policy, Programs and Evaluation*. Ottawa: Policy Planning and Development Branch, Department of Justice.

Hatch, A.J. 1991. "Historical Legacies in Canadian Criminal Law and Justice." In M.A. Jackson and C.T. Griffiths, eds. *Canadian Criminology: Perspectives on Crime and Criminality*. Toronto: HBJ-Holt. 19-47.

Hatch, A., and K. Faith. 1989-90. "The Female Offender in Canada: A Statistical Profile." 3 *Canadian Journal of Women and the Law*. 432-56.

Henderson, L.N. 1985. "The Wrong of Victims Rights." 37 *Stanford Law*

Review. 937-1021.

Himelfarb, A. 1990. "Public Opinion and Public Policy." 2 *FORUM on Corrections Research.* 20-22.

Hughes, S.P., and A.L. Schneider. 1989. "Victim-Offender Mediation: A Survey of Program Characteristics and Perceptions of Crime Effectiveness." *Crime and Delinquency.* 217-23.

Johnson, H. 1986. *Women and Crime in Canada.* Ottawa: Solicitor General of Canada.

_____. 1987. "Getting the Facts Straight: A Statistical Overview." In E. Adelberg and C. Currie, eds. *Too Few To Count: Canadian Women in Conflict with the Law.* Vancouver: Press Gang Publishers. 23-43.

Keane, C. 1992. "Fear of Crime in Canada: An Examination of Concrete and Formless Fear of Victimization." 34 *Canadian Journal of Criminology.* 215-24.

Kelly, D.P. 1987. "Victims." 34 *Wayne Law Review.* 69-86.

Kennard, K.L. 1989. "The Victim's Veto: A Way to Increase Victim Impact on Criminal Case Dispositions." 77 *California Law Review.* 417-53.

Kennedy, L.W., and D.G. Dutton. 1989. "The Incidence of Wife Assault in Alberta." 21 *Canadian Journal of Behavioural Science.* 40-54.

Kennedy, L.W., and R.A. Silverman. 1988. *The Elderly Victim of Homicide: Limitations of the Routine Activities Approach.* Edmonton: Centre for Criminological Research, University of Alberta.

Kennedy, L.W., R.A. Silverman, and D.R. Forde. 1988. *Homicide From East To West: A Test of the Impact of Culture and Economic Inequality on Regional Trends of Violent Crime in Canada.* Edmonton: Centre for Criminological Research, University of Alberta.

Kennedy, L.W., and R.A. Silverman. 1990. "The Elderly Victim of Homicide: An Application of the Routine Activities Approach." 31 *The Sociological Quarterly.* 307-19.

Krahn, H., and L.W. Kennedy. 1985. *Producing Personal Safety: Parallel Production, Police, Fear and Crime.* Edmonton: Centre for Criminological Research, University of Alberta.

Lachance, A. 1981. "Women and Crime in Canada in the Early Eighteenth Century, 1712-1759." In L.A. Knafla, ed. *Crime and Criminal Justice in Europe and Canada.* Waterloo: Wilfrid Laurier University Press. 157-97.

Langley, British Columbia Victim-Offender Reconciliation Program. 1988. *VORP — Victim Offender Reconciliation Program.* Langely, British Columbia.

MacLeod, R.C. 1988. *Lawful Authority: Readings on the History of Criminal Justice in Canada.* Toronto: Copp Clark Pitman.

McGahan, P. 1988. *Crime and Policing in Maritime Canada-Chapters from the Urban Record.* Fredericton: Goose Lane.

McLeod, L. 1987. *Battered But Not Beaten...Preventing Wife Battering in*

Canada. Ottawa: Canadian Advisory Council on the Status of Women.

McMullan, J.L., and P.D. Swan. 1989. "Social Economy and Arson in Nova Scotia." 31 *Canadian Journal of Criminology.* 281-308.

May, M. 1989. "Victims' Rights and the Parole Hearing." 15 *Journal of Contemporary Law.* 71-80.

Meredith, C. 1984a. *Access to Justice — Evaluation of the Ottawa Witness Co-ordinator Project.* Ottawa: Supply and Services Canada.

_____. 1984b. *Overview and Annotated Bibliography of the Needs of Crime Victims.* Ottawa: Solicitor General of Canada.

Moore, R.J. 1985. "Reflections of Canadians on the Law and the Legal System: Legal Research Institute Survey of Respondents in Montreal, Toronto, and Winnipeg." In D. Gibson and J.K. Baldwin, eds. *Law in a Cynical Society? Opinion and Law in the 1980s.* 41-87. Calgary and Vancouver: Carswell Legal Publications, Western Division.

Moylan, J. 1990. *Victim Services and Canadian Police Agencies — A Source Book.* Ottawa: Canadian Association of Chiefs of Police and Solicitor General of Canada.

Mundt, R.J. 1990. "Gun Control and Rates of Firearms Violence in Canada and the United States." 32 *Canadian Journal of Criminology.* 137-54.

Murphy, C., and D. Clairmont. 1990. *Rural Attitudes and Perceptions of Crime, Policing and Victimization: Preliminary Findings from a Survey of Rural Nova Scotians.* Unpublished paper. Halifax: Atlantic Institute of Criminology, Dalhousie University.

Norquay, G., and R. Weiler. 1981. *Services to Victims and Witnesses of Crime in Canada.* Ottawa: Solicitor General of Canada.

Ouimet, M., and E.J. Coyle. 1991. "Fear of Crime and Sentencing Punitiveness: Comparing the General Public and Court Practitioners." 33 *Canadian Journal of Criminology.* 149-62.

Pullyblank, J. 1986. *The Victim Services Unit of the Edmonton Police Department: An Evaluation.* Ottawa: Solicitor General of Canada.

Ranish, D.R., and D. Shichor. 1985. "The Victim's Role in the Penal Process: Recent Developments in California." 49 *Federal Probation.* 50-57.

Rattner, A., and C. McKie. 1990. "The Ecology of Crime and Its Implications for Prevention: An Ontario Study." 32 *Canadian Journal of Criminology.* 155-71.

Roberts. J.V. 1988. *Sentencing in the Media: A Content Analysis of English-Language Newspapers in Canada.* Ottawa: Department of Justice Canada.

Roberts, J.V., and N.R. White. 1986. "Public Estimates of Recidivism Rates: Consequences of a Criminal Stereotype." 28 *Canadian Journal of Criminology.* 229-41.

Roberts, J.V., and A.N. Doob. 1989. "Sentencing and Public Opinion: Taking

False Shadows for True Substances." 27 *Osgoode Hall Law Journal*. 491-515.

Rock, P. 1986. *A View From the Shadows: The Ministry of the Solicitor General of Canada and the Justice for Victims of Crime Initiative.* Oxford: Oxford University Press.

_____. 1991b. *Government Spending on Justice Services.* 11 Juristat Service Bulletin. Ottawa: Statistics Canada. 1988. "Governments, Victims, and Policies in Two Countries." 28 *British Journal of Criminology*. 44-66.

Rubel, H.C. 1986. "Victim Participation in Sentencing Proceedings." 28 *Criminal Law Quarterly*. 226-50.

Sacco, V.F. 1988. "Public Definitions of Crime Problems and Functionalist Processes: A Reassessment." 25 *Canadian Review of Sociology and Anthropology*. 84-97.

Sacco, V.F., and H. Johnson. 1990. *Patterns of Criminal Victimization in Canada.* Ottawa: Statistics Canada.

Silverman, R.A., and L.W. Kennedy. 1987. *The Female Perpetrator of Homicide in Canada.* Edmonton: Centre for Criminological Research, University of Alberta.

Sloan, J.H., A.L. Kellerman, D.T. Reay, J.A. Ferris, T. Koepsell, F.P. Rivara, C. Rice, L. Gray, and L. Logerfo. 1988. "Handgun Regulations, Crime, Assaults, and Homicide." 319 *New England Journal of Medicine.*

Smith, M.D. 1990. "Sociodemographic Risk Factors in Wife Abuse: Results from a Survey of Toronto Women." 15 *Canadian Journal of Sociology*. 39-58.

Solicitor General of Canada. 1984. *Canadian Urban Victimization Survey. Bulletin 3. Crime Prevention: Awareness and Practice.* Ottawa: Research and Statistics Group, Programs Branch.

_____. 1985a. *Canadian Urban Victimization Survey. Bulletin 4. Female Victims of Crime.* Ottawa: Research and Statistics Group, Programs Branch.

_____. 1985b. *Canadian Urban Victimization Survey. Bulletin 6. Criminal Victimization of Elderly Canadians.* Ottawa: Research and Statistics Group, Programs Branch.

Solicitor General of Canada and Department of Justice. 1990. *Directions for Reform. A Framework for Sentencing, Corrections and Conditional Release.* Ottawa: Supply and Services Canada.

Spencer, B.J. 1987. "A Crime Victim's Views on a Constitutional Amendment for Victims." 34 *The Wayne Law Review*. 1-6.

Sproule, C.F., and D.J. Kennett. 1989. "Killing With Guns in the USA and Canada 1977-1983: Further Evidence for the Effectiveness of Gun Control." 31 *Canadian Journal of Criminology*. 245-51.

Stuebing, W.K. 1984. *Crime Victims. Working Paper No. 9. Victims and Witnesses: Experiences, Needs, and Community/Criminal Justice Response.* Ottawa: Policy Planning and Development Branch, Department of Justice.

Van Ginkel, D.M. 1990. "Finally Compensating the Victim: *Harder v. Brown.*" 8 *Canadian Journal of Family Law*. 388-94.

Weaver, J. 1986. "Crime, Public Order, and Repression: The Gore District in Upheaval, 1832-1851." 78 *Ontario History*. 175-207.

Welling, S.N. 1987. "Victim Participation in Plea Bargains." 65 *Washington University Law Quarterly*. 310-56.

Young, M.A. 1987. "A Constitutional Amendment for Victims of Crime: The Victims' Perspective." 34 *The Wayne Law Review*. 51-68.

Zamble, E. 1990. "Public Support for Criminal Justice Policies: Some Specific Findings." 2 *FORUM on Corrections Research*. 14-19.

3 THE STRUCTURE AND OPERATION OF CANADIAN POLICING

In this chapter, we consider the structure and operation of Canadian policing. Our discussion will include an examination of the history and development of police forces in this country, the structure and role of contemporary police agencies, the occupation of policing, and the perceptions Canadians hold of their police forces.

POLICING IN EARLY CANADA

The development of policing in Canada was strongly influenced by the system of policing that emerged in England in the early 1800s, although as the following discussion will reveal, Canadian policing has its own unique history and evolved into a structure quite distinct from its counterparts in England and the United States. While a detailed examination of the factors — social, political, geographical, and cultural — that influenced the development of Canadian policing is beyond the scope of this text, we should consider the major events that served to shape the course of Canadian policing from the days of the early settlers to the present.[1] In recent years, the work of police observers such as Talbot, Jaywarden, and Juliani (1983; 1984) and others have contributed immensely to the historical record of policing in Canada.

Early Municipal Policing

Prior to Confederation in 1867, the arrangements for policing across Canada were as diverse as the peoples and the land on which they lived. In areas such as Newfoundland, which very early attracted fishermen on a seasonal basis, and French Canada, which was also settled early, there were pressures to make some provision for law enforcement. The western reaches of the country, on the other hand, remained sparsely settled until the mid to late 1800s.

The development of structures for maintaining order in Newfoundland provides an illustration of not only the types of problems that existed in the early settlements, but also the remedies that were offered for maintaining order. To counter the disorder that often existed among the fishermen, English authorities appointed "fishing admirals," captains of fishing vessels who were empowered to settle disputes among the fishermen (see Fox, 1971). However, these admirals, being untrained and perhaps as disorderly as those they sought to control, were largely ineffective. This led to the issuance in 1792 of a Royal Proclamation that authorized the governor of Newfoundland to appoint justices of the peace and constables, although no regulations governing their supervision were established until 1825.

French Canadians are generally credited with deploying the first police officers on the streets of Quebec City in 1651 (Dickson, 1987). It is likely that these officers served primarily as night watchmen, and it was not until the imposition of British laws and the creation of justices of the peace in 1673 that their role included law enforcement. During this time, commerce on the St. Lawrence River increased, bringing with it large numbers of immigrants and seamen. A system of policing was also introduced in Montreal during the mid-1600s, although its primary purpose was the protection of residents from the Iroquois.

The conquest of New France by the British in 1759 radically altered the French-influenced system of policing that had been developing in French Canada, and in 1787 an ordinance was passed that authorized justices of the peace to appoint people to assist in carrying out orders of the court and to maintain order in the cities of Montreal and Quebec. This legislation served to introduce the position of constable, which was to provide the model of policing throughout the province.

In Upper Canada (now the province of Ontario), the English settlers implemented a legal system similar to that of England. Sheriffs, constables, and justices of the peace formed the basis of the peacekeeping function. In 1792, the English common law was installed as the law of Upper Canada, and in 1793, the *Parish and Town Officers Act* was enacted and provided for the appointment of high constables for each provincial district, who, in turn, were to appoint citizens to act as unpaid constables in each parish and township in the district.

While this legislation was designed to expand the system of policing throughout Upper Canada, community officials and citizens did not regard crime as a serious problem, nor the development of crime control structures such as the police and jails as a high priority. Citizens were often reluctant to serve as constables, and while many of the charters establishing towns required the creation of systems of policing, communities were often reluctant to do so unless confronted with disorder.

During the early 1800s, however, a growing concern with crime and the "criminal classes" emerged. Whether this shift in attitude was due to an *actual* increase in the amount and seriousness of crime or merely to citizens' *perceptions* that crime was increasing has been the subject of considerable debate. What is clear is that Canadians became more interested in developing systems for the control of crime — including police forces.

Again, Newfoundland provides a good illustration of the changes that were occurring at this time. The police force in St. John's during the early 1800s consisted of tavern-keepers who performed police duties in return for being granted licences to operate their businesses. In 1848, the first night-watch system was established in the city, consisting of 16 special constables and four constables under the supervision of a high constable. These officers were the predecessors of the Royal Newfoundland Constabulary, which was formed in 1872.

Similar developments were occurring in Upper Canada, with a full-time police force of six men replacing the night-watch system in Toronto in 1835. In 1858, the *Municipal Institutions of Upper Canada Act* authorized towns and cities to form police forces and to create boards of commissioners to oversee the activities of the police.

It was not unusual for police officers in early Canada to perform a variety of duties in addition to law enforcement. Among the tasks assigned to the municipal police constable in Sudbury, Ontario, for example, were jailer, engineer of the fire department, caretaker of the fire hall, tax collector, sanitary inspector, truant officer, bailiff, chimney inspector, and animal caretaker. Today, only RCMP officers posted to remote northern communities continue to provide a wide variety of services in addition to their policing duties.

Given the patterns of settlement in Canada, municipalities in the areas west of Upper Canada did not have organized policing and municipal police forces until the late 1800s. Calgary hired its first constable in 1885, and the city of Lethbridge appointed its first officer in 1891. In the absence of police forces, most communities maintained order on a self-policing basis, similar to that employed by the villages in England prior to the Industrial Revolution. Aboriginal peoples, of course, did have in place systems of social control and mechanisms for sanctioning behaviour deemed to be in violation of customary and traditional "law," although these systems were gradually displaced by the imposition of British law.

The lack of serious crime was also a reason for the late development of policing systems in the West. With the exception of the disorder caused by fortune-seekers, the Canadian West was relatively violence-free as compared to its U.S. counterpart. While the landscape of the American West was often littered with the victims of battles between indigenous peoples and the U.S. Cavalry, and the streets of frontier towns the scene of "high noon" shoot-outs, the Canadian West and its Aboriginal peoples were subdued with considerably less bloodshed (although the outcome of this conflict was the same). There are few instances from the early Canadian West of train and bank robberies, of battles between the Mounted Police and Aboriginal peoples, or of shoot-outs at high noon.

One of the unique attributes of policing in the Canadian West was the role played by agents of the Hudson's Bay Company. As late as the 1860s, these agents performed a variety of roles, including coroner, jailer, sheriff, and medical officer. As settlements grew in size, provisions were made for the appointment of constables, who were paid a small sum of money for carrying out peacekeeping duties.

In 1858, the first organized police force was created in the area that is now the province of British Columbia. Modelled after the Royal Irish Constabulary, this force was created in response to the increasing violence and disorder that had occurred with the discovery of gold deposits in the area. (This police force was the predecessor of the provincial police force that was formed in 1871 when British Columbia joined Confederation.) The governor and British authorities were also concerned that the United States had territorial ambitions in the area. Officers carried out policing duties, collected revenue and excise taxes, and provided emergency services in communities.

Police historians have identified at least three major functions that early municipal police forces carried out: (1) preventing conflicts between ethnic groups and between labour groups and industry; (2) maintaining the moral order through the enforcement of puritanical laws, particularly in the areas of prostitution and drinking; and (3) apprehending individuals involved in criminal activity.

Municipal police officers often carried out their tasks with considerable tolerance. This was reflected in a policy of non-intervention: officers often elected not to intervene in labour disputes out of sympathy with the workers and exhibited considerable tolerance for prostitution and alcohol use. Further, there were numerous instances of corruption and criminal activity among municipal police forces. When corrupt police officers were removed from office, their behaviour was rarely mentioned as the reason for dismissal: "When the boozing, brawling chief of the Winnipeg police was caught 'in flagrante delicto' in a Colony Creek whorehouse, he was fired because he was stupid enough to get caught" (Juliani, Talbot, and Garden, 1984:337).[2]

Early Provincial and Federal Policing

The emergence of provincial police forces following Confederation in 1867 was closely intertwined with the establishment and growth of the federal police force, now known as the Royal Canadian Mounted Police (RCMP). Under the provisions of the *Constitution Act, 1867*, the federal government was given the authority to enact criminal law and procedure, while the enforcement of laws and the administration of justice were delegated to the provinces. Provincial governments, through the office of the Attorney-General, were required to establish law enforcement agencies, courts, and correctional institutions.

While it would appear that the *Constitution Act, 1867,* clearly delegated to the provinces the authority to enforce the criminal law, in 1868 the federal Parliament passed the *Police of Canada Act*. This authorized the federal government to establish the Dominion Police Force, which was granted Canada-wide jurisdiction. The force had as its primary mandate the protection of federal buildings, including Parliament, although it later became involved in enforcing laws in the area of counterfeiting and providing security for naval shipyards and other government properties. Although the Dominion Police Force was absorbed by the RCMP in 1920, it was the first time a police authority had been created with jurisdiction beyond the municipal level, a precedent that was to provide the basis for the modern-day RCMP.

The terms of the *Constitution Act, 1867,* provided that, upon entry into Confederation, provinces would enact legislation providing for the creation of provincial police forces. Legislation authorizing the creation of provincial police forces was passed in Manitoba and Quebec in 1870, British Columbia in 1871, Ontario in 1909, New Brunswick in 1927, Nova Scotia in 1928, and Prince Edward Island in 1930. In Newfoundland, where the Royal Newfoundland Constabulary had been operating since 1872, a second provincial police force, the Newfoundland Company of Rangers, was formed in 1935.

Provincial police forces often experienced considerable difficulties in carrying out their mandate (as did the early municipal forces), due in large measure to political interference. These difficulties led to a greater involvement of the federal forces in policing at the provincial and municipal levels.

In fact, the governments of Alberta and Saskatchewan disrupted the established procedure for the creation of provincial police forces under the *Constitution Act, 1867,* by negotiating the federal forces to serve as provincial police. Following their entry into Confederation in 1905, these governments, like the other provinces before them, enacted legislation providing for provincial police forces, but unlike the others, they then entered into negotiations with the federal government for the services of the Royal North-West Mounted Police (RNWMP). Under contracts signed between the federal and provincial governments, the RNWMP would act as the provincial police under a cost-sharing agreement. There is no evidence that this action by the governments of the two provinces was ever challenged, although it clearly represented a significant departure from the intent of the *Constitution Act, 1867.*

The North-West Mounted Police (NWMP) had been created under the *Act of 23 May 1873,* to police the vast area known as Rupert's Land, which had been purchased from the Hudson's Bay Company in 1869. In 1904, its name was changed to the Royal North-West Mounted Police. In 1920, the name changed again to its present-day name, the Royal Canadian Mounted Police (RCMP).

The reasons behind the creation of this federal force have been the subject of considerable debate. It is generally assumed that the NWMP was established to maintain law and order among the settlers and to protect the indigenous Aboriginal population from unscrupulous traders and whiskey runners.

Other observers have presented a different image of the role of the NWMP. According to Horrall (1972), Morrison (1985), and others, the NWMP served much the same function as the Canadian Pacific Railway and was used by the federal government to establish political and economic sovereignty over the far reaches of the country. This included ensuring the orderly settlement of indigenous lands by white settlers and guarding against any attempt by the United States to annex portions of the northern frontier. Police historians have also examined the role that the Mounties played in labour disputes, including the 1906 Lethbridge

Strike (Baker, 1991) and in policing the Doukhobors in the Prairie provinces (Betke, 1974).

While there may be disagreement over the role that the mounted police played in early Canada, there is little doubt that the RCMP has become the most widely recognized symbol of Canada in the world, outdistancing the beaver. The exploits and daring of the Mounties were immortalized by Canadian, American, and European authors in such books as *Morgan of the Mounted* (White, 1939), *Tales of the Mounted* (Brockie, 1949), *Yukon Patrol* (Douthwaite, 1936), and *Arctic Patrols* (Campbell, 1937). With the advent of motion pictures, these exploits soon appeared on the silver screen.

While the stature and popularity of the Mounties have been extensively documented, it is not generally known that the force was beset with numerous internal difficulties in the early days of its existence and that considerable hostility was directed toward it by both settlers and federal legislators. Walden (1982) points out that there were many reasons for citizens to dislike the Mounties, including the fact that officers exercised extraordinary legal powers, acting as both police officers *and* magistrates and justices of the peace. This resulted in officers not only arresting suspected offenders, but conducting the trial and imposing sentences as well.

Morgan (1973), drawing from the historical record, presents evidence suggesting that the Mounties experienced high rates of desertion, resignations, and improper conduct, including drunkenness and illicit sexual alliances with women. These difficulties were ascribed to the isolation and harsh conditions of the frontier, inadequate housing and medical attention, and the failure of officers to be paid, often for months at a time. There is also the likelihood that criticism of the Mounties was, at least in part, politically motivated, a consequence of conflicts that often occurred between the Mounties and the municipal police forces. These conflicts created situations in which members of each force were arrested by the other. Illustrative of one community's sentiment toward the Mounties was an editorial that appeared in the Regina *Leader*, charging that "many a scalawag and scoundrel, many an idle loafer, many a brainless young blood, has worn its uniform and fed at its trough" (Morgan, 1973:60).

With the assumption of provincial policing responsibilities in Alberta and Saskatchewan in 1905, a major expansion of the Mounties' policing activities occurred. In these provinces, members of the force acted as both federal and provincial law enforcement officers. Alberta and Saskatchewan were policed by the Mounties until 1916, when the services of the force were withdrawn by mutual agreement of the provinces and the federal government. Both provinces then created provincial police forces in 1917. Exactly why the arrangement was terminated is unclear. The official reason given was that the federal police should be employed only for federal purposes, although it is likely that the onset of World War I and the desire of provincial politicians to have more direct control over the police were also factors in the decision to terminate the agreement (see Robertson 1978).

While other provinces had apparently been successful in establishing police forces, Alberta and Saskatchewan did not fare as well. The misfortunes of the Saskatchewan Provincial Police (SPP) were so extensive as to constituted a major source of embarrassment for the provincial authorities. One police historian has noted that, while many of the men recruited for the SPP were capable and experienced, others were merely "filling the gap...Some barely understood the words of their oath, while others would have been stumped to spell some of them" (Anderson, 1972:18). The lack of qualified manpower, inadequate physical facilities, poor equipment, and the reluctance of many municipalities in the province to contract for the services of the SPP contributed to its dissolution in 1928. The Alberta Provincial Police remained in operation until 1932. The RCMP resumed provincial policing duties in both provinces.

Throughout the 1930s and into the 1950s, the RCMP continued to expand into provincial policing, absorbing police forces in New Brunswick, Nova Scotia, and Prince Edward Island in 1932, and in Newfoundland and British Columbia in 1950. Again, there is no evidence that this expansion and its implications for the structure of Canadian policing was either discussed or debated. The RCMP were also to become extensively involved in policing at the municipal level. With these developments, only three provincial police forces remained: the Ontario Provincial Police, the Quebec Police Force, and the Newfoundland Constabulary.

CONTEMPORARY CANADIAN POLICING

Policing in Canada today is carried out at three levels: municipal, provincial, and federal. In 1991, there were nearly 57,000 police officers in the country (Canadian Centre for Justice Statistics, 1992:5). This figure represents a continuing growth in the number of police officers.[3]

Among the trends in Canadian policing as we head into the 1990s are the following.

- ► While the number of police officers has doubled since 1962, the number of reported *Criminal Code* offences has increased fivefold and the ratio of offences per officer has risen from 20 to 51 during this time period, indicating an increasing workload for officers.
- ► The number of female police officers has continued to increase and female officers now represent 7% of the total number of officers.
- ► There is considerable variability across the country in the "population per police officer" figures, ranging from one officer for every 695 persons in Prince Edward Island (the highest) to one officer per every 230 citizens in the Yukon and the Northwest Territories (the lowest).
- ► Total expenditures on policing continued to increase, totalling $5.3 billion in 1991.

In addition to the police forces operating at the municipal, provincial, and federal levels, there are several other less well-known police services.[4] These include the National Harbours Board Police, who primarily protect property owned by the National Harbours Board, and the Canadian Pacific Railways Police and the Canadian Pacific Investigation Service, which fulfill similar roles for their organizations. Urban centres such as Montreal, Toronto, and Vancouver have also developed transit police forces that provide security and protection for property and passengers. There has also been an exponential growth in private security police, who now outnumber their "public" police counterparts.

Recent years have also witnessed the emergence of several "autonomous" Aboriginal police forces that are involved in providing a full range of policing services on reserves as well as to Aboriginal communities. Among the larger Aboriginal police forces are the Amerindian Police Service, which is involved in policing a number of communities in Quebec, and the Dakota-Ojibway Tribal Council Police Force, which operates on several reserves near Brandon, Manitoba. The emergence of Aboriginal police forces is part of a larger trend toward increasing

Aboriginal involvement in, and control over, all facets of the criminal justice system. We will consider these initiatives and the issues surrounding them in greater detail in Chapter 15.

Municipal Police Forces

There are currently 588 municipal police forces operating across Canada, and municipal officers constitute the largest body of police personnel in the country. This includes municipalities that have either contracted for police services from the RCMP (191) or that have their own "independent" non-contract police force (397) (Canadian Centre for Justice Statistics, 1992).

Municipal police forces range in size from units of one or two officers in remote RCMP detachments to the over 6,000 members of the Montreal Urban Community Police Force. Municipal police officers enforce all laws relating to their area of jurisdiction, including the *Criminal Code,* provincial statutes, municipal by-laws, and, in recent years, certain federal statutes such as the *Narcotic Control Act.* Those municipalities that operate their own policing services generally assume the majority of the policing costs, with some assistance provided by the provincial governments.

In many communities, police boards oversee the activities of the municipal police force. First established during the 1850s in what is now the province of Ontario, police boards are in operation across the country, although there is little uniformity in pattern of development and in their specific activities. While all municipalities with their own police forces in British Columbia are required to have a police board, in Manitoba, only Brandon and Winnipeg have boards. Such boards have never existed in Quebec and Newfoundland (see Stenning, 1981a; 1981b). Although some boards are extensively involved in the preparation and control of the municipal police budget, others have a much more limited range of activity (see Hann *et al.,* 1985).

Many municipalities, rather than establishing and maintaining their own police forces, have chosen to contract with the provincial police force for municipal policing services. In all provinces except Quebec, provincial police forces are involved in municipal policing. In Ontario, policing services in some communities are provided by the Ontario Provincial Police (OPP) under contract, while in the remaining provinces, the RCMP, acting as the provincial police force, contracts to provide municipal policing services. This contract policing is authorized by the *Royal Canadian Mounted Police Act* and by provisions in provincial police legislation.[5]

While municipal police forces remain a dominant feature of contemporary Canadian policing, two trends could, in the long term, have a significant impact on the delivery of policing services: (1) the increasing control being exercised by provincial governments over municipal policing; and (2) the regionalization of municipal police forces.

Over the past two decades, most provinces have passed provincial police acts that set uniform policing standards for municipal police forces; provide for the creation of provincial police commissions, which monitor the performance of municipal police forces; and authorize provincial subsidization of municipal policing services. The precedent-setting legislation was the *Ontario Police Act* of 1946, which standardized provincial regulations for policing, established uniform discipline codes and procedures for handling complaints against the police, and set up a system for monitoring the performance of municipal police forces.

In 1962, Ontario created the first provincial police commission, which now has counterparts in seven provinces. While the specific activities of provincial police commissions vary, their roles generally centre around developing policing standards, promoting research into police issues, and exercising appellate jurisdiction over internal disciplinary matters and over complaints against municipal police officers. Provincial police commissions are also involved in training programs for provincial and municipal police officers.

The Ontario Police Commission operates the Ontario Police College at Aylmer, Ontario, and the British Columbia Police Commission oversees the programs of the British Columbia Police Academy in Vancouver. In Quebec and Ontario, provincial police commissions monitor activities of both the provincial police forces and municipal police services, while in the remaining provinces, police commission activities are directed only toward non-RCMP municipal forces. RCMP officers involved in policing municipalities and provinces under contract are subject to a separate system of accountability, involving the RCMP Public Complaints Commissioner.

In addition, several provinces have established police academies to standardize the training of municipal police officers. The Atlantic Police Academy, located in Charlottetown, Prince Edward Island, serves the provinces of Prince Edward Island, Nova Scotia, and New Brunswick, and is funded by the provinces and the federal government. The training program, which began in 1971, includes a basic recruit training course as well as specialized courses.

In British Columbia, the British Columbia Police Academy, which is situated at the Justice Institute of British Columbia in Vancouver, operates a municipal recruit training program — a series of five "blocks" of training spread over three years. Under the *Police Act* of British Columbia, successful completion of this training course is a prerequisite for permanent admission to a municipal police force. L'Institut de police du Quebec provides basic training, in-service training, and specialized training for both provincial and municipal police officers in Quebec, while the Ontario Police College provides a similar training facility for police officers in Ontario.

Another trend that has the potential to reshape the structure of municipal policing in Canada is regionalization, which generally involves the amalgamation of a number of police forces in a metropolitan area into one police organization. The move to regionalization began in the early 1960s. From 1962 to 1977, 150 municipal police forces in Ontario were involved in amalgamation, the largest force created being the Peel Regional Police Force. Ten regional police forces provide policing services to more than 50% of Ontario's population. A similar regional police force, the Montreal Urban Community Police Force, was formed in 1972 to police Montreal and surrounding areas. Regionalization is currently under consideration in the Lower Mainland area of British Columbia (1990). In fact, regional policing is quite widespread across Canada. The Quebec and Ontario provincial police provide centralized policing services within their respective jurisdictions, and the RCMP have a centralized division headquarters in provinces where they serve as the provincial and municipal police. Regionalization of police forces will likely continue to be a viable option for jurisdictions seeking to increase cost-efficiency in recruitment, training, and the allocation of resources.

Proponents contend that regionalized police forces are more effective in providing a full range of services to the community, are less expensive in the long term than operating a number of smaller departments, and that regional police forces create an equity situation where everyone contributes to the costs of policing services and receives equal protection. Critics, however, contend that regionalization will result in higher police costs (particularly during the start-up phase) and that a large regional force would be distant from the community and not amenable to local control. The lack of research studies on the experiences with regionalization in Quebec and Ontario, however, preclude an assessment of whether the stated objectives have been achieved and of the validity of the concerns that have been expressed.

In British Columbia, a study of regional policing (British Columbia, 1990) found widespread support among police executives for some form of regionalized policing in the Vancouver metropolitan area and in the Capital Regional District surrounding Victoria, although mayors and police board members tended to oppose the move to regional policing. As of 1992, no specific plans for regionalization in either of the two areas had been developed.

Provincial Police Forces

As mentioned earlier, only three provincial police forces are operating in Canada today: the OPP, the Quebec Police Force, and the Newfoundland Constabulary, which today polices only the city of St. John's. Provincial police forces are responsible for policing areas outside of municipalities and for the enforcement of provincial laws and the *Criminal Code*.

Provincial police forces may also be involved in policing municipalities under contract. In all provinces except Quebec and Ontario, this is done by the RCMP. Under the *Ontario Police Act*, the OPP contract to provide municipal policing services, and in 1991 were policing in 13 communities. There is, however, no provision under law for the Quebec Police Force to contract to provide municipal policing services. The Ontario and Quebec provincial police also operate Native Special Constable programs, which involve the recruitment and training of Aboriginal peoples to police on reserves in these two provinces.

The Royal Canadian Mounted Police

Canada's federal police force, the RCMP, is organized under the authority of the *Royal Canadian Mounted Police Act* and is headed by a commissioner under the direction of the Solicitor General of Canada. The RCMP operates in all provinces and territories to enforce those federal statutes for which it is responsible, such as the *Narcotic Control Act*, the *Food and Drugs Act*, and the *Indian Act*. The RCMP also provides provincial and municipal policing services under contract. The RCMP is the only police force in the Yukon Territory and in the Northwest Territories and operates under agreements signed between the federal government and the territorial governments.

In 1991, the RCMP had 15,555 personnel, which was approximately 28% of all police personnel in Canada. These officers were deployed as follows: municipal policing (20%); provincial policing (34%); federal policing (30%); and other duties, including administration (16%) (Canadian Centre for Justice Statistics, 1992).

The RCMP is organized into 16 divisions (Figure 3.1), with headquarters usually located in the provincial and territorial capitals. When acting in the capacity of a federal police force, the RCMP does not normally enforce the *Criminal Code* unless it receives a request from a federal government department to investigate allegations of fraud connected with the use of public funds or when it lays a conspiracy charge in relation to a drug offence under the *Narcotic Control Act* or the *Food and Drugs Act*.

The RCMP provides a 12-month training program for its recruits. Basic recruit training is a 25-week course at the training depot in Regina, Saskatchewan, where recruits undergo a rigorous course structured around both physical activities and academic studies. Based on the British Cavalry model, the recruits train in groups of 32, and the training course stresses peer pressure and peer accountability. Academic courses range from the technical aspects of the police role (including report writing, identification processes, and the study of federal statutes) to courses in human relations. Following successful completion of the training course in Regina, the recruits enter a six-month practical component in a field training detachment.

It should be noted that the RCMP does not act in isolation, even when operating as a federal police force. The force operates several different branches that serve as an information resource for all police departments in the country. These include the Economic Crime Branch, which provides assistance in the investigation of economic crimes (such as money laundering and fraud), and the National Crime Intelligence Branch, which combats organized crime and cooperates with special units in municipal and provincial police forces.

Through its "L" Directorate, the RCMP provides the services of its Crime Detection Laboratories, which are located across the country, and Identification Services (fingerprints, criminal history files, etc.). The "V" Directorate includes the Canadian Police Information Centre (CPIC), a computerized information system providing police forces with instant

FIGURE 3.1
ORGANIZATION OF THE ROYAL CANADIAN MOUNTED POLICE

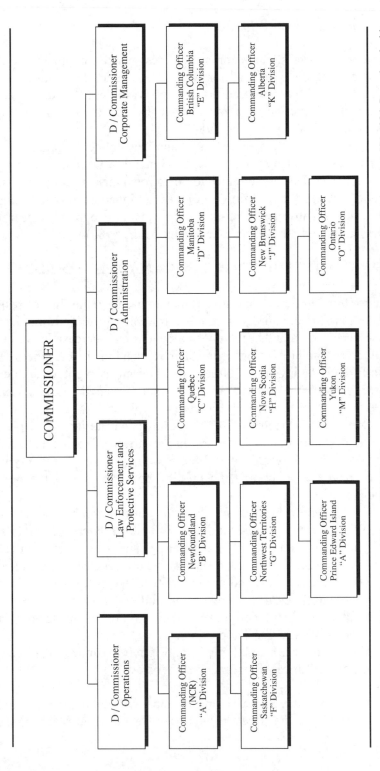

Source: Solicitor General of Canada. *Annual Report, 1988-89.* (Ottawa: Supply and Services Canada, 1990), p. 22. Catalogue no. JS1-1986. Reproduced with permission of the Minister of Supply and Services Canada.

information on criminal records, vehicles, wanted or missing persons, stolen property, and persons for whom there is an outstanding warrant. While the RCMP were traditionally responsible for internal security matters, this function was taken over by the Canadian Intelligence Service, a civilian agency, in 1984.

The RCMP also operates the Canadian Police College, a training facility that is funded by the Solicitor General of Canada. The programs at the police college are intended to be national in scope and purpose, and include education and training courses designed to provide Canadian police forces with upgrading and development programs, research and information, and advisory services (see Muir, 1986).[6]

THE ROLE OF THE POLICE IN CANADIAN SOCIETY

A major trend in Canadian criminal justice has been the shift of responsibility for maintaining order from the community level to formal agencies of social control, and that there was a concurrent decrease in community involvement in preventing crime and responding to offenders. While initially undertaking fairly limited tasks, such as night watchmen and watching for fires, policing agencies soon assumed a wider range of duties previously handled by the community.

One consequence of these trends has been the increased pressures upon modern-day police forces to play a variety of roles and to achieve a number of objectives. Today there is considerable uncertainty on the part of both the police and the public about the role of the police in Canadian society.

Police forces have a number of general goals, including: (1) preventing crime; (2) apprehending criminal offenders; (3) maintaining order in the community; (4) regulating and controlling traffic; (5) responding to non-law enforcement emergencies such as traffic accidents, lost and injured persons, and crowd control; and (6) providing information to the public on crime prevention and on various resources in the community, such as victim and witness programs, mental health resources, and social service programs.

These and the other activities that might be assigned to police forces can be grouped under three major categories:

> ▸ *crime control:* responding to and investigating crimes and patrolling the streets to prevent offences from reoccurring;

▶ *order maintenance:* preventing and controlling behaviour that disturbs the public peace, including quieting loud parties, responding to (and often mediating) domestic and neighbourhood disputes, and intervening in conflicts that arise between citizens; and

▶ *service:* the provision of a wide range of services to the community, often as a consequence of the 24-hour availability of the police, including assisting in the search for missing persons and acting as an information/referral agency.

Police officers are often called upon to do the "dirty work" of society: they are often the first to encounter social problems in the community, whether these centre on the homeless street people, conflicts between ethnic groups, the breakdown of families, drug and alcohol abuse, or violence.

While it is often the law enforcement/crime control role of the police that has traditionally assumed primacy in the minds of both police officers and the general public, research conducted in Canada and the United States indicates that crime control activities generally occupy less than 25% of police officers' time and, for most officers, this figure is considerably lower.

CALLING THE POLICE: PATTERNS OF CRIME REPORTING

The majority of crimes are brought to the attention of the police by the general public and are responded to by uniformed patrol officers.[7] In fact, the Canadian Urban Victimization Survey (CUVS) conducted in the early 1980s, found that only 3% of crime victimizations were discovered by the police without the assistance of the public (Solicitor General of Canada, 1983a; 1983b). The more recent General Social Survey (GSS) found that, in those instances in which the police did find out about a criminal victimization, it was a consequence of reporting action taken by the victim (Sacco and Johnson, 1988).[8]

In effect, crime victims, as well as others who may notify the authorities (bystanders, witnesses, relatives of the victims), are the gatekeepers of the criminal justice system. A considerable amount of research in North America has focused on the extent to which criminal behaviour is reported (and underreported) by the victims and witnesses of crime.

Studies that have examined the calls placed to the police by citizens have consistently revealed that the majority of requests made of the police relate to order maintenance, the provision of information, and other service-related activities (see Ericson, 1982). In his study of citizen mobilization of the police in an eastern Canadian city, Shearing (1984:20-22) found that calls to the police broke down into the following categories.

internal police business: 23.6%
accidents, collapses, illness: 16.3%
suspicious circumstances: 8.9%
traffic problems: 8.7%
public nuisance: 7.4%
other types of calls: 7.3%
services: 7.2%
reports of thefts: 6.7%
disputes: 5.5%
response of fire department and/or ambulance service: 3.4%
report of injury or damage to person or property: 2.5%
return calls: 2.2%
robbery or hold-up: 0.3%

Of particular interest in Shearing's findings is the high percentage of calls that were related to internal police business and the fact that, although the police department studied was in a large metropolitan area, only a small percentage of the calls related to law enforcement or order maintenance. However, Shearing (1984:29) points out that many of the calls that come in relating to order maintenance, for example, domestic disputes, have the potential to become law enforcement matters.

The findings of research conducted in Canada are generally consistent with those of studies done in the States. Among the more significant findings of the CUVS and the GSS relating to crime reporting are the following.

▸ *There is a "dark figure" of crime that is not reflected in official crime statistics.*

This "dark figure" is a consequence of the failure of the public to report a wide range of criminal offences to the police. The CUVS found that more than half (58%) of estimated incidents involving victims were never brought to the attention of the police. In the GSS, it was revealed that the police found out about only 40% of the incidents that had occurred among the sample surveyed.

▸ *The likelihood of victims calling the police is not related to the seriousness of the crime.*

The GSS found that the highest reporting rates were for incidents involving break and enters (70%) and the theft of motor vehicles (57%). Household incidents had a higher report rate (54%) than personal incidents (40%). Victims were least likely to call the police in incidents involving assault (30%) and robbery (32%). One of the highest report rates in the CUVS (70%) was for motor vehicle theft, providing us with some idea of the value that people attach to their cars (see Table 3.1).

Most disturbing was the finding that the police were called in less than half (44%) of incidents involving spousal assault. This finding suggests that the massive underreporting of crime extends to even more serious, personal offences. There is no evidence to indicate whether female victims of domestic assault are more willing to report incidents to the police in the early 1990s than they were ten years ago.

Among victims of spousal assault surveyed in the GSS, for example, the three most common reasons given for *not* calling the police were: (1) it was a personal matter and not a matter for the police (59%); (2) the police would not be able to do anything about it (52%); and (3) a fear of revenge from the offender (52%). For female victims of violence in the GSS, the fear of revenge was the primary factor (38% versus 4% for males) in non-reporting.

▸ *There are variations in reporting patterns across different regions of the country.*

The CUVS found significant differences in reporting rates between the seven cities included in the study (see Table 3.2). Specifically, there was a 7% difference between the city with the highest reporting rate (Montreal) and the city with the lowest reporting rate (Vancouver). The reporting rate differences between the cities were much larger for specific

TABLE 3.1

NUMBER OF INCIDENTS OF SELECTED TYPES AND PROPORTION NOT REPORTED TO POLICE IN SEVEN CITIES

Type of Incident	Estimated Incidents	Percent of Estimated Incidents	Percent Unreported	Percent Reported
Sexual Assault	17,200	1	62	38
Robbery	49,300	3	55	45
Assault	285,700	18	66	34
Break and Enter	227,400	14	36	64
Motor Vehicle Theft	40,600	3	30	70
Household Theft	417,300	26	71	29
Personal Theft	349,900	22	71	29
Vandalism	213,100	13	65	35
TOTAL	1,600,500	100	58	42

Source: *Bulletin No. 1. Canadian Urban Victimization Survey: Victims of Crime* (Ottawa: Programs Branch, Research and Statistics Group, Solicitor General Canada, 1983), p. 3. Reproduced with permission of the Minister of Supply and Services Canada, 1993.

TABLE 3.2
PERCENT OF INCIDENTS COMING TO ATTENTION OF THE POLICE, BY CITY

	Percent Reported in Seven Cities	Vancouver	Edmonton	Winnipeg	Toronto	Montreal	Halifax Dartmouth	St. John's	Reported Range
Sexual Assault	38	32(5)*	15(7)	33(4)	40(2)	50(1)	29(6)	40(3)	(15-50)
Robbery	45	43(6)	46(1)	42(7)	46(2)	45(3)	45(4)	44(5)	(42-46)
Assault	34	34(4)	32(6)	23(7)	36(2)	39(1)	35(3)	33(5)	(23-39)
Break and Enter	64	61(7)	62(5)	62(4)	65(3)	66(2)	61(6)	68(1)	(61-68)
Motor Vehicle Theft	70	71(6)	77(1)	73(4)	72(5)	67(7)	74(3)	74(2)	(67-77)
Household Theft	44	39(7)	46(4)	47(3)	46(5)	46(6)	48(1)	48(2)	(39-48)
Personal Theft	29	29(4)	30(3)	25(7)	30(2)	31(1)	28(5)	26(6)	(25-31)
Vandalism	35	29(6)	39(2)	38(3)	37(4)	36(5)	40(1)	27(7)	(27-40)
Overall Percentage Reported	42	38(7)	42(4)	40(5)	42(3)	45(1)	42(2)	39(6)	(38-45)
Overall Percentage Not Reported	58	62	57	60	58	55	58	61	

*Numbers in brackets indicate the rank-ordering of cities within offence categories. A "1" indicates the city with the highest percentage reported, and a "7" indicates the city with the lowest percentage of reported incidents.

Source: *Bulletin No. 2. Canadian Urban Victimization Survey: Reported and Unreported Crime* (Ottawa: Programs Branch, Research and Statistics Group, Solicitor General Canada, 1983), p. 5. Reproduced with permission of the Minister of Supply and Services Canada, 1993.

offence categories, suggesting regional differences in attitudes about particular crimes and differences in the perceived benefits to be gained from reporting. Note that this survey was conducted among urban residents. Few data exist on the patterns of victimization and reporting in remote areas of the country, particularly among Aboriginal peoples.

▸   *There are age and, perhaps, gender differences in reporting by crime victims.*

The GSS found that in only 20% of the personal incidents involving younger persons (15-24) were the police called, while the reporting rate for victims aged 45-64 was 54%. The GSS found no reporting differences between males and females, although women were more likely to report incidents in order to stop or prevent them from reoccurring and to receive protection from the criminal justice system. These findings are somewhat different from those of the CUVS, which found that women were more likely than men to telephone the police for both personal and property-related offences.

▸   *There appears to be a "utilitarian" factor at work in the decisions of victims to either mobilize or not to mobilize the police.*

While a high percentage of victims (70% in the GSS and 66% in the CUVS) did not report their victimization because they felt it was not serious enough to warrant official intervention, the second most frequent reason given in both studies was that the police could not do anything about it (see Table 3.3). While this finding might be interpreted as evidence of suspicion or distrust of the police, it may be that citizens have fairly accurate knowledge of the limits of the police in catching the perpetrator. Crime victims, through their decision making to report or not to report an incident, filter out a large number of relatively minor offences that may more effectively be resolved without police intervention. In Figures 3.2 and 3.3, the reasons for the failure to report personal violent offences and property offences are presented.

In exploring why victims *did* call the police following a victimization, the GSS found that the primary reasons were a desire to "stop the incident or prevent an occurrence" (77%) and to "catch and punish the offender" (80%). For property-related offences, particularly motor vehicle

TABLE 3.3

REASONS GIVEN BY VICTIMS FOR FAILURE TO REPORT INCIDENTS TO THE POLICE

Reasons	Percent of All Unreported Incidents
No Perceived Benefit	
Too Minor	66
Police Couldn't Do Anything	61
Nothing Taken/Items Recovered	19
Costs Outweigh Benefits	
Inconvenience	24
Fear of Revenge	4
Concern with Attitude of Police or Courts	8
Personal Reasons	
Protect Offender	6
Personal Matter	13
Reported to Another Official	12
Overall Percent Unreported	58

Percentages do not add to 100% since respondents could indicate more than one reason for failure to report any one incident.

Source: *Bulletin No. 2. Canadian Urban Victimization Survey: Reported and Unreported Crime* (Ottawa: Programs Branch, Research and Statistics Group, Solicitor General Canada, 1983), p. 3. Reproduced with permission of the Minister of Supply and Services Canada, 1993

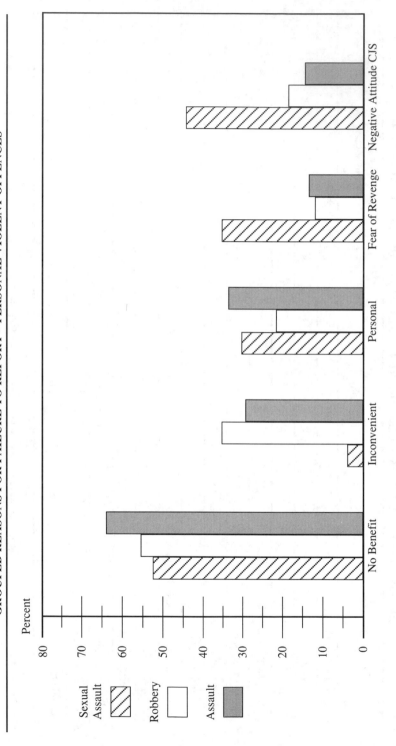

FIGURE 3.2

GROUPED REASONS FOR FAILURE TO REPORT – PERSONAL VIOLENT OFFENCES

Source: *Bulletin No. 2. Canadian Urban Victimization Survey: Reported and Unreported Crime* (Ottawa: Programs Branch, Research and Statistics Group, Solicitor General Canada, 1983), p. 5. Reproduced with permission of the Minister of Supply and Services Canada, 1993.

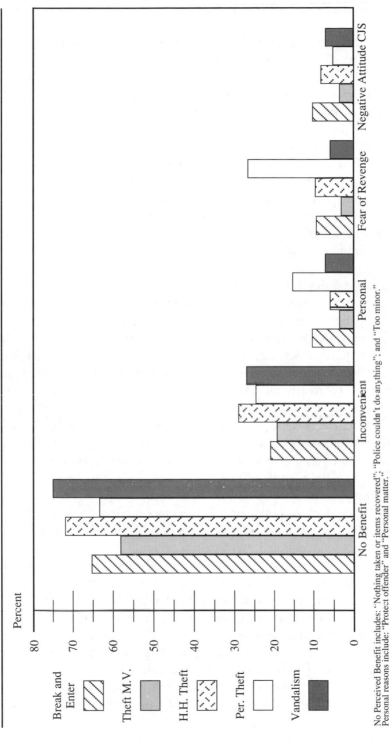

FIGURE 3.3

GROUPED REASONS FOR FAILURE TO REPORT — PROPERTY OFFENCES

No Perceived Benefit includes: "Nothing taken or items recovered"; "Police couldn't do anything"; and "Too minor."
Personal reasons include: "Protect offender" and "Personal matter."

Source: *Bulletin No. 2 Canadian Urban Victimization Survey: Report and Unreported Crime* (Ottawa: Programs Branch, Research and Statistics Group, Solicitor General Canada, 1983), p. 5.
Reproduced with permission of the Minister of Supply and Services Canada, 1992.

theft, a primary reason for reporting was the requirement of a police report when filing an insurance claim.

▸ *The victim's attitudes toward the police may have a significant impact on the decision to call the police.*

Having been a victim of a crime affected a person's attitudes toward the police, often in a negative fashion. Citizens' perceptions of the police also appear to affect reporting patterns. The CUVS found that citizens who rated police performance favourably were more likely to report victimizations. The findings suggest that it is contact with the police after a victimization that may create negative attitudes, which might mitigate against calling the police in future incidents.

The preceding discussion has revealed that a variety of factors influence the decision to mobilize the police. While in many instances crime victims, through their decision not to report, screen out minor cases for the police, there are some disturbing findings as well. First, many serious personal incidents go unreported, particularly those in which the victim is young. Second, it is clear that women who are victims of violence are reluctant to call the police for fear of revenge. Finally, many people feel (correctly, in many instances) that the police will not be able to do anything about their victimization, particularly in terms of capturing the perpetrator or recovering their lost property. These findings have significant implications not only for the police and their relationship to the community, but also for how the criminal justice system as a whole is viewed by the victims of crime.

Thus far, our discussion has centred on why citizens and victims choose to contact the police or not when a crime has occurred. However, it is also important to consider what happens if there is a delay in calling the police. Conventional wisdom in policing has long held that by reducing the response time — the amount of time it takes a patrol car to arrive at the "scene of the crime" — the police will increase their catch rate. Some evidence from studies in the United States (see Spelman and Brown, 1983), however, suggests that it is *citizen-reporting time*, and not police response time, that is the most critical factor in increasing the likelihood of arrests. Scholars and police agencies should focus on the reasons why people delay in calling the police.

Also, studies should be carried out to see whether the 9-1-1 emergency number system has reduced call delay. In one of the first studies conducted on the 9-1-1 system in the United States, Spelman and Brown (1983:166) found that 9-1-1 systems did not significantly improve citizen reporting times. Because of widespread police publicity that the 9-1-1 number was to be used only for emergencies, most callers took the time to look up the department's telephone number in the telephone book.

Demands on Police

In considering the demands that are placed on police officers, it is important to remember that there may be considerable variation between police departments in the activities of patrol officers. This may be due to the particular organizational priorities of the department and the demands placed upon the police by the task or policing environment in which they operate. The task environment of a police department is comprised of the community and the areas that are being policed, the demographic characteristics, including the size and composition (age, ethnicity, etc.) of the population, and the nature and extent of criminal activity in the area. It should not be automatically assumed, for example, that police officers in urban areas spend a greater proportion of their time on law enforce-ment-related activities, particularly since the highest rates of *Criminal Code* violations per 100,000 population in Canada occur in the more rural and remote areas of the country. In Chapters 4 and 5, we will consider further the mobilization of the police by the community, as well as the police response to citizen requests for assistance.

It is clear that many of the demands that are made upon police officers are of a "social problem" nature, and we must understand that the police, being reactive, have only a limited ability to address the underly-ing causes of conflicts to which they are called. Rather, they are largely limited to responding to the *symptoms* of deeper societal or personal problems. It is thus unrealistic to expect that the police, with certain exceptions, can actually prevent crime. Rather, they respond to crime.

With the advent of modern policing philosophies such as "commun-ity-based policing," police departments and their officers have been asked to adopt a much broader mandate and to expand their activities beyond the singular focus on law enforcement. In Chapter 5, we'll consider community-based policing, its basic principles, and the extent to which Canadian police departments have adopted this philosophy. There is little doubt that the implementation of community-based policing will result in significant changes in the organizational structure of police departments as well as in the manner in which patrol officers are trained, deployed, and evaluated.

There is, of course, a danger in continuing to organize and deliver police services as if crime control were the primary activity of the police. Such an approach places the police in the position of being responsible for crime control, even though it has been well established that the causes of crime, be they social, political, cultural, or psychological, are largely beyond the ability of the police to impact. In addition, past experience has indicated that the law enforcement model of policing has functioned to isolate the police from the community and to rob the police of access to the assistance of community groups, citizens, and organizations.

Among the arguments made by police scholars and progressive police leaders today is that a more holistic approach to policing is required in order for the police to become more effective. As we shall see, in a community-based policing framework, the police become one of many partners in responding not only to the symptoms of disorder, but also to the causes of such disorder.

As we head into the final decade of the twentieth century, there is little doubt that the environment within which Canadian police forces are carrying out their tasks is changing. Normandeau and Leighton (1990) identified the following trends that will have a significant impact on the demands placed upon the police.

- ▸ An aging Canadian population will result in a greater dependency upon non-crime-related police services, a slowing of the crime rate, but an increasing fear of crime.
- ▸ An increasing ethnic and cultural diversity in Canadian society will further enhance the cultural mosaic across the country. Two-thirds of arriving immigrants currently settle in the major urban centres of Vancouver, Toronto, and Montreal. These and other cities are also attracting increasing numbers of Aboriginal peoples from rural and remote areas. Police forces will need to adapt their recruitment, training, and delivery of services to reflect the diverse needs of multicultural communities and neighbourhoods.
- ▸ Economic, political, social, and cultural trends will result in more sophisticated types of crimes, the "globalization" of crime, and an increase in crime in the major metropolitan areas of the country due to increasing cultural and economic

diversity. In addition, there will be conflicts over environmental issues, such as logging, Aboriginal land claims, and deteriorating social conditions in urban areas. It is likely, for example, that police agencies will assume a much more proactive and expanded role in the enforcement of environmental law in the coming years (see Kwasniak, 1992).

These and other changes in Canadian society will place even greater demands upon police organizations and accelerate the adoption of new models of service delivery such as community-based policing. The pressures of societal and organizational change will perhaps be felt most intensely by line-level patrol officers — those who are on the "front lines" of the policing effort. This requires that we consider the occupational perspective of patrol officers and the conflicting demands that are often placed upon them.

THE POLICE OCCUPATION

For Canadian line-level patrol officers, a number of sources of conflict may have a significant impact on how they carry out their tasks and on their relations with the communities they serve. One major source of frustration for police officers is the discrepancy between the traditional conception of the police role as "crime fighters" and the actual requests that are made of the police by the community. In other words, the difference between what the police think they should be doing and what they are actually asked to do.

A second source of conflict for police officers is the uncertain and often conflicting expectations that communities have of the police. The relationship between the police and the public is critical, for the police rely heavily upon the public for mobilization. Unfortunately, the police often feel that the community is not clear and consistent in its expectations. This dilemma has been succinctly described by Weiner:

> On the one hand, the public expects the police to be the symbol of authority, to enforce the law, and to prevent crime. On the other hand, the public also expects the police to provide services and to maintain public order. At the same time, they resent the policeman's presence when he uses his authority, or when he inconveniences them, or when his response is not quick enough. And, they resent the policeman

when he intrudes upon them, at which point they often ask, "Why are you bothering honest people? Why don't you do something useful, like catch a crook?" (1976:16).

Evidence suggests that Canadians expect their police forces to perform a wide range of tasks. In their survey of Nova Scotians, Murphy and Clairmont (1990) found that citizens in both rural and urban areas wanted the police to perform a broad social role that included not only the traditional policing activities, but also such services as making school presentations, increased interaction with the community, and greater concern for the needs of minorities and victims of crime.

A third factor that often causes conflict is the problems associated with policing in a democratic society. In carrying out their tasks, police officers must balance the need to assert authority and maintain order while respecting the rights and freedoms of citizens. This issue has assumed even greater importance with the enactment of the *Canadian Charter of Rights and Freedoms.* In our discussion of police powers and decision making in Chapters 4 and 5, we will see that, while police officers have considerable powers at their disposal, the full force of the law is invoked infrequently. This requires officers to develop a variety of strategies for managing the conflicts and contingencies they encounter.

As a consequence of these and other conflicts surrounding the police occupation, many police observers have argued that police officers develop a "working personality," or a set of attitudes and behaviours that separate the police from the public. In his classic work *Justice Without Trial*, Jerome Skolnick proposed the existence of such a "working personality" and identified its source:

> The police, as a result of the combined features of their social situation, tend to develop ways of looking at the world distinctive to themselves, cognitive lenses through which to see situations and events. The strength of the lenses may be weaker or stronger depending upon certain conditions, but they are ground on a similar axis (1966:42).

Among the components of the working personality of the police that have been identified by police scholars are: (1) a preoccupation with danger; (2) excessive suspiciousness of people and situations; (3) a protective cynicism; and (4) the difficulties associated with exercising authority. While policing is less hazardous than many other occupations in society, including construction, transportation, and work associated with natural resources (for example, mining and logging), officers come to be preoccupied with danger largely because of the unpredictable nature of many of the people and events they encounter. This may lead to officers developing suspicious views of the community and the people they police.

An additional component of the police personality is cynicism toward the community or toward particular groups or neighbourhoods with which there is regular contact. This cynicism is largely a defensive mechanism and a response to the fact that the police tend only to see the negative side of the human condition.

In considering the working personality of police officers, we should remember that, in the final analysis, each patrol officer is an individual and there may be different types of working personalities among officers. An attempt to refine the concept of the working personality of the police has been made by Broderick (1987), who categorized officers in his study on the basis of the emphasis that they placed upon: (1) the needs for social order or (2) due process and the constitutional rights of citizens. (Again, one of the difficulties faced by police officers in a democratic society is the need to balance the control of crime and disorder with the rights of individual citizens.)

From his inquiry, Broderick (1987) identified four types of working personality among police officers: (1) *the idealists* (high emphasis on social order, high emphasis on due process); (2) *the enforcers* (high emphasis on social order, low emphasis on due process); (3) *the optimists* (low emphasis on social order, high emphasis on due process); and (4) *the realists* (low emphasis on social order, low emphasis on due process). While Broderick cautions us that these are only "ideal types"— that officers may only approximate one type of personality or another — his work nevertheless represents an important contribution to the policing literature and provides the basis for additional research on the concept of the working personality.

The working personality of police officers is a component of the larger occupational subculture of the police. Two major attributes of the occupation subculture of the police are: (1) the social isolation of police officers from the community, with a resulting solidarity among officers that includes a "blue shield" of secrecy and in-group support, and (2) police perceptions that the public is hostile and/or unappreciative and nonsupportive of their efforts.

A widely held view in policing literature is that police officers are isolated from the communities they serve. In his early work on the police, Westley (1953) used the term "pariah" to describe officers' feelings of social estrangement from the community. Contemporary police observers have characterized police-community relations such as the following:

> Because police officers are, by occupational prescription, inclined to be suspicious, they tend to isolate themselves from an unsympathetic, critical, untrustworthy, and uncomprehending community, and to form their own in-group alliances with fellow officers (Radalet, 1986:95).

Although the working personality and occupational subculture of the police appear throughout the policing literature, an emerging body of research in Canada and the United States has called these concepts into question. Research findings suggest that there may be considerable diversity in the extent to which officers exhibit the attributes of a working personality or adhere to an occupational perspective that includes feelings of social isolation and nonsupport by a hostile public.

A primary determinant appears to be the policing or "task environ-ment" in which police officers work. It might be expected that patrol officers working in large urban police departments, particularly those who are assigned to high crime/high trouble areas, might be more suspicious of the general public and perceive the community to be hostile toward them. Conversely, it is unlikely that officers policing in smaller towns and in remote settlements, where policing is more "personal," would display attitudes and behaviours similar to their urban counterparts. In our examination of public perceptions of the police, we will see that the majority of Canadians residing in both rural and urban areas have favourable images of the police, leading one to question the source of police perceptions that communities are hostile and nonsupportive.

Further questions about police officers as social isolates have been raised by Canadian research. In a study of an Ontario police department, Vincent (1990) found that while those officers who had been in police work for a long period of time and had a higher rank in the organization tended to socialize with other officers, this was not the case with the younger, more educated officers who had a wider circle of friends. While one high-ranking officer stated that he did not "feel at home with outsiders," a younger officer in the same department commented: "No, I don't go out with a lot of other cops...I'm getting tired of cop talk. I want a fuller life. I want to be accepted, not because I'm a cop, but because I am me" (Vincent, 1990:105).

Similarly, in a study of the Cape Breton Police Force, Poel (1985:10) found that only 36% of the officers expressed feelings of isolation from the public and other professionals in the criminal justice system. Interestingly, in Poel's (1985) sample, it was the younger officers and part-time constables that expressed the greatest feelings of isolation, a marked contrast from Vincent's study (1990). These conflicting findings suggest that there may be considerable variability between police departments, and between officers in the same police organization, in the extent to which there are feelings of isolation from the community. While the risk of isolation may be potentially acute in remote and rural areas, particularly in the case of non-Aboriginal officers policing an Aboriginal community, such a policing environment may also provide a unique opportunity for the development of positive police-community relations that is generally absent in urban areas.

Rather than viewing relations with the public in an "us versus them" perspective, it appears that police officers make a distinction between the general public, which is viewed as holding supportive (or at least neutral) attitudes toward the police, and a smaller segment of the population that has high rates of conflict with the police and is viewed as presenting difficulties for both the police and the community. Shearing (1981) found, for example, that officers made a distinction between the general public, whom they did things *for*, and the "dregs" or "scum" in the community, whom they did things *to*.

Among the officers interviewed by McGahan in St. John's, there was the perception that public respect for and cooperation with the police varied across the various districts in the city:

> Mount Pearl is excellent. Really good. No problems there. Mostly because it is residential and there's nothing much there to pose any problems, really. So people are fairly cooperative because you are not in there all the time...It's the type of people you are dealing with. These types that you have here and in Buckmaster Circle and Chalker Place, where the problems are, that's where you'll have no cooper-ation. They just go hand in hand (1984:165).

In fact, the above perceptions are supported by research conducted by Murphy and Lithopolous (1988) in Toronto that found variations in attitudes toward the police, not only across neighbourhoods in the city, but among various groups within neighbourhoods as well. In Chapter 5, we will examine how police officers categorize situations and people and how this has an impact on the decisions that officers make in encounter situations with the public.

It could be argued that line-level patrol officers constitute a distinct subculture within police organizations. Among the shared attributes of patrol officers are: (1) the relegation of patrol officers to the lowest levels of the police organization, often with little opportunity for upward mobility; (2) the fact that the discretionary powers of patrol officers are subject to greater scrutiny than are those exercised by police administrators, making line-level officers more vulnerable to public criticism; and (3) the fact that patrol officers are often the recipients of a one-way flow of communication from the administrative levels.

A major source of stress for patrol officers may be the senior leadership in the police department. As police organizations have grown in size and complexity, many line-level officers have become isolated and detached. Chris Braiden (1991:13), a superintendent with the Edmonton Police Service, argues that there has been a "flight from the front" whereby officers attempt to transfer out of line-level patrol work to specialized police units: "Taking calls-for-service...has become the lowest rung on the status ladder." Braiden (1991) argues that patrol officers have no sense of ownership in their work and "they don't see themselves as part of the problem, or the solution." The concerns raised by Braiden and other police observers have significant implications, not only for individual officers, but for the success of initiatives such as community-based policing (see also Braiden, 1990).

To this end, police scholars and police leaders are giving increased attention to job satisfaction among patrol officers. A survey (Rossmo and Glackman, 1991) of officers who had resigned from an urban police department in western Canada during a one-year period found that the majority of officers had joined another police department, indicating that a major reason for their departure was dissatisfaction with the organization itself. Among the reasons cited by the departed officers were the distant attitude of management, the centralization of bureaucratic power, and the department's promotion system.

As Rossmo and Glackman (1991:10) note: "A significant portion of those in the constable rank feel that their devotion to the job is not being reciprocated by management...[Officers] will endure a variety of dangers and harsh working conditions, but they must feel that they are being treated fairly." In a related survey of active police members in the department, Rossmo and Glackman (1991) found a drop in job satisfaction for all service-length groups and a decline in job satisfaction based on service length. These findings are similar to those of Crawford and Stark-Adamec (1988) who examined the reasons why women police officers left their positions as patrol officers. Among the primary reasons were a perceived lack of respect from supervisors and the absence of channels of communication between police managers and patrol officers.

Needless to say, the issue of job satisfaction is extremely important, not only for individual officers, but for the organization itself. For initiatives such as community-based policing to be effective, the commitment of linc-lcvel officers must be secured and lines of communication between police leaders and their officers developed.[9]

PUBLIC PERCEPTIONS OF THE POLICE

A very important part of understanding the role and activities of the police are the attitudes of the general public. Considering public perceptions of the police provides us with insights into potential problem areas in police-community relations as well as possible explanations as to why various initiatives sponsored by the police in communities and neighbourhoods may fall short of their objectives.

The findings of the research conducted on the public's attitudes toward the police can be generally summarized as follows.

► *The majority of adult and adolescent Canadians residing in rural and urban areas have favourable views of the police and express high levels of satisfaction with police services.*

In a wide-ranging study, Brillon, Louis-Guerin, and Lamarche (1984) found that 86% of urban and rural residents in Quebec, Ontario, and Manitoba expressed high levels of satisfaction with the police. In Nova Scotia, Murphy and Clairmont (1990) found that 80% of the residents in rural areas, in towns, and in the city of Halifax described police-community relations as "excellent," and police received high ratings for a variety of activities, including law enforcement activities, response to calls, being approachable, and providing the public with information (see also Loree, Richards, and Buckley, 1990). Yarmey (1991) also found generally high levels of public support for the police among a sample of citizens in Ontario.

▸   *The most positive ratings of the police are expressed by older Canadians, while youth and young adults have less favourable views of the police.*

The fact that younger Canadians tend to be less positive toward the police than older citizens may be due to the fact that young males, in particular, have a higher likelihood of having experiences with crime, being victimized, and having contact with the police. Related to the age-attitude correlation is the finding that single people tend to have less favourable attitudes toward the police. Even given this difference, however, the available research suggests that most Canadian youths have favourable images of the police (Griffiths and Winfree, 1983).

▸   *There may be considerable variability in citizen attitudes toward the police not only across different regions of the country, but also between neighbourhoods in the same city and even within subgroups in the same neighbourhood.*

Murphy and Lithopoulos (1988), in a study of attitudes toward the police in metropolitan Toronto, found considerable variation in residents' attitudes toward the police not only across different neighbourhoods but also among sub-groups *within* neighbourhoods. This finding suggests that police forces must not only be sensitive to the particular area being policed, but also to the needs of specific sub-groups (such as youth) within neighbourhoods.

▸   *A primary determinant of citizen attitudes toward the police is the type of contact they have had with police officers.*

For most Canadians, contact with the police is limited to either a class presentation by a police officer (for youths) or a brief encounter with a police officer in relation to a traffic infraction (for adults). Yet even these interactions can play a major role in determining the perceptions that citizens hold toward the police. In short, citizens who have negative encounters with the police tend to be more negative in their perceptions of police officers (Decker, 1981; Griffiths and Winfree, 1983).

▸ *Citizens who have been the victims of crime, particularly the victims of violent crime, tend to have less positive views of the police.*

While there is some inconsistency in the research findings regarding the impact of victimization on attitudes toward the police, there is substantial evidence that victims tend to be more dissatisfied with the police. In an Ontario study, Yarmey (1991) found that persons who had been the victims of violent crime held less favourable perceptions of the police than non-victims, were more likely than non-victims to feel that the police were not available when needed, and felt that the police did not provide them with sufficient feedback following their victimization.

The views of victims toward the police may be due in large measure to the particular police department involved. In a study conducted in the Yukon, McLaughlin (1984) found that 90% of the victims surveyed were satisfied with the help they received from the police, and Stuebing (1984) reported similar results in Red Deer, Alberta.

▸ *Many Canadians express concern with the quality of communication between the public and the police.*

It appears that many citizens are not well informed about the role and activities of the police, and the police are often felt to be unsuccessful in rectifying this situation (see Yarmey and Rashid, 1983; Amoroso and Ware, 1981). Police-citizen communication and mutual understanding may be particularly problematic on Aboriginal reserves, in urban areas among cultural and ethnic minorities, and in rural and northern Aboriginal communities policed by white police officers. As we will see in our consideration of Aboriginal policing in Chapter 15, police officers often have little understanding of the culture and community of the people they are policing.

▸ *Despite the overall positive ratings of the police by the Canadian public, many Aboriginal people and members of cultural and ethnic minorities hold negative perceptions of the police.*

The perceptions of cultural and ethnic minorities toward the police is perhaps one of the most critical, yet virtually unresearched, areas of Canadian policing. In a Metropolitan Toronto study, Murphy and Lithopoulos (1988) found that the most positive ratings of the police were held by Anglo-Saxons and the Northern and Eastern Europeans in the sample, while less favourable attitudes were held by East Indian and Italian citizens.

Within the past several years, several police shootings involving black suspects in Toronto and Montreal have heightened tensions between the police and the minority communities in these cities. Similarly, relations between Aboriginal peoples and the police in many urban, rural, and remote areas of the country are characterized by mutual distrust and suspicion. The Manitoba Aboriginal Justice Inquiry (Hamilton and Sinclair, 1991), for example, found widespread distrust of the police among Aboriginal peoples. We will explore police-Aboriginal relations in greater detail in Chapter 15. Suffice it to say that the multicultural context of Canadian policing places unique demands and requirements upon officers that they have often not been adequately prepared to meet.

In summary, it can be stated that, contrary to assertions made by many observers in the policing literature, the large majority of adults and adolescents in Canada appear to hold favourable attitudes toward the police. We must bear in mind, however, that the quality of police-citizen interaction and the resultant attitudes toward the police held by residents in a city, neighbourhood, or region will vary and that there are areas in Canada where police-citizen relations are strained and require attention.

NOTES

[1]Readers are encouraged to explore further the history of policing and, in particular, the events surrounding the formation of organized police forces in England in the early 1800s. Such an examination will reveal that not only are organized police forces a relatively recent development, but also that suggestions for creating such an authority were met with considerable resistance and opposition from those who feared the concentration of power in a single agency. Among the more valuable historical accounts are those by Critchley (1975; 1978) and McDougall (1988).

[2]There are numerous historical accounts of the development of policing in specific regions of the country. Peter McGahan's *Crime and Policing Maritime*

Canada (1988) also provides fascinating insights into policing in this region of the country from the 1830s to the 1930s. See also Gray (1971) for a description of early policing on the Prairies and Carrigan (1991) for a historical account of crime and punishment in Canada.

[3]For a statistical overview of policing operations in Canada, see the annual report *Policing in Canada*, published by the Canadian Centre for Justice Statistics.

[4]The New Brunswick Highway Patrol was disbanded in 1989. Established in 1980, this force had operated 16 detachments throughout the province, serving municipalities that did not have a RCMP detachment and outlying areas that were not covered by RCMP contracts. The RCMP has assumed the policing responsibilities of the New Brunswick Highway Patrol.

[5]In municipalities with a population under 15,000, the cost-sharing arrangement is split 70% (municipality) and 30% (federal government). In communities with a population over 15,000, the split is 90% (municipal) and 10% (federal). Most RCMP contracts for municipal policing are in communities of under 15,000 people, although there are notable exceptions — both Surrey and Burnaby, British Columbia, have detachments with more than 200 officers.

[6]In 1989, the RCMP undertook a most unusual assignment: serving as police monitors for elections held in Namibia, a country in West Africa. The RCMP became part of the United Nations Transition Assistance Group (UNITAG), and 100 members were stationed in various regions of the country in an observer/advisory role. This deployment represented one of the first instances in which a non-military force had been used by the United Nations and one of the few instances in which the RCMP have been involved in policing outside of Canada (Fowler, 1990). In 1992, RCMP officers were deployed in a peacekeeping role in Croatia and there were plans to send a group of officers to Cambodia as well.

[7]In his study of police patrol work in an eastern Canadian metropolitan area, Ericson (1982:74) found, contrary to previous investigations, that nearly 48% of police-citizen encounters were the result of proactive police mobilization. This finding may be a consequence of organizational policies and priorities of the particular department studied or may suggest that Canadian police are more aggressive in their policing styles than their U.S. counterparts, where most of the research has been conducted.

[8]Most victimization surveys, including the Canadian Urban Victimization Survey and the General Social Survey, suffer from severe methodological shortcomings that preclude the findings from being considered on any more than a general level. Both surveys, for example, gathered data via telephone interviews. While all but a few Canadian households have telephones, it can be anticipated that cultural and ethnic minorities, many of whom do not speak and/or understand English, will be excluded from the survey sample. This is

unfortunate, particularly given the multicultural fabric of Canadian society and the importance of understanding the particular difficulties experienced by minorities as victims of crime.

[9]See Burke and Kirchmeyer (1990a; 1990b), McGinnis (1991), and Kankewitt (1986) for additional material on the career patterns, sources of stress, and burnout among patrol officers. Police unions across the country have become increasingly involved in addressing the "human resource" issues facing their members. A study by Ellis (1991) provides key insights into how the perceptions of police officers about their role, the community, and the police organization change as they move from the recruit stage to being an experienced constable.

REFERENCES

Amoroso, D.M., and E.E. Ware. 1981. "Adolescent's Perceptions and Evaluation of the Police." 13 *Canadian Journal of Behavioural Science*. 326-35.

Anderson, F.W. 1972. *Saskatchewan's Provincial Police*. Calgary: Frontier Publishing Co.

Baker, W.M. 1991. "The Miners and the Mounties: The Royal North West Mounted Police and the 1906 Lethbridge Strike." 27 *Journal of Canadian Labour*. 55-96.

Betke, C. 1974. "The Mounted Police and the Doukhobors in Saskatchewan, 1899-1909." XXVII *Saskatchewan History*. 1-14.

Bennett, Lavrakas. 1989.

Braiden, C. 1991. "Who Washes a Rented Car?" Unpublished paper. Edmonton: Edmonton Police Service.

Braiden, C. 1990. "Policing: From the Belly of the Whale." Unpublished paper. Edmonton: Edmonton Police Service.

Brillon, Y., C. Louis-Guerin, and M.-C. Lamarche. 1984. *Attitudes of the Canadian Public Toward Crime Policies*. Montreal: International Centre for Comparative Criminology, University of Montreal.

British Columbia. 1990. *Policing British Columbia in the Year 2001. Report of the Regionalization Study Team*. Victoria, British Columbia: Police Services Branch, Ministry of Solicitor General.

Brockie, W. 1949. *Tales of the Mounted*. Toronto: Ryerson.

Broderick, J.J. 1987. *Police in a Time of Change*. 2nd ed. Prospect Heights, Illinois: Waveland Press.

Burke, R.J., and C. Kirchmeyer. 1990a. "Initial Career Orientations, Stress and Burnout in Policeworkers." 14 *Canadian Police College Journal*. 28-36.

_____. 1990b. "Present Career Orientations, Stress and Burnout in Police-workers." 14 *Canadian Police College Journal*. 50-57.

Campbell, W. 1936. *Arctic Patrols*. Milwaukee: Bruce Publishing.

Canadian Centre for Justice Statistics. 1992. "Police Personnel and Expenditures in Canada - 1991." 12 *Juristat Service Bulletin*. Ottawa: Statistics Canada.

Carrigan, D.O. 1991. *Crime and Punishment in Canada: A History*. Toronto: McClelland and Stewart.

Crawford, B.M., and C. Stark-Adamec. 1988. *Women in Canadian Urban Policing: Why Are They Leaving?* Unpublished report. Regina, Saskatchewan: University of Regina.

Critchley, T.A. 1975. "The New Police in London, 1750-1830." In W.T. McGrath and M.P. Mitchell, eds. *Police Function in Canada*. Toronto: Methuen. 37-52.

_____. 1978. *A History of Police in England and Wales*. London: Constable.

Decker, S.H. 1981. "Citizen Attitudes Toward the Police: A Review of Past Findings and Suggestions for Future Policy." 9 *Journal of Police Science and Administration*. 80-87.

Dickson, J.A. 1987. "Reflexions sur law police en Nouvelle-France." 32 *McGill Law Journal*. 497-522.

Douthwaite, L.C. 1936. *Yukon Patrol*. London and Glasgow: Blackie.

Ellis, R.T. 1991. "Perceptions, Attitudes and Beliefs of Police Recruits." 15 *Canadian Police College Journal*. 95-117.

Ericson, R.V. 1982. *Reproducing Order: A Study of Police Patrol Work*. Toronto: University of Toronto Press.

Fowler, K. 1990. "March South   The RCMP in Namibia." 52 *RCMP Gazette*. 1-9.

Fox, A. 1971. *The Newfoundland Constabulary*. St. John's: Robinson, Blackmore Printing and Publishing, Ltd.

Gray, J.H. 1971. *Red Lights on the Prairies*. Toronto: Macmillan.

Griffiths, C.T., and L.T. Winfree. 1983. "Adolescent Attitudes Toward the Police: A Comparison of Canadian and American Adolescents." 6 *International Journal of Comparative and Applied Criminal Justice*. 127-41.

Hamilton, Associate Chief Justice A.C., and Associate Chief Judge C.M. Sinclair. (Commissioners). 1991. *Report of the Aboriginal Justice Inquiry in Manitoba. The Justice System and Aboriginal People. Volume 1*. Winnipeg: Ministry of Justice, Province of Manitoba.

Hann, R. *et al.* 1985. "Municipal Police Governance and Accountability in Canada: An Empirical Study." 9 *Canadian Police College Journal*. 1-85.

Horrall, S.W. 1972. "Sir John A. Macdonald and the Mounted Police Force for the Northwest Territories." 53 *Canadian Historical Review*. 179-200.

Juliani, T.J., C.K. Talbot, and C.H.S. Jayewardene. 1984. "Municipal Policing in Canada: A Developmental Perspective." 8 *Canadian Police College Journal*. 315-85.

Kankewitt, B. 1986. *The Shattered Badge*. Toronto: Methuen.

Kwasniak, A.J. 1992. "Policing the Environment." 16 *Canadian Police College Journal*. 1-23.

Loree, D.J., B. Richards, and L. Buckley. 1990. "Sensing the Community: A Small Town Case Study." 13 *Canadian Police College Journal*. 128-36.

McDougall, A.K. 1988. *Policing: The Evolution of a Mandate*. Ottawa: Supply and Services Canada.

McGahan, P. 1984. *Police Images of a City*. New York: Peter Lang.

_____. 1988. *Crime and Policing in Maritime Canada*. Fredericton, N.B.: Goose Lane Editions, Ltd.

McGinnis, J.H. 1991. "Adaptation to Career Constable Status." 15 *Canadian Police College Journal*. 26-71.

McLaughlin, A. 1984. Crime Victims. *An Analysis of Victims/Victim Witness Needs in Yukon. Working Paper No. 11*. Ottawa: Policy Planning and Development Branch, Department of Justice.

Morgan, E.C. 1973. "The North-West Mounted Police: Internal Problems and Public Criticism, 1874-1883." 26 *Saskatchewan History*. 41-62.

Morrison, W.R. 1985. *Showing the Flag: The Mounted Police and Canadian Sovereignty in the North, 1894-1925*. Vancouver: University of British Columbia Press.

Muir, R.G. 1986. "The Canadian Police College: A Decade of Service." 10 *Canadian Police College Journal*. 169-88.

Murphy, C., and D. Clairmont. 1990. *Rural Attitudes and Perceptions of Crime, Policing and Victimization: Preliminary Findings from a Survey of Rural Nova Scotians*. Halifax: Atlantic Institute of Criminology, Dalhousie University.

Murphy, C., and S. Lithopoulos. 1988. *Social Determinants of Attitudes Towards the Police: Findings from the Toronto Community Policing Survey*. Ottawa: Solicitor General of Canada.

Normandeau, A., and B. Leighton. 1990. *A Vision of the Future of Policing in Canada: Police-Challenge 2000. Background Document*. Ottawa: Solicitor General of Canada.

Poel, D.H. 1985. "Dimensions of 'Hard' Policing: Competing Notions of Applied Justice within Local Police Cultures." Unpublished paper. Halifax: Department of Political Science, Dalhousie University.

Radalet, L.A. 1986. *The Police and the Community*. 3rd ed. New York: Macmillan.

Robertson, D.F. 1978. "The Saskatchewan Provincial Police, 1917-1928." 31 *Saskatchewan History*. 1-11.

Rossmo, D.K., and W. Glackman. 1991. "Police Organizational Surveys: Labour-Management Diagnostic Tools." Unpublished paper. Burnaby, British Columbia: School of Criminology, Simon Fraser University.

Sacco, V.F., and H. Johnson. 1990. *Patterns of Criminal Victimization in Canada*. Ottawa: Minister of Supply and Services Canada.

Shearing, C.D. 1981. "Subterranean Processes in the Maintenance of Power: An Examination of the Mechanisms of Coordinating Police Action." 18 *Canadian Review of Sociology and Anthropology*. 283-98.

Shearing, C.D. 1984. *Dial-A-Cop: A Study of Police Mobilization*. Toronto: Centre of Criminology, University of Toronto.

Skolnick, J.K. 1966. *Justice Without Trial: Law Enforcement in a Democratic Society*. New York: John Wiley and Sons.

Stenning, P.C. 1981a. "The Role of Police Boards and Commissions as Institutions of Municipal Police Governance." In C.D. Shearing, ed. *Organizational Police Deviance: Its Structure and Control*. Toronto: Butterworths. 161-208.

_____. 1981b. *Police Commissions and Boards in Canada*. Toronto: Centre of Criminology, University of Toronto.

Stuebing, W.K. 1984. *Crime Victims. Victims and Witnesses: Experiences, Needs, and Community/Criminal Justice Response*. Ottawa: Policy Planning and Development Branch, Department of Justice.

Talbot, C.K., C.H.S. Jayewardene, and T.J. Juliani. 1983. *The Thin Blue Line: An Historical Perspective of Policing in Canada*. Ottawa: CRIM-CARE, Inc.

_____. 1984. "Policing in Canada: A Developmental Perspective." 8 *Canadian Police College Journal*. 218-88.

Vincent, C.L. *Police Officer*. 1990. Ottawa: Carleton University Press.

Walden, K. 1982. *Visions of Order: The Canadian Mounties in Symbol and Myth*. Toronto: Butterworths.

Weiner, N.L. 1976. *The Role of the Police in Urban Society: Conflicts and Consequences*. Indianapolis: Bobbs-Merrill.

Westley, W.A. 1953. "Violence and the Police." 59 *American Journal of Sociology*. 34-41.

White, S.A. 1939. *Morgan of the Mounted*. New York: Phoenix Press.

Yarmey, A.D. 1991. "Retrospective Perceptions of Police Following Victimization." 15 *Canadian Police College Journal*. 137-43.

Yarmey, A.D., and S. Rashid. 1983. "Perceptions of the Public and Legal Professionals Toward Police Officers." 7 *Canadian Police College Journal*. 89-95.

4 THE POWERS AND DECISION MAKING OF THE POLICE

In this chapter, we will consider the powers of the Canadian police, the police exercise of discretion, and the factors that appear to influence the decision making of police officers in encounter situations with citizens and suspects.

The activities of patrol officers can be generally grouped into those that are reactive and those that are proactive. *Reactive policing* results from spontaneous or planned requests by citizens or groups for police intervention. In Chapter 3 we saw how the majority of crimes are brought to the police by the general public. *Proactive policing* occurs when officers, on their own, take the initiative to engage in various policing tasks. Among the more common (and visible) proactive police activities are conducting traffic stops to check for compliance with seatbelt laws, vehicle registration checks, roadblocks to detect impaired drivers, and identification checks of suspicious persons. Less visible proactive police activities include undercover surveillance of criminal suspects and the case investigation activities of plainclothes detectives.

POLICE EXERCISE OF DISCRETION

Once a victim or another citizen telephones the police, a series of decisions are made by the police department. While research has generally focused on the decision making of patrol officers in encounter situations with the victims and/or suspects of crime, there is an additional stage of discretionary decision making involving police telephone operators, complaint officers, and dispatch officers who receive citizen requests and assess whether police intervention is warranted. These decisions determine whether there will, in fact, be an encounter situation between a patrol officer and the victim or suspect. In Chapter 3, we noted that the public requests a wide range of services from the police, only a fraction of which are directly related to the enforcement of the law or crime control. Given limited organizational resources, the police must prioritize the requests they receive; this involves discretionary decision making by police personnel even before an officer is sent to the scene.

Perhaps the most extensive Canadian analysis of citizens' request for police service and the police response to such requests was undertaken by Shearing (1984). In a study of the Metropolitan Toronto Police Department, Shearing (1984:104) found that police complaint officers employed a system for determining the priority of calls, with those related to serious property damage and bodily injury being rated first, followed by alarms, fires, domestic disputes, and traffic parking violations.

Shearing (1984) also discovered that the decision of the complaint officer was strongly influenced by the officer's perception of the amount of trouble represented by the call, the degree of deference shown to the police by the caller, and the manner in which the "trouble" was presented by the caller. Those callers, for example, who exhibited deference toward the police in their telephone conversation with the complaint officer were more likely to receive a sympathetic consideration of their request for police intervention (see also Gilsinan, 1989; Jorgensen, 1981).

In those instances in which the complaint officer decided that the dispatch of a patrol unit was warranted, the request was forwarded to the dispatch officers in the department, who then engaged in additional discretionary decision making. The dispatch officers attempted to reconcile the "demands for police service with the resources available" (Shearing, 1984:161). Using two indicators — the number of units dispatched and the elapsed response time for the dispatch of a unit — Shearing (1984:166) found that dispatcher decisions were also affected by a priority system that was premised on the perceived probability that a suspect could be apprehended.

These research findings indicate that the discretionary decision making of the police begins long before the police officer arrives at the scene. However, note that there may be considerable variability between police departments in the criteria used in assessing citizen requests for intervention and in determining that the dispatch of a patrol car is warranted. The demands of the policing or "task" environment, available resources, and the policies and priorities of the senior administration in the department may all affect dispatch and response decisions.

Goldstein (1977) has identified the various forms of discretion exercised by police agencies: (1) prioritizing how resources will be allocated among a variety of competing demands that are placed on the department; (2) the discretion that senior administrators in the department exercise in setting and enforcing policies; (3) the choices that patrol officers make in determining how to respond to and gain control over a specific incident, for example, whether to use force or not; (3) the choice made by the officer as to how to dispose of a particular case, for example, whether to arrest, mediate, warn, or make a referral; and (4) the decisions that are made by police investigators in gathering evidence.

For the purposes of our discussion, we will focus on the discretion exercised by police patrol officers. Police discretion at the street level involves "the power to decide which rules to apply to a given situation and whether or not to apply them" (Ericson, 1982:11). A key attribute of the decision making of the police patrol officer is the power to exercise discretion. While patrol officers occupy the lowest level in the organizational hierarchy, they exercise the most discretion on a day-to-day basis in carrying out policing duties. When controversies erupt over the decisions of police officers, they are often related to how individual police officers have exercised discretion in a specific encounter incident and to whether the officers have abused their discretionary powers and violated the rights of suspects.

In Canada, there is no specific legislation that addresses the exercise of discretion by police officers. The *Criminal Code* appears to encourage the exercise of discretion by police officers, providing that a police officer *may* make an arrest in those instances in which there are reasonable and probable grounds to believe that an offence has been committed. In recent years, however, there has been a call for the development of guidelines to structure the broad discretionary powers of police officers. As we will see in our discussion of police powers, the Canadian courts have become a major mechanism by which the limits of police discretion are established, particularly in relation to cases involving the *Canadian Charter of Rights and Freedoms*.[1]

Throughout the policing literature, there is a considerable diversity of opinion regarding the exercise of discretion by the police and the extent to which such discretionary power should be structured and controlled. There are differing perspectives on how much discretion police officers actually have and whether such discretion is exercised in a fair and equitable manner.

In his classic treatise on police discretion, the American police observer Kenneth Culp Davis (1975) argued that, while police discretion should not (and could not) be eliminated, it should be structured, confined, and controlled. Also, there should be an acknowledgement by police forces that full enforcement of all laws, at all times, is not possible and that selective enforcement necessarily involves the exercise of discretion by police patrol officers. While officers must have the discretion to tailor their decision making to the requirements of each encounter, the issue becomes one of defining the parameters within which discretion is to be exercised. Police officers may be most effective in those instances in which they do not exercise their full enforcement powers, but rather use their discretion to mediate a situation and to resolve an incident in an informal manner.

Many police observers have expressed the concern that ethnic minorities and Aboriginal peoples in Canada, as well as citizens of lower socioeconomic status, are often the victims of police discrimination. While there is no evidence of systematic discrimination against specific groups across the country, there is no doubt that relations between the police and the public in certain jurisdictions have been coloured by the abuse of discretionary powers by police officers.

These abuses may be a consequence of the personal views and prejudices of individual police officers. However, the possibility that discrimination will occur is enhanced by the fact that officers rely upon their personal judgment and experience in dealing with situations, which may require the legitimate exercise of discretion, yet be interpreted as having been unfair and discriminatory by the suspect or members of the general public.

The potential for the abuse of discretion and/or the perception of discrimination on the part of a suspect by police officers may be higher in those encounters involving white police officers and members of cultural or ethnic minorities. The lack of knowledge by both parties to the encounter, as well as language differences and other cultural barriers, may lead to suspicion, misunderstandings, and distrust.

Among the more important questions that we must ask in considering police discretion are the following.

- ▶ How much discretion do police officers require to effectively carry out their tasks?
- ▶ What powers are Canadian police given under law to exercise discretion and make decisions, and how have these powers been affected by various court decisions?
- ▶ What factors affect how individual police officers exercise discretion in encounter situations?

- ▶ What is the fine line between the exercise of discretion in a positive fashion, which enhances the quality of policing, and the abuse of discretion, which may result in discrimination?
- ▶ What factors affect the exercise of discretion by police officers in encounter situations?
- ▶ What structures are in place across Canada to monitor the use (and abuse) of discretion by police officers and to hold police officers accountable for their actions?

POLICE POWERS

The Significance of the *Canadian Charter of Rights and Freedoms*

As the Law Reform Commission of Canada (1984b:6) has noted:

> The balance between law enforcement and effective protection of individual interests is, ultimately, a working definition of justice, and the prospect of agreement on this aspect of social policy is always elusive.

Historically, in Canada, the police have been given broad powers to carry out their function of law enforcement, and it is fair to say that the courts have generally leaned toward "crime control" rather than "due process" values in performing their difficult task of balancing the rights of individual citizens and the perceived needs of law enforcement (Cohen, 1984b:267). However, it may be contended that the balance between police powers and individual rights has shifted since the enactment of the *Charter* in 1982 (Alexander, 1990; Luther, 1987; Stuart, 1987).

The *Charter* entrenches a number of constitutional rights on behalf of an accused person in the criminal justice process and provides various remedies for the infringement of those rights. Section 24(1) provides that a court may grant "such remedy as the court considers appropriate and just in the circumstances" (see Roach, 1987; Trotter, 1989). It has been suggested[2] that possible remedies under this provision may include a notice to quash a search warrant, a stay of proceedings, an action for damages, a prosecution for an offence or for an infringement of the *Charter*, or a petition for an injunction or a declaration (for example, a declaration that certain criminal legislation is void because it infringes the guarantees of the *Charter*).[3] Any of these remedies may be sought in the situation where it is alleged that a police officer has infringed rights guaranteed by the *Charter*. In addition, section 24(2) of the *Charter* provides the courts with a totally new power; namely, the *discretion* to exclude evidence from the trial of an accused person where such evidence was obtained in a manner that infringed or denied any of the rights and freedoms protected by the *Charter*. However, the discretion to exclude such evidence will only be exercised where it is established that its admission "would bring the administration of justice into disrepute." This particular provision of the *Charter* created a considerable degree of concern among the police, who feared that the courts would be willing to release dangerous criminals back onto the streets because there had been a mere "technical violation" of the law. However, as we shall see, this fear is really unjustified since the *Charter* clearly does not establish a rule that automatically excludes illegally obtained evidence and, in practice, the courts have generally been somewhat reluctant to exercise their discretion to exclude evidence.

One important point that should be made about the rights and freedoms guaranteed by the *Charter* is that they are by no means absolute in nature. Indeed, section 1 states that such rights can be subject to "such reasonable limits prescribed by law as can be demonstrably justified in a free and democratic society." This means that a court may hold that a *Charter* right has been infringed but that such an infringement is nevertheless justified; in these circumstances, the person whose right has been infringed will have no remedy.

There is little doubt that the advent of the *Charter* has injected a totally new dimension into the debate over the extent of police powers vis-à-vis the individual citizen (Greenspan, 1989; Harvie and Foster, 1990). As we shall see, there have been some important decisions by the courts that have resulted in additional restrictions being placed on the police. However, there is a debate as to exactly how effective the *Charter* is likely to be in altering the real balance of power between the police and a suspect in a criminal case. At one end of the spectrum, there have been claims that the *Charter* has tilted the balance in favour of criminals. Certainly, at the time of its enactment, there was no shortage of police officers in Canada who were prepared to express the view that the *Charter* had left them to fight crime "with one hand tied behind their backs."[4] On the other hand, some commentators (Ericson, 1983; Glasbeek, 1989) have suggested that the *Charter* will have relatively little impact on criminal justice practices. Indeed, Ericson has contended that, in general, judicial decisions, have relatively little effect on police practices. In his view, it is the actions of the police rather than the decisions of judges that are most likely to affect average citizens in their day-to-day affairs:

> In sum, it is the law of arrest, the law of search and seizure, and the prison rules, more than the [*Charter*]; and, the police more than the judiciary; that make evident that the law is there more to restrict than liberate, more to regulate than to provide relief, more to deny the rights of many and grant privileges to a few (1983:53).

Ericson (1983:25) has dismissed as fiction the belief that the *Charter* will "profoundly alter" criminal procedure. He contends (1983:53-54) that the *Charter* has little direct impact in protecting the rights and freedoms of individual citizens and that its major function is to "guarantee a framework of official discretion" for the police and for "legitimating decisions about the restriction of rights in any given conflict." In his opinion, the *Charter* provides a "protective symbolic canopy for a statutory and common law scheme" that permits the police to "get on with their routine social control tasks."

In any event, there clearly are a number of sharply conflicting views as to the potential efficacy of the *Charter* as a means of setting boundaries to the exercise of police powers within the criminal justice system. Nevertheless, the initial decade's experience with the *Charter* suggests that there has been a significant shift in the balance between police powers and individual rights and freedoms, and that this shift has generally favoured the private citizen. On the other hand, it may well be the case that the 1990s will witness a tilt in the balance back toward the other direction. Indeed, it has been contended (Tanovich, 1992:205) that the Supreme Court of Canada has become convinced that it has gone too far in protecting the legal rights of accused persons under the *Charter* and is now moving to retrench its position by placing greater emphasis on the need to safeguard the interests of society in effective law enforcement.

Arrest

Perhaps the police power that first springs to most people's minds is that of arrest. The Law Reform Commission of Canada (1985a:27-28) states that the purposes of arrest or detention can be classified as being "either protective or repressive." Protective (or preventive) purposes include the use of the power to arrest or detain in order to prevent a commission of an offence or to terminate a breach of the peace. Repressive purposes include the use of the power to compel an individual's attendance in court or to collect evidence in relation to a criminal offence.

As the Law Reform Commission of Canada (1985a:7) has stated, "the principles governing arrest are a fundamental aspect of any legal system which give practical shape to relations between the state and individual citizens." Arrest represents one of the most far-reaching of the encroachments that the state makes upon the lives of citizens (Cohen, 1981; Leggatt, 1989; Pavlich, 1982); therefore, it is scarcely surprising that the exercise of the police power to make an arrest is hedged around with numerous legal restrictions. These restrictions are not only contained in the *Criminal Code* and in case law, but are also enshrined in the *Charter* (Friedland, 1982).

What is an "arrest"? This question has created a considerable amount of difficulty for Canadian courts. The "common sense" definition would appear to revolve around the *physical* taking into custody of a suspect against his or her will (Pavlich, 1982:III-56-60). However, it appears that Canadian courts are prone to adopt a somewhat more expansive definition. Indeed, the Law Reform Commission of Canada (1985a:31) has suggested that judicial authority has ruled that an arrest is one of two things: "(i) touching with a view to detention, even where the suspect may not submit voluntarily; or (ii) stating that the suspect is under arrest where the suspect submits." As we shall see, an arrest may take place either with or without the authority of a judicial warrant.

A number of statutory provisions, both federal and provincial, authorize the police to exercise a power of *detention*, which falls short of amounting to a full arrest in the sense outlined above. One striking example of such a power is the demand that a citizen blow into a breathalyzer. Individuals who are asked to carry out this request clearly suffer some restriction upon their liberty, but the degree of this restriction falls considerably short of that which would apply were they subjected to arrest. It is necessary to pay close attention to the power to detain because the *Charter* (sections 9 and 10) contains specific guarantees of the legal rights of those who have experienced arrest or detention. The Supreme Court of Canada has adopted a very broad definition of "deten- tion" for the purpose of the Charter.[5] In the view of the Court, there is a detention whenever a police officer "assumes control over the movement of a person by a demand or direction which may have significant legal consequence and which prevents or impedes access to (legal) counsel."[6] There must be an element of compulsion, the Court has ruled, but *psychological* compulsion, in the form of a "reasonable perception of suspension of freedom of choice,"[7] is sufficient for this purpose.

Most individuals do not have a working knowledge of the precise scope of police powers and, if they submit to a police demand because they believe they have no real choice but to do so, then there has been a detention and their rights are protected by sections 9 and 10 of the *Charter*. Section 9 protects the citizen from arbitrary detention, while section 10 gives an arrested or detained person the right to be informed promptly of the reasons therefor and the right to retain and instruct counsel and to be informed of that right. Infringement of these rights by the police may give the accused person a remedy (such as damages) under section 24(1) of the *Charter* or, under section 24(2), may lead to the exclusion of any evidence obtained as a consequence of such unlawful activity by the police.[8]

The power of a police officer to effect an arrest is derived from legislation, both federal and provincial (Law Reform Commission of Canada, 1985a:15-26). The most significant federal statute for this purpose is, of course, the *Criminal Code*. At the provincial level, powers of arrest are frequently specified by, for example, motor vehicle and liquor licensing and control legislation.

The primary purpose of arrest, in the Canadian system of criminal procedure, is to compel an accused person's attendance at trial (Law Reform Commission of Canada, 1985a:28). It is important, therefore, to underscore that arrest is only one of a number of alternative mechanisms for effecting this purpose. Indeed, the *Criminal Code* provides the police officer with the options of arresting an individual, issuing an appearance notice, or seeking a summons.

A police officer may arrest *without a warrant* any individual:

(a) who has committed an indictable offence or who the officer believes, on reasonable grounds, has committed or is about to commit an indictable offence; or

(b) whom the officer finds actually committing any criminal offence (whether it be an indictable or a summary conviction offence); or

(c)   for whom the officer has reasonable grounds to believe
that a warrant of arrest or committal is in force within the
jurisdiction in which he or she is found.[9]

(See Chapter 6 for further details on types of offences.)

Note that, in those cases where the police do not actually find the
accused committing an offence, they do not have to establish a *prima
facie* case for conviction before exercising their discretion to make an
arrest. All that they have to do is establish that they have *reasonable
grounds* to believe that, for example, an indictable offence has been or is
about to be committed by the person they arrest. In other words, they
need only establish that there is a reasonable basis for their suspicion that
the individual concerned has committed, or is about to commit, such an
offence. This clearly gives the police considerable leeway to make honest
mistakes without invalidating the arrest. In the Supreme Court of
Canada,[10] this situation was summarized in the following manner:

> ...the *Criminal Code* requires that an arresting officer must subjective-
> ly have reasonable and probable grounds on which to base the arrest.
> Those grounds must, in addition, be justifiable from an objective point
> of view. That is to say, a reasonable person placed in the position of
> the officer must be able to conclude that there were indeed reasonable
> and probable grounds for the arrest. On the other hand, the police
> need not demonstrate anything more than reasonable and probable
> grounds. Specifically, they are not required to establish a *prima facie*
> case for conviction before making an arrest.[11]

The *Criminal Code* grants police officers additional powers of arrest
without a warrant in relation to such *Code* offences as breach of the
peace[12] and being found in a common gaming or betting house.[13]

There are some significant restrictions upon the power of a police
officer to arrest a suspect without a warrant. The most important of these
restrictions was imposed as a consequence of certain recommendations
made by the Ouimet Committee (1969) and acted upon by Parliament in
the form of the *Bail Reform Act*, which came into force in January,
1972.[14] The *Act* amended the *Criminal Code* so as to require that, for the
less serious criminal offences, police officers *not* use their discretion to
make an arrest unless they have reasonable grounds to believe that the
"public interest" can only be satisfied by adopting such a course or they

have reasonable grounds to believe that, if an arrest is not made, the suspect will not show up in court.[15] The term "public interest" is made concrete by requiring the police officer to have "regard to all the circumstances including the need to (i) establish the identity of the person, or (ii) secure or preserve evidence of or relating to the offence, or (iii) prevent the continuation or repetition of the offence or the commission of another offence."

Even where the officer has decided to use the option of arrest without a warrant, the *Code* requires that the officer release the suspect "as soon as practicable" with the intention of compelling the suspect's later attendance in court by means of a summons or appearance notice, provided, of course, that such a release would be in the public interest and that there are no reasonable grounds for believing that the suspect will fail to show up in court in the absence of an arrest.[16] The *Bail Reform Act* further strengthened the presumption in favour of releasing arrested suspects from custody by permitting the officer in charge of a police "lock-up" to release them and to ensure their attendance by means of a summons or appearance notice.[17] The *Criminal Code* also contains provisions for the arrest of suspects under the authority of a judicial warrant (see Salhany, 1989:59-65). More specifically, a justice of the peace may issue a warrant for the arrest of an individual suspected of having committed either an indictable or a summary conviction offence.[18] A warrant may only be issued after someone (usually a police officer) lays a document, known as an "information," before a justice, alleging that he or she has reasonable grounds to believe that an offence has been committed.[19] Except insofar as the most serious offences are concerned, the justice is required to issue a summons, rather than an arrest warrant, unless the evidence available to him or her discloses reasonable grounds for believing that the "public interest" requires that an arrest be made.[20] Significantly, in relation to all but the most serious offences, the justice may endorse the arrest warrant so as to provide for the subsequent release of the suspect by the officer in charge of a lock-up.[21]

In order to ensure that a suspect is not detained in custody unnecessarily after arrest (whether or not this has been brought about by virtue of a warrant), the *Criminal Code* places the arresting police officer under a duty to bring the suspect before a justice "without unreasonable delay" and, in any event, within 24 hours (unless a justice is not available within this period, in which case the suspect must be brought before a justice "as soon as possible").[22] The justice may decide to release the suspect to the community, pending the suspect's later appearance in court, either unconditionally or upon conditions. Failure on the part of the police to bring a suspect before a justice as soon as possible will not only infringe the relevant provision of the *Code*, but may also represent a breach of the *Charter*, since section 9 of the *Charter* protects the citizen from arbitrary detention or imprisonment.[23] See Chapter 6 for further details of arrest and release.

Alternatives to Arrest

As noted earlier, instead of making an arrest, the police officer has the option to release suspects with the intention of securing their appearance in court by means of a *summons* or an *appearance notice* (Pavlich, 1982:III-41).

A summons is issued by a justice of the peace after an information has been laid before him or her alleging that the accused has committed an offence. The summons has been described as a "formal document which is directed to the accused and which sets out the charge as well as the time and place at which the accused is to appear in court" (Law Reform Commission of Canada, 1985a:43). It might also require the accused person to go to a designated place for fingerprinting and photographing (assuming the offence charged is indictable in nature).[24]

An appearance notice is similar to a summons, insofar that it is a mechanism geared toward compelling the attendance of a suspect without the necessity of an arrest (Pavlich, 1982:46-50). However, it differs from the summons since it does not require the intervention of a justice; in other words, the police officer can issue it "on the spot."[25] As is the case with a summons, an appearance notice may require the accused person to go to a designated place for fingerprinting, etc. Once an appearance notice has been issued, the police officer must "as soon as practicable" ensure that an information is laid before a justice of the peace.[26] In order to be effective, the notice must be confirmed by the justice. The justice may confirm the notice or cancel it outright (giving the suspect notice that this has been done); alternatively, the justice may decide to cancel the notice and issue a summons or an arrest warrant instead.[27]

With the advent of the *Charter*, the police have been placed under a duty to provide certain critical information to a suspect who has been arrested or detained. Indeed, section 10 provides that everyone who has been arrested or detained has the right: (a) "to be informed promptly of the reasons therefor"; and (b) "to retain and instruct counsel without delay *and to be informed of that right*" (emphasis added) (Conway, 1985). The first of these duties has existed for many years under the common law; failure to adhere to it may render an arrest unlawful (Law Reform Commission of Canada, 1985a:51). It is also enshrined in the *Criminal Code*, which states that it is the duty of an arresting officer, where it is feasible to do so, to give notice of the process or warrant under the authority of which he or she is acting or the reason for the arrest.[28] The second duty has been added by the *Charter* and failure to perform it will normally result in charges being dismissed or any statements made by the accused being excluded from their trials.[29]

The significance of this duty was dramatically illustrated in the *Therens* case,[30] where the accused, who had lost control of his vehicle and driven into a tree, was required by a police officer to take a breathalyzer test and to accompany the officer to the police station for that purpose. The accused duly supplied samples of his breath. However, the officer never informed Therens of his right to retain and instruct counsel. At his trial, the charge of driving with an excessive level of alcohol was dismissed because Therens's right, under the *Charter*, to be informed of his right to counsel had been violated by the police. The Supreme Court of Canada upheld the dismissal of the charge, noting that, although he had not been "arrested," Therens had certainly been "detained" within the meaning of section 10 of the *Charter* and that evidence obtained as a result of the violation of the accused's constitutional rights in this manner should be excluded from consideration by the courts because its admission would bring the administration of justice into disrepute within the meaning of section 24(2) of the *Charter*.[31]

In the later case of *Brydges*,[32] the Supreme Court of Canada expanded the scope of this duty even further. It was held that, where an accused person expresses a wish to obtain counsel but indicates a belief that he or she cannot afford it, then the police are under a duty to inform him or her of the availability of duty counsel or legal aid. In this case, too, the evidence obtained after the accused's constitutional rights had been violated (in this case an incriminating statement) was excluded at trial under section 24(2) of the *Charter*. In effect, the police have been placed under a duty to facilitate access to counsel, if an arrested or detained person requests it, and, as part of this duty, they are obliged to give that person a reasonable opportunity to gain such access before proceeding with their interrogation. Furthermore, it is essential that the police make a conscientious effort to fulfill this responsibility and must avoid, for example, giving any misleading information to a defendant who has expressed an interest in obtaining the assistance of a lawyer.[33]

Police officers' powers of arrest have also been circumscribed by other provisions of the *Charter*. Section 7 guarantees the "right to life, liberty and security of the person and the right not to be deprived thereof except in accordance with the principles of fundamental justice." This provision clearly affects the exercise of a variety of police powers (Law Reform Commission of Canada, 1985a:9-12). In addition, section 9 protects citizens from arbitrary detention or imprisonment, a provision that is also likely to serve as the basis for constitutional challenges to the use of the power of arrest by the police (Toselli, 1990; Young, 1991). For example, in one case,[34] the Court stayed the proceedings against a woman who had been arrested and charged with the summary conviction offence of soliciting for the purposes of prostitution. She had been held overnight in the police cells because of a departmental policy that all such persons should be held in custody overnight and taken to a justice in the morning. However, as we have seen, the *Criminal Code* provides that the police officer, who is considering whether to make an arrest for a less serious offence, must first consider whether the "public interest" or the possibility that the accused will not appear in court really require that an arrest actually be made or, even after an arrest has been made, whether the accused should be released from custody. Here the police had not even considered whether the accused should be given an appearance notice or be summonsed as an alternative to arrest and continuing custody. For these reasons, the conduct of the police was considered to be a clear breach of section 9 of the *Charter* as well as their duties under the *Criminal Code*.

Before we leave the issue of police powers of arrest, note that the police have the power to take photographs and fingerprints from suspects who have been charged with an indictable offence. This particular power arises under the terms of the *Identification of Criminals Act*. The police may take photographs and fingerprints while the accused is in custody or the accused may be ordered to attend the police station at a particular time, specified in an appearance notice or a summons. This power may be exercised even against those accused persons who are charged with what are known as "mixed offences" (offences that may be tried either on indictment or by summary conviction procedures), despite the fact that the prosecution may ultimately decide to proceed by way of summary conviction procedures rather than by indictment. This means that the intrusive powers granted to the police, under the *Identification of Criminals Act*, apply to a broad range of criminal charges. In *Beare*,[35] the Supreme Court of Canada held that compulsory fingerprinting under the *Identification of Criminals Act* did not infringe sections 7, 8, 9, 10, or 11 of the *Charter*. La Forest J. said:

> It seems to me that a person who is arrested on reasonable and probable grounds that he has committed a serious crime, or a person against whom a case for issuing a summons or warrant, or confirming an appearance notice has been made out, must expect a significant loss of personal privacy. He must expect that incidental to his being taken in custody he will be subjected to observation, to physical measurement and the like. Fingerprinting is of that nature. While some may find it distasteful, it is insubstantial, of very short duration, and leaves no lasting impression. There is no penetration into the body and no substance is removed from it.[36]

Police Use of Force

One controversial aspect of police powers in Canada concerns the use of force, particularly when the making of an arrest is concerned (Pavlich, 1982:III-176-180). Section 25(1) of the *Code* permits police officers to use "as much force as is necessary" for the purpose of carrying out what they are required or authorized to do in the administration or enforcement of the law, provided that they act "on reasonable grounds." Subsections (3) and (4) permit the use of deadly force in certain circumstances. Subsection (3) is unobjectionable and, indeed, clearly necessary since it permits police officers to use force that is intended to inflict death or grievous bodily harm where they believe, on reasonable grounds, that it is necessary to do so for the purpose of preserving themselves from death or grievous bodily harm. Subsection (4), however, is much more problematic since it provides that, where a suspect is bent on escape by fleeing from the police, then an officer who is seeking to make an arrest may use "as much force as is necessary to prevent the escape by flight, unless the escape can be prevented by reasonable means in a less violent manner."[37] The problem with this subsection is that it is not limited in its operation to suspects who pose a real danger either to the police or to the broader community at large. Therefore, the subsection permits the use of firearms by the police to prevent an escape even if the suspect is not really "dangerous." Although the police in Canada do not resort to the use of firearms nearly as frequently as many of their counterparts south of the border, some 119 citizens were shot to death by police officers in Canada between 1970 and 1981, and it has been suggested that perhaps three times as many individuals were injured as a result of the use of firearms by the police (Chappell and Graham, 1985:10, 33). According to Solomon (1985:333), an unpublished study by the Ministry of the Solicitor General of Canada "revealed that the police in Canada had used their guns mainly against unarmed fleeing suspects (some of whom turned out to be innocent) and that the guns did not usually help in their apprehension." Unfortunately, there is still a relative dearth of information concerning the nature of the use of deadly force by the police in Canada; however, one Canadian study in the area has recommended that it be limited to situations where it is necessary for the defence of life (Chappell and Graham, 1985:194). In the spring of 1992, the Federal Minister of Justice announced that there would be amendments to the *Criminal Code* to deal with this problem. It remains to be seen what shape these amendments will take.

What happens if the police wish to arrest someone who is in private premises, particularly their own home? Where the officers have a warrant for the arrest of a suspect, then they may forcibly enter private premises, even the suspect's home, in order to make the arrest, provided they have reasonable grounds to believe that the person named in the warrant is in those premises and provided that they have announced their presence, demanded entry, and have been refused (Law Reform Commission of Canada, 1984:55).

If police do not have an arrest warrant in their pockets, but believe on reasonable grounds that a suspect has or is about to commit an indictable offence and seek to make an arrest, the police may enter private premises, without the consent of the occupier, in order to carry out that arrest. However, there must be reasonable grounds for believing that the suspect is actually on the premises and the police must properly announce their presence and purpose before being refused entry.[38]

Can a citizen resist an unlawful arrest? In theory, this is certainly the case. In practice, however, resisting a police officer is a course of action that is fraught with many pitfalls and dangers (Law Reform Commission of Canada, 1984:56). Even where the citizen is, in fact, innocent of committing an offence, an arrest may still be lawful because a police officer has reasonable grounds to believe to the contrary. Furthermore, the Supreme Court of Canada has ruled that, where, for example, the *Criminal Code* permits the arrest of someone found "committing a criminal offence," this phraseology should be interpreted as meaning "*apparently*" committing an offence.[39] Clearly, both the *Code* and the courts give the police officer a considerable margin to make honest errors of judgment, and it would be a foolhardy citizen who decided to resist arrest except in the most blatant cases of abuse of police power (Pavlich, 1982:III-205). In addition, as Ericson and Baranek (1982:45) point out, the police have the ability to "worsen a situation through more charges (e.g., 'obstruct police,' 'assault police,' 'cause a disturbance')."

What remedies are available to a citizen who has been wrongfully arrested or detained? We have seen that a violation of a suspect's constitutional rights, under the *Charter*, may result in courts granting the citizen a variety of remedies, including the staying of a prosecution or the exclusion of evidence from the suspect's trial.[40] These are important remedies, from the citizen's point of view. However, bear in mind that, in theory, criminal charges could be laid against an errant police officer (Law Reform Commission of Canada, 1985a:57). Section 26 of the *Criminal Code* states that a person authorized to use force may be held criminally responsible for "any excess thereof according to the nature and quality of the act that constitutes the excess." Therefore, depending on the circumstances, a number of criminal charges (such as assault) may be laid against a police officer. However, as the Law Reform Commission (1985a:57) points out, a criminal proceeding may not be the most practical method for a wronged individual to pursue, unless the provincial authorities are willing to prosecute and it is widely believed that there is considerable reluctance, on their part, to publicize police wrongdoing. A citizen could lay an information himself or herself; however, the cost of pursuing a "private" prosecution might well be beyond his or her means and there is always the danger that the Crown may terminate such a prosecution by staying it. An unlawful arrest could also be the subject of a civil action for damages (Law Reform Commission of Canada, 1985a:58),[41] although such an action is clearly out of the question for many individuals because of the expense of pursuing a case in the courts. Finally, there is always the possibility of launching a complaint by using the particular procedures prescribed in the various provincial police acts or by approaching the RCMP Public Complaints Commission (Goldsmith, 1988; McMahon, 1988).

Search and Seizure

Police powers of search and seizure have been aptly described as "exceptional powers" because they permit the police to do "what an individual is, in ordinary circumstances, forbidden to do" (Law Reform Commission of Canada, 1983a:10). The Commission goes on to state:

> The ambit of these exceptional powers is of equally grave concern to society as a whole. For the interests with which these powers conflict are among the most critical accorded to individuals in a liberal democracy: interests involving the inviolability and dignity of the person, the concept of privacy, the security of possessions and self-expression (1983a:11).

The general rule is that the police powers of search and seizure are derived from specific legislative authority. There is, however, one major exception to this rule; namely, the power of the police to search an individual as part of the process of effecting an arrest (Cohen, 1988, 1990; Law Reform Commission of Canada, 1983a:48).[42] For this purpose, a suspect may be searched with a view both to discovering evidence that may be relevant to any charge(s) that might be laid and to seizing any weapon(s) that might be carried on his or her person. In the words of the Supreme Court of Canada, "the police have a power to search a lawfully arrested person and to seize anything in his or her possession or immediate surroundings to guarantee the safety of the police and the accused, prevent the prisoner's escape or provide evidence against him."[43]

The question of just how intrusive a personal search may be has acquired critical importance given the guarantee, enshrined in section 8 of the *Charter*, against unreasonable search and seizure. For example, the Supreme Court of Canada has held that a frisk search incidental to an arrest is justifiable since it is a "relatively non-intrusive procedure." The Court stated that such a search "reconciles the public's interest in the effective and safe enforcement of the law on the one hand, and on the other its interest in ensuring the freedom and dignity of individuals."[44]

What is the situation where the search procedures are more physically intrusive? The Supreme Court of Canada has held, for example, that grabbing suspects by the throat to prevent them from swallowing evidence (in this case a drug) is reasonable if the police officer is searching someone whom he or she believes on reasonable grounds to be a drug dealer.[45] Of course, it is well known that some drug dealers keep their "merchandise" in balloons or condoms in their mouths so that they can swallow them, without harm to themselves, if they are approached by the police; they can subsequently recover the drugs once they have excreted them. The "throat hold" is designed to prevent this method of concealing evidence. However, the Supreme Court also emphasized that the use of the throat hold would not be reasonable unless the police have very specific information that the person in question is in possession of drugs. For example, they cannot grab someone by the throat merely because he or she is in a bar where the police believe that drugs are being sold.

It has also been held that forcing a suspect, with medical assistance, to drink a substance that induces vomiting in order to cause the suspect to bring up a narcotic was reasonable as a means of gathering evidence and protecting the "health of the accused"[46] and that a search, performed by medical personnel, of the accused's bodily orifices for concealed cocaine was reasonable in the circumstances.[47]

All this would seem to indicate that the police may use extremely invasive procedures in the course of executing a search and that these procedures will generally be considered reasonable in terms of section 8 of the *Charter*. However, some limitations have been placed on the power of the police in this context. For example, in *Pohoretsky v. The Queen*,[48] the Supreme Court of Canada ruled that taking a blood sample from an "incoherent and delirious" accused person, lying in a hospital bed, constituted an unreasonable search in violation of section 8 of the *Charter*. Significantly, the Court declared that the evidence of intoxication, gained from the blood sample, could not be admitted at the accused's trial on a charge of driving a car while having a blood alcohol level of more than 80 mg. The Court stated that to admit such evidence would bring the administration of justice into disrepute (within the meaning of section 24(2) of the *Charter*). As Lamer J. said, the police had taken "advantage of the accused's unconsciousness to obtain evidence which they had no right to obtain from him without his consent had he been conscious."[49] In another case, the New Brunswick Court of Appeal ruled that the forcible removal of hairs from the head and beard of the accused without the accused's consent constituted an unreasonable seizure that infringed section 8 of the *Charter*.[50]

In addition to the powers of search and seizure that have been considered to be incidental to the process of arrest, it should also be remembered that the police may conduct a search, without any specific legislative authority, if a citizen *consents* to such an intrusion (Barton, 1993). However, it has been held that, at the accused's trial, the prosecutor is under a duty to establish that any such consent is both valid and effective. It is not enough for the prosecutor merely to show that the accused did not object to a search. Indeed, the Crown must establish that the accused had full knowledge of his or her right to be protected from an unreasonable search and realized the impact that a waiver of that right would have in his or her particular case.[51]

Of course, the issue of consent is a difficult one since individuals may feel compelled to cooperate with the police and may, in fact, be unaware of their right to refuse. As Ericson and Baranek (1982:47) noted in their observational study of the processing of defendants in the criminal process:

> ...accused people frequently explained compliance in terms of a belief that resistance would incur further assertions of police power. Police power is taken for granted by the accused so that its exercise becomes routine.

Apparently, some police forces (including the RCMP) have devised special procedures for handling "consent" searches, and some require the use of written consent forms that, in addition to offering subsequent evidence of an individual's consent, notify him or her of the right to refuse (Law Reform Commission of Canada, 1983a:52-53).

In general, however, the police have no powers of search and seizure except insofar as statute law clearly grants them such authority. Traditionally, such legislation gave the police these powers within the framework of a system of prior authorization by judicial warrants. However, the more recent legislative trend has been toward granting the police considerably greater powers to conduct searches without previously obtaining a warrant (Law Reform Commission of Canada, 1984b:4). Such a trend raises major concerns as to the protection of individual privacy since the increase of warrantless searches represents, in theory at least, a major reduction in the degree of formal legal control over the search power of the police (Law Reform Commission of Canada, 1983a:35). Instead of an independent justice deciding whether there are adequate grounds for a search, the system of permitting warrantless searches leaves that decision to the police themselves; this is a troublesome situation since the police clearly have a stake in the outcome of such a decision (Law Reform Commission of Canada, 1983a:35).

The most important *general* source of statutory powers of search and seizure is section 487 of the *Criminal Code*, which authorizes a justice to issue a search warrant in certain, clearly specified circumstances (Salhany, 1989:70). Basically, before a search warrant may be issued, an information must be sworn on oath before the justice, who may issue a warrant if he or she is satisfied (on the basis of the information sworn) that there are "reasonable grounds to believe that there is in a building, receptacle or place":

(1)   anything upon or in respect of which an offence has been, or is suspected to have been, committed against the *Criminal Code* or any other federal statute;

(2)   anything that might reasonably be considered will furnish evidence in relation to such an offence; or

(3)   anything that is reasonably believed is intended to be used to commit any offence against the person for which an individual may be arrested without a warrant.[52]

The intention underlying the *Code* procedures is to prevent the police from undertaking speculative "fishing expeditions" in the vague hope that they may turn up something illegal. Furthermore, should the police obtain a search warrant on the basis of incomplete or misleading information, then the warrant may be declared invalid and the trial court may refuse to admit any of the evidence that is seized in the course of the search.[53]

Normally, a warrant must be "executed" during daytime hours, although the justice can authorize a night-time search, if it is necessary to do so.[54] The warrant must state, with a reasonable degree of particularity, the articles to be searched for and must also indicate the alleged offence(s) involved (Salhany, 1989:72). Significantly, the *Criminal Code* provides that the police may seize not only the items specified in the warrant but also "anything that on reasonable grounds" they believe has been "obtained by or has been used in the commission of an offence."[55] The police officer named in the warrant must carry it with him or her and is required to produce it if requested to do so.[56] Should the occupants of the premises concerned refuse to let the officers in after the officers have made a formal request to enter, then the officers may make a forcible entrance in order to execute the warrant (Salhany, 1984:80). However, the police must not use an excessive amount of force in executing the warrant. They may take special measures if there is, for example, a threat of violence toward them but, as the Supreme Court of Canada has emphasized, this does not give them *"carte blanche"* to "ignore completely all restrictions on police behaviour."[57] Normally, the police must announce their presence before entering a person's residence in order to execute a search warrant. However, the Supreme Court of Canada has ruled that this requirement may be set aside where it is necessary to do so in order to prevent the destruction of evidence.[58] For example, illegal drugs may be flushed down a toilet in a matter of seconds, and requiring the police to announce their presence in every case could well render a search warrant useless as a means of enforcing the drug laws.

If police officers seize anything that is not required for the purposes of investigation or in connection with any court hearing and are satisfied that there is no dispute as to their ownership, then they must normally return them to the person lawfully entitled to possess them.[59] If the officers do not return the items seized, then they are required to bring them physically before a justice or to make a report to the justice that they have seized the items and are holding them pending the justice's decision as to what should be done with them.[60]

Although the procedures for obtaining a search warrant may appear to establish a formidable barrage of protective mechanisms, bear in mind that the "law in the books" might not always match the "law in action." The Law Reform Commission of Canada (1983a:83) conducted a survey of search warrant procedures and concluded that almost 60% of the warrants sampled were invalidly issued as they stood. This did not mean that the warrants could not have been issued legally, but rather that the strict legal procedures were not followed to the letter. The Commission, in fact, found that there were considerable differences across Canada in the extent to which warrant procedures were followed to the letter of the law. The Commission states (1983a:87) that:

> The more common apprehension, however, remains the suspicion that the justice treats search warrant issuance as a "formality." While obtaining a warrant was by no means a formality in all of the cities surveyed, there were some instances in which the detail presented in the publication to the issuer was so sketchy as to call into question whether the issuer really bothered to evaluate the documents he was given (1983a:87).

Ericson (1981) conducted an observational study of the activities of police detectives in one Ontario jurisdiction and demonstrated that they tended to develop long-term, cooperative relationships with individual justices and "relied on their routine cooperation to ease their tasks":

> Occasionally, this co-operation went well beyond the point of signing warrants without question. On one occasion, two detectives went to five addresses, mainly for the purpose of locating a suspect. Anticipating resistance from the various occupants, they took along unsigned search warrants and "left handed" them (signed a J.P.'s name). These warrants were later logged in the divisional records, and the two Justices of the Peace whose names were used were subsequently contacted and their collaboration gained (1983a:153-154).

There are other provisions in the *Criminal Code* that deal with the power of the police to conduct searches and to seize property in particular circumstances. For example, special provisions exist in relation to searches conducted under the authority of a warrant in relation to offences involving gaming houses, bookmaking, and common bawdyhouses.[61] These provisions generally grant slightly expanded powers of search and seizure to the police. Other provisions of the *Code*, however, go much further and permit searches *without a warrant* in certain circumstances; for example, a police officer may conduct a warrantless search for prohibited or restricted weapons, firearms or ammunition of a person, a vehicle, or any premises other than a dwelling house.[62]

Very broad powers of search and seizure may be granted to the police under other federal legislation. For example, both the *Narcotic Control Act* and the *Food and Drug Act* permit warrantless searches to be made in places other than dwelling houses.[63] The legislative trend toward granting the police greater powers to conduct searches *without* warrants is, as we have seen, quite troublesome. As the Law Reform Commission (1984b:4) pointed out in a report to the Minister of Justice:

> ...warranted searches remain relatively constrained compared to warrantless ones. In addition, the warrant procedure with its reliance on documentary authority facilitates review of the legality of the search or seizure...By way of contrast, a warrantless power of search and seizure represents a relatively discretionary mode of authorization, in respect of which accountability is impeded by the lack of any kind of documentary record.

However, as we shall see, the trend toward warrantless powers of search and seizure may well be dramatically reversed as a consequence of the enactment of section 8 of the *Charter*.

Telewarrants

One important change to the powers of the police in the areas of search and seizure was made by Parliament in 1985,[64] when the *Code* was amended so as to permit police officers to obtain search warrants, in certain circumstances, without the need for them to appear personally in front of a justice when they are making an application (Brodsky, 1987; Law Reform Commission of Canada, 1983b; McCalla, 1984). The availability of so-called "telewarrants" may be of particular advantage to police officers in drug cases where there may be an urgent need to conduct a search before the suspects concerned take advantage of an opportunity to destroy any relevant evidence (Brodsky, 1987:345). There is no space here to deal with the details of the relevant procedures connected with telewarrants. However, suffice it to say that a telewarrant may only be issued in respect of an indictable offence and there must be reasonable grounds for dispensing with the police officer's personal attendance. The officer will swear an information over the telephone. The statement will be recorded by the justice and, if it is decided that a warrant should be issued, the justice fills one out and signs it. The officer must then fill out a facsimile warrant, which he or she is required to produce at the scene of the search.[65]

The advent of telewarrants has rendered it relatively simple for the police to obtain *prior* judicial authorization for a search even in most situations of an emergency nature and, therefore, it could be argued that the justification for searches without warrants has been greatly reduced. It will be interesting to see to what extent the courts will be prepared to declare invalid statutory provisions that permit warrantless searches. Such a development may well occur in light of the requirement of section 8 of the *Charter* that searches be "reasonable," since it could well be contended that prior judicial authorization may readily be sought under the new telewarrant procedure (Brodsky, 1987). However, early evidence indicates that, in most provinces, the telewarrant procedure is not being used on a frequent basis.[66] It remains to be seen whether this situation will change in the years ahead.

Search and Seizure and the *Charter*

Prior to the *Charter*, relatively little attention needed to be paid, as a matter of practice, to the question of whether a search was illegal, because the fruits of an illegal search could be admitted as evidence in a criminal trial regardless of their tainted origins. The *Charter* has dramatically altered this unsatisfactory situation. Section 8 guarantees "the right to be secure against unreasonable search or seizure" (Connelly, 1985). There are two major consequences stemming from this development. First, evidence obtained as a result of an "unreasonable" search may be excluded from any subsequent trial if the Court feels that to admit it would bring the administration of justice into disrepute (according to the provisions of section 24(2) of the *Charter*). For example, in one case,[67] the police carried out an unlawful search of the accused person's yard. The officer concerned admitted that he did not have the reasonable grounds that would be necessary to obtain a search warrant so he went ahead regardless. The police suspected that the accused was cultivating marijuana and an attempt was made to peer into the windows of his house. The police saw nothing, but they detected the odor of marijuana. On the basis of these observations, a warrant was obtained and marijuana plants were later seized in the accused's home. The accused was charged with possession of marijuana for the purpose of trafficking and cultivating marijuana. The trial judge, however, refused to admit the evidence of the seized plants because the original perimeter search of the accused's home was an unreasonable search in light of section 8 of the *Charter* and he excluded the evidence under section 24(2). The Supreme Court of Canada later upheld this decision. As Sopinka J. remarked, "where the police have nothing but suspicion and no legal way to obtain other evidence, it follows that they must leave the suspect alone, not charge ahead and obtain evidence illegally and unconstitutionally."[68]

It should be emphasized that the exclusion of evidence is considered to be a course of action that is not to be taken lightly by the courts. As the Supreme Court of Canada has stated, "any denial of a Charter right is serious, but s. 24(2) is not an automatic exclusionary rule."[69] In other words, evidence will not be excluded automatically merely because an officer has blundered (see Jull, 1988; Mitchell, 1989). This principle is important since an excessive eagerness to exclude evidence may itself result in the administration of justice being brought into disrepute, and the public may lose all confidence in the judiciary if it feels that criminals are being routinely released on technicalities (Bryant *et al.*, 1990).

In *Collins v. The Queen*,[70] the Supreme Court of Canada emphasized that the accused is placed under the burden of establishing that the admission of illegally obtained evidence at his or her trial would bring the administration of justice into disrepute. Lamer J. suggested that the real question was whether the admission of the evidence would "bring the administration of justice into disrepute in the eyes of the reasonable man, dispassionate and fully apprised of the circumstances of the case."[71] Among the factors that the Supreme Court thought important to take into account when deciding whether to exclude evidence are the following.

> ▸ What kind of evidence was obtained?
> ▸ What *Charter* right was infringed?
> ▸ Was the *Charter* violation serious or was it of a merely technical nature?
> ▸ Was it deliberate, willful, or flagrant, or was it inadvertent or committed in good faith?
> ▸ Did it occur in circumstances of urgency or necessity?
> ▸ Were there other investigatory techniques available?
> ▸ Would the evidence have been obtained in any event?
> ▸ Is the offence serious?
> ▸ Is the evidence essential to substantiate the charge?
> ▸ Are other remedies available?[72]

In *Genest*,[73] the Supreme Court of Canada later held that, in deciding whether or not to exclude evidence under section 24(2), the court should consider such factors in the context of three separate questions: (1) the effect that the admission of unlawfully obtained evidence would have on the fairness of the trial; (2) the seriousness of the *Charter* violation and the reasons for it; and (3) the need to balance the effect of excluding such evidence against the effect of admitting it. In *Genest*, the Court excluded the evidence (weapons that had been seized by the police during a drug raid) because there had been a very serious violation of the accused's *Charter* rights. The warrant used by the police to search the accused's home was seriously defective, and this should have been obvious to the officers concerned. Furthermore, an excessive degree of force was used in conducting the search. Finally, whereas excluding evidence where there had been only a minor *Charter* violation could itself bring the administration of justice into disrepute, in this case, the violation was neither minor nor technical in nature. Indeed, the evidence had been obtained as a consequence of a flagrant and intentional breach of the accused's right to be free from unreasonable search and seizure. Dickson C.J. stated that while "the purpose of s. 24(2) is not to deter police misconduct, the courts should be reluctant to admit evidence that shows the signs of being obtained by an abuse of common law and *Charter* rights by the police."[74]

In deciding whether the fairness of the accused's trial has been compromised by the breach of the accused's *Charter* rights, the Supreme Court of Canada has drawn an important distinction between "real" evidence and "conscriptive" evidence.[75] Essentially, real evidence refers to tangible objects (such as drugs) that existed prior to the breach of the accused's *Charter* rights. On the other hand, "conscriptive" evidence refers to evidence that is only obtained by virtue of the fact that, in violation of their *Charter* rights, the accused persons concerned are "conscripted against themselves" through a confession or some other evidence emanating from them (such as a breath sample or blood sample). In other words, the Court has taken the view that the admission of real evidence obtained as a consequence of an infringement of the accused's *Charter* rights will rarely result in a finding of unfairness, while the admission of evidence obtained by conscripting accused persons against themselves will generally be considered to result in an unfair trial.

More specifically, the Supreme Court of Canada has ruled that narcotics[76] and weapons[77] can be considered real evidence and may generally be admitted at the accused's trial even though they have been obtained in the course of an unreasonable search that violated the accused's rights under section 8 of the *Charter*. By way of contrast, self-incriminating statements[78] and samples of blood[79] taken from an accused in violation of the right to counsel (under section 10(b) of the *Charter*) were considered to be "conscriptive" evidence and were not admitted in evidence. In one case,[80] for example, the accused was denied his right to counsel and was forced to participate in a police line-up. The Supreme Court of Canada ruled that the evidence obtained from the line-up should be considered as conscriptive evidence and was, therefore, inadmissible at the accused's trial. As Lamer J. said, "the use of any evidence that could not have been obtained but for the participation of the accused in the construction of the evidence for the purposes of the trial would tend to render the trial process unfair."[81] Clearly, in this particular case, the accused was forced to participate in the construction of incriminating evidence that could not be obtained in any other way. Again, to quote Lamer J.:

> An accused who is told to participate in a line-up before having had a reasonable opportunity to communicate with counsel is conscripted against himself since he is used as a means of creating evidence for the purposes of the trial. Line-up evidence is evidence that could not have been obtained but for the participation of the accused in the construction of the evidence for the purposes of the trial. In my view, the use of such evidence goes to the fairness of the trial process.[82]

The second consequence flowing from the *Charter's* guarantee against unreasonable search and seizure is that section 8 may be used to strike down statutory provisions that are deemed to give the police unreasonable powers of search or seizure. This development is of critical importance given the trend over the past few decades to grant the police increasing powers to conduct warrantless searches; indeed, section 8 could well reverse this trend, particularly because the advent of the telewarrant has greatly weakened the rationale for such warrantless searches. Indeed, in a seminally important case, the Supreme Court of Canada has unanimously ruled that, provided it is feasible to require it, prior authorization (namely, the granting of a warrant) is a *precondition* for a valid search or seizure,[83] and it struck down certain powers of search and seizure, under the *Combines Investigation Act*, on the basis that they infringed section 8 (Rosenberg, 1985). Dickson J. stated that:

> A requirement of prior authorization, usually in the form of a valid warrant, has been a consistent prerequisite for a valid search and seizure both at common law and under most statutes. Such a require-ment puts the onus on the State to demonstrate the superiority of its interests to that of the individual. As such it accords with the apparent intention of the Charter to prefer, where feasible, the right of the individual to be free from State interference to the interests of the State in advancing its purposes through such interference.[84]

Powers of Interrogation

The police may well wish to question criminal suspects in order to obtain information that may lead to the discovery of evidence that is relevant to their investigations. They may also seek to elicit incriminating statements that may later be used in court against the suspects concerned. In general, the police do not have any formal powers to compel suspects to answer their questions (Coughlan, 1985; Ratushny, 1983:182). Indeed, suspects have a right to choose whether or not to make a statement that might later be used against them in a criminal trial. In this sense, accused persons have a "right to silence" and, as we shall see, the Supreme Court of Canada has now declared that this right is protected by section 7 of the *Charter* (Watson, 1991).

Of course, in practice it may be very difficult for an accused person to resist answering police questions. A failure to provide an explanation when the accused is found in suspicious circumstances may well precipitate an arrest. It would be a foolhardy person who, when found with stolen goods in his or her possession, refused to give a reasonable explanation as to how the goods came to be there. Note that a right to remain silent does not extend so far as to permit a citizen to obstruct the police in the execution of their duties. For example, in *Moore v. The Queen*,[85] the Supreme Court of Canada demonstrated that it believes that the right to remain silent has some very definite limitations. Moore had ridden his bicycle through a red light and this infraction was witnessed by a police officer. The officer asked Moore to identify himself so that a highway traffic ticket could be written out. Moore ignored the request and continued his journey. He was subsequently stopped forcibly. After a bitter argument, Moore was arrested and charged with the *Criminal Code* offence of obstructing a police officer in the execution of his duty. Moore was not required by any statute to identify himself; however, the Supreme Court ruled that the police officer was required to issue an appearance notice rather than making an arrest whenever this was possible and, therefore, in requesting Moore to give his name, the officer was acting in the execution of his duty. This decision has been strongly criticized insofar as it weakens the right to remain silent:

> Due to this judgment social cooperation has been transformed into social coercion. The right to silence, long believed to be an inviolate cornerstone of just criminal procedure, has peripherally suffered an assault (Cohen, 1981:554).

Depending on the nature of the circumstances of any particular case, the police may need to engage in interrogation in order to obtain a confession. In many cases, as where there is independent evidence establishing the guilt of the accused, a confession is superfluous. However, in cases where there is no other available evidence to "clinch a conviction," then a confession may be the only means of making a charge stick in court. In their observational study, Ericson and Baranek (1982:50-52) noted that a clear majority of defendants (nearly 60%) gave verbal statements to the police "in field settings" during preliminary questioning and prior to their questioning in police custody. Furthermore, of those who were asked to give written statements to the police, while in custody, nearly 70% did so. The authors (1982:52) concluded that "most suspects do not successfully resist giving a confession."

There is a great potential for abuse of the ability of the police to obtain confessions from accused persons who are in their custody. In Canada, judicial scrutiny of the questioning process is exercised in a rather indirect manner. There is a special rule of evidence that operates to place confessions given to the police under close scrutiny before they may be introduced in evidence against the accused. The rule is that "no statement made out of court to a person in authority can be admitted into evidence against him unless the prosecution shows to the satisfaction of the trial judge that the statement was made freely and voluntarily."[86] A "person in authority" is generally "anyone who has authority or control over the accused or over the proceedings or prosecution against him" (Salhany, 1991:77); of course, a police officer is the prime example of a "person in authority." Where the prosecution seeks to rely upon a confession, the Court must hold a *voir dire* (or a trial-within-a-trial) in order to determine whether the confession is admissible (McWilliams, 1991:15-69). If there is a jury, then the *voir dire* will be held in their absence. It is up to the prosecution to prove that the confession was made voluntarily. The critical issue in this process is the manner in which the courts have fashioned a test for determining whether a statement has been made voluntarily.

For many years, the exclusive test was derived from a case decided by the English Law Lords in 1914[87] in which it was established that a statement would be considered to be voluntary if it was not obtained from the accused "either by fear of prejudice or hope of advantage exercised or held out by a person in authority." In other words, the court is limited to investigating whether the confession was obtained by threats or inducements (or, of course, actual violence). In recent years, this formulation of the test of voluntariness has been considered to be excessively technical, and the Supreme Court of Canada has indicated a willingness to expand the scope of the test (Conway, 1984). For example, it has been held that the accused must have an "operating mind" before a confession will be considered admissible at the accused's trial.[88] Therefore, a confession will not be admissible where a police interrogator unwittingly placed the accused in a light hypnotic trance.[89]

What is the situation where the police employ some form of trickery to obtain a confession? For example, is it acceptable for the police to place an undercover officer in a cell with the accused for the express purpose of encouraging him or her to make an incriminating statement? Until relatively recently, confessions obtained in this manner were routinely admitted into evidence at the accused's trial.[90] However, the advent of the *Charter* has changed this situation significantly. Indeed, in the case of *Herbert*,[91] the Supreme Court of Canada held that the police cannot employ such tactics to actively elicit a confession from an accused person who has refused to give a formal statement.

The Court ruled that the "right to silence" of an accused person who has been detained is one of the fundamental principles of justice and emphasized the fact that section 7 of the *Charter* guarantees that no one may be deprived of "life, liberty and security of the person," except in accordance with the principles of fundamental justice. As McLachlin J. stated, "a person in the power of the state's criminal process has the right to freely choose whether or not to make a statement to the police."[92] The scope of this right is broad enough to exclude any tricks that would effectively deny the accused the benefit of this choice. In Justice McLachlin's view, "to permit the authorities to trick the suspect into making a confession to them after he or she has exercised the right of conferring with counsel and declined to make a statement, is to permit the authorities to do indirectly what the Charter does not permit them to do directly."[93] Therefore, the *Charter* renders invalid any confession obtained by means of such trickery.

In this particular case, the accused had clearly chosen not to speak to the police and had informed them that he did not want to make a statement. When he subsequently spoke to an undercover police officer in his cell, he had no intention of changing his mind and making a decision to speak to the police. He merely thought he was talking to a fellow prisoner, which was "quite a different matter."[94] The police had essentially employed trickery to negate his choice not to speak to the police and, therefore, had violated his right to silence. The Court then ruled, on the basis of section 24(2) of the *Charter*, that a confession made in such circumstances should be excluded from the accused's trial on the basis that to permit its introduction would bring the administration of justice into disrepute. The *Hebert* case does not mean that all forms of trickery are prohibited in the quest to obtain incriminating statements from the accused. However, it does make clear that the police may not actively elicit confessions by placing undercover officers in the cells of accused persons who have refused to give them statements.[95]

The Law Reform Commission of Canada (1984a) has expressed considerable dissatisfaction with the existing rule relating to confessions and has suggested that the courts should exercise a much greater degree of control over the process of police questioning of suspects.[96] One of its recommendations to the Minister of Justice would represent a major shift in the balance of power between the police and the accused (Solomon, 1985); more specifically, the Commission has recommended that a general rule be introduced to the effect that no confession may be admitted in evidence "unless the prosecution establishes that the admission of evidence would not bring the administration of justice into disrepute" (1984a:13). This rule would clearly furnish the trial courts with considerable freedom to control police interrogation and would free them from the confines of the existing rule that focuses on only a few of the ways in which a statement may be obtained unfairly.

One technique that is increasingly being used by the police, during the course of questioning a suspect, is the videotaping of the whole process (Goldstein, 1984-85; Grant, 1987; Morton, 1988; McWilliams, 1991:15-49). The playing of the relevant videotape in court permits the trial judge to gain a much more complete understanding of the circumstances surrounding the making of a confession than is possible from a reading of a written statement alone. It is certainly possible that, while the use of videotaping may benefit the police in terms of their ability to contradict claims that they obtained a statement unfairly, it may also serve to reduce the possibility that the police will resort to illegal behaviour in order to extract a confession.

We noted earlier that the police are now placed under a number of significant duties as a consequence of section 10 of the *Charter*. Indeed, section 10(a) provides that the police must inform an accused promptly of the reasons for an arrest or detention. Furthermore, section 10(b) establishes that an accused person who has been arrested or detained has the right to "retain and instruct counsel without delay and to be informed of that right." This particular provision may well play an important part in regulating the questioning process (Cohen, 1984a:113; Conway, 1985; Skurka, 1992). If a confession is obtained in the situation where the accused has not been informed of his or her right to counsel or, worse still, where the right to counsel has been ignored, then it is possible that the confession may be excluded from consideration at the trial. This result would be possible as a consequence of the discretion, under section 24(2) of the *Charter*, to exclude evidence obtained in violation of an accused's rights under the *Charter* where the court considers that to admit the evidence would bring the administration of justice into disrepute. Such protection of the accused may well be necessary in light of the findings of Ericson and Baranek (1982:55), whose subjects suggested that their requests to see third parties (such as friends or relatives or lawyers) during questioning in custody were frequently refused by the police.

A good example of the combined effect of sections 10(b) and 24(2) of the *Charter* in this context is the case of *Manninen*.[97] Here, a police officer questioned the accused, who had already been arrested, and elicited an incriminating statement from him even after he had clearly stated that he did not want to say anything until he saw his lawyer. The Supreme Court of Canada ruled that the accused's right to counsel, as guaranteed by section 10(b), had been violated in two respects. First, the police did not give the accused an opportunity to contact counsel even though there was a telephone close at hand. Second, the police violated their duty to cease questioning the accused until he had been given a reasonable opportunity to retain and instruct counsel. In light of the flagrant breach of the accused's right to counsel, the Court ruled that the incriminating statement should never have been admitted at the accused's trial; to admit it following such a serious violation of his right to counsel would clearly bring the administration of justice into disrepute.[98] In a later case, it is noteworthy that the Supreme Court of Canada went so far as to say that, "*as a general rule*," any self-incriminating evidence obtained in violation of the accused's right to counsel is not admissible "because it would adversely affect the fairness of the trial and bring the administration of justice into disrepute."[99]

It appears that the courts are concerned to ensure that the accused actually comprehends his or her right to counsel. In one case,[100] an accused, who had been drinking and was possibly mentally unstable, was given a "potted version" of his rights (Conway, 1985:50) and the accused said that he understood these rights. The police immediately proceeded to ask questions about the incident that led to a charge of murder being laid against the accused. The trial court ruled that the accused's rights had been infringed and the statement was excluded. The Court held that the accused should have a "fair opportunity" to consider whether he or she wished to take advantage of the right to counsel. The police should not read a "potted version" of the accused's rights and then launch right into questioning. Given the accused's mental condition at the time and his limited educational background, it was held that the provisions of section 10(b) had not been properly complied with. Similarly, where the police know that an accused person has a limited mental capacity and has stated that he or she does not understand the nature of the right to counsel, then the police cannot rely on a "mechanical recitation" of his or her rights; instead, they must take steps to facilitate a real understanding of the accused's right to counsel.[101]

While section 10 of the *Charter* guarantees that the police will inform the accused of his or her right to retain and instruct counsel, there is no similar constitutional requirement that the accused be informed of the right to remain silent. However, it seems that the police in Canada almost invariably do inform the accused of such a right (Conway, 1985:41). At present, the absence of a caution (bringing the right to silence to the attention of the accused) is not, in itself, a reason to exclude a confession. However, it is considered to be a very important factor in determining whether a confession was given "freely and voluntarily" (Paciocco, 1987; McWilliams, 1991:15-11).[102]

Ericson and Baranek (1982:56-59) discovered that many defendants have difficulty understanding the "right-to-silence-caution." The authors also suggest that the existence of a rule requiring a police caution prior to questioning has little impact in practice:

> The accused left us with the impression that the right-to-silence caution is a legal formalism that they see as largely irrelevant to their circumstances, or is simply not mentioned at all. The accused certainly did not see it as a possible resource to be used to justify silence (1982:59).

This finding is significant since a failure to exercise the right to counsel may have important consequences for the accused person. Indeed, if a suspect does not make it clear to the police that he or she wishes to take advantage of the right to counsel, then it is likely that the courts will rule that he or she has *waived* this right and the police may proceed with their questioning (Coughlan, 1990; Tanovich, 1992).[103] Any statement the police elicit will then be admissible in evidence at the suspect's trial.

Electronic Surveillance of Private Communications

The inexorable march of modern technology has afforded police officers with a formidable array of electronic devices for monitoring the activities of criminal suspects. Electronic surveillance and the interception of private conversations have become standard weapons in the police armoury and have created considerable concern as to the implications of such technology for the civil liberties of those who may be subjected to such monitoring (see Burtch, 1979; Cohen, 1983; Fletcher, 1989).

The Canadian Committee on Corrections pointed out, in their 1969 report (Ouimet, 1969:85), that electronic surveillance of private communications was taking place on a widespread scale and that there was an urgent need to regulate it. The response of the Canadian government to this challenge was embodied in the *Protection of Privacy Act*, 1973-74, c. 50.[104] The *Act* was designed to meet two major objectives: (1) to criminalize unauthorized electronic surveillance with a view to protecting the privacy of individual citizens, and (2) to provide a formal set of procedures for authorizing the legitimate use of electronic surveillance by the police (see Law Reform Commission of Canada, 1986b:2-5). In fact, very few prosecutions have been launched against individuals for infringing upon the privacy of other citizens, whereas there have been literally thousands of authorizations for "wiretaps" since the legislation came into force in 1974 (Law Reform Commission of Canada, 1986b:7). In this sense, the legislation has, in practice, had much more to do with authorizing the use of police powers of surveillance than with the protection of individual freedoms (MacDonald, 1987; MacLean, 1987).[105] However, it is also important to bear in mind that the advent of the *Charter* in 1982 opened up a whole new area of jurisdiction in which Canadian courts have started to redress the deficiencies of the *Protection of Privacy Act* and have placed a greater emphasis on the need to safeguard the privacy rights of individual citizens. It is, therefore, vital that the provisions of the *Protection of Privacy Act* be considered in the same breath as the various *Charter* protections that have been identified and enforced by Canadian courts in recent years (Rabideau, 1991; Rauf, 1988; Rosenberg, 1990).

The *Protection of Privacy Act* provides safeguards in relation to private communications. According to the *Act*, a private communication "means any oral communication or any telecommunication made under circumstances in which it is reasonable for the originator thereof to expect that it will not be intercepted by any person other than the person intended by the originator thereof to receive it."[106] It is significant that under the terms of this definition, conversations carried on through the medium of cellular telephones are not considered "private communications" because the ordinary user of these devices is aware that transmissions may be intercepted by persons other than the intended recipient.[107] The *Act* renders it a criminal offence to intercept a private communication, although no offence is committed where either the originator of the message or its intended recipient consent to the interception.[108] Most important, from the police point of view, are the provisions of the *Act* that permit officers to intercept private communications if they have obtained prior judicial authorization to do so. The *Criminal Code*[109] states that such authorization may only be obtained in relation to a select list of criminal offences, although this list is quite extensive. In most circumstances, the police must request either the Solicitor General of Canada (for offences falling within the federal jurisdiction to prosecute), the Attorney-General of the particular province concerned (for any other offences), or specially designated agents of these officials to seek authorization from a judge of a Superior Court of Criminal Jurisdiction of the province in question.[110] Police investigators may only request a designated agent to seek authorization for a wiretap if they have received written approval of a senior officer in their respective police forces (Solicitor General of Canada, 1987:4).

A judge may give the "go ahead" for electronic surveillance in a particular case if he or she is satisfied that "it would be in the best interests of justice to do so" and that other investigative procedures have been tried and have failed, other methods of investigation are unlikely to succeed, or the urgency of the matter is such that it would be impractical to carry out the investigation of the offence concerned by using only other types of investigative procedures.[111] The judge may impose conditions on the conduct of the surveillance; indeed, during 1986, 57% of judicial authorizations included such conditions (Solicitor General of Canada, 1987:9). The authority for such surveillance is valid for up to 60 days,[112] although it is possible for a renewal of the authorization to be granted for a further period of up to 60 days.[113] A significant feature of the legislation is the requirement that the person, who is the object of police surveillance, be notified within 90 days that this has taken place,[114] although it is possible, if the police claim that their investigations are still going on, to extend this period up to a maximum of three years.

An important component of the *Protection of Privacy Act* is the provision that the contents of a wiretap that has been illegally made may not be used as evidence in a trial unless either the originator or the intended recipient of the private communication give their consent.[115] The intention of the legislation was to prohibit the introduction of illegal wiretap evidence in a criminal trial in those situations where neither of the parties involved consented to interception of their private communications. In other words, under the *Protection of Privacy Act*, the police must obtain prior judicial authorization for the surveillance of communications between parties who do not give their consent to such activity. If they do not obtain such judicial authorization, the wiretap evidence may not be admitted at a criminal trial. However, where one of the parties to the communications gave his or her consent, then the police do not have to obtain judicial authorization, under the terms of the *Act*, and the wiretap evidence may be introduced in a criminal trial. The *Act*, therefore, permitted a serious intrusion into the privacy of a citizen's private communications in those situations where the other party to those communications collaborated with the police; such an intrusion was permitted without there being any requirement of prior judicial authorization of police surveillance.

The Supreme Court of Canada has now ruled[116] that *any* surreptitious electronic surveillance of the individual by the police represents an unreasonable search and seizure under section 8 of the *Charter*. Such a search and seizure may only be justified under section 1 of the *Charter* if there has been a prior judicial authorization of such surveillance and it makes absolutely no difference whether or not one of the parties to the communications consents to their interception. Any wiretap evidence obtained without such a prior judicial authorization may, under section 24(2) of the *Charter*, be excluded at a criminal trial if its admission would bring the administration of justice into disrepute.[117] As La Forest J. stated in the Supreme Court of Canada:[118]

> The very efficacy of electronic surveillance is such that it has the potential, if left unregulated, to annihilate any expectation that our communications will remain private. A society which exposed us, at

the whim of the state, to the risk of having a permanent electronic
recording of our words every time we opened our mouths might be
superbly equipped to fight crime, but would be one in which privacy
no longer had any meaning.

He went on to say that it is "unacceptable in a free society that the
agencies of the state be free to use this technology at their sole discretion." The Court ruled that it is necessary to strike a balance between the
right of the individual to be left alone and the right of the state to intrude
on the individual's privacy in the pursuit of its law enforcement responsibilities. That balance can only be struck in an acceptable manner when
the police are required to seek prior judicial authorization for the
interception of private communications and to show reasonable cause for
making such an application (that is, they must have *reasonable grounds*
for believing an offence is being or has been committed and that the
interceptions proposed will yield evidence of such an offence).[119]

It is now clear that the police must seek judicial approval before they
intercept private communications, even if one of the parties consents to
electronic surveillance. If the police do not obtain such prior authorization, then, under section 24(2) of the *Charter*, the wiretap evidence that
they collect may be excluded from any criminal trial that ensues if the
court believes that to admit it would bring the administration of justice
into disrepute.

Under the *Protection of Privacy Act*, wiretap evidence that has been
obtained illegally cannot be introduced into evidence at a criminal trial.
However, what is the situation where the prosecution wish to introduce
not the communication itself but evidence derived from it (what is
referred to in the United States as the "fruit of the poisonous tree")? The
original legislation excluded such evidence on the same basis as the
communication itself. However, in 1977, a number of amendments were
made; among these was the provision that rendered such *derivative*
evidence admissible as evidence *unless* the trial judge is "of the opinion
that the admission thereof would bring the administration of justice into
disrepute." In effect, such evidence is now generally admissible, whereas
before 1977 it had been completely excluded from consideration by the
court (Burns, 1979; Law Reform Commission of Canada, 1986b:84-86).
Certainly, this view has been supported by judicial authority, which
emphasizes that the mere fact that a communication has been intercepted
unlawfully does not mean that the admission of evidence derived from it

will bring the administration of justice into disrepute.[120] In other words, there have to be other "aggravating factors" before such derivative evidence is excluded.

Of course, under section 24(2) of the *Charter,* the courts now have a similar power to exclude all evidence that has been obtained in violation of the accused's *Charter* rights. However, the power of section 24(2) is broader than that exercised under the *Protection of Privacy Act* because, as we have seen, it is not illegal under the *Act* to collect wiretap evidence without obtaining prior judicial authorization provided one of the parties consents to the surveillance. However, the Supreme Court of Canada has made it clear that such surveillance does infringe the accused's *Charter* right to be free from unreasonable search and seizure, and, therefore, evidence obtained from such surveillance may be excluded under section 24(2) of the *Charter*.

The Solicitor General of Canada is required[121] to prepare an annual report concerning requests for authorization to carry out electronic surveillance in relation to alleged offences *falling within federal prosecutorial jurisdiction*. This report provides only a partial picture of the use of electronic surveillance by the police in Canada. There were 408 applications for authorizations or renewals in 1989. Significantly, not even one of these requests was rejected by the judge concerned. In fact, between 1985 and 1989, only three applications out of 2,222 were rejected. The amazingly low number of refusals is attributable, in the view of the Solicitor General, to two factors. First, the strict procedural regime, which must be followed before an application is made, minimizes the possibility that an unwarranted request for an authorization will be made. Second, judges may "turn back" applications until the police can provide further information to convince them that an authorization should be granted (Solicitor General of Canada, 1991:9). Despite these explanations, it seems that requests for authorization to wiretap are practically always granted by the judges concerned. The numbers of authorizations or renewals granted show a steady downward trend from 603 in 1985 to 336 in 1988; however, in 1989, this trend was reversed and there was an increase to 408 (Solicitor General of Canada, 1991:8):

Year	1985	1986	1987	1988	1989
Total	603	460	412	336	408

The vast majority of the authorizations were granted in connection with "serious drug-related offences" and were in relation to alleged criminal conspiracies. Indeed, some 96.3% of the authorizations in 1989 concerned conspiracies to commit serious drug offences. On this basis, the Solicitor General of Canada (1991:16) claims that the use of electronic surveillance is focusing on "the more serious federal drug offences, and organized conspiracies to commit these offences."

It is claimed by the proponents of electronic surveillance that it is a vital tool for the control of organized crime and the illicit drug trade in Canada. For example, it has been pointed out (Solicitor General of Canada, 1991:31) that, although most crimes that come to the attention of the police do so as result of a complaint by a citizen, many drug-related offences would never come to their attention if it were not for their power to conduct electronic surveillance. Approximately 47% of those persons charged by federal authorities during 1985-89 had their criminal activities come to the attention of the police as the result of electronic surveillance, while some 76% of these individuals were charged with an offence specified in the authorization for surveillance.

Critics of the existing powers of the police to conduct electronic surveillance suggest that such powers may be easily exceeded and extend to the control of relatively petty crimes and that the efficacy of electronic eavesdropping in actually securing convictions has not been unequivocally established (Burtch, 1979:9). In the latter respect, although the statistics are notoriously difficult to interpret, it appears that, from 1985-89, 59% of federally laid charges, based on evidence derived from electronic surveillance, resulted in convictions; the remainder were disposed of by way of a dismissal, a withdrawal, or a stay of proceedings (Solicitor General of Canada, 1991:37). The most recent report of the Solicitor General, therefore, concludes with the observation that an analysis of the data "tends to suggest that electronic surveillance plays an important role in the successful conclusion of investigations, detecting criminality, stemming the illicit flow of drugs and obtaining convictions" (Solicitor General of Canada, 1991:36).

The Law Reform Commission of Canada (1986b) has strongly recommended that substantial reform of the existing *Protection of Privacy Act* be undertaken with some celerity. The Commission notes that there is an apparent "reticence on the part of the judiciary, at the application stage, to see their role as one of supervising the exercise of police discretion" (1986b:12). However, the Commission suggests that the

Charter clearly implies that judicial control of police discretion is entirely appropriate and recommends that Parliament spell out the circumstances in which the judiciary should and should not grant authorizations, as well as clarifying what the contents of such authorizations should be:

> The legislation must recognize that it is essentially unfair to expect a judge, who is used to being the impartial arbiter, in effect to accept a supervisory role over the prosecution, without some very clear guidelines as to the limits of his authority. We feel that it is primarily up to Parliament, rather than the judiciary, to strike the balance between a justifiable intrusion and an unwarranted invasion of privacy, although obviously in the particular case the ultimate decision must be for the judge to make (1986b:12).

The Police and Entrapment

A highly controversial matter relating to the exercise of police powers concerns the problem of entrapment (France, 1988; Stober, 1985, 1988, 1992). The police may well decide to use informers, *agents provocateurs*, or decoys in an attempt to enforce the law, particularly when victimless offences (such as drug-related crimes) are concerned. The police are unlikely to receive a citizen complaint in such cases and can rarely expect to catch a drug dealer "red-handed" unless they adopt the proactive techniques of employing informers, etc. It is, of course, difficult to decide when such techniques cross the borderline between legitimate law enforcement techniques, which must be considered necessary in all the circumstances, and unsavoury police misconduct, which should be soundly deprecated (Wool, 1985-86). In the United States in recent years, the issue of entrapment has assumed a high profile as the police have engaged in various "sting" operations in an attempt, for example, to suppress alleged corruption among high-placed officials.

Essentially, entrapment occurs when the police (usually in the form of an undercover agent) persistently harass an individual into committing an offence that he or she would not have committed, had it not been for the persistent inveigling by the police. More specifically, in the *Mack* case,[122] the Supreme Court of Canada stated that entrapment exists when:

> (a)   the authorities provide a person with an opportunity to commit an offence without acting on a reasonable suspicion that this

person is already engaged in criminal activity or pursuant to a *bona fide* inquiry; or

(b)   although having such a reasonable suspicion or acting in the course of a *bona fide* inquiry, they go beyond providing an opportunity and induce the commission of the offence.[123]

The Supreme Court also said that, when asking whether entrapment has actually occurred, it is "useful to consider whether the conduct of the police would have induced the average person in the position of the accused." The Court emphasized that the rationale underpinning the defence of entrapment was the need for the courts to preserve the "purity of the administration of justice." In this sense, entrapment must be regarded as an aspect of the doctrine of "abuse of process," whereby the courts have an inherent power to stay (or terminate) the proceedings where it is believed that the police or the prosecution have been using the judicial process for unfair purposes (Stuart, 1989). In the words of the Supreme Court of Canada:

> The court is, in effect, saying it cannot condone or be seen to lend a stamp of approval to behaviour which transcends what our society perceives to be acceptable on the part of the state. The stay of the prosecution of the accused is the manifestation of the court's disapproval of the state's conduct. The issuance of the stay obviously benefits the accused but the court is primarily concerned with a larger issue: the maintenance of the public confidence in the legal and judicial process.[124]

In the *Mack* case itself, the Supreme Court of Canada ordered that a stay of proceedings should be entered in relation to a charge of possession of narcotics for the purpose of trafficking. Mack had been a drug user and had been convicted of several drugs charges in the past. However, he had given up the use of drugs for quite a long period. Nevertheless, he was approached by a police informer and *repeatedly* asked to supply the informer with narcotics. This suggested that the police were trying to make the accused "take up his former life-style." The Court said that:

> The length of time, approximately six months, and the repetition of requests it took before [Mack] agreed to commit the offence also demonstrate that the police had to go further than merely providing

[Mack] with the opportunity once it became evident that he was unwilling to join the alleged drug syndicate.

Perhaps the most important and determinative factor...is [Mack's] testimony that the informer acted in a threatening manner...I believe that this conduct was unacceptable...I have come to the conclusion that the average person in the position of the appellant might also have committed the offence, if only to satisfy this threatening informer and to end all further contact.[125]

By way of contrast, in *Showman*,[126] the Supreme Court of Canada later refused to apply the defence of entrapment to a case that also involved trafficking in narcotics. In *Showman*, the police persuaded a friend of the accused to approach him with a request to supply him with narcotics. This request was made repeatedly over a period of a few days. At first, the accused refused to supply the drugs, but later he sold a package of marijuana to an undercover police officer brought to his home by the friend. The Supreme Court of Canada held that there had not been any entrapment in this case. The police were acting on reasonable suspicion that Showman was *already dealing in drugs* and "were fully entitled to provide [him] with an opportunity to commit the offence."[127] Unlike the *Mack* case, the phone calls made by the friend were made over a few days only, and the Court noted that the average person would not be induced into the commission of an offence purely as a consequence of such activity. In the view of the Court, therefore, the police had not crossed the fine line between, on the one hand, merely providing an opportunity for Showman to commit an offence and, on the other hand, employing "tactics designed to induce someone into the commission of an offence."

In *Barnes*,[128] the Supreme Court of Canada addressed the issue of whether the defence of entrapment may be raised where the police approach individuals at random and offer them the opportunity to commit a crime. Barnes was charged with a number of offences arising from the sale of *cannabis* to an undercover police officer. The officer had approached Barnes, whom she had never seen before, and asked him to sell her some *cannabis*. After a brief conversation, Barnes sold her some hashish. He was subsequently arrested and his defence was based on the allegation that he had been entrapped by the police. The incident had taken place within the confines of a six-block pedestrian mall in downtown Vancouver and evidence indicated that this one area was the source of almost one-quarter of all the drug charges laid in the city. The undercover officer indicated that she had approached Barnes because he fitted the description of a person who would be likely to be willing to deal in drugs. Barnes asserted that he was the victim of entrapment because the police had been engaged in "random virtue testing."

The Supreme Court of Canada rejected the entrapment defence in this case. Lamer C.J. accepted the argument that the police officer had no reasonable basis for suspecting that Barnes was involved in criminal activity. However, she was engaged in a *bona fide* inquiry. Her intention was to investigate and control drug dealing in an area where the police had clear evidence that such criminal activity was both frequent and widespread. It would not be entrapment, in light of the principles set out in the *Mack* case, if the officer merely presented Barnes with the opportunity to sell drugs in the course of a *bona fide* inquiry. In the Chief Justice's words:

> The basic rule articulated in *Mack* is that the police may only present the opportunity to commit a particular crime to an individual who arouses suspicion that he or she is already engaged in the particular criminal activity. An exception to this rule arises where the police undertake a *bona fide* investigation directed at an area where it is reasonably suspected that criminal activity is occurring. When such a location is defined with sufficient precision, the police may present *any* person associated with the area with the opportunity to commit the particular offence. Such randomness is permissible within the scope of a *bona fide* inquiry.[129]

Since Barnes was clearly in an area where it was reasonably believed that drug-related crimes were occurring, the officer's conduct was justified and could not be considered entrapment. Her conduct would only have been regarded as "random virtue testing" (and thus entrapment) if she had not had a reasonable belief that the area in which the incident took place was one in which drug-dealing was likely to be occurring.[130]

Despite these three important rulings on the nature and scope of the defence of entrapment, it is still a relatively novel defence and it remains to be seen just how restrictively Canadian courts will apply it in the future. The cases of *Mack*, *Showman*, and *Barnes* suggest that it will not be an easy defence to advance successfully. Most Canadians would agree that the individual citizen must be protected from overzealous (or even corrupt) law enforcement; however, the problem lies in deciding exactly where the courts should draw the line in any individual case. This is certain to be an onerous task for Canadian courts in the future.

In this chapter, we have attempted to present the more significant materials on police powers and the exercise of discretion. In Chapter 5, we will consider in further detail many of the issues raised in this chapter and in Chapter 3, including the decision making of the police, the effectiveness of the police, community policing and crime prevention, and the recruitment and training of police officers.

NOTES

[1]Hereinafter referred to as the *Charter*.

[2]See *R. v. Genest* (1986), 32 C.C.C. (3d) 8 (Que. C.A.).

[3]In *R. v. Charles* (1987), 36 C.C.C. (3d) 286 (Sask. C.A.), it was held that reduction of the accused's sentence might be an appropriate remedy under section 24(1).

[4]The Canadian Association of Chiefs of Police actively lobbied against the *Charter* during 1980 and 1981 (see Marquis 1991:403).

[5]See *R. v. Therens* (1985), 45 C.R. (3d) 97.

[6]*Ibid.*, at 124 per Le Dain J. Similarly, the Supreme Court of Canada has ruled that a person who has been required by a customs officer to submit to a strip search has been "detained" within the meaning of section 9; see *R. v. Simmons* (1988), 45 C.C.C. (3d) 296 (S.C.C.) and *R. v. Jacoy* (1988), 45 C.C.C. (3d) 46 (S.C.C.).

Individuals will not be considered to have been detained where they are merely talking to the police as potential *witnesses*. However, once they become *suspects* then they are considered to be in detention and the police must inform them of their right to counsel: see *R. v. Williams* (1992), 76 C.C.C. (3d) 385 (B.C. S.C.).

[7]*Ibid.*, at 125-126. See also *Regina v. Keats* (1987), 39 C.C.C. (3d) 358 (Nfld. C.A.). In this case, the Court ruled that there was a "detention" because there was an element of *psychological compulsion* in the accused's mind in spite of the fact that a police officer had told her that she was "free to leave" the police station. Since her original detention continued, in spite of her being told she could leave, the Court ruled that she should have been informed of her right to counsel.

In *R. v. Hawkins* (1992), 72 C.C.C. (3d) 524, the Newfoundland Court of Appeal stated that the phrase, "psychological detention," should be given a very broad interpretation. Indeed, Marshall J. suggested (at p. 543) that individuals are subject to psychological detention as soon as the police start to focus their inquiries on them with a view to laying charges against them. Any questioning beyond this point must be delayed until the police have informed the accused of their right to counsel. According to Marshall J. psychological detention may exist even though the accused persons concerned are unaware of any compulsion.

Random vehicle stops constitute a form of *detention*, although the Supreme Court of Canada has held that they are justifiable under section 1 of the *Charter* even though they might infringe on the accused's right not to be "arbitrarily" detained under section 9; see *R. v. Wilson* (1990), 56 C.C.C. (3d) 142 (S.C.C.); *R. v. Ladouceur* (1990), 56 C.C.C. (3d) 22 (S.C.C.); *R. v. Husky* (1988), 40 C.C.C. (3d) 398 (S.C.C.).

However, the Supreme Court of Canada later made clear that random roadside check stops are only justified insofar as they are limited to the task of reducing the "terrible toll of death and injury so often occasioned by impaired drivers or by dangerous vehicles." See *R. v. Mellenthin* (1992), 76 C.C.C. (3d) 481 (S.C.C.). In the view of the Court (at p. 487), "the primary aim of the (check-stop) program is...to check for sobriety, licenses, ownership, insurance and the mechanical fitness of cars." Random check "must not be turned into a means of conducting either an unfounded general inquisition or an unreasonable search." For example, they may not be used as a means of conducting a fishing expedition to see if motorists have any illegal drugs in their possession. See also Tanovich (1993).

[8]See, for example, *R. v. Duguay* (1989), 46 C.C.C. (3d) 1 (S.C.C.).

[9]Section 495(1) of the *Criminal Code*.

[10]*R. v. Storrey* (1990), 53 C.C.C. (3d) 316 (S.C.C.).

[11]*Ibid.*, at 324, *per* Cory J. (emphasis added). Note that the Court refers to "reasonable and probable grounds" even though the *Code* now mentions only "reasonable grounds." Prior to the R.S.C. 1985 version of the *Criminal Code,* the term "reasonable and probable grounds" was used in relation to the powers of arrest in the *Code*. Apparently, the change in terminology was not intended to alter the scope of the power to make an arrest.

[12]Section 31(1).

[13]Section 199(2).

[14]*Bail Reform Act*, R.S.C., 1970 (n Supp.), c.2.

[15]Section 495(2).

[16]Section 497. It has been held that, under the provision of section 497(1)(f), a police officer may continue to detain a motorist, arrested for impaired driving, until he or she has sobered up. Such a continuing detention does not infringe the Charter's guarantee against arbitrary detention (section 9). See *R. v. Williamson* (1986), 25 C.C.C. (3d) 139 (Alta. Q.B.) and *R. v. Pashowitz* (1987), 59 C.R. (3d) 396 (Sask. C.A.).

[17]Section 498.

[18]Sections 507, 512, and 795.

[19]Sections 504 and 795.

[20]Section 507(4).

[21]Section 507(6) and 499.

[22]Section 503.

[23]It was held to be an arbitrary detention, under section 9, where a suspect was kept in custody for eight hours for the purpose of interrogation, despite the fact that a justice was readily available; see *R. v. Reeves* (November 5, 1985), 15 W. C.B. 269 (N.S. Prov. Ct.). However, in *R. v. Storrey* (1990), 53 C.C.C. (3d) 316, the Supreme Court of Canada held that there was no breach of the accused's rights under section 9 in the situation where he had been arrested and held for 18 hours so that a line-up could be arranged. After the line-up, in which the accused was identified, he was formally charged, and only at that point was he taken before a justice. The Court held that 18 hours was not an unreasonable delay in the particular circumstances of the case (a line-up was the only practical method of identification) and in light of the fact that the accused was taken before the justice immediately after the line-up.

[24]Section 509.

[25]Sections 496 and 501.

[26]Section 505.

[27]Section 508.

[28]Section 29(2).

[29]See section 24(2) of the *Charter*; *R v. Elshaw* (1991), 67 C.C.C. (3d) 97 (S.C.C.); and *R. v. Finta* (1992), 73 C.C.C. (3d) 65 (Ont. C.A.).

[30]*R. v. Therens et al.* (1985), 45 C.R. (3d) 97 (S.C.C.).

[31]In *Regina v. Mohl* (1987), 34 C.C.C. (3d) 435, the Saskatchewan Court of Appeal ruled that evidence obtained from a breathalyzer test should be excluded (under section 24(2) of the *Charter*), where the accused had been required to blow at a time when he was too intoxicated to comprehend his right to counsel (as guaranteed by section 10(b) of the *Charter*). In exercising its discretion to exclude the evidence, the Court placed great emphasis on the fact that the police were well aware of the accused's extreme state of intoxication. On the other hand, in *Regina v. McAvena* (1987), 34 C.C.C. (3d) 461, the same Court of Appeal ruled that where the accused might not have understood his right to counsel because of a concussion, the evidence obtained from a breathalyzer test should be admitted even though it had been obtained in violation of section 10(b) of the *Charter*. Bayda C.J. said that the police officer concerned had "made an honest, dedicated and diligent attempt to comply with the requirements of the *Charter*" (at p. 472).

The issue, as to when evidence obtained in violation of the accused's rights under s. 10(b) should be declared inadmissible at the trial, was also considered by the Supreme Court of Canada in *Jacoy v. The Queen* (1988), 45 C.C.C. (3d)

46. Here the accused had been not informed of his right to counsel during a customs search that revealed the presence of cocaine on his person. Although the Court ruled that the accused's right to counsel had been infringed, it refused to exclude the evidence of narcotics. Dickson C.J. pointed out that the customs officers had acted in good faith (since they were acting on a policy directive based on a decision of the Ontario Court of Appeal) and they held no malice to Jacoy himself. Furthermore, Jacoy was not mistreated. In short, the violation of the accused's right to counsel was not "deliberate or flagrant."

Of course, accused persons may waive their right to counsel and cannot later claim that this right was infringed because they gave a statement to the police without consulting a lawyer. In *Regina v. Neaves* (1992), 75 C.C.C. (3d) 201 (N.S.C.A.), the accused was informed of his right to counsel but stated that he did not want to speak to a lawyer. He then made some statements that incriminated him. Meanwhile, the police had refused access to a family member and a lawyer. The accused was told that the lawyer wanted to see him but he stated that he did not want to speak to a lawyer. The Court of Appeal ruled that the accused's right to counsel under section 10(b) had not been violated by the refusal of the police to grant the lawyer access to him. The accused himself had voluntarily waived his right to counsel.

[32]*R. v. Brydges* (1990), 53 C.C.C. (3d) 330 (S.C.C.). In a later case, the Nova Scotia Court of Appeal stated that the right identified by the Supreme Court of Canada in the *Brydges* case does not require a province to establish a duty counsel system to provide legal assistance outside regular office hours: *Regina v. Prosper* (1992), 75 C.C.C. (3d) 1 (N.S.C.A.). In *Prosper*, the police demanded that the accused provide a breath sample and, at the same time, he was informed of his right to counsel and the availability of legal aid. The accused told the police that he wanted to speak to a lawyer. He was given a list of legal aid lawyers but, because it was outside normal office hours, he was unable to reach any of them. The police then gave the accused a list of all of the lawyers in Halifax but he stated that he could not afford a private lawyer. He then took the breathalyzer test. The trial judge acquitted the accused of the charge of being "above 80" on the basis that he had been denied his right to counsel. However, the Court of Appeal disagreed and entered a conviction. The view of the Court of Appeal was that the accused's right under section 10(b) of the *Charter* only amounts to a right to be granted a reasonable opportunity to retain and instruct counsel. The accused does not have a right to have a legal aid lawyer appointed for him or her. Therefore, the police in this case fulfilled their obligations under section 10(b) merely by informing the accused of his right to counsel and the availability of legal aid and by giving him a reasonable opportunity to contact a lawyer. The fact that he could not reach a legal aid lawyer was not relevant to the question of whether the police had infringed his right under section 10(b).

[33]*R. v. Bain* (1992), 69 C.C.C. (3d) 481 (S.C.C.).

[34]*R. v. Pithart* (April 3, 1987, B.C. Co. Ct.).

[35]*R. v. Beare* (1988), 45 C.C.C. (3d) 57 (S.C.C.).

[36]*Ibid.,* at 77.

[37]The offence, in connection with which the officer seeks to make an arrest, must be one for which the suspect can be arrested without a warrant.

[38]*R. v. Landry* (1986), 25 C.C.C. (3d) 1 (S.C.C.).

[39]*R. v. Biron* (1975), 23 C.C.C. (2d) 513.

[40]However, not every unlawful arrest amounts to a breach of the accused's *Charter* rights; see, for example, *R. v. Duguay* (1989), 46 C.C.C. (3d) 1 (S.C.C.), in which it was held that an unlawful arrest is not necessarily an arbitrary detention in violation of section 9 of the *Charter.*

[41]In *Campbell v. Hudyma* (1985), 42 Alta. L.R. 59 (Alta. C.A.), a civil action for false imprisonment, wrongful arrest, and assault was successful because the officer failed to inform the arrested person of the reasons for the arrest.

[42]The Law Reform Commission of Canada (1991: 22-24) has recommended that the police should be granted the general power to search a person in addition to their existing power to conduct such a search as part of an arrest. This additional power would be exercised only under the authority of a warrant (except in emergency situations). The Commission (1991:51) recommends that a search of the person be carried out in a manner that "respects the dignity of the person," preserves privacy as much as possible, and involves as little intrusion on bodily integrity as is reasonably practical. Special provisions would apply to the issue of warrants for intrusive searches of the person and for the conduct of forensic tests to obtain such items as hair and saliva samples (Law Reform Commission of Canada, 1985b and 1991:57-69).

[43]*Per* L'Heuruex-Dube J. in *Cloutier v. Langlois* (1990), 53 C.C.C. (3d) 257, at 274.

In *R. v. Garcia* (1992), 72 C.C.C. (3d) 240, the Quebec Court of Appeal emphasized that the right of the police to search suspects without a warrant and as an incident to their arrest is not an absolute power. Such a search can only be carried out for a "valid objective." Referring to Justice L'Hereux-Dube's judgment in *Cloutier v. Langlois, supra,* Justice Rousseau-Houle of the Quebec Court of Appeal held that a "valid objective" would be to search for a weapon or other object that might threaten the safety of the police, the accused or the public or that might facilitate an attempt to escape or to search for evidence relevant to the offence(s) for which the police are taking the accused into custody. The police may not go beyond these limited objectives and conduct a general fishing expedition. In Garcia, the accused was arrested for breach of probation (he had apparently broken his curfew). The police took him to the station and told him to empty his pockets. He did so and the police examined a cigarette package that he gave them. It turned out that it contained a small quantity of hashish. The Quebec Court of Appeal ruled that the police had no right to open the package since there was no concern that the accused had a weapon of any kind nor did they need to search the package as a means of obtaining evidence relevant to the charge of breach of probation. Since the Crown did not establish that the police had a "valid objective" to open the package as an incident to the accused's arrest, the Court ruled that they had carried out an unreasonable search and seizure, contrary to the terms of section 8 of the *Charter*. However, it is interesting to note that the Court nevertheless ruled that the evidence obtained by this search could still be admitted at the accused's trial for possession of narcotics because, even though it had been obtained in breach of the accused's *Charter* rights, it was "real evidence" and its admission would not bring the administration of justice into disrepute.

[44]*Ibid.*, at 277-278.

[45]*Collins v. The Queen* (1987), 33 C.C.C. (3d) 1. See also *R. v. Garcia-Guiterrez* (1991), 65 C.C.C. (3d) 15 (B.C.C.A.).

[46]*R. v. Meickle*, unreported, April 29, 1983, Ont. Co. Ct., Matlow Co. Ct. J. In another case, it was held that a search, performed by medical personnel, of the accused's bodily orifices for cocaine was reasonable in the circumstances.

[47]*R. v. McCready* (November 25, 1982), 9 W.C.B. 109 (B.C. Prov. Ct., Smith, Prov. Ct. J.).

[48](1987), 33 C.C.C. (3d) 398 (S.C.C.).

[49]*Ibid.*, at 402. See also *R. v. Dyment* (1988), 45 C.C.C. (3d) 244 (S.C.C.), in which the Supreme Court of Canada said that it was not reasonable for a police officer to take a blood sample from a physician who had removed it without the accused's consent and turned it over to the police without a warrant. In *R. v. Racette* (1988), 39 C.C.C. (3d) 289, the Saskatchewan Court of Appeal ruled that provincial legislation giving the police the right to demand blood samples or the taking of such samples without consent where the subject is unconscious was in violation of sections 7 and 8 of the *Charter*. It was also held that the legislation could not be rescued as a "reasonable limitation" within the meaning of section 1. However, note that, under section 254(3) of the *Code,* a police officer who has reasonable and probable grounds to believe that the accused has been driving while impaired or "above 80," may require that the accused provide a sample of breath or (in certain circumstances) blood. In *R. v. Altseimer* (1982), 1 C.C.C. (3d) 7 (Ont. C.A.) and *R. v. Gaff* (1984), 15 C.C.C. (3d) 126 (Sask. C.A.), it was held that the breath demand provisions did not infringe the *Charter*. In *R. v. Pelletier* (1989), 50 C.C.C. (3d) 22 (Sask. Q.B.), in a trial court decision, it was held that even if the blood sample provisions of the *Code* did infringe the *Charter,* they were justified as a reasonable limitation under section 1.

[50]*R. v. Legere* (1988), 43 C.C.C. (3d) 502 (N.B. C.A.).

[51]*R. v. Nielsen* (1988), 43 C.C.C. (3d) 548 (Sask. C.A.); *R. v. Wills* (1992), 70 C.C.C. (3d) 529 (Ont. C.A.). Of course, only the persons whose property is the subject of an investigation may give their consent to a search by the police. For example, a hotel manager may not give a valid consent to the search of a guest's room by the police; see *R. v. Mercer; R. v. Kenny* (1992), 70 C.C.C. (3d) 180 (Ont. C.A.).

[52]Note that the warrant will be invalid if the information does not set out the "reasonable grounds" required by the *Criminal Code*; see *R. v. Pastro* (1988), 42 C.C.C. (3d) 485 (Sask. C.A.).

[53]See, for example, *R. v. Silvestrone* (1991), 66 C.C.C. (3d) 125 (B.C.C.A.) and *R. v. Brassard* (1992), 77 C.C.C. (3d) 285 (Sask. Q.B.).

[54]Section 488.

[55]Section 489.

[56]Section 29(1).

[57]*Per* Dickson C.J.C. in *R. v. Genest* (1989), 45 C.C.C. (3d) 385, at 408.

[58]*R. v. Genest* (1989), 45 C.C.C. (3d) 385 (S.C.C.); *R. v. Gimson* (1991), 69 C.C.C. (3d) 552 (S.C.C.).

[59]Section 489.1.

[60]The ultimate disposition of the seized items, by the justice, is governed by section 490.

[61]See section 199.

[62]Section 101. There is a trial decision in which it was held that this provision was invalid in light of section 8 of the *Charter*; see *R. v. McDonough* (1988), 44 C.C.C. (3d) 370 (Ont. Dist. Ct.).

[63]Section 10 of the *Narcotic Control Act* and section 42 of the *Food and Drugs Act*. The police must have reasonable and probable grounds for making a warrantless search of this type; see *R. v. Debot* (1989), 52 C.C.C. (3d) 193 (S.C.C.); *Greffe v. The Queen* (1990), 55 C.C.C. (3d) 161 (S.C.C.); and Young (1990). Drug-related searches of dwelling houses require the issue of a warrant, obtained under the authority of the respective statutes.

In a recent case, the B.C. Court of Appeal ruled that, under the terms of section 10 of the *Narcotic Control Act,* the police may conduct a warrantless search of a motor vehicle, even though it is parked on private property that is located next to a dwelling house: *R. v. Zastowny* (1992), 76 C.C.C. (3d) 492 (B.C.C.A.).

[64]The new section 487.1 of the *Code* was proclaimed into force in December, 1985.

[65]"Facsimile" means a reasonable copy. Such a copy must be free from any significant or misleading errors; see *R. v. Skin* (1988), 13 M.V.R. (2d) 130 (B.C. Co. Ct.).

[66]Note that Pomerance (1990:324) contends that there is no longer a province-wide system of telewarrants in Ontario. The system was not continued

owing to excessive costs and marked underuse. Pomerance notes (1990:329) that telewarrant systems are in place in Alberta, New Brunswick, Manitoba, British Columbia, Quebec, Newfoundland, and the Yukon Territories. Only in Quebec, British Columbia, and the Yukon were the telewarrants reported to be in frequent use.

[67]*R. v. Kokesch* (1990), 61 C.C.C. (3d) 207 (S.C.C.).

[68]*Ibid.*, at 227.

[69]*R. v. Strachan* (1988), 46 C.C.C. (3d) 479 (S.C.C.), per Dickson C.J.C. However, see Paciocco (1990) for the view that the Supreme Court of Canada has gone too far in permitting the exclusion of evidence under section 24(2).

[70](1987), 33 C.C.C. (3d) 1. See Delsisle (1989).

[71]*Ibid.*, at 18.

[72]*Ibid.*, at 18-19.

[73]*Genest v. The Queen* (1989), 45 C.C.C. (3d) 385 (S.C.C.).

[74]*Ibid.*, at 409. The fact that the police acted in good faith, believing that they were acting in accordance with the law, may be a strong factor in persuading the trial court to admit illegally obtained evidence: see *R. v. Kokesch* (1990), 61 C.C.C. (3d) 207 (S.C.C.); *R. v. Charbonneau* (1992), 74 C.C.C. (3d) 49 (Que. C.A.); *R. v. Grant* (1992), 73 C.C.C. (3d) 315 (B.C.C.A.).

[75]See, for example, *R. v. Collins* (1987), 33 C.C.C. (3d) 1 (S.C.C.); *R. v. Wise* (1992), 70 C.C.C. (3d) 193 (S.C.C.).

[76]*R. v. Jacoy* (1988), 45 C.C.C. (3d) 46 (S.C.C.); *R. v. Debot* (1989), 52 C.C.C. (3d) 193 (S.C.C.); *R. v. Genereux* (1992), 70 C.C.C. (3d) 1 (S.C.C.); *R. v. E.* (G.A.) (1992), 77 C.C.C. (3d) 60 (Ont. C.A.).

[77]*R. v. Black* (1989), 50 C.C.C. (3d) 1 (S.C.C.).

[78]*R. v. Manninen* (1987), 34 C.C.C. (3d) 385 (S.C.C.); *R. v. Chartrand* (1992), 74 C.C.C. (3d) 408 (Man. C.A.); *R. v. Proulx* (1992), 76 C.C.C. (3d) 316 (Que. C.A.).

[79]*R. v. Pohoretsky* (1987) , 33 C.C.C. (3d) 398 (S.C.C.). However, there may be some exceptional cases where, although a blood sample is taken in violation of an accused person's *Charter* rights and is considered to be "conscriptive evidence, it may nevertheless be admitted because its admission in all of the circumstances of the case would not affect the fairness of the trial; see, for example, *R. v. Brown* (1991), 69 C.C.C. (3d) 139 (N.S.C.A.).

If the police seize information from medical personnel concerning a blood analysis originally conducted for strictly medical purposes, then the information will be considered "real" rather than "conscriptive" evidence because it existed before the infringement of the accused's *Charter* rights; this evidence may, therefore, be admissible at the accused's trial; see *R. v. Erickson* (1992), 72 C.C.C. (3d) 75 (Alta. C.A.); *R. v. Tessier* (1990), 58 C.C.C. (3d) 192 (S.C.C.). However, there have been cases where such evidence was excluded because, for example, it was felt that the public's confidence in, and trust of, hospitals might be diminished if the police were granted ready access to personal information concerning blood samples taken for medical purposes; see *R. v. Dyment* (1988), 45 C.C.C. (3d) 244 (S.C.C.).

[80]*R. v. Ross* (1989), 46 C.C.C. (3d) 129 (S.C.C.).

[81]*Ibid.*, at 139.

[82]*Ibid.*, at 139-140.

[83]*Hunter et al. v. Southam Inc.* (1984), 14 C.C.C. (3d) 97.

[84]*Ibid.*, 109.

[85][1979] 1 S.C.R. 195.

[86]*Per* Dickson J. in *Erven v. The Queen* (1978), 44 C.C.C. (2d) 76 (S.C.C.).

[87]*Ibrahim v. The Queen*, [1914] A.C. 599 (P.C.).

[88]*Ward v. The Queen*, [1979] 2 S.C.R. 30.

[89]*Horvath v. The Queen*, [1979] 2 S.C.R. 376.

[90]*Rothman v. The Queen* (1981), 20 C.R. (3d) 97 (S.C.C.).

[91]*R. v. Hebert* (1990), 57 C.C.C. (3d) 1 (S.C.C.). See also *R. v. Jackson* (1991), 68 C.C.C. (3d) 385 (Ont. C.A.).

[92]*Ibid.*, at 32.

[93]*Ibid.*, at 38

[94]*Ibid.*, at 43.

[95]The *Hebert* decision was later applied by the Ontario Court of Appeal in a case where the police sought to elicit incriminating statements from an accused person by sending an undercover, female police officer to visit him in jail. The accused formed a romantic attachment to the officer, who then asked him questions that led to the accused making some incriminating remarks. The Court of Appeal ruled that these statements should have been excluded in violation of the principles of fundamental justice (which included the accused's right to silence); see *R. v. Jackson and Davy* (1991), 68 C.C.C. (3d) 385 (Ont. C.A.). By way of contrast, it has been held that a statement made by the accused to an undercover officer in his cell may be introduced in evidence provided the latter did not actively elicit information from the accused. In other words, passive listening does not infringe the accused's right to silence. See *R. v. Graham* (1991), 62 C.C.C. (3d) 128 (Ont. C.A.). Similarly, confessions made to police informers who have been placed in the cells of accused persons may be admitted into evidence if the informers act independently of the police. See *R. v. Johnston* (1991), 64 C.C.C. (3d) 233 (Ont. C.A.) and *R. v. Naldzil* (1991), 68 C.C.C. (3d) 350 (B.C. C.A.).

Informers act independently of the police where they merely tell the authorities about incriminating statements that have already been made to them by other inmates. Any confessions obtained in this way will be admissible evidence at trial. On the other hand, if informers are deliberately planted by the police to elicit information from specific individuals then they are clearly acting as "agents of the police" and any incriminating statements obtained by such informers will normally be excluded at trial because they have been obtained in violation of the right to silence. In *R. v. Broyles* (1991), 68 C.C.C. (3d) 308 (S.C.C.), the Supreme Court of Canada articulated general principles as a means of determining when the use of informers violates the accused's right to silence (*per* Iacobucci J. at 318-319).

In the *Broyles* case, the police used a friend of the accused to obtain incriminating statements. The friend was wearing a recording device when he visited the accused in prison and asked him questions about the murder with which the accused had been charged. The Supreme Court ruled that the statements should have been excluded from the accused's trial because his right to silence had been infringed. The friend was being used by the police to actively elicit incriminating statements and was clearly acting as an agent of the police. "If the authorities had not intervened, the conversation between [the friend] and [the accused] would either not have occurred at all, or else would have taken a materially different course" (at 322).

[96]Another mechanism for the regulation (or structuring) of police interrogation procedures is the development by the police authorities themselves of formal guidelines that must be followed whenever a suspect is questioned; see Freedman (1988).

[97]*R. v. Manninen* (1987), 34 C.C.C. (3d) 385 (S.C.C.). A confession may also be excluded if it was obtained during a period of "arbitrary detention" (contrary to section 9 of the *Charter*); see *R. v. Spence* (1988), 41 C.C.C. (3d) 354 (Man. C.A.).

[98]See also the similar case of *R. v. Black* (1989), 50 C.C.C. 1 (S.C.C.).

[99]*R. v. Elshaw* (1991), 67 C.C.C. (3d) 97 (S.C.C.), *per* Iacobucci J., at 129. See also *R. v. Broyles* (1991), 68 C.C.C. (3d) 308 (S.C.C.).

[100]*R. v. Nelson* (1982), 3 C.c.C. (3d) 147 (Man. Q.B.).

[101]*R. v. Evans* (1991), 63 C.C.C. (3d) 289 (S.C.C.). In this case, the accused, who was described as being of "subnormal intelligence," was not informed of his right to counsel in terms that he could understand. The Supreme Court held that incriminating statements that he made during his interrogation should have been excluded from the trial under section 24(2) of the *Charter*.

It should be noted that the police may be required to repeat their statement to the accused that he or she has a right to counsel. For example, in *R. v. Chartrand* (1992), 74 C.C.C. (3d) 409 (Man. C.A.), the accused was arrested on a robbery charge and was informed of his right to counsel. However, later on, the police changed their focus of inquiries and asked the accused if he had been involved in any other offences. The accused was not reinformed of his right to counsel at this stage and he then confessed to a break and enter offence. The Court of Appeal ruled that, since there had been a "fundamental and discrete change in the purpose of the investigation" when the police shifted the thrust of their interrogation away from the robbery charge, the police were under a duty to reinform the accused of his right to counsel. Since the police did not do so, the confession was considered to have been obtained in violation of section 10(b) and was not admissible evidence at the accused's trial.

[102]See also *R. v. Hebert* (1990), 57 C.C.C. (3d) (S.C.C.), *per* McLachlin J., at 26-27.

[103]See, for example, *R. v. Smith* (1989), 50 C.C.C. (3d) 308 (S.C.C.) and *R. v. Smith* (1991), 63 C.C.C. (3d) 313 (S.C.C.).

[104]Note that there were some major changes to this *Act* in 1977 (Bill C-51). The legislation is contained in the *Criminal Code,* Part VI.

[105]In *R. v. Wong* (1990), 60 C.C.C. (3d) 460 (S.C.C.), the Supreme Court of Canada ruled that Part VI of the *Criminal Code* does not apply to electronic video surveillance. However, the Court held that such surveillance could constitute a search and seizure within the meaning of section 8 of the *Charter*. Therefore, the subjects of such surveillance are protected by the *Charter* guarantees against unreasonable search and seizure. Such surveillance will only pass *Charter* scrutiny when the police have previously obtained a warrant. Evidence that has been obtained without the authorization of a warrant may be excluded from a criminal trial under section 24(2) of the *Charter*.

[106]Section 183 of the *Criminal Code*.

[107]*R. v. Solomon* (1992), 77 C.C.C. (3d) 264 (Que. Mun. Ct.).

[108]Section 184.

[109]Section 183.

[110]Section 185. The precise name of the court concerned will vary from province to province; however, the judge, from whom authorization is sought, will be a federally appointed judge.

[111]Section 186(1). The Law Reform Commission of Canada (1991:130-135) has recommended that the test for issuing a warrant should be tightened up so to reduce the number issued.

[112]Section 186(4). Note that section 188 of the *Code* contains provisions for an "emergency" authorization, which is valid for up to 36 hours only.

[113]Section 186(6) and (7).

[114]Section 196.

[115]Section 189(1). In an important decision, the Supreme Court of Canada has ruled that a surreptitious entry by the police in order to install a listening device did not render the evidence inadmissible because authorization had been duly obtained for the "interception"; see *Lyons et al. v. The Queen* (1984), 15 C.C.C. (3d) 417. This particular section of the *Code* refers only to the requirement that the "interception" be lawfully made before it may be admissible in evidence. See also *R. v. Chesson* (1988), 43 C.C.C. (3d) 353 (S.C.C.).

However, in *R. v. Thompson* (1990), 59 C.C.C. (3d) 225, the Supreme Court of Canada held that there is a violation of an accused person's rights under section 8 of the *Charter* if a surreptitious entry is made without specific, prior authorization from a judge. In the situation where there has been prior authorization for the interception, then the wiretap evidence is not automatically excluded under section 189(1) of the *Code.* Instead, the Court has a discretion to exclude it, under section 24(2) of the *Charter,* if it believes that to admit it would bring the administration of justice into disrepute.

In an important case, *R. v. Paterson et al.* (1985), 18 C.C.C. (3d) 137, the Ontario Court of Appeal held that the use of so-called "basket clauses" in wiretap authorizations was invalid. Such clauses purported to give the police the authority not only to eavesdrop on parties who were specifically named in the authorization, but also any other persons (unspecified) for whom there are "reasonable and probable grounds to believe that the interception of such private communications may assist the investigation." The Court held that such clauses were invalid because they, in effect, delegated the judge's responsibility to decide who should be the object of surveillance to the police themselves. This judgment was later affirmed by the Supreme Court of Canada in *R. v. Paterson et al.* (1987), 39 C.C.C. (3d) 575. See also *R. v. Chesson* (1988), 43 C.C.C. (3d) 353 (S.C.C.).

[116]*R. v. Duarte* (1990), 53 C.C.C. (3d) 1 (S.C.C.). See also *R. v. Wiggins* (1990), 53 C.C.C. (3d) 475 (S.C.C.).

[117]See, for example, *R. v. Proulx* (1992), 76 C.C.C. (3d) 316 (Que C.A.).

[118]*Ibid.,* at 11.

[119]See *R. v. Garofoli* (1990), 60 C.C.C. (3d) 161 (S.C.C.).

[120]*R. v. Dennison* (1984), 15 C.C.C. (3d) 510 (Ont. C.A.).

[121]Section 195.

[122]*Mack v. The Queen* (1988), 44 C.C.C. (3d) 513. The Supreme Court of Canada had apparently recognized the existence of the defence of entrapment in *Amato v. R.* (1982), 69 C.C.C. (2d) 31, but did not apply it in that particular case. *Mack* was the first case in which the Supreme Court actually applied the defence and entered a stay of proceedings.

[123]*Ibid.,* 559.

[124]*Ibid.,* 542.

[125]*Ibid.,* 569-57 (emphasis added).

[126]*Showman v. The Queen* (1988), 44 C.C.C. (3d) 289 (S.C.C.).

[127]*Ibid.,* 295. On this point, see also *R. v. Rousseau* (1991), 70 C.C.C. (3d) 445 (Que. C.A.).

[128]*Barnes v. The Queen* (1991), 63 C.C.C. (3d) 1 (S.C.C.).

[129]*Ibid.,* 10-11.

[130]Entrapment was successfully advanced as a defence in a case where a police officer asked a customer in a tavern to purchase drugs from the accused on the officer's behalf. The customer did facilitate such a sale. The officer did not have any prior reason to suspect that the accused was involved in drug-dealing activity, nor did the officer have any prior reason for believing that the tavern was being used as a location for drug dealing. In these circumstances, the

officer was indeed engaging in "random virtue testing" and, therefore, the B.C. Court of Appeal held that the officer did entrap the accused. See *R. v. Kenyon* (1990), 61 C.C.C. (3d) 538 (B.C. C.A.).

REFERENCES

Alexander, E.R. 1990. "The Supreme Court of Canada and the Canadian Charter of Rights and Freedoms." 40 *University of Toronto Law Journal*. 1-73.

Brodsky, D.J. 1987. "Telewarrants." 29 *Criminal Law Quarterly*. 345-67.

Brooks, L.W. 1989. "Police Discretionary Behavior: A Study of Style." In G.P. Alpert and R.G. Dunham, eds. *Critical Issues in Policing: Contemporary Issues*. Prospect Heights, Illinois: Waveland Press. 121-45.

Brown, M.K. 1981. *Working the Street: Police Discretion and the Dilemmas of Reform*. New York: Russell Sage Foundation.

Bryant, A.W. *et al.* 1990. "Public Attitudes Toward the Exclusion of Evidence: Section 24(2) of the Canadian Charter of Rights and Freedoms." 69 *Canadian Bar Review*. 1-45.

Burns, P.T. 1979. "A Retrospective View of the Protection of Privacy Act; a Fragile Rede is Recked." 13 *U.B.C. Law Review*. 123-57.

Burtch, B.E. 1979. "Electronic Eavesdropping and Legal Civil Liberties." 1 *Canadian Criminology Forum*. 1-12.

Chappell, D., and L.P. Graham. 1985. *Police Use of Deadly Force: Canadian Perspective*. Toronto: Centre of Criminology, University of Toronto.

Cohen, S.A. 1981. "The Investigation of Offences and Police Powers." 13 *Ottawa Law Review*. 549-70.

_____. 1983. *Invasion of Privacy: Police and Electronic Surveillance in Canada*. Toronto: Carswell Co.

_____. 1984a. "Controversies in Need of Resolution: Some Threshold Questions Affecting Individual Rights and Police Powers under the Charter." 16 *Ottawa Law Review*. 97-116.

_____. 1984b. "The Impact of Charter Decisions on Police Behaviour." *39 Criminal Reports (3d Series)*. 264-80.

_____. 1988. "Search Incident to Arrest: How Broad an Exception to the Warrant Requirement?" 63 *Criminal Reports (3d)*. 182-93.

_____. 1990. "Search Incident to Arrest." 32 *Criminal Law Quarterly*. 366-92.

Connelly, P. 1985. "The Fourth Amendment and Section 8 of the Canadian Charter of Rights and Freedoms. What has been Done? What has to be Done?" 27 *Criminal Law Quarterly*. 182-211.

Conway, R. 1985. "The Right to Counsel and the Admissibility of Evidence." 28 *Criminal Law Quarterly*. 28-63.

Conway, R. 1984. "No Man's Land: Confessions not Induced by Fear of Prejudice or Hope of Advantage." 42 *University of Toronto Faculty Law Review*. 26-49.

Coughlan, S. 1985. "Police Detention for Questioning: a Proposal." 28 *Criminal Law Quarterly*. 64-90 and 170-202.

_____. 1990. "When Silence Isn't Golden: Waiver and the Right to Counsel." 33 *Criminal Law Quarterly*. 43-60.

Crank, J.P. 1990. "The Influence of Environmental and Organizational Factors on Police Style in Urban and Rural Environments." 27 *Journal of Research in Crime and Delinquency*. 166-89.

Davis, K.C. 1975. *Police Discretion*. Minneapolis: West Publishing Co.

Delisle, R.J. 1989. "The Exclusion of Evidence Obtained Contrary to the Charter: Where are we now?" 67 *Criminal Reports (3d)*. 288-93.

Dunham, R.G., and G.P. Alpert. 1988. "Neighborhood Crime Differences in Attitudes Toward Policing: Evidence for a Mixed-Strategy Model of Policing in a Multi-Ethnic Setting." 79 *Journal of Criminal Law and Criminology*. 504-23.

Ericson, R.V. 1981. *Making Crime: A Study of Detective Work*. Toronto: Butterworths.

_____. 1982. *Reproducing Order: A Study of Police Patrol Work*. Toronto: University of Toronto Press.

_____. 1983. *The Constitution of Legal Inequality*. Ottawa: Carleton University.

Ericson, R.V., and P.M. Baranek. 1982. *The Ordering of Justice: A Study of Accused Persons as Dependants in the Criminal Process*. Toronto: University of Toronto Press.

Fletcher, J.F. 1989. "Mass and Elite Attitudes about Wiretapping in Canada: Implications for Democratic Theory and Politics." 53 *Public Opinion Quarterly*. 225-45.

Friedland, M.L. 1982. "Legal Rights under the Charter." 24 *Criminal Law Quarterly*. 430-54.

France, S. 1988. "Problems in the Defence of Entrapment." 22 *U.B.C. Law Review*. 1-20.

Frankel, S.D. 1981. "Interception of Private Communications." In *Criminal Procedure: Canadian Law and Practice*, VIII-i to VIII-81. Vancouver: Butterworths.

Freedman, C.D. 1988. "Structuring Investigative Discretion in Canada: Recommendations and Guidelines for Police Questioning." 11 *Police Studies*. 139-53.

Gilsinan, J.F. 1989. "They Is Clowning Tough: 911 and the Social Construction of Reality." 27 *Criminology*. 329-44.

Glasbeek, H.J. 1989. "A No-Frills Look at the Charter of Rights and Freedoms or How Politicians and Lawyers Hide Reality." 9 *Windsor Yearbook of Access to Justice*. 293-352.

Goldsmith, A.J. 1988. "New Directions in Police Complaints Procedures: Some Conceptual and Comparative Departures." 11 *Police Studies*. 60-71.

Goldstein, E. 1984-85. "Using Videotape to Present Evidence in Criminal Proceedings." 27 *Criminal Law Quarterly*. 369-84.

Goldstein, H. 1977. *Policing a Free Society*. Cambridge, Massachusetts: Ballinger Publishing Company.

Grant, A. 1987. "Videotaping Police Questioning: A Canadian Experiment." (June) *Criminal Law Review*. 375-83.

Greenspan, B.H. 1989. "Toward a Distinctively Canadian Jurisprudence: The Charter's Impact on the Criminal Law." In F.E. McArdle, ed. *The Cambridge Lectures 1987*. Montreal: Les Editions Yvon Blais. 349-65.

Harvie, R., and H. Foster. 1990. "Ties that Bind? The Supreme Court of Canada, American Jurisprudence, and the Revision of Canadian Criminal Law Under the Charter." 28 *Osgoode Hall Journal*. 729-88.

Hogarth, J. 1982. "Police Accountability." In R. Donelan, ed. *The Maintenance of Order in Society*. Ottawa: Supply and Services Canada. 111-25. (Catalogue No. JS66-2/1982E.). Reproduced with permission of the Minister of Supply and Services Canada, 1989.

Jorgensen, B. 1981. "Transferring Trouble — The Initiation of Reactive Policing." 23 *Canadian Journal of Criminology*. 257-78.

Jull, K. 1988. "Exclusion of Evidence and the Beast of Burden." 30 *Criminal Law Quarterly*. 178-89.

Law Reform Commission of Canada. 1983a. *Police Powers — Search and Seizure in Criminal Law Enforcement. Working Paper No. 30*. Ottawa: Minister of Supply and Services Canada.

_____. 1983b. *Writs of Assistance and Telewarrants. Report No. 19*. Ottawa: Law Reform Commission of Canada.

_____. 1984a. *Questioning Suspects. Report No. 23*. Ottawa: Minister of Supply and Services Canada.

_____. 1984b. *Search and Seizure. Report No. 24*. Ottawa: Minister of Supply and Services Canada.

_____. 1985a. *Arrest. Working Paper 41*. Ottawa: Law Reform Commission of Canada.

_____. 1985b. *Obtaining Forensic Evidence. Report No. 25*. Ottawa: Law Reform Commission of Canada.

_____. 1986a. *Arrest. Report No. 29*. Ottawa: Law Reform Commission of Canada.

_____. 1986b. *Electronic Surveillance. Working Paper 47*. Ottawa: Law Reform Commission of Canada.

_____. 1988. *Compelling Appearance, Interim Release and Pre-Trial Detention. Working Paper No. 57.* Ottawa: Law Reform Commission of Canada.

_____. 1991. *Recodifying Criminal Procedure, Volume 1. Police Powers. Report No. 33.* Ottawa: Law Reform Commission of Canada.

Leggatt, S. 1989. "Power of Arrest Revisited." 47 *The Advocate.* 555-61.

Lundman, R.J. 1980. *Police and Policing — An Introduction.* New York: Holt, Rinehart, and Winston.

Luther, G. 1987. "Police Power and the Charter of Rights and Freedoms: Creation or Control?" 51 *Saskatchewan Law Review.* 217-27.

MacDonald, N. 1987. "Electronic Surveillance in Crime Detection: An Analysis of Canadian Wiretapping Law." 10 *Dalhousie Law Journal.* 141-66.

McCalla, W. "Telewarrants." 1984. 16 *Ottawa Law Review.* 425-30.

MacLean, S.C. 1987. "Video Surveillance and the Charter of Rights." 30 *Criminal Law Quarterly.* 88-123.

McGahan, P. 1984. *Police Images of a City.* New York: Peter Lang.

McMahon, M. 1988. "Police Accountability: The Situation of Complaints in Toronto." 12 *Contemporary Crises.* 301-27.

McWilliams, P.K. 1991. *Canadian Criminal Evidence, Third Edition.* Aurora, Ontario: Canada Law Book Limited.

Marquis, G. 1991. "Canadian Police Chiefs and Law Reform: The Historical Perspective." 33 *Canadian Journal of Criminology.* 385-406.

Mastrofski, S. 1981. "Policing the Beat: The Impact of Organizational Scale on Patrol Officer Behavior in Urban Residential Neighborhoods." 9 *Journal of Criminal Justice.* 343-58.

Meagher, M.S. 1985. "Police Patrol Styles: How Pervasive is Community Variation?" 13 *Journal of Police Science and Administration.* 36-45.

Mitchell, G.E. 1989. "Exclusion from High: The Supreme Court of Canada on s. 24(2) of the Charter." 70 *Criminal Reports (3d).* 118-38.

Morton, J. 1988. "Towards Video Recording." 4 *Policing* 256-63.

Murphy, P.V., and T. Pate. 1977. *Commissioner.* New York: Simon and Schuster.

Ouimet, R. (Chairman). 1969. *Report of the Canadian Committee on Corrections — Toward Unity: Criminal Justice and Corrections.* Ottawa: Information Canada.

Paciocco, D.M. 1987. "The Development of Miranda-Like Doctrines under the Charter." 19 *Ottawa Law Review.* 49-70.

Paciocco, D.M. 1990. "The Judicial repeal of s. 24(2) and the Development of the Canadian Exclusionary Rule." 32 *Criminal Law Quarterly.* 326-65.

Pavlich, D.J. 1982. "Law of Arrest." In J. Atrens, P.T Burns and J.P. Taylor, eds. *Criminal Procedure: Canadian Law and Practice.* Vancouver: Butterworths. III-1 to III-211.

Pomerance, R.M. 1990. "The Demise of the Telewarrant System in Ontario: Blood Samples Seizure Alternatives." 2 *Journal of Motor Vehicle Law*. 323-56.

Ratushny, E. 1983. "Emerging Issues in Relation to the Legal Rights of a Suspect under the Canadian Charter of Rights and Freedoms." 61 *Canadian Bar Review*. 177-89.

Rabideau, M. 1991. "*Duarte v. R.*: In Fear of Big Brother." 49 *University of Toronto Faculty Law Review*. 171-85.

Rauf, M. N. 1988. "Recent Developments in Wire-Tap Law." 31 *Criminal Law Quarterly*. 208-39.

Roach, K. 1987. "Section 24(1) of the Charter: Strategy and Structure." 29 *Criminal Law Quarterly*. 222-72.

Rosenberg, M. 1985. "Unreasonable Search and Seizure: *Hunter v. Southam Inc.*" 19 *U.B.C. Law Review*. 271-95.

Rosenberg, M. 1990. "Controlling Intrusive Police Investigative Techniques under Section 8." 1 *Criminal Reports (4th Series)*. 32-44.

Sacco, V.F., and H. Johnson. 1990. *Patterns of Criminal Victimization in Canada*. Ottawa: Statistics Canada.

Salhany, R.E. 1984. *Canadian Criminal Procedure*. 4th ed. Aurora, Ontario: Canada Law Book.

Salhany, R.E. 1989. *Canadian Criminal Procedure, Fifth Edition*. Aurora, Ontario: Canada Law Book Inc.

Salhany, R.E. 1991. *A Basic Guide to Evidence in Criminal Cases*. 2nd ed. Scarborough, Ontario: Thomson Professional Publishing Canada.

Shearing, C.D. 1984. *Dial-A-Cop: A Study of Police Mobilisation*. Toronto: Centre of Criminology, University of Toronto.

Sherman, L.W. 1980. "Causes of Police Behavior: The Current State of Quantitative Research." 17 *Journal of Research in Crime and Delinquency*. 69-100.

_____. 1986. "Policing Communities: What Works?" In A.J. Reiss and M. Tonry, eds. *Crime and Justice: An Annual Review of Research. Volume 8*. Chicago: University of Chicago Press. 343-86.

Skurka, S. 1992. "When the Telephone Rings: Advising the Arrested Client." 34 *Criminal Law Quarterly*. 349-61.

Smith, D.A. 1986. "The Neighborhood Context of Police Behavior." In A.J. Reiss and M. Tonry, eds. *Crime and Justice: Annual Review of Research. Volume 8*. 131-41.

Smith, D.A., and J. Klein. 1984. "Police Control of Interpersonal Disputes." 31 *Social Problems*. 468-81.

Solicitor General of Canada. 1983a. *Canadian Urban Victimization Survey. Bulletin No. 1 — Victims of Crime*. Ottawa: Programs Branch, Research and Statistics Group.

_____. 1983b. *Canadian Urban Victimization Survey. Bulletin No. 2 — Reported and Unreported Crimes*. Ottawa: Programs Branch, Research and Statistics Group.

_____. 1987. *Annual Report on Electronic Surveillance (Section 178.22 of the Criminal Code), 1986*. Ottawa: Programs Branch, Research and Statistics Group.

_____. 1991. *Annual Report on Electronic Surveillance As Required under Subsection 195(1) of the Criminal Code 1989*. Ottawa: Minister of Supply and Services Canada.

Solomon, P.H. 1985. "The Law Reform Commission of Canada's Proposals for Reforms of Police Powers: An Assessment." 27 *Criminal Law Quarterly* 321-51.

Spelman, W.G., and D.K. Brown. 1983. "Response Time." In C.B. Klockars, ed. *Thinking About Police: Contemporary Readings*. New York: McGraw-Hill. 160-66.

Stober, M.I. 1985. *Entrapment in Canadian Law*. Toronto: Carswell Legal Publications.

Stober, M. 1988. "Persistent Importuning for a Defence of Entrapment." 33 *McGill Law Journal*. 400-21.

Stober, M.I. 1992. "The Limits of Police Provocation in Canada." 34 *Criminal Law Quarterly*. 290-48.

Stuart, D. 1987. "Four Springboards from the Supreme Court of Canada: *Hunter, Therens, Motor Vehicle Reference* and *Oakes* — Asserting the Basic Values of our Criminal Justice." 12 *Queen's Law Journal*. 131-54.

Stuart, D. 1989. "Mack: Resolving Many But Not All Questions of Entrapment." 67 *Criminal Reports (3d)* 68-73.

Tanovich, D.M. 1992. "To Be or Not to Be": Doctrinal Schizophreni and the Right to Counsel." 34 *Criminal Law Quarterly*. 205-17.

Toselli, V.C. 1990. "Arbitrary Detention and Judicial Stay of Proceedings." 80 *Criminal Reports (3d)*. 86-96.

Trotter, G.T. 1989. "Judicial Termination of Criminal Proceedings Under the Charter." 31 *Criminal Law Quarterly*. 409-30.

Van Maanen, J. 1973. "Observations on the Making of Policemen." Reproduced by permission of the Society for Applied Anthropology from 32 *Human Organization*. 407-18.

Watson. J. 1991. "Talking about the Right to Remain Silent." 34 *Criminal Law Quarterly*. 106-23.

Wilson, J.Q. 1968. *Varieties of Police Behavior: The Management of Law and Order in Eight Communities*. Cambridge, Massachusetts: Harvard University Press.

Wool, G.J. 1985-86. "Police Informants in Canada: The Law and Reality." 50 *Saskatchewan Law Review*. 249-70.

Young, A. 1990. "Greffe: A Section 8 triumph or a Thorn in the Side of Drug Law Enforcement?" 75 *Criminal Reports (3d)*. 293-06.

Young, A. 1991. "All Along the Watchtower: Arbitrary Detention and the Police Function." 29 *Osgoode Hall Law Journal*. 329-97.

5 CRITICAL ISSUES IN CANADIAN POLICING

There is little doubt that Canadian police administrators and patrol officers carry out their tasks in social, cultural, and political environments considerably more complex than those faced by their predecessors just 25 years ago. Many of the critical issues confronting Canadian policing during the 1990s are related to how police departments provide services to the community, the limits of traditional police strategies, and the need for a new model of policing in which there is a partnership between the police and the community. The particular approach to policing taken by a police department will have significant implications for the recruitment, training, and deployment of police officers, as well as for the development of police-community relations programs and crime prevention initiatives. The debate over the delivery of police services has assumed even greater importance with the increasing multicultural diversity of Canadian society.

In the following discussion, we consider some of the issues surrounding the delivery of policing services, including the decisions made by police, the traditional approach to policing, the move in recent years to community policing, and the programs that have been developed in an attempt to better prevent and respond to crime.

POLICE DECISION MAKING

In the policing literature, there is a considerable amount of research on the decision making of police patrol officers — far more than we are able to consider within the space limitations of this text. Nevertheless, we will endeavour to identify the potential sources of influence on the exercise of discretion by patrol officers, as well as the findings of specific research studies that have examined the decision making of the police. Our discussion of police decision making is confined to the exercise of discretion by uniformed patrol officers in encounter situations where either the suspect or the victim/complainant, or both, are present.

Chapter 3 noted that the majority of police activity does not involve crime control, but rather the response to requests for order maintenance or service. Further, the exercise of discretion by patrol officers in encounter situations occurs only after the decision has been made by the victim or another citizen to telephone the police, and the police operators and dispatchers have decided to dispatch a patrol car to the scene. It is also important to remember that the decision to arrest a suspect is only one of many alternatives available to patrol officers, and in the majority of incidents, the situation is resolved through mediation between the disputing parties or by referring the complainant to another source of assistance. Most of the encounter situations in which police officers find themselves can be classified as "minor," that is, of relatively low risk and not involving either danger or the threat of violence.

While the actions of patrol officers are constrained by the provisions of the *Criminal Code*, the protections afforded citizens under the *Canadian Charter of Rights and Freedoms*, and departmental policies, officers do have considerable discretion and many factors influence their decision making in encounter situations. For purposes of our discussion, we will group these into three major categories, with the recognition that there may well be others in any specific incident:

1) the policing environment in which the encounter occurs;
2) the organizational polices of the police department or detachment of which the officer is a member;
3) the participants in the encounter situation, including the police officer(s), the complainant, and the suspect.

A number of factors, other than the offence alleged to have been committed by the suspect, may determine the actions taken by the police (see Brooks, 1989). Our discussion is limited, however, by the lack of recent empirical research studies on police decision making in Canada. Much of the police decision-making research in North America has focused on police-young-offender encounters, and these findings may not be directly transferrable to police encounters with adult suspects.

The Policing Environment

The policing environment of a police department includes the physical environment (the geographic boundaries that establish the size and shape of the area policed), the demographic features of the area policed (including population size and the ethnicity and socioeconomic status of the population policed), and human-made features, such as the presence of industry, farms, parks, and waterfront. The attributes of the policing environment determine, in large measure, the demands placed on policing services by the community and the ability of the police to address adequately community concerns and expectations.[1]

In Chapter 3, we noted that public perceptions of the police may vary across neighbourhoods within the same urban area. Research in the United States suggests that how the police manage their resources and how patrol officers exercise discretion may be significantly influenced by the racial composition of a neighbourhood, the socioeconomic status of its residents, the degree of heterogeneity of the population, the crime rate in the area, and citizen attitudes toward the police (see Dunham and Alpert, 1988). Smith and Klein (1984) found, for example, that in high-income neighbourhoods, the police were more receptive to requests for an arrest of a suspect than in low-income areas. There is also evidence that police officers are more aggressive in their enforcement practices in neighbourhoods that are heterogeneous and that have high crime rates (see Mastrofski, 1981; Sherman, 1986; Smith, 1986).

An important feature in Canadian policing is the wide variety of policing environments across the country, from small Inuit villages in the Arctic to large urban areas of the "south." There may also be differing environments within a particular urban area. In Vancouver, for example, members of the Vancouver City Police Department are involved in policing the area known as Chinatown; the fashionable Point Grey district near the University of British Columbia; the Skid Row area of the city; and the West End, an area of high density apartment blocks near English Bay. Toronto also has several distinct policing environments, including the Jane-Finch community in the northwest sector, which is comprised of high density public housing, mixed ethnic and racial groups, a population that tends to be young and transient, and which has a high crime rate; Parkdale, which has a high elderly population; the Chinatown area between Dundas Street and the CNR tracks; and Rosedale, a fashionable area similar to Vancouver's Point Grey. In any municipality (of size), there are distinct environments distinguished by the socioeconomic status and ethnicity of the residents, and each area produces different demands upon the police as well as a variety of police-citizen encounter situations.[2] This has led police scholars such as Sherman (1986) to argue for a "mixed strategy" of policing, adapted to meet the needs of individual neighbourhoods and communities.

The particular attributes of the community or area within the community being policed may also have a substantive impact on the nature of police-community relations, the willingness of the citizens to telephone the police, and the extent to which citizens cooperate with police officers when they arrive on the scene. It is well known, for example, that ethnic minorities, such as the Chinese, are often reluctant to involve the police in difficulties that arise in their communities. We can assume that such a hesitancy may also exist on the part of many Aboriginal peoples across the country.

A critical issue in policing is the extent to which the police, in their enforcement patterns and decision making, should take into account the customs, practices, and standards of conduct of different groups in the community or of communities in certain geographical locations. This is particularly true in the multicultural context of Canadian society. Should, for example, the Chinese community be policed in the same fashion as other districts of an urban area? Similarly, to what extent should policing and enforcement practices vary in Aboriginal communities and in remote, northern villages where many of the laws appropriate to "southern," urban areas may be inappropriate or even irrelevant?

One of the major sources of influence on patrol officer decision making that arises from the policing environment is community expectations. Given that the police, by necessity, engage in selective enforcement of the law, it is unlikely that any police department or detachment in Canada is free from community pressures that will affect official and unofficial departmental policy and actual patrol officer practice. Increased police visibility and level of enforcement in a given area — commonly known as a "crackdown" — may occur as a consequence of a media exposé, the protests of an organized group or petitions from citizens about activities such as prostitution, drug dealing, speeding vehicles, or young persons "hanging out" in a particular area of the community.[3]

The Police Organization

Another potential source of influence on the decision making of patrol officers in encounter situations are the policies of the particular police organization in which the officer works. From a study of patrol work in an eastern Canadian city, Ericson concluded: "...what happens inside a police organization influences the initiation of encounters with citizens and what happens in those encounters. Available manpower, organizational priorities, production expectations, 'recipe' rules for 'targeting' segments of the population, and many other elements influence transactions and the production of case outcomes" (1982:21).

In a U.S. study, Smith and Klein (1984) found that the probability of arrest in encounter situations increased as police departments become more professional and more bureaucratic. Research also suggests that police officers in larger departments tend to have fewer constraints placed on their exercise of discretion by their supervisors, and these officers have fewer links with the communities they police. Officers in smaller departments, on the other hand, were found to spend more time on patrol and to be more lenient in their enforcement practices (see Mastrofski, 1981; Brown, 1981). Similarly, in those departments that frequently rotated officers from one policing area to another, encounter situations tended to be characterized by "stranger policing" and a lack of empathy and understanding on the part of officers in encounter situations (Mastrofski, 1981; Murphy and Pate, 1977).

Similarly, the management "style" of the leadership in a police department will affect the development and implementation of policies and procedures within the department, how the competing demands that are placed upon the agency are prioritized, and the extent to which patrol officers are encouraged to exercise discretion and seek solutions to problems they encounter. Police leaders today carry out their roles in an increasingly complex society that places a myriad of demands and pressures upon them.

In what has become a classic study in the policing literature, Wilson (1968) attempted to assess the impact of the police organization on the decision making of patrol officers. From extensive observation in eight departments in the United States, three "ideal types" of police organization were identified: (1) watchman; (2) legalistic; and (3) service. Each of the eight departments "more or less" fit one of these three types.

In the *watchman* departments, police officers were recruited locally and were very much a part of the community they served. With low salaries and minimum training, officers in the watchman-style departments attempted to avoid work as much as possible, and in carrying out their duties, officers exhibited a considerable amount of personal judgment and discretion rather than a strict adherence to the law and to departmental policies. Order maintenance was preferred to law enforcement, and there was considerable tolerance of illegal activities, such as gambling, in the community.

In the *legalistic* departments, on the other hand, there was a strong professional orientation among the officers, who had high levels of education and training. Cases were decided "by the book," and the informal resolution of disputes was not encouraged. In carrying out their daily tasks, officers adhered to the formal policies of the department, and enforcement was the dominant characteristic of the officers' work.

A *service* style of policing was evident in departments operating in affluent suburbs — in areas with homogeneous populations where clear standards of behaviour existed. Officers in the service departments were less likely to use arrest as a formal sanction, and they were oriented toward community relations. Leniency characterized the decision making of officers in encounter situations, and officers engaged in a considerable amount of counselling and referral.

Although Wilson's (1968) study was conducted 25 years ago and is based on an examination of police departments in the United States, the findings are instructive for us here in Canada. Basically, they suggest that individual police organizations will have a particular "style" that will affect the decision making of its officers. In a U.S. study, Crank (1990) found significant differences in policing styles between rural and urban police departments, and it is likely that similar differences would be found in Canada. To date, the majority of research studies conducted on policing have focused on urban police organizations. There is a pressing need for research that captures the diversity of settings in which police organizations function across Canada and the impact of this on the particular organizational style that a department exhibits. Regardless of whether such research uncovers the three types identified by Wilson (1968), it would nonetheless highlight the potential influence of police organization on patrol officer decision making.

The Encounter

In our discussion of the police role in Canadian society, we noted that, given limited resources, police departments must prioritize requests from the community. But perhaps the greatest burden for handling cases efficiently falls upon the individual patrol officers who are dispatched to encounter situations throughout the community. Given the demands on police officers' time, Lundman has noted that "Individualizing policing is a luxury most police officers cannot afford" (1980:104). Rather, in response to external community and internal organizational pressures to

handle cases efficiently, police officers employ two methods of conceptual shorthand: *typifications* and *recipes for action*.[4]

Typifications are constructs or formulations of events based on
experience and involve what is typical or common about routinely
encountered events. Lundman (1980:110) argues that officers use their
experience to classify or typify situations into one of two general
categories: those that require "real" police work and those that are
"bullshit." Situations of "real" police work refer to those situations
"where you figure you may have to use the tools of the trade" (Van
Maanen, 1973:413).

Most requests made of the police are not viewed as real police work,
says a U.S. police officer confiding to Van Maanen (1973:414): "You
could give most of what we do around here to any idiot who could put
up with the insanity that passes for civilized conduct." Neighbourhood
disputes, minor traffic accidents, and noisy parties are examples of
situations that many officers feel have little to do with real police work.
It might be anticipated that, in contrasts to the majority of public-initiated
requests for service that are responded to reactively by patrol officers, a
higher percentage of those encounter situations that are the result of
proactive policing (discovered by the police themselves) may be of the
"real police work" variety. As we will see in our consideration of the
police-citizen encounter, it is not only the officers who typify events, but
also the people involved in them.

Recipes for action constitute the actions taken and the decisions that
are normally made in certain types of incidents. In a study of police
patrol in a major Canadian city, Ericson (1982:100) found that officers
based their judgment of whether or not a criminal offence had occurred
not on the views of the citizens involved, but rather on "recipe" rules,
legal rules, and/or community rules to decide whether the matter could
or should be transformed into police property.

Some evidence suggests that the typifications and recipes for action
employed by patrol officers are non-negotiable and may be based on
stereotypes and discriminatory views of people and circumstances
(Lundman, 1980). While a portion of the information that officers use to
formulate typifications and recipes for action may be learned during their
initial recruit training, most is learned "on the street" from fellow officers
and acquired through personal experience. Once the new police officer
has graduated from the police academy, he or she is assigned a training
officer who plays a major role in introducing the new recruit to the

intricacies and complexities of police work. Recruits may be admonished to "forget" what they have learned in the academy and to learn what policing is really like on the streets.

It is also apparent that police officers, using typifications and recipes for action, tailor their decision making to the particular area and population they are policing. Ericson (1982:86) found that "Patrol officers develop and use cues concerning (1) individuals out of place, (2) individuals in particular places, (3) individuals of particular types regardless of place, and (4) unusual circumstances regarding property." Thus, a poorly dressed, dishevelled individual in a fashionable residential district would draw police attention, as would a well-dressed person loitering in a Skid Row area. Similarly, McGahan (1984) found that patrol officers in St. John's, Newfoundland, held specific mental images of different sections of the city, which influenced the manner in which they carried out their tasks.

Research studies, carried out primarily in the United States, have also examined the potential influence of officer attributes, including age, length of service, ethnicity, and level of education on the exercise of discretion. While the findings of this research are generally inconclusive, there is some evidence to suggest that those officers with less experience tended to make more arrests, while those arrests made by more experienced officers were more likely to result in convictions (see Sherman, 1980). College-educated officers have been found to be more active in detecting offences, to make more arrests, to suffer fewer injuries from assaults, and to generate fewer citizen complaints than their less-educated colleagues. The role of gender has been explored in studies comparing male and female police officers and will be presented in our discussion of police women later in this chapter. There is a clear need for Canadian research on the impact that individual officer attributes have in the exercise of discretion and on decision making in encounter situations.

The Complainant

A consistent finding from the studies of police decision making is that the preferences of the complainant have a significant impact on the decision making of police officers in encounter situations. In his study of patrol officers in an eastern Canadian city, Ericson (1982:103) found that the socioeconomic status, age, gender, demeanour, and the ethnicity of the complainant influenced officer decision making. Further, the impact of the attributes of the complainant varied between encounters involving minor incidents and those in which a serious offence was alleged to have occurred. In minor complaint situations, the police were more likely to provide advice and assistance to lower-status persons and to complainants who were cooperative. Higher-status and uncooperative complainants, on the other hand, were less likely to receive assistance from the police.

In encounters involving major incidents, complainants who were older, male, and non-white were more likely to receive assistance and advice from the police. Ericson (1982:111) also found that the police officer was more likely to write a formal report on the incident if the complainant was of a high socioeconomic status or male, but less likely to prepare such a report if the situation involved an interpersonal dispute. It is unknown whether these findings would apply in other policing jurisdictions across the country and, in the absence of corroborating findings, the research findings to date should only be taken as suggestive and not conclusive. They do, however, suggest that the complainant may play an important role in the decision-making process of patrol officers.

The Suspect

Suspects are the primary targets of police officer typifications. Police officers distinguish between the general public, who are to be protected, and the "dregs" or "scum," who are to receive police attention. Research has focused on the role of the seriousness of the offence alleged to have been committed by the suspect and on sociobiographical attributes of the suspect, including ethnicity, age, relationship to the victim, and attitude or demeanour exhibited toward the officer.

There is no conclusive evidence that Canadian police officers discriminate in their arrest practices on the basis of the ethnicity of the suspect. However, the high arrest rates of Aboriginal peoples in many areas of the country, and the ongoing conflicts between ethnic minorities and the police in many urban areas of the country, warrant close examination. In this Canadian study, Ericson (1982:152,159) found that male suspects, those in the age group 16 to 24, and suspects of lower socioeconomic status were more likely to be checked by patrol officers through the national Canadian Police Information Centre (CPIC) as well as to be searched by officers. In addition, formal action was more likely to be taken against suspects of lower socioeconomic status who were non-white and in those instances where property loss or damage had occurred.

Police research has consistently reported a relationship between the attitude or demeanour of the suspect and police decision making. All other factors being equal, those suspects who are disrespectful toward the police or who are uncooperative are more likely to be arrested than those who behave in a deferential and civil manner. The relational distance between the suspect and the victim/complainant may also influence the action taken by patrol officers. The more distant the relationship, the more likely the police are to arrest. This may be changing in some areas of enforcement, however. While traditionally the female victims of domestic assault have been reluctant to press charges (and the police often reluctant to get involved in a "private matter"), over the past decade there have been policy changes that require police officers to take formal action, even in those instances in which the victim does not want such action taken.

As would be expected, the seriousness of the alleged offence is strongly related to the action taken by police officers in encounter situations, with those suspects who are alleged to have committed serious crimes being more likely to be arrested than those alleged to have committed minor offences. As the seriousness of the alleged crime increases, the amount of discretion available to officers is diminished as is the influence of complainant preference and other "extra-legal" factors such as the suspect's ethnicity and demeanour. In considering the potential role that suspect characteristics play in police decision making, we should remember that the exercise of discretion in encounter situations takes place against the backdrop of organizational policies and pro- cedures, the environment in which the encounter takes place, and the style of policing of the individual officer(s) involved in the encounter. All of these may significantly affect the role and impact of suspect attributes on the decision that are made.

Insuring Police Accountability

In our discussion of the police occupation in Chapter 3, we noted that policing in a democratic society requires officers to balance the need to assert authority with the requirement that the rights and freedoms of citizens be protected. There is little doubt that the enactment of the *Charter of Rights and Freedoms* and other legislation such as the *Young Offenders Act* (to be discussed in Chapter 14) have had a significant impact upon the powers of the police and their exercise of discretion. Yet, increasingly, citizens and their governments are asking the question "who polices the police?," a query that often arises after a widely publicized incident involving what is perceived to be a misuse of police force. Citizen complaints against the police generally involve allegations of officer dereliction of duty, including the excessive use of force or disrespectful behaviour.

In recent years, a number of initiatives have been undertaken to insure police accountability, and many of these have centered on establishing procedures and structures to provide citizens with the opportunity to complain about police behaviour and for governments to assume some measure of control over police misconduct. While provincial police commissions and municipal police boards have played a major role in establishing complaint procedures, considerable diversity exists in systems that are in place across the country.

The complaint system in British Columbia, encompassing four stages, is illustrative of the review systems currently in place across the country. Initially, an attempt is made to resolve the complaint informally between the officer and the complainant. The majority of complaints against the police are resolved in this fashion. For those cases not resolved informally, a police investigation and disciplinary hearing may occur. In the third and fourth stages, the complaint is brought before the municipal police board and the British Columbia Police Commission.

There are also complaint systems that involve an ombudsman and external review boards. In Metropolitan Toronto, the Public Complaints Commissioner oversees the police handling of complaints and may intercede in the investigation at any time. Should a citizen be dissatisfied with the outcome of the police investigation into the complaint, a public inquiry may be held before a 24-person tribunal (civilian review board), comprised of judges, lawyers, police, and citizens. Where officers are found to have engaged in serious misconduct, the board may dismiss the officer from the force, while a finding of responsibility for lesser offences may result in a period of suspension.

The creation of civilian review boards such as the Toronto tribunal is an attempt to provide for the external review of police activities. Patrol officers and senior administrators have generally been opposed to civilian review on the grounds that the public does not understand the complexities of police work and is therefore not in a position to evaluate police conduct. The RCMP has traditionally been even more resistant to external review of its officers' behaviour than have municipal police agencies. In

1986, amendments to the *Royal Canadian Mounted Police Act* resulted in the creation of two external boards of review. The Public Complaints Commission reviews complaints made by citizens against members of the RCMP who are policing under contract. The External Review Committee hears appeals from RCMP members who have been disciplined for an infraction of force regulations.[5]

Hogarth has noted that the dilemma surrounding police accountability in Canada "is to try to ensure the accountability of the police and at the same time protect the police from unwarranted political interference in their day to day professional decisions and discharge of their duties" (1982:113).

TRADITIONAL POLICE PRACTICE

In Chapter 2, we noted that one of the "outcomes" of the criminal justice system in Canada was that, while there has been a steady increase in the numbers of police officers and in the amount of expenditures for policing services, the rates of crime and, as importantly, the *fear* of crime by the general public, has also steadily increased. As a result, we must reconsider the "more is better" formula that has been the basis of traditional police practice: more police personnel, increased operating budgets, and more sophisticated equipment equals more effectiveness in crime prevention and crime control.

In fact, citizens are often surprised to learn that, with a few exceptions, the police can do very little to prevent much of the crime and other difficulties that arise in the community. As we'll see, the catch rate of offenders after a crime has been committed is lower than one might expect. This suggests that in order to improve the effectiveness of the police, changes are required in how police departments are organized and in how they deliver policing services to the communities they serve. Such reform becomes even more critical in a time of increasing fiscal restraint. But before we can chart a course for change, we need to know where we have been in terms of traditional police practice.

Within the traditional crime control model of policing, the primary strategy for deploying police officers is the *watch system*, or preventive patrol. In watch policing, officers are assigned to patrol, in a random fashion, large districts on a rotating basis under the supervision of higher-level officers, who also rotate. The underlying assumption of watch policing is that, by being visible in the community, the police can deter potential offenders as well as reduce citizens' fear of crime. A growing body of research, however, has challenged the basic assumptions of watch policing and raised questions about its effectiveness as a crime prevention/criminal apprehension strategy.

A project that became known as the Kansas City study is perhaps the most extensive evaluation of the effectiveness of preventive mobile police patrol ever conducted and was the first attempt to empirically assess traditional policing strategies (see Kelling *et al.*, 1974). In the project, fifteen police beats in the city were divided into five groups of three precincts each. Each group included beats that were as similar as possible in population, crime level, and calls for police service. Within each group, three different patrol strategies were used for one year. One beat was patrolled in the customary fashion by a single patrol car, the second beat received patrol activity two to three times the normal level, and in the third beat, preventive patrol was eliminated and service was provided only in response to specific citizen requests. Prior to and following the experiment, citizens in the beat areas were interviewed regarding their perceptions of police service, whether they had been victimized, and their level of fear of becoming a victim of crime.

Among the major findings of the Kansas City study were that the levels of reported crime, citizen fears about crime, community attitudes toward the police, police response time to incidents, and the rate of traffic accidents were *not* affected by increasing or decreasing the level of routine preventive patrol in the beat areas (Kelling *et al.*, 1983:160). Needless to say, these findings generated considerable debate within the policing community and precipitated further research on the effectiveness of various policing strategies as well as providing the basis for a move toward community policing.

Since the early 1970s, there has been an increasing chorus of criticism by police scholars and enlightened police administrators, centering on the structure and operation of police forces and their ineffectiveness in addressing community problems. This criticism is reflected in the view of Bayley (1991:22), who argued that police forces tend to be "governed by tradition" and "driven by instinct," rather than being organized around clearly articulated goals and well-defined policies for successfully responding to the multiple demands placed upon them by society.

Questions have also been raised about other strategies employed in traditional policing. Despite the widespread use of two-officer patrol cars, for example, some research evidence suggests that one-officer patrol cars may be more productive, less expensive, and safer than two-officer patrols (Kessler, 1985; Hickling-Johnston, 1982). As well, while it has often been assumed that the response time of a mobile patrol unit was closely related to the catch rate, we saw in Chapter 3 that it is *citizen-reporting time* — not police response time — that increases the likelihood of apprehending offenders at the scene of a crime. In fact, in their study of citizen delay in reporting and police response time in several U.S. cities, Spelman and Brown (1983:162) found that in only 2.9% of serious crime cases were arrests made that could be attributed to a fast police response time. There may also be limits to the contribution that high technology can make to the effectiveness of traditional police service delivery. Despite the widespread use of computers for record keeping, policy and planning projects, and in mobile patrol units, it is not clear that such innovations have increased the ability of the police to prevent or respond to crime. In fact, there is some evidence that the increased reliance upon technology may widen the distance between the police and the community. This concern has led one progressive police leader (Braiden, cited in Appleby, 1992:A7) to call for a "moratorium on gadgetry" until there is a more clearly defined objective for its use.

Inspector Braiden's concerns are supported by Palys, Boyanowsky, and Dutton (1984), who studied the impact of the Mobile Radio Data System (MRDS) following its installation in Vancouver City police patrol cars. This system is comprised of computer terminals located in the patrol cars through which officers can gain immediate access to information on suspects. While many officers felt that the system provided them with greater amounts of information, which (they felt) increased their efficiency and effectiveness on patrol, there was concern that younger officers, in particular, would come to rely too extensively on the MRDS for primary rather than supportive information. It was feared that an overreliance upon the computers would widen the communication gap between mobile patrol officers and community residents, further isolating the police and decreasing their effectiveness. Expanding the use of high technology without a corresponding change in how policing services are delivered will not produce increased efficiency or effectiveness.

Assessing Police Effectiveness: An Elusive Goal

A long-standing problem within traditional policing is how to assess the "effectiveness" or "productivity" of the police. While these terms are often used in discussing the delivery of police services, developing techniques to measure accurately the extent to which police activities are effective or productive has proven to be quite elusive. Given the complexity of the police role in Canadian society and the wide variety of tasks that police officers perform, it is important to have measures of effectiveness that accurately assess the various tasks police departments and patrol officers perform. Unfortunately, this has not been the case.

The most common method of measuring the effectiveness of police departments is by clearance rates, which are the proportion of offences known to the police that are cleared by a charge or other means. Crime rates may also indicate how well the police department is fulfilling its mandate. The following points, however, show that crime and clearance rates fall far short of providing accurate measures of the adequacy of police services on a number of counts.

▸   *Crime rates are a function of many factors other than police activity.*

Murphy (1985:5) reminds us that police forces have little control over the conditions that produce high rates of crime in their jurisdiction. Social and economic factors may play a more significant role in determining the level of crime than activities of the police (see also Koenig, 1991).

▸   *Depending on how they are viewed, rising crime rates can reflect either good or poor police performance.*

When official crime rates go down, the police are seen as doing a good job; when crime rates go up, the police are seen as doing a poor job and are under pressure to reduce them. However, it can be argued the other way: when crime rates go up, the police are doing a *good* job, both in terms of having a supportive public that reports more crimes and in apprehending more offenders.

▸   *Clearance rates are in part a function of the willingness of the public to report crimes to the police.*

Given the large figure of unreported crime, official crime rates and clearance rates relate only to those crimes that *are* reported. While clearance rates may provide an indication of the quantity of police performance, they tell us little about the *quality* of police service.

▸   *Clearance rates tend to be quite low, but vary by type and serious-
      ness of offence.*

Figure 5.1 reveals the clearance rates for major categories of *Criminal
Code* offences during 1991. The data, drawn from the Uniform Crime
Reporting System (Canadian Centre for Justice Statistics, 1992a:31)
indicate that the clearance rates for violent crimes are higher (74.6%) than
those for property offences (24.7%), a trend that has existed historically
in Canada. Violent crimes are most often committed by acquaintances of
the victim, making apprehension of the offender more likely. Property
offences, on the other hand, generally involve offenders and victims who
are strangers to one another.

▸   *Clearance rates may depend upon the resources a department has
      at its disposal and the specific nature of the policing environment.*

There is considerable variability across police departments in terms of the
resources available to prevent and respond to crime and other demands
that are placed upon the police. Some departments, for example, may
have the resources to engage in more proactive policing, which may
result in high rates of arrest for certain categories of crime. As noted in
Chapter 4, there is considerable variability in the policing environments
in which departments operate: one police department may police a "high
crime" area that has a large number of offences of a type that generally
have low clearance rates, while another department may police an area
with a low incidence of offences.

The performance of individual patrol officers may be measured by
the number of arrests made or appearance notices issued. Those officers
who issue a higher number of appearance notices or make a large number
of arrests are often seen as performing their duties more effectively than
those who do not. As we saw in our discussions in Chapter 3, however,
the role of the police in Canadian society is complex, and police officers
are asked to perform a myriad of order maintenance and service-related
activities in addition to those involving the detection and apprehension of
criminal offenders. Crime control activities account for only a small
portion of a police officer's time.

We have noted that in many encounter situations, patrol officers do not
take official action, but rather mediate a resolution to the particular

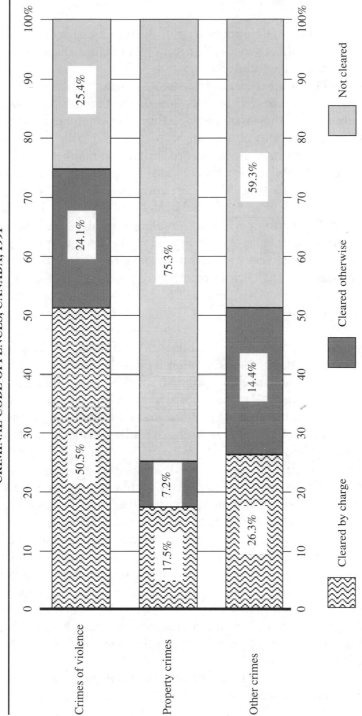

FIGURE 5.1
CLEARANCE RATES FOR THE MAJOR CATEGORIES OF
CRIMINAL CODE OFFENCES, CANADA, 1991

Crimes of violence

Property crimes

Other crimes

Cleared by charge

Cleared otherwise

Not cleared

Source: Adapted from Canadian Centre for Justice Statistics. *Canadian Crime Statistics, 1991* (Ottawa: Statistics Canada, 1992a), p. 31. Catalogue no. 85-205. Reproduced with permission of the Ministry of Industry, Science, and Technology, 1993.

conflict. Measures of performance premised on official action (arrests) do not measure the effectiveness of officers in mediating disputes, reducing tensions, and avoiding violence.

A number of measures can be used to assess the effectiveness and productivity of police departments and their officers that would more accurately reflect the tasks they perform. These include surveys of community perceptions of the police, satisfaction with police services among those requesting assistance, recording the number of complaints filed against a police department and its officers, and developing techniques for assessing officer performance in non-crime control activities (see Murphy, 1985; Schneider, 1991). The difficulties in assessing police performance and the reliance on measures focusing on crime control contributed to the argument for a move toward a new model of service delivery — community policing — and the adoption of a problem-solving approach to community problems, including crime.

COMMUNITY POLICING

Increasing concerns with the inability of traditional policing services based on mobile patrol to affect either the levels of crime or the fear of crime provided the impetus during the 1970s and 1980s for a new approach to policing. All of these initiatives can be loosely grouped under the term "community policing," although, as we shall see, this term has been overused to the point of being of little assistance in describing police policies and programs.

One of the first attempts to move away from the traditional watch system of policing was "zone" or "team" policing, introduced in Canada in the early 1970s. Team policing was designed to restructure the organization and delivery of policing services, shifting the focus from traditional "call-oriented" enforcement to community service and crime prevention. The intent was to increase police contact with the community by having officers concentrate their efforts in well-defined neighbour-hoods on a permanent basis. Despite the fanfare that accompanied the introduction of team policing in many jurisdictions in Canada and the United States, it met with mixed success and has been largely discarded. At present, mobile watch patrol remains the basis of service delivery in most communities.

Many factors hindered efforts to implement team policing. Organizationally, team policing involved a decentralization of authority and decision making in the police force, with an accompanying reduction in the power of many mid-management officers. Uniformed officers became "generalists" and were involved in all phases of case investigation. In short, team policing required a change in the organizational structure of the police department and this was resisted by many officers at the mid-management level. So too was there resistance on the part of patrol officers, many of whom felt that the traditional crime control mandate of the police was being compromised in favour of a focus on community relations.

While the full potential of team policing was never realized in Canada, it did serve as a precursor for a much broader notion: community policing. Community policing is the new "buzz-word" in policing circles throughout North America, and an extensive literature is developing on it (see Greene and Mastrofski, 1991; Trojanowicz and Bucqueroux, 1990). The key principles of community policing have been set out by Murphy and Muir (1985:81-95).

▶ The community has a key role to play in the development of the philosophy, management, and delivery of police services.
▶ The objectives of policing should be community-defined and include service and order maintenance as well as crime control.
▶ The diverse functions that the police perform in the community are legitimate elements of the police role.
▶ The police are but one component of the informal and formal network of social control in the community and must share with the community the responsibility for solving community policing problems.
▶ The police, in assuming a proactive stance toward community problems, must place greater emphasis on prevention, referral, and education.

Community policing, then, involves a shift away from traditional approaches to service delivery, involving the community as an active participant in the identification of and response to problems. It attempts to reverse the historical trend of increasing police responsibility (and, many would argue, decreasing police effectiveness) for crime and disorder in the community and the corresponding decrease in community responsibility and involvement. Under a community policing scheme, the police and the community comprise a partnership that brings together the resources and talents of each to identify and solve problems. No longer are the police assumed to have sole proprietary interest in or control over the identification of and response to crime and disorder. In actuality, as Inspector Chris Braiden of the Edmonton Police Service (1989a:21;24) has pointed out, community policing is not really new, but rather involves a return to a philosophy upon which policing was originally premised: that the police are to function only as a reflection of the interests and needs of the community.

The move to community policing, however, has profound implications for how police organizations are structured, how resources are allocated, and for the recruitment, training, and role of patrol officers, who under many community policing schemes are called "community policing officers" (CPOs). It also holds the potential to address the low morale, widespread job dissatisfaction, and burnout that afflicts officers in many police departments. Officers are able to use their talents to address a full range of community concerns and become proactive problem-solvers rather than merely reacting to calls for service. With the active participation of community residents in programs such as Neighbourhood Watch (discussed later), police officers are able to tackle underlying causes of crime and disorder, rather than just responding to symptoms. Community policing holds the promise of providing a model of service delivery that is most appropriate for the multicultural nature of Canadian society.

Common strategies associated with community policing are problem-solving/problem-oriented policing, police storefront offices located in neighbourhoods, foot patrol, and various crime prevention initiatives.

Problem-Oriented Policing

A key component of community policing is problem-oriented policing, which was first implemented on a trial basis in the United States in the early 1980s, but which has yet to be widely adopted by Canadian police departments. The term "problem-oriented policing" was first coined by Goldstein (1979), and, while its basic tenets may seem commonsensical, it represents a sharp departure from traditional police practice.

Traditional watch policing is incident driven; that is, the police spend the majority of time responding to calls from the general public. These calls are often treated in isolation from one another, and there is little or no effort to gather information on the larger context within which the incident occurs. Problem-oriented policing, on the other hand, is a process with several clearly defined stages:

> ▸ *scanning:* officers consider whether the issue at hand is a problem — their concern may be the result of a series of incidents, for example, break and enters in a particular neighbourhood or business area, or a series of assaults or robberies;
> ▸ *analysis:* information on the problem is gathered from as many sources as possible, including the police department and the community, in order to understand the nature, extent, and probable cause of the problem;
> ▸ *response:* officers develop a plan to address and solve the problem in collaboration with other police members, community leaders, residents, and organizations; and
> ▸ *assessment:* the effectiveness of the response in addressing the problem is evaluated and, if required, adjustments to the response are made (see Eck and Spelman, 1989:103-104).

Inspector Braiden (1989b:10) makes the distinction that "'Community policing' is the vision that tells us the right things to do. 'Problem-oriented policing' is *how* we get those things done right." The Calgary Police Service and the Halton Regional Police are two Canadian police forces that have undertaken training programs to provide their patrol officers with the skills to do problem-oriented policing.

Foot Patrol: Turning Back the Clock

Concerns about the effectiveness of mobile "watch" police patrol have led progressive police departments to seek ways to improve police-community relations and police effectiveness. A prominent image of early Canadian policing was the police officer walking the beat. Now, in the late twentieth century, foot patrol is being heralded as a "breakthrough" and as one of the key components of community policing. We seem to have come full circle in policing and have begun to see the importance of police-community links and the limits of mobile patrol.

Experiences with foot patrol in urban areas across North America have produced some interesting results that suggest that this strategy should be given more serious consideration (see Greene and Taylor,

1991). Two studies of foot patrol — in Newark, New Jersey, and in Flint, Michigan — found that, while foot patrol did not have a significant impact on crime rate (a finding similar to that of the Kansas City study of mobile patrol), it did reduce citizen fear of crime, increase feelings of personal safety among residents, and reduce the number of calls for service. In Newark, community residents were more satisfied with police services delivered via foot patrol than those provided by mobile patrol (Police Foundation, 1981). In Flint, foot patrol officers were found to have higher levels of familiarity with the neighbourhoods in which they worked, felt safer in their work, and perceived higher levels of community support than did their motor patrol counterparts (Trojanowicz, 1983; Trojanowicz and Banas, 1985). Despite these encouraging results, very few Canadian police departments use foot patrol as a strategy for deploying patrol officers in the community on a full-time basis. The most notable exception is the foot patrol program operated by the Edmonton Police Service.

POLICE-COMMUNITY RELATIONS PROGRAMS

Community relations programs are specific initiatives designed to improve contact and communication between the police and the public and are a basic building block of community policing. The objective of these programs is to increase the effectiveness of the police by building bridges of communication and understanding between the police department and the community. Because many community relations programs have as a major objective the prevention of crime, it is often difficult to separate the two types of programs, although we will discuss them in separate sections for purposes of clarity. Community relations programs may be directed toward specific groups of citizens in the community, such as youth, minorities, the victims of crime (see Chapter 2), and the elderly. Police-school liaison programs are a primary example of a community relations effort directed toward a specific target group.

The established link between the nature and types of contact between youth and the police and the formation of adolescent attitudes toward the police (see Chapter 3) has provided the impetus for the development of a wide range of non-residential and residential police-school programs. These programs vary considerably in their structure and operation, but are generally designed to improve relations between the police and youth and to control youthful misbehaviour.

Non-residential police programs involve visits by police officers to schools on a regular basis to make class presentations, generally of an informational nature. In addition, youths may participate in sports activities or accompany officers on patrol. Residential police programs involve a police officer in residence in a school on a full-time basis during school hours. The Vancouver City Police School Liaison Program and the St. John, New Brunswick, School Liaison Program are two examples of residential programs in which officers not only patrol school property, but participate in extra-curricular activities and make formal presentations on a variety of subject areas including drug use, criminal law, and the operation of the criminal justice system.

It would be inappropriate to evaluate police-school programs within a traditional "crime control" framework. It is unlikely, for example, that these programs will reduce the incidence of youth crime in a neighbourhood, as the youths who are involved in the most serious types of crime are most likely not in school in the first place and therefore would not be exposed to the program. Evaluations of non-residential police-school programs suggest that such initiatives increase positive police-adolescent interaction and create a more favourable view of the police among youths. Whether these favourable attitudes toward the police result in actual behavioural changes on the part of youths is unclear. However, if the programs function to increase positive communication and contact between youth and the police, this is an important contribution to a community policing strategy (see Griffiths, 1982).

With the emergence of youth gangs and conflicts that often occur between rival factions, as well as the efforts to recruit gang members on school grounds, the role of the police-school liaison officer has assumed even greater importance. Many police departments also operate prevention, counselling, and diversion programs for young offenders in conflict with the law. This will be considered further in Chapter 14.

Crime Prevention Programs

Crime prevention programs, also an important component of community policing, are designed to reduce the levels of crime and to increase citizens' perceptions of safety (see Lab, 1992; Rosenbaum, 1986). There are three approaches to crime prevention: primary, secondary, and tertiary, each of which comes into play at different stages (see Brantingham and Faust, 1976).

Primary crime prevention programs are the most common. They seek to identify opportunities for criminal offences and to alter these conditions so as to reduce the likelihood of a crime being committed. Since the majority of offences committed in Canada are property related, most crime prevention programs are oriented toward these crimes. Among the more well-known primary crime prevention programs are Operation Identification (for residences), Operation Provident (for businesses), Neighbourhood Watch, and various Block Parent and Blockwatch programs (see Lab, 1992). Operation Identification and Operation Provident involve citizens and businesspeople marking property with identification numbers to make the disposal of stolen goods more difficult and to assist in the recovery of items by the police. Neighbourhood Watch involves mobilizing the "eyes and ears" of citizens in the community in the crime prevention effort and is also designed to forge a sense of community among neighbourhood residents — neighbours keep an eye on each other's property and watch out for anything unusual. Citizen patrols, both mobile and on foot, have also developed in recent years. Perhaps the most well known of the citizen patrol groups is the Guardian Angels, who are most active on the streets of U.S. cities but who have also had a presence in many Canadian cities. They wear distinctive clothing and a red beret as a "uniform" and often ride the subways, keeping an eye out for disturbances.

Crime Prevention Through Environmental Design (CPTED) is also a primary crime prevention program used by many police departments. The basic premise of CPTED is that many criminal acts, particularly property offences such as break and enters, are the result of a cost/benefit decision by the offender and that such offences can be prevented when offenders have a high risk of apprehension and there is a corresponding lack of potential payoff. To this end, the focus of CPTED is on altering elements in the physical environment to discourage offenders. This includes controlling access to areas to make victimization more difficult and employing architectural designs incorporating such features as improved lighting that allow for better surveillance.

In recent years, television has offered crime prevention/criminal apprehension programming. Many of these programs are designed to educate the public about crime, while others, often called "crime time" programs, solicit the public's assistance in locating known criminals. Police forces have developed a myriad of "hot tip" lines and televised re-enactment programs such as "Crime Stoppers," which offer cash rewards for information leading to the arrest and conviction of offenders.

Secondary crime prevention programs focus on areas that produce crime and other problems and are often based on crime area analysis, including targeting high crime areas and the use of neighbourhood dispute resolution; diversion of offenders; crime prevention initiatives in schools; and programs that provide intervention for youth in conflict. Examples of secondary crime prevention are MADD (Mothers Against Drunk Driving) and SADD (Students Against Drunk Driving).

Tertiary crime prevention programs are designed to intervene with youth and adult offenders so as to reduce the likelihood of their committing further offences. Most of these programs are operated by the criminal justice system and are designed to deter, incapacitate, and/or rehabilitate offenders. We'll be considering tertiary crime prevention programs in greater detail in our discussion of correctional programs in Chapters 11 and 12.

Police departments are most extensively involved in primary crime prevention programs, although they do participate in secondary and, to a lesser extent, tertiary crime prevention as well.

Do Crime Prevention Programs Prevent Crime?

A primary impetus for the move toward community-oriented policing has been the less-than-positive results obtained by police crime prevention programs operated within the traditional model of policing (see Lab, 1992; Rosenbaum, 1986). Determining whether crime prevention programs actually "work" is a difficult task. Research studies have examined programs operating in different types of policing environments (rural/urban; Canada/ United States/Europe), and studies have used different measures of program "success," for example, reduction in the crime rate and reduction in citizen fear of crime. Typically, as would be expected in police departments following a traditional style of service delivery, success is measured by a reduction in the crime rate for the targeted offence category. However, within a community policing framework, other measures would be as appropriate, including whether the program increased police-community contact and whether citizens felt safer in their neighbourhoods.

Another major problem is that, particularly in Canada, there have been very few controlled evaluations of crime prevention initiatives, a surprising fact given the widespread use of crime prevention programs across the country. This means we can only provide a very general overview of research findings, with the caveat that much more research remains to be done on crime prevention programs operated by Canadian police departments.

Citizen Patrols

While there have been no published evaluations of citizen patrols in Canada, research in the United States and Europe suggests that citizen patrols may reduce property crime and levels of violence, and decrease the fear of crime among neighbourhood residents (see Troyer and Wright, 1985; Van Andel, 1989). An evaluation of the Guardian Angels in the United States (Pennell *et al.*, 1989) found that while the patrols did not reduce violent crime, they did have an impact on property crime and, as importantly, citizens (particularly transit riders), felt safer when the Angels were on patrol.

Operation Identification and Operation Provident

The impact of these two widely used primary prevention programs on property crime is unclear. Research on similar property-marking programs in the United States has generally found that they do not reduce the number of break and enters or property loss. However, the programs may function to increase police-community interaction and to make community residents aware of the crime prevention activities of the police (Heller *et al.*, 1975). A more recent evaluation (Laycock, cited in Lab, 1992:26-27) of a property-marking program in Wales found a short-term reduction in break-ins; however, over time, as media publicity about the project diminished, so did the impact of the program.

An evaluation (Solicitor General of Canada, 1984) of Operation Identification and Operation Provident programs operated by the RCMP in Portage La Prairie, Manitoba, found that, seven months following the implementation of the programs, there had been a 68% decrease in business break and enters and a 48% reduction in residential break and enters. The long-term success of the program is not known; however, over the following two-year period, business break-ins had continued to decline, while residential break and enters had increased.

A key question for these types of programs is whether or not they merely "displace" crime, rather than prevent it. This means that criminals travel to an adjacent area that is not participating in the program and the crime rate in that area increases.

Neighbourhood/Block Watch

While most police departments in Canada participate in Operation Identification and Operation Provident (or variations thereof), there are few controlled evaluations of their impact on crime. Those studies done on programs operating in the United States have produced mixed results: in some areas, the programs have reduced the number of residential break and enters; in others, there was either no change in the property crime rate or an increase was recorded (see Johnson and Merker, 1992). While some Neighbourhood Watch programs have been found to reduce the fear of crime (Bennett and Lavrakas, 1989), others have found that participation in a Neighbourhood Watch program *increased the fear of crime* (Rosenbaum, 1987).

Crime Prevention Through Environmental Design (CPTED)

Although many communities have attempted to implement the basic principles of CPTED, there is no clear evidence that altering the physical environment through such measures as installing better lighting or designing cul-de-sacs instead of through streets has a significant impact on the crime rate.

Media-Based Crime Prevention/Criminal Apprehension Programs

Despite their proliferation, very few of the crime prevention/criminal apprehension programs have been evaluated to assess the degree to which they lower crime rates, reduce the fear of crime, or increase the catch rate. There is some evidence from Canada (Carriere, 1987) and the United States (Rosenbaum *et al.*, 1989) that these types of programs have widespread public support and that citizens in both countries perceive them to be effective in apprehending offenders. Further, Rosenbaum *et al.* (1989) found in an overview survey of Crime Stoppers programs in the United States that the programs were cost effective, with businesses and the media contributions offsetting most of the expenses.

Among the more ingenious initiatives to solicit community participation in the apprehension of offenders are television programs such as "America's Most Wanted," which profile cases of "at large" criminals. This is one instance in which Canadian exposure to American television has produced positive results: many of America's "most wanted" have escaped to Canada and have been identified by Canadian viewers for capture by Canadian police forces. There is little doubt that the use of the electronic media holds great potential (while presenting potential dangers, such as the "Big Brother" syndrome) to bring together the police and the public in a cooperative effort to prevent crime and apprehend offenders (see Sacco and Trotman, 1990).

Our brief review of the effectiveness of crime prevention programs suggests that these initiatives have been much less successful than is commonly assumed by both the police and the general public. Remember, however, that the research findings are from studies that examine programs operating in a wide variety of policing environments and each program has its unique attributes. Despite this, we can identify some reasons why crime prevention programs may not achieve their full potential and what can be done to increase their effectiveness.

THE RHETORIC AND REALITY OF COMMUNITY POLICING

In their discussion of the current status of community policing in Canada, Normandeau and Leighton (1990:46) state that community policing has become the "conventional wisdom among executives and police constables in more progressive urban police services." This conclusion, however, is not supported by any clear evidence that there has been a profound shift in the manner in which policing services are organized and delivered across the country.

There are, at present, no established criteria as to what constitutes a "community" policing strategy and what the requirements would be for community input and participation in an initiative before it can properly be labelled a "community" policing strategy. At this point, it is not possible to ascertain the extent to which there have been significant structural changes in policing organizations; the extent to which there have been improvements in police-community relations; or the degree to which police organizations have altered their policies and practices for allocating resources and personnel. Community policing can take many forms and is really "an 'umbrella term' to describe any approach to policing that encourages involvement with the community" (Murphy and Muir, 1985:81).

Community relations programs and crime prevention initiatives have suffered because they have been implemented with a traditional "crime control" model of service delivery. In order to realize the full potential of these programs, police departments must move toward community policing. Generally speaking, we can identify at least two major reasons why crime prevention programs have not been effective and also why attempts to move toward a community policing model may encounter difficulties: (1) resistance on the part of police departments to adopt a community policing model of service delivery and to develop a partnership with the community; and (2) the failure of police departments to solicit and maintain community involvement in crime prevention programs (a factor directly related to the persistence of the crime control model of policing).

A major obstacle to the implementation of effective community relations/crime prevention programs has been the resistance of police departments themselves. This is due to the fact that, for so many years, the police have assumed full responsibility for identifying and responding to crime and other problems in the community. It is now hard for them to pass along some of this responsibility to the community. Other reasons why the police may resist developing and implementing community programs include police dissatisfaction with or mistrust of the community, opposition to altering the crime control mission, and the failure of senior police administrators to recognize and reward officers' efforts in community relations and crime prevention.

The opposition from within the department experienced by officers involved in police-community relations and crime prevention units is aptly illustrated by the comments of an officer in St. John's, Newfoundland:

> It has changed my attitude and my image toward the public...It changed what I think about people...But the only thing that saddens me is your own fellow police officers sometimes I won't say look down on you but they think you're running a bluff...It's not real police work (to them). They see you in the hallways, and say, "How many crimes did you prevent today?" (McGahan, 1984:182).

In many police organizations, there is no clear-cut conception of where the community relations or crime prevention unit "fits," and organizational support for its program initiatives by both senior adminis- tration and patrol officers is often lacking. Murphy (1991:184) has argued that, despite the proliferation of crime prevention programs and other initiatives under the rubric of "community policing" in Canada:

> ...they remain in most cases isolated police strategies, unrelated to the general philosophy or operational policies of the department as a whole...most police departments remain committed to crime control and mobile rapid response to calls for service as their basic oper- ational philosophy, while community policing strategies remain a specialized adjunct to the core crime control model.

Senior police administrators have also been a major source of resistance to organizational change. Many police leaders have adopted the rhetoric of community policing, while continuing to manage their organizations within a traditional service delivery model. Sykes (1985:64) has argued that "...reform movements may have succeeded to some extent in creating the appearance without the substance of fundamental reform." Inspector Braiden of the Edmonton Police Service has argued that, in their preoccupation with paperwork, procedures, and politics, many police administrators have become isolated from front-line policing, further hindering the reform process (1990). As Clairmont concludes in his dis- cussion of the challenges that will confront attempts to implement community-based policing:

> ...it remains to be seen whether the proactive and problem-solving activity will ultimately be left to a few officers working with volunteers and advisory groups while the rest of the members carry on a conventional, basically reactive, incident-driven style of policing" (1992:481).

Community Involvement in Community Relations/Crime Prevention Programs

For the full potential of community relations and crime prevention initiatives to be realized, it is essential that the public participate in a substantive fashion. Needless to say, this is also a prerequisite for the community policing model. The research to date, however, suggests that not only is there limited community participation in many crime prevention and community relations programs, but that those citizens who do participate may be those least at risk from victimization (see Roberts and Grossman, 1990). Lab (1992:55) reports that citizens who participate in crime prevention initiatives are "more often males, middle-to-upper income, owners of their own homes, live in single-family dwellings, are more highly educated, white, and living in homogeneous areas." Rosenbaum (1987) concluded from a review of Neighbourhood Watch programs that residents in high crime areas were less likely to participate in this initiative than their counterparts in less crime-ridden areas. Another major issue confronting crime prevention initiatives is continuity and stability. Garofalo and McLeod (1989) found that many Neighbourhood Watch programs in the United States were dormant and that it was difficult to sustain community interest and participation.

Municipal governments also have an important role to play in crime prevention activities. Among the findings of a survey of 464 Canadian municipalities conducted by Hastings and Melchers (1990) were that involvement in crime prevention programs was a high priority. The most prevalent type of involvement was in providing crime prevention education and in participating in programs such as Operation Identification. However, these authors (1990:114) also discovered that municipalities rarely took a lead role in these initiatives, relying instead upon the police to assume the leadership role. There would seem to be considerable potential for the substantive involvement of municipal governments as a partner in crime prevention activities.

COMMUNITY POLICING: RECENT INNOVATIONS

Despite the glacial pace at which police departments in Canada are moving away from traditional models of policing, a number of innovative projects across the country give us reason to be at least cautiously optimistic that substantial changes will occur before the end of the century. All of the following examples represent the efforts of the police departments involved to move away from the "watch" system of policing and toward community policing (see Loree and Murphy, 1987). Among the more high profile initiatives that have been implemented in recent years are the following.

▸   *The Victoria Community Police Station Program (Co.P.S.)*

The Community Police Station Program (Co.P.S) was established by the Victoria City Police in 1987 and is comprised of several storefront-style police stations staffed by one uniformed police constable who is assisted by citizen volunteers. The community police stations deliver crime prevention programs such as Neighbourhood Watch and Operation Identification, as well as programs and services tailored to the specific needs of local neighbourhoods. Ideally, each community police station reflects the community that it serves.

A preliminary evaluation (Walker and Walker, 1989:75) found that officers in the Victoria Police Department viewed the program with "cautious optimism," with many officers expressing the concern that the program was draining resources from the more important patrol function of the department. There was also a high level of awareness of the program among community residents (see also Walker and Walker, 1990). It remains to be seen, however, whether the community police stations will become an integral part, rather than merely an appendage to, the Victoria Police Department.

▸   *Community-Based Zone Policing in Halifax*

The primary mechanism by which community policing services are delivered in Halifax is through "zone" or "team" policing. The city is divided into three zones, each of which is policed by four units under the direction of a "zone commander." The units work as a team to identify the problems in their particular area and to formulate policing strategies to address them. Each zone also has a "crime prevention coordinator" whose job it is to maintain ties between the police and the community and to solicit the concerns of residents and encourage public participation in problem solving. Under the zone policing scheme, uniformed constables are involved in all stages of the investigative process.

A survey (Clairmont, 1990) of patrol officers who had volunteered to be assigned to the first policing zone found that a majority felt that the strategy improved police-community relations. Support was also expressed by the officers for the "constable-generalist" role, which many felt increased their responsibilities and accountability. The officers also perceived that both the police and the public benefitted from the implementation of zone policing.

► *Edmonton Police Service Neighbourhood Foot Patrol Project*

The Neighbourhood Foot Patrol Project began in 1987 when officers were assigned to 21 areas of the city, selected for their high number of crime and incident occurrences and repeat calls for service. The project was designed to provide policing services on a proactive, rather than a reactive, basis; to improve public attitudes toward the police; to increase the level of job satisfaction among police officers; and to involve the police and neighbourhood residents in a collaborative effort to identify and resolve problems that arise in the community. In each of the neighbourhood areas, constables patrol on foot from a storefront office. The storefront offices, staffed by patrol officers and assisted by community volunteers, are designed to make the police visible and accessible to community residents.

An evaluation of the Foot Patrol Project (Hornick *et al.*, 1990) found that foot patrol resulted in a reduction of repeat calls for service in high incidence areas; an increase in levels of community satisfaction with the police; an increased level of job satisfaction among foot patrol officers; and evidence that foot patrol officers employed creative approaches to problem-solving in their neighbourhoods, often involving collaboration with community residents, leaders, and organizations.

The Future of Community Policing in Canada

The move toward community policing by Canadian police forces, however, has been a very uneven process. For many senior police administrators, the commitment to community policing is only rhetorical, and in many departments both senior administrators and their patrol officers remain resistant to substantive change.

Anticipating the resistance of many police officials to making organizational changes required to implement community policing (and perhaps hearing the ghost of team policing), Braiden (1989a:24) warns his police colleagues that it will not be sufficient merely to "stick a new box on the edge of the organizational chart, put a few people in it and announce the birth of 'Community Policing.'" He argues: "It's not a hors d'oeuvre, or dessert. It's the main course. It's the meat and spuds of what policing was supposed to be from the beginning" (1989a:24).

While problem-oriented policing, community relations programs, and crime prevention initiatives are a vital component of community policing, they must be implemented in conjunction with broader organizational changes in service delivery in order to be effective. Community policing is a *model* for service delivery that contains several key ingredients. It is within a community policing framework that such strategies as problem-oriented policing, police-community relations programs, and crime prevention programs will be most successful. Merely creating specific programs without changing the overall model of policing will limit their effectiveness. Police departments across Canada must make the necessary organizational and operational changes required to implement community policing strategies and to conduct evaluations of the effectiveness of these initiatives in preventing and responding to crime and other problems in the community (see Kennedy, 1991).

HUMAN RESOURCE ISSUES

With the move away from traditional models of police practice, there has been an increased focus on the human resource issues in policing. In order for community policing to be successful, police departments must reflect in their ranks a gender balance and the multicultural diversity of Canadian society. The manner in which police recruits are trained and the development of standards for police professionalism are also issues that must be addressed.

Women in Policing

Women have been employed in Canadian police forces since the early 1900s, although traditionally their duties were confined to specific areas such as clerical work, handling youths and women, and serving as jail matrons. The past decade, however, has seen a steady rise in the number of women police officers from 2% of total police officers in 1980 to 7% in 1991 (Canadian Centre for Justice Statistics, 1992b:7). A study (Ontario Police Commission, 1986) of recruitment methods and the status of women on Ontario regional and municipal police forces found that women represented only 2.7% of the total uniformed police force and that only nine of the 121 police forces surveyed made special attempts to hire female officers. The majority of women in policing, however, are still confined to non-policing roles: in 1990, women comprised 64% of non-police personnel. Similar increases in women police officers have also occurred in police departments across the United States, although their numbers as an overall percentage of officers are similar to those in Canada (Martin, 1989).

Traditionally, a number of arguments have been advanced in opposition to women becoming involved in general-duty policing: (1) the perception of male police officers that the image of policing will suffer if women are hired; (2) concern by male police officers that women are less committed to policing as a career; (3) the threat that women would pose to the social world of male police officers; and (4) the perception that women are unable to cope with the violent and physical aspects of police work (see Balkin, 1988; Hale, 1992). The findings of research studies conducted on women in policing in Canada and the United States, however, suggest that these concerns are largely unfounded. In fact, there is some evidence that women may be more effective in the police role than their male counterparts.

In terms of carrying out the policing role, Linden (1980) found no significant differences between male and female police officers in their patterns of arrests, and officers of both genders tended to handle similar types of calls (see also Morash and Greene, 1986). There were also no differences between male and female officers in their abilities to carry out general police duties. From observations of police-citizen encounters, Linden (1980) found the public very positive toward and respectful of female police officers. Linden (1980) also found that women police officers were more effective in their interactions with the general public than their male counterparts. Research (Martin, 1989:316) in the United States has found that female police officers made fewer arrests than their male counterparts, carried out their tasks in a less aggressive fashion, and were less likely than male officers to become involved in serious misconduct. In interviews with supervisory personnel and an examination of departmental records, Linden (1980;1983) found no significant differences in the job performance assessment of Canadian male and female officers. Both municipal and RCMP supervisory personnel held positive views of the work of female officers. Positive perceptions of the capabilities of female officers were also provided by police leaders interviewed for the Ontario Police Commission study (1986).

Despite evidence of positive performance in the field, there are sources of organizational resistance to women in policing. While it can be assumed that changes have occurred since Linden conducted his work over a decade ago, his studies uncovered several disturbing factors that must be addressed. Many male patrol officers in the municipal department and the RCMP detachment surveyed by Linden expressed strong reservations and negative attitudes toward female police officers.

Of particular concern is the high attrition rate for women police officers. Linden (1985) found that female RCMP officers left the force in greater numbers than their male counterparts. This was due to marriage and family-related reasons rather than dissatisfaction with policing or difficulties in the job. The transfer policy of the RCMP, whereby officers are relocated to a new detachment every two or three years, was identified by many women as the major reason for their having left the force.

It is crucial that the organizational and attitudinal barriers that have hindered the recruitment, performance, and promotion of women police officers fall in the coming years. This will allow women officers to play a significant role in policing communities and to move beyond their current "token" status. Given that much of the opposition to women in policing is rooted in traditional views of gender roles, the increased emphasis on employment equity and affirmative action in hiring will assist in this process. It will be a much longer-term process to change the attitudes of many police personnel.

Visible Minorities in Policing

Discussions surrounding women in policing have a longer history than those relating to visible minorities and Aboriginal peoples. Many of the issues, however, are similar. The need to recruit Aboriginal peoples and members of visible minorities into policing has assumed even greater urgency in view of increasing conflicts (often sparked by police shootings of black suspects) between the municipal police forces and minorities in Montreal, Toronto, and Halifax and between the Quebec Police Force and Aboriginal peoples in the crisis that erupted at Oka in 1990. The furor over the decision by the RCMP to allow a Sikh recruit to wear a turban as part of the official police uniform illustrates the types of controversies that will surround the movement toward multicultural policing (see Fleras *et al.*, 1989; Jaywardene and Talbot, 1990).

The most extensive work on the recruitment of visible minorities by police forces in Canada has been done by Jain (1987;1988). In a survey of 14 Canadian police departments, Jain (1988) found that, while visible minorities comprise approximately 7% of the country's population, their representation in the departments surveyed ranged from zero to 3.4%. A further finding was that nearly all of the visible minority police officers were males. In 1990, Jain (1991) found that these same departments had increased the number of visible minorities and that most of the departments had visible minorities in positions above the rank of constable. Among the barriers to attracting visible minorities into policing are the perceptions held of the police in their country of origin, distrust of the police, and the view held by many visible minorities that policing is not an honourable profession.

Police forces are taking more proactive steps to increase the numbers of minorities in their ranks. During 1988-89, the RCMP created a national recruiting team with the specific purpose of increasing recruits from visible minorities, indigenous peoples, Francophones, and women. In a further development (to be discussed in Chapter 15), the RCMP in 1991 phased out the Indian Special Constable program, making these officers "regular" members and created the Aboriginal Constable Development Program. Under this program, indigenous peoples are hired as regular members and then, over a two-year period, receive physical and educational training to meet the requirements to enter recruit training. Our discussion in Chapter 15 will also reveal that many reserve-based Aboriginal groups are not waiting for "outside" police forces to recruit Aboriginal members; rather, they are creating their own autonomous police forces on the reserves.

Training and Education: Professionalization of the Police

In our discussion in Chapter 3, it was noted that provincial governments, through the development of police commissions, have become extensively involved in the training of police officers for municipal and provincial police forces. The increased concern with training is reflected in the establishment of various police colleges and central training facilities and the provision, in many jurisdictions, of university- or college-based education programs.

The education and training of police officers is closely related to the concept of professionalization of the police. Professionalization has been viewed as the mechanism for increasing the effectiveness and efficiency of police organizations, as a way to gain public confidence, and as the foundation for police reform. On an operational level, however, the term "professionalization" has not been clearly defined, and the specific role and nature of education and training in this process has not been clearly established (see Buckley, 1991).

Defining what actually is meant by a "professional" police officer and a "professional" police organization, however, is difficult. Canadian police forces have not developed uniform standards of admission, training, promotion, or transfer of certification and rank across jurisdiction. There is considerable variation in the standards for the recruitment and training, and there is little opportunity for officers to move laterally between departments without a loss of rank. In addition, in most police organizations in Canada, officers are required to advance through the ranks of a paramilitary structure. There is little lateral entry of officers into police departments from the outside. However, we can anticipate that increasing the education and training levels of police officers within a traditional model of service delivery may not accomplish these objectives.

Police education can be divided into basic training and ongoing training. Normandeau and Leighton (1990:94) have identified four models of basic training.

1) *Police training offered in independent facilities apart from the adult education mainstream:* this is the model used by the RCMP, where all recruits are trained at Depot in Regina, Saskatchewan, and by the province of Ontario, which trains recruits at the Ontario Police College in Alymer, Ontario.

2) *Police training offered in a university campus setting, but apart from the education mainstream:* in this model, practiced at the Saskatchewan Police College at the University of Regina and by the Atlantic Police Academy at Holland College in Prince Edward Island, academic and police personnel teach courses to recruits.

3) *Police training as part of a general criminal justice training facility:* municipal police recruits in British Columbia are trained at the Police Academy, which is part of the Justice Institute in British Columbia, a training facility for probation officers, correctional personnel, and court staff.

4) *Police training integrated into mainstream adult education:* in the province of Quebec, police recruits in the Quebec Police Force enroll in a two-and-one-half-year program at a community college, which includes law, policing, criminology, as well as other liberal arts and science courses.

Ongoing training for full-time police personnel is available in a number of forums across the country. The Police Academy, Justice Institute of British Columbia offers courses for mid- and senior management officers, and the Canadian Police College in Ottawa offers specialized courses for police officers.

A notable trend in Canadian policing is toward recruiting officers with higher levels of education. There is some evidence, primarily from studies conducted in the United States, that officers with higher levels of education are more culturally sensitive to visible minorities, exhibit greater flexibility in carrying out policing tasks, and generate fewer complaints from citizens than their less-educated counterparts (see Fischer, Golden, and Heininger, 1985). More research remains to be done not only on the impact of education on police officer performance in Canada, but also on what *types* of educational experiences are most beneficial to police officers operating in various policing environments (see Tomovich and Loree, 1989).

This chapter has looked at the critical issues surrounding police, from the actual decisions made by the police to the involvement of the community in policing. Chapter 6 looks at the court system and what happens to people after they have been arrested.

NOTES

[1]Although one can expect that different task environments will result in variability in the demands that are placed upon police departments, it appears that there may be a core of activities that are common to most patrol officers. In a U.S. study, Meagher (1985) discovered that officers in small, medium, and large municipal police departments shared the following common tasks: (1) general patrol tasks; (2) offender processing; (3) traffic accident tasks; and (4) driving tasks. However, while the types of tasks performed by officers may be similar across departments, the level of demand for these tasks may vary considerably, as may the settings in which the encounters between police and citizens take place.

[2]One unique attribute of Canadian policing is the frequent transfer (often every two years) of officers in the RCMP. During their policing careers, RCMP officers are likely to be exposed to a variety of policing environments, with the concurrent requirement that adjustments be made in their policing style. One rationale offered for this transfer policy is to prevent officers from becoming involved in the community to the extent that it adversely affects their ability to

perform their duties. Ironically, as we will see in our discussion of Aboriginal peoples and the police in Chapter 15, a major complaint of many communities is that the frequent transfer of officers prevents the development of police-community relations that would improve the delivery of policing services.

[3]A major issue in policing is the extent to which policing is the extent to which police practice reflects community sentiments. Police observers have argued that there must be more direct lines of communication between the general public and police agencies and the creation of mechanisms to ensure public input into police policy and practice on an ongoing basis. This may be particularly important in communities where the RCMP is acting as the municipal police force, as policies for the RCMP detachment are set at the division level and at RCMP headquarters in Ottawa.

In the United States, county sheriffs, who are responsible for policing areas that lie outside of incorporated cities and towns, are elected by popular vote. It might be argued that this increases the likelihood that enforcement policies and practices of the Sheriff's Department may more accurately reflect community expectations and standards, or at least the needs of certain groups in the community. To the contrary, it might be argued that electing policing officials interjects politics into the policing function, which may not be desirable. There are no elected policing officials in Canada.

[4]Researchers in the United States have explored the impact of the officer's age, experience, level of education, rank, and ethnicity on decision making. Some evidence from this research suggests that these variables may affect officer decision making, although the relationship remains to be empirically examined in the Canadian context.

[5]The activities of the RCMP Public Complaints Commission are documented in an annual report available from the Minister of Supply and Services.

REFERENCES

Appleby, T. 1992. "Embattled Police Seek Solutions." *The Globe and Mail* (May 9):A1, A7.

Balkin, J. 1988. "Why Policemen Don't Like Policewomen." 16 *Journal of Police Science and Administration*. 29-38.

Bayley, D.H. 1991. *Managing the Future: Prospective Issues in Canadian Policing*. Ottawa: Solicitor General of Canada.

Bennett, S.F., and P.J. Lavrakas. 1989. "Community-Based Crime Prevention: An Assessment of the Eisenhower Foundations Neighborhood Program." 25 *Crime and Delinquency*. 345-64.

Braiden, C. 1989a. "The Origin of Community Policing." 1.9 *Blue Line Magazine*. 21, 24.

_____. 1989b. "The Realities of Community Policing — Bringing the Village to the City." 1.10 *Blue Line Magazine*. 10-11.

_____. 1990. "Policing from the Belly of the Whale." Unpublished paper. Edmonton: Edmonton Police Service.

Brantingham, P.J., and F.L. Faust. 1976. "A Conceptual Model of Crime Prevention." 22 *Crime and Delinquency*. 284-296.

Brown, M.K. 1981. *Working the Street: Police Discretion and the Dilemmas of Reform*. New York: Russell Sage Foundation.

Buckley, L.B. 1991. "Attitudes Toward Higher Education Among Mid-Career Officers." 15 *Canadian Police College Journal*. 257-73.

Canadian Centre for Justice Statistics. 1992a. *Canadian Crime Statistics, 1991*. Ottawa: Minister of Industry, Science and Technology Canada.

_____. 1992b. "Police Personnel and Expenditures in Canada — 1991." 12 *Juristat Service Bulletin*. Ottawa: Statistics Canada.

Carriere, K.D. 1987. "Crime Stoppers Critically Considered." 8 *Canadian Criminology Forum*. 104-115.

Clairmont, D. 1990. *To the Forefront: Community-Based Zone Policing in Halifax*. Ottawa: Canadian Police College.

Clairmont, D. 1992. "Community-based Policing: Implementation and Impact." 33 *Canadian Journal of Criminology*. 469-484.

Cryderman, B.K., C.N. O'Tolle, and A. Fleras. 1992. *Police, Race and Ethnicity — A Guide for Police Services*. Toronto: Butterworths.

Dunham, R.G., and G.P. Alpert 1988. "Neighborhood Crime Differences in Attitudes Toward Policing: Evidence for a Mixed-Strategy Model of Policing in a Multi-Ethnic Setting." 79 *Journal of Criminal Law and Criminology*. 504-23.

Eck, J., and W. Spelman. 1989. "A Problem-Oriented Approach to Police Service Delivery." In D.J. Kenny, ed. *Police and Policing: Contemporary Issues*. New York: Praeger. 95-111.

Ericson, R.V. 1982. *Reproducing Order: A Study of Police Patrol Work*. Toronto: University of Toronto Press.

Fischer, R.J., K.M. Golden, and B.L. Heininger. 1985. "Issues in Higher Education for Law Enforcement Officers: An Illinois Study." 13 *Journal of Criminal Justice*. 329-338.

Fleras, A., F.J. Desroches, C. O'Toole, and G. Davies. 1989. "'Bridging the Gap': Towards a Multicultural Policing in Canada." 13 *Canadian Police College Journal*. 153-164.

Garofalo, J., and M. McLeod. 1989. "The Structure and Operation of Neighborhood Watch Programs in the United States." 35 *Crime and Delinquency*. 326-344.

Goldstein, H. 1979. "Improving Policing: A Problem-Oriented Approach." 25 *Crime and Delinquency*. 236-258.

Greene, J.R., and S.D. Mastrofski. 1991. *Community Policing: Rhetoric or Reality*. New York: Praeger.

Greene, J.R., and R.B. Taylor. 1991. "Community-Based Policing and Foot Patrol: Issues of Theory and Evaluation." In J.R. Greene and S.D. Mastrofski, eds. *Community Policing: Rhetoric or Reality*. New York: Praeger. 195-223.

Griffiths, C.T. 1982. "Police School Programs: The Realities of the Remedy." 24 *Canadian Journal of Criminology*. 329-340.

Hale, D.C. 1992. "Women in Policing." In G.W. Cordner, and D.C. Hale, eds. *What Works in Policing? Operations and Administration Examined*. Cincinnati, Ohio: Anderson Publishing Co. 125-142.

Hastings, R., and R. Melchers. 1990. "Municipal Government Involvement in Crime Prevention in Canada." 31 *Canadian Journal of Criminology*. 433-446.

Heller, N.B., W.W. Stenzel, A.D. Gill, R.A. Kolde, and S.R. Shimerman. 1975. *Operation Identification Projects: Assessment of Effectiveness*. Washington, D.C.: Law Enforcement Assistance Administration.

Hickling-Johnston. 1982. *Metropolitan Toronto Police Management Study: Productivity Improvements — Delivery of Cost Effective Police Services to Metropolitan Toronto Citizens*. Toronto: Hickling-Johnston, Ltd.

Hogarth, J. 1982. "Police Accountability." In R. Donelan, ed. *The Maintenance of Order in Society*. Ottawa: Supply and Services Canada. 111-25. (Catalogue No. JS66-2/1982E.). Reproduced with permission of the Minister of Supply and Services Canada, 1989.

Hornick, J.P., B.A. Burrows, I. Tjowvold, and D.M. Phillips. 1990. *An Evaluation of the Neighborhood Foot Patrol Program of the Edmonton Police Service*. Ottawa: Solicitor General of Canada.

Jain, H.C. 1987. "Recruitment of Racial Minorities in Canadian Police Forces." 42 *Relations Industrielles/Industrial Relations*. 790-805.

_____. 1988. "The Recruitment and Selection of Visible Minorities in Canadian Police Organizations, 1985 to 1987." 31 *Canadian Public Administration*. 463-482.

_____. 1991. "An Assessment of Strategies of Recruiting Visible Minority Police officers in Canada: 1985-1990." Unpublished paper. Hamilton, Ontario: McMaster University.

Jaywardene, C.H.S., and C.K. Talbot. 1990. *Police Recruitment of Ethnic Minorities*. Ottawa: Canadian Police College.

Johnson, K.W., and S.L. Merker. 1992. "Crime Prevention." In G.W. Cordner and D.C. Hale, eds. *What Works in Policing? Operations and Administration Examined*. Cincinnati: Anderson Publishing Company. 63-84.

Kelling, G.L., T. Pate, D. Dieckman, and C.E. Brown. 1974. *The Kansas City Preventive Patrol Experiment: A Summary Report.* Washington, D.C.: Police Foundation.

_____. 1983. "The Kansas City Preventive Patrol Experiment." In C.B. Klockars, ed. *Thinking About Police: Contemporary Readings.* New York: McGraw-Hill,. 136-160.

Kennedy, L.W. 1991. "The Evaluation of Community-Based Policing in Canada." 15 *Canadian Police College Journal.* 275-89.

Kessler, D.A. 1985. "One-or Two Officer Cars? A Perspective from Kansas City." 13 *Journal of Criminal Justice.* 49-64.

Koenig, D.J. 1991. *Do the Police Cause Crime? Police Activity, Police Strength and Crime Rates.* Ottawa: Research and Program Development Branch, Canadian Police College.

Lab, S.P. 1992. *Crime Prevention: Approaches, Practices and Evaluations.* Cincinnati, Ohio: Anderson Publishing Company.

Linden, R. 1980. *Women in Policing: A Study of the Vancouver Police Department.* Ottawa: Solicitor General of Canada.

_____. 1983. "Women in Policing: A Study of Lower Mainland R.C.M.P. Detachments." 7 *Canadian Police College Journal.* 217-229.

_____. 1985. "Attrition Among Male and Female Members of the RCMP." 9 *Canadian Police College Journal.* 86-97.

Loree, D., and C. Murphy. 1987. *Community Policing in the 1980's: Recent Advances in Police Programs.* Ottawa: Supply and Services Canada.

Lundman, R.J. 1980. *Police and Policing — An Introduction.* New York: Holt, Rinehart, and Winston.

McGahan, P. 1984. *Police Images of a City.* New York: Peter Lang.

Martin, S.E. 1989. "Female Officers on the Move? A Status Report on Women in Policing." In R.G. Dunham and G.P. Alpert, eds. *Critical Issues in Policing: Contemporary Issues.* Prospect Heights, Illinois: Waveland Press. 312-330.

Mastrofski, S. 1981. "Policing the Beat: The Impact of Organizational Scale on Patrol Officer Behavior in Urban Residential Neighborhoods." 9 *Journal of Criminal Justice.* 343-58.

Morash, M., and J.R. Greene. 1986. "Evaluating Women on Patrol: A Critique of Contemporary Wisdom." 10 *Evaluation Review.* 230-255.

Murphy, C. 1985. *Assessing Police Performance: Issues, Problems and Alternatives.* Ottawa: Solicitor General of Canada.

Murphy, C.R. 1991. "The Development, Impact, and Implications of Community Policing in Canada." In J.R. Greene and S.D. Mastrofski, eds. *Community Policing: Rhetoric or Reality.* New York: Praeger. 177-189.

Murphy, C., and R.G. Muir. 1985. *Community-Based Policing: A Review of the Critical Issues.* Ottawa: Solicitor General of Canada.

Murphy, P.V., and T. Pate. 1977. *Commissioner.* New York: Simon and Schuster.

Normandeau, A., and B. Leighton. 1990. *A Vision of the Future of Policing in Canada: Police-Challenge 2000.* Ottawa: Minister of Supply and Services.

Ontario Police Commission. 1986. *Report on the Study of Female Police Officers, Ontario Regional and Municipal Police Forces.* Toronto: Ontario Ministry of the Solicitor General.

Palys, T.S., E.O. Boyanowsky, and D.G. Dutton. 1984. "Mobile Data Access Terminals and Their Implications for Policing." 40 *Journal of Social Issues.* 113-127.

Pennell, S., C. Curtis, J. Henderson, and J. Tayman. 1989. "Guardian Angels: A Unique Approach to Crime Prevention." 35 *Crime and Delinquency.* 378-400.

Police Foundation. 1981. *The Newark Foot Patrol Experiment.* Washington, D.C.: Police Foundation.

Roberts, J.V., and M.G. Grossman. 1990. "Crime Prevention and Public Opinion." 32 *Canadian Journal of Criminology.* 75-90.

Rosenbaum, D.P. 1986. *Community Crime Prevention? Does It Work?* Beverly Hills, California: Sage Publications.

Rosenbaum, D.P. 1987. "The Theory and Research Behind Neighborhood Watch: Is It a Sound Fear and Crime Reduction Strategy? 33 *Crime and Delinquency.* 103-134.

Rosenbaum, D.P., A.J. Lurigio, and P.J. Lavrakas. 1989. "Enhancing Citizen Participation and Solving Serious Crime: A National Evaluation of the Crime Stoppers Program." 35 *Crime and Delinquency.* 401-20.

Sacco, V.F., and M. Trotman. 1990. "Public Information Programming and Family Violence: Lessons from the Mass Media Crime Prevention Experience." 32 *Canadian Journal of Criminology.* 91-105.

Schneider, F.W. 1991. "Police Organization Effectiveness: The Manager's Perspective." 15 *Canadian Police College Journal.* 153-165.

Sherman, L.W. 1986. "Policing Communities: What Works? In A.J. Reiss and M. Tonry, eds. *Crime and Justice: An Annual Review of Research. Volume 8.* Chicago: University of Chicago Press. 343-86.

_____. 1980. "Causes of Police Behavior: The Current State of Quantitative Research." 17 *Journal of Research in Crime and Delinquency.* 69-100.

Smith, D.A., and J. Klein. 1984. "Police Control of Interpersonal Disputes." 31 *Social Problems.* 468-81.

Solicitor General of Canada. 1984. *Selected Trends in Canadian Justice.* Ottawa: Research and Statistics Group, Programs Branch.

Spelman, W.G., and D.K. Brown. 1983. "Response Time." In C.B. Klockers, ed. *Thinking About Policing: Contemporary Readings*. New York: McGraw-Hill. 160-166.

Sykes, G.W. 1985. "The Functional Nature of Police Reform — The 'Myth' of Controlling the Police." 2 *Justice Quarterly*. 52-65.

Tomovich, V.A., and D.J. Loree. 1989. "In Search of New Directions: Policing in Niagara Region." 13 *Canadian Police College Journal*. 29-54.

Trojanowicz, R.C. 1983. "An Evaluation of a Neighborhood Foot Patrol Program." 11 *Journal of Police Science and Administration*. 410-419.

Trojanowicz, R.C., and D. Banas. 1985. *Perceptions of Safety: A Comparison of Foot Patrol versus Motor Patrol Officers*. East Lansing, Michigan: National Neighborhood Foot Patrol Center, Michigan State University.

Trojanowicz, R., and B. Bucqueroux. 1990. *Community Policing: A Contemporary Perspective*. Cincinnati, Ohio: Anderson Publishing Company.

Troyer, R.J., and R.D. Wright. 1985. "Community Response to Crime: Two Middle-Class Anti-Crime Patrols." 13 *Journal of Criminal Justice*. 227-242.

Van Andel, H. 1989. "Crime Prevention That Works: The Care of Public Transport in the Netherlands." 29 *British Journal of Criminology*. 47-56.

Van Maanen, J. 1973. "Observations on the Making of Policemen." Reproduced by permission of the Society for Applied Anthropology from 32 *Human Organization*. 407-18.

Walker, C.R., and S.G. Walker. 1989. *The Victoria Community Police Stations: An Exercise in Innovation*. Ottawa: Canadian Police College.

Walker, C.R., and S.G. Walker. 1990. "The Citizen and the Police: A Partnership in Crime Prevention." 31 *Canadian Journal of Criminology*. 125-35.

Wilson, J.Q. 1968. *Varieties of Police Behavior: The Management of Law and Order in Eight Communities*. Cambridge, Massachusetts: Harvard University Press.

6 THE STRUCTURE AND OPERATION OF CANADIAN CRIMINAL COURTS

The criminal courts occupy a special place at the heart of the criminal justice system.[1] The courts are responsible for determining the guilt or innocence of accused persons and for imposing an appropriate sentence upon those who are convicted. In this sense, they are part of the vast criminal justice apparatus that plays a major part in maintaining social control in Canada. However, unlike the police or corrections components of the criminal justice system, the critical function of the courts is to protect the rights of those individuals who become enmeshed in the criminal justice process. In this respect, the courts are responsible for monitoring the activities of the various agents of the criminal justice system with a view to enforcing the rights of accused persons (Friedland, 1988-89). The courts are, therefore, responsible for protecting the rights of those persons who may well be intensely unpopular in the arena of public opinion. As Friedenberg (1985:417) notes: "The law derives its moral authority, as distinct from its legal authority, from its commitment to protect as well as to control or punish those who come before it and especially those whom public opinion would condemn."

The extent to which the courts should balance the competing demands of social control and protection of individual accused persons is a matter that will fuel continuing debate in the indefinite future. The advent of the *Charter* in 1982 has raised expectations that the courts will place considerably more emphasis on the protection of individual rights in the years immediately ahead (Friedenberg, 1985).

As Pink and Perrier (1988:141) point out, the courts must be considered as a distinct branch of Canadian government; in particular, they are quite separate from those who are elected to make laws (Russell, 1987). The courts perform a governmental function because they are charged with the enforcement of the laws made by legislators in the Canadian Parliament and the various provincial and territorial legislatures across the country (Tardi, 1992). According to Pink and Perrier:

> ...in our society, the concept of having different and parallel author-
> ities making and enforcing the law is so strongly established that it is
> now the right of anyone in this country who is charged with an

offence to be treated in accordance with principles of fundamental justice, and it rests with the courts to ensure that that occurs (1988:141-142).

The courts are also entirely distinct from the executive branch of government in Canada (the federal, provincial, and territorial governments, represented by the prime minister, premiers, government leaders, and their respective cabinets). The concept of judicial independence implies that Canadian citizens enjoy the right to have their cases tried before tribunals that are fair, impartial, and immune from political pressure exerted by the executive branch of government (Colvin, 1986-87; Lederman, 1987; Pink and Perrier, 1988). This principle is of vital importance when it is remembered that it is the executive branch that is responsible for the activities of the police, the prosecutors, and correctional officials.

It is interesting to note that all levels of government in Canada spent almost $640 million for the operation of the court system in 1988-89, representing an expenditure of $25 for every Canadian (Canadian Centre for Justice Statistics, 1991b:3).[2] In spite of the central role of the courts in the criminal justice system, they only receive a relatively small proportion of the total funds dedicated to criminal justice expenditures. For example, in 1989-90, court expenditures represented only 8% of total expenditures on justice in Canada, as compared with 61% for policing and 26% for corrections (Canadian Centre for Justice Statistics, 1991b:4).[3] These figures arguably raise some critical questions as to whether enough priority is being given to the funding of Canada's court system.

THE CRIMINAL COURT SYSTEM

In order to illustrate the structure of the criminal court system, we will follow the progress of a criminal case through the various stages of the court process, from the laying of a charge right through to the final appeal that may be made. Before doing this, however, it is necessary to set the stage by outlining both the basic structure of the system of criminal courts and the nature of the classification of criminal offences in Canada.

The Canadian criminal court system has two important distinctions. First, there is a sharp distinction between the *trial* and the *appellate* functions of the courts. The trial function, as the name suggests, is concerned with the actual trial of criminal cases, while the appellate function is concerned with the hearing of appeals from the decisions of courts that are lower in the judicial hierarchy. As we shall see shortly, some courts may exercise *both* trial and appellate functions in relation to criminal cases. Second, there is a distinction between *provincial* and *federal* courts: in effect, there are two separate court systems in Canada, with the Supreme Court of Canada serving as the tribunal of ultimate resort for both systems.

Provincial Court System

The *Constitution Act, 1867,*[4] grants to the provinces the power to make laws in relation to "the administration of justice in the province," and this power expressly includes the "constitution, maintenance, and organization of provincial courts, both of civil and criminal jurisdiction."

Until relatively recently, it was possible to identify a complex, four-tiered court system in every province except Quebec (Hogg, 1985:134). This system consisted of: (1) the courts of appeal; (2) the superior courts; (3) the county or district courts; and (4) the provincial courts. However, beginning in the late 1970s, there was a move in a number of provinces to amalgamate the county or district courts with the superior courts (Canadian Centre for Justice Statistics, 1991a:7-8). The form that the amalgamation took was the abolition of the county or district courts and a consequent expansion of the jurisdiction of the superior courts (Hogg, 1985:134). This process of amalgamation has now occurred in nine provinces (British Columbia, Alberta, Saskatchewan, Manitoba, Ontario, New Brunswick, Prince Edward Island, Nova Scotia, and New-foundland).[5] The county or district courts never existed in the province of Quebec. In essence, the provincially established court systems across all of Canada now consist of just three tiers: the courts of appeal, the superior courts, and the provincial courts.[6] A similar three-tiered system exists in the Yukon and Northwest Territories.

In each province and territory, a court of appeal sits at the very top of the judicial hierarchy. In British Columbia, Alberta, Saskatchewan, Manitoba, Ontario, Quebec, New Brunswick, Nova Scotia, Newfoundland, the Yukon, and the Northwest Territories, it is known, simply, as the Court of Appeal. However, in Prince Edward Island it is known as the Appeal Division of the Supreme Court (Waddams, 1987:129). Depending on the nature of the offence concerned, the courts of appeal may hear appeals from the superior courts and, in some circumstances, from the provincial courts (Lederman, 1988-89).

Immediately below the Court of Appeal in the judicial hierarchy is the Superior Court. The precise name of the Superior Court varies from province to province (Canadian Centre for Justice Statistics, 1989; Waddams, 1987:129). In Manitoba, Saskatchewan, Alberta, and New Brunswick, it is known as the Court of Queen's Bench, and, in Quebec, it is known as the *Cour Superieur.* In Ontario, the Superior Court is known as the Court of Justice, General Division. In the other provinces and territories, it is known simply as the Supreme Court, which, in Prince Edward Island, is divided into a *trial division* and an *appellate division* (called the Court of Appeal in the other provinces). The superior courts, as we shall see, try the more serious indictable offences and hear appeals from the provincial courts in relation to summary conviction offences.

At the bottom of the hierarchy of courts in the provincial system are the so-called provincial (and territorial) courts. (In Ontario it is called the Ontario Court of Justice, Provincial Division, and, in Quebec, the Court of Quebec.) These courts deal with an enormous workload of criminal cases. In fact, all criminal cases enter the provincial courts, and the vast majority are tried and finally disposed of there. The most serious criminal cases, however, will be tried in the "higher courts" (the superior courts). Where the nature of the case is such that it cannot be tried in the Provincial Court, a judge of this court will hold a preliminary inquiry to determine whether there is enough evidence to warrant sending the accused for trial in a higher court. The provincial courts are also responsible for holding the great majority of bail hearings.

The provincial courts are usually organized in a number of separate divisions or, in some provinces, in separate courts. Common divisions are small claims, family, youth, traffic, and criminal. As far as criminal cases are concerned, the Criminal Division of the Provincial Court deals with the offences committed by persons aged 18 or above, and the Youth Court or Division deals with the offences committed by young persons under the age of 18. In some jurisdictions, there may also be a Traffic Division that deals with minor traffic violations arising under provincial legislation. In most jurisdictions, there is also a Family Division of the Provincial Court, which deals with various family issues such as the maintenance and custody of children; in some provinces, it may also deal with the cases of young persons under the *Young Offenders Act* instead of leaving this to a separate Youth Court or Division.[7]

In Quebec, there is yet another tier of courts at the municipal level. Municipal Court judges are appointed by the provincial government and, *inter alia*, they deal with infractions of municipal by-laws and minor traffic offences under the *Highway Code*. In Montreal, Quebec City, and Laval, these courts may also deal with minor (summary conviction) offences arising under the *Criminal Code*. Regina and Saskatoon, Saskatchewan, also have municipal courts, which hear only parking cases and municipal by-law infractions and are presided over by senior justices of the peace (Canadian Centre for Justice Statistics, 1991a:7).

Under the Canadian Constitution (Hogg, 1985:136-137), the federal government appoints and pays the judges of the courts of appeal and the superior courts.[8] On the other hand, the various provincial governments appoint and pay the judges of the provincial courts.[9]

Figure 6.1 shows the organization of provincially established courts in British Columbia. The system of courts in British Columbia is now very similar to that in most other provinces. Figure 6.1 provides a useful graphic summary of the discussion in the preceding paragraphs.

Even though the provincially established system of courts has been simplified in recent years, it is possible that the process of streamlining the court system will gather even further momentum in the years ahead. The Law Reform Commission of Canada (1989:49) has recommended that the criminal court system in Canada be simplified even further by establishing a single court or court division called the Criminal Court in each province and territory. Significantly, the Ontario Government has announced its intention to do just that in the near future (Ontario, Ministry of the Attorney-General, no date).

Federal Court System

The tribunal of last resort in Canada is the Supreme Court of Canada. Insofar as its criminal jurisdiction is concerned, the Supreme Court hears appeals from the provincial courts of appeal in relation to both indictable and summary conviction offences (see "The Classification of Offences" below). Since the Supreme Court is a federal court, the justices are appointed by the federal government (albeit from lists prepared by the provinces), and the salaries of the justices and the operations of the court are paid for by the federal government.

The other court in the federal system is the Federal Court of Canada, which is divided into a Trial Division and a Court of Appeal. The Federal

FIGURE 6.1
BRITISH COLUMBIA'S LAW COURTS

APPEAL COURT

- reviews decision of the lower courts when requested to do so
- normally 3 judges sit on an appeal
- not a trial court

SUPREME COURT

- hears civil cases involving money over $10,000
- hears divorce matters
- hears serious criminal cases

PROVINCIAL COURT

Family Division	Traffic Division	Small Claim Division	Criminal Division
• hears family matters	• hears traffic cases	• hears civil cases involving money under $10,000	• hears 90% of criminal cases
Youth Court			
• hears criminal cases of young people between the ages of 12 and 17 years			

Source: *British Columbia's Legal System: A Guide to the Wall Charts* (Vancouver: Law Courts Education Society of British Columbia, 1992), p. 10.

Court is not involved in the trial of criminal cases; it deals with actions brought against the federal government and federal agencies, and, therefore, may hear cases involving criminal justice agencies (such as the Correctional Service of Canada). In this respect, the Trial Division of the Federal Court of Canada may hear, for example, cases challenging the disciplinary practices of federal correctional institutions or the constitutionality of their regulations. Appeals from the decisions of the Trial Division may be made to the Federal Court of Appeal (from which the tribunal of last resort is the Supreme Court of Canada).

Justices of the Peace

Justices of the peace also play a critically important role in the criminal justice process in Canada. The major functions of the office of justice of the peace are in the pre-trial process. All criminal charges are laid before a justice of the peace, who is also responsible for reviewing the status of those accused persons held in custody and, in most cases, who has the power to release such persons on bail. The justice of the peace is also the official charged with the task of issuing search or arrest warrants to police officers and may secure the attendance of an accused person at his or her trial by confirming the appearance notice issued by a police officer or by issuing a summons. Furthermore, in many Canadian jurisdictions, the justices retain a judicial role in addition to their pre-trial functions. In some provinces (as well as both of the territories), they may try summary conviction offences in certain circumstances, although in order to do this they may be required to sit in groups of two or more.[10] They may also try minor traffic violations. In certain jurisdictions, they may also conduct the preliminary inquiries that are held in order to establish if there is enough evidence to send an accused person to one of the higher courts (the superior courts) for trial on one of the more serious criminal charges.

The jurisdiction of justices of the peace is different from the jurisdiction of Provincial Court judges. Provincial Court judges have all the powers of a justice of the peace *in addition* to those that flow from their appointment to the Provincial Court (such as the power to try all but the most serious criminal cases).[11]

Figure 6.2 gives an overview of the organization of the various courts in Canada. The figure includes not only those courts dealing with criminal cases, but also those handling civil (or non-criminal) matters.

THE CLASSIFICATION OF OFFENCES

The classification of offences is a vital aspect of the procedure that dictates the manner in which cases flow through the criminal justice system in Canada (Atrens, 1988; Law Reform Commission of Canada, 1986; Salhany, 1989; Shetreet, 1979). The classification of offences determines, for example, the nature of the powers of arrest that the police may exercise in any specific case, the type of court before which the accused must be tried, whether the accused has any choice as to the method of trial, the severity of the maximum penalty that may be imposed upon conviction, and the nature of the appeal process.

In 1892, the *Criminal Code* created three categories of criminal offences: (1) summary conviction offences; (2) indictable offences; and (3) so-called "hybrid" offences, which are both summary conviction and indictable offences. Summary conviction offences are the least serious and carry the most lenient penalties, while indictable offences are the most serious and carry the most severe penalties.

Typical summary conviction offences in the *Criminal Code* are: wilfully committing an indecent act, causing a disturbance in or near a public place, soliciting for the purpose of engaging in prostitution or obtaining sexual services from a prostitute, driving a motor vehicle without the consent of the owner, and fraudulently obtaining food from a restaurant. Typical indictable offences include: murder, treason, obtaining money or property by false pretences, possession of stolen goods, dangerous driving, assault, and sexual assault.

The "dual" or "hybrid" offences lie somewhere between the other two categories of offence in terms of the scale of seriousness (Atrens, 1988:I-6). Hybrid offences include theft and fraud under the value of $1,000, impaired driving or driving with more than 80 milligrams of alcohol per 100 millilitres of blood, assault, sexual assault, and assaulting a police officer.

There is an important distinction to be drawn between summary conviction offences and indictable offences. The *Criminal Code*[12] provides that summary conviction proceedings shall not be "instituted more than six months after the time when the subject matter of the proceedings arose." There is no time limit, however, for the initiation of proceedings in relation to indictable offences. Summary conviction offences may only be tried by a Provincial Court judge sitting alone. On the other hand, indictable offences may be tried in a number of different

FIGURE 6.2
ORGANIZATION OF COURTS IN CANADA

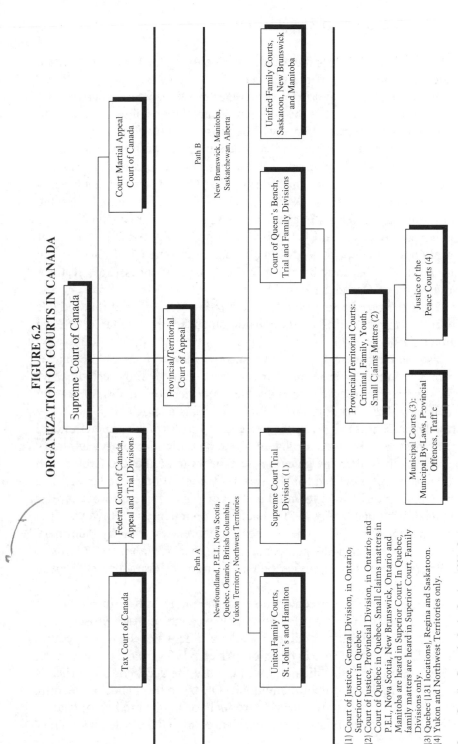

(1) Court of Justice, General Division, in Ontario;
    Superior Court in Quebec
(2) Court of Justice, Provincial Division, in Ontario; and
    Court of Quebec in Quebec. Small claims matters in
    P.E.I., Nova Scotia, New Brunswick, Ontario and
    Manitoba are heard in Superior Court. In Quebec,
    family matters are heard in Superior Court, Family
    Divisions only.
(3) Quebec (131 locations), Regina and Saskatoon.
(4) Yukon and Northwest Territories only.

Source: Canadian Centre for Justice Services, 1991a:5.

courts, depending on a number of factors, including the seriousness of the offence and the choice of the accused.

The category of hybrid offences has given rise to a considerable degree of concern because the prosecutor has the absolute discretion to decide whether a hybrid offence will be prosecuted by way of indictment or by way of summary conviction procedures. Some time ago, Cohen (1977:140) estimated that there were at least 30 sections in the *Criminal Code,* as well as provisions in some 40 other federal statutes that created hybrid offences. Atrens (1988:1-7) has more recently noted that the number of such offences is ever increasing, as Parliament places more reliance on the procedural flexibility and opportunity for the exercise of discretion that they provide. All in all, there are some 65 offences in the *Criminal Code* that may be classified as hybrid offences (Law Reform Commission of Canada, 1986:30).

Until the prosecutor actually elects the method of trial that will be employed, a hybrid offence is considered to be an indictable offence (Salhany, 1989:3). This is critical because it means that the police may exercise the expanded rights that exist in relation to indictable offences and may require, for example, that suspects undergo fingerprinting and photographing in accordance with the *Identification of Criminals Act* (procedures that are not required for individuals charged with summary conviction offences).[13] Where the prosecutor fails to make an election and a trial proceeds in a court that has the jurisdiction to try summary conviction cases, then the general rule appears to be that the Crown will be deemed to have elected trial by summary conviction procedures.[14] The Crown may even change its mind and reverse its choice of procedure as long as this is done before the trial actually commences.[15] However, it is important to remember that if the Crown elects trial by summary conviction procedures, the proceedings have to start within six months of the offence. If the six-month period has expired, the Crown must proceed by way of indictment.

The right of the prosecutor to select the mode of trial in relation to hybrid offences represents a powerful weapon in the prosecutor's armoury. The prosecutor's choice will determine which set of procedural rules will apply to the case in question (Atrens, 1988). Most dramatically, proceeding by way of indictment will expose the accused to the risk of a more severe penalty upon conviction. On the other hand, proceeding summarily may prevent the accused from choosing the method of trial — a right that exists in relation to a number of indictable offences.

Given the enormous degree of discretionary power vested in the prosecutor in relation to hybrid offences, it is somewhat surprising that the courts have generally shown a marked reluctance to interfere with the exercise of that discretion (Rosenthal, 1990-91). The courts have traditionally held that it is not open to either the defence or the court to decide how a hybrid offence is to be dealt with (Stenning, 1986:216). Indeed, it has been said in the Ontario Court of Appeal that:

> The Crown Attorney, when exercising the discretion to prosecute by way of indictment, is acting as an officer of the Crown and performing a function inherent in the office of the Attorney-General whose agent he is for that purpose. He is not acting pursuant to a statutory power and is not exercising a statutory discretion and accordingly his decision is not subject to review by the courts.[16]

Significantly, the advent of the *Charter* has apparently had relatively little effect on the courts' unwillingness to interfere with the manner in which the Crown exercises its power to choose the method of trial for hybrid offences. To date, the courts have almost always rejected any *Charter* assaults launched against the exercise of such discretion. In one case,[17] for example, the Ontario High Court ruled that the accused's right, under section 11(a) of the *Charter*, to "be informed without unreasonable delay of the specific offence," did *not* give him or her the right to be informed in advance as to how the Crown will elect to proceed with a hybrid offence. It was ruled that the accused's rights in this case were not infringed despite the fact that the Crown only made its choice of procedure on the day of the trial. Similarly, in another case,[18] the Ontario Court of Appeal held that the accused's right to a trial by jury where the maximum penalty is more than five years in prison (guaranteed by section 11[f] of the *Charter*) was not infringed by the Crown's power to elect summary conviction procedures, which do not permit the presence of a jury. In this particular case, if the Crown had decided to proceed by indictable procedures, then the accused would have had the option to select trial by jury.

However, the case of *Quinn*[19] illustrates the rare circumstances in which the court was willing to stay criminal proceedings on the basis that the exercise of prosecutorial discretion in relation to a hybrid offence constituted an infringement of the accused's *Charter* rights. In this case, Quinn was charged with the possession of a small amount of cocaine, under the provisions of the *Narcotic Control Act*. The evidence was absolutely clear that the Crown counsel originally intended to proceed on this hybrid offence by way of summary conviction procedures. However, the six-month limitation period that applies in relation to summary conviction offences expired before the Crown had received the required certificate of analysis. Crown counsel realized that it was too late to prosecute the accused by way of summary conviction procedures and refused to proceed with the case. However, some months later a different Crown counsel agreed to prosecute the accused by way of indictment. Here, the Quebec Court of Appeal ruled that it was contrary to the principles of fundamental justice, enshrined in section 7 of the *Charter*, that the accused person's position should be prejudiced solely because the Crown had allowed the six-month limitation period to expire. The Court entered a stay of proceedings, which terminated the case against the accused. The Court indicated that, as a general rule, the courts should not interfere with the exercise of the prosecutor's discretion as to how a hybrid offence should be tried; however, the present case was seen as being "quite exceptional."

The courts may also be willing to use their inherent power to prevent the abuse of their process as a means of controlling the prosecutor's discretion to choose the method of proceeding in the case of a hybrid offence (Atrens, 1988). This power exists quite apart from the powers of the courts under the *Charter* and gives them the option to stay proceedings against an accused person where the Crown has exercised its discretion in an abusive manner. For example, it appears that the courts are prepared to use the doctrine of abuse of process to prevent the Crown from trying to change its mind after a summary conviction trial has actually commenced solely in order to avoid the effect of the limitation period that applies to summary conviction cases. In the Ontario case of *Parkin*,[20] the Crown had decided to proceed on a charge of sexual assault by way of summary conviction procedures. During the presentation of the Crown's evidence it became clear that the events in question had occurred more than six months before the laying of the information and, therefore, the limitation period applicable to summary conviction offences barred prosecution in these circumstances. The Crown withdrew the charge with the approval of the trial judge and presented a new information with a view to proceeding by way of trial on indictment (to which the limitation period would not apply). The Ontario Court of Appeal held that the proceedings should be "stayed" (or terminated) on the basis that the

Crown's actions constituted an abuse of the court's process. The circumstances were most unusual, given the fact that the trial had already started when the Crown sought to change its mind as to how to proceed in relation to a hybrid offence. However, it will be interesting to see whether, in the future, the courts will be prepared to exercise a greater degree of control over the Crown's discretion, as to the method of trial in hybrid offences, through use of the abuse of process doctrine.

Given the various ways in which hybrid offences may be considered to give the prosecutor an unfair advantage over the accused, it is not surprising that the Law Reform Commission of Canada (1986:33) recommended the elimination of these offences from the *Criminal Code*.

BRINGING A CASE TO THE CRIMINAL COURT

The essential first step in launching a prosecution against a suspect is the laying of an information before a justice of the peace (Atrens, 1986:IX-4).[21] The Supreme Court of Canada has referred to "the citizen's fundamental and historical right to inform under oath a justice of the peace of the commission of a crime,"[22] and it appears that the origins of this procedure may be traced back to early sixteenth-century England (Stenning, 1986:17). The *Criminal Code* provides that anyone who "on reasonable grounds" believes that a person has committed an offence may lay an information in *writing and under oath* before a justice of the peace.[23] As the Law Reform Commission of Canada (1987a:3) has pointed out, "an accusation of crime lodged against an accused is one of the most serious steps our society can take against an individual," and since the "mere fact of being charged can have enormous repercussions on the accused's life," we therefore require that such an accusation be made in writing and under oath.

"Laying an information" basically means that an individual must present a formal, written accusation that an offence has been committed to a justice of the peace for the latter to sign (Salhany, 1989:55). Of course, several different charges may well be contained in one information, although it is important to remember that each charge must be contained in a separate "count" (Atrens, 1986:IX-12). If insufficient details of the alleged offence appear in the information, it is possible that a court will rule that there has been a breach of section 11(a) of the *Charter,* which guarantees any person charged with an offence "the right to be informed without unreasonable delay of the specific offence."[24]

In practice, the informant is usually a police officer, although there is nothing in the *Code* that requires that an information must be laid by someone acting in any sort of official capacity (Atrens, 1986:IX-7). In some jurisdictions, the police lay charges under the direct supervision of Crown counsel (the prosecutors), while, in other jurisdictions, it appears that the police perform this function without much consultation with Crown counsel (except for the most serious cases).[25] Clearly, the choice of the specific charge(s) to lay is a critical one, since it will determine how the particular case is dealt with in the criminal court system.

The justice of the peace is required to "receive" the sworn information provided certain jurisdictional requirements are met; in other words, the justice has no discretion to refuse to receive it. However, once the information has actually been laid, then the justice does have the discretion to decide whether the accused will be required to appear in court for trial to answer the charge(s) laid against him or her. At this point, therefore, the justice is considered to be acting in a judicial capacity. The justice must hear the allegations of the informant and, if he or she thinks it is desirable or necessary to do so, may hear the evidence of witnesses.[26] However, this process is nothing like a criminal trial; the hearing is conducted *ex parte* or, in other words, in the absence of the accused person and must be conducted *in camera* (in private).[27]

If the justice determines that the accused *should* be required to attend court for a trial, then the question arises as to how the accused should be compelled to appear in court. The justice may issue a *summons*, requiring that the accused attend for trial at a certain date and, if the offence is indictable, that he or she appear at a police station for photographing and fingerprinting under the *Identification of Criminals Act*.[28] On the other hand, the justice may issue a warrant for the *arrest* of the accused, but this procedure is only to be used where there are "reasonable grounds to believe that it is necessary in the public interest to issue a warrant for the arrest of the accused."[29] Therefore, a justice is much more likely to compel the attendance of the accused by means of a summons rather than an arrest warrant.[30]

It may be the case that the accused has already been given an appearance notice by a police officer or has been arrested and then released by the officer in charge of the police lock-up. In the latter case, the officer in charge will have released the accused in one of two ways: (1) either by obtaining the accused's "promise to appear" or (2) by requiring that the accused enter into a "recognizance" (see the next section on bail). In these circumstances, once the information has been laid, the justice of the peace must decide whether to confirm the appearance notice, promise to appear, or recognizance, or to cancel them and issue a summons or arrest warrant instead.[31] The *Criminal Code* requires that, where the police have released the accused in this manner, they must lay an information before a justice "as soon as practicable."[32]

The procedure for laying a charge and obtaining the accused person's attendance in court has been considerably simplified in the case of the vast number of traffic offences that arise under provincial motor vehicle legislation.[33] In place of the rather cumbersome procedure discussed above, a "traffic ticket" system has been instituted under which a traffic violator can be given a ticket and then given the opportunity to mail in the penalty to the court unless he or she wishes to dispute liability. As Atrens (1986:IX-6) points out, the "traffic ticket fulfills the function of both information and summons" and, thus, significantly streamlines a system that might otherwise collapse under the strain of the flood of traffic violations that appear to be an inevitable consequence of a society that is dominated by the automobile.

Figure 6.3 shows a general overview of the early stages of the criminal court process.

THE BAIL PROCESS

When the police have decided to arrest a suspect, or a justice of the peace has decided to issue a warrant for the arrest of a person who has been charged, the critical question arises as to whether the suspect or accused person should be detained in custody pending trial or whether he or she should be granted bail (see Law Reform Commission of Canada, 1988). The *Bail Reform Act*[34] (implemented in 1972) established a legal framework in which an accused person may be released from custody either by the officer in charge of a police lock-up or by a justice or a judge at a formal bail hearing.

A lengthy period of pre-trial detention may well prove to be disastrous to accused persons, who may lose their jobs, thus rendering it impossible for them to fulfill their obligations to either their family or their community (Ouimet, 1969:101-102). Furthermore, pre-trial incarceration may render it more difficult for accused persons to engage the services of a lawyer and to assist in the assembling of evidence for their defence (Hagan and Morden, 1981:14). Particularly disturbing is the

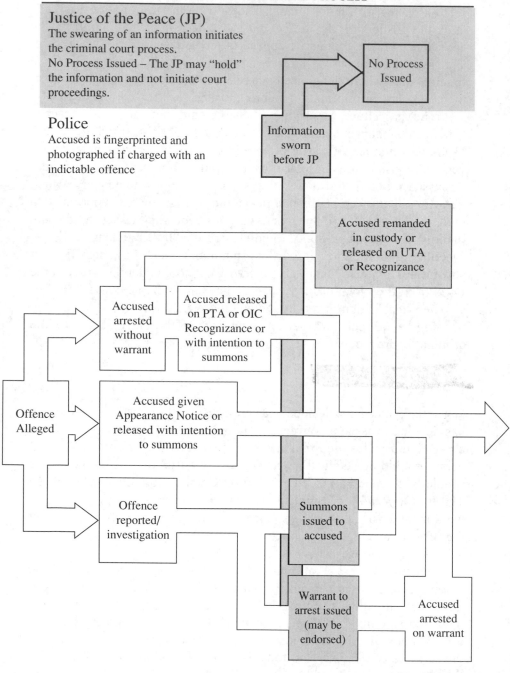

FIGURE 6.3
OVERVIEW OF THE LEGAL PROCESS

Justice of the Peace (JP)
The swearing of an information initiates
the criminal court process.
No Process Issued – The JP may "hold"
the information and not initiate court
proceedings.

No Process
Issued

Police
Accused is fingerprinted and
photographed if charged with an
indictable offence

Information
sworn
before JP

Accused remanded
in custody or
released on UTA
or Recognizance

Accused
arrested
without
warrant

Accused released
on PTA or OIC
Recognizance or
with intention to
summons

Offence
Alleged

Accused given
Appearance Notice or
released with intention
to summons

Offence
reported/
investigation

Summons
issued to
accused

Warrant to
arrest issued
(may be
endorsed)

Accused
arrested
on warrant

FIGURE 6.3
OVERVIEW OF THE LEGAL PROCESS

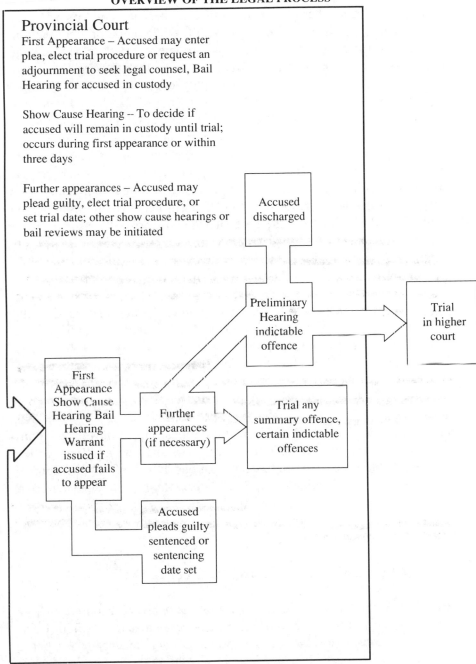

Provincial Court

First Appearance – Accused may enter plea, elect trial procedure or request an adjournment to seek legal counsel, Bail Hearing for accused in custody

Show Cause Hearing -- To decide if accused will remain in custody until trial; occurs during first appearance or within three days

Further appearances – Accused may plead guilty, elect trial procedure, or set trial date; other show cause hearings or bail reviews may be initiated

Accused discharged

Preliminary Hearing indictable offence

Trial in higher court

First Appearance Show Cause Hearing Bail Hearing Warrant issued if accused fails to appear

Further appearances (if necessary)

Trial any summary offence, certain indictable offences

Accused pleads guilty sentenced or sentencing date set

Source: *British Columbia's Legal System: A Guide to the Wall Charts* (Vancouver: Law Courts Education Society of British Columbia, 1992). Reprinted with permission.

conclusion of a number of Canadian studies that the denial of bail to a suspect has a significant effect upon both the likelihood of a conviction and the severity of any sentence that is ultimately meted out (Friedland, 1965:124; Hagan and Morden, 1981; Koza and Doob, 1975a; Doob and Cavoukian, 1977). For example, in a study conducted in Peel County, Ontario, Hagan and Morden (1981) found that being held for a bail hearing increased both the possibility of a conviction and the likelihood that, if convicted, the accused person would ultimately be incarcerated. It is not exactly clear how the suspect's bail status exerts such an impact upon the trial and sentencing processes; however, there is certainly a strong possibility that an aura of suspicion may surround a defendant who appears in custody before the court and that this negative impression may well affect the outcome of the case (Koza and Doob, 1975a).

The *Bail Reform Act* was enacted primarily as a response to the recommendations of the Ouimet Committee (1969), which strongly asserted that suspects should not be detained in custody unless it was necessary to do so as a means either of ensuring their appearance at trial or of protecting the public. In turn, the Ouimet Committee was strongly influenced by a major study conducted by Friedland (1965), who concluded that a considerable proportion of arrested suspects (40%) were being kept in custody pending their trial. It was generally felt that reforms needed to be introduced in order to reduce the incidence of pre-trial detention in Canada, and the *Bail Reform Act* was, therefore, explicitly conceived as a device for achieving this goal. Indeed, the very fact that the *Act* appeared to place stringent limitations on the power to detain suspects engendered a considerable degree of opposition among police officers at the time of its passage (Koza and Doob, 1977). Of course, since 1982, the application of the *Bail Reform Act* must be considered in light of the enactment of section 11(e) of the *Charter*, which guarantees the right of a person charged with an offence "not to be denied reasonable bail without just cause."

Release by the Officer in Charge of a Police Lock-Up

As we saw in Chapter 4, the *Bail Reform Act* placed a police officer under a duty, in certain circumstances, to release a suspect whom he or she has arrested. However, if the police officer decides to keep the suspect in custody, then the officer in charge of the police lock-up is required to consider whether or not the suspect should be released. As a general rule, if the offence with which the suspect is charged carries a penalty of imprisonment for five years or less,[35] then the officer in charge is under a duty to release the suspect "as soon as practicable" *unless*:

- ► he or she has "reasonable grounds" to believe that it is necessary in the "public interest"[36] that the suspect be detained in custody, or
- ► he or she has "reasonable grounds" to believe that if the suspect is released, the latter will fail to show up in court.[37]

There are four different methods by means of which the officer in charge may release a suspect from police custody. The officer may:

- ► release the suspect with a view to compelling his or her attendance in court by way of a summons;
- ► release the suspect upon the latter giving a "promise to appear" (the suspect signs a formal document);
- ► release the suspect upon the latter entering into a recognizance (or a formal acknowledgement of debt to the Crown) for any amount up to $500 without requiring any deposit;
- ► release the suspect (if he or she does not ordinarily live in the province where the arrest occurred or within 200 kilometres of where he or she is being held in custody) upon the suspect's entering into a recognizance for any amount up to $500 and, if the officer in charge requires it, upon the suspect's depositing a sum of money or some other form of valuable security not exceeding $500 in value.[38]

Upon releasing the suspect, the officer in charge may require that he or she be fingerprinted or photographed at a later date in accordance with the *Identification of Criminals Act*. If the suspect fails, without a lawful excuse, to attend for trial or to appear for fingerprinting or photographing, then he or she may be guilty of an offence,[39] and any recognizance or security will be forfeited. In addition, a warrant may be issued for the arrest of the suspect.[40]

These rules for the release of a suspect by the officer in charge apply to all those cases where the suspect was arrested *without a warrant*. If the accused was arrested *with a warrant*, then the officer in charge may only release the suspect if the justice of the peace has endorsed the warrant so as to permit this to occur.[41]

Hagan and Morden (1981) have pointed out that these release provisions grant a considerable degree of discretionary power to the police. Indeed, they suggest (1981:10) that the *Bail Reform Act* "seems intentionally vague and ambiguous." In particular, the *Act* does not specify what types of circumstances may provide the officer in charge with "reasonable grounds" to conclude that the suspect would fail to attend for trial in the event of his or her release. These authors found that prior convictions, prior incarceration, employment status, and the suspect's behaviour toward the police had a significant impact on the decision to release, as did the seriousness of the offence charged, the type of victim, whether a warrant had been issued, and whether a statement had been taken. Their finding that employment status affects the police decision to release a suspect gives rise to considerable concern. This may be a significant way in which the criminal justice system may discriminate against the poor, even though there is little evidence to suggest that the unemployed are more likely to abuse the granting of bail. Furthermore, the impact of this form of discrimination may be compounded at a later stage of the criminal justice process because the accused's bail status appears to exert a significant impact upon the ultimate outcome of a criminal case (in terms of both verdict and sentence).

Another cause for concern is the finding that suspects who were deemed to be "uncooperative" with the police were more likely to be retained in custody. Hagan and Morden consider this to be an example of "police deviance" insofar as the *Bail Reform Act* provides no legal basis for using the threat of detention as a means of making suspects more cooperative with the police or, alternatively, as a method of punishing those who are deemed to be uncooperative. This finding becomes even more troublesome in light of the observation by Ericson and Baranek (1982:61) that the police may engage in so-called "bail bargaining," in the course of which threats of continued detention or of police opposition to bail at a judicial hearing may be used as a device to extract confessions or information from a suspect in their custody.

Despite the philosophy of liberal release in the *Bail Reform Act*, it appears that, soon after its passage, the police continued to retain a considerable proportion of arrested suspects in their custody prior to their appearance before a justice or a Provincial Court judge. Mackaay

(1976:8) found that some 53% of accused persons were in custody prior to their first appearance before the Montreal Municipal Court.

Release by a Justice or a Judge (Judicial Interim Release)

If the police decide *not* to release a suspect whom they have arrested, then the suspect must, in normal circumstances, be brought before a justice or a Provincial Court judge within 24 hours of the arrest.[42] If a suspect is not brought before a justice or judge within 24 hours, then it is possible that this might constitute arbitrary detention under section 9 of the *Charter*.[43] At this stage, the justice or judge may immediately consider the question of bail, although the proceedings may be adjourned for periods of up to three days, upon the application of the prosecutor or the accused.[44] Although the great majority of bail decisions are made by a justice or a Provincial Court judge, there are certain circumstances in which only a judge of the Superior Court of Criminal Jurisdiction may release an accused person on bail.[45] More specifically, only a Superior Court judge may release a suspect who has been charged with such serious offences as murder, treason, sedition, and piracy.[46]

Bail hearings are called "show cause" hearings because either the prosecutor or the accused must "show cause" why the latter should be released or not, as the case may be.[47] In the vast majority of cases, the *Bail Reform Act*[48] clearly places the burden of justifying the continued detention of the accused squarely upon the shoulders of the prosecution (Hamilton, 1990:IV-5). Furthermore, if the suspect *is* ultimately released on bail, the onus is placed on the prosecution to justify the imposition of any conditions upon his or her release, the presumption being that a suspect should normally be released merely upon giving an undertaking to appear for trial.

In 1976, the *Bail Reform Act* was amended[49] so as to reverse the onus in certain situations and to require the accused to justify why he or she should be released by the justice or Provincial Court judge. In brief, the burden of justifying release is placed upon the accused's shoulders when he or she is charged with:

> ▸ an indictable offence alleged to have been committed while the accused was at large after having been released on bail in connection with another indictable offence;

- an indictable offence and the accused is not ordinarily a resident in Canada;
- an offence connected with failing to show up in court or to fulfill the conditions attached to the accused's bail while he or she was waiting to be tried for another offence; or
- trafficking in or exporting/importing narcotics or conspiring to commit these offences.

In addition, the *Bail Reform Act* specifies that a suspect, charged with one of the offences in relation to which only a Superior Court judge may grant bail, must justify his or her release.[50]

Until recently, there was considerable debate as to whether these "reverse onus" provisions, which place the burden on the accused persons to justify their release, are valid in light of their *Charter* right "not to be denied reasonable bail without just cause"[51] or the presumption of innocence enshrined in the *Charter*[52] (Kiselbach, 1988-89). In two very important decisions, *Morales*[53] and *Pearson*,[54] the Supreme Court ruled that at least some of the "reverse onus" provisions are valid because they do not infringe the *Charter* rights of accused persons. In *Morales,* the Supreme Court examined the special requirement that accused persons must show cause why they should be granted bail if they have been charged with an indictable offence committed after having been released on bail for a separate indictable offence. As Lamer C.J. pointed out, this requirement merely establishes "an effective bail system in circumstances where there are reasonable grounds to believe that the normal bail system is permitting continuing criminal behaviour."[55] By requiring the accused to justify the granting of bail, the special requirement seeks to ensure that the "objective of stopping criminal behaviour will be achieved,"[56] and, therefore, that the right to reasonable bail is not infringed.

Similarly, in *Pearson,* the Court dealt with a *Charter* challenge to the special requirement that the accused must shoulder the onus of establishing that they should be granted bail where they have been charged with trafficking in or importing narcotics. Once again, the Court ruled that this requirement did not infringe the *Charter* rights of the accused. In particular, Lamer C.J. stated that the presumption of innocence was not infringed because this presumption has no application to the bail process where the guilt or innocence of the accused is not the issue and where punishment is not imposed. The Chief Justice noted that the drug trafficking business is "highly lucrative, creating huge incentives for an offender to continue criminal behaviour even after arrest and release on bail."[57] Since the normal bail rules are unlikely to be effective in stopping such criminal activity, special rules, such as those requiring the accused to justify their release, were clearly necessary.

The *Morales* and *Pearson* cases have removed the uncertainty surrounding these particular "reverse onus" provisions in the bail system and have made it easier for the courts to respond to the public's concern that people on bail not continue to commit serious offences while they are "out on bail." It remains to be seen whether the Supreme Court of Canada will uphold the validity of the other reverse onus provisions discussed above.

Continued detention of the accused is justified only on the following grounds:

(i) on the primary ground that it is necessary to ensure the accused's attendance at trial; and

(ii) on the secondary ground that it is necessary for the protection or safety of the public, "having regard to all the circumstances including any substantial likelihood that the accused will, if he is released from custody, commit a criminal offence or an interference with the administration of justice."[58]

The secondary ground may only be considered once the justice or judge has determined that detention is not justified on the basis of the need to ensure that the accused will show up at trial. In determining the likelihood that the accused will appear for trial, the justice or the judge will take into account a broad range of personal circumstances, including whether the accused has a fixed address, his or her employment and marital or family status, any prior record of criminal convictions, and his or her relationships with friends and relatives in the community (Hamilton, 1990:IV-14). As noted earlier, the attention paid to factors such as employment status raises a considerable degree of concern insofar as it almost inevitably results in discrimination against those of low socioeconomic status.

One situation in which a court may decide to detain an accused on the secondary ground (for the "protection or safety of the public") arises where an accused is alleged to be a major trafficker in drugs (Hamilton, 1990:IV-18). Similarly, the courts have ruled that major drug traffickers may also be detained on the basis that there would be a "substantial likelihood of [their] committing a criminal offence" if they were to be released (Hamilton, 1990:IV-19).

If the justice or judge decides to release the accused, then he or she may do so according to one of five different methods. The accused may be released:

(a)   upon giving an undertaking to appear together with such conditions (if any) as the justice or judge directs;

(b)   upon entering into a recognizance in such amount and with such conditions as the justice or judge may direct;

(c)   upon entering into a recognizance in such amount and with such conditions as the justice or judge may direct together with the requirement of sureties (friends or relatives who assume responsibility for ensuring that the accused shows up for trial);

(d)   (provided the prosecutor consents) upon entering into a recognizance in such amount and with such conditions as the justice or judge may direct together with a deposit of cash or other valuable security; or

(e)   (if the accused is not ordinarily resident in the province or within 200 kilometres of the place in which he or she is in custody) upon entering into a recognizance either with or without sureties in such amount and upon such conditions as the justice or judge may direct together with the requirement of a deposit of cash or some other valuable security.[59]

The relevant *Criminal Code*[60] provisions set out these five methods according to a "ladder of increasing severity." The Crown is required to progress up the ladder of severity in recommending the specific form of release that should be made; in other words, the prosecutor must justify the imposition of a requirement of a recognizance, as opposed to the requirement of a simple undertaking to appear, and so on "up the ladder" (Hamilton, 1990:IV-8; Salhany, 1989:108).

Obviously, taking on the responsibility of being a surety is a serious matter. As Salhany (1989:133) points out, it is a "fundamental principle of the law of bail that the surety's prime obligation is to ensure the appearance of the accused at the proper time and place." Therefore, if the accused fails to show for trial or breaches the conditions of bail, then the surety's recognizance may be forfeited, either in part or in whole, to the Crown.[61] In determining whether the surety should forfeit his or her recognizance, the courts generally consider the extent to which the surety was personally responsible for the accused's failure to live up to his or her obligations (Salhany, 1989:134). If the surety wishes to back out of his or her commitment, the *Code* establishes procedures that may accomplish this objective.[62] In some cases, the accused may have to be taken into custody once the surety has been released from his or her recognizance. However, it is possible for a justice or a judge simply to substitute another surety without the necessity for taking the accused into custody again.[63]

The conditions that may be imposed when an accused person is released on bail include regular reporting to a police officer, remaining in a particular area, notifying the police of a change in address or employment, refraining from communicating with any witness or other person named in the release order, and depositing one's passport. The *Criminal Code* also contains a general provision that requires the released suspect to "comply with such other reasonable conditions specified in the order as the justice considers desirable."[64] This particular provision has been interpreted very broadly by the courts (Salhany, 1989:109).[65] For example, it was held to be legitimate for a justice to impose a condition that an alleged prostitute stay away from that part of the city where the alleged offence had occurred in order to prevent the commission of further offences while she was on bail.[66]

To what extent have the provisions of the *Bail Reform Act* encouraged the release of accused persons pending their trial? The great majority of accused persons are released on some form of bail once they have made an initial appearance in court. A national survey (Canadian Centre for Justice Statistics, 1986) indicated that, on a Canada-wide basis, only about one out of every fifteen persons (7%) charged with an offence is remanded in custody by a court pending their trial.

Is there any evidence that bail courts "rubber stamp" the recommendations of the police and prosecutors? A study of bail hearings in Toronto by Koza and Doob (1975b) suggests that the judges in the study were quite willing to apply the philosophy of liberal release that underlies the *Bail Reform Act*, even in the face of opposition from the prosecutor. In those cases where the prosecutor urged that the accused should remain in custody, the court nevertheless released 43% of the accused persons concerned. On the other hand, where the prosecutor made a positive recommendation for release, then the court was much more likely to implement the recommendation (which it did in 95% of cases). This study suggests that, in this jurisdiction at least, the judges did not simply endorse the restrictive recommendations of the prosecutor and the police, but rather they appeared to apply the liberal spirit of the *Bail Reform Act*.

In recent years, a number of provinces have established programs to facilitate the granting of bail in urban areas. For example, Toronto established a bail program in 1979 (Morris, 1981) designed to provide two types of service: *bail verification* and *bail supervision*.

Bail verification is designed to prevent the unnecessary detention of accused persons who would be released if only fuller and more accurate information about their background were available to the courts earlier in the process. Bail verification interviewers ask accused persons, who are in police custody, a series of questions as soon as the police have completed their interrogation of them. The interviewers then make the information available to the appropriate bail court.

Bail supervision, however, is designed to deal with those accused persons for whom bail has been set but who do not have a surety who will enter into a recognizance for them. Impecunious accused persons, who cannot come up with a surety who will stand bail for them, may just stay in jail merely because of their lack of financial resources (Morris, 1981:158). If an accused person is eligible for release with the require-ment of a surety, but he or she is unable to find someone to take on this responsibility, then bail supervision may be proposed as an alternative. The accused may be released on his or her own recognizance but would be required to be subject to the supervision of the bail program. Similar programs exist elsewhere in Ontario[67] and in British Columbia, Alberta, Saskatchewan, and the Yukon (see Madden and Carey [1982]).

What happens if an accused person fails to live up to the conditions of his or her bail? The *Criminal Code* provides that where an accused person on bail has (a) violated or is about to violate the terms of his or her release or (b) committed an indictable offence while on bail, then he or she may be arrested either by the police on their own initiative or on the basis of a warrant signed by a justice.[68] In these circumstances, the suspect's bail will be cancelled unless he or she "shows cause" why he or she should not be detained.[69]

In general, a bail order remains in effect until the accused's trial has been completed and, if he or she is convicted, the trial court has the discretion to extend the order pending sentence.[70] However, the courts do have the power to order that the accused be detained in custody at any stage in the trial process or to make any variation in the order that they deem appropriate.[71] There are also provisions giving courts the power to grant or continue bail pending an appeal of a conviction or sentence.[72]

The *Criminal Code*[73] makes provision for either the accused or the prosecutor to apply for a review of the bail decision made by a justice or Provincial Court judge to a judge of the Superior Court of Criminal Jurisdiction. Similarly, a review of the bail decision made by a Superior Court judge may be undertaken by the Court of Appeal.[74]

Review of the Accused's Detention Where the Trial is Delayed

The *Criminal Code*[75] provides for an automatic review of the continuing detention of an accused person whose trial has been delayed.[76] The purpose of this provision is clearly to ensure that a detained suspect does not become "lost in the system." The review must generally be conducted within 90 days of the accused first coming before a justice in the case of an indictable offence and 30 days in the case of a summary conviction offence. The review is conducted by a judge of the Superior Court of Criminal Jurisdiction. In deciding whether or not to release an accused person, the judge may take into consideration whether the accused or the prosecutor has been responsible for "any unreasonable delay in the trial of the charge."[77] If the judge does not think that continued detention is necessary, then the accused may be released on bail. The *Code*[78] also provides that, where such an automatic review takes place, then the judge shall give directions for speeding up the accused's trial.[79]

THE TRIAL OF CRIMINAL CASES

The classification of offences determines how individual cases will be tried within the criminal court system. The *Criminal Code* provides for only one method of trial for summary conviction offences, but as many as three alternative methods for indictable offences.

The Trial of Summary Conviction Offences

Part XXIV of the *Criminal Code* lays out the procedures for the trial of summary conviction offences arising either under the *Code* itself or under other federal statutes (Salhany, 1989:324-342). Similar procedures exist to deal with the summary conviction offences created by provincial statutes.[80] Of course, where the Crown has elected to proceed with a hybrid offence summarily, then that offence will be tried according to summary conviction procedures.

In general, summary conviction offences may only be tried before a Provincial Court judge sitting without a jury, although the *Criminal Code* does permit such offences to be tried, in certain circumstances, before a justice of the peace sitting alone or before two or more justices sitting together.[81] Although accused persons, if they so wish, may appear in person at their trial for a summary conviction offence, they may also send their lawyer to represent them in their absence.[82] Nevertheless, the court does have the power to require their attendance and may issue an arrest warrant for that purpose. If an accused person, who has been given an appearance notice or a summons, fails to attend for trial in accordance with the written instructions provided, then the court may conduct a trial in his or her absence (an *"ex parte"* trial) or may issue an arrest warrant and adjourn the trial until the accused appears.[83] Although a trial in the accused's absence may seem somewhat drastic, the courts have ruled that it does not infringe the accused's right to be treated in accordance with the fundamental principles of justice or the right to a fair trial, protected by sections 7 and 11(d), respectively, of the *Charter*.[84] It is likely, of course, that a court would not conduct a trial in the accused's absence if the accused were prevented from attending by forces beyond his or her control (for example, adverse weather conditions).[85]

As the term suggests, "summary conviction" procedures were meant to provide "summary" justice, and there is some evidence that the provincial courts, whose workload consists to a large extent of summary conviction cases, do provide exactly that. In a study of the provincial courts in Toronto, for example, Hann (1973, vol. 1) discovered that the courts devoted, on average, a mere five minutes to each appearance by an accused person and that more than 75% of all cases were dealt with in only three or less court appearances. This certainly suggests that, in this jurisdiction at least, justice was dispensed swiftly when summary conviction offences were involved. Perhaps this swiftness is inevitable given both the heavy caseload faced by the provincial courts and the relatively minor nature of summary conviction cases. However, it is at least questionable whether due process is being served by what appears to be "assembly-line justice."

The Trial of Indictable Offences

Historically, a trial on indictment meant that the accused would be tried before a judge and jury (Atrens, 1988:1-22). Indeed, the *Criminal Code*[86] states that "except where otherwise expressly provided by law, every accused who is charged with an indictable offence shall be tried by a court composed of a judge and jury." In fact, the exceptions provided for in the *Code* itself have grown to be so numerous that, as Atrens (1988:1-23) notes, "while any indictable offence *may* be tried by judge and jury, only a *few* must be so tried." The *Code* provides for a number of different forms of trial depending upon the classification of the offence(s) concerned. There are three major categories of indictable offence for determining the form of trial.

A. *Offences that may only be tried by a judge of the Superior Court sitting with a jury.*

In this category are the most serious offences, such as murder, treason, and piracy.[87] However, the *Code*[88] provides that an accused person charged with one of these offences may be tried by a Superior Court judge *without* a jury, provided both he or she and the Attorney-General of the province give their consent.[89]

B. *Offences that may only be tried by a Provincial Court judge.*

Into this category fall the least serious of the indictable offences. They are said to fall within the "absolute jurisdiction" of a Provincial Court judge.[90] They include such offences as theft (other than theft of cattle), obtaining money or property by false pretences, possession of stolen goods, and keeping a common bawdy-house.[91]

C. *Offences for which the accused person may elect the method of trial.*

If a person is charged with an offence falling within categories A or B, he or she has no choice as to the method of trial. However, if the accused is charged with an offence falling within this third category, then he or she has the right to "elect" the mode of trial.[92] This category is a residual category in that it contains all those indictable offences not falling within categories A or B. Among the "electable" offences are robbery, dangerous driving, assault, sexual assault, breaking and entering, and attempted murder. The accused person may choose between three different methods of trial: (1) trial by a Provincial Court judge; (2) trial by a Superior Court judge and jury; or (3) trial by a Superior Court judge.

If the accused fails to make an election, he or she will be deemed to have chosen to be tried by a court composed of a judge and jury.[93]

However, the right to elect the method of trial is not absolute (Salhany, 1989:7) since the Attorney-General of the province can override an accused's election to be tried by Provincial Court judge or by a Superior judge sitting alone. The *Criminal Code*[94] provides that the Attorney-General may require that the accused be tried by a judge and jury, provided that the offence charged carries a maximum penalty of more than five years' imprisonment. Similarly, if the Provincial Court judge believes that a case should be heard in a higher court, then a preliminary inquiry will be held and, if the judge feels there is sufficient evidence, may refer the case to the Superior Court of Criminal Jurisdiction for trial by judge alone, regardless of the accused's wish to be tried in the Provincial Court.[95] In general, however, such exceptional procedures are rarely resorted to, and the accused has a right to determine how he or she will be tried for the less serious indictable offences.

The whole process of trial election is complex because the *Criminal Code* allows the accused to change his or her mind and to "re-elect" the mode of trial in certain circumstances (Taylor and Irvine, 1986:XIV-16). The right to re-elect is nevertheless subject to important restrictions.[96]

▸   *Re-election where the accused originally chose to be tried by either a Superior Court judge alone or a Superior Court judge and jury.*

An accused person who originally elected to be tried by the Superior Court (either with or without a jury) has the absolute right to change his or her choice from judge and jury to judge alone or *vice versa*, provided the re-election is made within 14 days of the completion of the preliminary inquiry. After the 14 days have elapsed, the accused may only make such a re-election with the written consent of the Crown. If the accused wishes to re-elect in favour of trial by Provincial Court judge, then Crown counsel must give his or her written consent, no matter how many days have passed since the completion of the preliminary inquiry.[97] The *Code* also provides that on or after the 15th day following the completion of the preliminary inquiry, the accused can re-elect in favour of any mode of trial but can only do so with the written consent of the prosecutor.[98]

▸ *Re-election where the accused originally chose trial before a Provincial Court judge.*

An accused person who initially chose to be tried by a Provincial Court judge has an absolute right to re-elect in favour of trial before the Superior Court of Criminal Jurisdiction (either with or without a jury), provided the re-election takes place no later than 14 days before the day first appointed for trial. After this period has elapsed, re-election is only permitted with the written consent of the prosecutor.[99] There are certain other restrictions on the right to re-elect, but they are too complex to consider here (see Taylor and Irvine, 1986:XIV-16-XIV-17).

The fairly generous provisions permitting re-election are somewhat problematic given the fact that they offer the accused and his or her lawyer a golden opportunity to delay court proceedings (albeit not indefinitely). Amendments to the *Criminal Code* made in 1985 tightened up the pre-existing re-election provisions quite considerably by imposing stricter time limits. In an interesting study conducted in Montreal before the 1985 amendments, Mackaay (1976) found that a very high proportion of accused persons who decided to plead not guilty took advantage of the re-election provisions. Significantly, some 86% of defendants initially chose trial by judge and jury, but the great majority of them later changed their minds and re-elected in favour of trial by judge alone. Indeed, it turned out that only 4% of those defendants who pleaded not guilty were ultimately tried by a judge and jury, while 90% of them were tried by judge alone. In Mackaay's view (1976:94), the generous system of re-election contributed directly to the problem of excessive delays in the court system. Whether the 1985 restrictions will improve the situation remains to be seen.

Trying Indictable Offences

All accused persons make their first appearance in the Provincial Court. While some cases involving indictable offences will finally be disposed of in the Provincial Court, others will be moved on to the Superior Court of Criminal Jurisdiction for trial. If the accused is charged with an offence that falls within the so-called "absolute jurisdiction" of a

Provincial Court judge, then the latter may proceed to try the accused immediately or set a later date for trial. The trial proceeds on the basis of the information that is before the Provincial Court judge (Salhany, 1989:5). The same situation exists where the accused has elected to be tried by a Provincial Court judge (in relation to that category of offences that give the accused a right to elect). In such a case, the Provincial Court judge must endorse the election on the information and then try the accused immediately or fix a date for trial in the future.[100] Unlike cases tried in the Superior Court, no indictment needs to be drawn up for the trial of indictable offences in the Provincial Court.

If the accused is charged with an offence that may only be tried by the Superior Court or if he or she has elected trial by judge sitting alone or by judge and jury, the trial will be conducted in the Superior Court. However, before such a case may proceed to the Superior Court, the Provincial Court judge must first conduct a preliminary inquiry to determine whether there is sufficient evidence to warrant committing the accused for trial.

The Preliminary Inquiry

The preliminary inquiry may be conducted either by a Provincial Court judge or, in some circumstances, by a justice of the peace. A preliminary inquiry is not a trial. The Provincial Court judge or the justice is not concerned with establishing the guilt or innocence of the accused. Indeed, no plea to the charge may be taken at the preliminary inquiry. The preliminary inquiry's function is to determine whether there is "admissible evidence that could, if it were believed, result in a conviction."[101] The Crown may call whatever witnesses it wishes; the Provincial Court judge or the justice of the peace does not have any power to order the Crown to call any particular witnesses.[102] If witnesses are called by the Crown, the accused's counsel may cross-examine them. Those witnesses who *are* called must give their evidence on oath and may be cross-examined.[103] The accused may also call witnesses and give evidence him or herself, but there is no obligation to do so.[104] However, it would appear that witnesses are actually summoned in less than half of the preliminary inquiries that are conducted across Canada. A federal Department of Justice study of preliminary inquiries in 13 judicial districts across Canada (cited in Law Reform Commission of Canada, 1984:11) found that witnesses were summoned and heard in only 46% of cases in which preliminary inquiries were conducted. In 80% of the cases, moreover, the preliminary inquiry lasted for less than a day.

The Provincial Court judge or justice of the peace may impose a ban on the publication of the evidence taken at a preliminary inquiry. This provision is necessary for ensuring that the accused has a fair trial because pre-trial publicity may prove to be very prejudicial, particularly in a jury trial. The ban will continue until either the accused is discharged or, if he or she is ordered to stand trial, the trial has been completed.[105]

When all the evidence has been taken at the preliminary inquiry, the Provincial Court judge or the justice of the peace has two options:

1) "if in his [or her] opinion there is sufficient evidence to put the accused on trial for the offence charged or any other indictable offence in respect of the same transaction, order the accused to stand trial" or

2) "discharge the accused, if in his [or her] opinion on the whole of the evidence no sufficient case is made out to put the accused on trial for the offence charged or any other indictable offence in respect of the same transaction."[106]

The Provincial Court judge or justice of the peace may commit the accused where there is sufficient evidence to warrant committal for trial. The Crown does not have to establish guilt or innocence at the preliminary inquiry; instead, the Crown must merely "make a *prima facie* case" (Holmes, 1982:263).

It is noteworthy that, when Crown counsel prefers an indictment against an accused person who has been committed for trial at the conclusion of a preliminary inquiry, he or she may not only include any charge on which the accused was ordered to stand trial by the Provincial Court judge or justice of the peace, but also add or substitute "any charge founded on the facts disclosed by the evidence taken on the preliminary inquiry."[107] In one case,[108] for example, the accused was charged with assault causing bodily harm. After the preliminary inquiry, the Provincial Court judge ordered the accused to stand trial on the lesser charge of simple assault. However, Crown counsel then preferred an indictment in which the original charge of assault causing bodily harm was laid against the accused. When the accused challenged the prosecutor's decision, he was ultimately unsuccessful because it was ruled that the Crown has the power to substitute charges in this manner just as long as the facts revealed at the preliminary inquiry would provide some basis for such a substitution. This case is a good example of the broad discretionary power enjoyed by prosecutors in Canada and raises serious questions about the importance of the preliminary inquiry as a screening device.

To what extent does the preliminary inquiry serve as an "effective filter" in the sense of weeding out those cases that are not strong enough to warrant a trial? Empirical evidence would appear to suggest that relatively few accused persons are discharged after a preliminary inquiry. Mackaay (1976:38), in his study of the Montreal court system, concluded that only one in nine cases resulted in a discharge as opposed to a committal for trial. Similarly, in a study of thirteen judicial districts across Canada conducted by the federal Department of Justice in 1980, it was found that only 10% of those cases that went to a preliminary inquiry resulted in withdrawal of the charges or discharge of the accused (Law Reform Commission of Canada, 1984:11). The small percentage of cases in which the accused is discharged as the result of a preliminary inquiry would appear to suggest that the latter serves as a rather inadequate filter. On the other hand, the Department of Justice study did find that 71% of the cases that led to a committal for trial after a preliminary inquiry ultimately resulted in a plea of guilty; this suggests that the Crown must have possessed reasonably strong evidence against the accused in the clear majority of cases where a committal for trial was ultimately made by the Provincial Court judge or justice of the peace.

There are two circumstances in which a preliminary inquiry will *not* be held even though the accused is to be tried in the "higher courts." First, the prosecutor and the accused may jointly agree to waive the preliminary inquiry.[109] In the Department of Justice study (cited in Law Reform Commission of Canada, 1984:11), a preliminary inquiry was held in only 30% of the cases in which it was available, while Mackaay (1976) found in his study of the Montreal courts that an inquiry was held in only 37% of eligible cases at the court house and 50% at the Municipal Court. These studies appear to suggest that a considerable proportion of defendants waive their right to a preliminary inquiry.

Second, it is possible for the Attorney-General or the Deputy Attorney-General of the province to bypass the preliminary inquiry and prefer a so-called "direct indictment."[110] This procedure is very rare (Taylor and Irvine, 1986:XIV-7), and it is contended that it is most likely to be employed in cases involving major drug conspiracies. This right may not be questioned by the courts unless there is an abuse of process in some respect or there is a violation of an accused person's *Charter* rights.[111] "Ordinary" Crown counsel do not have the power to prefer a direct indictment (Atrens, 1986:IX-41). The use of the direct indictment procedure raises a considerable degree of concern since it can deprive an accused of his or her right to a preliminary inquiry. Nevertheless, it has been held that the preferring of a direct indictment, where no preliminary inquiry has been held, does *not* infringe the accused's right to be treated in accordance with the "principles of fundamental justice" guaranteed by section 7 of the *Charter*.[112] On the other hand, it has been held that a remedy may be available under the *Charter* where the use of the direct indictment procedure results in unfairness to the accused.[113] A direct indictment may be preferred not only in the situation where there has not been a preliminary inquiry, but also in the situation where the accused has been discharged as a consequence of a preliminary inquiry, although the courts would be unlikely to permit this drastic step unless new evidence had been uncovered since the accused's discharge or different charges were concerned.[114]

The Preliminary Inquiry and the Issue of Discovery

Although the sole purpose of the preliminary inquiry is to determine whether there is sufficient evidence to commit an accused person for trial,[115] traditionally, it was widely recognized that an extremely important function of the preliminary inquiry was to permit the accused to obtain "discovery" of the prosecution's case against the accused (Ferguson, 1991:XIII-75). "Discovery" refers to "the accused's actions of searching for and obtaining any information or evidence that may be relevant to the conduct of the accused's defence" (Ferguson, 1991:XIII-1).

The *Criminal Code* obliges the Crown to reveal relatively little of the evidence that it intends to bring against the accused at the latter's trial (Ferguson, 1991; Law Reform Commission of Canada, 1984), although provincial guidelines for Crown counsel as well as ethical principles[116] have operated, in practice, to persuade prosecutors to reveal more than they have to under the *Code*.

The preliminary inquiry does afford the accused the opportunity to gain a reasonable degree of knowledge concerning the Crown's case against him or her, although the prosecutor only has to introduce sufficient evidence to warrant a committal for trial (in other words, the prosecutor does not have to introduce *all* the evidence that he or she later intends to use at the accused's trial).

Ferguson (1991:XIII-5-6) has contended that discovery is essential to the "effective working of our adversarial system of justice":

> The adversary system is based on the assumption that a legally correct verdict is most likely to arise if opposing parties devote their full attention to marshalling and presenting all evidence favourable to their position before an impartial judge. However, this assumption is hardly realistic unless the evidence favourable to either side is accessible. Since the evidence most favourable to the accused may not be accessible to him because of his lesser opportunities, capacities and resources to conduct investigations, this assumption of the adversary system will not work unless the State at least discloses all the results of its investigation to the accused.

Clearly, in the absence of a *Criminal Code* requirement that the Crown disclose the substance of its case against the accused, the preliminary inquiry was frequently the only means by which the accused could obtain such information and mount an effective defence. In this respect, therefore, the preliminary inquiry could be considered to have fulfilled a very important purpose in many criminal cases. However, this particular function of the preliminary inquiry may now have been superceded by a decision of the Supreme Court of Canada that has finally placed Crown counsel under a duty to disclose all *relevant* information in his or her possession.

In *Stinchcombe*,[117] the Supreme Court of Canada held that the Crown is under a duty to disclose all the material it proposes to use at trial and, in particular, all evidence that may assist the accused in mounting his or her defence *even if the Crown does not propose to place such evidence before the court*.[118] However, it is significant that the Court also ruled that there was no reciprocal obligation on the accused to disclose the basis of his or her case:

> ...the fruits of the investigation which are in the possession of counsel for the Crown are not the property of the Crown for use in securing a conviction but the property of the public to be used to ensure that justice is done. In contrast, the defence has no obligation to assist the prosecution and is entitled to assume a purely adversarial role toward the prosecution.[119]

The Supreme Court stated that there were some exceptions to the duty of the Crown to disclose all the relevant evidence in its possession. In other words, the duty is not an absolute one. For example, the Crown may well be justified in temporarily *delaying* disclosure of information where such disclosure may impede the completion of a criminal investigation. Similarly, the Crown does not have to release information that a court might consider to be "privileged" at trial; for example, the identity of police informers is regarded as "privileged," and a trial court will generally not force a police witness to disclose the identity of an informant (McWilliams, 1991:35-53). Finally, the Court emphasized that the Crown's duty is only to disclose information that is *relevant* and, therefore, the Crown may refuse to disclose information that does not meet this basic requirement. However, the Court emphasized that the Crown's decision to refuse to disclose information to the accused in any particular case may be reviewed by the trial judge, who has the power to overrule the Crown and order the disclosure of the information in question. In general, said the Supreme Court, "information should not be withheld if there is a reasonable possibility that the withholding of information will impair the right of the accused to make full answer and defence, unless the non-disclosure is justified by the law of privilege."[120] In the view of the Supreme Court, the Crown should generally make initial disclosure of its case before the accused is called upon to elect the method of trial that will apply in his or her case or before the accused is required to enter a plea to the charge(s) against him or her. The duty of the Crown to make disclosure is a continuing one, however, and new information must be disclosed as, and when, it becomes available.

It remains to be seen exactly how the courts will interpret the *Stinchcombe* case in the future. However, a subsequent decision by the British Columbia Court of Appeal provides some guidance as to the scope of the Crown's duty of disclosure.[121] The Court noted that the *Stinchcombe* case was predicated on the principle that the Crown must disclose all of the evidence that the accused needs to "make full answer and defence." In this respect, the B.C. Court of Appeal made the following comments:

> What then is "full answer and defence"? It is, first, the ability to probe the evidence of the Crown so that the jury can judge if it be credible, by which I mean both honest and accurate — "the truth, the whole truth and nothing but the truth." Secondly, it is the right to adduce all

evidence not known to be false that may raise in the minds of the jurors either a conviction of innocence or a reasonable doubt of guilt. Thirdly, it is the right to make submissions to the trier of fact on the law and on the evidence.[122]

Clearly, this approach requires the Crown to disclose all of the evidence that is necessary for the purpose of determining "the truth," including evidence that may be favourable to the accused. If the Crown does not disclose the evidence that the accused needs, the Crown counsel may be ordered to do so by the trial judge. In extreme cases, where the Crown's refusal to disclose evidence has effectively made it impossible for there to be a fair trial, then the trial court may enter a stay of proceedings, thereby terminating the trial altogether.[123]

With the establishment of a system of discovery by the Supreme Court of Canada, the question will no doubt arise as to whether the preliminary inquiry should be abolished now that (what is arguably) its major function no longer appears to be necessary. Some years ago, the Law Reform Commission (1974) suggested that the preliminary inquiry could be abolished if a formal system of discovery were introduced. The rationale for this approach was the Commission's belief that the most important function of the preliminary inquiry was to provide the accused with a form of discovery and that, if this function were to be pre-empted by a formal system of discovery, then the preliminary inquiry would no longer have a *raison d'être*. However, in a more recent report on discovery, the Law Reform Commission (1984) abandoned its advocacy of the abolition of the preliminary inquiry. The commission (1984:13-15) proposed that the accused should be entitled to specific rights of discovery and contended (1984:11) that a system of full disclosure by the Crown would reduce the length and number of preliminary inquiries. In the Commission's view, "if there is full disclosure, the preliminary inquiry will survive to perform its true function as a screen against an insufficient case." It remains to be seen whether the Canadian Parliament will take steps to modify, or even abolish, the preliminary inquiry as an important component in the pre-trial procedures that are applicable to those indictable offences that proceed to the Superior Court of Criminal Jurisdiction for trial. Perhaps the efforts of Parliament should be directed toward rendering the preliminary inquiry a more effective screening process rather than abolishing it outright.

Trial on Indictment

Once the preliminary inquiry has been completed and the accused committed for trial, the next step in the process is for the Crown to prefer an indictment (Atrens, 1986:IX-28). An indictment is merely a formal, written accusation of a crime made by either the Attorney-General personally or by the Crown counsel. An indictment may be preferred against an accused person either in relation to the charge on which he or she was committed for trial or any charge "founded on the facts disclosed by the evidence taken on the preliminary inquiry, in addition to or in substitution for any charge on which that person was ordered to stand trial."[124] As noted earlier, the normal procedure of committal for trial after a preliminary inquiry may be bypassed by the so-called "direct indictment procedure." In this situation, the Attorney-General may prefer an indictment either where there has been no preliminary inquiry or where the accused has been discharged after such an inquiry. The trial by judge only or judge and jury in the Superior Court of Criminal Jurisdiction will then take place on the basis of the indictment.

In order to save precious trial time, the *Criminal Code* provides for a pre-trial conference to be held between the prosecutor and the accused or counsel for the accused before a judge of the court in which the trial is to take place.[125] The hearing is to "consider such matters as will promote a fair and expeditious trial." In the pre-trial conference, the Crown and the accused will attempt to locate those areas where there may be agreement between the parties and thereby avoid the need to deal with such issues in the courtroom. It may well be the case, for example, that the pre-trial conference will serve as an opportunity for the accused to obtain discovery of the Crown's case or to discuss the possibility of making an agreement to plead guilty in return for some concession from the Crown (so-called "plea bargaining"). The *Code* requires that all jury trials be preceded by a pre-trial conference. In non-jury trials, the pre-trial hearing would not be mandatory but would be held only with the consent of both the prosecutor and the accused.

Figure 6.4 illustrates the organization of a typical courtroom used for the trial of indictable offences. The intricate details of the trial process in relation to indictable offences cannot be dealt with in this book. However, one or two general comments are certainly in order.

FIGURE 6.4
CRIMINAL COURT SETTING

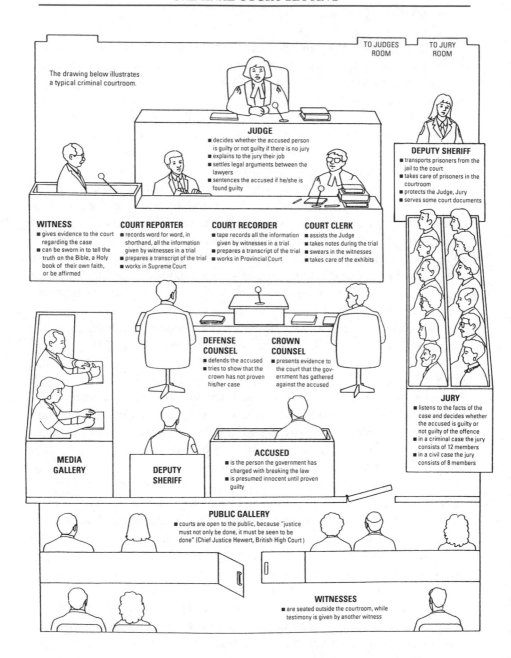

The drawing below illustrates a typical criminal courtroom.

TO JUDGES ROOM

TO JURY ROOM

JUDGE
- decides whether the accused person is guilty or not guilty if there is no jury
- explains to the jury their job
- settles legal arguments between the lawyers
- sentences the accused if he/she is found guilty

DEPUTY SHERIFF
- transports prisoners from the jail to the court
- takes care of prisoners in the courtroom
- protects the Judge, Jury
- serves some court documents

WITNESS
- gives evidence to the court regarding the case
- can be sworn in to tell the truth on the Bible, a Holy book of their own faith, or be affirmed

COURT REPORTER
- records word for word, in shorthand, all the information given by witnesses in a trial
- prepares a transcript of the trial
- works in Supreme Court

COURT RECORDER
- tape records all the information given by witnesses in a trial
- prepares a transcript of the trial
- works in Provincial Court

COURT CLERK
- assists the Judge
- takes notes during the trial
- swears in the witnesses
- takes care of the exhibits

DEFENSE COUNSEL
- defends the accused
- tries to show that the crown has not proven his/her case

CROWN COUNSEL
- presents evidence to the court that the government has gathered against the accused

JURY
- listens to the facts of the case and decides whether the accused is guilty or not guilty of the offence
- in a criminal case the jury consists of 12 members
- in a civil case the jury consists of 8 members

MEDIA GALLERY

DEPUTY SHERIFF

ACCUSED
- is the person the government has charged with breaking the law
- is presumed innocent until proven guilty

PUBLIC GALLERY
- courts are open to the public, because "justice must not only be done, it must be seen to be done" (Chief Justice Hewert, British High Court)

WITNESSES
- are seated outside the courtroom, while testimony is given by another witness

Source: *British Columbia's Legal System: A Guide to the Wall Charts* (Vancouver: Law Courts Education Society of British Columbia, 1992), p. 14.

First, unlike the situation that exists in relation to the trial of summary conviction offences, the accused is required to be present during his or her trial for an indictable offence[126] (Proulx, 1983).

Second, it is important to bear in mind that the realities of the trial process may be at considerable odds with the popular image of how serious criminal offences are dealt with in the courts. As Hagan (1984:167) notes, the "media image of the court process is that of a trial by jury, with prosecution and defence attorneys assuming adversarial roles in a battle for justice." In reality, the great majority of cases involving indictable offences are dealt with in a very different manner. Jury trials are relatively rare in Canada, despite the fact that section 11(f) of the *Charter* guarantees the accused person's right to a jury trial for any offence that carries a maximum sentence of five years' or more imprisonment. Insofar as the *Charter* guarantee of a jury trial is concerned, the Supreme Court of Canada has ruled[127] that the accused person may waive this right and, in many cases, this is precisely what the accused does. Indeed, according to Hagan (1984:167), there are less than 2,000 jury trials in Canada in any given year.[128]

The reality is that the great majority of criminal cases are actually tried in the provincial courts. For example, in British Columbia during 1986, about 96% of all cases entering the Provincial Court system were finally disposed of within this system; that is, only some 4% of criminal cases were subsequently sent on to the "higher courts" for trial.[129]

A significant proportion of defendants plead guilty to the charges laid against them rather than participate in an adversarial trial. The percentage of guilty pleas varies from jurisdiction to jurisdiction across Canada. However, it is difficult to make direct comparisons. A plea of guilty may be entered at different stages of the trial process, and published statistics do not always make it clear whether the percentage of guilty pleas quoted refers to guilty pleas entered at any stage of the trial process or only to guilty pleas entered at one particular stage of the process. In British Columbia, for example, during 1986, about 46% of all defendants before the Provincial Court entered a plea of guilty on their very first appearance in court.[130] Almost 70% of the defendants studied by Ericson and Baranek (1982:157) pleaded guilty at some stage in the trial process. Mackaay (1976:32) found that 63.5% of defendants pleaded guilty at the Montreal Municipal Court and 31.4% at the Montreal Court House. No matter what the variation between jurisdictions may be, it is clear that a very considerable proportion of criminal cases are disposed of without a trial of the innocence or guilt of the accused person. This observation has important implications for the image of the criminal courts held by many Canadians. Figure 6.5 provides an overview of the whole process by means of which cases flow through the Canadian system of criminal courts.

THE SYSTEM OF APPEALS

Once the trial has been concluded, it is always possible that either the accused or the Crown may wish to appeal against the verdict or the sentence meted out. Until 1923, there was only a very limited system of appeals in existence in Canada (Salhany, 1989:402). However, at the present time, a fairly elaborate system of appeals operates in relation to criminal cases. There is a marked difference between the system of appeals available in relation to summary conviction offences and the system that operates in relation to indictable offences.

Appeals in Relation to Summary Conviction Offences

While the trial process in relation to summary conviction offences is relatively straightforward, the appeal process is quite complex (Atrens, 1988:I-31). This compares sharply with the situation applicable to indictable offences where, although the various trial options are almost labyrinthine in their complexity, the system of appeals is relatively simple in its basic structure.

Basically, two forms of appeal are available in relation to a summary conviction offence: an "Appeal to a Section 812 Appeal Court"; and a "Summary Appeal on Transcript or Agreed Statement of the Facts."[131]

Appeal to a Section 812 Appeal Court

In this appeal procedure, either the Crown or the accused may appeal from a decision of the Provincial Court of the province to a court designated by section 812 of the *Code*. The appeal may cover a broad range of issues, including questions of fact as well as matters relating to the sentence meted out by the trial court.

Until 1976, this form of appeal took the shape of a completely new trial, or "trial *de novo*" (Salhany, 1989:445). One of the reasons for this rather costly form of appeal procedure was to remedy the possibility that

FIGURE 6.5
CRIMINAL TRIAL PROCEDURES

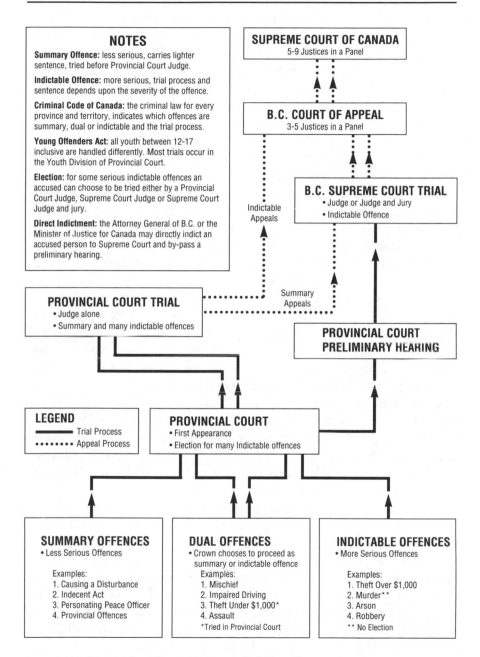

NOTES

Summary Offence: less serious, carries lighter sentence, tried before Provincial Court Judge.

Indictable Offence: more serious, trial process and sentence depends upon the severity of the offence.

Criminal Code of Canada: the criminal law for every province and territory, indicates which offences are summary, dual or indictable and the trial process.

Young Offenders Act: all youth between 12-17 inclusive are handled differently. Most trials occur in the Youth Division of Provincial Court.

Election: for some serious indictable offences an accused can choose to be tried either by a Provincial Court Judge, Supreme Court Judge or Supreme Court Judge and jury.

Direct Indictment: the Attorney General of B.C. or the Minister of Justice for Canada may directly indict an accused person to Supreme Court and by-pass a preliminary hearing.

SUPREME COURT OF CANADA
5-9 Justices in a Panel

B.C. COURT OF APPEAL
3-5 Justices in a Panel

Indictable Appeals

B.C. SUPREME COURT TRIAL
• Judge or Judge and Jury
• Indictable Offence

Summary Appeals

PROVINCIAL COURT TRIAL
• Judge alone
• Summary and many indictable offences

PROVINCIAL COURT PRELIMINARY HEARING

LEGEND
—— Trial Process
••••••• Appeal Process

PROVINCIAL COURT
• First Appearance
• Election for many Indictable offences

SUMMARY OFFENCES
• Less Serious Offences

Examples:
1. Causing a Disturbance
2. Indecent Act
3. Personating Peace Officer
4. Provincial Offences

DUAL OFFENCES
• Crown chooses to proceed as summary or indictable offence

Examples:
1. Mischief
2. Impaired Driving
3. Theft Under $1,000*
4. Assault

*Tried in Provincial Court

INDICTABLE OFFENCES
• More Serious Offences

Examples:
1. Theft Over $1,000
2. Murder**
3. Arson
4. Robbery

** No Election

Source: *British Columbia's Legal System: A Guide to the Wall Charts* (Vancouver: Law Courts Education Society of British Columbia, 1992), p. 18.

there would not be a proper record of the original trial in the magistrates' courts (the predecessors of the modern provincial courts). Another reason for adopting this procedure was that many of the magistrates did not have any formal legal training. However, by the mid-1970s, magistrates were being appointed exclusively from the ranks of professional lawyers and proper transcripts were being taken at all criminal trials. In light of these developments, it seemed unnecessary to require the expense of an entirely new trial, together with the concomitant inconvenience that such an appeal procedure thrust upon witnesses; therefore, in 1976, the *Code* was amended so as to require that this form of appeal be conducted on the basis of the transcript taken in the original trial. However, the *Code* does preserve the option of a full trial *de novo* in exceptional cases. The trial *de novo* will now be held only in the situation where, "because of the condition of the record" or for "any other reason," the appeal court "is of the opinion that the interests of justice would be better served" by staging a completely new trial.[132] Clearly, the trial *de novo* procedure is intended to be used only in rare situations.

What is meant by a "section 812 appeal court"? Until relatively recently, this form of appeal was made to the County or District Court in those provinces that had this tier in their court system. However, as we saw earlier in this chapter, this tier of courts has now disappeared across Canada. An appeal to a "section 812 appeal court" now means an appeal to the Superior Court of Criminal Jurisdiction. In New Brunswick, Manitoba, Alberta, and Saskatchewan, this court will be the Court of Queen's Bench; in Newfoundland and P.E.I., the Trial Division of the Supreme Court; in Quebec, the Superior Court; in Ontario, the Ontario Court (General Division); in the Yukon Territory and Northwest Territories, a judge of the Supreme Court; and in British Columbia and Nova Scotia, the Supreme Court.

Who may appeal and in what circumstances? Defendants may appeal either from a conviction or order made against them or against the sentence passed on them. On the other hand, the prosecutor may appeal either from an order that stays proceedings on an information or dismisses an information or, alternatively, against the sentence passed on the accused.[133] Clearly, the Crown has very broad powers of appeal under these provisions of the *Code*; indeed, the prosecutor can launch an appeal not only on questions of law, but also on questions of fact. Nevertheless, these extensive powers of appeal by the Crown have been held to be valid under the *Charter*.[134]

What are the powers of the appeal court insofar as the disposition of the appeal is concerned? Very briefly, in the case of an appeal by the accused against conviction, the appeal court may allow the appeal, set aside the verdict, and either direct a judgment or verdict of acquittal be entered or order a new trial.[135] If a new trial is to be held, then it will normally be held in a different court than the one that entered the original conviction.[136] On the other hand, of course, the appeal court could find that the appeal does not have sufficient merit and will dismiss it. Where the prosecutor is appealing against an "acquittal," the court may just dismiss the appeal if it does not feel that it has adequate merit. Or it may decide to allow the appeal and set aside the verdict of the trial court. In this case, the appeal court has two options: (1) it may order a new trial or (2) it may enter a verdict of guilty with respect to the offence of which the accused should have been found guilty by the trial court. In the latter situation, the appeal court may pass sentence itself or hand the case back to the trial court for sentencing.[137] In the case of an appeal against sentence (either by the accused or by the prosecution), the appeal court has the power to vary the sentence "within the limits prescribed by law" or it may just dismiss the appeal altogether.[138] It is critical to remember that the court has the power either to decrease or to increase the sentence meted out at the trial level.[139]

Summary Appeal on Transcript or Agreed Statement of Facts

This form of appeal is much more restricted in its scope than its companion form of appeal. It is concerned exclusively with questions of law; in other words, unlike the appeal to a section 812 appeal court, the summary appeal on transcript or agreed statement of facts cannot be concerned with the facts of a case or the appropriateness of the sentence handed down.

Historically, this form of appeal represented an efficient method of resolving questions of law where there was agreement on the facts of the case. It provided a comparatively inexpensive alternative to the trial *de novo*, which was, until 1976, the process that was required where questions of fact were in dispute. Now that a trial *de novo* is the rare exception, rather than the rule, in section 812 appeals, the rationale for maintaining two distinct appeal procedures has been seriously diminished. Nevertheless, the summary appeal on transcript or agreed statement of facts continues as a distinct procedure in the current *Criminal Code*.

Under this form of appeal, either the accused or the prosecution may appeal to the Superior Court of Criminal Jurisdiction for the province concerned. Either party may appeal, as the case may be, "against a conviction, judgment or verdict of acquittal or other final order or determination of a summary conviction court" on the basis that:

- ▸ it is erroneous in point of law;
- ▸ it is in excess of jurisdiction; or
- ▸ it constitutes a refusal or failure to exercise jurisdiction.[140]

An appeal launched in this way will be made on the basis of either a transcript of the trial court proceedings or, if both parties give their consent, an agreed "statement of facts." Since the issues raised are much more narrow than those raised in an appeal to a section 812 court, the Superior Court has fewer options to summon in disposing of a case. The appeal court may either "affirm, reverse or modify the conviction, judgment or verdict of acquittal or other final order or determination" or, alternatively, it may send the case back to the trial court with the appeal court's opinion on the matter of law raised and "may make any other order in relation to the matter" that it "considers proper."[141] Note that the appeal court does *not* have the power to order a new trial.[142]

Now that the county and district courts have disappeared from the Canadian criminal court system and *all* appeals in summary conviction cases go to the Superior Court of Criminal Jurisdiction, it is questionable whether it is necessary to retain two separate forms of appeal. The present system is unnecessarily complicated, and presumably the *Criminal Code* could be amended to provide for one simple avenue of appeal from the trial court in summary conviction cases. When the two forms of appeal were heard by two different courts and many cases involved a complete re-trial, it made sense to provide for two distinct appeal procedures. However, with the elimination of the county and district courts and the disappearance of the need for a trial *de novo* in summary conviction cases, the present appeal procedures have become hopelessly outdated.

Appeal to the Provincial Court of Appeal

Once an appeal has been dealt with by the Superior Court of Criminal Jurisdiction, there is the possibility of a further appeal by either party to the Provincial Court of Appeal. However, such an appeal may only be made in relation to a question of law (not a question of fact).[143] Since the appeal is limited to questions of law, there is no appeal against sentence in the sense that neither party can raise the issue of the appropriateness of the sentence. However, a question as to the legality of any particular sentence could be the subject of an appeal on the basis that it constitutes a genuine question of law (Salhany, 1989:469).[144] Similarly, an appeal could be made on the question of whether a sentence infringed any of the provisions of the *Charter*.

Appeal to the Supreme Court of Canada

The *Criminal Code* does not make any provision for an appeal from the decision of a Provincial Court of Appeal to the Supreme Court of Canada insofar as summary conviction offences are concerned. However, according to Salhany (1989:471):

> ...under section 40(1) and (3) of the Supreme Court of Canada Act, an appeal lies to the Supreme Court of Canada with leave of that court from the judgment of the highest court of final resort in the province acquitting or convicting an accused, or setting aside or affirming a conviction or acquittal on any question of law or jurisdiction.

The system of appeals in relation to summary conviction offences is summarized in Figure 6.6 for the purpose of easy reference.

Appeals in Relation to Indictable Offences

Appeal to the Provincial Court of Appeal

Unlike the situation that exists in relation to summary conviction offences, the *Criminal Code*[145] has established only one method of appeal insofar as indictable offences are concerned. All appeals from the decisions of trial courts are to be taken to the Provincial Court of Appeal.[146] Both the accused and the prosecutor may appeal, but the prosecutor's rights of appeal are more limited than those of the accused.

The accused may appeal against conviction in the following circumstances:

(i) (as a matter of right) on a question of law alone;

    (ii) on a question of fact or a question of mixed fact and law provided he or she first obtains the permission ("leave") of the Court of Appeal or if the trial judge issues a certificate indicating that the case is a "proper case for appeal" (however, it is worth noting that, at present, the trial judge's certificate is almost never used as a means of bringing an appeal);

    (iii) on any ground other than those mentioned in (i) and (ii) above provided that the court of appeal considers it to be "a sufficient ground of appeal" and gives the accused leave to appeal.[147]

The accused may also appeal against the sentence meted out provided he or she first obtains the leave of either the Court of Appeal or a single judge of that court (unless, of course, the sentence is fixed by law such as is the case, for example, in first-degree murder).[148]

The prosecutor (either the Attorney-General or counsel appointed by him or her) may appeal in the following circumstances only:

    (i) against acquittal on any ground that involves a question of law alone;

    (ii) against an order of a Superior Court of Criminal Jurisdiction that quashes an indictment or in any manner refuses or fails to exercise jurisdiction on an indictment;

    (iii) against an order of a trial court that stays proceedings on an indictment or quashes an indictment; or

    (iv) against the sentence passed by the trial court provided either the Court of Appeal or a single judge of that court give their "leave" (unless, of course, the sentence is one fixed by law).[149]

The major difference between the rights of appeal enjoyed by the accused and the Crown lies in the fact that, in general, the prosecution may only appeal against an acquittal *if it involves a question of law,* whereas the accused can appeal against conviction not only on a question of law but also on a question of fact (or mixed law and fact). In order for the Crown to launch a successful appeal on a question of law, it must establish that the trial judge was under a misapprehension as to the correct legal principle or misapplied it.[150] It has been suggested that the

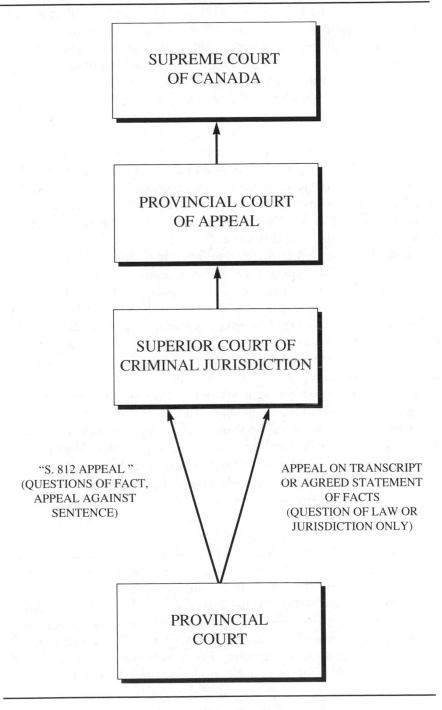

FIGURE 6.6
THE SYSTEM OF APPEALS: SUMMARY CONVICTION OFFENCES

SUPREME COURT
OF CANADA

PROVINCIAL COURT
OF APPEAL

SUPERIOR COURT OF
CRIMINAL JURISDICTION

"S. 812 APPEAL "
(QUESTIONS OF FACT,
APPEAL AGAINST
SENTENCE)

APPEAL ON TRANSCRIPT
OR AGREED STATEMENT
OF FACTS
(QUESTION OF LAW OR
JURISDICTION ONLY)

PROVINCIAL
COURT

Crown and the accused should be on the same footing when it comes to their rights of appeal. However, the Crown already has more extensive rights of appeal than exist in certain other countries. For example, in England, a country whose legal system has many affinities with the Canadian legal system, the Crown does not even have the right to appeal against an acquittal. To allow the Crown, in Canada, to appeal against an acquittal on a question of fact as well as a question of law would place a very considerable burden on the shoulders of every accused person who has been acquitted at trial. Such a person would be constantly subjected to the threat of prolonged uncertainty and continuing expense until the appeal process had run its protracted course. Perhaps limiting the Crown's right of appeal to questions of law is a more satisfactory compromise, always assuming that it is desirable for the Crown to be able to appeal against an acquittal in the first place.[151]

Even if the accused does exercise the right to appeal on a question of fact, the Court of Appeal is generally reluctant to second-guess the trial judge's findings, particularly on such issues as the credibility of witnesses; after all, the trial judge and jury actually see the witnesses "in the flesh," whereas the appellate justices can only read what they said in the trial record. The major concern of the Court of Appeal, in this respect, is whether the verdict was "reasonable" and, provided the jury or judge acted reasonably, then the justices of appeal will not overturn that verdict merely because they might have arrived at a different decision had they been the finders of fact at the accused's trial.[152] As well, the Court of Appeal will not hear new evidence unless it could not have been obtained at the time of the trial through the "exercise of due diligence."[153] In other words, new evidence will not be considered unless it is truly "fresh," that is, it was not reasonably available at the time of the trial.

In an important provision, the *Criminal Code*[154] states that the Court of Appeal or a judge of that court may assign a lawyer to act on behalf of an accused person, who has brought an appeal, where in their opinion "it appears desirable in the interests of justice that the accused should have legal aid and where it appears that the accused has not sufficient means to obtain that aid." However, it is important to recognize that this provision gives the Court of Appeal a discretion as to whether to assign counsel to the accused and it has been held that the *Charter* does not require that there be an absolute right to counsel in such circumstances.[155]

Where the accused is appealing against conviction, the Court of Appeal may decide to allow his or her appeal where in its opinion:

   (i) the verdict should be set aside on the ground that it is unreasonable or cannot be supported by the evidence;

  (ii) the judgment should be set aside on the ground that there was a wrong decision on a question of law; or

(iii) on any ground there was a miscarriage of justice.[156]

On the other hand, of course, the Court of Appeal may dismiss the accused's appeal. It may take this course of action where:

   (i)   the court is of the opinion that the accused, even though he or she was not properly convicted on one count or part of the indictment, was properly convicted on another count or part of the indictment;

  (ii)   the appeal is not decided in the accused's favour on the basis of any of the three grounds for allowing an appeal that are set out above;

(iii) even though the court is of the opinion that there was a mistake of law made by the trial court, it is nevertheless of the opinion that no substantial wrong or miscarriage of justice has occurred; or

(iv) even though there was a procedural irregularity at the trial, the trial court had the necessary jurisdiction over the class of offences of which the accused was convicted and the appeal court is of the opinion that the accused did not suffer any prejudice as a consequence of the irregularity.[157]

Where the Court of Appeal decides to allow the accused's appeal, it has two options. It may:

  (a) direct that a judgment or verdict of acquittal be entered; or

  (b) order a new trial.[158]

On the other hand, where the appeal court decides to dismiss the accused's appeal, it may substitute the verdict that in its opinion should have been found and either:

  (a) affirm the sentence passed by the trial court; or

   (b)   impose a sentence itself or send the matter back to the trial court with a direction to impose the appropriate sentence.[159]

Where the prosecution is appealing against acquittal, the Court of Appeal may just dismiss the appeal or, alternatively, it may allow the appeal, set aside the verdict, and either:

   (i)   order a new trial; or

   (ii) except where the acquittal was made by a jury, enter a verdict of guilty with respect to the offence of which, in its opinion, the accused should have been found guilty but for the error in law, and either impose a sentence itself or send the case back to the trial court for the imposition of an appropriate sentence.[160]

Even though the Crown establishes that there was an error at the trial level, the Court of Appeal will not order a new trial unless the Crown can demonstrate "with a reasonable degree of certainty" that the outcome might have been affected by the error.[161] In other words, only legal errors that might have had an impact on the decision to acquit the accused can serve as a justification for subjecting the accused to the hardships associated with a new trial.

    Where an appeal has been made against the sentence imposed by the trial court, then the Court of Appeal may (provided, of course, that the sentence is not fixed by law) either:

   (a)   vary the sentence within the limits permitted by law; or

   (b)   dismiss the appeal.[162]

    The court may vary a sentence upward (in terms of severity) as well as downward, even in the situation where it is the accused who has appealed against his or her sentence.[163] However, as a matter of basic justice, the Crown must give reasonable notice that it wishes to seek an increased sentence and the accused be given the opportunity to be heard on this issue. Nevertheless, the threat of the possibility that a sentence could be increased is likely to have a chilling impact upon an accused person contemplating an appeal against his or her sentence.

Appeal to the Supreme Court of Canada

The *Criminal Code*[164] makes provision for an appeal from the decision of the Court of Appeal to the Supreme Court of Canada. A person who has been convicted of an indictable offence and whose conviction has been upheld by the Provincial Court of Appeal may appeal to the Supreme Court of Canada:

(a) *(as a matter of right)* on any question of law on which a judge of the Court of Appeal has dissented;[165] or
(b) on any question of law if the accused obtains the leave of the Supreme Court of Canada or a judge of that court.

In addition, a person who has been acquitted of an indictable offence at trial and whose acquittal has been set aside by the Court of Appeal may appeal (as a matter of right) to the Supreme Court of Canada on a question of law.[166]

The Crown may appeal against the decision of the Court of Appeal in the following circumstances:

(a) (as a matter of right) on a question of law on which a judge of the Court of Appeal has dissented; or
(b) on any question of law with the leave of the Supreme Court of Canada.[167]

The powers of the Supreme Court of Canada in relation to indictable offences are the same as those available to the provincial courts of appeal, as discussed earlier.

Power of the Minister of Justice to Refer a Case to the Court of Appeal or the Supreme Court of Canada

Even though the appeal process may have been exhausted, there is one provision of the *Criminal Code*[168] that may be used to "re-open" an accused person's case. This provision gives the federal Minister of Justice, who has received an application by or on behalf of the accused person "for the mercy of the Crown," the power to:

(i) order a new trial;

(ii) refer the case to the Court of Appeal for a hearing (as though it were an appeal by the accused person); or

(iii) "refer to the Court of Appeal at any time, for its opinion, any question upon which he desires the assistance of that court, and the court shall furnish its opinion accordingly."

Where the Minister of Justice refers a case to the Court of Appeal, it is likely that the court will be presented with fresh evidence that was not available at the original trial and the associated appeals.[169] It appears that the Court of Appeal, dealing with a reference from the Minister of Justice, may be willing to be more flexible in receiving new evidence than it would be if it was dealing with an "ordinary" appeal.[170]

Perhaps the most famous exercise of the minister's power to order a new trial occurred in the case of Dr. Henry Morgentaler during the mid-1970s. Dr. Morgentaler was acquitted by a Quebec jury of the charge of unlawfully procuring a miscarriage (abortion). However, the Crown appealed and the Court of Appeal upheld this appeal and substituted a verdict of guilty. This was the first occasion upon which a Court of Appeal had used its power to substitute a verdict of guilty for an acquittal by a jury.[171] The Supreme Court of Canada ultimately upheld the Court of Appeal's decision.[172] The Minister of Justice then ordered a new trial at which Morgentaler was again acquitted by a jury (Dickens, 1976).

It should also be noted that the Governor General of Canada, on the recommendation of the Minister of Justice, has the power, under section 53 of the *Supreme Court Act*,[173] to refer a case directly to the Supreme Court of Canada for its opinion as to whether there has been a miscarriage of justice. The importance of this rarely used power is well illustrated by the *Milgaard* case. In 1991, the Honourable Kim Campbell (then Minister of Justice) referred the case of David Milgaard to the Supreme Court of Canada. Milgaard had been in prison for 22 years after having been convicted of the murder of Gail Miller in Saskatoon. Milgaard consistently claimed that he was innocent. In light of the information she received, the Minister of Justice eventually asked the Supreme Court to consider whether the conviction of Milgaard constituted a miscarriage of justice and to indicate what remedial action (if any) should be taken. In April, 1992, the Supreme Court, after hearing evidence from various witnesses, ruled that in light of the new evidence available to the Court the continued conviction of Milgaard would indeed constitute a miscarriage of justice.[174] The Supreme Court recommended

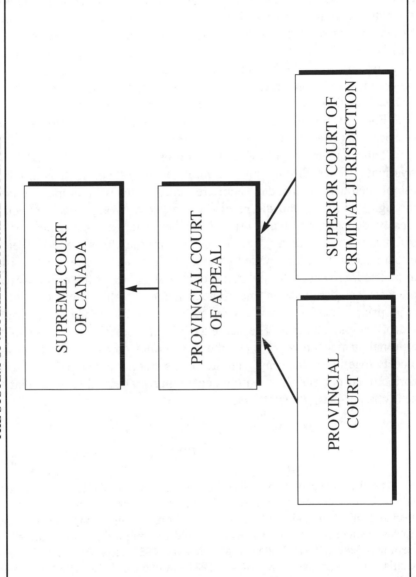

FIGURE 6.7
THE SYSTEM OF APPEALS: INDICTABLE OFFENCES

SUPREME COURT
OF CANADA

PROVINCIAL COURT
OF APPEAL

SUPERIOR COURT OF
CRIMINAL JURISDICTION

PROVINCIAL
COURT

that there be a new trial, but the Attorney-General of Saskatchewan later announced that the charges against Milgaard would be stayed (primarily on the basis that it would be impossible to bring an effective prosecution after the lapse of so many years since the commission of the offence). Milgaard was released shortly after the decision of the Supreme Court was issued. Obviously, this was a dramatic use of the power to refer a case directly to the Supreme Court of Canada, and it is clear that this power may well constitute the last resort of a person who claims that he or she is a victim of injustice in the criminal trial process.

For easy reference, the process of appeals in relation to indictable offences has been summarized in Figure 6.7.

This chapter has followed the progress of a person charged with a criminal offence through the elaborate maze of courts that has been established across Canada. There are many pathways that may be taken through this maze, and the precise route taken by any specific accused clearly depends on many critical factors, such as the nature of the offence, the discretionary decisions made by the Crown, and (in certain circumstances) choices made by the accused as to how he or she wishes to be tried. However, to this point, one vital aspect of the criminal court process has barely been mentioned: namely, the imposition of an appropriate sentence once the accused has been found to have committed the offence(s) charged. The sentence of the court is the phase of the criminal justice process where the courts and corrections are brought closely together in the sense that the courts assign the clientele to various correctional options. It is on the sentencing process, therefore, that the next chapter casts its spotlight.

NOTES

[1]The historical evolution of the criminal courts followed different paths in the various provinces and territories of Canada. The complexity of this process precludes an examination of the history of the criminal courts in this book. However, there is a rapidly burgeoning field of literature in this area. See, for example, Banks, 1981; Bindon, 1981; Flaherty, 1981; Hett, 1973; Knafla, 1986; Knafla and Chapman, 1983; Risk, 1981; Williams, D.C., 1962 and 1963; Williams, D.C., 1963, 1964, 1965, and 1966; Williams, D.R., 1986.

[2]This amount excludes expenditures on prosecution services and legal aid.

[3]Approximately 4% of total expenditures are devoted to legal aid.

[4]Section 92(14).

[5]In Ontario, the system will eventually be collapsed into one court: the Ontario Court of Justice (Ontario, Ministry of the Attorney-General, no date).

[6]Where the county or district courts existed, they used to try the more serious (indictable) offences, although the most serious offences of all (such as murder, treason, and piracy) could only be tried by the superior courts. They also heard most appeals from the provincial courts in relation to minor (summary conviction) offences.

[7]In some areas, so-called "unified family courts" have been established in order to try and bring all matters relating to the family within one court building. In jurisdictions where such courts do not exist, some family matters are dealt with in the superior courts and others in the provincial courts. The Unified Family Court allows family matters to be settled in an integrated manner and eliminates the necessity of going to different courts to have them resolved (Canadian Centre for Justice Statistics, 1991a:7). Such courts currently exist in St. John's, Newfoundland; Hamilton, Ontario; and Saskatoon, Saskatchewan. In Quebec, all family law matters are dealt with in the Family Division of the *Cour Superieur*. Similarly, the Family Divisions of the Courts of Queen's Bench in Manitoba and New Brunswick function as unified family courts, as does the Family Section of the Prince Edward Island Supreme Court (Trial Division). See also Canadian Centre for Justice Statistics, 1990.

In Ontario, it is planned that there will be a province-wide Unified Family Court, which will be part of the Ontario Court of Justice (Ontario, Ministry of the Attorney-General, no date).

[8]Sections 96 to 101 of the *Constitution Act, 1867*.

[9]Section 92(4) of the *Constitution Act, 1867*.

[10]Section 790 of the *Criminal Code*.

[11]Section 2 of the *Criminal Code*.

[12]Section 786(2).

[13]See Pavlich (1982:III-172-75).

[14]*R. v. Robert* (1973), 13 C.C.C. (2d) 43 (Ont.C.A.).

[15]*R. v. German* (1974), 3 C.R. 516 (Ont.C.A.).

[16]*Re Abarca and The Queen* (1980), 57 C.C.C. (2nd) 410, *per* Lacourciere J.A., at 416.

[17]*Re Warren et al. and The Queen* (1983), 10 W.C.B. 146.

[18]*R. v. Darbishire* (1983), 11 W.C.B. 5.

[19]*R. v. Quinn* (1989), 54 C.C.C. (3d) 157 (Que. C.A.).

[20]*Re Parkin and The Queen* (1986), 28 C.C.C. (3d) 252 (Ont. C.A.).

[21]The exception to this general rule is the rarely used direct indictment procedure that is discussed later in this chapter.

[22]*Per* Lamer J. in *Re Dowson and The Queen* (1983), 7 C.C.C. (3d) 527, at 536.

[23]Section 504.

[24]See *R. v. Myhren* (1986), 48 C.R. (3d) 270 (N.W.T.S.C.), for example. The Supreme Court of Canada has ruled that there must be a reasonable degree of specificity in an information; see *R. v. WIS Development Corp. Ltd.* (1984), 12 C.C.C. (3d) 129.

[25]It has been argued that in Toronto, Ontario, for example, the police lay most of the routine criminal charges without consultation with Crown counsel (Wheeler, 1987).

[26]Sections 507 and 508.

[27]The Supreme Court of Canada has ruled that section 507 requires that such hearings be held *in camera*. The Court also ruled that, while this form of hearing violates the *Charter* guarantee of freedom of expression (section 2[b]), it is nevertheless justified under section 1 of the *Charter* as a "reasonable limit" on the right of the public to have free access to court proceedings in Canada. See *Southam et al. v. Coulter et al.* (1990), 60 C.C.C. (3d) 267 (S.C.C.). For further discussion of the rationale for holding this inquiry *in camera*, see Law Reform Commission of Canada (1987b:73-75).

[28]The Supreme Court of Canada has ruled that requiring an accused person to submit to fingerprinting before he or she has been convicted of an indictable offence does not contravene his or her rights under section of the *Charter*: *R. v. Beare* (1988), 45 C.C.C. (3d) 57 (S.C.C.).

[29]Section 507(4).

[30]Even where an arrest warrant is issued, the *Code* gives the justice the discretion, in relation to most offences, to endorse the warrant so that the officer in charge of a police lock-up may later release the accused on bail (sections 510 and 499). The details of the bail procedures are discussed in the next section.

[31]Section 508. It has been held that, while it is preferable for the justice of the peace to ask the person laying the information to "briefly divulge the factual basis of the charge," this is not always necessary in order for the requirements of section 508 to be met; see *Re Morton and The Queen* (1991), 70 C.C.C. (3d) 244 (Ont. Ct., Gen. Div.).

[32]Section 505. In any event, the information must be laid before the court date specified in the appearance notice, promise to appear, or recognizance. In *R. v. Brown* (1982), 44 Nfld. & P.E.I.R. 38 (Nfld. C.A.), it was held that laying an information some 25 days after issuing an appearance notice was not "as soon as practicable."

[33]See, for example, section 14 of the *Offence Act*, RSBC 1979, c. 305, which sets out the traffic ticket scheme for the province of British Columbia.

[34]R.S.C. 1970, c.2 (2nd Supp.). The *Bail Reform Act* has now been incorporated into the *Criminal Code*, Part XVI.

[35]*Criminal Code,* section 498(1).

[36]In deciding whether the "public interest" requires that the suspect be kept in custody, the officer in charge is required to have regard to "all the circumstances," including the need to (i) establish the identity of the suspect, (ii) secure or preserve evidence relating to the offence, or (iii) prevent the continuation or repetition of the offence or the commission of another offence (section 498[1][i]).

[37]Section 498(1) (i) and (j).

[38]Where a police officer has arrested a suspect under a warrant issued by a justice of the peace, then the officer in charge may release the suspect *provided the justice has endorsed the warrant so as to permit this course of action* (section 499). The suspect may be released upon giving a promise to appear, a simple recognizance, or (in the case of a non-resident) a recognizance and some form of security.

[39]Section 145(5).

[40]Section 502.

[41]Section 499.

[42]Section 503(1).

[43]*R. v. Charles* (1987), 36 C.C.C. (3d) 286 (Ont. C.A.). However, the Supreme Court of Canada held that an 18-hour delay (for the purpose of arranging a line-up) did not infringe section 9 of the *Charter*; see *R. v. Storrey* (1990), 53 C.C.C. (3d) 316 (S.C.C.).

[44]Section 516. Adjournments of more than three days may not take place without the consent of the accused.

[45]Section 522.

[46]Section 469.

[47]It should be noted that, upon the application of the accused, the justice or the judge will impose a press and media blackout on the evidence presented at a bail hearing (section 517). This provision is intended to protect the accused from the impact of publicity that may prejudice him or her at trial.

[48]See section 515(1) of the *Criminal Code*.

[49]S.C. 1974-75-76, c. 93.

[50]Section 522(2).

[51]Section 11(e).

[52]Section 11(d).

[53]*R. v. Morales* (1992), 77 C.C.C. (3d) 91 (S.C.C.).

[54]*R. v. Pearson* (1992), 77 C.C.C. (3d) 124 (S.C.C.).

[55](1992), 77 C.C.C. (3d) 91, at 113.

[56]*Ibid.,* at 113.

[57](1992), 77 C.C.C. (3d) 124, at 144.

[58]Section 515(10). In *Regina v. Lamothe* (1990), 58 C.C.C. (3d) 530 (Que. C.A.), it was held that, although the judge has a broad discretion in deciding whether detention is justified for the protection of the public, that discretion must

be exercised in light of the presumption to innocence (section 11[d] of the *Charter*) and the right to reasonable bail (section 11[e]). In *Lamothe*, the Court ruled that the judge had made an error in making the decision to detain the accused solely on the basis of the seriousness of the offence and the likelihood of conviction.

The *Criminal Code* also directs the courts to consider the "public interest" in determining whether the accused should be detained on the second ground; however, in the *Morales* case, the Supreme Court of Canada ruled that public interest criterion should be deleted on the basis that it was so vague as to infringe the fundamental principles of justice guaranteed by the *Charter*. See *R. v. Morales* (1992), 77 C.C.C. (3d) 91 (S.C.C.).

[59]These five methods of release (and the conditions that may be imposed in connection with them) are also applicable to those cases involving the serious charges that may only be dealt with by a judge of a Superior Court of Criminal Jurisdiction (section 522[3]).

[60]Section 515(2).

[61]As to the approval of sureties, note Trotter (1987-88).

[62]Sections 766 and 767.

[63]Section 767.1.

[64]Section 515(4).

[65]An Ontario court decision has held that section 11(e) of the *Charter* requires that each bail application must be considered on an individual basis, in terms of the offence and the accused person, and that the *justice must inquire as to the ability of the accused person to meet the conditions that may be imposed: Re R. and Brooks et al.* (1982), 1 C.C.C. (3d) 506 (Ont. H.C.J.).

[66]*R. v. Bielefeld* (1981), 64 C.C.C. (2d) 216 (B.C.S.C.).

[67]In 1985, the various organizations providing bail verification and supervision services in Ontario formed the Association of Pre-Trial Services of Ontario.

[68]Sections 524(1) and (2).

[69]Section 524(4)

[70]Section 523.

[71]Section 523(2).

[72]Sections 679(1), 816, and 831.

[73]Section 520.

[74]Section 680.

[75]Section 525.

[76]This provision does not apply, however, to those accused persons whose offences are so serious that their bail status can only be determined by a judge of the Superior Court of Criminal Jurisdiction.

[77]Section 525(3).

[78]Section 525(9).

[79]It has been held that a failure to hold the review within the 90-day period (for indictable offences) does not *automatically* render the accused person's continuing detention "arbitrary" within the meaning of section 9 of the *Charter*. Whether the accused has a *Charter* remedy in such a case depends on the specific circumstances that exist (such as whether the failure was deliberate on the part of the jailer). See *R. v. Pomfret* (1990), 53 C.C.C. (3d) 56 (Man. C.A.).

[80]These procedures are normally contained in the applicable provincial *Summary Convictions Act*.

[81]Section 785.

[82]Section 800(2).

[83]Section 803(2).

[84]*R. v. Tarrant* (1984), 13 C.C.C. (3d) 219 (B.C.C.A.); *R. v. Rogers*, [1984] 6 W.W.R. 89 (Sask. C.A.).

[85]*R. v. McLeod* (1983), 36 C.R. (3d) 378 (N.W.T.S.C.).

[86]Section 471.

[87]Section 469.

[88]Section 473.

[89]In *R. v. Turpin* (1989), 48 C.C.C. (3d) 8, the Supreme Court of Canada held that section 11(f) of the *Charter*, which enshrines the right to jury trial for the most serious offences, does not give an accused person, charged with an offence mentioned in section 469 of the *Code*, a corresponding right to be tried by a judge without a jury. In other words, *both the Crown and the defence must agree* before there may be a trial by judge alone when the accused is charged with one or more of the serious offences mentioned in section 469 of the *Code*.

[90]Technically, the word "absolute jurisdiction" is misleading because the Superior Court of Criminal Jurisdiction in each province has the jurisdiction "to try any indictable offence" (section 468). However, it would be very rare indeed for a Superior Court to try an offence falling within the so-called "absolute jurisdiction" of a Provincial Court judge.

[91]Section 553.

[92]Section 536(2).

[93]Section 536(2).

[94]Section 568. It has been held that this provision does not infringe either section 7 or section 11(f) of the *Charter*; see *Re Hanneson and The Queen* (1987), 31 C.C.C. (3d) 560 (Ont.H.C.J.).

[95]Section 555.

[96]Section 561.

[97]Section 561(1)(a) and (b). It has been held that the requirement of the Crown's consent in section 561(1)(a) does *not* violate guarantees enshrined in sections 7 and 15 of the *Charter*; see *Re Koleff and The Queen* (1987), 33 C.C.C. (3d) 460 (Man.Q.B.).

[98]Section 561(1)(c).

[99]Section 561(2).

[100]Section 536(3)

[101]*U.S.A. v. Sheppard* (1976), 30 C.C.C. (2d) 424 (S.C.C.).

[102]*Re R. and Brass* (1981), 64 C.C.C. (2d) 206 (Sask.Q.B.).

[103]Section 540(1)(a).

[104]Section 541(1).

[105]Section 539(1). It has been held that this section does not infringe the guarantee of freedom of the press contained in section 2(b) of the *Charter*; see *R. v. Banville* (1983), 3 C.C.C. (3d) 312 (N.B.Q.B.).

[106]Section 548(1). In *R. v. Cancor Software Corp.* (1990), 58 C.C.C. (3d) 53, the Ontario Court of Appeal held that section 548(1)(a), which permits the presiding judge to order the accused to stand trial for the offence charged *or any other indictable offence in respect of the same transaction*, does not infringe the accused's right under section 11(a) of the *Charter* to be informed without unreasonable delay of the specific offence charged.

[107]Section 574(1) (b). See, for example, *R. v. Rosebush* (1992), 77 C.C.C. (3d) 241 (Alta. C.A.).

[108]*R. v. Tapaquon* (1992), 71 C.C.C. (3d) 50 (Sask. C.A.).

[109]Section 549.

[110]Section 577. In the case of private prosecutions, the written consent of a judge is required for the direct indictment procedure; see section 577(d).

[111]*R. v. Ertel* (1987), 35 C.C.C. (3d) 398 (Ont. C.A.); *R. v. Moore* (1986), 26 C.C.C. (3d) 474 (Man.C.A.) and R. V. Light (1993), 78 C.C.C. (3d) 221 (B.C.C.A.).

[112]*Re Regina and Arviv* (1985), 19 C.C.C. (3d) 395 (Ont. C.A). This ruling was predicated on the assumption that the accused must be given a full disclosure of the Crown's case. See also *R. v. Stolar* (1983), 4 C.C.C. (3d) 333 (Man. C.A.).

[113]*R. v. Rosamond* (1983) 5 C.C.C.(3d) 523 (Sask. Q.B.).

[114]In *Re Oshaweetok and The Queen* (1984), 16 C.C.C. (3d) 392 (N.W.T.S.C.), for example, it was held that laying an identical charge after the accused has been discharged in the course of a preliminary inquiry constitutes an abuse of process and violates the "fundamental principles of justice" guaranteed by section 7 of the *Charter* unless there is some new evidence that has been uncovered since the preliminary inquiry.

[115]*Patterson v. The Queen*, [1970] S.C.R. 409; *Caccamo v. The Queen*, [1976] 1 S.C.R. 786.

[116]See, for example, *Cunliffe v. Law Society of B.C.; Bledsoe v. Law Society of B.C.*, [1984] 4 W.W.R. 451 (B.C.C.A.).

[117]*Stinchcombe v. The Queen* (1991), 68 C.C.C. (3d) 1 (S.C.C.).

[118]*Ibid.*, p. 11, *per* Sopinka J., on behalf of the whole court.

[119]*Ibid.*, p. 7.

[120]*Ibid.*, p. 12. In 1974, the Law Reform Commission of Canada (1974: 35) recommended that a formal system of discovery should be introduced on a uniform basis across the country. At that time, the Commission recommended that the system should be based on a requirement of full disclosure of the Crown's case coupled with a special pre-trial court hearing to ensure that the disclosure was adequate. Following this recommendation, there were a number of experimental projects designed to introduce a system of disclosure in certain Canadian cities (such as Montreal, Ottawa, Toronto, Winnipeg, Edmonton, and Vancouver). The pilot project in Montreal conducted in the mid-70s, which implemented the Commission's specific recommendations, was formally evaluated and was considered to be successful (Law Reform Commission of Canada, 1984:7-9).

[121]*R. v. Ford* (1993), 78 C.C.C. (3d) 481 (B.C.C.A.).

[122]*Ibid.*, at 498, *per* Southin J.

[123]See *R. v. W.J.V.* (1992), 72 C.C.C. (3d) 97 (Nfld. C.A.).

[124]Section 574. See *R. v. Tapaquon* (1992), 71 C.C.C. (3d) 50 (Sask. C.A.) for a discussion of the power to prefer an indictment on a charge that is different from the charge on which the Provincial Court judge has committed the accused for trial after holding a preliminary inquiry.

[125]Section 625(1).

[126]Section 650(1).

[127]*R. v. Turpin* (1989), 48 C.C.C. (3d) 8 (S.C.C.).

[128]The Law Reform Commission of Canada (1980:22) noted that there were 1,370 jury trials across Canada in 1976-77. Various issues concerning the jury are discussed in Law Reform Commission of Canada (1980 and 1982).

[129]Unpublished statistics from the "Disposition Report: Provincial Adult Criminal Court, Jan. 01, 1986 to Dec. 31, 1986," made available by Ministry of Attorney-General, Policy Planning Branch. The percentage cited does not include the vast number of provincial motor vehicle offences. At the time of the study, British Columbia maintained both the Supreme and the County courts; they have since been amalgamated.

[130]*Ibid.*

[131]*Criminal Code*, Part XXVII.

[132]Section 822(4).

[133]Section 813.

[134]*R. v. Century 21 Ramos Inc.* (1987), 32 C.C.C. (3d) 353 (Ont. C.A.).

[135]Section 822, incorporating section 686.

[136]Section 822(2).

[137]Section 686(4).

[138]Section 687(1).

[139]*Hill v. R. (No .2)* (1975), 25 C.C.C. (2d) 6 (S.C.C.).

[140]Section 830(1).

[141]Section 834(1).

[142]*R. v. Giambalvo* (1982), 70 C.C.C. (2d) 324 (Ont. C.A.).

[143]Section 839.

[144]On this point, see *R. v. Loughery* (1992), 73 C.C.C. (3d) 411 (Alta. C.A.). Note that it is also considered an error in law if the trial judge applied the wrong principles in deciding whether a particular sentence should be imposed. For example, the Quebec Court of Appeal allowed the accused's appeal against the imposition of a fine for shoplifting because the trial judge had applied too narrow a test in deciding whether a discharge was appropriate; see *R. v. Moreau* (1992), 76 C.C.C. (3d) 181.

[145]Part XXI.

[146]Section 673.

[147]Section 675(1)(a).

[148]Section 675(1)(b).

[149]Section 676.

[150]See *R. v. Morin* (1992), 76 C.C.C. (3d) 193 (S.C.C.).

[151]The Ontario Court of Appeal has ruled that the right of the Crown to appeal against an acquittal does not offend the *Charter*'s guarantee against double jeopardy (section 11[h] of the *Charter*); *R. v. Morgentaler, Smoling and Scott* (1985), 22 C.C.C. (3d) 353. However, it should be noted that, if the Crown keeps appealing against the acquittal of the accused, then it is possible that the trial court will eventually enter a stay of proceedings on the basis that there has been an abuse of its process; for example, in *R. v. Mitchelson* (1992), 71 C.C.C. (3d) 471 (Man. C.A.), it was ruled that a fourth trial for an accused person charged with a summary conviction offence constituted an abuse of process in all the circumstances of the case.

[152]For a case where the Court of Appeal did overturn the trial judge's findings of fact, see *R. v. J.H.H.P.L.* (1992), 75 C.C.C. (3d) 165 (Man. C.A.).

[153]See, for example, *R. v. P.S.M.* (1992), 77 C.C.C. (3d) 402 (Ont. C.A.).

[154]Section 684.

[155]*R. v. Robinson* (1989), 51 C.C.C. (3d) 452 (Alta.C.A.).

[156]Section 686(1)(a).

[157]Section 686(1)(b). If the Court of Appeal decides that there was a legal error at the accused's trial, this does not mean that he or she is automatically entitled to a new trial or an acquittal. Indeed, as the text indicates, the Court may rule that the error did not result in a "substantial wrong or miscarriage of justice" and refuse to allow the accused's appeal. However, the Court will not take this approach unless the Crown can establish that there is no "possibility that a trial judge would have a reasonable doubt on the admissible evidence." If there is any basis for such a reasonable doubt, then the Court of Appeal should not affirm the conviction of the accused and must order a new trial or enter an acquittal. See,

generally, *Broyles v. The Queen* (1991), 68 C.C.C. (3d) 308 (S.C.C.); *R. v. Wong* (1992), 71 C.C.C. (3d) 490 (B.C.C.A.).

[158]Section 686(2).

[159]Section 686(3).

[160]Section 686(4).

[161]*R. v. Mackenzie* (1993), 78 C.C.C. (3d) 193 (S.C.C.), at 218.

[162]Section 687.

[163]*Hill v. R. (No.2)*, (1975), 25 C.C.C. (2d) 6 (S.C.C.).

[164]Sections 691-695.

[165]A judge of the Court of Appeal dissents when he or she disagrees with the decision of the court in any particular case and provides his or her reasons in a separate opinion.

[166]Section 691(2). This subsection also provides for an appeal (as a matter of right) on a question of law in the situation where the accused was tried jointly with another, was convicted, and his or her conviction was upheld on appeal while his co-accused was acquitted at trial and his or her acquittal was set aside by the Court of Appeal.

[167]Section 693.

[168]Section 690.

[169]*Reference re Regina v. Gorecki (No.2)* (1976), 32 C.C.C. (2d) 135 (Ont. C.A.). An example of the impact of new evidence in prompting a referral to the Court of Appeal is provided by the case of *R. v. Nepoose* (1992), 71 C.C.C. (3d) 419 (Alta. C.A.). In *Nepoose,* after a referral by the Minister of Justice, the Alberta Court of Appeal ordered a new trial primarily on the basis that the police failed to inform either the Crown or the defence at the first trial that they had evidence that might cast serious doubt on the credibility of the principal Crown witness. If the jury had heard this evidence at the first trial, it might have arrived at a different decision.

[170]*R. v. Marshall* (1983), 57 N.S.R. (2d) 286 (N.S. C.A.).

[171]This power has now been removed and the Court of Appeal is now restricted to ordering a new trial where it allows an appeal against acquittal. See section 613(4)(b)(ii).

[172]*Morgentaler v. The Queen*, [1976] 1 S.C.R. 616.

[173]R.S.C. 1985, c. S-26.

[174]*Reference re Milgaard* (1992), 71 C.C.C. (3d) 260 (S.C.C.).

REFERENCES

Atrens. J. 1986. "The Charging Procedure." In Atrens, J., P.T. Burns, and J. Taylor, eds. *Criminal Procedure: Canadian Law and Practice.* Vancouver: Butterworths & Co. (Western Canada). IX-i - IX-51.

_____. 1988. "The Classification of Offences." In J. Atrens, P.T. Burns, and J.P. Taylor, eds. *Criminal Procedure: Canadian Law and Practice.* Vancouver: Butterworths & Co. (Western Canada). I-1, I-32.

Banks, M.A. 1981. "The Evolution of the Ontario Courts 1788-1981." In D.H. Flaherty, ed. *Essays in the History of Canadian Law, Volume II.* Toronto: University of Toronto Press. 492-572.

Bindon, K.M. 1981. "Hudson's Bay Company Law: Adam Thom and the Institution of Order in Rupert's Land 1839-54." In D.H. Flaherty, ed. *Essays in the History of Canadian Law, Volume I.* Toronto: University of Toronto Press. 44-87.

Canadian Centre for Justice Statistics. 1986. *Custodial Remand in Canada — A National Survey.* Ottawa: Statistics Canada.

_____. 1989. *Profile of Courts in Canada,* 1987-88. Ottawa: Statistics Canada.

_____. 1990. *Family Courts in Canada.* Juristat Service Bulletin, Vol 10(3). Ottawa: Statistics Canada.

_____. 1991a. *Court Services in Canada.* Juristat Service Bulletin, Vol 11(3). Ottawa: Statistics Canada.

_____. 1991b. *Government Spending on Justice Services.* Juristat Service Bulletin, Vol. 11(7). Ottawa: Statistics Canada.

Cohen, S.A. 1977. *Due Process of Law: The Canadian System of Criminal Justice.* Toronto: Carswell.

Colvin, E. 1986-87. "The Executive and the Independence of the Judiciary." 51 *Saskatchewan Law Review.* 229-249.

Dickens, B. 1976. "The *Morgentaler* Case: Criminal Process and Abortion Law." 14 *Osgoode Hall Law Journal.* 229-273.

Doob, A.N., and A. Cavoukian. 1977. "The Effect of the Revoking of Bail: *R. v. Demeter.*" 19 *Criminal Law Quarterly.* 196-202.

Ericson, R.V., and P.M. Baranek. 1982. *The Ordering Of Justice: A Study of Accused Persons as Dependants in the Criminal Process.* Toronto: University of Toronto Press.

Ferguson, G. 1991. "Discovery in Criminal Cases." In Atrens, J., P.T. Burns, and J. Taylor, eds. *Criminal Procedure: Canadian Law and Practice.* Vancouver: Butterworths & Co. (Western Canada). XIII-i - XIII-195.

Flaherty, D.H. 1981. "Writing Canadian Legal History: An Introduction." In D.H. Flaherty, ed. *Essays in the History of Canadian Law, Volume I.* Toronto: University of Toronto Press. 3-42.

Friedenberg, E.Z. 1985. "Law in a Cynical Society." In Gibson, D., and J.K. Baldwin, eds. *Law in a Cynical Society: Opinion and Law in the 1980's.* Vancouver: Carswell Legal Publications. 417-426.

Friedland, M. 1965. *Detention Before Trial.* Toronto: University of Toronto Press. XIII-i – XIII-195.

Friedland, M. 1988-89. "Controlling the Administrators of Criminal Justice." 31 *Criminal Law Quarterly*. 280-317.

Gall, G.L. 1983. *The Canadian Legal System*. 2nd. ed. Toronto: Carswell Legal Publications.

Hagan, J. 1984. *The Disreputable Pleasures: Crime and Deviance in Canada*. 2nd. Ed. Toronto: McGraw-Hill Ryerson Ltd.

Hagan, J., and C.P.Morden. 1981. "The Police Decision to Detain: A Study of Legal Labelling and Police Deviance." In C.D. Shearing, ed. *Organizational Police Deviance: Its Structure and Control*. Toronto: Butterworths. 9-28.

Hamilton, K.R. 1990. "Judicial Interim Release." In Atrens, J., P.T. Burns, and J. Taylor, eds. *Criminal Procedure: Canadian Law and Practice*. Vancouver: Butterworths & Co. (Western Canada). IV-i - IV-91.

Hann, R. 1973. *Decision-Making in a Canadian Criminal Court System: A Systems Approach*. Two Volumes. Toronto: Center of Criminology, University of Toronto.

Hett, R. 1973. "Judge Willis and the Court of King's Bench in Upper Canada." LXV *Ontario History*. 19-30.

Hogg, P.W. 1985. *Constitutional Law of Canada*. 2nd ed. Toronto: The Carswell Company Limited.

Holmes, R.D. 1982. "The Scope of Judicial Review of Preliminary Hearings and Committals for Trial." 16 *U.B.C. Law Review*. 257-294.

Kiselbach, D. 1988-89. "Pre-Trial Criminal Procedure: Preventive Detention and the Presumption of Innocence." 31 *Criminal Law Quarterly*. 168-196.

Knafla, L.A., and T.L. Chapman. 1983. "Criminal Justice in Canada: A Comparative Study of the Maritimes and Lower Canada 1760-1812." 21 *Osgoode Hall Law Journal*. 245-274.

Knafla, L.A. 1986. "From Oral to Written Memory: The Common Law Tradition in Western Canada." In L.A. Knafla, ed. *Law and Justice in a New Land. Essays in Western Canadian Legal History*. Toronto: Carswell. 31-77.

Koza, P., and A.N. Doob. 1975a. "The Relationship of Pre-Trial Custody to the Outcome of a Trial." 17 *Criminal Law Quarterly*. 391-400.

_____. 1975b. "Some Empirical Evidence on Judicial Interim Release Proceedings." 17 *Criminal Law Quarterly*. 258-272.

_____. 1977. "Police Attitudes Toward the *Bail Reform Act*." 19 *Criminal Law Quarterly*. 405-414.

Law Reform Commission of Canada. 1974. *Working Paper No. 4: Criminal Procedure: Discovery*. Ottawa: Information Canada.

_____. 1980. *Working Paper No. 27: The Jury in Criminal Trials*. Ottawa: Minister of Supply and Services Canada.

_____. 1982. *Report No. 16: The Jury*. Ottawa: Minister of Supply and Services Canada.

_____. 1984. *Report No. 22: Disclosure by the Prosecution.* Ottawa: Minister of Supply and Services Canada.

_____. 1986. *Working Paper No 54: Classification of Offences.* Ottawa: Law Reform Commission of Canada.

_____. 1987a. *Working Paper No. 55: The Charge Document in Criminal Cases.* Ottawa: Law Reform Commission of Canada.

_____. 1987b. *Working Paper No. 56: Public and Media Access to the Criminal Process.* Ottawa: Law Reform Commission of Canada.

_____. 1988. *Working Paper No. 57: Compelling Appearance, Interim Release and Pre-Trial Detention.* Ottawa: Law Reform Commission of Canada.

_____. 1989. *Working Paper No. 59: Toward a Unified Criminal Court.* Ottawa: Law Reform Commission of Canada.

Lederman, W.R. 1987. "Judicial Independence and Court Reforms in Canada for the 1990's." 12 *Queen's Law Journal.* 385-398.

MacKaay, E. 1976. *The Paths of Justice: A Study of the Operation of the Criminal Courts in Montreal.* Montreal: Groupe de Recherche en Jurimetrie, Universite de Montreal.

McWilliams, P.K. 1991. *Canadian Criminal Evidence.* 3rd. ed. Aurora, Ontario: Canada Law Book Inc.

Madden, P., and C. Carey. 1982. Bail Verification and Supervision in Ontario. Toronto: Ontario Ministry of Correctional Services.

Morris, R. 1981. "Toronto Bail Program." 25 *International Journal of Offender Therapy and Comparative Criminology.* 156-167.

Ontario, Ministry of the Attorney-General. No Date. *Court Reform in Ontario.* Toronto: Ministry of the Attorney-General.

Ouimet, R. (Chairman). 1969. *Report of the Canadian Committee on Corrections — Toward Unity: Criminal Justice and Corrections.* Ottawa: Information Canada.

Pavlich, D. 1982. "Law of Arrest." In J. Atrens, P.T. Burns, and J.P. Taylor, eds. *Criminal Procedure: Canadian Law and Practice.* Vancouver, Butterworths & Co. (Western Canada). III-1 to III-211.

Pink, J.E., and D. Perrier. 1988. *From Crime to Punishment: An Introduction to the Criminal Law System.* Toronto: Carswell.

Proulx, M. 1983. "The Presence of the Accused at Trial." 25 *Criminal Law Quarterly.* 179-205.

Risk, R.C.B. 1981. "The Law and the Economy in Mid-Nineteenth-Century Ontario: A perspective." In D.H. Flaherty, ed. *Essays in the History of Canadian Law, Volume I.* Toronto: University of Toronto Press. 88-131.

Rosenthal, P. 1990-91. "Crown Election Offences and the Charter." 33 *Criminal Law Quarterly.* 84-126.

Russell, P.H. 1987. *The Judiciary in Canada: The Third Branch of Government.* Toronto: McGraw-Hill Ryerson Ltd.

Salhany, R.E. 1989. *Canadian Criminal Procedure, Fifth Edition*. Aurora, Ont.: Canada Law Book Inc.

Shetreet, S. 1979. "The Administration of Justice: Practical Problems, Value Conflicts and Changing Concepts." *13 U.B.C. Law Review*. 52-80.

Sinclair, W.R. 1988-89. "Structural Reform: The Creation of Provincial Supreme Courts: A View from Alberta." 31 *Criminal Law Quarterly*. 43-54.

Statistics Canada. 1985. "Manpower, Resources and Costs of Courts and Criminal Prosecutions in Canada 1983-84." 5(2) *Juristat Service Bulletin*. 1-6.

Stenning, P.C. 1986. *Appearing for the Crown: A Legal and Historical Review of Criminal Prosecutorial Authority in Canada*. Cowansville, Que.: Brown Legal Publications.

Tardi, G. 1992. *The Legal Framework of Government: A Canadian Guide*. Aurora, Ontario: Canada Law Book.

Taylor, J.P., and F.M. Irvine. 1986. "The Preliminary Inquiry and the Election." In Atrens, J., P.T. Burns, and J. Taylor, eds. *Criminal Procedure: Canadian Law and Practice*. Vancouver: Butterworths & Co. (Western Canada). XIV-i - XIV-52.

Trotter, G.T. 1987-88. "Fundamental Justice and the Approval of Sureties by the Crown." 30 *Criminal Law Quarterly*. 238-250.

Waddams, S.M. 1987. *Introduction to the Study of Law*. 3rd. ed. Toronto: Carswell.

Wheeler, G. 1987. "The Police, the Crowns and the Courts: Who's Running the Show?" (February 1987) *Canadian Lawyer*. 27-31.

Williams, D.C. 1962 and 1963. "The Dawn of Law on the Prairies." 26 and 28 *Saskatchewan Bar Review*. (vol. 26) 126-133; (vol. 28) 17-27, 63-69.

Williams, D.C. 1963, 1964, 1965 and 1966. "Law and Institutions in the North West Territories (1869-1905)." 28, 29, 30, and 31 *Saskatchewan Bar Review*. (vol. 28) 109-118; (vol. 29) 83-101; (vol. 30) 51-66; (vol. 31) 1-26, 137-161.

Williams, D.R. "The Administration of Criminal and Civil Justice in the Mining Camps and Frontier Communities of British Columbia." In L.A. Knafla, ed. *Law and Justice in a New Land. Essays in Western Canadian Legal History*. Toronto: Carswell. 215-232.

7 CURRENT ISSUES CONCERNING THE COURT PROCESS

This chapter addresses four of the current issues that are frequently raised in connection with the operation of the court process in Canada: (1) the right to counsel and legal representation in court; (2) the right to a trial within a reasonable time; (3) prosecutorial discretion; and (4) plea bargaining. Each of these issues raises some fundamental questions about the degree to which the criminal courts are capable of ensuring that each accused person is treated in accordance with the rights enshrined in the *Canadian Charter of Rights and Freedoms.*

THE RIGHT TO COUNSEL AND LEGAL REPRESENTATION IN COURT

The immensely complex structure of the court process, together with the intricate set of procedural and evidential rules that govern the conduct of a criminal trial, place the accused person at a considerable disadvantage vis-à-vis the professional lawyer who conducts the prosecution on behalf of the Crown. It is not surprising that considerable emphasis has been placed upon the need to ensure that accused persons are treated with "due process of law" by providing them with legal representation when they appear in court. Indeed, Greenspan (1985:207) has contended that "due process without the right to counsel is as empty as democracy without free elections."

It has often been suggested that the right to counsel is an essential component of a criminal court system that is based on an adversarial approach to matters of justice. As a former chief justice of British Columbia remarked in a case before the Court of Appeal:

> Our criminal justice system is administered under the adversary system; that is to say, a system where when a conflict arises between a citizen and the state the two are to be regarded as adversaries. The conflict is to be resolved by fighting it out according to fixed, sometimes rather arbitrary, rules. The tribunal trying the matter settles the dispute on the basis of only such evidence as the contestants choose to present.[1]

The chief justice went on to point out that the rules of procedure and evidence employed in a criminal trial are so complex that they can only be understood after a long period of training and experience. It is for this reason, he said, that the Crown employs counsel who are well versed in the law and are knowledgeable about the techniques of advocacy. Prosecutors also have the resources of both the government and the police to support them in presenting their cases. It would be unrealistic to expect the defendant in a criminal case to be able to compete with Crown counsel if he or she is unrepresented by a lawyer (Griffiths, Cousineau, and Verdun-Jones, 1980:217).

The Right to Counsel

A number of provisions in both the *Charter* and the *Criminal Code* have a direct bearing on the right to counsel (Friedland, 1989:297-301). Section 10(b) of the *Charter*, as we saw in Chapter 4, guarantees a person who has been arrested or detained the right to "retain and instruct counsel without delay and the right to be informed of that right." Furthermore, the Supreme Court of Canada has ruled in *Brydges*[2] that an accused person's right to counsel under section 10(b) of the *Charter* places a duty on the police to inform those persons who have been detained and who express a concern that they cannot afford a lawyer of their right to apply for legal aid (Elman, 1990; Michalyshin, 1990).

Section 10(b) of the *Charter*, however, does not apply specifically to the representation of an accused person in the courtroom setting. Section 11(d) of the *Charter*, on the other hand, is of considerable relevance to the trial situation since it protects the right to a "fair and public hearing by an independent and impartial tribunal." It can well be argued that a necessary component of a "fair hearing" is that an accused person should be represented by legal counsel of his or her choice[3] (Osborne, 1986). Similarly, section 7 ensures that accused persons may not be deprived of their right to life, liberty, and security of the person except in accordance with the fundamental principles of justice, which may include the right to counsel during the trial process.

In addition, the *Criminal Code*[4] provides that an "accused is entitled, after the close of the case for the prosecution, to make full answer and defence personally or by counsel." Thus the courts have ruled that a lawyer cannot be forced upon an unwilling defendant[5] and that a court cannot proceed with a trial where the accused's lawyer fails to show up in court.[6] Furthermore, it has been held that, where the accused is unrepresented, the trial judge has a special duty to ensure that there is a fair hearing.[7] If an accused person is not granted his or her right to counsel at trial, then a new trial may be ordered by the appropriate appeal court (Egleston, 1990:XIX-58).

An important provision of the *Code*[8] empowers the Provincial Court of Appeal, or a judge of that court, to assign counsel to act on behalf of a defendant who is involved in an appeal, "where, in the opinion of the court or judge, it appears desirable in the interests of justice that the accused should have legal aid and where it appears that the accused has not sufficient means to obtain aid" (Epstein, 1988; MacFarlane, 1990:463-465; Moon, 1989). This statutory provision applies only to appeals to the Court of Appeal, and the question arises whether a court may use its inherent jurisdiction to appoint counsel for an indigent defendant at the trial stage.

A considerable body of case law supports the view that trial courts may have a residual power to assign counsel to act on behalf of an accused person who lacks the means to engage counsel.[9] Two major cases addressed this issue prior to the enactment of the *Charter*. In *White* (1976),[10] a judge of the Supreme Court of Alberta ruled that there may be certain exceptional circumstances in which a trial court has the power to assign counsel to a defendant. According to this decision, the factors that would need to be taken into account in deciding whether counsel should be assigned might include the financial position and educational level of the accused, the complexity of the case, and the possibility that the accused may be imprisoned if convicted (see Mossman, 1985:25). The Court also stated that if there is a possibility that the relevant legal aid authority may be willing to grant a legal aid certificate, then there should be an adjournment to permit the accused to apply to the authority in question. However, note that the court in this case did not go so far as to suggest that *all* indigent accused are entitled to have counsel appointed for them, nor did it express the view that there can never be a fair trial where the accused is unrepresented.

The second pre-*Charter* case was *Ewing and Kearney*,[11] in which the British Columbia Court of Appeal ruled that indigent accused persons were not entitled to have counsel appointed for them, *as a general rule*. However, at least one of the judges suggested that the duty of the trial judge to ensure that there was a fair trial might require the appointment of counsel in special circumstances, for example, where the case is exceedingly complex (Egleston, 1990:XIX-11).

Court decisions made after the enactment of the *Charter* have consolidated the earlier case law and have suggested that the residual power of the trial courts to appoint counsel for an indigent accused is enshrined in sections 7 and 11(d) of the *Charter*. For example, the first major decision that reflects this trend is the case of *Deutsch* (1986).[12] Craig J. of the Ontario Divisional Court clearly rejected the contention that the *Charter* had entrenched a general "right to funded counsel." Indeed, he said:

> ...the right to a funded counsel has not been entrenched by s.7 and/or s.11(d) of the *Charter*. With the exception of the language provisions, most of the rights guaranteed by the *Charter* are expressed in negative terms in the sense that they require that the state refrain from certain activities. To impose a constitutionally entrenched positive duty on the government to expend public funds on the defence of persons accused of crimes would require a specific guarantee in express language.

However, he also stated that there may be certain exceptional cases in which legal counsel must be appointed by the court if the accused is to be accorded a fair trial.

> Pursuant to s. 7 of the *Charter,* the accused has an entrenched right not to be deprived of his or her liberty except in accordance with the principles of fundamental justice. Also pursuant to s. 11(d), he [or she] has an entrenched right to a "fair and public hearing..." The right to fundamental justice and a fair public hearing includes the right to a fair trial. There may be rare cases where legal aid is denied to an accused person facing trial, but where the trial judge is satisfied that, because of the seriousness and complexity of the case, the accused cannot receive a fair trial without counsel. In such a case it seems to follow that there is an entrenched right to funded counsel under the *Charter*.[13]

A number of appellate courts have built on this approach and have added further pieces to the emerging puzzle. In the case of *Rowbotham* (1988),[14] the Ontario Court of Appeal made the point that those who have the funds to pay for a lawyer are not entitled to ask the state to pay for their defence.

As a matter of common sense, an accused who is able to pay the costs of his or her defence is not entitled to take the position that he or she will not use personal funds, but still to require Legal Aid to bear the cost of his or her defence. A person who has the means to pay the costs of his or her defence but refuses to retain counsel may properly be considered to have chosen to defend himself or herself.[15]

What is the situation where the accused clearly lacks the funds to pay for a lawyer? The Ontario Court of Appeal took the view that the *Charter* does not expressly enshrine the right of an indigent accused to be provided with state-funded counsel because those who drafted it assumed that the existing legal aid systems across the country were adequate to provide counsel to all those accused persons who were facing serious charges but were unable to afford to hire a lawyer. However, the Court went on to state that:

> ...*in cases not falling within provincial legal aid plans,* ss. 7 and 11(d) of the Charter, which guarantee an accused a fair trial in accordance with the principles of fundamental justice, require funded counsel to be provided if the accused wishes counsel, but cannot pay a lawyer, and representation of the accused is essential to a fair trial.[16]

In *Robinson* (1989),[17] the Alberta Court of Appeal also held that, although the *Criminal Code* gave an appellate court the discretion to order that an indigent accused be provided with funded counsel, there was no absolute right to funded counsel nor was the accused entitled to be provided with the transcripts of the trial at state expense. Furthermore, the Court emphasized that the *Charter* cannot be interpreted in such a manner as to provide an unqualified right to state-funded counsel either at trial or on appeal, whether it be as a matter of fundamental justice (under section 7) or as part of the guarantee to a fair trial (under section 11[d]).

A significant question is whether the Supreme Court of Canada's decision in the *Brydges* case has had any impact on the right to counsel at trial. The *Brydges* case apparently left open the question of whether the accused had an absolute constitutional right to state-funded counsel.[18] Nevertheless, some defence lawyers tried to contend that the *Brydges* case had broadened the scope of the right to counsel at trial. However, in *Prosper* (1992),[19] the Appeal Division of the Nova Scotia Court of Appeal held that the *Brydges* case had *not* changed the pre-existing principle that, while section 10(b) of the *Charter* ensures that accused persons have a right to be informed as to the availability of legal aid, it does not provide them with a constitutional right to have a state-funded lawyer appointed to handle their case. According to the Nova Scotia court, the *Brydges* case is only authority for the principle that, in order to fulfill their duty under section 10(b) of the *Charter* to grant a detained person a reasonable opportunity to exercise his or her right to retain and instruct counsel, the police must inform the accused of the existence of legal aid and duty counsel — where such programs exist.

Even if an accused person receives legal aid and a lawyer is provided, the Legal Aid Plan may impose a limit on the funding earmarked for the case. Does the setting of such a limit infringe the accused's right to counsel under the *Charter*? The Nova Scotia Court of Appeal has ruled that placing such limits on funding does *not* constitute a denial of the accused's *Charter* rights.[20] In similar vein, this Nova Scotia Court of Appeal has held that an accused person is not entitled, under the *Charter*, to demand that the Legal Aid Plan appoint the counsel of the accused's choice.[21] As Chipman J.A. stated:

> In order to render the *Charter* rights meaningful, I believe counsel provided must be sufficiently qualified to deal with the matter at issue with a reasonable degree of skill. Again, however, the case-law on the *Charter* aspect of this appeal does not go so far as to give the indigent a right of choice beyond those counsel willing to serve within the constraints of the Legal Aid Programme...to extend the *Charter* right to the point contended for by the appellant could introduce chaos into the administration of justice.[22]

Where do we now stand insofar as the right to counsel at trial is concerned? MacFarlane (1990:463) has summarized the situation:

> ...it is clear that the *Charter of Rights and Freedoms* does not entrench a general right to a publicly funded trial, irrespective of circumstances. Put at its highest, where an accused has been denied legal aid and the trial judge is satisfied that (a) the accused cannot afford a lawyer and (b) the nature of the case is such that the accused cannot have a fair hearing without counsel, the court is entitled to grant a remedy to the accused by directing the appointment of counsel...Thus, at the trial level, the right to counsel...*is inextricably linked to the facts of the*

case and the background of the accused. It is clearly not a *general right* applicable to all cases, irrespective of circumstances.

It remains to be seen whether, in the future, the Supreme Court of Canada will be willing to give a broader interpretation of the right to a fair trial. Nevertheless, the present position is that, while accused persons have an absolute right to counsel, they do not have the absolute right to have counsel appointed for them and paid for by government funds.[23]

Legal Aid in the Criminal Courts

In order to ensure that the poorest members of the community are not denied access to counsel because of lack of funds, legal aid programs have been established across Canada (Canadian Centre for Justice Statistics, 1991).

The first comprehensive legal aid system was introduced in Ontario in 1967 (Wilkins, 1975; Zemans, 1986:47). Today, legal aid plans are based on provincial and territorial legislation and are administered independently of government departments, although the federal government makes substantial contributions to the plans (Canadian Centre for Justice Statistics, 1992:2).[24] In 1990-91, legal aid plans received $398 million to provide legal services across Canada. The federal, provincial, and territorial governments contribute the lion's share of funding for legal aid (84%). More specifically, $333.8 million was provided by governments; $42.2 million (11%) from the legal profession (including the interest earned by lawyers' trust accounts in some provinces); $13.3 million (or 3%) from clients' contributions; and $9.1 million (2%) from various other sources (Canadian Centre for Justice Statistics, 1992:3).

In recent years, the costs of providing legal aid have sky-rocketed. In 1987-88, the total cost of the various legal aid plans in Canada was $258.7 million (Canadian Centre for Justice Statistics, 1989:7). Since 1987, spending on legal aid has consistently increased at a pace well above the rate of inflation (Canadian Centre for Justice Statistics, 1992:5). In 1990-91, total expenditures were $412 million, which represented a massive 21% increase over the previous year (Canadian Centre for Justice Statistics, 1992:5). The federal government is now paying a smaller percentage of the overall bill for legal aid, thus placing the major burden on the provincial and territorial governments (Canadian Centre for Justice Statistics, 1992:4-5). At a time when provincial and territorial governments are struggling with deficits and accumulated debts, it is highly unlikely that legal aid plans will continue to receive the significant increases that they have enjoyed in the recent past. This expected crisis in funding during the next few years will constitute one of the most profound challenges that legal aid plans have been forced to confront since they were introduced to Canada in the 1960s (Cawley, 1991).

Legal aid agencies provide a range of services, from legal representation to referral and information services. These services cover not only the criminal law, but also various areas of civil law (such as family law). In 1990-91, almost 860,000 applications for legal aid were approved in Canada (about 88% of the total number of applications received). In 1990-91, about 54% of the total expenditures on legal aid went to criminal matters and 46% to civil matters (Canadian Centre for Justice Statistics, 1992:6).

As far as criminal cases are concerned, legal aid is generally provided for all indictable offences and for summary conviction offences where there is a reasonable chance that the accused will go to jail or will lose his or her livelihood (for example, through the revocation of a driving licence).[25] However, it should be emphasized that, even if accused persons should qualify in terms of these general criteria of eligibility, they will not be granted legal aid unless they also meet certain financial requirements, designed to limit the award of legal aid to the most needy citizens. These requirements vary from province to province. However, in general, applicants will not be eligible to receive legal aid unless they are either receiving social assistance or their family incomes are at or below social assistance levels (Canadian Centre for Justice Statistics, 1992:8; Hutchison and Marks, 1991). An evaluation conducted in British Columbia suggests that, in that province at least, only the most impoverished members of the community were likely to qualify (Brantingham and Brantingham, 1984:171; Cormier, 1990; Morrison, 1990).

Legal aid services are not provided in a uniform manner across Canada. There are three models for delivering such services across the country (Canadian Centre for Justice Statistics, 1992:3). In New Brunswick, Alberta, and the Yukon, legal aid services are provided by private lawyers on a fee-for-service basis with the legal aid plan bearing all or most of the costs; this model, which gives each client the choice as to which lawyer will represent him or her, is known as the "judicare model." On the other hand, in Prince Edward Island, Nova Scotia, and Saskatchewan, legal aid is provided through a "staff system" in which staff lawyers are employed directly by the legal aid plan.[26] In this system, the individual client does not have the opportunity to choose his or her lawyer.[27] This system is based on the so-called "public defender" model. In Newfoundland, Quebec, Ontario, Manitoba, British Columbia, and the Northwest Territories, the judicare and public defender models are combined in one system for the delivery of legal aid. In this combined model, legal services are provided by both staff lawyers and private lawyers on a fee-for-service basis. Taking Canada as a whole, about 60% of the total amount expended on legal aid in 1990-91 went to private law firms (Canadian Centre for Justice Statistics, 1992:9).

What are the comparative advantages of the judicare and public defender models for delivering legal aid services? According to Burns and Reid (1981:412-414), the advantages of the judicare system include the following:

- the client has the choice of lawyer;
- the ordinary lawyer-client relationship that exists in non-legal aid cases is extended to the poor in the judicare system;
- the judicare lawyer is independent and owes a duty only to the client and the court;
- the judicare system is better equipped to deal with rural and remote areas because it is decentralized in nature; and
- the judicare system is no more costly than the public defender system.

On the other hand, according to Burns and Reid (1981:414-416), the advantages of the public defender system include the following:

- public defenders are specialists in their particular area of law;
- they are less costly than judicare lawyers;
- the public defender system is more efficient because it is centralized;
- public defenders become spokespeople for the poor; and
- since public defenders are salaried they do not have any incentive to adopt tactics that are in their own financial interest rather than in the interests of their clients.

Without the necessary research, it is not possible to evaluate all of the relative claims made in support of one system or the other. However, a few studies have attempted to evaluate the two systems in order to determine their relative cost efficiency and whether there are any differences in the results achieved by lawyers in the two systems.

During the 1980s, there were two major studies of the costs of the public defender and judicare systems. An evaluation, over three years, of a relatively small public defender program in a suburb of Vancouver (Burnaby) found that there was very little difference between the costs of services provided by the public defender system and the costs of services delivered by private lawyers on a fee-for-service basis (Brantingham and Burns, 1981). However, an evaluation conducted in the province of Quebec by the Commission des Services Juridiques indicated that the public defender model was more cost effective than the judicare system (Zemans, 1986:54). The reason underlying the difference in the outcome of these studies seems to lie in the different nature of the public defender programs evaluated. The B.C. study was based on a small public defender project employing only three lawyers and a paralegal, and it dealt almost exclusively with criminal cases. The Quebec study, on the other hand, was concerned with both civil and criminal legal aid cases and involved a greater number of lawyers, thereby permitting economies of scale.

While this research is equivocal about the relative cost efficiency of the two systems, it is interesting to note that, insofar as criminal cases are concerned, the evaluation of the B.C. public defender project did indicate that there were significant differences between the results obtained by public defenders and private lawyers operating on a fee-for-service basis. Brantingham (1985) found that there were no significant differences between public defenders and private lawyers insofar as findings of guilt or innocence were concerned. However, it was found that there were strong differences in the *sentencing outcomes* obtained by private lawyers and public defenders. Convicted clients of the public defenders were much less likely to be incarcerated (24.5%) than the clients of the private lawyers (40.4%), although there were no major differences in the length of the jail terms or the size of the fines imposed on the two groups. The reason for the differences in the incarceration rates was to be found in "differences in discussion patterns between defence counsel and Crown counsel" (Brantingham, 1985:76). Clients of the private lawyers received similar sentences whether or not discussions were held with the Crown (about 40% of the sentences involved imprisonment). On the other hand, when public defenders had discussions with the Crown their clients were much less likely to be imprisoned (17%). However, when no such discussions occurred, the incarceration rates of clients of the public defenders were similar to those of the clients of the private lawyers (36% versus 40%, respectively). It seems that the public defenders found it relatively easy to discuss cases with the Crown because they were in daily contact with the Crown counsel. Although this study might well suggest that the public defender system may be more effective in terms of achieving a more satisfactory sentencing outcome, it also raises serious questions about the desirability of a system that appears to deny many of the benefits of plea bargaining to private lawyers while offering such benefits to the public defender lawyers who happen to interact frequently with Crown counsel.

A more recent comparison of the judicare and public defender models of delivering legal aid in British Columbia (Ministry of the Attorney-General [B.C.], 1991) concluded that the "staff system" was considerably more cost-efficient than its judicare counterpart. The report (1991:i) suggested that "the annual cost of a staff model large enough to handle 95% of Young Offender, Adult Summary Conviction, Family, and Immigration cases in the Vancouver area is projected to be $6.3 [million]," while the "cost of providing equivalent service through the tariff system is estimated at $11.4 [million]." It was suggested that the average cost for a staff lawyer to handle a case would be $400, whereas under the judicare system, it would be closer to $1,000. The report (1991:ii) also suggested that adoption of the staff model would result in a significant decrease in the time spent on each case because there would be a "greater degree of specialization, more negotiated settlements, fewer trials, and less travel time." Of course, this kind of approach appears oriented more toward bureaucratic considerations of efficiency than to the best interests of the individual client and may be vulnerable to criticism on that score.

As far as case outcome is concerned, the report (1991:ii) found that the rate of guilty verdicts was similar for both staff and judicare lawyers; however, staff lawyers were more likely to plead their clients guilty and the judicare lawyers were more likely to go to trial. The clients of judicare lawyers were more likely to go to prison, while the clients of staff lawyers were more likely to be sentenced to probation, fines, or other dispositions. Overall, the report took the view that the quality of the service provided by staff lawyers was equivalent, or superior, to that provided by judicare lawyers. However, private lawyers in British Columbia have sharply criticized the conclusions drawn in the report (Zapf, 1992), and it remains to be seen whether plans to place a much greater degree of reliance on staff lawyers will be implemented in the province in the years ahead. Nevertheless, given the present financial problems facing legal aid systems in Canada, it is reasonable to assume that, if the staff lawyer system is perceived to be more cost-efficient, it will swiftly become the dominant model for delivery of legal aid services.

Renner and Warner (1981) addressed the complex question of whether the presence or absence of legal representation had any impact on the outcome of a criminal case. They found that accused persons who pleaded guilty were *less* likely to have a lawyer (34%) than those who pleaded not guilty (61%). However, there were no significant differences in the conviction rates of those accused persons who pleaded not guilty. On the other hand, there were significant differences in the treatment of represented and unrepresented defendants at the sentencing stage. Even when the variables of plea and prior record were controlled, it was found that first offenders who were legally represented and pleaded guilty to summary charges were more likely to receive more lenient treatment, such as a discharge or a suspended sentence (64%), than persons who appeared in court without a lawyer (20%) (Renner and Warner, 1981:69).

The researchers also investigated whether there were any differences in the outcome of cases in which the accused was represented by a private lawyer as opposed to a legal aid lawyer. They found that private lawyers were more successful in obtaining an acquittal for their clients than were legal aid lawyers.[28] Privately represented defendants were found guilty in 54% of their trials while the equivalent figure for defendants represented by legal aid lawyers was 72% (Renner and Warner, 1981:70). As far as sentencing was concerned, defendants represented by legal aid lawyers were more likely to receive punitive sentences in relation to summary conviction offences (although this did not apply in the case of indictable offences). Privately represented first offenders were more likely to receive a discharge (50%) than legal-aid-represented first offenders (15%) (Renner and Warner, 1981:71). In a separate article, Warner and Renner (1981:91) note that 54% of all defendants in their study were unrepresented and state that "this observation alone calls into serious question the reality of the adversary model of justice." They conclude (1981:91) that "most defendants, who are largely the poor and marginal, are not represented and do not experience the benefits of a legal adversary system."

Carrington and Moyer (1990) examined the impact of legal representation on the outcome of cases decided in the juvenile courts of five major Canadian cities in 1981 (that is, before the implementation of the *Young Offenders Act* in 1984). In most courts, the presence of a lawyer increased the likelihood of a not guilty plea, and it was found that private lawyers were more likely than public defenders or duty counsel to advise their clients to enter such a plea (Carrington and Moyer, 1990:633).

In addition to appointing lawyers to represent individual accused persons, both the judicare and public defender systems generally provide duty counsel to assist in the representation of accused persons, particularly before they make their first appearance in court. Duty counsel are either private lawyers paid by the legal aid plan or staff lawyers (if the province concerned is based on the public defender model) who give summary advice primarily to those who are held in custody. They may ensure that the accused applies for legal aid and that bail is applied for where appropriate. They may also represent the accused at the sentencing hearing if the latter should plead guilty on first appearance in court. The provision of duty counsel is an extremely cost effective method of offering legal services to a large number of clients and is particulary useful as a means of bringing legal advice to those accused who are held in custody by the police prior to their first appearance in court. However, it is not a system that is able to provide close personal attention to the problems of individual clients. Indeed, in their interviews of 101 defendants in an Ontario municipal jurisdiction, Ericson and Baranek (1982:85) found that most of their subjects talked negatively of duty counsel because of their being simultaneously involved in a large number of cases. However, Ericson and Baranek (1982:201) also point out that duty counsel are so over-burdened with cases that it is not surprising that they cannot gain a complete understanding of the client's circumstances.

In addition to making the services of duty counsel available, most Canadian jurisdictions provide funding for various organizations to offer the services of courtworkers to accused persons caught up in the criminal court process (Brantingham and Brantingham, 1984:65). Courtworkers help accused persons understand the court process and ensure that they are aware of their legal rights and their entitlement to apply for legal aid. Courtworkers may also be called upon to provide information to the court, particularly on matters relevant to sentencing. Among the organizations that may provide services primarily (but by no means exclusively) to clients from specific "minority groups" are the Elizabeth Fry Society and various Native courtworker organizations (such as the Native Courtworker and Counselling Association of British Columbia and the Native Counselling Services of Alberta). One organization that may provide courtworker services on a more general basis in the provincial courts is the Salvation Army.

One of the most significant of the recent developments in the provision of legal aid services is the emergence of paralegals — non-lawyers who provide various legal services to low-income persons under the supervision of lawyers (Zemans, 1986:57). They may offer services directly to clients or may operate in a support role to lawyers in a community legal aid clinic setting. The emergence of paralegals as important contributors to the system for delivering legal services to the poor may well permit legal aid authorities to meet some of the ever-increasing demand for such services at a time when governments are implementing policies of financial restraint. Indeed, paralegals not only provide a cost-effective service but also tend to be particularly responsive to the needs of the local community (Zemans, 1986:61).

The Nature and Extent of Legal Representation in the Criminal Courts

Canadian research shows that most defendants in a criminal case obtain legal representation where the charge is indictable, but that a significant proportion are unrepresented when the charge relates to a summary conviction offence. For example, in a study of a Toronto Provincial Court, Taman (1975) found that only 48% of those persons charged with summary offences were represented, while 72% of those charged with indictable offences did enjoy the services of legal counsel. In a more comprehensive study, Renner and Warner (1981) studied defendants appearing before three magistrates' courts and two county courts in Halifax. They found (1981:69) that 90% of the defendants charged with indictable offences were represented while a majority of persons facing summary conviction charges were unrepresented (59%).

Carrington and Moyer (1992) found large variations in the nature and extent of legal representation for young persons tried in 1981 under the old *Juvenile Delinquents Act* in five major Canadian cities. In Montreal and Toronto, between 92% and 99% of accused juveniles had some kind of legal representation at some stage of the court proceedings, while in Edmonton and Vancouver more than 70% were represented at some phase of the process. In Winnipeg, however, less than half of the accused were represented. In Montreal, most juveniles were provided with staff lawyers, while in Toronto and Edmonton, most accused were represented by duty counsel. In Winnipeg and Vancouver, however, most juveniles appeared in court with private lawyers (Carrington and Moyer, 1992:57). However, these findings are now of historical interest only since the *Young Offenders Act*[29] mandates the appointment of counsel for any young person who requests it when appearing in Youth Court.

Ericson and Baranek (1982) have presented some fascinating data as to the reasons why defendants either do or do not decide to seek the assistance of legal counsel. According to Ericson and Baranek, from the point of view of an accused person:

> The potential benefits of engaging a lawyer include his or her superior specialist and "recipe" knowledge and his or her access to other criminal control agents to negotiate settlements. The potential costs include the obvious financial burden if a private lawyer is chosen and the loss of control over decision-making (1982:76).

Three-quarters of the 101 accused, whom they interviewed, decided to engage a lawyer (1982:76). Of those who did not retain counsel, 17 of the 25 said that they had made this decision because they felt that a lawyer would be of no benefit in influencing the outcome of the case (1982:79). Such a decision is understandable when relatively minor charges are involved, since it will probably cost defendants more to invoke their rights in such circumstances than it would to plead guilty at the earliest opportunity (1982:79). Eleven of the accused who were interviewed said that they could not afford a lawyer (1982:80), a finding that raises serious questions about the extent to which legal aid was available to those who needed it.

Of those who were represented by lawyers, 32 retained private lawyers, 29 retained legal aid lawyers, and 12 retained duty counsel (Ericson and Baranek, 1982:84). What were the reasons given for deciding to retain a lawyer? Of the 75 interviewees who retained a lawyer, 54 felt that there was some "strategic advantage" in having a lawyer, for example, that a lawyer could obtain a more lenient disposition of the case than the accused could on his or her own (Ericson and

Baranek, 1982:81). According to the researchers, lawyers were considered to be in possession of two major assets that gave them a "strategic advantage" in the criminal court system: "superior knowledge" and "superior credibility" in the eyes of the judge and other criminal justice officials (Ericson and Baranek, 1982:82).

Paradoxically, Ericson and Baranek suggest that obtaining the services of a lawyer does not put accused persons in a position where they have much of an opportunity to influence the course of events in the criminal trial process. In essence, they are placed in a dependent position with little grasp of what is taking place around them. Most defendants, particularly those without extensive prior experience of the criminal justice system, find it very difficult to understand what is happening to them in the courtroom. Ericson and Baranek suggest:

> The regular courtroom participants, who are well versed in the legal rhetoric used to orchestrate the rules, have a monopoly on use of them. The accused seldom acquires this knowledge in time. His inability to participate reaffirms his dependent status. As a result, his definitions and interpretations are given less acknowledgment (1982:193).

Accused persons lack the specialist knowledge to evaluate the performance of their lawyer in court and, furthermore, they are excluded from the discussions that are frequently held between Crown and defence counsel and may result in the arrangement of a so-called "plea bargain" (Ericson and Baranek, 1982:77). Indeed, according to Ericson and Baranek (1982:99), the lawyer has a "godfather" quality to his or her role vis-à-vis the defendant in a criminal case. This quality is particularly marked where the defendant is making critical decisions because the lawyer often presents the "choices" open to the accused in terms of "an offer you can't refuse." Ericson and Baranek found, in this respect, that many accused persons felt that their lawyer was making the really critical decisions as to the conduct of their case. For example, the majority of accused persons who had the option to elect the mode of their trial believed that this critical decision was made by their lawyer rather than by themselves (Ericson and Baranek, 1982:101). Certainly, the perspective advanced by Ericson and Baranek raises some provocative questions as to the real nature of the adversarial system in the criminal trial process.

THE RIGHT TO A TRIAL WITHIN A REASONABLE TIME

Solomon (1983:51) states that, in the decade before the enactment of the *Canadian Charter of Rights and Freedoms* in 1982, there was "growing public concern about the 'crisis of the courts,' as manifested by congestion, backlogs, and delays in the processing of criminal cases." There is no doubt that excessive court delays may impose harsh costs, in human terms, on defendants, victims, and witnesses alike (Feeley, 1979), and considerable concern has been expressed as to the need for governments to take some action to remedy this problem (Osborne, 1980; Solomon, 1983; Walker, 1984; Wilson, 1987; Zuber, 1987).

Significantly, section 11(b) of the *Charter* now guarantees the right of an accused person to "be tried within a reasonable time" (Levesque, 1988). This important right, which was not recognized in Canadian jurisprudence prior to the enactment of the *Charter* in 1982, has brought an added urgency to the task of coping with court delays (Code, 1992). Indeed, section 11(b) has already had a substantial impact on the day-to-day functioning of the criminal courts in Canada; judges have stayed a considerable number of charges against defendants in criminal cases owing to unreasonable delay (Walker, 1984:83), and this, in turn, has caused prosecutors to place greater emphasis on processing their cases more expeditiously.

Section 11(b) of the *Charter* deals with the delay between *the laying of the charge* and *the time that a person is tried*.[30] The reason for this approach is that a person's liberty and security are not impinged upon until a charge is laid against him or her.[31] However, it may be open to an accused person who feels that he or she has been prejudiced by the long time that it has taken the police to lay charges to argue that their rights to a fair trial under sections 7 and 11(d) of the *Charter* have been infringed or that they are entitled to a remedy for abuse of process (MacIntosh, 1991). However, the mere length of the delay would not be the critical issue in an argument under sections 7 and 11(d) or in relation to abuse of process; instead, it must be shown that the effect of the delay was to bring about a situation in which the accused could not obtain a fair trial. It is difficult to prove such prejudice and, in general, the courts have not been willing to grant a remedy purely because of long pre-charge delays.[32] This is important because, for example, many victims of sexual abuse do not bring their cases to court until many years after the alleged incidents took place, and a long delay between these incidents and the laying of charges should not automatically be a reason to deny such victims of the opportunity to gain justice in the courts.[33] In one case,[34] it was held that even a 30-year delay in laying charges involving various sexual offences against children did not, *per se*, violate the accused's rights under the *Charter*. The delay would only constitute such a violation where the accused could prove that the delay had actually rendered it impossible for him or her to have a fair trial.

For the purposes of section 11(d), what is considered to be a "reasonable time" between the laying of a charge and the holding of the accused's trial? The courts will decide this issue in light of the particular circumstances of each case — there is no arbitrary period for completion of all cases in the court process. However, the Supreme Court of Canada has, in a number of critical cases, gradually developed a set of criteria for determining whether there has been an unreasonable delay.[35]

In the pivotal *Askov* case (1990),[36] the Supreme Court held that a number of critical factors should be considered in determining whether or not the accused's right to a speedy trial has been infringed: (1) the length of the delay; (2) the explanation for the delay; (3) whether the accused has waived (or renounced) his or her right by agreeing to the delay; and (4) the extent (if any) to which the accused has actually been prejudiced by the delay. Cory J. summarized the impact of these factors in the following fashion.

(i) The length of the delay

The longer the delay, the more difficult it should be for a court to excuse it. Very lengthy delays may be such that they cannot be justified for any reason.

(ii) Explanation for the delay

(a) Delays attributable to the Crown

Delays attributable to the actions of the Crown or officers of the Crown will weigh in favour of the accused...

Complex cases which require longer time for preparation, a greater expenditure of resources by Crown officers, and the longer use of institutional facilities will justify delays longer than those acceptable in simple cases.

(b) Systemic or institutional delays

Delays occasioned by inadequate resources must weigh against the Crown. Institutional delays should be considered in light of [a comparison with the delays experienced in similar communities elsewhere in Canada]...The burden of justifying inadequate resources resulting in systemic delays will always fall upon the Crown. There may be a transitional period to allow for a temporary period of lenient treatment of systemic delay.

(c) Delays attributable to the accused

Certain actions of the accused will justify delays. For example, a request for adjournment or delays to retain different counsel.
    There may, as well, be instances where it can be demonstrated by the Crown that the actions of the accused were undertaken for the purposes of delaying the trial.

(iii) Waiver

If the accused waives his [or her] rights by consenting to or concurring in the delay, this must be taken into account. However, for a waiver to be valid it must be informed, unequivocal and freely given. The burden of showing that a waiver should be inferred falls upon the Crown. An example of a waiver or concurrence that could be inferred is the consent by counsel for the accused to a fixed date for trial.

(iv) Prejudice to the accused

There is a general and in the case of very long delays an often virtually irrebuttable presumption of prejudice to the accused resulting from the passage of time.
    Where the Crown can demonstrate that there was no prejudice to the accused flowing from the delay, then such proof may serve to excuse the delay. It is also open to the accused to call evidence to demonstrate actual prejudice to strengthen his position that he [or she] has been prejudiced as a result of the delay.[37]

How are these criteria applied in practice? In *Askov*, the accused were charged with a number of serious offences and, although some of them were kept in custody for about six months, eventually they were all released on bail prior to the completion of their preliminary inquiry in the Provincial Court. After their committal for trial in a higher court, the trial date was set for one year later. However, because of inadequate resources in the court system, it was not possible to proceed with the case and the trial was postponed for yet another year. The trial was to be held in Brampton, Ontario, which falls within the judicial district of Peel, and it appears that the postponement of the accused's trial was a consequence of the policy in that district to give priority to cases where the accused were in custody or where the charges had been laid at an even earlier date. The upshot of these events was that the accused in the *Askov* case were not tried until some two years had elapsed since their committal for trial after the preliminary inquiry. When the accused did eventually make it to court, they brought an application to have the proceedings stayed on the basis that their right under the *Charter* to be tried within a reasonable time had been infringed.

The trial judge granted the application and eventually the Supreme Court of Canada ruled that the trial judge had been perfectly correct in entering the stay of proceedings, given the particular circumstances of this case. In applying the criteria, set out above, Cory J. looked first at the length of the delay and concluded that a two-year delay was "so lengthy that unless there is some very strong basis for justifying the delay, which becomes clear from an examination of the other factors, then it would be impossible for a court to tolerate such a delay."[38] He also concluded that the accused had suffered prejudice by the two-year delay. Some of them had been incarcerated for a significant period and all of them had eventually been subjected to onerous conditions on their bail. The Crown could not prove that they had not been prejudiced by the protracted delay and, therefore, could not justify it on this basis. Cory J. then examined the explanations given for the delay. In terms of delays attributable to the Crown, he noted that the Crown had not taken any particular steps that had contributed to the delay (by, for example, requesting an adjournment). However, Cory J. indicated that the case was not so inherently complex or difficult as to justify a lengthy delay. In this case, it was clear that the real culprit was systemic or institutional delay.

Evidence was presented to the Supreme Court that showed that, insofar as waiting periods were concerned, Peel District was one of the worst in Canada. This was attributed to a shortage of prosecutors, court space, and judges. The Supreme Court compared the delays in Peel

District with those in comparable, metropolitan districts in the province of Quebec. The evidence showed that the usual delays in Peel were more than four times as long as those in the comparable districts in Quebec, and the delay in the *Askov* case itself was more than eight times as long. Taking into account these comparisons, Cory J. suggested that a "period of delay in a range of some six to eight months between committal and trial might be deemed to be the outside limit of what is reasonable in Peel District." He concluded that more resources should be made available to the district (more prosecutors and courtrooms) and emphasized that "some solution must be found to eradicate this malignant growth of unreasonable trial delay that constitutes such an unacceptable blight upon the administration of justice in Peel District."[39]

The Court also examined whether any of the delay was attributable to the accused themselves. In this respect, the Court noted that they had not done anything to contribute to the delay; they had not been given any choice as to the date for their trial. The last criterion to be explored was whether the accused had waived their right to a speedy trial. The Court noted that the silence of the accused or their failure to raise any objection was not enough to permit a conclusion that they had waived their rights. Clearly, the Crown could not show that they had, in any way, agreed to the delay of their trial date.[40]

In light of all these considerations, the Supreme Court of Canada ruled that the delay in the trial of the accused in *Askov* could not be justified and that the stay of proceedings should be implemented (Coughlan, 1991; Jubinville, 1990).

Askov was interpreted initially as setting very severe limits on the extent to which a shortage of court resources could be used as a justification for delay in bringing an accused person to trial. It was a widespread belief that the Supreme Court had ruled that there must be a stay of proceedings, based on the application of section 11(b) of the *Charter*, whenever the limit of six to eight months' delay had been exceeded (Ledgerwood, 1992).[41] In Ontario, Crown counsel, faced with a backlog of criminal cases caused by a lack of court resources, decided that the *Askov* decision left them no alternative but to clear the backlog by staying or withdrawing over 47,000 charges between October 22, 1990, and September 6, 1991.[42] This response aroused a considerable amount of criticism from those who believed that the *Askov* decision had resulted in the granting of a virtual amnesty to criminals, many of whom were perceived to have beaten the rap in spite of having been charged with serious crimes. Furthermore, this course of action was considered to have caused considerable injustice to many victims of crime who had suffered considerably at the hands of individuals who were now excused from ever "facing the music" in court.

In *Morin* (1992), the justices of the Supreme Court of Canada quickly seized the opportunity to correct any misinterpretation of their intentions in the *Askov* case. *Morin* was also a case that originated in Ontario. The accused had been charged with impaired driving and being "over 80." More than 14 months elapsed from the time of her first appearance in court and the time at which her case came on for trial in the Oshawa Provincial Court. It was clear that the main cause for the delay was the lack of court resources (at least 12 months of the overall delay was attributed to this cause).[43] The question arose as to whether the accused was entitled to a stay of proceedings on the basis that her rights under section 11(b) of the *Charter* had been infringed.

Ultimately, the Supreme Court of Canada ruled that the accused's rights under section 11(b) were *not* infringed. While "account must be taken of the fact that the state does not have unlimited funds and other government programs compete for the available resources, this consideration cannot be used to render s. 11(b) meaningless." It went on, "there is a point in time at which the court will no longer tolerate delay based on the plea of inadequate resources."[44] This point is reflected in an "administrative guideline" that is set by the Court. This guideline is not to be interpreted as a fixed ceiling or limitation period (as some courts had done after the *Askov* case), and it can, therefore, not be applied in a "purely mechanical fashion."[45] In *Askov*, the guideline had been set as a range of six to eight months between the accused's committal for trial and the trial itself in a higher court. In *Morin*, the accused was to be tried in the Provincial Court so there was no preliminary inquiry. Sopinka J. held that, as far as cases to be tried in the Provincial Court were concerned, the guideline should indicate that a period of delay from eight to ten months of "purely systemic delay" would not be unreasonable. However, this guideline can be adjusted where, for example, there is a sudden and temporary strain on court resources — as was the case in *Morin*.[46] Taking into account this temporary situation and the fact that the accused was not prejudiced by the delay in any significant way (she had not been held in custody or subjected to bail conditions), the Court held that the delay in this case was not unreasonable.

In *Sharma* (1992),[47] there was a 13-month delay between the accused's arrest and the date of his trial on charges of impaired driving causing bodily harm, being "over 80," and obstructing a police officer. The question arose as to whether his rights had been infringed under section 11(b). The trial judge thought they had and entered a stay of proceedings, but the Ontario Court of Appeal disagreed and ordered a new trial. The Supreme Court of Canada agreed with the Court of Appeal and ruled that the accused's right to be tried within a reasonable time had not been infringed. Three months of delay was attributable to the need for the Crown and the accused to prepare for the case; thus, this was justified by the "inherent time requirements of the case." Nine months of the delay was attributable to limits on court resources. The guideline set in the *Morin* case for delay in the provincial courts was between eight and ten months. The Supreme Court stated that in *Sharma*, a case that was tried in the District of Peel (Ontario), the local court system had experienced problems with delay for a considerable period and had had plenty of time to adjust to the problem; therefore, the lower range of the guideline should be adopted (eight months). In *Sharma*, the institutional delay was about nine months but this, in itself, was not unreasonable unless the accused suffered prejudice thereby. In *Sharma*, although the accused had suffered some prejudice as a result of the conditions of his bail (which included a prohibition against driving), the prejudice was "minimal" and the accused and his counsel had done nothing to try to engineer an earlier trial date. For these reasons, the Supreme Court ruled that the accused's right to a speedy trial had not been infringed.

Although the *Morin* and *Sharma* cases represent a major retreat by the Supreme Court of Canada from the apparently tough stance it adopted in the *Askov* case (Coughlan, 1992), there is no doubt that the impact of section 11(b) of the *Charter* on the operation of the Canadian criminal court system during the 1990s has already been profound. The *Askov* case initially sparked the dismissal of thousands of charges by judges across Canada who believed that it required a strict application of the right to a speedy trial under section 11(b) (Canadian Centre for Justice Statistics, 1993:10) and this judicial action, in turn, caused prosecutors (particularly in Ontario) to drop tens of thousands of charges where it was not possible to pursue a case within the deadlines apparently set by the Supreme Court of Canada in *Askov*.

In order to respond to the challenge set by the *Askov* case, particular emphasis was placed on effective caseflow management within the

Canadian criminal court system (Lessard, 1990; Mitchell, 1990; Scott, 1989). Newfoundland, Nova Scotia, Quebec, Manitoba, Alberta, and British Columbia all established case management committees with a membership drawn from officials working in the justice system (Canadian Centre for Justice Statistics, 1993:10).

In Ontario, where there have been major problems with court delay in the past, standing committees were set up to keep an eye on, and ultimately to reduce, court delay. A Central Caseflow Management Unit was initiated by the Provincial Court to achieve a more efficient processing of cases throughout the whole court system. Similarly, at the level of the local community, Delay Reduction Committees were established to identify the causes of delay in a local area, review the way in which cases are processed, identify and implement solutions, and evaluate their impact (Canadian Centre for Justice Statistics, 1993:10).

In 1991, the Canadian Judicial Council, chaired by the Chief Justice of Canada, launched a court delays project that resulted in recommendations from various committees as to how to handle the challenge of delay (Canadian Centre for Justice Statistics, 1993:10).

Some provinces addressed the challenge posed by *Askov* by allocating additional resources to the court system. For example, in Ontario, 27 new judges were appointed to the provincial division of the new Ontario Court of Justice in 1991, while three additional judges were appointed to the Alberta Provincial Court. In Edmonton and Calgary, special traffic commissioners were created in 1991 to hear all traffic trials (Canadian Centre for Justice Statistics, 1993:11).

Many jurisdictions have made greater use of modern technologies to manage the processing of cases in the criminal court system. For example, in Newfoundland, Prince Edward Island, Quebec, Ontario, British Columbia, and the Northwest Territories, a number of courts have turned to the computer in order to establish automated information systems that can schedule and keep track of cases in an effective manner (Canadian Centre for Justice Statistics, 1993:11).

Overall, it is fair to say that the establishment of a right to be tried within a reasonable time constitutes an aspect of the enactment of the *Charter* that has exerted an extremely profound influence on the operation of the system of criminal courts in Canada. It will be interesting to monitor the impact of this provision during the rest of the 1990s and to ascertain whether *Morin* and *Sharma* truly represent a major easing of the standards that the courts will apply in determining whether there has been an unreasonable delay in particular cases.[48]

PROSECUTORIAL DISCRETION

It is still theoretically possible for private citizens to conduct prosecutions of criminal cases in Canada, although this is rarely done at the present day (Burns, 1975 and 1991; Law Reform Commission of Canada, 1986; Stenning, 1986:c.12). In the great majority of cases, prosecutions are conducted by public officials. Furthermore, even where a private citizen has laid an information alleging an offence, the Attorney-General of the jurisdiction concerned can either take over the prosecution him or herself or bring it to an end; thus the so-called right of a private citizen to prosecute an offence is really little more than the right to lay an information[49] (Burns, 1991:V-11; Stenning, 1986:263).

Prosecutions under the *Criminal Code* are conducted by the Attorney-General or Minister of Justice of the province concerned or by one of his or her agents since, under the *Constitution Act*, the provinces are responsible for the administration of justice.[50] The Minister of Justice of Canada or his or her agents are responsible for the conduct of prosecutions of offences arising under federal statutes other than the *Criminal Code* (for example, the *Narcotic Control Act* and the *Food and Drugs Act*) as well as conspiracies to commit such offences. The precise degree of overlap between the federal and provincial prosecuting powers, however, is a matter of some uncertainty (see Burns, 1991:V-28; Stenning, 1986:c.10).[51]

It has been contended in traditional literature that the prosecutor is not a partisan advocate, but rather a "minister of justice" (Gourlie, 1982:32; Sutherland, 1990a; Stenning, 1986:240). In a passage from a decision in the Supreme Court of Canada, Rand J. said:

> ...the purpose of a criminal prosecution is not to obtain a conviction, it is to lay before a jury what the Crown considers to be credible evidence relevant to what is alleged to be a crime. Counsel have a duty to see that all available legal proof of the factors is presented: it should be done firmly and pressed to its legitimate strength but it must also be done fairly. The role of prosecutor excludes any notion of winning or losing; his [or her] function is a matter of public duty than which in civil life there can be none charged with greater

personal responsibility. It is to be efficiently performed with an ingrained sense of the dignity, the seriousness and the justness of judicial proceedings.

Stenning (1986:241) points out that there may well be a sharp discrepancy between the theoretical role of the prosecutor as a minister of justice and the reality of everyday practice in the courts (see Grosman, 1969). However, regardless of the accuracy of this conception of the prosecutor as a "minister of justice," Stenning (1986:241) suggests that it has, nevertheless, strongly influenced the Canadian judiciary in its "hands off" approach toward defining and supervising the exercise of prosecutorial discretion.

The Canadian prosecutor enjoys a formidable degree of discretion in carrying out his or her duties in the court process. For example, the prosecutor has such discretionary powers as: selecting how to proceed on a dual or hybrid offence; restricting an accused person's right to elect the method of trial in relation to an indictable offence by laying a direct indictment or by insisting on a trial by judge and jury where an offence carrying a maximum penalty of more than five years' imprisonment is concerned; deciding whether or not to oppose bail; deciding whether to grant discovery of the prosecution's case against the accused and to what extent; and deciding whether to appeal against an acquittal.

The Discretionary Power to Lay Charges

The *Criminal Code* says nothing about the discretion of a prosecutor to lay criminal charges. However, as Stenning (1986:243) points out, Canadian courts have long been willing to accept that prosecutorial powers are derived from the common law (or the law developed by judges in specific cases) as well as from statutory provisions (Rosenthal, 1990). Furthermore, the courts have emphasized that, in general, they are not prepared to investigate the manner in which a prosecutor decides to exercise his or her discretion whether or not to lay charges in specific cases (Morgan, 1986:24ff.; Sutherland, 1990b). However, it appears that there are, nevertheless, some restrictions that may be imposed on the exercise of this discretionary power in exceptional circumstances. For example, while prosecutors are perfectly free to decide not to lay charges in individual cases, they cannot preclude prosecution in relation to a whole category of offences or offenders without considering the specific facts in each case. If prosecutors were permitted to adopt such a policy, it would be tantamount to permitting Crown counsel to override the will of the legislature (Stenning, 1986:244). For example, in one case,[52] an Aboriginal was prosecuted for illegal hunting. The defendant claimed that the prosecution was an abuse of process and sought to have the prosecution stayed since there was an explicit policy on the part of both the federal and provincial governments not to prosecute Aboriginals for such offences within the province of Manitoba. The Court of Appeal ruled that there was no abuse of process because, while the prosecuting authorities have the power to refuse to prosecute in light of the particular facts of an individual case, they had no power to adopt a blanket policy of refusing to prosecute any of the members of a particular group. Indeed, the Court said that a blanket dispensation in favour of a particular group must always be considered invalid:

> Today the dispensing power may be exercised in favour of Indians. Tomorrow it may be exercised in favour of Protestants, and the next day in favour of Jews. Our laws cannot be so treated. The Crown may not by executive action dispense with laws. The matter is as simple as that, and nearly three centuries of legal and constitutional history stand as the foundation for that principle.[53]

On the other side of the coin, it has been held that the Attorney-General may not order that every violation of the law be prosecuted regardless of the circumstances of individual cases. For example, in a Manitoba case,[54] the Minister of Justice had decreed that every case involving domestic violence should be prosecuted and that, once started, criminal proceedings could not be stopped. The accused was charged with assault following the administration of physical discipline to his eight-year-old son. The accused's wife complained to the authorities and an arrest was made. She later attempted to reconcile with her husband and wrote him an apology. However, the prosecution was not halted. The Court of Appeal allowed the accused's appeal against his conviction of assault and ordered that a stay of proceedings be entered. In the view of the Court:

> In my opinion, this is a case which should never have come to the courts. I do not understand the policy of the Ministry of Justice which apparently believes that the full force of the criminal law should be

brought to bear against a father who in good faith administers punishment to his son in a manner which the trial judge deemed to be excessive, but which was well within the range of what has been generally accepted by parents in this province over the years. It sounds nice to say we will have zero tolerance for domestic violence, but the result of such a policy is a case such as we have here where a family is torn apart by judicial proceedings...

In my opinion, it is not sound policy to mandate that every violation of the law requires the laying of charges. That policy has the undesirable effect of nullifying prosecutorial discretion; such discretion should be exercised in favour of values in society such as family life. In my opinion, such prosecutorial discretion is subject to judicial review.[55]

One of the parties who might object to the refusal of the prosecutor to lay charges is the victim of an alleged offence. Under the existing system, the victim has no avenue by means of which he or she can challenge the failure of the prosecutor to act. However, The Law Reform Commission of Canada (1988:32) has recommended that, where Crown counsel declines to charges, the victim should "not feel shut out of the criminal justice system." In the commission's view (1988:33), the Canadian citizen should be granted an expanded role in private prosecutions; subject to the "overriding right of the Attorney-General to supervise all prosecutions," private prosecutors should enjoy exactly the same rights as Crown counsel in pursuing their cases through the criminal courts.

A possible limitation on the prosecutor's discretionary power to lay charges may be the emergence of a defence to criminal charges where there has been selective prosecution (Allen, 1992). In the United States, a defence has been recognized in the federal courts where an accused person can show that he or she was singled out for prosecution in a discriminatory manner (Allen, 1992:422-440). In a recent decision,[56] the Ontario Court of Appeal seemed to recognize that such a defence could exist in Canada, although it declined to apply it in the particular circumstances of the case. The accused had challenged some 59 charges under the (Ontario) *Retail Business Holidays Act*, which prohibited the Sunday opening of stores (except in certain circumstances that did not apply to the accused). He contended that many other retailers broke the law by opening their stores on Sunday but were not prosecuted. He, therefore, claimed he was the victim of discriminatory prosecution. The Ontario Court of Appeal ruled that the accused could not claim the benefit of the defence of selective prosecution because he had failed to provide evidence that the other stores that opened on Sundays had not, in fact, been prosecuted. However, the door appears to have been left open for other defendants in the future to claim the benefit of the defence where they can show not only that others in the same situation as themselves have not been prosecuted but also that the discriminatory prosecution was based on impermissible grounds, such as race, sex, or religion (Allen, 1992:415).

The Discretionary Power to Stay Proceedings

The prosecutor has the discretionary power to *stay* (or suspend) criminal proceedings in relation to both indictable and summary conviction offences (Cohen, 1977:150; Sun, 1974; Salhany, 1989:238-243).[57] The exercise of this power may sometimes be controversial because the victims of alleged offences may well feel that they have been denied justice, and accused persons may believe that they have been deprived of their "day in court" and denied the opportunity to establish their innocence in a conclusive manner. According to Salhany (1989:238), the right to stay criminal proceedings:

> ...is based upon the principle that since all criminal prosecutions are carried out in the name of the Queen, the Queen may, through her Attorney-General, intimate to the officer of the court that proceedings are stayed by her direction.

A stay can be entered at any time after an information has been laid[58] and before the judgment in the case is delivered (Salhany, 1989:238). In order to stay proceedings, the prosecutor merely instructs the clerk of the court to enter the stay on the record; neither the clerk nor the judge has any discretion over the matter (Burns, 1991:V-6; Morgan, 1986:29). An extreme example of the ability of the Crown to enter a stay at the last possible moment occurred in a case that came before the B.C. Court of Appeal in 1967.[59] In this case, the Crown had entered a stay of proceedings *after* the trial judge had charged the jury and directed them to find the accused not guilty but *before* the jury had actually returned with their verdict. Despite the fact that the Crown was using the stay merely to avoid the impact of an adverse ruling that would have resulted in the accused being acquitted,[60] the appeal court nevertheless ruled that the Crown's entry of the stay of proceedings was perfectly valid. Bull J.A. said that "the entry of a stay is a statutory administrative discretion given to the Attorney-General, and, if exercised, his direction is to the Clerk of the Court as such and is outside any control of the Judge."[61]

This is undoubtedly an extreme case; however, the courts' reluctance to exercise control over the power of the Crown to enter a stay of proceedings has clearly placed a powerful, tactical weapon in the armoury of the prosecutor. The Ontario Court of Appeal, for example, has ruled that the courts should not interfere with the Attorney-General's decision to stay proceedings unless there is some form of "flagrant impropriety."[62] Nonetheless, it is significant that, in one case before the Quebec Court of Appeal,[63] one of the justices of appeal suggested that the courts do have the power to review a decision to stay proceedings where the Attorney-General has "violated the law or abused his powers through corruption in favour of the accused, through prejudice against the victim or against the law which creates the offence, or finally through an obviously unreasonable decision."[64] Furthermore, the Court made it clear that the Attorney-General's discretion to enter a stay of proceedings could be reviewed if he or she has used it to override rights guaranteed by the *Charter* (Salhany, 1989:241).

The effect of a stay of proceedings is to suspend them rather than to terminate them altogether (Stenning, 1986:232). The *Code*[65] provides that, insofar as indictable offences are concerned, the prosecutor can recommence the proceedings within one year of entering the stay merely by giving notice to the clerk of the court. As far as summary conviction offences are concerned, the *Code* states that the proceedings must be recommenced either within one year of the entry of the stay or "before the expiration of the time within which the proceedings could have been commenced, whichever is the earlier." The latter restriction refers to the fact that summary conviction offences normally have a limitation period of six months. Therefore, in most cases, a stay in relation to a summary conviction offence will only suspend court proceedings until the end of this six-month period. Once the specified periods have elapsed, the Crown cannot revive the proceedings; indeed, "the proceedings shall be deemed never to have been commenced." However, there is nothing to prevent the prosecutor from initiating fresh proceedings for the same offence, provided that (as far as summary conviction offences are concerned), this is done within the appropriate limitation period (Stenning, 1986:233).

Sun (1974:488) has noted that there is a marked disparity in the use of the stay in different provinces across Canada. In provinces such as British Columbia and Manitoba, she found that the stay was used frequently, while in others it was rarely used (the withdrawal of charges mechanism was apparently used instead).

The Discretionary Power to Withdraw Charges

Although the *Code* does not expressly give prosecutors the right to withdraw charges, once an information has been laid or an indictment preferred, the courts have nevertheless recognized that this right does indeed exist (Burns, 1991:V-3; Salhany, 1989:238; Stenning, 1986:245).[66] Osborne (1983:57) indicates that from 20% to 30% of criminal cases in Canada are terminated by a withdrawal or staying of charges.

It is important to distinguish between the staying and the withdrawal of charges. As we have seen, entering a stay of charges merely suspends them, whereas the withdrawal of charges results in their termination (after a withdrawal of charges, the Crown cannot continue the prosecution without laying completely new charges).

As Osborne (1983:58) points out, "the withdrawal of charges does not put the stamp of finality on a case although such a disposition may reasonably give rise to an expectation in the mind of an accused that the matter is closed." Indeed, provided the court does not consider it to be an abuse of process, the prosecutor may always lay new charges and thereby reactivate a case in which charges had previously been withdrawn.[67]

To what extent does the power to withdraw charges fall within the discretion of the Crown? The generally accepted view (Burns, 1991:V-4; Osborne, 1983:58) is that the Crown has an absolute right to withdraw a case before a plea is taken but that the trial judge has a discretion whether to grant the Crown's request to withdraw charges as soon as any evidence has been heard following the entry of the accused's plea.[68] In theory, it appears that the necessity of obtaining judicial approval renders withdrawal a much more palatable device with respect to the civil liberties of the individual citizen (Cohen, 1977:59). However, in practice, judges very rarely withhold their consent to the withdrawal of charges (Osborne, 1983:58).

Osborne (1983) discovered that charges were frequently withdrawn because the victim or other witnesses did not appear in court. Similarly, in certain cases that stemmed from so-called "domestic disputes," the charges had to be withdrawn because the complainant was unwilling to proceed with the prosecution of a spouse. It was also found that charges were likely to be withdrawn where the police had laid charges before obtaining the necessary supporting evidence (for example, where analysis of a blood sample failed to indicate that the accused had the prohibited level of alcohol required in order to sustain the charge). Osborne concluded that the reasons for withdrawing charges were varied and, in most cases, were beyond the personal control of Crown counsel:

> His [or her] options are limited by the willingness of victims and witnesses to co-operate; the preferences of the police; the strategies of the accused and his [or her] counsel; the willingness of the judge to grant remands and the state of the day's court lists. These factors are above all unpredictable. The decision to withdraw is a heavily contingent one (1983:73-74) .

Accountability of Prosecutors

The scope of prosecutorial discretion is very broad in Canada and that Canadian courts are generally somewhat reluctant to interfere with the exercise of that discretion. However, this does not mean that there are absolutely no limits to what a prosecutor can or cannot do in the exercise of his or her discretionary powers. The Attorney-General or Minister of Justice of a province is ultimately accountable to the legislature for the conduct of prosecutions; individual Crown counsel are accountable to the Attorney-General or Minister of Justice for their decisions; and the courts are gradually developing mechanisms for controlling the most excessive abuses of prosecutorial powers.

Accountability of the Attorney-General or Minister of Justice to the Legislature

Each Attorney-General or Minister of Justice — the chief law officer of the Crown — is a member of the legislature and, therefore, is ultimately accountable to the members of that legislature for the exercise of prosecutorial discretion in criminal proceedings (Stenning, 1986:301). The Attorney-General or Minister of Justice must answer questions about the exercise of prosecutorial discretion, but only *after* a decision not to prosecute has been made or when a prosecution has been completed (Law

Reform Commission of Canada, 1990:11; Stenning, 1986:303). Further-more, as Stenning (1986:305) points out, since the Attorney-General or Minister of Justice is a member of both the government and the party with the largest number of seats in the legislature, it is unlikely that this responsibility to the legislature will represent a significant method of controlling prosecutorial discretion.[69]

Accountability of Crown Counsel to the Attorney-General or Minister of Justice

Of course, Attorney-Generals or Ministers of Justice do not conduct prosecutions themselves except in the most exceptional cases. Crown counsel are accountable to the Attorney-General or Minister of Justice for the conduct of individual prosecutions. Stenning (1986:312) points out that, since the Attorney-General or Minister of Justice is not involved personally in the day-to-day administration of justice, the individual prosecutor has a considerable degree of autonomy in practice; however, this does not prevent the Attorney-General or Minster of Justice from getting involved in particular cases, if need be.[70] In addition to issuing directions to Crown counsel in specific cases, the Attorney-General or deputy may issue general guidelines indicating the broad principles that should be applied in exercising prosecutorial discretion in relation to particular types of offences or offenders or in relation to such matters as plea bargaining (Law Reform Commission of Canada, 1990:17; Stenning, 1986:316-317; Verdun-Jones and Cousineau, 1979:239-240).

Accountability of Crown Counsel to the Individual Citizen

Until recently, it was generally accepted that, in most provinces, a private citizen could not sue the Attorney-General or deputy for damages sustained as a result of the conduct of their prosecutorial functions (Law, 1990; Law Reform Commission of Canada, 1990:24). Indeed, the Attorney-General and Crown counsel were considered to enjoy an "absolute immunity" from such lawsuits. The rationale for this approach appears to have been the belief that such an immunity was necessary to maintain the independence of the Crown and to protect it from harass-ment; clearly, these concerns were considered to outweigh the interests of accused persons who claimed that they had been wrongly prosecuted.[71] Undoubtedly, this sweeping immunity from law suits rendered private citizens quite powerless in the face of potentially malicious prosecutions by leaving them without a remedy in the courts.

However, in *Nelles v. Ontario* (1989),[72] the Supreme Court of Canada ruled that the Attorney-General does not, after all, enjoy an immunity from being sued for malicious prosecution. The Court stated that public confidence in the criminal justice system is diminished when private citizens are unable to sue prosecutors who abuse their powers. Lamer J. noted that it would be no easy task for a citizen to bring a successful action for malicious prosecution because he or she would have to prove "deliberate and malicious use of the office for ends that are improper and inconsistent with the traditional prosecutorial function."[73] Therefore, it is highly unlikely that dispensing with the prosecutor's immunity will open the floodgates to a wave of lawsuits that will divert prosecutors from their customary duties in the criminal courts (Law Reform Commission of Canada, 1990:24). The fact that they are available as a last resort does protect the individual citizen to some degree against the abuse of the prosecutor's discretion to lay criminal charges.

It should also be pointed out that aggrieved citizens may seek a remedy under section 24(1) of the *Charter* whenever they believe that their *Charter* rights have been violated as a consequence of a prosecutor's abuse of power. The remedies available under section 24(1) may include an award of damages (Law Reform Commission of Canada, 1990:24-25).

Accountability of the Prosecutor to the Courts

Historically, the Canadian courts have been quite reluctant to exercise any control over prosecutorial discretion (Morgan, 1986:24). According to Morgan, the major reason for this approach is the courts' view of "how the criminal justice system best operates":

> It is apparently thought, for various reasons, to work most effectively through a very broad grant of prosecutorial discretion, and conversely, with a minimum of judicial interference. Courts have seemingly concluded that virtually any form of challenge could hamper the independence and fearlessness of the prosecutor, regarded as vital to the efficacy of the prosecutorial process generally (1986:31).

Morgan's views are well reflected in the judgment of the Supreme Court of Canada in the case of *R. v. V.T.* (1992).[74] The Court noted that "there is no doubt that the Crown acting through the Attorney-General, and in turn through his or her prosecutors, has a wide amount of discretion in the carriage of criminal cases."[75] The Court stated that it had recognized this principle numerous times in the past. For example, the Court quoted from one of its earlier judgments, in which it stated that the existence of such broad prosecutorial discretion did not, *per se*, infringe principles of fundamental justice guaranteed by the *Charter*:

> The existence of the discretion conferred by the statutory provisions does not, in my view, offend principles of fundamental justice. A system that attempted to eliminate discretion would be unworkably complex and rigid. Police necessarily exercise discretion in deciding to lay charges, to arrest and to conduct incidental searches, as prosecutors do in deciding whether or not to withdraw a charge, enter a stay, consent to an adjournment, proceed by way of indictment or summary conviction, launch an appeal and so on.[76]

The Supreme Court took the view that the judicial and executive functions in the criminal justice system should not be mixed. Except in cases of flagrant impropriety, the courts should not cross over into the realm of executive decisions and start to interfere with the "administrative and accusatorial functions" of the Attorney-General or his or her prosecutors. In justifying the need for the courts to maintain deference to prosecutorial discretion, the Supreme Court quoted a passage from a decision of the English House of Lords:

> A judge must keep out of the arena. He should not have or appear to have any responsibility for the institution of a prosecution. The functions of prosecutors and judges must not be blurred. If a judge has power to decline to hear a case because he does not think it should be brought, then it soon may be thought that the cases he allows to proceed are cases brought with his consent or approval.[77]

Nonetheless, the Court commented that "while the principle of prosecutorial discretion is an important precept in our criminal law, and exists for good reason, it is by no means absolute in its operation."[78] In particular, the Court underscored the fact that a stay of proceedings may prevent a violation of *Charter* rights and abuse of the court's process.

The principle that a court could stay criminal proceedings in the event that the judge believed there had been an abuse of the court's process developed in the early 1970s — well before the advent of the *Charter* (Morgan, 1986; Salhany, 1989:241-243; Trotter, 1989; Taylor, 1985). The legal doctrine of "abuse of process" refers to the courts' inherent jurisdiction to protect their process from abuse by the prosecution. Courts may enter a stay of proceedings in those cases where it is felt that there has been an exceptional abuse of the court process on the part of the prosecution and that this abuse has resulted in "an unacceptable degree of unfairness to an accused" (Morgan, 1986: 35).[79] As Trotter notes, "the imposition of a stay of proceedings due to an abuse of process is a 'self-protecting' mechanism as far as the courts are concerned" and "the focus is not so much upon the rights of an aggrieved accused person inasmuch as it is protecting the integrity of the court" (1989:414).

For many years, the extent to which the Supreme Court of Canada was prepared to embrace the doctrine of abuse of process, as it had been developed by the lower courts, was left in a considerable degree of doubt. That doubt was largely dispelled in the critical case of *Jewett*.[80] In this case involving entrapment of the accused, the Supreme Court unequivocally endorsed the doctrine that a trial court has the residual jurisdiction to stay proceedings if forcing the accused to stand trial would violate "those fundamental principles of justice which underlie the community's sense of fair play and decency and to prevent the abuse of a court's process through oppressive or vexatious proceedings."[81] However, it was emphasized that this power may only be exercised in the "clearest of cases."[82] In a later case, the Ontario Court of Appeal stated that, in effect, the accused must prove, on the balance of probabilities, that the Crown acted in an oppressive or vexatious manner or that the prosecution was offensive to the principles of fundamental justice and fair play.[83]

Since the doctrine of abuse of process emerged prior to the enactment of the *Charter*, it is not entirely clear whether it will continue to exist as a separate common law remedy or whether it will be gradually subsumed into the various remedies available under the *Charter* (Morgan, 1986:43ff.). As noted elsewhere, section 24 of the *Charter* provides the courts with the power to invoke a number of alternative remedies whenever there has been a violation of an accused person's rights under the *Charter*. The courts can enter a stay of proceedings where there has been a violation of the right to be tried within a reasonable time, as guaranteed by section 11(b) of the *Charter*. It is quite likely that section 7, which guarantees the right not to be deprived of "life, liberty and security of the person" except in accordance with "the principles of fundamental justice," will provide the basis for the courts to move beyond the narrow scope of the doctrine of abuse of process in controlling prosecutorial excesses. Indeed, the Ontario Court of Appeal[84] has already ruled that section 7 does, in fact, incorporate some degree of protection against "abuses of process" (Morgan, 1986:52). In this sense, it is possible that section 7 may well be used to broaden most significantly the impact of the doctrine of abuse of process in Canada in the years ahead.

In *Kearney* (1992),[85] a case decided by the New Brunswick Court of Appeal, it appears that the Court took the view that the doctrine of abuse of process, developed by the judges, had been swallowed up by the remedies now made available by the *Charter*. The accused was a Crown prosecutor who had been suspended during a police investigation of his conduct. The Deputy Attorney-General was given the police report, which contained allegations of sexual abuse and breach of trust in relation to his position as a prosecutor. This official fired the accused and informed the Attorney-General, who did not give any indication that he disagreed with this course of action. Some radio newscasts reported that Kearney had been dismissed and the Attorney-General confirmed that Kearney was "no longer with the Department." Subsequently, some newspaper accounts of the dismissal appeared in New Brunswick.

After charges were laid against the accused, he sought a stay of proceedings on the grounds that there had not only been an abuse of process but also a violation of his *Charter* rights under sections 7 (principles of fundamental justice) and 11(d) (presumption of innocence and guarantee of a fair trial). The trial judge granted the application because he believed that to allow the proceedings to continue would constitute an abuse of process. The Attorney-General's Department had permitted the news of Kearney's dismissal to be leaked to the media and, as a consequence, he would be deprived of a fair trial since prospective jurors would be affected by the knowledge that "the chief law officers of the province must have believed Mr. Kearney to be guilty, otherwise he would not have been dismissed."[86] The Court of Appeal affirmed the trial judge's decision. Interestingly, both the trial judge and the Court of Appeal appeared to assume that the common law doctrine of abuse of process had been subsumed into the individual rights guaranteed by the *Charter*.[87] In other words, the abuse of process was held to constitute a violation of the accused's *Charter* rights and the appropriate remedy was granted under section 24(1) of the *Charter*. Abuse of process was not seen as a separate basis for granting the stay of proceedings.

The Court of Appeal made some interesting comments on the extent to which the conduct of the Attorney-General should be subjected to judicial scrutiny under the *Charter*. Ryan J.A. stated that:

...the Attorney-General's function involves more than just an exercise of powers. His function encompasses corresponding duties and I reiterate that the office holder must exclude and appear to exclude any notion of winning or losing. Here, the firing could be taken as self-confirming confirmation of the decision to prosecute or could be interpreted as an attempt to mask the shortcomings of the Attorney-General in carrying out his supervisory responsibilities of prosecutors in general and of this prosecutor in particular.[88]

Ryan J.A. went on to make the point that "courts are not liberal in their dispensation of judicial stays, and rightly so." However, in this case, the entering of a stay was well justified:

Here, the trial judge found as a fact that the Minister and the highest official in his office committed an abuse of process that could not be rectified by the usual safeguards. They had failed to uphold the fundamental rights of an accused person as guaranteed by the Charter. To continue would be an abuse of process. He held that in view of the rare and exceptional circumstances of this case that the ends of justice would only be served by a stay of proceedings. In effect he was also saying that the general public have a vested interest in the integrity of the legal system.[89]

However, the *Kearney* case is not the final word on the question of whether the remedy furnished by the abuse of process doctrine has maintained its independence from the sweeping remedies available under the *Charter*. Other cases have suggested that the "exact relationship between the common law doctrine of abuse of process and the operation of s. 7 of the *Charter* has not yet been finally resolved."[90] The Ontario Court of Appeal[91] has suggested that, while the doctrine of abuse of process and the constitutional requirement of fundamental justice under section 7 of the *Charter* are "closely related," they are "independent of each other." By way of example, the Court suggested that, in cases involving charges of summary conviction offences, it may be difficult for the accused to rely on section 7 of the *Charter* because the "right to life, liberty and security of the person" is not likely to be infringed where the probable outcome of a conviction is only a relatively small fine. However, the conduct of the police or the Crown might nevertheless have been so oppressive as to constitute an abuse of process. It may well be the case that the difference between the doctrine of abuse of process and the remedies available under the *Charter* is that the doctrine of abuse of process is more focused on the allegedly oppressive or vexatious nature of police and prosecutorial misconduct while sections 7 and 11(d) of the *Charter* are more focused on the issue of whether such conduct has, in fact, brought about substantial prejudice to the accused's right to a fair trial (Trotter, 1989:415).[92] Obviously, it will remain to the Supreme Court of Canada to determine whether abuse of process survives as a remedy that is independent of the individual rights guaranteed by the *Charter*. Unfortunately, to date, it deliberately left this issue open.[93] In any event, the criminal courts in Canada do have the authority to control the abuse of prosecutorial powers by granting a stay of proceedings and that this authority will only be invoked in the "clearest cases" of abuse.

PLEA BARGAINING

Plea bargaining has, for some time, been one of the most controversial, and perhaps least understood, aspect of the Canadian criminal justice system (Berzins, 1990; Chevalier, 1990; Cousineau and Verdun-Jones, 1979; Genova, 1981; Law Reform Commission of Canada, 1989; Verdun-Jones and Cousineau, 1979; Verdun-Jones and Hatch, 1985 and 1987). At first, the idea of accused persons bargaining for lenience behind closed doors is singularly unattractive. However, the reality of the situation is much more complex than this popular image would lead one to believe.

The Law Reform Commission of Canada (1975b:45) once defined a plea bargain (also called "plea negotiation") as "any agreement by the accused to plead guilty in return for the promise of some benefit." Subsequently, the Commission (1989:3-4) indicated that it preferred the term "plea agreement," which it defined as "an agreement by the accused to plead guilty in return for the prosecutor's agreeing to take or refrain from taking a particular course of action." However, the term "plea bargain" is generally used in a much broader sense by those involved in criminal justice research. As Verdun-Jones and Hatch (1985:1) note, plea bargaining is really a compendious term used to describe a wide diversity of behaviours that occur among actors in the court system. The police, the Crown, and defence counsel may engage in behaviours ranging from simple discussions through negotiations to agreements. Clearly, discussions and negotiations may not ultimately lead to any form of agreement between the parties; however, these behaviours have generally been considered by researchers as falling within the concept of plea bargaining (Cousineau and Verdun-Jones, 1979).

Some researchers have questioned whether the terms, plea negotiations and plea bargains, are appropriate given the so-called "realities" of the criminal justice process. For example, Ericson and Baranek (1982) question whether the word "negotiate" is meaningful in light of the stark imbalance of power between the police and the Crown, on the one hand, and the defendant, on the other. Furthermore, they argue that it is more realistic to view the accused's decisions within the criminal justice system as being "coerced" or "manipulated" and that, therefore, any accommodation with the Crown will scarcely be perceived by the accused as being a genuine "bargain." Furthermore, even where an agreement is actually reached, it is perhaps a little misleading to refer to it as a "plea bargain" because, as we shall see, neither the Crown nor the defendant has any guarantee that such an agreement will ultimately be carried into effect by the sentencing judge, who is not bound by anything that has been agreed to by the parties concerned. In any event, we shall use the term plea bargaining in the following discussion because of its widespread use in the criminal justice research literature (just keep in mind that the term covers a broad range of potential interactions that may occur between the Crown and the defence in Canada).

If plea bargaining is concerned with reaching an agreement to secure a concession from the Crown in return for the accused pleading guilty, what concessions may the defence seek from Crown counsel? Broadly speaking, these benefits may be considered to fall into three overlapping categories: (1) promises relating to the charges to be laid; (2) promises relating to the ultimate sentence to be meted out by the court; and (3) promises relating to the facts that the Crown is willing to bring to the attention of court (assuming that the trial judge's knowledge of such facts will have a significant impact on the sentencing decision). Verdun-Jones and Hatch (1985:3) suggested the Crown might promise the following list of potential benefits.

Charge bargaining:

(a)   reduction of the charge to a lesser or included offence;

(b)   withdrawal or stay of other charges or the promise not to proceed on other possible charges; and

(c)   promise not to charge friends or family of the defendant.

Sentence bargaining:

(a)   promise to proceed summarily rather than by way of indictment;

(b)   promise that the Crown will make a particular recommendation in relation to sentence;

(c)   promise not to oppose defence counsel's sentence recommendation;

(d)   promise not to appeal against sentence imposed at trial;

(e)   promise not to apply for a more severe penalty (under section 665 of the *Code*);

(f)   promise not to apply for a period of preventive detention under section 753 of the *Code*;

(g)   promise to make a representation as to the place of imprisonment, type of treatment, etc.; and

(h)   promise to arrange sentencing before a particular judge.

Fact bargaining:

(a)   promise not to "volunteer" information detrimental to the accused (for example, not adducing evidence as to the defendant's previous convictions under section 255 of the *Code*); and

(b)   promise not to mention a circumstance of the offence that may be interpreted by the judge as an aggravating factor (and, therefore, deserving a greater degree of severity of punishment).

The Official Response to Plea Bargaining

While it has probably been practiced for many years, plea bargaining was traditionally frowned upon, and most individuals involved in the criminal justice system would not openly admit that it took place (Verdun-Jones and Cousineau, 1979). Until relatively recently, plea bargaining was held in such low regard that the Law Reform Commission of Canada (1975a:14) contended that it was "something for which a decent criminal justice system has no place." However, such attitudes now appear to be undergoing a significant degree of change. Only a decade after its extremely negative comment on the practice, the Law Reform Commission (1984) referred to plea bargaining, in one of its working papers, almost as a routine part of the court process and, by 1989, the Commission (1989:8) contended that "plea negotiation is not an inherently shameful practice" and recommended that the practice become more open and accountable.

A similar evolution of thought is apparent on the part of the judiciary, who were very critical of the practice until fairly recently (Verdun-Jones and Cousineau, 1979). In a case decided in 1979, a justice of the Supreme Court of Canada mentioned, without any apparent disapproval (and, indeed, almost as an afterthought) that the guilty plea had been obtained as a result of a plea bargain.[94] Even professional bodies, such as the Canadian Bar Association, appear to have sanctioned certain forms of plea bargaining. The *Code of Professional Conduct* of the Canadian Bar Association (1988) recognizes the legitimacy of a defence lawyer entering into a "tentative" plea agreement with the Crown and sets out ethical guidelines for the regulation of such conduct (Verdun-Jones and Hatch, 1985:22-23).

While they have not openly endorsed the practice of plea bargaining, Canadian courts have nevertheless offered a subtle condonation and even a certain degree of encouragement of the practice by establishing an atmosphere that permits it to flourish unchecked (Verdun-Jones and Hatch, 1985:29). In most cases, Canadian courts do not actively investigate the circumstances surrounding the entry of a guilty plea before they accept it. If the accused is represented by defence counsel, the trial judge will normally refrain from conducting a meticulous inquiry into the circumstances surrounding a guilty plea (Verdun-Jones and Cousineau, 1979; Watson, 1991:174).[95] In these circumstances, it is unlikely that there will be any investigation into the nature of the inducements offered to an accused person to plead guilty or any inquiry into whether the accused really understands the full implications of any plea bargain into which he or she may have entered. Indeed, it may well be argued that the lack of a requirement under Canadian law that a judge ferret out the critical factors that may have led to the defendant's decision to plead guilty has effectively created an environment in which it is possible for Crown and defence counsel to enter into plea bargains behind the inscrutable veil of secrecy.

The courts may also give some tacit encouragement to the practice of plea bargaining as a consequence of the widespread belief that accused persons entering guilty pleas may legitimately expect to receive a more lenient sentence than if their guilt had been determined by a trial (Fitzgerald, 1990; Watson, 1991:198-200). This form of "sentence discounting" has been referred to as "tacit plea bargaining." A more lenient sentence may be justified on the basis that the guilty plea indicates remorse,[96] that the community is spared the cost of a trial,[97] that the victim does not have to undergo the trauma of testifying,[98] or that the accused has cooperated with the police.[99] These justifications are necessary in order to avoid the impression that accused persons may be penalized for exercising their right to a trial. In one case, for example, the judge stated:

> It is a fundamental concept of our system of justice that a person accused of crime is entitled to demand that the Crown prove his guilt by a fair and impartial trial. There is nothing that the court should ever do to whittle down or undercut that fundamental principle. At the same time, it would be unrealistic not to recognize that if everyone demanded a full and complete trial our system of justice would come to an abrupt halt. It is for that reason that those who are guilty, and wish to so plead, should be given special consideration when they appear before the court.[100]

By encouraging guilty pleas in this manner, the courts appear to be facilitating the practice of plea bargaining. However, there is, to date, little evidence to establish that those who plead guilty do, in fact, receive more lenient sentences than those who go to trial. Solomon's analysis of data taken from a study of the fictionally titled "Robert County," Ontario, did not reveal any evidence to support the notion that there was a penalty imposed for pleading not guilty. Solomon (1983:39) notes that in only one of the seven cases in which there was a conviction after a fully contested trial did the offender receive a more severe punishment than that received by those who had pleaded guilty to the same offences. However, Solomon (1983:39) rightly notes that these data are "too scanty to be conclusive." Nevertheless, most of the defence lawyers in Robert County did genuinely believe that there was a discount for pleading guilty (Solomon, 1983:41) and this belief may well have exerted a strong influence over their clients' decision as to whether or not to plead guilty. Certainly, lawyers interviewed by Ericson and Baranek (1982) noted that the promise of a more lenient sentence can be extremely persuasive in convincing a reluctant client to plead guilty.

The courts have also facilitated plea bargaining practices by encouraging the submission of sentence recommendations by the Crown and defence (Verdun-Jones and Hatch, 1985:34). There is evidence that some Canadian courts are prepared to encourage joint sentence recommendations by the Crown and defence.[101] Since many Canadian courts appear to permit, and frequently accept, such sentencing recommendations, they encourage plea bargaining by giving Crown counsel a valuable commodity to bargain with: in other words, a favourable sentence recommendation may be exchanged for a guilty plea. However, the courts have consistently emphasized that they have absolute discretion in sentencing matters, and no particular recommendation, even one made as part of a plea bargain, is binding on the sentencing judge.[102] Nevertheless, as Ruby (1987:74) points out, such sentencing recommendations are "customarily given considerable weight," and the Quebec Court of Appeal has stated that, while judges are in no way bound by a joint recommendation of Crown and defence counsel as to sentence, they "usually pay a good deal of attention to a common recommendation by experienced and competent counsel."[103]

Empirical Research into Plea Bargaining in Canada

The empirical research conducted in Canada suggests that plea bargaining does occur at least in certain jurisdictions in this country. However, a number of these studies are affected by major methodological problems (Cousineau and Verdun-Jones, 1979). Research into plea bargaining in Canada has taken three forms: interviews, analysis of official documents, and observations of the practice itself.

Two of the pioneering studies of plea bargaining in Canada were based on interviews. Grosman (1969) drew upon both his own experience as a prosecutor and upon a series of interviews with 45 Crown attorneys in the County of York, Ontario. He suggested that plea bargaining occurred routinely as part of a well-established pattern of accommodations and concessions that were exchanged between prosecutors and certain, "favoured" defence counsel. While the impact of Grosman's trailblazing study should not be underestimated, it must nevertheless be noted that his analysis was based on impressions and hearsay rather than systematic observation of the actual practices associated with plea bargaining. It has also been pointed out that Grosman's findings, which related to a jurisdiction that contained the massive metropolitan area of Toronto, would not necessarily be applicable to other jurisdictions (Bowen-Coulthurst, 1970:496).

Another fascinating study based on interviews was conducted by Klein, who interviewed some 115 inmates in a maximum- security federal penitentiary in 1972. Klein (1979:132) concentrated on the types of "deals" that the offenders had struck "in interaction with the agents in the criminal justice system to minimize the possible punitive consequences" of their illegal activities. Slightly more than half the inmates claimed that they had been involved in deals with the police or prosecutors.

The Grosman and Klein studies were exploratory in nature and, as is the case with all research that relies upon interviews as the major source of data, there is a question as to the accuracy with which they represent the phenomenon studied.

Another group of studies involved an examination of official court documents as an indication of the nature and extent of plea bargaining. The first of these quantitative studies was undertaken by Hartnagel and Wynne (1975) and Wynne and Hartnagel (1975)[104] in a Prairie city during 1972 and 1973. The researchers examined the files of all those persons charged with *Criminal Code* offences where they believed that there was "evidence" of plea bargaining between the Crown and defence counsel. The factors they found to affect plea bargaining, as they defined it, were the existence of multiple charges against the accused and the specific nature of the offence(s) charged (for example, plea bargaining did not customarily occur in relation to summary conviction offences). The researchers found that those who were unrepresented did not share in the benefits of plea bargaining and that Aboriginal peoples were less likely to gain any advantages from this process than their white counterparts.

In similar vein, Hagan (1975) studied the role played by legal, procedural, and extra-legal factors in the sentencing process using data from court files and, incidentally, offered a number of significant observations in relation to the practice of plea bargaining. The study was conducted in Edmonton and involved the examination of the files of some 1,018 offenders. The researcher concluded that the sentence imposed by a court was primarily a reflection of the seriousness of the initial charge and the defendant's prior record rather than of such procedural variables as charge alteration and initial plea (which may be closely related to the existence of plea bargaining). Hagan also found that plea bargaining is much more likely to occur where the Crown has laid multiple charges. However, he suggested that the accused's race did not appear to have any significant effect upon the incidence of plea bargaining.

Both these studies, based on court documents, provide very valuable insights into the operation of the court process. However, they are not entirely satisfactory as studies of plea bargaining since the researchers did not observe the phenomenon itself but rather inferred that plea bargaining had taken place on the basis of indicators identified in court files. For example, Hagan concluded that plea bargaining had occurred whenever the record indicated a reduction in the charge against the accused; however, charges may be reduced for many reasons and there is no reason to suppose that all charge reductions are in fact the consequence of plea bargaining. Hartnagel and Wynne, on the other hand, only considered plea bargaining to have taken place where there were, *inter alia*, correspondence or written comments in the file that indicated a deal had occurred. Clearly, it is a somewhat doubtful assumption that all plea bargains will be recorded in writing in the official court files.

More recently, a group of researchers at the University of Toronto's Centre of Criminology conducted a major study of discretionary decision-making in the criminal justice process in the course of which a wealth of data based on a variety of research methods, including direct observation of the plea bargaining process, was uncovered. One hundred and one accused persons were tracked through the criminal justice system from arrest to sentence. The data from this study have been reported in several sources,[105] the most comprehensive of which is a book by Ericson and Baranek (1982). A number of different research techniques were employed in the collection of the data. Verbatim transcripts were kept of interviews with the accused and interviews with lawyers; recordings were also made of conversations in the Crown attorney's office. Researchers also observed the court appearances of the defendants in the sample. This study represents the first time researchers have actually been able to document the dynamics involved in the process of plea bargaining.

In their book, Ericson and Baranek (1982:117) employ the term "plea discussions" rather than "plea bargaining" because the former expression renders it clear that discussions may be entered into without an agreement ever being reached. They concluded (1982:121) that "plea discussions were a widespread and integral part of the order out of court." In this respect, they found (1982:117-118) that of the lawyers for 80 accused persons who were interviewed, lawyers for as many as 57 accused said that they had entered into plea discussions. Furthermore, they found (1982:121) that participation in plea discussions was not confined to Crown and defence counsel; indeed, the police were frequently involved at various stages in the plea discussion process.

Ericson and Baranek suggest that the existence of multiple charges appears to constitute a major element in the circumstances that lead to plea discussions taking place. Of the 23 accused whose lawyers did *not* engage in such discussions, 17 had only one charge laid against them (as compared with only 9 of the 57 accused whose lawyers were involved in plea discussions). The authors suggest that this underlines the importance of multiple charging as a vital component of the plea discussion process in Canada; without the existence of multiple charges, the defence could not negotiate for the withdrawal of some charge(s) in return for the entry of a guilty plea to others. Lawyers who engaged in discussions with the Crown said that withdrawal of charges was the major topic of conversation (Ericson and Baranek, 1982:119).

Given that there was widespread involvement in plea discussions, what was the outcome of such involvement? The striking finding made by Ericson and Baranek (1982:143) was that, although many of the lawyers engaged in plea discussions, only about a quarter of them stated that they had reached an agreement that could be considered a bargain. For this group of lawyers, the most frequently mentioned bargain was one that included a sentence concession. Of the remaining lawyers who entered plea discussions, 12% stated that they had not reached an agreement, while lawyers for the remaining 88% claimed that the agreement reached brought no real advantage for the accused. More than half of the lawyers (representing 23 accused) who thought that an agreement had brought no tangible benefit stated that the charges withdrawn or reduced in their cases did not represent a concession because such charges were merely the result of overcharging by the police in the first place (Ericson and Baranek, 1982:145).

Solomon (1983) also analyzed the data gathered from the study conducted by the Centre of Criminology at the University of Toronto. He contends that the data suggest that plea bargaining occurred more frequently in the provincial courts of Robert County than might have been expected from a reading of the Canadian literature on the topic.[106] However, as is the case with Ericson and Baranek, he contends that plea bargaining "did not result in important concessions for the accused." In the Provincial Court, almost 80% of the criminal cases that were not withdrawn by the Crown terminated with guilty pleas, and 60% of these cases involved plea discussions. It appears that the discussions between defence counsel and the Crown and/or police usually focused on the charges to which the accused would plead guilty rather than the sentence (although there was some discussion of the approach that the Crown would adopt at the sentencing stage). Plea agreements resulted in the dropping of charges (which were often not justified in the first place) and at least a tacit agreement about the Crown's recommendation as to sentence. However, Solomon (1983:37) points out that there was no clear relationship between the charges to which the accused ultimately pleaded guilty and the sentence handed down by the Court. Furthermore, the sentencing recommendations made by the Crown had no direct impact upon the sentence actually handed down by the court. In these circumstances, an accused person who entered into a plea arrangement with the Crown had no guarantee that his or her guilty plea would make any difference whatsoever to the ultimate outcome of the case.

If the defendant does not normally gain any special advantages from the plea discussion process, what is the rationale for the participation of so many defence counsel in the practice? In Solomon's view (1983:43), the data from Robert County are consistent with the view that the "primary responsibility of defence counsel in plea bargaining...consists not in seeking special advantages, but in assuring that the outcome of the case is no worse than the local norms dictate." He also contends that, from the point of view of the accused, plea bargaining may have some tangible benefits as an alternative means of disposing of his or her case. Although accused persons did not seem to gain more lenient sentences for themselves as a consequence of entering into a plea agreement, they did nevertheless derive a "procedural gain":

> More than anything else, plea bargaining offered the accused through his counsel a forum for presenting a defence of the case informally without the need to bear the costs (in money, time, and emotional strain) associated with contesting trial. From the defence counsel's presentation in plea discussions two tangible benefits did emerge. First, he [or she] could ensure that the interpretation of the evidence reflected in the final charges and the crown attorney's sentencing recommendation (if any) would be no worse than the local norm for that genre of case. Secondly, in some cases counsel could also obtain

the prosecutor's agreement to consider, if not a lenient sentence, then suggesting a particular kind of sentence (1983:48).

Conditions that Facilitate Plea Bargaining in Canada

Many factors in the structure of the Canadian system of criminal justice facilitate the practice of plea bargaining. Among the more significant of these are, as we have seen, the very broad discretionary powers enjoyed by the prosecution coupled with the essentially passive role adopted by the judiciary who rely upon the Crown and the defence to present the relevant facts of the case instead of conducting their own inquiries into the facts (Feeley, 1982). By way of comparison, Feeley (1982:347) points out that, in Germany, where the prosecutor does not have such broad discretionary powers and where the judge plays an active role in the criminal trial, plea bargaining is virtually unknown.

Other major factors that facilitate plea bargaining are the close relationships that develop between the court actors (Brantingham, 1985; Champion, 1989; Grosman, 1969). The existence of salaried prosecutors and the availability of professional lawyers for the representation of the accused permits trusting relationships to develop between these professionals. Ericson and Baranek (1982:13-14) note that this sense of trust also extends to the police. Individuals making "deals" have to be reasonably confident that the other party will honour his or her part of the bargain and such trust can evolve during the course of a number of plea discussions. In this context, it appears that defendants who are not members of this "bargaining unit" are precluded from participating directly in pre-trial negotiations (Hartnagel and Wynne, 1975). Having a lawyer, therefore, appears to be a necessary condition for plea bargaining to occur (Verdun-Jones and Hatch, 1985:41).[107]

The relationship with the other court actors poses major problems for defence lawyers. As Ericson and Baranek (1982) point out, the various court actors have a vested interest in maintaining mutually beneficial relationships between themselves and other court actors, even if the latter are ostensibly on the "other side." Defence counsel are in a particularly precarious position because they are attempting to serve the best interests of their clients while simultaneously maintaining a harmonious relationship with the Crown.

> The lawyer has a particularly complex set of stakes. These involve a balance between doing a job which appears competent to his client and maintaining the professional respect and collaboration of crime control officials (Ericson and Baranek, 1982:26).

It has been argued that the existence of such a rapport between the court actors is contrary to the notion of the adversary system of justice (Warner and Renner, 1981). Warner and Renner examined cases heard by three magistrate's courts and two county courts in Halifax. They found little evidence of the operation of a vigorous adversary system; rather, they suggested that the court system operated as a bureaucracy that was geared primarily to the processing of criminal cases in the most efficient manner possible. The majority of defendants were unrepresented. However, in those cases where the accused were represented, there was evidence of a lack of adversariness. The judge usually accepted the sentencing recommendation made by one of the lawyers with the other usually manifesting tacit acceptance by remaining silent or else both the lawyers agreed and the judge concurred (Warner and Renner, 1981:91).

However, it has been questioned whether the rise of plea bargaining truly represents a retreat from a golden past in which criminal cases were fought out between aggressive adversaries in the crucible of a full trial of the issues. Feeley, for example, strongly rejects the notion that plea bargaining is a cooperative practice that strikes at the heart of the adversarial system of criminal justice:

> Plea bargaining is not a cooperative practice that undermines or compromises the adversary process; rather, the opportunity for adversariness has expanded in direct proportion to, and perhaps as a result of, the growth of plea bargaining. As the requirements of due process have expanded, as resources have become more accessible to both the prosecution and the criminally accused, as the substantive criminal law has developed, and as the availability and role of defence counsel have expanded, the opportunity for both adversariness and negotiations has increased (1982:340).

In Feeley's view (1982:346), there never was a "golden era" or "high noon" of the adversary process in the United States, and one can perhaps extend the force of his comments to the Canadian situation as well. Even in the distant past, when there was a greater reliance upon the trial rather than the guilty plea as a means of deciding criminal cases, the trial process was generally very brief and perfunctory, and the accused was unlikely to be represented by defence counsel. In short, although there may have been a greater proportion of "trials," these tended to be rushed affairs with none of the adversarial protections that are claimed by defendants in the contemporary criminal trial process. In these circumstances, Feeley suggests that the access of accused persons to defence counsel has greatly enhanced the adversarial nature of the criminal justice process, even if much of the work of defence lawyers is concentrated upon the task of plea bargaining. Indeed, he feels (1982:352) that the very presence of a lawyer who can negotiate with the prosecution represents an increase in adversariness.

Solomon is equally sceptical of the contention that the close relationships between Crown and defense counsel necessarily represent a threat to the adversarial underpinnings of the criminal justice system. In his view (1983:42), "maintaining a working relationship with Crown attorneys did not call for abdication of defence responsibilities, but for avoiding unreasonable and unproductive tactics." According to Solomon, there was a "marked convergence of interest" between defence lawyer and client and the former tended to reserve his or her main efforts for the process of plea discussions on behalf of his or her clients.

A vital element in facilitating the plea bargaining process is the power of the police to lay multiple charges in relation to the same basic incident. In addition, with a view to future bargaining, the police may lay a more serious charge than the facts really warrant. Ericson and Baranek discovered some evidence for this proposition in their study:

> ...the police decide to charge with an eye towards outcomes in court. They "frame" the limits to what is negotiable, and produce conviction and sentence outcomes, by "overcharging," "charging up," and laying highly questionable charges (1982:71).

Solomon (1983:45) draws the same conclusions from this data when he states that, in Robert County, overcharging was the normal practice of the police, who laid every conceivable charge on the assumption that some of the excess charges could be bargained away for a guilty plea. Since the extra charges do not appear to have an impact on the ultimate sentence handed down by the Court, their abandonment did not inflict a particularly high "cost" upon the police.

The ability of the police to lay more charges than may reasonably be expected to result in convictions is an important facilitating condition of plea bargaining. Brannigan and Levy state that:

> Such a looseness of fit between the police latitude in laying charges and limitations on the Crown's ability to secure convictions on them is probably the single most important source of charge reductions and one of the most important factors in so-called plea bargaining (1983:404).

Unlike Ericson and Baranek or Solomon, however, Brannigan and Levy (1983:403) are reluctant to characterize this process as "overcharging" since they state that the police do not make up facts to justify additional charges. Instead, they contend that the police "are being technical in their charging behaviour."

The Supreme Court of Canada has indirectly encouraged the laying of multiple charges by the police by ruling in the *Kienapple* case (1974) that, while an individual cannot be *convicted* of more than one offence for exactly the same incident, he or she can still be *charged* with more than one offence.[108] In *Kienapple*, the accused had been convicted of both rape and unlawful sexual intercourse with a girl under the age of 14 years. The Supreme Court quashed the second conviction on the basis that he could not be convicted more than once for the same crime. However, the Court also ruled that more than one charge can be laid in such circumstances and that these charges should be treated as alternative counts. As Brannigan states:

> ...the application of the Kienapple doctrine is frequently quite ambiguous. Typically the police will lay whatever charges seem appropriate, leaving the question of double jeopardy for the lawyers to sort out. This affects plea discussions quite directly (1984:149).

One possible danger in such circumstances is that the defendant may be induced to plead guilty on the basis of the Crown dropping a charge in a situation where he or she could not have been convicted of more than one offence in any event. Such a plea agreement would be an "illusory" bargain since the accused has gained nothing from his or her decision to enter a plea of guilty (Verdun-Jones and Hatch, 1985:20).[109]

A further facilitating factor for plea bargaining is the ability of the police as well as the Crown and defence counsel to control the information that is ultimately introduced to the court, thereby having some impact on the sentence meted out (for example, not mentioning an accused person's prior record during the sentencing hearing). This has been called fact bargaining and has been extensively documented by Ericson and Baranek (1982:19-23, 66, 120-121).

Regulating Plea Bargaining

At present, plea bargaining operates without any substantial controls to protect the interests of society, the victim, and the offender. A study that focused on the responses to questionnaires mailed to defence lawyers and Crown counsel in six provinces found that over 77% of the defence lawyers and over 56% of Crown counsel indicated that they frequently engage in plea negotiations, while 20% and 32%, respectively, stated that they engaged in the practice "sometimes" (Landau, 1988:38). Given the extremely widespread existence of the practice, it is highly probable that any attempt to abolish plea bargaining would be fraught with insurmountable difficulties (Cousineau and Verdun-Jones, 1979; Verdun-Jones and Cousineau, 1979; Verdun-Jones and Hatch, 1985; 1987). Some U.S. studies suggest that attempting to abolish the practice does not eradicate it but rather changes its nature and/or displaces it to a different point in the criminal process (Carns and Kruse, 1992; Church, 1976; McCoy, 1984). In this respect, Verdun-Jones and Hatch (1985:14-15) note that research in the United States suggests that "plea bargaining is pervasive, tenacious and very adaptable." It appears that some form of discretionary decision-making is a necessary component of any criminal justice system (Easterbrook, 1992). Indeed, as Verdun-Jones and Hatch point out:

> Given the fact that criminal justice systems are characterised by attempts to achieve many varied and often conflicting goals, then it seems reasonable to assume that these systems will always generate and perpetuate discretionary decision-making processes as adaptations to these multiple ends. Plea bargaining appears to allow and facilitate the accommodation of these multiple purposes of criminal justice systems (1985:15).

If outright abolition is not feasible, what steps can be taken to ensure that plea bargaining is not abused? Perhaps the first step is to accept the legitimacy of the practice and to establish formal controls to monitor the conduct of those involved in it. As the Canadian Sentencing Commission stated:

> ...it would be far more realistic to recommend methods of enhancing the visibility and accountability of plea bargaining decisions than to recommend the abolition of the practice (1986:415).

To this end, the Commission (1986:417) recommended that a sentencing judge should inquire of a defendant whether he or she fully understands the nature and implications of a plea agreement and that, if he or she does not, then the judge should be granted the discretion to set aside the plea or sentence. The judiciary could, for example, take special care to ensure that a defendant does not plead guilty when there are doubts about his or her guilt. Ericson and Baranek (1982:158) found that 16 of the 101 defendants whom they interviewed pleaded guilty despite claiming that they were innocent. The Sentencing Commission (1986:422-423) also recommended that the appropriate federal and provincial authorities should devise, and attempt to enforce, guidelines concerning the ethics of plea bargaining and that the Crown should normally be required to "justify in open court a plea bargain agreement reached by the parties." The Commission (1986:425) further recommended that the judiciary not become involved in the plea negotiation process itself and that the *Criminal Code* should be amended so as to provide that the court is not bound by any joint sentencing submission made by the Crown and the defence or any other arrangement by the parties concerning a particular charge or sentence.

The Law Reform Commission of Canada (1989) made a series of similar recommendations. In summarizing the principles underlying its approach, the Commission stated that:

> ...we believe that the process needs to be more open; that it should be subject to judicial supervision; that the absence of improper inducements should be ensured with respect to pleas resulting therefrom; that the accuracy and appropriateness of pleas resulting therefrom should be monitored; that equal treatment of accused persons should be made

a general goal and that enforceability of plea agreements should be the
rule (1989:12).

No matter what the ultimate outcome of the Canadian Sentencing
Commission's recommendations may turn out to be, it should be noted
that plea bargaining may well become more institutionalized as a
consequence of an amendment to the *Criminal Code* that establishes pre-
hearing conferences between the Crown, defence counsel, and the trial
judge in order to try and settle certain issues before they come to trial.
Section 625.1 of the *Criminal Code* makes such hearings mandatory in
the case of jury trials and optional in other cases (provided the prosecutor
and accused agree). The section envisages the pre-trial hearing as a
method of promoting a "fair and expeditious" hearing or trial. Clearly,
such hearings could well provide a forum for plea bargaining with the
judge ensuring that the outcome is fair from the points of view of both
the accused, the victim (if any), and society at large. In British Columbia,
a number of so-called "disclosure courts" have been established to deal
with serious and/or complex criminal cases. Part of the function of these
courts is to provide an opportunity for the prosecution and the defence to
get together before a judge and see if there is a way to dispose of the
case before it goes to trial. The prosecutor can indicate the basis on
which it is prepared to dispose of the case and the range of sentence that
it is prepared to recommend, should there be a guilty plea. If the accused
is agreeable to this disposition, then he or she may plead guilty and
arrangements can be made for sentencing. If this aspect of the Disclosure
Court Process is successful, then it clearly has the potential to save a
considerable amount of court time and resources and to provide a
judicially supervised forum in which plea agreements can be presented to,
and accepted by, defence counsel.

Even if the courts are given greater power to supervise the plea
bargaining process, there is always a danger that the Crown and defence
may fail to present the "full facts" of the case to the judge, thereby
influencing whether or not a proposed plea agreement is accepted. One
method by means of which the dangers of "fact bargaining" could be
reduced would be to ensure that the sentencing judge is made aware of
the impact of the offence upon the victim (if there is one). The use of
victim impact statements (Clarke, 1986:39-40) by the Crown may ensure
that the facts presented to the court by the Crown and defence are not too
far removed from the victim's perception of what actually took place.

Dubious behaviour on the part of lawyers involved in the plea bargaining process may also be controlled by the application of ethical principles by the various provincial law societies in the course of disciplinary proceedings. The Canadian Bar Association's *Code of Professional Conduct* (1988) already contains specific guidelines concerning plea agreements, and the *Code* has been adopted by most provincial law societies. Unethical conduct might well be found to have occurred, for example, where a lawyer has persuaded a client to plead guilty despite the client's belief that he or she is not guilty.[110] In addition, the behaviour of Crown counsel is very likely to be controlled, at least to some extent, by principles established by the Attorney-General, usually in written form.[111]

Public Opinion and Plea Bargaining

In its 1989 working paper, the Law Reform Commission addressed the question of public attitudes towards plea bargaining in Canada and noted that "the plea negotiation process has not generally enjoyed a very flattering public image" (1989:7). The Commission (1989:84) indicated that it had developed a survey that was eventually administered by the Gallup organization in February, 1988. In discussing the results obtained from this survey, Cohen and Doob (1989:96) note that, in general, Canadians disapprove of the practice. Indeed, some 68% of adult Canadians (or 79% of those who had some opinion on this matter) expressed their disapproval of plea bargaining. Cohen and Doob (1989:97) suggest that this disapproval was strongly linked to the belief that plea bargaining leads to excessively lenient sentences. The study suggested that Canadians assumed that judges were generally not given all the relevant information when sentencing someone who had made a plea bargain with the Crown. However, the public appeared to view sentencing decisions in a more favourable light if they believed that the judge had been informed of the existence of a plea bargain and had full knowledge of the reasons that prompted it.

In summarizing the study results, Cohen and Doob suggest:

> Most Canadians disapprove of the process of plea bargaining. It may lower the public's confidence in the ability of the sentencing judge to deal with the case in a fair and appropriate manner. However, much of this detrimental impression is removed if the full explanation of the

process is given in open court. Enhancing the awareness of the judge of the facts of the process or actually having the judge present at key stages of the process appears to foster greater public confidence and render the outcome more acceptable than would be the case if the judge is not so involved (1989:103).

This research clearly tends to lend support to the recommendations of the Canadian Sentencing Commission and the Law Reform Commission of Canada that the process of plea negotiation should be rendered open, accountable and subject to judicial supervision.

This chapter has provided a glimpse of the sheer complexity of this critical stage in the criminal justice system. The analysis of the right to counsel and legal representation as well as the right to be tried within a reasonable time reveals the critical impact that the *Charter* may have on the day-to-day operations of the criminal justice system. However, the application of the *Charter* can create some daunting challenges for those who work in the system, for example, the attempts of the courts to enforce the right of accused persons to be tried within a reasonable time.

The discussion of prosecutorial discretion and plea bargaining also illustrates the impact of the *Charter* on the functioning of the court process. However, in addition, it provides a conspicuous example of the increased trend toward demanding more accountability on the part of criminal justice officials, such as the Crown counsel. In the case of prosecutors, this accountability may be achieved by expanding the supervisory role of the courts (through the application of the abuse of process doctrine as well as the enforcement of individual rights guaranteed by the *Charter*) and the adoption of clear guidelines for the exercise of prosecutorial discretion. These guidelines may be enshrined not only in legislation but also in codes of professional ethics or policy statements issued by the Office of the Attorney-General (or Minister of Justice). Discretion is clearly necessary if the criminal justice system is to operate in a manner that reflects the ever-changing context in which decisions are made about matters that may deeply affect the lives of accused persons, victims, and their respective families. Nevertheless, discretion that is exercised in an arbitrary manner will ultimately destroy the citizens' faith in the criminal justice system itself. Therefore, the challenge facing criminal justice policy makers and the courts in the future is to devise methods of structuring discretion without unduly handcuffing those who must make discretionary decisions. Clearly, their goal must be to encourage the exercise of discretion in conformity with guiding principles that will attract the support of the average Canadian.

NOTES

[1]Farris CJBC in *R. v. Ewing and Kearney,* [1974] 5 W.W.R. 232 (B.C.C.A.) at 233-234.

[2]*Regina v. Brydges* (1990), 53 C.C.C. (3d) 330 (S.C.C.).

[3]*Joplin v. Chief Constable of the City of Vancouver* (1983), 2 C.C.C. (3d) 396 (B.C.S.C.).

[4]Section 650(3). This particular section applies in the case of indictable offences. However, section 802(1) provides for a similar right to make a "full answer and defence" in the case of summary conviction offences. Section 802(2) also provides that the accused "may examine and cross-examine witnesses personally or by counsel or agent."

[5]*R. v. Bowles and Danylak* (1985), 21 C.C.C. (3d) 540 (Alta. C.A.).

[6]*Barrette v. The Queen* (1976), 29 C.C.C. (2d) 189 (S.C.C.).

[7]*R. v. Huebschwerlen,* [1965] 3 C.C.C. 212; *R. v. Hardy* (1991), 69 C.C.C. (3d) 190 (Alta.C.A.).

[8]Section 684.

[9]Note that section 672.24 of the *Code* provides that, where "the court has reasonable grounds to believe" that a mentally disordered accused is "unfit to stand trial and the accused is not represented by counsel, the court *shall* order that the accused be represented by counsel" (emphasis added).

[10]*Re White and The Queen* (1976), 32 C.C.C. (2d) 478 (Alta. S.C.T.D.)

[11]*R. v. Ewing and Kearney,* [1974] 5 .W.W.R. 232 (B.C.C.A.). This ruling was followed in the Ontario case of *R. v. Ciglen* (1979), 10 C.R. (3d) 226 (Ont. H.Ct.).

[12]*Deutsch v. Law Society of Upper Canada* (1986), 47 C.R. (3d) 166 (Ont. Div.Ct.).

[13]A very similar view was expressed by McDonald J. of the Alberta Court of Queen's Bench three years later; *Panacui v. Legal Aid Society of Alberta* (1987), 40 C.C.C. (3d) 459.

[14]*R. v. Rowbotham et al.* (1988), 41 C.C.C. (3d) 1 (Ont.C.A.).

[15]*Ibid.,* at 64.

[16]*Ibid.,* at 66.

[17]*R. v. Robinson et al.* (1989), 51 C.C.C. (3d) 452 (Alta.C.A.).

[18]Justice Lamer said that the issue was not before the Court (53 C.C.C. (3d) 330, at 351).

[19]*R. v. Prosper* (1992), 75 C.C.C. (3d) 1 (N.S.S.C., App.Div.).

[20]*R. v. Munroe* (1990), 59 C.C.C. (3d) 446 (N.S.C.A.).

[21]*R. v. Rockwood* (1989), 49 C.C.C. (3d) 129 (N.S.C.A.). See also *Panacui v. Legal Aid Society of Alberta* (1987), 40 C.C.C. (3d) 459 (Alta.Q.B.).

[22]*Ibid.*, at 134.

[23]An important issue that will probably be considered with increasing frequency under the *Charter* is the whole question of the effectiveness of defence counsel and whether the incompetence of counsel should be a ground for ordering a new trial where it is claimed that the accused was convicted as a consequence of such incompetence. After all, there is little point in the courts recognizing a right to counsel if they do not also ensure that defendants receive effective assistance from their counsel. However, it appears that there is considerable reluctance on the part of the courts to set aside a trial verdict on this basis. For example, in *R. v. Garofoli* (1988), 41 C.C.C. (3d) 97, the Ontario Court of Appeal rejected the accused's claim that his constitutional right to the effective assistance of counsel (under sections 7, 10(b) and 11(d) of the *Charter*) had been infringed. Justice Martin emphasized that, in order to use the *Charter* right to effective assistance from counsel as a means of overturning the trial decision, not only must the accused prove that counsel was incompetent but also that, but for counsel's errors, the result of the trial would have been different. The accused had been unable to prove these two elements so the Court was unwilling to give him a remedy. It is clear that this approaches places a heavy burden on the shoulders of defendants who claim that their *Charter* rights have been infringed because they were the victims of ineffective representation by counsel. A number of such claims have been rejected because the defendants concerned have not been able to meet these demanding criteria; see *R. v. E.J.B.* (1992), 76 C.C.C. (3d) 530 (Sask. C.A.); *R. v. Collier* (1992), 77 C.C.C. (3d) 570 (Ont. C.A.); *R. v. Sarson* (1992), 77 C.C.C. (3d) 233 (N.S. C.A.).

However, the same court ruled that, where the accused's counsel had been in a conflict of interest situation that deprived him of a fair trial, then he was entitled to a new trial; see *R. v. Silvini* (1991), 68 C.C.C. (3d) 251 (Ont.C.A.).

[24]The federal government paid about 42% of the total government contributions to the legal aid plans in 1990-91. It paid $86.9 million for criminal legal aid and $52.9 million for civil legal aid (Canadian Centre for Justice Statistics, 1992:4).

[25]See, for example, the discussion in *Mountain v. Legal Services Society*, [1984] 2 W.W.R. 438 (B.C. C.A.).

[26]However, in exceptional circumstances, lawyers may be retained from private firms to deal with legal aid cases.

[27]In this "staff system," the legal aid authority may also operate a number of community law offices or community legal aid clinics. For example, in British Columbia, community law offices are governed by community boards and contract annually for funds from the legal aid authority (Brantingham and Brantingham, 1984:31).

[28]In a study conducted in three U.S. states, Champion (1989) also found a difference in outcome based on the nature of legal representation. He discovered that private defence attorneys were much more likely to succeed in having charges dropped against their clients than was the case with public defenders. Furthermore, the clients of private attorneys fared better in terms of the punishment ultimately imposed on them.

[29]Section 11. An important question that arises in relation to the Youth Court is whether children have the necessary knowledge about the legal system to be able to give competent instructions to their lawyers. For discussion of this issue, see Peterson-Badali and Abramovitch (1992).

[30]*R. v. Kalanj* (1989), 48 C.C.C. (3d) 459 (S.C.C.). See also *R. v. Padfield* (1992), 79 C.C.C. (3d) 53 (Ont. C.A.).

[31]*Carter v. The Queen* (1986), 26 C.C.C (3d) 572 (S.C.C.).

[32]*R. v. Mills* (1986), 26 C.C.C. (3d) 481 (S.C.C.); *R. v. Gatley* (19920, 74 C.C.C. (3d) 468 (B.C.C.A.).

[33]*W.K.L. v. The Queen* (1991), 64 C.C.C. (3d) 321 (S.C.C.).

[34]*R. v. D.A.* (1992), 76 C.C.C. (3d) 1 (Ont. C.A.). See also *R. v. D.L.D.* (1992) 77 C.C.C. (3d) 426 (Man. C.A.) where a 20-year delay in laying a charge of sexual assault was not considered to constitute a violation of the accused's right to a speedy trial.

[35]Among the early cases were *R. v. Mills* (1986), 26 C.C.C. (3d) 481 (S.C.C.); *R. v. Rahey* (1987), 33 C.C.C. (3d) 289 (S.C.C.); *R. v. Conway* (1989), 49 C.C.C. (3d) 289 (S.C.C.); *R. v. Smith* (1989), 52 C.C.C. (3d) 97 (S.C.C.).

[36]*R. v. Askov* (1990), 59 C.C.C. (3d) 449 (S.C.C.).

[37]*Ibid.*, at 483-484.

[38]*Ibid.*, at 484-485.

[39]*Ibid.*, at 492.

[40]An example of a waiver of the right to a speedy trial occurred in the case of *R. v. Slaney* (1992), 75 C.C.C. (3d) 385 (Nfld. C.A.). In this case, there had been a 16-month delay between the laying of the charges and the date of the accused's trial. Approximately eleven months of this period passed between the committal for trial (after a preliminary inquiry) and the actual trial itself. However, since the accused's counsel had agreed to this date (by not asking for an earlier date when the judge had set the trial date), the Newfoundland Court of Appeal ruled that he had waived the delay between the setting of the trial date and the actual trial of the case (some seven months). The court concluded that the remaining delay of nine months (sixteen minus seven) was reasonable and did not infringe the accused's rights under section 11(b) of the *Charter*.

[41]For example, in *Bennett*, the trial judge granted a stay of proceedings because the thirteen-month delay (of which some nine months was due to "systemic delay") exceeded the six-to-eight-month guideline set in the *Askov* case. The Ontario Court of Appeal later overturned the stay and ordered a new

trial, stating that the Supreme Court had never intended to impose a rigid time-limit of six to eight months; rather, the Court must examine all the circumstances to determine whether the delay was, in fact, unreasonable. See *R. v. Bennett* (1991), 64 C.C.C. (3d) 449 (Ont. C.A.); affirmed, (1992), 74 C.C.C. (3d) 384 (S.C.C.).

[42]Figures quoted by Justice Sopinka in *R. v. Morin* (1992), 71 C.C.C. (3d) 1 (S.C.C.), at 7.

[43]*Ibid.*, at 27.

[44]*Ibid.*, at 19.

[45]*Ibid.*, at 20.

[46]In a similar case, the Supreme Court of Canada later ruled that a nine-month delay between arrest date and trial was not unreasonable where systemic delay had been brought about by reorganization of the Youth Court in Ontario; *R. v. M.A.J.* (1992), 75 C.C.C. (3d) 128 (S.C.C.).

[47]*Sharma v. The Queen* (1992), 71 C.C.C. (3d) 184 (S.C.C.).

[48]A very recent decision of the B.C. Court of Appeal suggests that the *Morin* and *Sharma* cases have, indeed, been interpreted as a major threat from the *Askov* case. In *R. v. Light* (1993), 78 C.C.C. (3d) 221 (B.C. C.A.), the Court ruled that a two-year lapse between the date of charging and the date of trial was not unreasonable given the circumstances; namely, that this was a complex narcotics case involving numerous defendants and congested calendars that affected both the courts and the lawyers concerned. Justice Wood, on behalf of the Court (at p. 251), stated that the *Morin* case required that the "length of the delay in any case must be viewed against a backdrop of the reasons for that delay, including the so-called 'inherent time requirements' of the case, the actions of the accused, the actions of the Crown and the limits on institutional resources." The *Light* decision clearly recognizes the inherent complexity of a case as a reason that would justify what would otherwise be considered an excessive delay. In similar vein, a 23-month delay was not considered to be unreasonable in a complex fraud case in which there were allegations involving fraud of millions of dollars and requiring the police to interview hundreds of witnesses and to review thousands of documents: *R. v. Atkinson et al.* (1991), 68 C.C.C. (3d) 109 (Ont. C.A.), affirmed (1992), 76 C.C.C. (3d) 288 (S.C.C.).

However, the "retreat from *Askov*" does not mean that the courts will not enter a stay of proceedings where the delay involved is very substantial in nature and cannot be justified by special circumstances. For example, the Quebec Court of Appeal, in a case decided after *Morin*, did enter a stay of proceedings where there was a delay of 27 months between the laying of several charges of sexual assault and the accused's trial; see *R. v. Trudel* (1992), 78 C.C.C. (3d) 169. Here the major factor appears to have been the fact that the trial judge suffered a heart attack and his subsequent absence caused a delay of six months. Since the Crown made no effort to apply for another judge to take the case, this component of the delay was considered unreasonable. In *Trudel*, therefore, at least part of the lengthy delay in bringing the accused to trial could have been avoided had the Crown had the will to do so. Similarly, in *R. v. Padfield* (1992), 79 C.C.C. (3d) 53, the Ontario Court of Appeal agreed with the view of the trial judge that a 32-month delay was unreasonable in light of all the circumstances and, in *R. v. Brassard* (1992), 78 C.C.C. (3d) 329, the Quebec Court of Appeal held that a two-year delay was unreasonable given the circumstance that a major proportion of this delay stemmed from the unavailability of a judge to hear the case. Clearly the delays in *Brassard, Padfield,* and *Trudel* were much more substantial than the delays in *Morin* and *Sharma*.

[49]See *Attorney of Quebec et al. v. Lechasseur* (1981), 63 C.C.C. (2d) 301 (S.C.C.) and *Re Dowson and The Queen*, [1983] 2 S.C.R. 144 (S.C.C.).

[50]In Saskatchewan, Quebec, Prince Edward Island, and Newfoundland, the chief law officer of the Crown is known as the Minister of Justice or the Minister of Justice *and* Attorney-General. In other provinces, he or she is simply known as the Attorney-General. In the Yukon and the Northwest Territories, prosecutions are the responsibility of the federal Department of Justice. See Stenning, 1986:c.9.

[51]A number of important cases concerning this constitutional issue have been decided by the Supreme Court of Canada. However, many matters still have not been resolved; see *R. v. Hauser*, [1979] 1 S.C.R. 984; *R. v. Aziz*, [1981] 1 S.C.R. 188; *A.-G. Can v. Canadian National Transportation, Ltd.*; *A.-G. Can v. Canadian Pacific Transport Co. Ltd.*; *R. v. Wetmore and A.-G. Ont. et al.*, [1983] 2 S.C.R. 284.

[52]*R. v. Catagas* (1978), 38 C.C.C. (2d) 296 (Man.C.A.).

[53]*Ibid.*, at 301.

[54]*R. v. M.K.* (1992), 74 C.C.C. (3d) 108 (Man.C.A.).

[55]*Ibid.*, at 109, 110.

[56]*R. v. Paul Magder Furs Ltd.* (1989), 49 C.C.C. (3d) 415 (Ont. C.A.).

[57]Sections 579(1) and 795.

[58]See *Re Pardo and The Queen* (1990), 62 C.C.C. (3d) 371 (Que. C.A.). In this case, it was held that a stay may be entered after the information has been laid but before the justice of the peace decides whether or not to issue process.

[59]*R. v. Beaudry*, [1967] 1 C.C.C. 272 (B.C. C.A.).

[60]Crown counsel immediately preferred a new indictment for a different offence and the accused was ultimately convicted.

[61]*Ibid.*, at 275. On this point, the authority of *Beaudry* was re-affirmed by the B.C. Court of Appeal in the more recent case of *R. v. Smith* (1992), 79 C.C.C. (3d) 70. It was also held, in the *Smith* case, that accused persons cannot challenge the entry of a stay as a violation of their *Charter* rights because, the moment a charge is dropped, they are no longer in jeopardy and, therefore, there

can be no possible violation of their *Charter* rights. See also *R. v. Fortin* (1989), 47 C.R.R. 348 (Ont. C.A.).

[62]*Campbell v. Attorney-General of Ontario* (1987), 35 C.C.C. (3d) 480 (Ont. C.A.).

[63]*Re Attorney-General of Quebec and Chartrand* (1987), 40 C.C.C. (3d) 270 (Que.C.A.).

[64]*Ibid.*, at 271, *per* Beauregard J.A.

[65]Section 508(2).

[66]In this respect, Stenning (1986:246) refers to a case before the Ontario High Court, in which Justice Lieff said:

> Once it is premised that the Attorney General is under a duty to decide whether or not to prosecute in any given case and, if it is decided to prosecute, to carry out that task, it must follow as a corollary thereof that, in the absence of special circumstances, he not only has the right, but is also under a duty to withdraw a charge, where, in his opinion, the decision to prosecute has, in the light of later factors, turned out to be ill-conceived.

See *R. v. Dick*, [1969] 1 C.C.C. 147 at 156.

[67]*R. v. Karpinski*, [1957] S.C.R. 343 (S.C.C.).

[68]See *R. v. Osborne* (1975), 25 C.C.C. (2d) 405 (N.B. C.A.).

[69]In 1956, one federal Minister of Justice (Mr. Guy Favreau) did resign after questions in the House of Commons and after a report was issued following a public inquiry in which the manner in which he had exercised his prosecutorial discretion was strongly criticized. See Stenning (1986:305).

[70]*Vogel v. Canadian Broadcasting Corporation. Bird and Good*, [1982] 3 W.W.R. 97 (B.C.S.C.).

[71]See, for example, the judgment of the Ontario Court of Appeal in *Nelles v. The Queen in right of Ontario* (1985), 46 C.R. (3d) 289.

[72][1989], 2 S.C.R. 170.

[73]*Ibid.*, at 196-197.

[74]*R. v. T.(V.)* (1992), 71 C.C.C. (3d) 32 (S.C.C.).

[75]*Ibid.*, at 38.

[76]*Ibid.*, at 39, citing *R. v. Beare* (1988), 45 C.C.C. (3d) 39 (S.C.C.), at 76.

[77]*Ibid.*, at 40, citing *Director of Public Prosecutions v. Humphrys*, [1976] 2 All E.R. 497 (H.L.), at 511, *per* Viscount Dilhorne.

[78]*Ibid.*, at 41.

[79]The Supreme Court of Canada has emphasized that the doctrine of abuse of process only applies to the activities of the Attorney-General and his or her agents. It does not apply to the conduct of other ministers of the Crown (such as

the premier of a province); see *R. v. Vermette* (1988), 41 C.C.C. (3d) 523 (S.C.C.).

[80]*R. v. Jewett* (1985), 21 C.C.C. (3d) 7.

[81]*Ibid.*, at 31.

[82]See, for example, *Scott v. The Queen et al.* (1990), 61 C.C.C. (3d) 300 (S.C.C.).

[83]*R. v. D. (T.C.)* (1987), 38 C.C.C. (3d) 434 (Ont. C.A.), at 447 (emphasis added).

[84]*R. v. Young* (1984), 13 C.C.C. (3d) 1.

[85]*R. v. Kearney* (1992), 70 C.C.C. (3d) 507 (N.B.C.A.).

[86]*Ibid.*, at 511.

[87]This was the view expressed by Justice Hoyt in a dissenting judgment (at 511). The majority of the Court of Appeal treated the matter as a straightforward *Charter* issue, in which the abuse of process was held to constitute a violation of the accused's *Charter* rights under sections 7 and 11(d).

[88]*Ibid.*, at 523-524.

[89]*Ibid.*, at 528.

[90]*R. v. D.L.D.* (1992), 77 C.C.C. (3d) 426 (Man. C.A.), *per* Scott, C.J.M., at 431.

[91]*R. v. Miles of Music Ltd.* (1989), 48 C.C.C. (3d) 431 (Ont. C.A.), *per* Krever J.A., at 108.

[92]*Ibid.*, at 437.

[93]*R. v. Keyowski* (1988), 40 C.C.C. (3d) 481 (S.C.C.), at 484. In a dissenting judgment (with which two other Supreme Court of Canada agreed), Justice McLachlin contended that the doctrine of abuse of process and the jurisdiction of the Court under section 7 of the *Charter* are quite independent of each other; see R. v. Scott (1990), 61 C.C.C. (3d) 300. The majority of the Court did not express an opinion. However, it is significant that the B.C. Court of Appeal, in one of the latest cases to address this issue, threw in its lot with Justice McLachlin; see (*R. v. Light* 1993), 78 C.C.C. (3d) 221 (B.C. C.A.). Indeed, Justice Wood (at p. 245) stated that the abuse of process doctrine is intended to "preserve the integrity of the process through which justice is administered in the community," whereas the section 7 jurisdiction is concerned with providing a remedy for the breach of individual rights.

[94]*R. v. Zelensky et al.* (1979), 41 C.C.C. (2d) 97, at 116, *per* Pigeon, J.

[95]In the Youth Court, the judge is required to satisfy her/himself that the facts of the case support a charge before accepting a plea of guilty (*Young Offenders Act*, R.S.C. 1985, C. Y-1, s. 19(1)). In adult proceedings, the court is not obliged to do so, although it certainly has the discretion to conduct an inquiry if it so wishes; see *Adgey v. The Queen* (1973), 13 C.C.C. (2d) 177 (S.C.C.).

[96]*R. v. Ikalowjuak* (1980), 27 A.R. 492 (N.W.T.S.C.); *R. v. Beriault* (1982), 26 C.R. (3d) 396 (B.C. C.A.).

[97]*R. v. Johnson and Tremayne*, [1970] 4 C.C.C. 64 (Ont. C.A.).

[98]*R. v. Shanower* (1972), 8 C.C.C. (2d) 527 (Ont. C.A.); *R. v. Traux* (1979), 22 Crim. L.Q. 157 (Ont. C.A.); *R. v. Pineau* (1979), 24 A.R. 176 (Alta. S.C).

[99]*R. v. Bartlett; R. v. Cameron* (1961), 13 C.C.C. 119 (Man. C.A.).

[100]*R. v. Layte* (1983), 38 C.R. (3d) 204 (Ont. Co.Ct.), *per* Salhany Co.Ct.J.

[101]*R. v. Greene* (1971), 20 C.R.N.S. 238 (Ont.Co.Ct.); *R. v. Simoneau* (1978), 40 C.C.C. (2d) 307 at 316, *per* Matas J.A. (Man.C.A.).

[102]*R. v. Mouffe* (1971), 16 C.R.N.S. 257 (Que. C.A.); *R. v. Wood* (1988), 43 C.C.C. (3d) 570 (Ont. C.A.); *R. v. Valiquette* (1990), 60 C.C.C. (3d) 325 (Que. C.A.); *R. v. Abbott* (1992), 71 C.C.C. (3d) 444 (Newfld. C.A.).

The potential danger, inherent in the process of joint sentencing submissions, is well illustrated by the case of *R. v. Rubinstein* (1987), 41 C.C.C. (3d) 91. The accused had entered a plea of guilty to charges of "wash trading" and fraud, apparently after a plea bargain of some sort. Crown and defence counsel put forward a joint sentencing submission that recommended a suspended sentence with probation and the making of restitution to two of the accused's victims in the sum of $85,000. The trial judge refused to accept this recommendation and sentenced the accused to five years' imprisonment. The Ontario Court of Appeal (although it reduced the sentence to a period of two years less a day) held that the trial judge had acted correctly in refusing to allow the accused to withdraw his guilty plea once he had discovered that the joint sentencing recommendation was going to be rejected. Justice Zuber said:

> To permit an accused to withdraw his plea when the sentence does not suit him puts the court in the unseemly position of bargaining with the accused.

[103]*R. v. Valiquette* (1990), 60 C.C.C. (3d) 325 (Que. C.A.), at 330. See also *R. v. Wood* (1988), 43 C.C.C. (3d) 570 (Ont. C.A.), at 574.

[104]The data from this article were re-analyzed by Taylor (1982).

[105]See, for example, Brannigan (1984); Brannigan and Levy (1983); Osborne (1983); Solomon (1983); Wilkins (1979).

[106]Solomon (1983:37-38) points out, however, that this pattern of plea bargaining might not be applicable to the "higher courts."

[107]However, note that both Ericson and Baranek (1982:c.2) and Klein (1979) indicate that accused persons claimed to have bargained with the police. Klein reported that some inmates even claimed to have negotiated directly with Crown counsel.

[108]*Kienapple v. The Queen* (1974), 15 C.C.C. (2d) 524.

[109]Another form of "illusory bargaining" can occur if the Parole Board decides to compensate for the plea bargain by delaying release of an individual on parole (Shin, 1973). The bargain is illusory, in such circumstances, because

any gain made during sentencing is lost at the parole stage of the criminal justice process.

[110]The potential for abuse is evident in the light of Ericson and Baranek's finding (1982:159-160) that the defence lawyer plays a critically important role in convincing an accused person to plead guilty.

[111]For example, the British Columbia *Crown Counsel Policy Manual* (1991) entry on plea discussion states that:

> Crown Counsel may facilitate discussions with defence counsel to resolve issues and encourage their resolution. However, in considering what is in the best interests of the administration of justice, Crown Counsel must balance the rights of the accused, the public interest and the interests of the victim...The following considerations are relevant to all plea discussions:
>
> 1. Crown Counsel should not approve excessive counts on an information merely to influence an accused to plead guilty to some of the counts. The quality control standards...always apply.
> 2. Crown Counsel should accept a plea of guilty to an offence only where the evidence discloses a substantial likelihood of conviction.
> 3. Crown Counsel should not accept a plea of guilty that cannot be prosecuted due to limitation periods.
> 4. Crown Counsel may advise defence counsel of the position Crown will take before the court with respect to sentence. Crown Counsel should advise the court of any mitigating circumstances that appear relevant and must not agree to withhold from the court any significant aggravating fact if there is a substantial likelihood that this fact can be proved.
> 5. All representations to the judge pertaining to judicial exercise of discretion concerning the guilty plea should be made, or placed on record, in open court. Where attendance in the judge's chambers is dictated by the circumstances, Crown Counsel should request that defence counsel be present.
> 6. Before entering into an arrangement to accept a guilty plea to a lesser offence than charged in a serious and sensitive case..., Crown counsel should refer the matter to Regional Crown Counsel. Regional Crown Counsel should decide the appropriateness of the arrangement in consultation with the Assistant Attorney-General.

REFERENCES

Allen, R.K. 1992. "Selective Prosecution: A Viable Criminal Defence in Canada." 34 *Criminal Law Quarterly*. 414-442.

Berzins, A. 1990. "Plea Bargaining; A Crown Counsel View." 7 *Justice Report*. 6-7.

Bowen-Coulthurst, T.G. 1970. "Book Review." 20 *University of Toronto Law Journal.* 494-496.

Brannigan, A. 1984. *Crimes, Courts and Corrections: An Introduction to Crime and Social Control in Canada.* Toronto: Holt, Rinehart and Winston.

Brannigan, A., and J.C. Levy. 1983. "The Legal Framework of Plea Bargaining." 25 *Canadian Journal of Criminology,* 399-419.

Brantingham, P.L. 1985. "Judicare Counsel and Public Defenders: Case Outcome Differences." 27 *Canadian Journal of Criminology.* 67-81.

Brantingham, P.L., and P.J. Brantingham. 1984. *An Evaluation of Legal Aid in British Columbia.* Ottawa: Department of Justice.

Brantingham, P.L., and P. Burns. 1981. *The Burnaby, British Columbia Experimental Public Defender Project: An Evaluation.* Ottawa: Department of Justice.

Burns, P. 1975. "Private Prosecutions in Canada: The Law and a Proposal for Change." 21 *McGill Law Journal.* 269-297.

Burns, P. 1991. "The Power to Prosecute." In J. Atrens, P. Burns, and J.P. Taylor, eds. *Criminal Procedure: Canadian Law and Practice.* Vancouver: Butterworths, V-1 - V-43.

Burns, P., and R.S. Reid. 1981. "Delivery of Criminal Legal Aid Services in Canada: An Overview of the Continuing 'Judicare Versus Public Defender' Debate." 15 *UBC Law Review.* 403-429.

Canadian Bar Association. 1988. *Code of Professional Conduct.* Ottawa: Canadian Bar Association.

Canadian Centre for Justice Statistics. 1989. *Legal Aid in Canada: Resource and Caseload Statistics, 1987-88.* Juristat Service Bulletin, vol. 9, no. 2. Ottawa: Statistics Canada.

Canadian Centre for Justice Statistics. 1991. *Legal Aid in Canada: The 1980's in Review.* Juristat Service Bulletin. vol. 11. no. 11. Ottawa: Statistics Canada.

Canadian Centre for Justice Statistics. 1992. *Legal Aid in Canada: 1990-91.* Juristat Service Bulletin. vol 12. no. 23. Ottawa: Statistics Canada.

Canadian Centre for Justice Statistics. 1993. *Court Services in Canada.* Juristat Service Bulletin. vol. 13. no. 2. Ottawa: Statistics Canada.

Canadian Sentencing Commission. 1986. *Sentencing Reform: A Canadian Approach. Report of the Canadian Sentencing Commission.* Ottawa: Minister of Supply and Services Canada.

Carns, T.W., and J.A. Kruse. 1992. "Alaska's Ban on Plea Bargaining Reevaluated." 75 *Judicature.* 310-317.

Carrington, P.J., and S. Moyer. 1990. "The Effect of Defence Counsel on Plea and Outcome in Juvenile Court." 32 *Canadian Journal of Criminology.* 621-638.

Carrington, P.J., and S. Moyer. 1992. "Legal Representation in Canadian Juvenile Courts: Its Nature, Extent and Determinants." 34 *Canadian Journal of Criminology*. 51-74.

Cawley, J.M. 1991. *The Evolution of Legal Aid Policy in British Columbia 1950-1976: A Structuralist Analysis.* Ph.D. Dissertation. Burnaby, B.C.: Simon Fraser University.

Champion, D.J. 1989. "Private Counsels and Public Defenders: A Look at Weak Cases, Prior Records, and Leniency in Plea Bargaining." 17 *Journal of Criminal Justice*. 253-263.

Chevalier, P. 1990. "Plea Bargaining; A Defence Counsel View." 7 *Justice Report*. 7-9.

Church, T. 1976. "Plea Bargains, Concessions and the Courts: Analysis of a Quasi-Experiment." 10 *Law & Society Review*. 377-401.

Clarke, P. 1986. "Is There a Place for the Victim in the Prosecution Process?" 8 *Canadian Criminology Forum*. 31-44.

Code, M.A. 1992. *Trial Within a Reasonable Time: A Short History of Recent Controversies Surrounding Speedy Trial Rights in Canada and the United States.* Scarborough: Carswell.

Cohen, S.A. 1977. *Due Process of Law: The Canadian System of Criminal Justice.* Toronto: Carswell.

Cohen, S.A., and A.N. Doob, 1989. "Public Attitudes to Plea Bargaining." 32 *Criminal Law Quarterly*, 85-109.

Cormier, M. 1990. "Legal Aid in Ontario: The Function of Charity." 6 *Journal of Law and Social Policy*. 102-132.

Coughlan, S.G. 1991. "R. v. Askov — A Bold Step Not Boldly Taken." 33 *Criminal Law Quarterly*. 247-252.

Coughlan, S.G. 1992. "Trial Within a Reasonable Time: Does the Right Still Exist?" 12 *Criminal Reports*. (4th series). 34-44.

Cousineau, F.D., and S.N. Verdun-Jones. 1979. "Evaluating Research into Plea Bargaining in Canada and the United States: Pitfalls Facing the Policy Makers." 21 *Canadian Journal of Criminology*. 293-309.

Easterbrook, F.H. 1992. "Plea Bargaining as Compromise." 101 *Yale Law Journal*. 1969-1978.

Egleston, D.J. 1990. "Right to Counsel." In J. Atrens, P. Burns, and J.P. Taylor, eds. *Criminal Procedure: Canadian Law and Practice.* Vancouver: Butterworths. XIX-i - XIX-62.

Elman, B.P. 1990. "Supreme Court of Canada in Brydges Expands Right to Counsel." 1 *Constitutional Forum*. 15-17.

Epstein, M.H. 1988. "The Guiding Hand of Counsel: The Charter and the Right to Counsel on Appeal." 30 *Criminal Law Quarterly*. 35-53.

Ericson, R.V., and P.M. Baranek. 1982. *The Ordering of Justice: A Study of Accused Persons as Dependants in the Criminal Process.* Toronto: University of Toronto Press.

Feeley, M.M. 1979. *The Process is the Punishment: Handling Cases in a Lower Criminal Court.* New York: Russell Sage.

Feeley, M.M. 1982. "Plea Bargaining and the Structure of The Criminal Process." 7 *The Justice System Journal.* 338-354.

Ferguson, G., and D. Roberts. 1974. "Plea Bargaining: Directions for Canadian Reform." 52 *Canadian Bar Review.* 498-576.

Fitzgerald, O.E. 1990. *The Guilty Plea and Summary Justice.* Toronto: Carswell.

Friedland, M.L. 1989. "Controlling the Administrators of Criminal Justice." 31 *Criminal Law Quarterly.* 280-317.

Genova, L.R. 1981. "Plea Bargaining: In the End, Who Really Benefits?" 4 *Canadian Criminology Forum.* 30-44.

Gourlie, W.C. 1982. "Role of the Prosecutor: Fair Minister of Justice with Firm Convictions." 12 *Manitoba Law Journal.* 31-42.

Greenspan, E.L. 1985. "The Future Role of Defence Counsel." In A.N. Doob, and E.L. Greenspan, eds. *Perspectives in Criminal Law: Essays in Honour of John L.L.J. Edwards.* Aurora, Ont.: Canada Law Book, 204-225.

Griffiths, C.T., D.F. Cousineau, and S.N. Verdun-Jones. 1980. "Appearance Without Counsel: Self-Representation in the Criminal Courts of the United States and Canada." 4 *International Journal of Comparative and Applied Criminal Justice.* 213-231.

Grosman, B.A. 1969. *The Prosecutor.* Toronto: University of Toronto Press.

Hagan, J. 1975. "Parameters of Criminal Prosecution: An Application of Path Analysis to A Problem of Criminal Justice." 65 *Journal of Criminal Law, Criminology and Police Science.* 536-544.

Hartnagel, T.H., and D.F. Wynne. 1975. "Plea Negotiations in Canada." 17 *Canadian Journal of Criminology and Corrections.* 45-56.

Hutchison, S.C., and J.G. Marks, J.G. 1991. "Let Them Eat Cake or the Poor Person's Right to Counsel." 3 *Journal of Motor Vehicle Law.* 63-72.

Jubinville, R. 1990. "Trial Delays — The *Askov* Decision." 7 *Justice Report.* 4:1-4.

Klein, J.F. 1979. *Let's Make a Deal; Negotiating Justice.* Lexington, Massachusetts: Lexington Books.

Landau, T. 1988. *Views of Sentencing: A Survey of Crown and Defence Counsel.* Ottawa: Department of Justice, Research and Development Directorate, Policy, Programs and Research Branch.

Law, J.M. 1990. "A Tale of Two Immunities: Judicial and Prosecutorial Immunities in Canada." 28 *Alberta Law Review.* 468-520.

Law Reform Commission of Canada. 1975a. *Fourth Annual Report.* Ottawa: Information Canada.

_____. 1975b. *Working Paper no. 15: Criminal Procedure: Control of the Process.* Ottawa: Information Canada.

_____. 1984. *Report no. 22. Disclosure by the Prosecution.* Ottawa: Ministry of Supply and Services Canada.

_____. 1986. *Working Paper no. 52: Private Prosecutions.* Ottawa: Law Reform Commission of Canada.

_____. 1988. *Report no. 32: Our Criminal Procedure.* Ottawa: Law Reform Commission of Canada.

_____. 1989. *Working Paper no. 60: Plea Discussions and Agreements.* Ottawa: Law Reform Commission of Canada.

_____. 1990. *Working Paper no. 62: Controlling Criminal Prosecutions; The Attorney General and the Crown Prosecutor.* Ottawa: Law Reform Commission of Canada.

Ledgerwood, L.N. 1992. "The Dangers of *R. v. Askov.*" 1 *National Journal of Constitutional Law.* 395-408.

Lessard, J. 1990. "Trial Delay Reduction." 14 *Provincial Court Judges Journal.* 18-23.

Levesque, J.F.R. 1988. "Trial Within a Reasonable Time." 31 *Criminal Law Quarterly.* 55-75.

MacFarlane, B.A. 1990. "The Right to Counsel at Trial and on Appeal." 32 *Criminal Law Quarterly.* 440-466.

McCoy, C. 1984. "Determinate Sentencing, Plea Bargaining Bans, and Hydraulic Discretion in California." 9 *The Justice System Journal.* 256-275.

McDonald, W.F. 1987. "Judicial Supervision of the Guilty Plea Process: A Study of Six Jurisdictions." 70 *Judicature.* 203-215.

MacIntosh, D.A. 1991. "Pre-Charge Delay." 1 *National Journal of Constitutional Law.* 260-273.

Michalyshin, P.B. 1990. "*Brydges*: Should the Police be Advising of the Right to Counsel?" 74 *Criminal Reports.* (3rd series). 151-160.

Ministry of the Attorney General (B.C.). 1991. *Legal Aid Models: A Comparison of Judicare and Staff Systems.* Victoria: Ministry of the Attorney General, Policy and Program Services Division.

Mitchell, G.G. 1990. "Beyond Systemic Delay: The Saskatchewan Experience." 79 *Criminal Reports.* (3rd series). 328-331.

Moon, R. 1989. "The Constitutional Right to State Funded Counsel on Appeal." 14 *Queen's Law Journal.* 171-197.

Morgan, D.C. 1986. "Controlling Prosecutorial Powers — Judicial Review, Abuse of Process and Section 7 of the Charter." 29 *Criminal Law Quarterly.* 15-65.

Morrison, I. 1990. "Poverty Law and the Charter: The Year in Review." 6 *Journal of Law and Social Policy.* 1-29.

Mossman, M.J. 1985. "The Charter and the Right to Legal Aid." 1 *Journal of Law and Social Policy.* 21-41.

Osborne, J.A. 1980. *Delay in the Administration of Criminal Justice: Commonwealth Developments and Experience. London: Commonwealth Secretariat Publications.*

Osborne, J.A. 1983. "The Prosecutor's Discretion to Withdraw Criminal Cases in the Lower Courts." 25 *Canadian Journal of Criminology.* 55-78.

Osborne, J.A. 1986. "Delay, Contempt of Court and the Right to Legal Representation." 28 *Canadian Journal of Criminology.* 31-45.

Peterson-Badali, M., and R. Abramovitch. 1992. "Children's Knowledge of the Legal System: Are they Competent to Instruct Legal Counsel?" 34 *Canadian Journal of Criminology.* 139-160.

Purdy, D.A., and J. Lawrence. 1990. "Plea Agreements Under the Federal Sentencing Guidelines." 26 *Criminal Law Bulletin.* 483-508.

Renner, K.E., and A. H. Warner. 1981. "The Standard of Social Justice Applied to An Evaluation of Criminal Cases Appearing before the Halifax Courts." 1 *The Windsor Yearbook of Access to Justice.* 62-80.

Rosenthal, P. 1990. "Crown Election Offences and the Charter." 33 *Criminal Law Quarterly.* 84-126.

Ruby, C.C. 1987. *Sentencing, 3rd Edition.* Toronto: Butterworths.

Salhany, R.E. 1989. *Canadian Criminal Procedure, 5th ed.* Aurora, Ontario: Canada Law Book.

Schulhofer, S.J., and I.H. Nagel. 1989. "Negotiated Pleas under the Federal Sentencing Guidelines: The First Fifteen Months." 27 *American Criminal Law Review.* 231-288.

Scott, I. 1989. "Court Management and Delay Reduction." 23 *Gazette.* 293-299.

Shin, H. 1973. "Do Lesser Pleas Pay? Accomodations in the Sentencing and Parole Processes." 1 *Journal of Criminal Justice.* 27-42.

Solomon, P.H., Jr. 1983. *Criminal Justice Policy, from Research to Reform.* Toronto: Butterworths.

Sun, C. 1974. "The Discretionary Power to Stay Criminal Proceedings." 1 *Dalhousie Law Journal.* 482-525.

Sutherland, J. 1990a. *The Role of Crown Counsel: Advocate or Minister of Justice.* LL.M. Thesis. Toronto: University of Toronto, Faculty of Law.

Sutherland, J. 1990b. "Some Comments on the Decision to Prosecute." 4 *Crown's Newsletter.* 31-44.

Taman, L. 1975. "The Adversary Process on Trial: Full Answer and Defence and the Right to Counsel." 2 *Osgoode Hall Law Journal.* 251-277.

Taylor, J.P. 1985. "Division of Responsibility Between Crown and Judiciary: Abuse of Process." In J. Atrens, P. Burns, and J.P. Taylor, eds. *Criminal Procedure: Canadian Law and Practice*. Vancouver: Butterworths. VI-1 - VI-42.

Taylor, K.W. 1982. "Multiple Analysis of Race and Plea Negotiations: The Wynne and Hartnagel Data." 7 *Canadian Journal of Sociology*. 391-401.

Trotter, G.T. 1989. "Judicial Termination of Criminal Proceedings Under the Charter." 31 *Criminal Law Quarterly*. 409-430.

Verdun-Jones, S.N., and F.D. Cousineau. 1979. "Cleansing the Augean Stables: A Critical Analysis of Recent Trends in the Plea Bargaining Debate in Canada." 17 *Osgoode Hall Law Journal*. 227-260.

Verdun-Jones, S.N., and A.J. Hatch. 1985. *Plea Bargaining and Sentencing Guidelines*. Ottawa: The Canadian Sentencing Commission.

Verdun-Jones, S.N., and A.J. Hatch. 1987. "An Overview of Plea Bargaining in Canada: Cautionary Notes for Sentencing Reform." In Dumont, J., ed. *Sentencing*. Cowansville, Quebec: Yvon Blais Inc. 71-106.

Walker, M.D. 1984. "Congestion and Delay in the Provincial Court (Criminal Division)." 42 *University of Toronto Faculty Law Review*. 82-104.

Warner, A.H., and K.E. Renner. 1981. "The Bureaucratic and Adversary Models of the Criminal Courts: The Criminal Sentencing Process." 1 *The Windsor Yearbook of Access to Justice*. 81-93.

Watson, J. 1991. "Guilty Pleas." 33 *Criminal Law Quarterly*. 163-203.

Wilkins, J. 1979. *The Prosecution and the Courts*. Toronto: Centre of Criminology, University of Toronto.

Wilkins, J.L. 1975. *Legal Aid in the Criminal Courts*. Toronto: University of Toronto Press.

Wilson, D. 1987. "Delay in the Criminal Justice System." 8 *Canadian Criminology Forum*. 116-130.

Wynne, D.F., and T.F. Hartnagel. 1975. "Race and Plea Negotiation: An Analysis of Some Canadian Data." 1 *Canadian Journal of Sociology*, 147-155.

Zapf, M. 1992. "B.C. Bar Raps Discussion Paper on Public Defender Feasibility." 11 *Lawyer's Weekly*. 21.

Zemans, F.H. 1986. "Recent Trends in the Organization of Legal Services." 11 *Queen's Law Journal*. 26-89.

Zuber, T. 1987. *Ontario Royal Commission: Report of the Ontario Courts Inquiry*. Toronto: Queen's Printer.

8 SENTENCING OPTIONS IN CANADA

THE SENTENCING PROCESS

The Canadian Sentencing Commission (1987:115) defines sentencing as "the judicial determination of a legal sanction to be imposed on a person found guilty of any offence."

The sentencing process is an extremely critical component of the criminal justice system; it single-handedly determines the flow of cases through the various correctional services offered by the federal, provincial, and territorial governments in Canada. However, it would be very misleading to examine the sentencing process in isolation from the other components of the criminal justice system. For example, as we saw in the last chapter, plea bargaining exerts a major influence on the sentencing process since cases may be presented to the courts in a manner that predetermines the maximum severity of the sanctions that may be imposed (Canadian Sentencing Commission, 1987:401ff.; Verdun-Jones and Cousineau, 1979; Verdun-Jones and Hatch, 1985). Consider the case where, as the result of a plea bargain, the Crown agrees to proceed summarily rather than by way of indictment in relation to a so-called "mixed offence." Here, the decision to proceed summarily clearly limits the sentencing discretion of the court to the relatively minor sanctions that may be imposed for summary conviction offences as opposed to the more substantial penalties for indictable offences. Similarly, it is highly probable that the sentencing process is affected by such matters as prison capacity (Blumstein, 1982; Canadian Sentencing Commission, 1987:132). Of course, the sentence imposed by the court may bear relatively little resemblance to the sentence actually served by an offender since remission and parole may substantially reduce the ultimate length of a sentence of imprisonment.

The Canadian Sentencing Commission (1987:105ff.) emphasized the need to distinguish between *sentencing* and *punishment*. While punishment may be regarded as the actual "imposition of *severe* deprivation on a person found guilty of wrongdoing" (1987:109), sentencing may be considered as a "*statement* ordering the imposition of a sanction and determining what it should be" (1987:111). (The word "sentencing" is derived from the Latin, *sententia*, which may be translated as an "opinion" or the "expression of an opinion" [Canadian Sentencing Commission, 1987:111]). In the Commission's view (1987:111), even if it is assumed that sentencing is a punitive process, it should still be viewed "above all" as the "subordination of punishment to fundamental justice." Furthermore, certain sentencing options (such as an absolute discharge, for example) cannot really be considered "punitive" in the normal sense of that word; therefore, it is important to distinguish between the concepts of sentencing and punishment.

As with most criminal justice processes, sentencing is characterized by the exercise of a considerable degree of discretionary power (Cressey, 1980; Ehecke, 1990). Indeed, the very breadth of this discretionary power renders sentencing one of the most difficult tasks that confronts the judge in a criminal case (Blumstein, 1982:307). The courts exercise discretion in relation to at least three critical questions: (1) the general nature of the sanction to be imposed (whether it is to be custodial or community in nature); (2) the specific type of sanction to be imposed (what type of custody or community disposition); and (3) the "quantum" of the sanction (the length of custody or the specific "amount" of the community disposition chosen) (Canadian Sentencing Commission, 1987:120ff.).

The following options are available to the sentencing court: (1) fine; (2) suspended sentence and probation; (3) imprisonment; (4) declaration that the accused is a dangerous offender; (5) discharge (either absolute or conditional); (6) order for compensation; and (7) prohibitions and forfeiture. These options are set out in Figure 8.1.

THE SENTENCING OPTIONS

The Fine

The fine is the most commonly imposed disposition in the sentencing armoury of the courts (Canadian Sentencing Commission, 1987:374ff.; Mitchell-Banks, 1983; Verdun-Jones and Mitchell-Banks, 1986). Unlike other sentencing options, the fine actually generates revenue for the public purse rather than inflicting extra expense upon the taxpayer. It is a simple, straightforward penalty that spares the offender from the harmful consequences of imprisonment and results in a considerably lesser degree of stigma than many other criminal sanctions (Ruby, 1987:256). According to Nadin-Davis (1982:425), a fine is generally imposed where a "deterrent or punitive" sentence is deemed to be

FIGURE 8.1
FEDERAL AND PROVINCIAL SENTENCING AND PEROLE

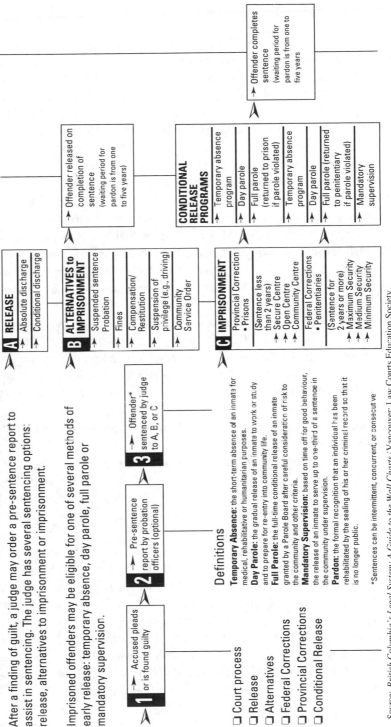

After a finding of guilt, a judge may order a pre-sentence report to assist in sentencing. The judge has several sentencing options: release, alternatives to imprisonment or imprisonment.

Imprisoned offenders may be eligible for one of several methods of early release: temporary absence, day parole, full parole or mandatory supervision.

☐ Court process
☐ Release
☐ Alternatives
☐ Federal Corrections
☐ Provincial Corrections
☐ Conditional Release

1 Accused pleads or is found guilty

2 Pre-sentence report by probation officers (optional)

3 Offender* sentenced by judge to A, B, or C

A RELEASE
→ Absolute discharge
→ Conditional discharge

→ Offender released on completion of sentence (waiting period for pardon is from one to five years)

B ALTERNATIVES to IMPRISONMENT
→ Suspended sentence Probation
→ Fines
→ Compensation/ Restitution
→ Suspension of privilege (e.g., driving)
→ Community Service Order

C IMPRISONMENT
→ Provincial Correction • Prisons
(Sentence less than 2 years)
→ Secure Centre
→ Open Centre
→ Community Centre
→ Federal Corrections • Penitentiaries
(Sentence for 2 years or more)
→ Maximum Security
→ Medium Security
→ Minimum Security

CONDITIONAL RELEASE PROGRAMS
→ Temporary absence program
→ Day parole
→ Full parole (returned to prison if parole violated)
→ Temporary absence program
→ Day parole
→ Full parole (returned to penitentiary if parole violated)
→ Mandatory supervision

→ Offender completes sentence (waiting period for pardon is from one to five years)

Definitions

Temporary Absence: the short-term absence of an inmate for medical, rehabilitative or humanitarian purposes.
Day Parole: the gradual release of an inmate to work or study and to prepare for re-entry into community life.
Full Parole: the full-time conditional release of an inmate granted by a Parole Board after careful consideration of risk to the community and other criteria.
Mandatory Supervision: based on time off for good behaviour, the release of an inmate to serve up to one-third of a sentence in the community under supervision.
Pardon: the formal recognition that an individual has been rehabilitated by the sealing of his or her criminal record so that it is no longer public.

*Sentences can be intermittent, concurrent, or consecutive

Source: *British Columbia's Legal System: A Guide to the Wall Charts* (Vancouver: Law Courts Education Society of British Columbia, 1992), p. 38.

necessary, but either the offence itself is not sufficiently serious to warrant incarceration or the presence of mitigating factors militates against the imposition of imprisonment. Ruby (1987:256) has asserted that one of the more significant uses of the fine is to prevent an offender from making a profit from his or her crime; it may well be the only feasible sanction where a corporation is the offender (Nadin-Davis, 1982:425) or where the offence is victimless in nature (Ruby, 1987:256).

In certain cases, the *Criminal Code* and related legislation set out minimum and/or maximum fines that may be imposed for specific offences. The *Criminal Code* also provides that a fine may be imposed in addition to or in lieu of any other punishment where the offender has been convicted of an indictable offence punishable with a maximum term of imprisonment of five years or less; however, where a minimum term of imprisonment has been prescribed by Parliament, a fine may only be imposed in addition to (and not as a substitute for) such a minimum term.[1] Similarly, if the offender has been convicted of an indictable offence punishable with imprisonment for more than five years, a fine may be imposed only in addition to, but not in lieu of, "any other punishment that is authorized."[2] In line with its emphasis on the need for the courts to make greater use of community sanctions, the Canadian Sentencing Commission has recommended (1987:374) that the *Criminal Code* should be amended so as to permit the imposition of a fine *alone* even for those offences punishable by a term of imprisonment of more than five years.

A sentencing court, when dealing with a conviction for an indictable offence, is generally not restricted as to the amount of a fine that may be imposed;[3] however, as Salhany (1989:368) aptly points out, it is always presumed that the "amount imposed will be reasonable in relation to the offence committed." As far as summary conviction offences are concerned, the *Criminal Code* provides that a fine may be levied either alone or in addition to any term of imprisonment that the court may decide to impose.[4] However, the *Code* limits the amount of the fine to $2,000 in the case of an individual[5] and to $25,000 in the case of a corporation (except where otherwise provided by law).[6]

The major problem with the fine is that, if unpaid, it may ultimately turn into a sentence of imprisonment. The *Criminal Code*[7] provides that the sentencing court may, if it so wishes, impose a term of imprisonment in case the offender should default in payment of a fine.[8] If a period of imprisonment is ordered in default of payment and the offender finds it impossible to come up with the money, then the sentence imposed is, in reality, a term of imprisonment (Jobson and Atkins, 1986; Ruby, 1987:261). Considerable concern has been expressed that the device of imposing a term of imprisonment in default of payment of a fine may be perceived as being discriminatory against the poor and particularly against women (Status of Women, Canada, 1986:132) and Aboriginal peoples. For example, Schmeiser has written that:

> Imprisonment for non-payment of fines appears to be an inconsistent and negative technique in the criminal process. It does not rehabilitate the offender...It destroys the deterrent value of prison. It is very expensive, being the most costly form of supervision, and actually penalizes society for the wrongs of the offender. It also gives the appearance of being discriminatory against the poor (1974:69).

There is considerable evidence that at least some of Schmeiser's concern is well-founded. For example, it is clear that fine-defaulters presently comprise a significant proportion of the populations of provincial correctional institutions. In 1983, for example, fine defaulters constituted 14% of the prison population in British Columbia and as high as 32% and 48% in Ontario and Quebec, respectively (Verdun-Jones and Mitchell-Banks, 1986:72). A somewhat disturbing study has suggested that as high as 69% of the fine default admissions in Quebec were for failing to pay fines originally imposed for traffic violations (Quebec, Ministere du Solliciteur General, 1986). A study by Hagan (1974) of admissions to provincial institutions in Alberta (during a period in the spring of 1973) underscores the implications of the fine default provisions for Aboriginal peoples. It was revealed that incarceration resulting from default in fine payment was nearly twice as common for Aboriginal persons as for non-Aboriginals (see also Hagan, 1976).

The courts, however, have increasingly emphasized the principle that the *Criminal Code* does not provide for the "routine imprisonment" of those offenders who default in payment of their fines. The sentencing court is under a clear duty to investigate the offender's ability to pay.[9] For this reason, Nadin-Davis has commented that "...the default period is, perhaps, one of the most misunderstood devices in penal law. Its proper purpose, it is submitted, is to enable the court to give alternatives to an accused who has the means to pay a fine" (1982:435).

A court has the authority to require payment of a fine immediately (at the time of the sentencing) in three situations identified by the *Criminal Code*: (1) if it is satisfied that the offender has the ability to do so; (2) if the offender does not request further time when asked if he or she needs it or if the offender declines the option of entering a fine option program (see below) as an alternative to payment; or (3) if the court "for any other special reason...deems it expedient that no time should be allowed." Alternatively, the court may grant the offender time to pay and, if it does so, the offender may always apply for further time.[10] An important provision of the *Criminal Code* states that, where an offender between the ages of 16 and 21 has been granted time to pay, then he or she may not be imprisoned until the court has obtained and considered a report concerning his or her conduct and ability to pay.[11]

Where the sentencing court does decide to impose a term of imprisonment in default of payment, it is assumed that the length of such a term should not be out of proportion to the size of the fine (Salhany, 1989:369). If the offender has managed to pay a part of his or her fine, the *Criminal Code* provides that the term of imprisonment shall be reduced proportionately.[12]

In a comprehensive study of the problem of fine default, Mitchell-Banks (1983) discovered that in British Columbia, there was a marked disparity between the periods of imprisonment imposed as an alternative to payment of a fine. For example, offenders convicted of impaired driving were serving "in default" prison terms at an average *per diem* rate of $22.90. However, among this group, some offenders were serving "in default" prison terms at a rate of less than $4 a day, while the highest rate was as much as $50 a day (Mitchell-Banks, 1983:182). Not surprisingly, the author concludes:

> ...it is difficult to justify a twenty-four hour period of incarceration being served at a rate approximate to one hour's minimum wage regardless of the offender's means. Surely one day of liberty is worth more than this? One cannot help but wonder if the judiciary is aware of this kind of sentencing disparity... (1983:206)

To eliminate this type of sentencing disparity, Verdun-Jones and Mitchell-Banks (1986:9) recommended that the length of an "in-default" prison sentence be commensurate with the size of the fine imposed and that a formula should be devised to reduce the significant variations in the *per diem* rates at which offenders are serving these sentences. The Canadian

Sentencing Commission subsequently recommended the adoption of a table for the calculation of default periods where incarceration is imposed for wilful non-payment of a fine (1987:386-7).

Mitchell-Banks (1983:194) also discovered that, in British Columbia, during the period 1977-83, 17% of fine defaulters served sentences of one week or less, 33% two weeks or less, 16% three weeks or less, and 22% four weeks or less. These figures would prompt the conclusion that "fine default" periods of imprisonment are relatively brief in the jurisdiction studied. Another interesting finding of this study is that only a very small proportion of persons fined are actually imprisoned for default. Mitchell-Banks (1983:179) estimated that, in any given year within British Columbia, approximately 100,000 cases will result in fines. However, from these cases, only 1,500 to 1,600 offenders will ultimately be imprisoned for non-payment of their fines. That the threat of imprisonment may well serve as a particularly effective technique of enforcing payment of a fine is illustrated by Mitchell-Banks's finding that the vast majority of people pay their fines in full when presented with a warrant for committal to prison. The author concludes that:

> Many people, it would seem, will only fully pay their fines when directly confronted with the threat of immediate imprisonment; in which case, imprisonment for fine default may be a necessary evil. If such people can further pay off their fines on a few hours notice, it would suggest that the fines imposed by the courts were not disproportionate to these offenders' means and that the delay in payment was a consequence of something other than poverty (1983:179).

The Canadian Sentencing Commission was particularly concerned to reduce the extent of imprisonment for fine default, and it strongly recommended that this device only be used for the *wilful* failure to pay a fine (1987:381). According to the Commission, other methods of attempting to collect payment of a defaulted fine should be tried before resorting to imprisonment; such methods might include attaching the offender's wages or salary, seizing his or her property, registering the offender in a fine option program (see below), or enrolling him or her in a community service program (1987:384).

An innovative response to the problem of fine default is the establishment of "fine option" programs in such provinces as Alberta, New Brunswick, Quebec, and Saskatchewan (Ekstedt, 1986:20; Mitchell-

Banks, 1983:18). These programs permit an offender to perform community service work instead of paying his or her fine. In addition to the benefits bestowed upon the community by the work undertaken, fine option programs spare the taxpayers the immense cost of incarcerating a fine defaulter. For example, in Saskatchewan during the fiscal year 1977-78, it was reported that 4,909 offenders performed the equivalent of $400,000 worth of community services. On the other side of the ledger, 75,795 days of incarceration were avoided at an estimated savings of $2 million to the taxpayers (Mitchell-Banks, 1983:120). In 1985, Parliament gave its unequivocal approval to fine option programs by enacting (what is now) section 718.1 of the *Criminal Code*, which established a legislative framework for the use of such programs. Under this amendment to the *Code*, an offender may earn credits for work performed toward discharging a fine, either in whole or part, for any period up to two years.

An inherent problem besetting the fine is the flagrant inequity arising from the differential impact of this disposition upon the rich and poor. While a fine of $200 may be regarded as "peanuts" by a wealthy person, it may well exert real hardship in the case of a poor citizen. One potential solution to this injustice is the introduction of a "day-fine" system. This system has been adopted in a number of countries, such as Denmark, Finland, Sweden, West Germany, and Austria (Verdun-Jones and Mitchell-Banks, 1986:42). The purpose of the day-fine system is to develop a method of imposing fines that ensures that the fines levied will exert a similar impact upon both rich and poor alike (Mitchell-Banks, 1983:81). In a day-fine system, the amount of any particular fine is determined by the size of the offender's income. Instead of setting a dollar amount for a fine, the sentencing judge imposes a specific number of day-fines. For example, in Sweden, it appears that one day-fine is equivalent to 1/1000th of the yearly gross income of the offender (after certain deductions have been made). If an offender with an income of $10,000 were sentenced to 20 day-fines, then he or she would actually pay $200. On the other hand, a more wealthy offender with an income of $100,000 would be required to pay $2,000 (Thornstedt, 1975; Law Reform Commission of Canada, 1974a:33-34, 43-48). In 1976, the Law Reform Commission of Canada (1976b:25) recommended that "any fine of $50 or more be stated in terms of a day-fine." More recently, the Canadian Sentencing Commission (1987:378-9) suggested that the Swedish day-fine system should be studied and that the various provinces should be encouraged to institute pilot projects on the use of day-fines. The Commission was not prepared to recommend the use of the day-fine on a national basis before such a study of the device had been undertaken. In the Commission's view, certain aspects of the Swedish system were significantly different from the Canadian situation (for example, information concerning the financial status of an offender is much more accessible in Sweden than it is in Canada).

Suspended Sentence and Probation

The suspended sentence and probation are, *par excellence*, dispositions that reflect a concern for what has been called the "individualization" of the sentencing process (Nadin-Davis, 1982:440).

The theory underlying probation is that offenders are given the opportunity to rehabilitate themselves under the supervision of a probation officer as well as the sentencing court. Most people consider probation as "getting off easy." However, offenders must observe a number of conditions (some of which may be quite onerous in nature) while they are on probation; if these conditions are not observed, offenders can be convicted of wilful breach of probation and, perhaps, be imprisoned for the offence for which they were originally placed on probation. As Ruby (1987:232) has observed, perhaps "the principal virtue of probation lies not in probation itself, but in the contrast which it provides for the inflexibility of imprisonment, and the impersonal nature of the fine" (see also Boyd, 1978; Ekstedt and Griffiths, 1988:261-268; Parker, 1976; Barnett, 1977).

A probation order may be imposed in a variety of situations. Foremost among these is the situation in which a probation order accompanies a suspended sentence. However, a probation order may also be imposed in connection with a conditional discharge or in addition to a fine, a sentence of imprisonment (provided the term does not exceed two years),[13] or an intermittent sentence.[14]

The *Criminal Code*[15] provides that a sentencing court has the power to suspend the passing of sentence and to direct that an offender be released upon the conditions prescribed in a probation order; however, this power may *not* be exercised in relation to an offence for which a minimum punishment has been prescribed by Parliament. In Canada, it is the *passing* of sentence that is suspended rather than the *execution* of a sentence that has already been imposed (Nadin-Davis, 1982:441). In other words, unlike the situation in England and Wales, a Canadian court does not have the power to impose a term of imprisonment and then suspend its execution; instead, it must suspend the very process of sentencing itself.[16] In deciding whether to impose a probation order, a court is likely to take into account a number of factors that bear upon the issue of whether an "individualized disposition" is appropriate. For example, if an offender is young and/or is being sentenced for the first time, then the court will give very serious consideration to the possibility of making a probation order (Ruby, 1987:232). On the other hand, the court may well feel that the offence is so serious in nature that it demands a term of imprisonment for the purposes of deterrence and/or denunciation.[17] Similarly, the offender's prior criminal record may disqualify him or her from receiving probation (Nadin-Davis, 1982:441). A further consideration is the likelihood of an offender benefiting from probation. It is most probable that the court will request a pre-sentence report (from a probation officer) in order to assist it in making its decision (Ekstedt and Griffiths, 1988:263-264; Salhany, 1989:373).[18]

The *Criminal Code*[19] provides that every probation order shall contain the following conditions:

> ...that the accused shall keep the peace and be of good behaviour and shall appear before the court when required to do so by the court.

However, the *Code* also states that the court, *in its discretion*, may also impose one or more of the following conditions (see Barnett, 1989):

[that the offender]

(a) report to and be under the supervision of a probation officer or other person designated by the Court;

(b) provide for the support of his [or her] spouse or any other dependents whom he [or she] is liable to support;

(c) abstain from the consumption of alcohol either absolutely or on such terms as the Court may specify;

(d) abstain from owning, possessing or carrying a weapon;

(e) make restitution or reparation to any person aggrieved or injured by the commission of the offence for the actual loss or damage sustained by that person as a result thereof;

(f) remain within the jurisdiction of the Court and notify the Court or the probation officer...of any change in his [or her] address or his [or her] employment or occupation;

(g) make reasonable efforts to find and maintain suitable employment; and

(h) comply with such other reasonable conditions as the Court considers desirable for securing the good conduct of the accused and for preventing a repetition by him [or her] of the same offence or the commission of other offences (section 737[2]).

The last provision (paragraph [h]) grants the court broad discretionary power to devise conditions that are specifically tailored for the individual offender, although note that excessively broad conditions are likely to be considered in breach of the *Canadian Charter of Rights and Freedoms*.[20] Perhaps the most ingenious use of this discretionary power has been the imposition of so-called "community service orders" (see Canadian Sentencing Commission, 1987:351-52; Griffiths, 1988:84; Nadin-Davis, 1982:458-62; Ruby, 1987:251-2; Grover, 1976; Stortini, 1979).[21] For example, in one celebrated case involving the conviction of a rock star for possession of heroin, an Ontario court imposed the condition that the offender perform a free concert for the benefit of charity.[22] Another example of a condition that has been developed on the basis of this broad discretionary power is the requirement that an offender who has been convicted of an alcohol-related offence and subjected to a probation order attend an impaired drivers' program (Vingilis, Adlaf and Chung, 1981). Similarly, offenders who have committed theft may be placed on probation and be required to attend counselling programs for shoplifters, and assaultive spouses may be required to attend treatment programs (Daubney, 1988:107).

In the past, a not infrequent condition imposed under this general power was that the offender participate in a treatment program for a psychiatric problem or drug dependency (Nadin-Davis, 1982:465). However, the future of such conditions is now in considerable doubt since the B.C. Court of Appeal ruled, in 1990, that any condition of a probation order that compels an offender to take psychiatric treatment or medication without his or her consent represents an unreasonable intrusion upon personal liberty and security.[23] In the Court's view, such a condition contravenes the fundamental principles of justice and, therefore, infringes section 7 of the *Charter*. Furthermore, according to the court, such a condition cannot be saved by section 1 of the *Charter* as a "reasonable limit" on an offender's *Charter* rights (unless there are "exceptional circumstances"). Although the Court of Appeal's decision represents a strong affirmation of the offender's right to personal autonomy, one potential problem with it is that sentencing courts may become more likely to impose terms of imprisonment on mentally disordered offenders rather than taking the risk of releasing them on probation with no guarantee that they will take treatment.[24] It remains to be seen how other appellate courts will approach this issue in the future.

Another significant development, in recent years, has been the establishment of several so-called "victim-offender reconciliation projects" (VORPs) — most notably in Ontario, although such projects have also emerged in British Columbia, Saskatchewan, Manitoba, and Quebec (Ekstedt, 1986; Ekstedt and Griffiths, 1988). The precise nature of these programs varies quite considerably; however, one form of victim-offender reconciliation revolves around the inclusion of a condition, in a probation order, that an offender meet with the victim (under the auspices of the project staff) in order to make an agreement as to the appropriate restitution.[25] At least in some jurisdictions, when such an agreement is completed, the term of the probation order is also deemed to have been completed (Norquay and Weiler, 1981:62-64). The Daubney Committee (1988:97) was particularly impressed with the evidence that was presented to it concerning the existing VORPs in Canada. The Committee (1988:98) recommended that the federal and provincial/territorial governments should work together to:

> ...support the expansion and evaluation throughout Canada of victim-offender reconciliation programs at all stages of the criminal justice process which:
>
> (a)   provide substantial support to victims through effective victim services; and
> (b)   encourage a high degree of community participation.

The *Criminal Code*[26] permits a court, at any time, to vary or add to the conditions included in a probation order or to relieve the offender of any of the optional conditions specified in such an order. It may also decrease the length of the period of probation.

What happens if an offender wilfully fails to fulfill the conditions of his or her probation? The *Code*[27] renders it a summary conviction offence wilfully to disobey the terms of a probation order.[28] However, a conviction of this offence may well constitute only the beginning of the offender's troubles. The court that originally imposed the probation order may vary or add to the conditions of the order and may extend it for a period of up to 12 months.[29] More drastically, the court also has the power to revoke the probation order and "impose any sentence that could have been imposed if the passing of sentence had not been suspended."[30]

Imprisonment

In recent years, the courts have repeatedly emphasized that imprisonment is a sanction that is to be employed only as a "last resort" (Nadin-Davis, 1982:388-389). In an influential report, the Law Reform Commission of Canada (1976b:26) advocated the adoption of sentencing guidelines that would further reduce the courts' use of imprisonment. The Commission contended that:

> Imprisonment is an exceptional sanction that should be used only:
>
> (a) to protect society by separating offenders who are a serious threat to the lives and personal security of members of the community; or
> (b) to denounce behaviour that society considers to be highly reprehensible, and which constitutes a serious violation of basic values; or
> (c) to coerce offenders who wilfully refuse to submit to other sanctions.

The Commission also articulated the principle that imprisonment should be resorted to only when the sentencing court is "certain that a less severe sanction cannot achieve the objective set out by the legislator." Despite public opposition to what is *perceived* to be excessive judicial "lenience" (Fattah, 1982b), the Government of Canada apparently endorsed the gist of the Commission's proposals and sought to embody them in amendments to the *Criminal Code* in 1984 with Bill C-19. Unfortunately, this bill was never enacted, owing to the dissolution of Parliament for the election of September, 1984. Subsequently, the Canadian Sentencing Commission also recommended that sentencing guidelines be adopted and that the thrust of the guidelines should be to ensure a greater reliance upon community sanctions as opposed to the penalty of imprisonment (1987:366).

The Daubney Committee (1988:55-56) also made very similar recommendations just one year later. The Committee also advocated the adoption of the sentencing principle that imprisonment should not be imposed until the court has canvassed the appropriateness of such alternatives as victim-offender reconciliation programs or what it called "alternative sentence planning."

All of these recommendations have found partial expression in the two principles articulated in Bill C-90, introduced to the Canadian Parliament in June 1992.[31] Bill C-90 clearly states that "an offender should not be deprived of liberty, if less restrictive alternatives may be appropriate in the circumstances," and "all available alternatives to imprisonment that are reasonable in the circumstances should be considered, particularly in relation to aboriginal offenders."[32] If Bill C-90 is ultimately passed into law, these principles will be adopted as part of the *Criminal Code*, and they will surely strengthen the resolve of the courts to avoid the ultimate sanction of imprisonment whenever possible.

Clearly, there seems to be an increasing degree of acceptance that imprisonment serves no rehabilitative functions and, on the contrary, may well achieve precisely the opposite results (Fattah, 1982a; Ruby, 1987:274). As one Canadian judge has suggested, the penitentiary "has often been described as a college offering a post-graduate course in crime" (Ruby, 1980:275). It is, therefore, a well-recognized principle of sentencing that, except in unusual circumstances, a sentence of imprisonment should normally not be imposed upon a first or youthful offender (Nadin-Davis, 1982:388-89). Nevertheless, there are many cases in which Canadian courts make the decision that a term of imprisonment is an appropriate disposition given the necessity for deterrence, denunciation, or incapacitation of the offender (Nadin-Davis, 1982:387).

The *Criminal Code* has five categories of *maximum* terms of imprisonment for indictable offences: life, fourteen years, ten years, five years and two years.[33] If the offender is convicted of a summary offence, then the maximum term of imprisonment may not exceed six months, unless otherwise provided by statute (Salhany, 1989:357). As might be expected, it has been recognized by the courts that the maximum penalty fixed by Parliament is intended to be applied only to the "worst case" of the particular offence concerned; worst case refers not only to the offence but also to the offender, whose prior criminal record may well exert a strong influence in the direction of increased severity of sentence (Nadin-Davis, 1982:44-45). In Canada, with the exception of life sentences and the sentences of "preventive detention" imposed upon so-called "dangerous offenders,"[34] prison sentences are determinate (or of fixed length), although, as will be shown in Chapter 11, such sentences may subsequently be reduced by the award of remission and the granting of parole to offenders.

In line with the general policy of allowing a broad range of sentencing discretion to the judiciary, the *Criminal Code* contains few examples of mandatory minimum prison sentences (namely, sentences that *must* be imposed regardless of the particular circumstances of the case).[35] The most important offences, in relation to which the courts are required to impose a minimum sentence of incarceration, are high treason, first- and second-degree murder (life),[36] use of a firearm during the commission of an indictable offence (one year upon a first conviction and three years upon subsequent convictions to be served consecutively to the sentence imposed for the main offence itself),[37] and driving while impaired or with more than 80 mg. of alcohol in the blood or refusing to provide a breath or blood sample (14 days on a second conviction and 90 days for each subsequent conviction).[38] The *Narcotic Control Act* (section 5) provides for a seven-year minimum sentence upon conviction of importing or exporting a narcotic; however, the Supreme Court of Canada struck down this provision as being in violation of the *Charter*.[39] The Canadian Sentencing Commission (1987:189) has recommended the abolition of all mandatory minimum periods of incarceration, except for the offences of murder and high treason. In the words of the Commission:

> If the punishment is to fit the crime, there can be no pre-determined sentences since criminal events are not themselves pre-determined. Although the offence should be the focus in determining the appropriate penalty, the circumstances of the offender must also have some weight (1987:186).

The length of a prison sentence is of considerable significance to the offender since the *Criminal Code*[40] provides that a sentence of imprisonment for two years or more or a sentence of life imprisonment must be served in a federal correctional institution (except in Newfoundland), whereas a sentence of less than two years must be served in a provincial correctional facility.

If an offender is convicted of multiple offences and is sentenced to more than one term of imprisonment, the court *may* order that the terms of imprisonment be served consecutively (the sentences coming one after another, for example, a four-month sentence followed by a six-month sentence) or concurrently (the sentences being served at the same time, for example, a four-month sentence included within a six-month sentence). It is fair to say that it is comparatively rare for a court to impose consecutive sentences. However, it is interesting that one of the leading commentators upon sentencing in Canada (Nadin-Davis, 1982:396) has written that:

> Few matters in the whole of sentencing law have caused as much difficulty as defining precisely when consecutive or concurrent sentences should be imposed. Running through all such considerations is the overriding principle, referred to as the "totality principle", that the total of sentences imposed should not be excessive in relation to the offender's overall culpability.[41]

It seems that a court is likely to exercise its discretion to impose consecutive sentences where the offences concerned are unrelated to each other and occurred at different times and in different places.[42] Conversely, a court is unlikely to impose consecutive sentences where the offences concerned were committed within a short period and can be perceived as constituting "in reality one transaction" (Salhany, 1989:362-363).[43] Significantly, Bill C-90 contains the following statement of principle on this issue: "where consecutive sentences are imposed, the combined sentence should not be unduly long or harsh."[44] If enacted, this provision of Bill C-90 would serve as a valuable guideline to the courts.

A noteworthy provision of the *Criminal Code*[45] grants courts the discretionary power to order that a term of imprisonment be served intermittently — provided that such a term does not exceed 90 days.[46] If it makes such an order, the court must specify the times at which the offender will serve the sentence (for example, on consecutive weekends) and must direct the offender to comply with the terms of a probation order during those periods when he or she is not in custody. The great advantage of the intermittent prison sentence is that it permits offenders to retain their employment, which might well be lost if a conventional, "straight" term of imprisonment were to be imposed (Nadin-Davis, 1982:423). Similarly, it may be used in an effort to avoid a number of other harmful effects of continuous imprisonment. For example, an intermittent sentence may be imposed in order to enable a spouse to care for the offender's children or to permit continued attendance at an educational institution (Ruby, 1987:284).

One problem that has arisen in relation to the intermittent term of imprisonment is that its frequent use may well result in the overcrowding of provincial correctional institutions at certain "peak periods" (Dombek and Chittra, 1984). Interestingly, in 1978, a bill was presented to Parliament, in 1978, that would have prevented the imposition of an intermittent sentence if no facilities were available (Chasse, 1980). However, the bill was never passed, and the Ontario Court of Appeal has ruled that the trial judge must not take into account the views of the provincial correctional authorities concerning the overloading of their facilities; in short, the judge must impose the sentence that he or she deems to be "fit and proper" in light of all the circumstances.[47]

Declaration that the Accused Is a Dangerous Offender

One sentencing option that has aroused an increasing degree of concern among commentators on the criminal justice system is the power of a court to declare a convicted person a "dangerous offender" and to impose a term of indefinite incarceration in a penitentiary in lieu of any other punishment that may have been inflicted for the offence(s) of which the offender was convicted (Grant, 1985).

The dangerous offender provisions in the *Criminal Code* have their roots in legislation enacted just after the World War II. In 1947, Parliament enacted legislation to deal with the habitual criminal and, in 1948, it followed with legislation directed toward the so-called "criminal sexual psychopath," later replaced by the term, "dangerous sexual offender" (Greenland, 1984; Webster, Dickens, and Addario, 1985:3). In 1977, Parliament did away with the habitual criminal legislation altogether and replaced the category of "dangerous sex offender" with a new category, known as "dangerous offender."

Crown counsel must make a formal application before the court may hold a hearing to determine whether the convicted offender should be designated a dangerous offender. The provincial Attorney-General must give his or her consent to any such application and, furthermore, the offender must be given at least seven days' notice of the prosecution's request for such a hearing.[48] The *Criminal Code* provides that the offender must normally be present when the hearing is held[49] and that the trial of the issue is to be held before the judge sitting without a jury.[50] If an accused person is ultimately found to be a dangerous offender, then the Court *may* decide to sentence him or her to an indeterminate period of incarceration in a penitentiary in lieu of any other sentence that might be imposed for the offence(s) of which the offender has been convicted.[51] The offender may only be released *on parole* by the National Parole Board, which examines the offender's case initially after a period of three years has elapsed since he or she was taken into custody and, thereafter, at intervals of two years.[52]

What are the criteria for dangerous offender status? The first requirement is that the offender must have been convicted of a "serious personal injury offence." This is defined in the following way:[53]

> (a) an indictable offence (other than high treason, treason, first degree murder or second degree murder) involving:
>
>   (i)   the use or attempted use of violence against another person, or
>   (ii) conduct endangering or likely to endanger the life or safety of another person or inflicting or likely to inflict severe psychological damage upon another person, and for which the offender may be sentenced to imprisonment for ten years or more, or
>
> (b)   an offence or attempt to commit an offence mentioned in section 271 (sexual assault), 272 (sexual assault with a weapon, threats to a third party or causing bodily harm), or 273 (aggravated sexual assault).

Once it has been established that a "serious personal injury offence" has been committed, the Crown must prove, insofar as category (a) "serious personal injury" offenders are concerned, that they constitute "a threat to the life, safety or physical or mental well-being of other persons."[54] Insofar as category (b) offenders are concerned, the *Code*[55] provides that the Crown must prove that:

> ...the offender, by his conduct in any sexual matter including that involved in the commission of the offence for which he has been convicted, has shown a failure to control his sexual impulses and a likelihood of his causing injury, pain or other evil to other persons through failure in the future to control his sexual impulses...

Since these criteria require that predictions be made as to the offender's future conduct, Parliament (rightly or wrongly) assumed that psychiatric evidence would be necessary before a determination could be made to the effect that the offender is a dangerous offender. The *Criminal Code*,[56] therefore, provides that the court may order the offender to attend an examination at a specific location or it may remand him or her in custody for observation. The *Code*[57] makes it mandatory for the court to hear the evidence of at least two psychiatrists (one for the Crown and one for the defence). The court may also hear other evidence from any "psychologist or criminologist," provided it considers such evidence to be relevant. In short, the underlying assumption of the dangerous offender provisions is that predictions as to the offender's future conduct should be clinical in nature (see Coles and Grant, 1991; Jackson, 1990).

In a comprehensive analysis of the Canadian dangerous offender provisions, Webster, Dickens, and Addario (1985) address some major problems surrounding the concept of sentencing individual offenders to indeterminate detention on the basis of psychiatric predictions as to their future behaviour. Empirical research has not established that clinical predictions of dangerousness *in relation to specific individuals* can attain a respectable degree of accuracy (Webster, Ben-Aron, and Hucker, 1985). Indeed, it appears that such a prediction is never likely to reach much more than 40% accuracy (see Menzies, Webster, and Sepejak, 1985; Monahan, 1981). In other words, when psychiatrists make predictions as to future dangerous conduct, there will always be a substantial number of so-called "false positives" (namely, offenders of whom it will be *wrongly* predicted that they will commit serious offences in the future) (see Webster, 1990:556-557). According to Webster, Dickens, and Addario:

> Predicting violence at the level of the individual prisoner is practically impossible without an almost inconceivable degree of control over key environmental, treatment, and biomedical variables. It is imperative to recognize that the most any clinician or researcher can *ever* offer is a probability estimate of future violent behaviour (1985:xviii).

Webster, Dickens, and Addario (1985:38ff.) suggest that statements as to the probability of an individual committing a serious crime in the future may be made in terms of a technique known as "risk assessment." However, this is not a technique in relation to which psychiatrists have any particular expertise as opposed to other professionals since at the heart of this technique is a consideration of such variables as age, number of previous convictions, and degree of force used in the commission of the offence, rather than the variables customarily employed in the clinical assessments made by psychiatrists.

Clearly the dangerous offender provisions raise serious ethical issues for those mental health professionals who engage in the assessment of individuals who may be designated as dangerous offenders. These ethical problems are so profound that Rogers and Lynett suggest that, given the inherent frailties of their predictive abilities, mental health professionals should refuse to participate in dangerous offender hearings altogether:

> The most prudent course would be for psychiatrists and other mental health experts to decline participation in dangerous offender determinations. As an analogy, how many experts would commit *their* lives to a risky enterprise, such as mountain climbing, when all technical information concur that the methods are more likely to fail than succeed? This analogy is offered not out of a crusading interest in the welfare of dangerous offenders but rather to emphasize the extraordinary consequences of a wrong decision (1991:82).

Given the fact that psychiatrists cannot predict, with any degree of certainty, whether a specific individual will commit a serious personal injury offence in the future, it is clear that the dangerous offender provisions in the *Criminal Code* are difficult to justify on a logical basis (Webster, Dickens, and Addario, 1985:142). Even if a well-informed judgment is made by an expert as to the degree of probable risk that an offender may commit another serious personal injury offence if he or she is released, is Canadian society justified in sentencing that offender to a very lengthy period of indeterminate detention based on the mere *probability* that he or she may commit such an offence in the future? Such a question is clearly a moral and social policy issue of great gravity (Petrunik, 1982). The answer depends on the extent to which society is willing to deprive individuals of their liberty in the name of the protection of the community. No doubt, if there is a high degree of probability that an offender may commit a serious personal injury offence if released, then it might be considered justifiable to detain that individual for the protection of society. However, such a grave decision should only be taken in accordance with procedures that are seen to be as fair as possible in all circumstances. Unfortunately, there is little doubt that there is a considerable degree of arbitrariness in the manner in which the existing dangerous offender provisions are applied and that the current use of them represents a severe challenge to the value that Canadians place on basic fairness in the system of criminal justice.[58]

A federal study (Jakimiec *et al.,* 1986) found that only some 60 persons were found to be dangerous offenders between October, 1977, and December, 1985. Of those found to be dangerous offenders, 78% had committed sexual offences that led to the Crown applying for a dangerous offender hearing (Jakimiec *et al.,* 1986:11). However, it is disturbing to note that, at the time of the study, the dangerous offender provisions had been used most unevenly across Canada (Jakimiec *et al.,* 1986:9-10). While Ontario had successfully used the provisions most frequently (29 times), the province of Quebec had not resorted to the provisions at all, despite its relatively large population. British Columbia had used the provisions successfully 16 times and Alberta, nine times. In other words, just three provinces were responsible for 90% of the successful applications. Unless one hypothesizes that there were a much greater number of dangerous people in these three provinces, as opposed to the rest of Canada, it is hard to resist the conclusion that those offenders who were selected for dangerous offender hearings were the hostages of such ephemeral factors as the attitudes of individual prosecutors and local community sentiment against sex offenders. However, the drastic consequences of a dangerous offender designation surely underscores the need to eliminate such arbitrariness.

The great majority of dangerous offenders are detained in protective custody in order to protect them from the other inmates in the prison population (Jakimiec *et al.,* 1986:14). Since dangerous offenders are usually convicted of sexual offences, they are inevitably stigmatized by the label of dangerous offender and become the target for the aggression of other inmates (Webster, Dickens, and Addario, 1985:143).

A number of other, weighty criticisms can be made against the dangerous offender provisions. Webster, Dickens, and Addario (1985:142) point out that the very indeterminate nature of the sentence can hinder the rehabilitation of offenders since the removing hope can cause serious deterioration in their mental state. These authors also assert (1985:145) that the dangerous offender provisions give a false impression that treatment will be provided. However, such treatment is unlikely to be given until a number of years have elapsed in the indeterminate sentence. In a situation reminiscent of "Catch-22," prison authorities realize that the parole board is unlikely to release a "dangerous" individual early in his or her sentence regardless of any progress in treatment and, therefore, the initiation of treatment is delayed until there is some prospect of release on parole.[59] Of course, the Parole Board is unlikely to consider releasing an offender who has not been "treated." In any event, Webster, Dickens, and Addario (1985:146) suggest that it is "highly questionable whether any methods exist that have sizeable demonstrable effects on Dangerous Offenders, including sex offenders." In the view of the authors:

> ...if in fact there are many offenders who are not receiving treatment and many whom treatment will not help, then the Dangerous Offender provisions operate for purely punitive or protectionary purposes.

Another major problem with the dangerous offender provisions is the degree of discretionary power that is placed in the hands of the prosecutor. Jakimiec *et al.* (1986:17-18) suggest that dangerous offender legislation is most likely to be applied when there is some uncertainty as to the offender's dangerousness. Where the offender commits a particularly brutal act, it is most likely that the court will impose a heavy, determinate sentence or, in particularly extreme cases, life imprisonment. However, according to these authors, where the "prosecutors sense themselves on insecure terrain they are apt to want psychiatric support in reaching decisions" and "it is well known that, generally, the courts find sex offenders to be hard to deal with." It has also been pointed out that the power to invoke the dangerous offender provisions places an excessive discretion in the hands of the prosecutor since he or she may be in a position to induce a plea of guilty by threatening to make a dangerous offender application if the offender does not plead guilty (Klein, 1973; Verdun-Jones and Cousineau, 1979).

In light of the harshness of the dangerous offender provisions, it is not surprising that they have been the subject of a number of legal challenges under the provisions of the *Charter* (Gordon and Verdun-Jones, 1987:192-3). However, the constitutionality of the provisions has been consistently upheld by the courts, despite the apparent recognition that psychiatric predictions as to future dangerousness are highly speculative at best.[60] Significantly, this approach was recently endorsed by the Supreme Court of Canada.[61] Indeed, the Supreme Court stated that society was justified in subjecting those individuals who are designated as "dangerous" to a regime of indeterminate detention even if it is known that, because the predictive techniques of psychiatrists are not totally reliable, some of those labelled as dangerous offenders will be "false positives" (that is, individuals who are wrongly predicted to be dangerous). Justice La Forest specifically approved the following articulation of the issues:

> There is a risk of harm to innocent persons at the hands of an offender who is judged likely to inflict it intentionally or recklessly — in any case culpably — in defiance or disregard of the usual constraints. His being in the wrong by virtue of the risk he represents is what entitles us to consider imposing on him the risk of unnecessary measures to save the risk of harm to innocent victims.[62]

The Canadian Sentencing Commission has recommended that the dangerous offender provisions of the *Criminal Code* be repealed (1987: 213). The Commission believed that these provisions offend against the basic principles of criminal law in two major respects: (1) the indeterminate nature of the sentence and (2) the "primary focus on the offender rather than the offence." In place of these provisions, the Commission recommends that the courts should be given the power to impose an "exceptional sentence" in the case of a particularly heinous crime (such as an unusually brutal attempted murder). The "extended sentence" would exceed the normal maximum for the offence of which the offender has been convicted by up to 50%. However, the Commission stated unequivocally that the "procedure for enhancement should be reserved for only the most heinous crimes which demand a longer period of incapacitation for security reasons" (1987:217). Of course, the Commission's proposal would abolish the indeterminacy that is such a controversial feature of the existing dangerous offender provisions.

The Commission's recommendations have been ignored and, in recent times, there has, in fact, been strong public pressure to keep a greater number of violent offenders and sexual offenders incarcerated on an indefinite basis. In May 1993, the Solicitor General of Canada (1993) responded to this public pressure by announcing his intention to introduce legislation that would permit Crown counsel, on the recommendation of the National Parole Board, to request the courts to apply the dangerous offender provisions of the *Criminal Code* to "high risk" offenders who are approaching the end of their sentences. If successful, such an application would result in an offender being kept in custody on an indefinite basis or being released to the community only on the basis of long-term, intensive supervision. The rationale advanced in favour of these proposals is that high-risk offenders (those who pose a substantial threat to re-offend) cannot be identified by the correctional authorities until shortly before they are released from the penitentiary. It is highly unlikely that this proposed legislation will pass through Parliament before the federal election, which must be held before the end of 1993. However, the reforms presented by the Solicitor General clearly reflect an increasing public demand for a greater use of the dangerous offender provisions to keep both violent and sexual offenders in a state of indefinite incarceration.

Of course, there is a very real question as to the fairness of sentencing offenders to a fixed term of imprisonment and, once they have almost served their sentence, taking their case back to court to turn their sentence into one of indefinite incarceration. No doubt, the reforms (if implemented) would be subjected to serious challenges under the *Charter*, and it would be left to the courts to decide if they infringe the individual *Charter* rights of the offenders concerned and, if they are held to do so, whether the danger posed to the public by violent and sexual offenders justifies such an infringement.

Absolute and Conditional Discharge

In 1969, the Ouimet Report (1969:194) advocated the introduction of provisions that would permit a sentencing court to "deal with first offenders charged with a minor offence in such a way that would avoid the damaging consequences of the existence of a criminal record." Hard on the heels of this recommendation, Parliament amended the *Criminal Code*[63] and, for the first time, courts were granted the power to impose an absolute or conditional discharge for certain offences (Greenspan, 1973; Nadin-Davis, 1982:474-89; Ruby, 1987:207-19; Salhany, 1989:382-85; Swabey, 1972; Wilkinson, 1977). Under the provisions of the *Criminal Code*,[64] instead of convicting an offender who has either pleaded guilty to or been found guilty of an offence, the sentencing court may order that he or she be discharged either absolutely or upon the conditions prescribed in a probation order. As Nadin-Davis (1982:475) points out, these provisions create two, quite different, dispositions. Where an absolute discharge is imposed, then the offender "is removed thereby entirely from correctional authority, and has no further obligation to the penal system." On the other hand, "the recipient of a conditional discharge is made subject to a probation order." An offender who fails to fulfill the conditions of a probation order or who commits a subsequent offence may find that his or her conditional discharge is revoked by the court that made the order. If this should happen, the court will convict the offender of the original offence for which he or she was granted a discharge, and is then empowered to impose any sentence that could have been selected at the time of the discharge.[65] Alternatively, the court may, instead of revoking the discharge, decide merely to change or add to the conditions specified in the probation order.

The court's power to impose an absolute or conditional discharge is by no means unfettered. Indeed, a discharge may not be granted where the offence concerned is one for which the *Criminal Code* imposes a minimum punishment or is one that is punishable by a prison term of 14 years or life. Furthermore, the court, before making its decision whether or not to discharge an offender, must consider such a discharge to be "in the best interests of the accused and not contrary to the public interest."[66]

It is clear that the courts have a considerable degree of discretion in determining whether or not to impose a discharge. However, over the past two decades, some general guidelines have emerged as to the circumstances in which such a disposition will be deemed appropriate (Nadin-Davis, 1982:479).

Perhaps the most significant principle is that the discharge should be imposed with a certain degree of "frugality" and that it should never be employed "routinely" in relation to any particular offence.[67] For example, if a discharge were to be imposed in relation to *all* cases of possession of marijuana, then the courts would effectively be inviting citizens to break the law of the realm. Therefore, it has been emphasized that the courts must consider each case on an individual basis. As Ruby (1987:208) points out, a sentencing court "must consider all the circumstances of the offence against the background of proper law enforcement in the community." Another general principle that has frequently been articulated by the judiciary is that discharges should not be confined merely to "trivial" cases.[68] Indeed, the courts have emphasized that there is a broad range of offences for which a discharge may be deemed to be appropriate, depending upon the individual circumstances of the particular case concerned.[69]

In addressing the "best interests of the accused," one leading decision of the B.C. Court of Appeal suggests that this requirement:

...would presuppose that the accused is a person of good character without previous conviction, that it is not necessary to enter a conviction against him in order to deter him from future offences or to rehabilitate him, and that the entry of a conviction against him may have significant adverse repercussions.[70]

In making its decision, the court will pay particular attention to whether the entry of a conviction will result in repercussions that are out of proportion to the guilt of the accused. For example, an important consideration in favour of granting a discharge is the possibility that a conviction will result in the loss of a job or the likelihood that the accused's criminal record will bar him or her from entering a profession.[71] Similarly, the possibility that a conviction will result in the deportation of a non-citizen has been considered.[72] As far as the "public interest" is concerned, the courts have emphasized that a discharge should not be imposed where there is a particular need to deter others from committing a similar offence.[73] For example, it may not be appropriate to grant a discharge for an offence (such as shoplifting) that happens to be particularly prevalent in an individual community.[74] Similarly, the seriousness of an offence might be a factor that militates against the granting of a discharge. Finally, a court may refuse to grant a discharge where it believes that the accused's offence should be brought to the attention of his or her potential employers in the future (Nadin-Davis, 1982:486). For example, this policy might be followed where a bank official has committed an offence involving an abuse of his or her trust.[75]

The *Criminal Code*[76] states that the recipient of a discharge "shall be deemed not to have been convicted of the offence," although there must be a "determination of guilt" before a discharge may be imposed. Clearly, the policy underlying this provision is to shield the offender from the stigmatizing consequences of a criminal record. As Davis (1980a; 1980b) has demonstrated, the existence of such a record may have potentially devastating consequences in relation to such critical matters as employment, immigration, and travel to other countries. The offender, who has obtained a discharge, may "truthfully say that he or she has never been convicted of a criminal offence" (Ruby, 1987:208).

Although an offender who has been granted a discharge is not considered to have been convicted, a record is kept of the discharge. After all, it may be argued that it is necessary to maintain some kind of record to ensure that a sentencing court considering granting a discharge for a subsequent offence will be aware that the offender has already received such a disposition in the immediate past. Indeed, the courts have held that the offender's receipt of a discharge in relation to a previous offence is a highly relevant factor in determining whether a subsequent discharge should be granted.[77] However, recent amendments to the *Criminal Records Act*[78] prohibit the custodian of the record from disclosing it to "any person" after one year has elapsed since the offender was given an *absolute* discharge, or after three years have passed since the offender was given a *conditional* discharge. The amendments not only prohibit disclosure of the record itself but also prevent release of the information that such a record even exists or that a discharge was ever granted in the first place.[79] In addition, the amendments require the Commissioner of the RCMP to remove all references to a discharge from the automated criminal convictions records system at the Canadian Police Information Centre (CPIC) maintained by the RCMP after the expiration of the periods referred to above. Clearly, these amendments to the *Criminal Records Act* ensure that a person given a discharge will be essentially free of the burden of a record after a minimal period has elapsed since his or her encounter with the criminal court system. A prior discharge will, therefore, only be relevant to the sentencing of an offender on a subsequent appearance before the courts when the discharge was granted in the recent past.

Although an offender given a discharge is "deemed not to have been convicted," he or she may still appeal from the determination of guilt "as if it were a conviction." Similarly, the prosecution may appeal from the decision not to convict the offender as if this decision were an acquittal or a dismissal of the information against the offender.[80]

Compensation

It has already been noted that a probation order may include a condition relating to restitution or reparation for any actual loss or damage inflicted as a consequence of the commission of a criminal offence.[81] However, specific provisions of the *Criminal Code* are concerned with the compensation of the victims of crime (see Ruby, 1987:327ff.). Of considerable significance is the *Criminal Code* provision[82] that empowers a sentencing court to order an offender who has been convicted of an offence or who has been given an absolute or conditional discharge to pay his or her victim compensation for "loss of or damage to property" suffered by the latter as a consequence of the commission of the offence. However, the victim must personally make an application for such compensation; the sentencing court may not make a compensation order on its own initiative. According to Hagan (1983:178), this provision has primarily been taken advantage of by "organization victims" (for example, retail stores) rather than by private individuals.

The *Criminal Code*[83] also makes provision for the situation where an innocent person purchases property that has been obtained by the commission of an offence and has subsequently been returned to its rightful owner. In this situation, the court is empowered to order that the offender reimburse the innocent purchaser in an "amount not exceeding the amount paid by the purchaser for the property." Once again, the purchaser is required to make a specific application to the court in order to obtain this form of relief.

What if the police have discovered "hot" property in the hands of an accused person and that property is before the court at the time the accused is tried? The *Code*[84] provides that, where the court determines that an offence has indeed been committed, then it is required to order the return of any property that has been obtained as the consequence of the commission of such an offence to the rightful owner or possessor of the property in question (assuming such a person can be ascertained).

The *Criminal Code* presently makes no provision for the compensation of a victim who has been subjected to bodily injury by an offender. In order to obtain such compensation, the victim of a violent crime must turn to the criminal injuries compensation schemes that currently exist in all provinces and territories in Canada. These schemes permit an administrative body to make compensatory payment to victims and are supported by cost-sharing agreements between the provinces and territories, on the one hand, and the Canadian Government, on the other (see Department of Justice, Canada, 1985:3). In 1990-91, the federal government gave $9,151,476 to the provinces and territories for expenditure on compensation to the victims of crime (Department of Justice, 1991:41). The extent of compensation and the rules of eligibility vary considerably from jurisdiction to jurisdiction. In British Columbia, for example, some 4,466 new applications were made in 1991 to the Workers' Compensation Board (which administers the scheme in this province) for compensation for criminal injuries. Of the 2,503 awards made during 1991, 44% involved assaults (including spousal assaults) and 43% involved sexual offences. A total of $15,989,661 was paid out in compensation awards in 1991 (Ministry of the Attorney-General of British Columbia, 1992).

At present, it appears that restitution and/or compensation orders are made in only a relatively small minority of cases (Hagan, 1983:194; Chretien, 1982:30). On the basis of a comprehensive empirical study, Hagan (1983:194-195) has suggested that the "public remedies" (such as restitution orders) that are available to victims of crime:

> ...may be serving a symbolic more than an instrumental function. That is, the existence of these remedies symbolizes a concern on the part of the State for the plight of victims, but it is a concern that is infrequently translated into action.

Over the past 15 years or so, an increasing degree of concern has been expressed as to the plight of the victims of crime (see Law Reform Commission of Canada, 1976a; Norquay and Weiler, 1981). In response to this concern, a strong demand for more emphasis to be placed upon restitution within the context of the sentencing process has arisen (Hudson and Galaway, 1989). For example, the Law Reform Commission of Canada was an enthusiastic advocate of such a policy:

> ...there are offences in respect of which reconciliation is useless and where the most rational sanction may be prolonged imprisonment. For the great majority of offences, however, restitution would appear to be appropriate. Restitution involves acceptance of the offender as a responsible person with the capacity to undertake constructive and socially approved acts. It challenges the offender to see the conflict in values between himself, the victim, and society. In particular, restitution invites the offender to see his conduct in terms of the damage it has done to the victim's rights and expectations. It contemplates that the offender has the capacity to accept his full or partial responsibility for the alleged offence and that he will in many cases be willing to discharge that responsibility by making amends (1974a).

Subsequently, in an influential report to Parliament, the Commission (1976b:24-25) recommended that the sentencing court should give priority to restitution, where the offence concerned involves a victim and where "restitution as a provision of conditional discharge is not appropriate." The Commission suggested that restitution may be "in symbolic form, by apologies, or the payment of a sum of money, or work done for the benefit of the victim." During the 1980s, Canadian governments started to ride the wave of public opinion in favour of victim-oriented sentencing options. In August, 1982, for example, the Government of Canada issued a significant document that articulated the principles that, in its opinion, should guide the ongoing process of criminal law review. A major principle espoused by the government (Chretien, 1982:62) was that:

> ...wherever possible and appropriate, the criminal law and the criminal justice system should also promote and provide for:
>
> (i)   opportunities for the reconciliation of the victim, community and offender;
> (ii) redress or recompense for the harm done to the victim of the offense...

The influence of this principle was clearly evident in the enactment of amendments to the *Criminal Code* in 1988 (Viens, 1989). These amendments introduced some very significant gains for victims in the process of sentencing. Unfortunately, not all of the amendments have yet been proclaimed in effect — although the Government of Canada has recently indicated its intention to attempt to put these amendments into effect as soon as possible (Department of Justice, 1990:3).

One of the critical reforms that has been proclaimed into effect is the victim impact statement.[85] The new *Criminal Code* provisions give the sentencing court the power to consider a written statement by victims concerning the harm done to, or the loss suffered by, them as a consequence of the offences committed against them (Young, 1993).[86] Such a statement must be completed according to the procedures established in each province and territory since the *Criminal Code* amendments do not include a standard form for the presentation of information by the victims of crime (Skurka, 1993).[87] These new provisions should do much to reduce the sense of alienation shared by many victims who feel that they are frequently of only tangential interest to the sentencing court.[88] The victim impact statement will, of course, be of considerable value to the court in determining *any* sentence that may ultimately be imposed on the offender. However, it will be of particular value to the sentencing court in helping it to decide whether compensation is appropriate and, if so, the specific amount that should be awarded.

Another major reform that was enacted in 1988 and immediately declared to be in effect is the victim fine surcharge. This reform, which had been strongly recommended by the Law Reform Commission of Canada, permits the sentencing courts to impose a fine surcharge on those individuals convicted of any offence under the *Criminal Code*, Parts III or IV of the *Food and Drugs Act,* or the *Narcotic Control Act.*[89] The order to pay the surcharge is *in addition to* any other punishment that may be imposed by the court. The *Code* provides that the amount of the surcharge will be a sum not exceeding 15% of any fine imposed or, if there is no fine, $10,000 or, alternatively, such "lesser amounts" as may be prescribed by federal regulations.[90] The proceeds of the fine surcharge are to be dedicated to the provision of victim assistance programs in the various provinces and territories.[91]

At the time the amendments to the *Code* were announced by the Minister of Justice, a commitment was made to double the federal government's contributions to provincial criminal injuries compensation programs, to establish a victim assistance fund to develop a "broader range of victim services and programs," and to provide funding for research and projects that would "enhance the development of innovative approaches for victims' programs." Overall, the federal government committed itself to allocating some $27.2 million over a three-year period to services and programs for the victims of crime (Hnatyshyn, 1987:3).

As noted earlier, some of the reforms were not proclaimed into effect immediately. An important component of the unproclaimed reforms is the abolition of the requirement that the victim of a crime has to make a specific application for restitution. Instead, under the terms of the unproclaimed amendments to the *Code*, the sentencing court will now have the power to impose restitution either on its own initiative or on the application of the Attorney-General of the province or territory concerned. The court will be able to impose an order for restitution in cases that involve not only damage to, or loss or destruction of, property stemming from the commission of a criminal offence, but also pecuniary damages caused by bodily injury to the victim (for example, loss of income or support attributable to the offence).[92] Before making any order for restitution, the court will be required to inquire into the extent of the victim's loss as well as the offender's ability to pay.[93] Significantly, if the court is also considering imposing a fine and has doubts as to the ability of the offender to pay both the amount of restitution ordered and the fine, then it will be required to give *priority to the restitution order over the fine.*[94] Finally, another significant feature of the unproclaimed amendments is the establishment of a procedure to enforce a restitution order if the offender does not comply with it voluntarily. In certain cases, the enforcement procedure may involve the imposition of a prison sentence of up to two years in the case of an indictable offence and up to six months in the case of a summary conviction offence.[95]

When these unproclaimed provisions eventually come into effect, they will greatly enhance the lot of those who are victims of offences that cause them financial losses. However, there are some weaknesses in the 1988 reforms (Daubney, 1988:99). In particular, the reforms only permit the sentencing court to impose a restitution order *in addition to* some other sentence; in other words, restitution cannot be imposed as the sole sanction. Furthermore, the amendments do not require the court to give reasons for failing to order restitution — a requirement advocated by a number of victim groups across Canada.

Although there is clearly a strong wave of reform in the direction of establishing restitution as a key element in the sentencing process, there have nevertheless been some harsh critics of this approach.[96] For example, Klein (1978) has raised serious questions as to the practicality of requiring restitution in a broad range of criminal cases. Klein (1978:393) contends that criminal courts may balk at the prospect of becoming "debt collectors" and that, in any event, such courts do not always represent an appropriate forum for the settling of minor disputes relating to property; indeed, he suggests that the civil courts (particularly small claims courts) are better equipped to deal with such matters (1978:394-396). The author also raises the thorny issue of the inherent dangers associated with appearing to "trade dollars for lenience." Finally, he (1978:399-401) suggests that there is insufficient empirical evidence to support the claims of the proponents of restitution that this sentencing option contributes significantly to the rehabilitation of offenders.

Nevertheless, in its most recent statement on the purpose and principles of sentencing, the Government of Canada has strongly re-affirmed the view that "providing for redress for the harm done to individual victims or to the community" is an important objective to be considered in sentencing (Government of Canada, 1990:16).

Similarly, the courts, no doubt influenced by the recent victim-oriented amendments to the *Criminal Code*, have started to emphasize the critical importance of compensation as a goal of sentencing, and the benefits that the courts feel are associated with this approach are not limited to the obvious advantages to the victim of receiving just compensation from the offender. For example, in the case of *Hoyt* (1992),[97] Justice Wood of the B.C. Court of Appeal stated that, in addition to the positive impact that compensation orders may have on offenders in terms of forcing them to take responsibility for their actions, there are also some very practical considerations that should encourage trial judges to make a greater use of this sentencing option:

> ...society has an interest, not only in recovering some of the real costs of crime, but also in avoiding some of the costs involved in maintaining large jail populations. And Parliament has expressly provided for [compensation] orders. Thus the courts have a responsibility to utilize the jurisdiction to make such orders, limited though it is by both statutory and practical considerations.[98]

Prohibitions and Forfeiture

In certain circumstances, the sentencing court is empowered to order that an offender, convicted of a particular offence, be prohibited from engaging in certain activities for a specified period (Ruby, 1987:303 ff.). For example, an offender may be prohibited from possessing a firearm,[99] from operating or navigating a car or boat,[100] or from owning or having the custody or control of an animal or bird.[101] These prohibitions may only be imposed in addition to some other sentence. The best known of these prohibitions, of course, is that which may be made after an offender has been convicted of an offence related to drunken driving.

It is also important to note that conviction of a criminal offence will, in certain instances, result in the forfeiture to the Crown of property that is involved in the case (MacFarlane, 1985). For example, the *Criminal Code* provides for the forfeiture of explosives,[102] obscene publications,[103] electronic "bugging" equipment,[104] money or other items seized in a gaming house or brothel,[105] as well as hate literature.[106] Perhaps the most severe form of forfeiture may be imposed under the provisions of the *Narcotic Control Act*; section 16(2) of this *Act* provides that, if a person has been convicted of either trafficking in or importing or exporting a narcotic, and if an aircraft, motor vehicle, or vessel was used in connection with the offence, then such a "conveyance" may be forfeited. In most cases, forfeiture is dependent upon the issuance of a judicial order; however, in some instances, the *Code* provides for automatic forfeiture upon the conviction of the offender concerned.

In 1988, the *Criminal Code* was amended in order to deal with the problem of preventing offenders from benefiting from the "proceeds of crime" (Rook and Leising, 1989).[107] Among the new amendments is a provision that empowers the court to order the forfeiture of the proceeds of crime where it is sentencing an offender who has committed "an enterprise crime offence" (for example, theft, robbery, fraud, extortion, and making counterfeit money).[108] The *Code* also permits the sentencing court to impose a fine on such offenders where it is no longer possible to obtain possession of the property in question (because, for example, it has been transferred out of Canada or cannot be found).[109] The fine will be in an amount equal to the value of the property that is considered to constitute the "proceeds of crime."

THE USE OF THE SENTENCING OPTIONS

As the Canadian Sentencing Commission (1987:60) has pointed out, there is a dearth of systematic information about sentencing in Canada.[110]

Hann *et al.* (1983) analyzed data concerned exclusively with defendants convicted of offences under the *Criminal Code*. They, therefore, relate to the more serious criminal offences since they do not include the many quasi-criminal offences arising under federal and provincial legislation; in particular, they exclude the numerous minor driving offences that are covered by the provincial motor vehicle acts. Figures 8.2 and 8.3 show the overall proportions of convicted defendants who were sentenced to four major forms of disposition: discharge, fine, probation, and custody. Figure 8.2 focuses on indictable offences alone, while Figure 8.3 turns the spotlight upon both indictable and summary offences combined (Hann *et al.*, 1983:11-12).

Custody is the most frequent form of sentence for indictable offences (from 43% to 55% of all cases), while the fine is most frequently resorted to when both indictable and summary offences are combined (from 40% to 55% of all cases).[111] The researchers chose probation as the most serious sentence in 35% to 39% of indictable offences and in only 15% to 21% of cases when summary and indictable offences are combined.

Mitchell-Banks (1983), on the other hand, analyzed the sentencing practices of B.C. courts in relation to *all* criminal offences (including the various quasi-criminal offences and, in particular, the numerous driving offences arising under provincial legislation). Therefore, her analysis includes a considerably greater proportion of the less serious criminal

FIGURE 8.2

PERCENTAGE DISTRIBUTION BY SENTENCE TYPE OF CASES WHERE DEFENDANT WAS FOUND GUILTY OF SELECTED OFFENCES FOR JURISDICTIONS REPORTING INDICTABLE CASES ONLY

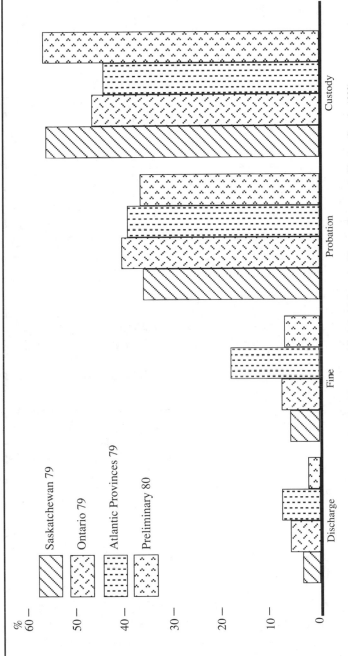

Source: R.G. Hann et al. Sentencing Practices and Trends in Canada: A Summary of Statistical Information (Ottawa: Department of Justice, Canada, 1983). Reproduced with permission of the Minister of Supply and Services Canada, 1993.

FIGURE 8.3

PERCENTAGE DISTRIBUTION BY SENTENCE TYPE OF CASES WHERE DEFENDANT WAS FOUND GUILTY OF SELECTED OFFENCES FOR JURISDICTIONS REPORTING INDICTABLE AND SUMMARY CASES COMBINED

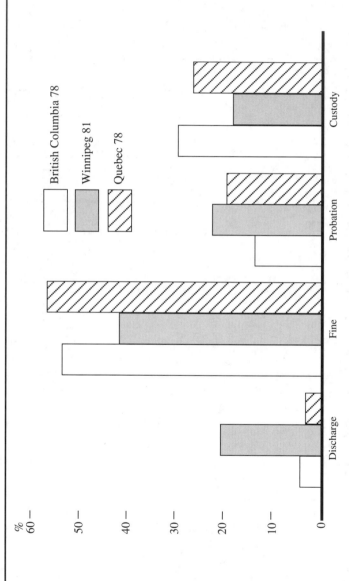

Source: R.G. Hann *et al. Sentencing Practices and Trends in Canada: A Summary of Statistical Information* (Ottawa: Department of Justice, Canada, 1983), p. 12. Reproduced with permission of the Minister of Supply and Services Canada, 1993.

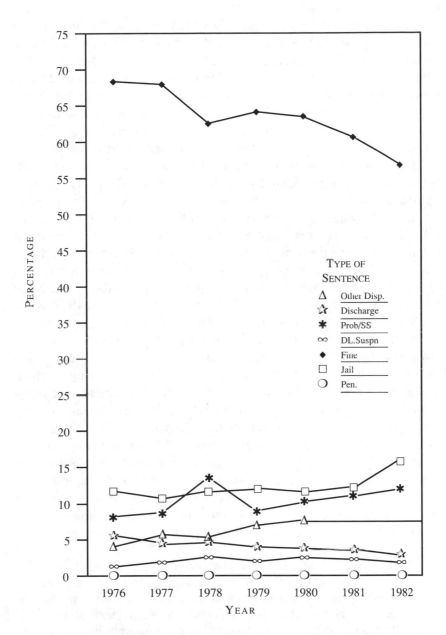

FIGURE 8.4
PERCENTAGE OF SENTENCES IMPOSED BY B.C. COURTS
DURING THE YEARS 1976-1982

Source: T.R. Mitchell-Banks. "The Fine: An Enigma." M.A. thesis (Burnaby, B.C.: School of Criminology, Simon
    Fraser University, 1983), p. 153.

offences than does the Hann *et al.* study. Figure 8.4 clearly indicates the predominance of the fine as the disposition of choice over the period between 1976 and 1982.

According to Mitchell-Banks (1983:152), in 1976, the fine was the most serious penalty[112] imposed by the B.C. courts in 68.6% of all cases; however, by 1982, this percentage had fallen to 56.1%. Mitchell-Banks points out (1983:152-153) that the apparent decline in the use of the fine is largely a consequence of a significant shift toward the use of "other dispositions" in relation to traffic offences.[113] She discovered that as many as 52.5% of all cases resolved by the B.C. courts were traffic offences and, when these offences were removed from her sample, it was revealed (1983:155-156) that the use of the fine had remained fairly constant over the seven-year period (from 54.9% in 1976 to 50.4% in 1982). It is significant that there was a slight increase in the use of jail (custody for less than two years in a provincial facility) from 12% in 1976 to 16% in 1982. On the other hand, Figure 8.4 indicates that the percentage of sentences involving the incarceration of offenders in federal penitentiaries (sentences of two or more years) remained at a relatively low level (from 0.2% in 1976, to 0.06% in 1982). The rates of imposition of probation and suspended sentence rose from 8.5% in 1976 to 11.7% in 1982, while the rates for discharge declined from 5.4% to 2.9% over the same period.

What conclusions can be drawn concerning the use of the various sentencing options by Canadian courts? The Canadian Sentencing Commission has argued that an analysis of Canadian sentencing practices reveals an over-reliance on imprisonment (1987:xxiii). Indeed, it has been pointed out that, with an imprisonment rate of 108 per 100,000 inhabitants, Canada can be considered to have one of the highest rates of imprisonment among all Western countries (Correctional Service of Canada, 1986).[114] As noted above, the Commission's response to this disturbing situation was to recommend that imprisonment be used only in very limited circumstances and that much greater emphasis be place upon community sanctions. The Commission's opinion of the excessive use of imprisonment in current sentencing practice is worth repeating.

> Besides the incalculable human costs to a person removed from society, there are easily calculable economic costs. Incarceration costs between 10 and 15 times as much as do alternative sanctions...The average annual cost of keeping a prisoner in a maximum security penitentiary is $50,000. In medium or minimum security institutions

the cost is $35,000. The cost per bed of building a new institution is now $200,000. One does not have to look far, then, for reasons to support the exercise of restraint in the use of incarceration (1987:233).

INNOVATIONS IN SENTENCING PROCEDURE: "CIRCLE SENTENCING"

In recent years, some Canadian courts have shown an increasing interest in adapting the sentencing process to meet the needs of particular communities, victims, and offenders. One fascinating example of this trend is the adoption of "circle sentencing procedures" in a case tried in the Yukon Territory Territorial Court.[115] In this case, the sentencing judge carried on the sentencing hearing in a "circle." The chairs in the courtroom were re-arranged so that everyone involved, including the judge, lawyers, accused, police, and members of the local community sat facing each other in an attempt to arrive at a consensus as to what was the appropriate disposition in this particular case. According to the sentencing judge, the circle promoted an intense discussion of what might best protect the community and rehabilitate the offender. The circle broke the dominance that the judge and lawyers usually enjoy in the traditional sentencing process, encouraged the free flow of information, and stimulated participation by laypersons. In addition, the sentencing judge believed that the circle inspired a more creative search for new sentencing options, promoted a greater sharing of responsibility with the community, encouraged the offender to participate, and actively involved the victim in the sentencing process. In the words of Stuart J.:

> The circle discussions highlighted the severe limitations of the justice system and the consequent value and necessity of community members assuming responsibility for community well-being. These discussions can promote a recognition that many community objectives in sentencing can either best be or only be carried out by the community.[116]

In addition, the circle in this case was found to have particular value as a means of according a greater degree of recognition of Aboriginal values by creating a less confrontational and less adversarial procedure for fixing the appropriate sentence.

It remains to be seen whether the "sentencing circle" is a device that will be used extensively in the future. It clearly permits a greater degree of community involvement in the sentencing process and lays the basis for a more meaningful participation in the process on the part of the victims of crime. However, the use of such innovative sentencing procedures does raise other questions that must be addressed. For example, it is clear that if the courts give the victims of crime and the local community a greater say in determining the appropriate sentence in any given case, then there is a possibility that this will lead to more sentencing disparity in Canada. That is, similar cases may be dealt with very differently depending on where the offence occurred and the specific approach favoured in individual communities across Canada. The extent to which Canadians are prepared to individualize the sentencing of offenders at the expense of the principle that fairness demands that like cases should be treated alike is a question that will be raised with increasing frequency over the next decade in Canada.

Sentencing procedures in Canada are increasingly being influenced by the desire to grant the victims of crime a more powerful voice in the determination of the appropriate sentence and by the willingness to recognize the need to provide compensation and redress not only to victims but also, where appropriate, to the community in which the offences occurred. Similarly, while there is currently a demand for longer periods of incarceration for those who commit violent and/or sexual offences, there is also a wish to reduce the extent of unnecessary imprisonment for other types of offender in favour of greater reliance on community options (such as community service orders). The implications of these trends for sentencing in the future are more fully explored in the next chapter.

NOTES

[1]Section 718(1).
[2]Section 718(2).
[3]Sections 717(2) and 719(a).
[4]Section 787(1).
[5]Section 787(1).
[6]Section 719(b).
[7]Sections 718(3)(a) and (b).

[8]For indictable offences, the term is limited to a maximum of five years if the offence is one for which a term of five years or more may be imposed, or to a maximum of two years, where the maximum punishment for the offence is less than five years: section 718(3)(a) and (b). For summary conviction offences, the term is (unless otherwise authorized) up to a maximum of six months: section 787(2).

[9]*R. v. Natrall* (1972), 9 C.C.C. 390 (B.C. C.A.); *R. v. Tracy* (1992), 71 C.C.C. (3d) 329 (B.C. C.A.).

[10]Sections 718(4), (5), and (11).

[11]Section 718(10). It has been held by the Supreme Court of Nova Scotia that this provision is invalid in light of the *Charter* guarantee against discrimination on the basis of age and should be read as though the age-limiting phrase was not present: *R. v. Hebb* (1989), 47 C.C.C. (3d) 193 (N.S.S.C.). However, the B.C. Supreme Court arrived at the opposite conclusion in *Williams v. Canada (Attorney-General)* (1990), 61 C.C.C. (3d) 198. See MacDougall (1989).

[12]Section 722(1).

[13]Section 737(1)(b). The courts have made it clear that probation may not be imposed in addition to imprisonment if the prison sentence or *total* of different prison sentences exceed a period of two years; see *R. v. Amaralik* (1984), 16 C.C.C. (3d) 22 (N.W.T. C.A.); *R. v. Miller* (1987), 36 C.C.C (3d) 100 (Ont. C.A.).

[14]Section 737(1)(c).

[15]Section 737(1).

[16]For example, the Ontario Court of Appeal has ruled that, while a court has the power to impose a suspended sentence together with probation, it may not also impose a disposition such as a fine; see *R. v. Polywjanyj* (1982), 1 C.C.C. (3d) 161. A suspended sentence necessarily implies that no sentence is imposed, but rather that the trial judge suspends the passing of sentence altogether. The making of a probation order is not seen as the imposition of a "sentence."

[17]For example, robbery is generally regarded as an offence in relation to which the courts have emphasized that the principle of deterrence must override the goal of individual rehabilitation; see *R. v. Johnas et al.* (1982), 2 C.C.C. (3d) 490 (Alta. C.A.).

[18]Section 735 of the *Code* sets out the authority for the court to request a pre-sentence report. The section does not *require* the court to order such a report.

[19]Section 737(2).

[20]For example, in *R. v. Fields* (1985), 42 C.R. (3d) 398 (Ont. Co. Ct.), it was held that a condition prohibiting the accused from participating in any strike or lock-out, unless he was an employee of the premises concerned, should be struck down on the basis that it infringed the offender's right of freedom of peaceful assembly, guaranteed by section 2(c) of the *Charter*. The condition was varied so as to apply only to the particular strike concerned.

[21]In *R. v. Shaw* (1977), 36 C.R.N.S. 358 (Ont. C.A.), it was held that section 737(2)(h) does authorize the imposition of a community service order.

[22]*R v. Richards* (1979), 49 C.C.C. (2d) 517 (Ont. C.A.).

[23]*R. v. Rogers* (1990), 61 C.C.C. (3d) 481 (B.C. C.A.).

[24]In the *Rogers* case, the Court of Appeal managed to preserve the probation order by imposing the following condition on the accused:

> You will take reasonable steps to maintain yourself in such condition that:
>
> (a)   your chronic schizophrenia will not likely cause you to conduct yourself in a manner dangerous to yourself or anyone else; and
> (b)   it is not likely you will commit further offences.

This approach clearly places the responsibility on the accused to maintain his or her mental health. However, it would not be entirely cynical to suggest that the only way that a mentally disordered accused can realistically fulfill this condition is by taking some form of treatment. If this is so, the Court of Appeal was *indirectly* imposing a requirement of treatment, while simultaneously stating that a sentencing court may not do this *directly*.

[25]A study by Ditenhoffer and Ericson (1983) suggests that the victim-offender reconciliation program does not appear to be operating as an *alternative* to imprisonment (as it was apparently designed to do). The authors conclude (1983:346) that "...on the whole VORP has contributed little to sparing offenders imprisonment. Instead of avoiding problems created by the use of the prison system, another sentencing option has been implemented which pulls a different set of offenders deeper into the system of social control and inevitably increased cost."

[26]Section 738(3).

[27]Section 740.

[28]Under the terms of Bill C-90 (first reading, June 23rd, 1992), provision is made for increasing the severity of the penalty that may be imposed on those who are convicted for a second (or more) time of having wilfully failed to comply with the terms of a probation order. Such individuals would be tried on indictment and would be subject to a maximum term of two years in prison (section 733.1).

[29]Section 738(4)(e).

[30]Section 738(4)(d). It is significant that there is judicial authority to the effect that the power of the court to revoke a probation order and impose a sentence does not infringe the *Canadian Charter of Rights and Freedoms*; see *R. v. Linklater* (1983), 9 C.C.C. (3d) 217 (Yuk. T.C.A.). See also *R. v. Elendiuk (No. 2)* (1986), 67 A.R. 221 (Alta. C.A.).

[31]First reading, June 23rd, 1992.

[32]Section 718.2.

[33]According to the Canadian Sentencing Commission (1987:29-30), the basic elements of the structure of penalties contained in the *Criminal Code* dates back to 1869, when Parliament passed the *Canadian Consolidation Acts*: "They provided the main articulations of the penalty structure, including: arbitrariness of design; heavy penalties; wide judicial discretion; few minimum sentences and prison terms based on the number seven."

When the *Criminal Code* was enacted in 1892, this basic structure was left untouched. The penalty scale of six months, two, five, seven, ten, and fourteen years of imprisonment, of life imprisonment, and capital punishment had been in use since the *1869 Acts*. The penalty structure appeared to be based on a rationale of retribution and deterrence (Canadian Sentencing Commission, 1987:32). After 1982, numerous amendments have been made to the maximum penalties set out in the *Criminal Code*; however, there has been no attempt to follow any kind of consistency (Dandurand, 1982).

[34]See *infra*.

[35]Minimum prison sentences may also be imposed by provincial legislation in certain (relatively rare) instances. For example, in B.C., under the *Motor Vehicle Act*, R.S.B.C. 1979, C. 288, section 88, a person who is convicted of the offence of driving a motor vehicle knowing that he or she has been prohibited from driving is liable to a fine of not less than $300 and not more than $2,000 and to imprisonment for not less than 7 days and not more than six months. In *R. v. Goltz* (1991), 67 C.C.C. (3d) 481, the Supreme Court of Canada held that this provision did not infringe the *Charter* guarantees against cruel and unusual punishment, provided the prohibition was based on the accused's poor driving record.

[36]See sections 47, 235, and 742. Where the accused is convicted of first-degree murder, he or she is not eligible for parole for a period of 25 years (10 to 25 years in the case of second-degree murder, as determined by the trial judge). The mandatory minimum sentences applicable to murder have been ruled valid under the *Charter*; see *R. v. Luxton* (1990), 58 C.C.C. (3d) 449 (S.C.C.); *R. v. Bowen* (1990), 59 C.C.C. (3d) 515 (Alta. C.A.); *R. v. Mitchell* (1987), 39 C.C.C. (3d) 141 (N.S.C.A.).

[37]See section 85. The *maximum* term that may be imposed is 14 years. The requirement that there be an additional term of imprisonment for use of the firearm does not violate the *Charter*; see *Krug v. R.* (1985), 21 C.C.C. (3d) 193 (S.C.C.).

[38]See section 255. These mandatory minimum terms have been held to be valid under the *Charter*; see *R. v. Aucoin* (1987), 48 M.V.R. 154 (N.S. C.A.); *R. v. Tardif* (1983), 9 C.C.C. (3d) 223 (Sask. C.A.). The *maximum* terms that may be imposed are six months (if tried summarily) and five years (if tried on

indictment).

[39]*Smith v. The Queen* (1987), 34 C.C.C. (3d) 97 (S.C.C.).

[40]Section 731.

[41]The application of this "totality principle" is illustrated in the case of *R. v. Johnas et al.* (1982), 2 C.C.C. (3d) 490 (Alta. C.A.). The Supreme Court of Canada has discussed some of the general principles, applicable to consecutive sentences, in *Paul v. The Queen* (1982), 67 C.C.C. (2d) 97.

[42]See, for example, *R. v. Munilla* (1986), 38 Man. R. 79 (Man. C.A.).

[43]See, for example, *R v. Desmarest* (1986), 2 Q.A.C. 151 (Que. C.A.).

[44]Section 718.2(c).

[45]Section 737(1)(c).

[46]A court has no power to impose *consecutive* 90-day prison terms to be served intermittently. Thus, an appeal court ruled that the imposition of two consecutive intermittent sentences, each of 90 days, constituted an illegal sentence; see *R. v. Fletcher* (1982), 2 C.C.C. (3d) 221 (Ont. C.A.).

[47]*Wortzman v. R.* (1979), 12 C.R. (3d) 115 (Ont. C.A.).

[48]Section 754.

[49]Section 758.

[50]Section 754(2).

[51]Section 753.

[52]Section 761.

[53]Section 752.

[54]Section 753(a). That the offender is such a threat can only be proved on the basis of evidence establishing:

    (i)   a pattern of repetitive behaviour by the offender, of which the offence for which he has been convicted forms a part, showing a failure to restrain his behaviour and a likelihood of his causing death or injury to other persons, or inflicting severe psychological damage upon persons, through his failure in the future to restrain his behaviour;

    (ii)   a pattern of persistent aggressive behaviour by the offender, of which the offence for which he has been convicted forms a part, showing a substantial degree of indifference on the part of the offender as to the reasonably foreseeable consequences to other persons of his behaviour; or

    (iii)   any behaviour by the offender, associated with the offence for which he has been convicted, that is of such a brutal nature as to compel the conclusion that his behaviour in the future is unlikely to be inhibited by normal standards of behavioural restraint.

[55]Section 753(b).

[56]Section 756.

[57]Section 755.

[58]As far as arbitrariness is concerned, it is interesting to note one rather disturbing study that suggests that the perceived physical unattractiveness of offenders may play a role in the process by means of which they are labelled "dangerous offenders"; see Esses and Webster, 1988.

[59]For a discussion of the treatment programs available, see Borzecki and Wormith, 1987; Wormith and Borzecki, 1985.

[60]*Re Moore and The Queen* (1984), 10 C.C.C. (3d) 306 (Ont. H.C.J.).

[61]*R v. Lyons* (1987), 37 C.C.C. (3d) 1 (S.C.C.).

[62]*Ibid.*, at p. 51. The passage that Justice La Forest approved is taken from Floud and Young (1981), at pp. 48-49.

[63]S.C. 1972, c.13, section 57.

[64]Section 736.

[65]Section 736(4). It has been held that the revocation of a conditional discharge and subsequent conviction and sentencing of the offender on the original charge does not infringe the *Charter*'s guarantee against double jeopardy — at least, where the offender has been convicted of another offence while on probation; see *R. v. Elendiuk* (1986), 27 C.C.C. (3d) 94 (Alta. C.A.).

[66]Section 736(1).

[67]*R. v. Derksen* (1972), 9 C.C.C. (2d) 97 (B.C. Prov. Ct.).

[68]*R. v. Vincente* (1975), 18 Crim. L. Qtrly. 292 (Ont. C.A.); *R. v. Bram* (1982), 30 C.R. (3d) 398 (Alta. C.A.).

[69]*R. v. Webb* (1975), 28 C.C.C. (2d) 456 (P.E.I. C.A.).

[70]*R. v. Fallowfield* (1973), 13 C.C.C. (2d) 450 (B.C. C.A.). See also *R. v. Stewart* (no.2) (1983), 11 C.C.C. (3d) 92 (Ont. H.Ct.).

[71]*R. v. Meneses* (1974), 25 C.C.C. (2d) 115 (Ont. C.A.).

[72]*R. v. Wing Shee Au Yeung* (1976), 19 Crim. L. Qtrly. 22 (Alta C.A.); *R. v. Melo* (1975), 30 C.R.N.S. 328 (Ont C.A.).

[73]*R. v. Macfarlane* (1976), 3 Alta. L.R. (2d) 341 (C.A.).

[74]*R. v. Sanchez-Pino* (1973), 11 C.C.C. (2d) 53 (Ont. C.A.).

[75]Similarly, a court is unlikely to grant a discharge where a serious offence is committed by an official, in whom a high degree of public trust has been placed. For example, a discharge was not granted to a police officer who was convicted of assaulting a suspect; see *R. v. Wigglesworth* (1983), 7 C.C.C. (3d) 170 (Sask. Q.B.); affirmed (1984), 11 C.C.C. (3d) 27 (Sask. C.A.).

[76]Section 763(3).

[77]*R. v. Tan* (1975), 22 C.C.C. (2d) 184 (B.C.C.A.).

[78]R.S.C. 1985, c. C-47, as amended by Bill C-71, 1992.

[79]Section 6.1(2). The *Act* apparently grants the Solicitor General the discretion to disclose information since the prohibition against disclosure is only operative if there has been no "prior approval" by the minister. However, it is not clear in what circumstances (if any) that this discretion would be exercised in favour of disclosing information about a discharge.

[80]Section 736(3).

[81]However, a court has no power to order compensation for the victim's "pain and suffering" under the provisions of section 737(2)(e). For a discussion of some of the practical problems caused by the failure of an offender to fulfill such a condition of his or her probation, see Zapf and Cole (1985).

[82]Section 725. It should be noted that the Supreme Court of Canada, in *R. v. Zelensky* (1978), 41 C.C.C. (2d) 97, ruled that compensation orders should only be made with "restraint and caution." In particular, such an order should not be made where complicated issues of law or fact are involved; otherwise, the sentencing court would be usurping the civil law process, which falls under provincial jurisdiction. For a discussion of some of the factors relevant to the court's decision whether to make a compensation order, see *R. v. Scherer* (1984), 16 C.C.C. (3d) 30 (Ont. C.A.) and *R. v. Fitzgibbon* (1990), 55 C.C.C. (3d) 449 (S.C.C.).

[83]Section 726.

[84]Section 491.1.

[85]For the history of the evolution of the victim impact statement in the United States, see Erez, 1990.

[86]Section 735(1.1).

[87]Section 735(1.2). The victim impact statement may only be made by the direct victim him or herself (except where he or she is dead, ill, or otherwise incapable of making a statement); see *Regina v. Curtis* (1992), 69 C.C.C. (3d) 385 (N.B. C.A.).

[88]An important question that must now be addressed by the courts concerns the extent to which they should take the views of victims into account when determining the appropriate sentence. There are some situations in which the courts have clearly stated that such considerations as general deterrence and denunciation should be given more weight than the wishes of a victim who urges that the offender be treated leniently. An obvious example of such a situation is where there has been domestic violence against women. In *R. v. Brown; R. v. Highway; R. v. Umpherville* (1992), 73 C.C.C. (3d) 242, the Alberta Court of Appeal unanimously endorsed (at pp. 250-251) the following statement of principle that had been articulated by Justice Hetherington (dissenting) in the earlier case of *R. v. Coston* (1990), 108 A.R. 209 (C.A.):

> Domestic violence is not in any way different from violence in the street except that frequently the victim, because of his or her emotional involvement with the offender, does not want to see the offender punished. If courts give effect to the wishes of the victims in this regard, persons inclined to assault family members will feel that they can do so with impunity. In my view, in the interest of general and specific deterrence, domestic violence must be treated in the same way as violence outside the family (at 210).

[89]Section 727.9(1).

[90]Section 727.9(1).

[91]Section 727.9(4).

[92]Section 725 (unproclaimed). Section 726 (also unproclaimed) authorizes the court to require restitution to an innocent party who, for example, purchased stolen goods from the offender in good faith or lent money to the offender on the security of such property and the property has been returned to its lawful owner, leaving the innocent party out of pocket. Unlike the existing section 725, the amended section does not require a specific application from the innocent party as a precondition for the imposition of a restitution order.

[93]Section 727 (unproclaimed).

[94]Section 727.3 (unproclaimed).

[95]Section 727.6 (unproclaimed).

[96]For a discussion of the pros and cons of restitution, see Barnett (1982).

[97]*R. v. Hoyt* (1992), 77 C.C.C. (3d) 289 (B.C.C.A.).

[98]*Ibid.*, at 298-299.

[99]Section 100(1).

[100]Section 259.

[101]Section 446(5).

[102]Section 492(1).

[103]Section 164(4).

[104]Section 192.

[105]Section 199(3).

[106]Section 320.

[107]Part XII.2 of the *Code*.

[108]Section 462.37. Once such an order has been made, it cannot be modified; see *Re Regina v. Sterling and Armstrong and Meyer* (1992), 71 C.C.C. (3d) 222 (B. Canadian Sentencing Commission).

[109]Section 462.37(3).

[110]Because of this dearth, this section uses studies and figures from 1983. There are, however, some more recent sentencing data that have been analyzed by Hann *et al.* (1987) and Programs and Research Section, Department of Justice, Canada (1987), but these studies deal only with custodial dispositions and probation.

[111]It should be emphasized that Figures 8.2 and 8.3 provide an analysis only of the "most serious" disposition imposed. In many cases, a fine may be imposed in addition to imprisonment; however, since imprisonment is regarded as the "most serious" disposition, the fine would be ignored in the analysis, undertaken in the two figures.

[112]As is the case with the Hann *et al.* data, the analysis deals solely with the "most serious" disposition imposed by the British Columbia courts.

[113]Mitchell-Banks indicates that it was not possible to ascertain precisely what forms of disposition are included in the category of "other" (1983:167).

[114]As to some of the problems associated with making comparisons between the incarceration rates of different countries, see Lynch (1988). According to the Daubney Committee (1988:49), among 16 European countries and the United States, only Poland and the United States have higher rates of incarceration than Canada.

[115]*R. v. Moses* (1992), 71 C.C.C. (3d) 347 (Stuart Terr. Ct.J.).

[116]*Ibid.*, at 364.

REFERENCES

Barnett, C.C. 1977. "Probation Orders under the Criminal Code." 38 *Criminal Reports* (New Series). 165.

_____. 1989. "Probation Order Guideline Conditions." 66 *Criminal Reports* (3rd series). 181-188.

Barnett, R.E. 1982. "Restitution: A New Paradigm of Criminal Justice." In C.L. Boydell and I.A. Connidis, eds. *The Canadian Criminal Justice System.* Toronto: Holt, Rinehart and Winston of Canada. 232-247.

Blumstein, A. 1982. "Research on Sentencing." 7 *Justice System Journal.* 307-330.

Borzecki, M., and J.S. Wormith. 1987. "A Survey of Treatment Programmes for Sex Offenders in North America." 28 *Canadian Psychology.* 1-44.

Boyd, N. 1978. "An Examination of Probation." 20 *Criminal Law Quarterly.* 355-382.

Canadian Sentencing Commission. 1987. *Sentencing Reform: A Canadian Approach.* Ottawa: Minister of Supply and Services Canada.

Chasse, K.L. 1980. "Intermittent Sentences: A Question of Judicial Independence." 12 *Criminal Reports* (3rd series). 117-120.

Chretien, J. 1982. *The Criminal in Canadian Society.* Ottawa: Government of Canada.

Coles, E.M., and F.E. Grant. 1991. "The Role of the Psychiatrist in Dangerous Offender Hearings." 36 *Canadian Journal of Psychiatry.* 534-543.

Correctional Service of Canada. 1986. *Basic Facts About Corrections in Canada.* Ottawa: Minister of Supply and Services and Canada.

Cressey, D.R. 1980. "Sentencing: Legislative Rule versus Judicial Discretion." In B. Grosman, ed. *New Directions in Sentencing.* 51-69.

Dandurand, Y. 1982. *Description de l'evolution de la partie positive du Code Criminel Canadien, 1892-1955*. Ottawa: Ministere de la Justice.

Daubney, D. (Chair). 1988. *Taking Responsibility: Report of the Standing Committee on Justice and Solicitor General on its Review of Sentencing, Conditional Release and Related Aspects of Corrections*. Ottawa: Queen's Printer for Canada.

Davis, R.P. 1980a. "Employer Stigmatization of Ex-Offenders and the Pardon under the Criminal Records Act." 22 *Canadian Journal of Criminology*. 343-353.

Davis, R.P. 1980b. "The Mark of Cain: Some Subliminal Effects of Criminal Process." 44 *Saskatchewan Law Review*. 219-260.

Department of Justice, Canada. 1985. *Criminal Injuries Compensation in Canada*. Ottawa: Department of Justice, Canada.

_____. 1987. *Sentencing Patterns in Canada: An Overview of the Correctional Sentences Project*. Ottawa: Programs and Research Section, Department of Justice, Canada.

_____. 1990. *Sentencing: Directions for Reform*. Ottawa: Minister of Supply and Services Canada.

_____. Canada. 1991. *Justice: Annual Report 1990-1991*. Ottawa: Ministry of Supply and Services Canada.

Ditenhoffer, T., and R.V. Ericson. 1983. "The Victim/Offender Reconciliation Program: A Message to Correctional Reformers." 33 *University of Toronto Law Journal*. 315-347.

Dombek, C.F., and M.W. Chittra. 1984. "The Intermittent Sentence in Canada — the Law and its Problems." 26 *Canadian Journal of Criminology*. 43-64.

Ehecke, W.F. 1990. "Letting the Punishment Fit the Crime." 48 *The Advocate*. 545-553.

Ekstedt, J.W., and C.T. Griffiths. 1988. *Corrections in Canada: Policy and Practice*. (2nd ed.). Toronto: Butterworths Canada Ltd.

Ekstedt, J.W., and M.A. Jackson. 1986. *A Profile of Canadian Alternative Sentencing Programmes: A National Review of the Policy Issues*. Ottawa: The Canadian Sentencing Commission.

Erez, E. 1990. "Victim Participation in Sentencing: Rhetoric and Reality." 18 *Journal of Criminal Justice*. 19-31.

Esses, V.M., and C.D. Webster. 1988. "Physical Attractiveness, Dangerousness, and the Canadian Criminal Code." 18 *Journal of Applied Social Psychology*. 1017-1031.

Fattah, E.A. 1982a. "Making the Punishment Fit the Crime: The Case of Imprisonment. The Problems Inherent in the Use of Imprisonment as a Retributive Sanction." 24 *Canadian Journal of Criminology*. 1-12.

Fattah, E.A. 1982b. "Public Opposition to Prison Alternatives and Community Corrections: A Strategy for Action." 24 *Canadian Journal of Criminology*.

371-386.

Floud, J., and W. Young. 1981. *Dangerousness and Criminal Justice*. London: Heinemann.

Gordon, R.M., and S.N. Verdun-Jones. 1987. "The Impact of the Canadian Charter of Rights and Freedoms upon Canadian Mental Health Law: The Dawn of a New Era or Business as Usual?" 14 *Law, Medicine & Health Care*. 190-197.

Government of Canada. 1990. *Directions for Reform in Sentencing, Corrections and Conditional Release*. Ottawa: Minister of Supply and Services Canada.

Grant, I. 1985. "Dangerous Offenders." 9 *Dalhousie Law Journal*. 349-382.

Greenland, C. 1984. "Dangerous Sexual Offender Legislation in Canada, 1948-1977: An Experiment that Failed." 26 *Canadian Journal of Criminology*. 1-12.

Greenspan, E.L. 1973. "Absolute and Conditional Discharge." In Canadian Bar Association, *Studies in Criminal Law and Procedure*. Agincourt, Ontario: Canada Law Book Co. 65-76.

Groves, P. 1976. "A Report on Community Service Treatment and Work Programs In British Columbia." In Law Reform Commission of Canada. *Community Participation in Sentencing*. Ottawa: Minister of Supply and Services, Canada. 119-150.

Hagan, J. 1974. "Criminal Justice and Native People: A Study of Incarceration in a Canadian Province." (Special Issue). *Canadian Review of Sociology and Anthropology*. 220-36.

Hagan, J. 1976. "Locking Up the Indians: A Case for Law Reform." 55 *Canadian Forum*. 16-18.

Hagan, J. 1983. *Victims Before the Law: The Organizational Dominance of the Criminal Law*. Toronto: Butterworths.

Hann, R.G. *et al.* 1983. *Sentencing Practices and Trends in Canada: A Summary of Statistical Information*. Ottawa: Department of Justice, Canada.

Hnatyshyn, R. 1987. *Notes for the Honourable Ray Hnatyshyn At a News Conference on November 5th, 1987*. Ottawa: Department of Justice, Canada.

Hudson, J., and B. Galaway. 1989. "Financial Restitution: Toward an Evaluable Program Model." 31 *Canadian Journal of Criminology*. 1-18.

Jackson, M.A. 1990. "The Clinical Assessment and Prediction of Violent Behaviour: Toward a Scientific Analysis." In N.Z. Hilton, M.A. Jackson, and C.D. Webster, eds. *Clinical Criminology: Theory, Research and Practice*. Toronto: Canadian Scholars' Press Inc. 516-528.

Jakimiec, J. *et al.* 1986. *A Descriptive Study of Incarcerated Dangerous Offenders*. Ottawa: Solicitor General Canada.

Jobson, K., and A. Atkins. 1986. "Imprisonment in Default and Fundamental Justice." 28 *Criminal Law Quarterly*. 251-271.

Klein, J.F. 1973. "Habitual Offender Legislation and the Bargaining Process." 15

Criminal Law Quarterly. 417-436.

Klein, J.F. 1978. "Revitalizing Restitution: Flogging a Horse that may have been Killed for Good Cause." 20 *Criminal Law Quarterly.* 383-408.

Law Reform Commission of Canada. 1974a. *Restitution and Compensation and Fines* (Working Papers 5 & 6). Ottawa: Information Canada.

_____. 1974b. *The Principles of Sentencing and Dispositions* (Working Paper 3). Ottawa: Information Canada.

_____. 1976a. *Community Participation in Sentencing.* Ottawa: Minister of Supply and Services, Canada.

_____. 1976b. *A Report on Dispositions and Sentences in the Criminal Process: Guidelines.* Ottawa: Information Canada.

Lynch, J.P. 1988. "A Comparison of Prison Use in England, Canada, West Germany, and the United States: A Limited Test of the Punitive Hypothesis." 79 *Journal of Criminal Law and Criminology.* 180-217.

MacDougall, A.J. 1989. "Are There No Prisons? *Hebb*: Imprisonment in Default of Fine Payment and S. 7 of the Charter." 69 *Criminal Reports* (3rd series). 23-36.

MacFarlane, B.A. 1985. "Confiscating the Fruits of Crime." 27 *Criminal Law Quarterly.* 408-432.

Menzies, R.J., C.D. Webster, and D.S. Sepejak. 1985. "Hitting the Forensic Sound Barrier: Predictions of Dangerousness in a Pretrial Psychiatric Clinic." In C.D. Webster, M.H. Ben-Aron, and S.J. Hucker, eds. *Dangerousness: Probability & Prediction, Psychiatry & Public Policy.* Cambridge: Cambridge University Press. 115-144.

Ministry of the Attorney General of B.C. 1992. *The Twentieth Annual Report of the Criminal Injury Compensation Act of British Columbia.* Victoria: Attorney General of B.C.

Mitchell-Banks, T.R. 1983. *The Fine: an Enigma.* Burnaby, B.C.: M.A.(Crim) Thesis, Simon Fraser University.

Monahan, J. 1981. *The Clinical Prediction of Violent Behavior.* Rockville, Md.: National Institute of Mental Health.

Nadin-Davis, R.P. 1981. "Canada's Criminal Records Act: Notes on How Not to Expunge Criminal Convictions." 45 *Saskatchewan Law Review.* 221-257.

Nadin-Davis, R.P. 1982. *Sentencing in Canada.* Toronto: Carswell.

Norquay, G., and R. Weiler. 1981. *Services to Victims and Witnesses of Crime in Canada.* Ottawa: Minister of Supply and Services, Canada.

Ouimet, R. (chairman). 1969. *Report of the Canadian Committee on Corrections. Toward Unity: Criminal Justice and Corrections.* Ottawa: Information Canada.

Parker, G. 1976. "The Law of Probation." In Law Reform Commission of Canada, *Community Participation in Sentencing.* Ottawa: Minister of Supply and Services Canada. 51-118.

Petrunik, M. 1982. "The Politics of Dangerousness." 2 *International Journal of Law and Psychiatry*. 225-253.

Quebec, Ministère du Solliciteur General. 1986. *Rapport du Comite d'étude sur les Solutions de Rechange a L'Incarceration.* Quebec: Ministère du Solliciteur General.

Rogers, R., and E. Lynett. 1991. "The Role of Canadian Psychiatry in Dangerous Offender Testimony." 36 *Canadian Journal of Psychiatry.* 79-84.

Rook, J.F., and J.W. Leising. 1989. "Canada's Seize and Freeze Legislation (Part I)." 6 *Business & The Law.* 30-32.

Ruby, C.C. 1987. *Sentencing* (Third Edition). Toronto: Butterworths.

Salhany, R.E. 1991. *Canadian Criminal Procedure* (5th ed.). Toronto: Canada Law Book.

Schmeiser, D.A. 1974. *The Native Offender and the Law.* Ottawa: Supply and Services Canada.

Skurka, S. 1993. "Two Scales of Justice: The Victim as Adversary." 35 *Criminal Law Quarterly.* 334-354.

Solicitor General of Canada. 1993. *News Release: Proposed New Law to Protect Public from Dangerous Offenders* (May 25th, 1993). Ottawa: Solicitor General of Canada.

Statistics Canada. 1983. *Criminal Injuries Compensation 1983.* Ottawa: Minister of Supply and Services, Canada.

Status of Women, Canada. 1986. *A Feminist Review of Criminal Law. Report.* Ottawa: Minister of Supply and Services Canada.

Stortini, R. 1979. "Community Service Orders." 21 *Criminal Law Quarterly.* 503-507.

Swabey, T.R. 1972. "Absolute and Conditional Discharge Under the Criminal Code." 20 *Criminal Reports* (New Series). 132.

Thornstedt, H. 1975. "The Day-Fine System in Sweden." 1975 *Criminal Law Review.* 307-312.

Verdun-Jones, S.N., and F.D. Cousineau. 1979. "Cleansing the Augean Stables: a Critical Analysis of Recent Trends in the Plea Bargaining Debate in Canada." 17 *Osgoode Hall Law Journal.* 227-260.

Verdun-Jones, S.N., and A.J. Hatch. 1985. *Plea Bargaining and Sentencing Guidelines.* Ottawa: Canadian Sentencing Commission.

Verdun-Jones, S.N., and T.R. Mitchell-Banks. 1986. *The Fine as a Sentencing Option in Canada.* Ottawa: Canadian Sentencing Commission.

Viens, C. 1989. "Le Projet de Loi C-89: Justice pour les victimes d'actes criminels." In Formation permanente Barreau du Quebec, ed., *Developpements recents en droit criminel.* Cowansville, Quebec: Les editions Yvon Blais. 133-168.

Vingilis, E., E. Adlaf, and L. Chung. 1981. "The Oshawa Impaired Drivers Programme: An Evaluation of a Rehabilitation Programme." 19 *Canadian*

Journal of Criminology. 93-102.

Webster, C.D. 1990. "The Clinical Prediction of Dangerousness." In N.Z. Hilton, M.A. Jackson, C.D. Webster, eds. *Clinical Criminology: Theory, Research and Practice.* Toronto: Canadian Scholars' Press Inc. 555-574.

Webster, C.D., M.H. Ben-Aron, and S.J. Hucker, eds. 1985. *Dangerousness: Probability & Prediction, Psychiatry & Public Policy.* Cambridge: Cambridge University Press.

Webster, C.D., B. Dickens, and S. Addario. 1985. *Constructing Dangerousness: Scientific, Legal and Policy Implications.* Toronto: Centre of Criminology, University of Toronto.

Wilkinson, J.L. 1977. "Absolute and Conditional Discharge." 19 *Criminal Law Quarterly.* 454-470.

Wormith, J.S., and M. Borzecki. 1985. *A Survey of Treatment Programs for Sexual Offenders in Canada.* Ottawa: Ministry of the Solicitor General of Canada.

Young, A.N. 1993. "Two Scales of Justice: A Reply." 35 *Criminal Law Quarterly.* 355-375.

Zapf, M.K., and B. Cole. 1985. "Yukon Restitution Study." 27 *Canadian Journal of Criminology.* 477-490.

9 CRITICAL ISSUES IN SENTENCING: THE GOALS OF SENTENCING

This chapter examines four critical issues concerning sentencing: (1) the goals of sentencing; (2) public opinion and sentencing; (3) sentencing disparity and discrimination; and (4) reform of the sentencing process — new directions in the 1990s. All of these issues are of particular importance in light of the fact that Canada is currently passing through an era in which not only has a fundamental reappraisal of the nature and function of sentencing been undertaken by a number of federal commissions and committees, but also an ambitious program of far-reaching sentencing reforms has been initiated by the Government of Canada.

TRADITIONAL SENTENCING GOALS

As the Canadian Sentencing Commission (1987:133) pointed out, it is important, when discussing the goals of sentencing, not to confuse the process of sentencing with the criminal law or with the entire criminal justice system. While the latter may have the overall goal of "protection of the public," it would surely overburden the judiciary if the same goal were given to the sentencing process. As the Sentencing Commission indicated (1987:119, 147), the aims of sentencing must be limited by the fact that only a small fraction of offences reported to the police ever result in actually sentencing a specific offender.

The Commission recommended the adoption of a fundamental goal that it considered to be appropriate to the specific functions of sentencing within the context of the overall criminal justice system:

> It is further recognized and declared that in a free and democratic society peace and security can only be enjoyed through the due application of the principles of fundamental justice. In furtherance of the overall purpose of the criminal law of maintaining a just, peaceful and safe society, the fundamental purpose of sentencing is to preserve the authority of and promote respect for the law through the imposition of just sanctions (1987:151).

The Commission's approach was based on the notion that a formally identified offender should not be seen by his or her fellow citizens as "getting away scot-free." If this were to happen, then the very legitimacy of the rules, embodied in the criminal law, would be seriously undermined. According to the Commission, the average citizen should not be "demoralized" by the perception that those who break the law are not accountable for their behaviour. In this sense, the Commission's recommended approach would ensure that the *just* imposition of sanctions in the sentencing process would promote general respect for the underlying community values embodied in the criminal law. It would also strengthen the belief that individual citizens will be held accountable for their criminal misconduct and that the perceived costs of indulging in such misconduct outweigh any benefit that may be apparently derived from it. In the Commission's view, their recommended goal was both realistic and achievable since:

> Sentencing is not committed to eradicate crime but to prevent it increasing beyond a threshold where freedom, peace and security can no more be enjoyed on the whole by a community (1987:152).

Given the considerable range of sentencing options available to Canadian criminal courts, one would assume that Parliament would have long ago set out a series of sentencing goals or objectives to guide judges in making the most appropriate choice of sentence. Curiously, the *Criminal Code* contains no statement of sentencing goals or objectives, thus leaving Canadian judges effectively rudderless in waters that are constantly being agitated by conflicting currents of thought. Appellate courts in the various provinces and territories have, from time to time, established goals for sentencing within their own specific jurisdictions, but since the Supreme Court of Canada does not deal with appeals against sentences, it has not been possible for that court to articulate sentencing goals that are applicable to the country as a whole (Roberts, 1990b; Young, 1988).

This unfortunate situation is apparently about to change. The Minister of Justice introduced Bill C-90[1] to the Canadian Parliament in June of 1992, and this Bill proposes that, for the first time, a formal statement of "the purpose and principles of sentencing" be included in the *Criminal Code*. The relevant provisions of this Bill are discussed in detail in the final section of this chapter.

However, until the *Criminal Code* is amended so as to include a formal statement of the specific sentencing objectives that must be followed by the courts, both Canadian judges and those who analyze the system of criminal justice in Canada will continue to refer to a broad range of goals that have traditionally been attributed to the sentencing process. These traditional sentencing goals may be divided into two groups: utilitarian and retributive.

Utilitarian goals focus on deterrence (both individual and general), incapacitation, and rehabilitation. Proponents of these goals contend that criminal sanctions may be justified by social benefits such as the deterrence of those who are convicted of offences, the deterrence of the general population, the incapacitation through imprisonment of those who would otherwise commit crimes, or the rehabilitation of offenders resulting in a cessation of their criminal activities. In this sense, the utilitarian approach looks to the future as a means of justifying the imposition of legal sanctions.

Retributive goals focus on retribution, the philosophy of "just deserts" and denunciation. They look primarily to the past, fixing upon the blameworthiness of the offence committed rather than the future consequences of punishment.

Of course, a major problem that becomes apparent immediately is that many of these traditional goals relate primarily to punishment in general rather than to the sentencing process *per se*. Furthermore, these goals may conflict, providing little assistance to the decision maker in the sentencing process. For example, rehabilitation may require that an offender be given a community sanction while deterrence may dictate that he or she be given a sentence of imprisonment. In this sense, therefore, these goals are really no more than considerations that the judge should take into account in determining a sentence in any particular case.

Deterrence

Much has been written about deterrence, although very few solid conclusions can be drawn from the criminological literature on this subject. In theory, deterrence should be an important goal of sentencing since, according to its proponents, legal sanctions prevent the commission of crimes by making potential offenders fearful of the threat of punishment. Deterrence may be specific or general in nature. *Specific deterrence* occurs when a convicted offender is deterred from committing further offences as a consequence of his or her personal experience of punishment. *General deterrence* is achieved when the threat of legal sanctions prevents the commission of potential crimes by people other than punished offenders (Conklin, 1992:435-437). Of course, it is not just threats of legal sanctions alone that may exert a deterrent effect. For example, the threat of shame or embarrassment following involvement in illegal behaviour may have an equally, if not greater, deterrent effect — particularly in relation to offences such as drunk driving, which are perceived to be socially unacceptable (Braithwaite, 1989; Grasmick and Bursik, 1990; Grasmick, Bursik, and Arneklev, 1993).

Although "common sense" appears to indicate that punishment must have some effect in preventing crime (Miller and Anderson, 1986:418), it is very difficult to conduct empirical research into the specific deterrent effects of legal sanctions (Hagan, 1982). Most research has focused upon general deterrence and, as yet, the results are still inconclusive.

After conducting an extensive review of the research literature, the Canadian Sentencing Commission (1987:137) concluded with the rather enigmatic statement that "legal sanctions have an overall deterrent effect which is difficult to evaluate precisely." While the Commission (1987:138) believed that it is "plausible to argue" that legal sanctions have a general deterrent effect, it also doubted whether the literature supported the proposition that these sanctions could be used to achieve very specific results in the sense of deterring a particular category of offenders, such as impaired drivers, or suppressing a crime wave in a particular neighbourhood.

An important point made by the research literature revolves around the observation that it is the *certainty* rather than the *severity* of punishment that is most likely to exert a deterrent impact (Friedland, 1990; Gibbons, 1992:487). Some studies suggest that the perceived risk of arrest has a significant deterrent effect on certain types of offenders (Decker, Wright, and Logie, 1993; Nagin and Paternoster, 1991), although the perception of the degree of risk will vary to the extent that a person has actual experience of being caught and convicted (Horney and Marshall, 1992). According to Miller and Anderson (1986:438), increasing the probability that an offender will be convicted and punished is likely to be more efficacious than lengthening the term of imprisonment under a system of punishment based on deterrence. A closely related issue concerns the question of the deterrent effect of the *swiftness* (or *celerity*) of punishment (Howe and Brandau, 1988). Gibbons (1992:489) notes that virtually nothing is known about this factor, although social learning theory suggests that the more swiftly punishment follows the commission of a crime, the less likely it will be that this deviant act will be repeated (Akers, 1990). On the other hand, some commentators (for example, Paternoster, 1987) suggest that we should not overestimate the extent to which people make rational choices based on their perception of the risk of being caught and punished.

One factor that is frequently overlooked is that legal sanctions cannot exert any sort of deterrent impact unless they are widely known. After all, the person to be deterred must actually perceive that there is a significant threat of punishment should he or she break the law (Siegel, 1983:99; Vingilis *et al.*, 1988; Webb, 1980; Williams and Hawkins, 1986). Gibbons (1992:488) notes that what evidence there is suggests that many people are relatively ignorant of the nature and severity of criminal penalties — a suggestion supported by the Canadian Sentencing Commission's research into Canadians' awareness of sentencing laws and practices (1987:89ff.). This ignorance on the part of the general public may well explain why it has been difficult to furnish unequivocal evidence of the effectiveness of punishment in deterring others from committing offences.

The Canadian Sentencing Commission's research suggests that the media may well undercut the deterrent impact of the law by focusing on sentences that are lenient rather than severe and by publicizing the low clearance rates for many crimes (1987:137). In this sense, the media contribute to public ignorance about the severity of legal sanctions and the likelihood that they will be applied. On the other hand, there is evidence that a widely publicized campaign warning the public of increased police enforcement of a particular law (such as that requiring the wearing of seat belts) can result in a substantial change in citizens' behaviour (Watson, 1986).

Of course, the impact of deterrence is likely to vary with the nature of the individual and the nature of the particular crime involved (Chambliss, 1967; Conklin, 1992:437-442). Many crimes are committed by individuals who are affected by alcohol or other drugs or who are acting in a state of extreme emotion (such as anger or rage); clearly, these are people who are not likely to be able to weigh calmly the potential benefits and drawbacks associated with the commission of a crime (Siegel, 1983:101). On the other hand, economically motivated offenders, such as "professional burglars," may be much more amenable to the impact of deterrence (Decker, Wright, and Logie, 1993). Miller and Anderson (1986:438) suggest that the threat of punishment is a "central and multi-dimensional factor of information processed by individuals faced with perceived economically motivated crime opportunities" and recommend that, to be effective, crime control programs must "neutralize or discount the value of financial gain from crime." The differential amenability of individual offenders and types of crime to deterrence obviously renders the task of the judge immensely difficult if deterrence is a major aim of sentencing.

With regard to specific deterrence, the Canadian Sentencing Commission (1987:135) found that there is little evidence to suggest that deterrence has much impact upon those offenders who are convicted and sentenced to terms of imprisonment in the federal correctional system. Between 1975 and 1985, 60% of those offenders released on mandatory supervision from federal institutions were subsequently re-admitted to a penitentiary, while 49% of federal parolees were subsequently re-admitted to a federal institution. It has been suggested that imprisonment can actually *increase* the likelihood of subsequent re-offending since offenders will be placed in an environment that is supportive of criminal activity (Bridges and Stone, 1986).

One interesting study of the impact of punishment upon convicted offenders (Bridges and Stone, 1986:230) found that:

> ...experiences with crime and criminal sanctions have few "eye-opening" effects. The effects are greatest among naive offenders, for whom punishment increases perceived threat. Among experienced offenders, the effects of punishment run counter to the prediction of specific deterrence. Punishment has no substantial direct effect on perceived threat and may actually lower perceived threat by increasing approval of criminal behavior.

In light of what little is known about deterrence, it is clear that sentencing courts adopting it as a goal should do so with extreme caution.

Incapacitation

The theory underlying the sentencing strategy of incapacitation rests on the premise that offenders who are incarcerated are unable to commit crimes in the community and that, therefore, adoption of this strategy should result in the reduction of crime. There are at least two major strategies of incapacitation: collective incapacitation and selective incapacitation (Cohen, 1983b; Conklin, 1992:460-464). *Collective incapacitation* refers to a sentencing strategy that imposes a prison sentence on all those offenders convicted of a particular category of serious offence (for example, offenders convicted of robbery would be sentenced to, say, five years' imprisonment). *Selective incapacitation*, on the other hand, refers to a strategy that relies on individualized sentences based on predictions that particular offenders would commit serious offences at a high rate if they were not incarcerated.

One major problem with such strategies is that any incapacitative effect is significantly reduced by the extent to which the crimes that would have been committed by incarcerated offenders are replaced by those of other offenders (Blumstein, 1982). Crimes committed by a violent sex offender, for example, are not likely to be replaced by those of other offenders so that, for this category of crime, there is a strong, incapacitative effect when such an offender is incarcerated. However, there are certain crimes that, as Blumstein (1982:315) notes, are the "work of a criminal labor market," and these are very likely to be replaced. For example, the crimes of those convicted offenders involved in the sale of illicit drugs will most likely be replaced since their sales will be "picked up either by an increase in the activity of those still out or by recruitment of an additional seller to take his place."

Cohen (1983a) suggests that the research literature demonstrates that collective incapacitation strategies do not appear to achieve large reductions in crime. At most, such strategies see only a 10% to 20% reduction. As Cohen points out, this is not insubstantial. However, she contends that "incapacitation does not make the dent in crime that might have been expected from a 'lock-em-up' strategy." More significantly, however, the research suggests that collective incapacitation strategies would result in a massive build up in the prison population, thus rendering such strategies impractical.

The theory of selective incapacitation is that a relatively small number of offenders commit a disproportionately large number of crimes (Blumstein, 1983; Cohen, 1983a). Locking up this group of offenders would, if this strategy were to be adopted, result in a significant decrease in the crime rate while avoiding overcrowding in the prisons. The strategy hinges on the ability to identify such offenders early in their criminal careers and to imprison them for substantial periods. One major problem with this approach is that many people consider it unjust to give one individual a more severe sentence than another who has committed exactly the same offence, solely on the basis of a prediction as to what he or she may do in the future (Conklin, 1992:462-463; Von Hirsch, 1984). Punishment for what one *may do* hardly seems fair. Furthermore, as Cohen (1983a) points out, past efforts at predicting future criminality have not been very successful. Without an adequate technique for making such predictions, Cohen contends that there is no sound basis for implementing selective incapacitation sentencing strategies. Even if reliable prediction techniques were to become available to the courts, a serious ethical problem would arise because such techniques would most likely place some reliance on socioeconomic variables and, by so doing, would discriminate against various minority groups (Blumstein, 1984:135).

It has been suggested that an emerging, more sophisticated form of selective incapacitation may hold greater promise for the future. Cohen (1983a) has labelled this approach "criminal career incapacitation." It is based upon the identification of individual "criminal careers," defined as the "pattern of offending engaged in by various categories of offenders" (Blumstein, 1984:133). The object of this strategy is to use the information gathered about criminal careers in an attempt to identify those categories of offenders who, if released, would commit a large number of crimes (Conklin, 1992:463). For example, it appears that robbery and burglary offenders commit these crimes at relatively high rates and yet have relatively short careers (Cohen, 1983a). Therefore, it would make sense to incarcerate such offenders for a relatively short period at the point in their careers when they are most likely to commit a large number of offences; the result should be a significant reduction in the level of robberies and burglaries. Instead of locking up all those individuals who commit serious offences (collective incapacitation) or attempting to identify dangerous individuals on the basis of predictions as to their future misconduct (selective incapacitation), the criminal career incapacitation strategy estimates, on the basis of information concerning the nature of criminal careers, the *probability* that certain categories of offenders will commit more crimes at a high rate of frequency. Using such estimates of probability, the strategy would incarcerate such categories of convicted offenders for a period that is adequate to prevent them from re-offending. However, this approach is still at a relatively early stage of development in the United States, and it seems reasonable to conclude that there is such uncertainty about the whole sentencing strategy of incapacitation that it would be unwise for Canadian courts to adopt it as a major goal of sentencing in the foreseeable future.

Rehabilitation

During the last 20 years or so, the goal of rehabilitation has undergone a remarkable eclipse (Von Hirsch, 1990:402-403). The utilitarian notion that punishment can be justified by its rehabilitative effects has been overwhelmed by an increasing public clamour for punishment rather than treatment (Gibbons, 1992:484) and by the belief that empirical research has failed to demonstrate that correctional programs are effective in reducing recidivism on the part of convicted offenders (Doob and Brodeur, 1989; Lipton, Martinson and Wilks, 1975; Lab and Whitehead, 1988). Indeed, in the mid-1970s, Martinson (1974) coined the phrase, "nothing works," which has had a major impact on criminal justice policy both in the United States and Canada. The problem is that most of the criticism of the goal of rehabilitation originally stemmed from the strong belief that imprisonment can, by no stretch of the imagination, be considered a strategy for reducing the rate of recidivism on the part of convicted offenders (Morris, 1974; Waller, 1974). Therefore, it has been accepted by Canadian courts that offenders should never be given a longer period of imprisonment than they would otherwise deserve, solely on the basis that such a term of imprisonment is allegedly necessary for the treatment or rehabilitation of the offender (Ruby, 1987:26).

However, while few (if any) would argue that imprisonment *per se* has rehabilitative effects, it by no means follows that correctional programs will not have any rehabilitative effects on at least some of those offenders who participate in them. But those evaluation researchers who seek to determine exactly what those effects might be face daunting methodological problems (Andrews, 1990; Gendreau and Andrews, 1990; Gendreau and Ross, 1979; Gendreau and Ross, 1987).

If rehabilitation is a goal that a sentencing court *ought* to take into consideration, then it is clear that it may well conflict with other goals, such as deterrence. Nadin-Davis (1982) has contended that the first step taken by judges in deciding upon an appropriate sentence is to resolve this conflict between goals. Nadin-Davis, therefore, suggests that sentencing courts are faced with a "primary decision" as to whether they should pursue the goal of deterrence and impose a sentence of imprisonment or a fine (according to the prevailing "tariff") or the goal of rehabilitation and impose an *individualized* sentence. In the view of the Canadian Sentencing Commission (1987:139), if a judge feels that a particular offender can be rehabilitated, then that offender should be given an individualized sentence that should be "neither a custodial sentence nor a fine."

Retribution

The doctrine of retribution has undergone considerable changes over the centuries. Historically, retribution was closely associated with simple revenge and was best encapsulated by the phrase, "an eye for an eye and a tooth for a tooth," a doctrine that can be traced back to passages in the Bible and the Code of Hammurabai (Conklin, 1992:469; Reid, 1991:97). Under this doctrine, those who transgressed the law were liable to be treated in the same fashion as they had treated their victims. Very few people would advocate this approach in the context of a modern criminal justice system, although some of those who advocate a return to the death penalty would be likely to use the approach as a means of justifying the imposition of this ultimate penalty for the crime of murder. However, it is an approach that can only be applied to homicide since no one would seriously argue that we should burn down the houses of convicted offenders as a punishment for arson or mutilate those who have injured others in criminal assaults.

The notion of an eye for an eye is, therefore, really only of historical interest rather than a current statement of the nature of the theory of retribution. Under this theory, punishment is imposed for its own sake, not because it is supposed to achieve any particular result such as deterrence or rehabilitation. The offender is made to pay for his or her wrongdoing and is made to suffer by way of legal retaliation even if the punishment does not benefit anyone (Conklin, 1992:469-470). In other words, the focus of retribution is clearly upon what has been done because it is not at all concerned with the *outcome* of punishment as a relevant issue in the sentencing process (Canadian Sentencing Commission, 1987:128).

Siegel notes that it is an essential tenet of retribution that punishment is necessary in a "just society." In this perspective, punishment is viewed as a necessary method of maintaining the social equilibrium, which is disturbed when a crime is committed:

> If a person acquires an unfair advantage by disobeying rules law-abiding citizens respect, then matters cannot be set straight until this advantage is erased (1983:110).

Historically, retribution was advanced as a justification for punishment because it emphasized the obligation placed upon society to punish those who committed crimes. However, as the Canadian Sentencing Commission has pointed out (1987:141), retribution does not really provide a well-articulated rationale for imposing punishment since the question, "Why should a person be punished?" is answered by the rather lame statement that the offender has done something that *deserves* punishment — a classic example of circular reasoning!

In more recent years, proponents of retribution have advanced it as a reason for *limiting* the amount of punishment justified on other grounds such as deterrence or rehabilitation (Hart, 1968; Ruby, 1987:12). In particular, they contend that an offender should not be given a longer sentence of imprisonment than he or she "deserves" simply because such a sentence may have a deterrent value or because a lengthy period of incarceration is required in order to ensure rehabilitation. In other words, the "offender should not be treated as more (or less) *blameworthy* than is warranted by the character of his or her offence" (Siegel, 1983:112). Most of the literature concerning this approach has originated in the United States, primarily because, until the mid-1970s, most U.S. jurisdictions operated a system of indeterminate sentences that placed great power in the hands of correctional authorities rather than the courts. It was strongly contended that such a system was basically unfair since offenders who committed similar offences would be released at the end of vastly different periods purely on the basis of the parole board's predictions as to their future behaviour (American Friends Service Committee, 1971; Kittrie, 1980; Reid, 1991:104). In Canada, there are no indeterminate sentences (other than life sentences and the indeterminate detention of individuals who have been declared to be dangerous offenders), although the possibility of release on parole does represent an element of indeterminacy in the actual execution of the sentence handed down by the court. Although the U.S. sentencing context is markedly different from the Canadian, the modern retributive approaches that have evolved south of the border are still of considerable significance to the evolution of criminal justice policy in Canada.

"Just Deserts"

The "just deserts" perspective is the most influential of the attempts to use a form of retributivism as a means of limiting excessive punishment

(Canadian Sentencing Commission, 1987:143; Conklin, 1992:472-482; Siegel, 1983:110). The most influential statement of this perspective was made in 1976 by Andrew Von Hirsch (1976). This scholar's main concern was not to justify the imposition of punishment but rather to limit the quantum of punishment meted out to the offender (Von Hirsch, 1990:398). For Von Hirsch, while sanctions must be justified by their preventive effects, those sanctions must nevertheless be commensurate with the degree of the offender's blameworthiness. In other words, punishment in an individual case should never exceed the level that is appropriate for the crime that has been committed. For example, suppose that two offenders have been convicted of offences of equal seriousness. It would be unjust, in light of the just deserts theory, to sentence one offender to a greater degree of punishment than the other simply because it is contended that a longer sentence of imprisonment will have a deterrent effect in the first case but not in the second. Therefore, it would be unjust to impose a significantly greater punishment than is "normal" merely because the court feels that such a sentence will have a strong deterrent effect in a particular local community that is experiencing a so-called "crime wave."

It seems fair to suggest that the just deserts doctrine is beset by some major problems of a practical nature. While the general principle that punishment must be commensurate with the degree of blameworthiness of the offence is attractive in the abstract, applying it to specific cases is a complicated task (Durham, 1988). As Blumstein notes:

> Offense seriousness is an extremely complex notion. At a minimum, it involves consideration of harm to the victim, malevolence of intent, degree of involvement, victim precipitation, prior relationship between the offender and the victim, premeditation, and many other factors associated with a combination of culpability and victim injury. Any demand for strict proportionality is thus far more difficult to implement than to articulate (1982:310).

According to Blumstein (1982:311-12), therefore, the just deserts principle can only be applied in a general sense because there is no *precisely calculable* sentence for any given crime. However, Blumstein suggests that, for any specific offence, there is instead a "band of reasonable width to accommodate the variety of special circumstances associated with a particular offence and offender and any sentence within that band can reasonably be viewed as a 'just desert'." Therefore, the task of the sentencing process is to find the appropriate band so as to avoid imposing an "unjust" desert.

The just deserts doctrine is not a goal of sentencing as much as it is a restraining principle that limits the *quantum* of punishment that may be imposed. The notion that the penalty imposed should be commensurate with the degree of the offender's blameworthiness clearly had a considerable influence upon the approach adopted by the Canadian Sentencing Commission, which in formulating its overall goal for the sentencing process, noted that:

> If the fundamental purpose of sentencing is to preserve the authority of the law and to promote respect for it through the imposition of *just sanctions*, it follows that the principle of proportionality is given highest priority (1987:152).

Denunciation

Denunciation has been identified as a goal of sentencing with increasing frequency; however, there are at least two quite different forms that this goal has assumed. One form is based on the view that the sentencing process should serve an *educative function*. According to the Law Reform Commission of Canada (1974; 1976), the solemn imposition of a penalty in open court provides an undoubted opportunity for society to underline its basic values by strongly denouncing behaviour that is unacceptable. In this sense, it has been contended that the sentencing process has an educative effect that should consciously be taken advantage of by the courts. According to this view, therefore, the sentencing process can actually influence people's behaviour by indicating that unacceptable conduct will be punished.

The Canadian Sentencing Commission (1987:142-43) made the telling point that the denunciatory (or educative) aspect of sentencing can only be effective insofar as sentences are actually publicized. According to the Commission (1987:98), evidence appears to suggest that Canadians receive rather inadequate information about the nature of the sentencing process and, therefore, suffer from fundamental misconceptions as to the nature of the process. The Commission also contended (1987:142-43) that there is no empirical evidence to suggest that the degree of disapproval of any particular crime on the part of the public is either raised or lowered by information about sentencing. Indeed, it suggested that public views about the seriousness of particular offences are moulded by such factors as the public's perception of the harm done or the offender's intent rather than by knowledge of the severity of the sentence imposed in court or the maximum penalty set by the *Criminal Code*.

Ruby (1987:14) has contended that another form of the denunciation rationale is beginning to influence Canadian courts and that it is closely linked to the theory of retribution. This approach focuses on the need for sentences to express the abhorrence that society feels for certain types of serious crimes. As the Ontario Court of Appeal stated in one case:[2]

> The degree of repudiation to be expressed must itself be governed by the degree of disapproval which should be manifested by an average, high principled, intelligent citizen or, more accurately, by such a person's view of the gravity of the offence, not by what we judge as individuals with varying moral and religious opinions might reasonably consider proper.

As Ruby points out (1987:14), the nature of the sentence meted out under this rationale is "inevitably harsh" because it is supposed to represent the revulsion of society in the face of what are, by definition, horrible crimes. However, it is very difficult for the courts to determine what the average, "high principled" Canadian really feels about any particular crime and, furthermore, there is the very real danger that emotional public reaction, as expressed in the press and the electronic media at the time of a trial, may result in a much more severe sentence than would be imposed if a just deserts philosophy were being applied.

There is little doubt that none of the traditional justifications for punishing offenders can be converted into a single, overall goal of sentencing. To date, research into the deterrent, incapacitative, and rehabilitative effects of punishment has been relatively inconclusive. Furthermore, there are serious doubts as to the efficacy of the sentencing process as an educative or denunciatory device. Finally, the philosophies of retribution and just deserts are not so much aims of sentencing as principles that limit the quantum of punishment meted out by the courts. As the Canadian Sentencing Commission (1987:145) concluded, we know much more about what punishment *cannot do* than about what it *can actually achieve* and what should really justify its imposition. In these circumstances, the Commission recommends that there is a strong need for restraint in the use of punishment since pain and deprivation are its direct consequence, and society is uncertain as to its benefits either to the offender or society in general.

The Commission (1987:145) raised the question as to why such goals as deterrence, rehabilitation, and incapacitation figure so prominently in most discussions about the justification for punishment when it is increasingly clear that the sentencing process can have at best only a very limited capacity to prevent crime. The Commission suggested that punishment meets some deep-seated needs in our psychological makeup:

> Even if punishment cannot ultimately be justified, it apparently satisfies a strong desire, seated both in moral thinking and human emotions, and it cannot be renounced. There is consequently a natural tendency to compensate for the limits of retributivism by attributing to penal sanctions an efficiency in preventing crime which they do not really possess.

Although there are major problems associated with the adoption of any of the traditional goals of sentencing and justifications for punishment, they have continued to figure prominently both in the sentencing literature and in the opinions of the courts (Ruby, 1987:c.1). Without a clear statement of the purpose and principles of sentencing, the sentencing process will continue to be affected by conflicting goals and a lack of knowledge as to the wisdom of pursuing such goals. As we shall see at the end of this chapter, however, such a statement has finally been articulated in Bill C-90 (1992) and, if it is ultimately enacted, it will effect a profound change on the whole process of sentencing.

PUBLIC OPINION AND SENTENCING

Canadians consider the courts to be too lenient in their sentencing practices (Doob and Roberts, 1984). On the basis of a nation-wide gallup poll, Doob and Roberts (1983:1) found that 79.5% of Canadians believed that sentences in criminal courts were "too mild." The negative evaluation of the judiciary, in this respect, obviously creates a major problem for the public's overall confidence in the criminal justice system. The question clearly arises as to why there should be such a major discrepancy between the views of the judges and the views of the public.

Doob and Roberts (1983) have demonstrated that this discrepancy is the result not so much of a basic philosophical difference between the public and the courts as of an "information deficit."[3] On the basis of a number of empirical studies, these researchers concluded that, when members of the public were given background information concerning both offences and offenders, they were much more likely to recommend sentences that paralleled those imposed by the courts. In other words, there is a world of difference between answering a totally abstract question as to whether the courts are dealing too leniently with offenders, and being asked to consider an appropriate sentence while knowing the detailed circumstances surrounding the particular offence and the individual offender. Clearly, the alleged public demand for more punitiveness can be overstated (Roberts and Doob, 1989:515).

Doob and Roberts (1983:11-12) suggest that the press plays an important role in shaping the public's perception that sentences are too lenient. As they point out, public opinion concerning sentencing is more likely to be moulded by what is reported in the media than by direct knowledge of what is actually happening in the courts. Unfortunately, it appears that the media provide inadequate and selective information about sentencing. In particular, it is unlikely that the media will report "run-of-the-mill" cases, choosing instead to focus on those that are in some way exceptional or sensational (Canadian Sentencing Commission, 1987:96). Furthermore, the press and television tend to accentuate violent crime, thereby creating the impression that there is more violence in crime than there really is (Canadian Sentencing Commission, 1987:97; Roberts, 1988; Roberts and Doob, 1990). Indeed, a majority of Canadians in a gallup poll seriously overestimated the extent to which violence is involved in crime in Canada (Doob and Roberts, 1984:271), and this preoccupation with violent crime probably influenced their perception that sentences were, in general, too lenient (Roberts and Edwards, 1989).

Doob and Roberts (1983:19) emphasize that one's first "gut reaction" to a report of a serious criminal offence is almost certain to be one of "moral outrage." However, this initial reaction would probably be modified once the various mitigating circumstances that are usually present in most criminal cases are made known. Unfortunately, media reports of sentencing practices are more likely to refer to the heinousness of a particular offence than to dwell on the mitigating factors. Doob and Roberts, therefore, urge decision makers to place relatively little weight on the public clamour for more harshness in sentencing:

Those, then, who urge that the policy maker and the court follow the one-dimensional cry for judicial harshness in sentencing are not taking into account the willingness of Canadians to consider the complexity of each case on its own and the willingness of Canadians to temper their calls for harshness if the full facts of the case warrant it.

Public opinion about the criminal justice system is important, but only the naive politician or judge would urge that a badly informed public be followed blindly.[4]

Indeed, Roberts and Doob (1990:466) suggest that the Canadian public are prepared to support the increased use of *intermediate sanctions* (punishments that are less severe than imprisonment and more severe than simple probation) rather than the building of new prisons.

An important implication of this type of research is that there is a pressing need for more effective education of the public concerning this vital, albeit complex, process in the Canadian criminal justice system. The Canadian Sentencing Commission (1987:98) points out, quite correctly, that media reports are only one of many reasons why the public has formed the view that sentencing practices in Canada are too lenient, and it would be unfair to place all the blame for public misperceptions about sentencing upon the shoulders of reporters. However, the Commission concluded that:

...the analyses reported here do suggest that with little additional effort newspapers might present a more informative picture to their readers. In terms of public reactions to individual cases, the public might respond quite differently if it had reference points such as the maximum penalty and the average sentence.

The Commission also takes account of the fact that more systematic and adequate information has to be made available to reporters if they are to fulfill their responsibilities to the public. For example, it is still quite difficult to obtain information about average sentences because there are still no comprehensive, national statistics on sentencing. According to the Commission, however, its recommendations for the reform of the sentencing process in Canada will render it much more understandable to both reporters and the public alike, thus contributing to the gradual elimination of some of the fundamental misconceptions that currently plague public attitudes to sentencing in Canada.

SENTENCING DISPARITY AND DISCRIMINATION

The problem of sentencing disparity has been identified as one of the major issues that should be addressed in any contemporary proposal for reform of the Canadian criminal justice system (Linden, 1986:3). This concern has been given new impetus by the advent of the *Charter*, which might well be interpreted in such a manner as to render excessive sentencing disparity unconstitutional (Jobson and Ferguson, 1987:18).

Canada is a geographically immense country, with significant differences between the various provinces, territories, and regions. Since the *Criminal Code* generally leaves an enormous degree of discretion in the hands of the courts, it is, therefore, scarcely surprising that there is a considerable degree of sentencing disparity across the country. The maximum penalties in the *Criminal Code* provide little real guidance to the courts since they are set at a level that is generally far too high except for the most serious cases (Canadian Sentencing Commission, 1987:63ff.). Furthermore, the lack of guidance available to judges has been exacerbated by the complete absence of comprehensive court statistics gathered on a "national and continuing basis" (Canadian Sentencing Commission, 1987:61). Indeed, the last comprehensive, national sentencing data were released by Statistics Canada as long ago as 1978 (Canadian Sentencing Commission, 1987:60). As the Commission points out:

> In the present system, where there are no formal "standards" against which to judge a sentence, the lack of systematic sentencing information accessible to judges in their determination of sentences almost ensures that there will be unwarranted variation in sentences (1987:62).

Although both the Crown and the offender have the right to appeal against the sentence handed down by a trial judge, the system of appeal courts is not really suited to establishing uniformity of sentencing on a *national* basis. Although the Supreme Court of Canada has the power to hear appeals on all sentencing matters, its policy is to deal only with sentencing matters raising questions of law (Canadian Sentencing Commission, 1987:70). Therefore, the ten provincial courts of appeal effectively serve as the final tribunal on sentencing matters: instead of one court attempting to achieve sentencing uniformity on a national basis, there are ten different courts attempting to achieve such uniformity on a purely provincial basis. Furthermore, only a few of the appeal courts have, to date, given trial courts specific guidance as to the appropriate range of sentences that should be imposed in relation to different categories of offence. In other words, the appeal courts in most provinces have not shown a preference for the formulation of a sentencing "tariff" that gives concrete guidance as to what the "going rate" is for specific offences (Canadian Sentencing Commission, 1987:70).

Given this background, it is almost inevitable that there should be evidence of sentencing disparity across Canada. There are significant variations in the manner in which different offence categories are assigned sentences in the various provinces (Hann *et al.*, 1983; Hann and Kopelman, 1986). Furthermore, evidence shows that there are significant sentencing variations within the various provinces themselves. For example, Murray and Erickson (1983) found widespread disparity in the sentencing of offenders charged with the possession of cannabis in five locations in Ontario. Similarly, in his classic study of magistrates' courts in Ontario, Hogarth concluded that these courts varied "immensely" in terms of their sentencing practices:

> In the course of one year, one court used probation in nearly half of the cases coming before it, while another never used this form of disposition. Similarly, the use of suspended sentence without probation ranged from 0 to 34 per cent, fines from 2 to 39 per cent, short-term gaol sentences from 4 to 60 per cent, reformatory sentences from 1 to 37 per cent and long-term penitentiary sentences from 0 to 23 per cent. These differences appear to be too large to be explained solely in terms of differences in the types of cases appearing before courts in different areas (1971:12).

Nevertheless, it is clear that a wide disparity in the sentencing of similar cases offends the basic notions of fairness held by most Canadians (Nadin-Davis, 1982:8). As one Canadian Provincial Court judge put it:

> The notion of uniformity of sentence...is an essential consideration in the fair and just administration and enforcement of the criminal law in any democratic society.[5]

Indeed, it is primarily because of the need to control disparity in sentencing that, as we shall see, the Canadian Sentencing Commission (1987:269ff.) strongly recommended the introduction of a system of sentencing guidelines in Canada.

However, before discussing the research concerning unwarranted variations in sentencing practices, it is necessary to clarify the whole notion of disparity. In an excellent discussion of this issue, Forst (1982) emphasizes that the "essence of disparity is variation from some norm or standard" (1982:24). However, in his view, the problem is that there are differing views as to the exact nature of the norm or standard from which the alleged variation may be measured. Forst contends that there are two main approaches in this respect. The first views disparity as being a variation from some norm of *proportionality*, while the second conceptualizes disparity in terms of variations from *statistical patterns* of sentencing. Suppose, for example, that a trial judge imposes a sentence of life imprisonment upon a first offender for a "simple" breaking and entering of a dwelling house. While this punishment is permitted by the *Criminal Code*,[6] most people would regard it as being disproportionate to the inherent seriousness of the offence; therefore, the sentence could be regarded as being disparate in the first sense of the word. On the other hand, suppose that a researcher analyzed the dispositions of the court concerned and discovered that all first offenders convicted of breaking and entering a dwelling house were sentenced to life imprisonment. In these circumstances, although there is disparity in terms of there being a variation from a norm of proportionality, there is no deviation from the statistical patterns observed in the particular jurisdiction; therefore, there is no disparity in the second sense of the word. As Forst (1982:25) indicates, offenders in a certain offence category (such as breaking and entering) may well be treated uniformly but not with proportionality. Conversely, a judge could well impose a disposition that, while clearly deviating from a statistical pattern, nevertheless does conform to a norm of proportionality. In the second sense of the word, the inherent justice or proportionality of a sentence is irrelevant; all that matters is whether or not it deviates from the statistical pattern.

Most researchers have adopted the second approach to the conceptualization of disparity. Within this approach, the focus is upon the issue of whether "similar" cases are treated *differently* by the courts. However, while there is considerable agreement that unjustified disparity occurs when similar cases are treated differently, there is remarkably little consensus as to the criteria that should be employed in determining whether or not cases can be considered similar in the first place. Should the court consider only the nature of the offence committed or should it also take into account the prior record of the offender? Should the court consider the likelihood of the offender repeating the offence, his or her employment status, etc.? While, in the United States, there has been an increasing desire to limit the scope of a sentencing court's consideration to the seriousness of the offence and the prior record of the offender, in Canada the courts have continued to take a whole range of factors into account (Ruby, 1987:c.6; Vining and Dean, 1980). Unfortunately for the researcher who attempts to investigate the issue of sentencing disparity, the greater the number of factors that may be taken into account, the more difficult it is to determine whether there has been dissimilar treatment of similar cases.

Nadin-Davis (1982) has contended that the sentencing process should really be analyzed in terms of two distinct decision-making stages. The first decision is concerned with the *type* of sentence (for example, imprisonment, fine, probation, etc.) that should be imposed. Nadin-Davis (1982:3-6) suggests that this decision really boils down to a choice between a "tariff" disposition (such as imprisonment or a fine) and an "individualized" disposition (such as probation). The second decision-making stage deals with the exact details of the decision made in the first stage, for example, fixing the exact length of the prison term or probation order or the precise amount of the fine. Where a "tariff" sentence is imposed, then, according to Nadin-Davis (1982:4) the sentencing court may turn for guidance to an appropriate "range of sentence" that has emerged in the evolution of the relevant case law. The precise placement of the particular case in the "range" for the offence concerned will be affected by certain aggravating or mitigating factors recognized in the case law (for example, the presence of a lengthy prior record or the fact that the offender abused a position of trust may be regarded as aggravating factors while the absence of a prior record, the youth, or the mental illness of the offender may be considered mitigating factors). In Nadin-Davis's words:

> This choice between individualized and tariff sentencing may be phrased in a number of ways: treatment v. punishment, subjective sentencing v. objective sentencing, or sentencing the offender v. sentencing the offence (1982:5).

In the view of Nadin-Davis (1982:4), while there is considerable uniformity in the length of prison terms or size of fines imposed in relation to a "tariff" sentence, such uniformity will necessarily be absent where the central focus is upon the individual offender rather than the offence (namely, in relation to an "individualized" sentence). However, Nadin-Davis (1982:14) contends that Canadian courts still apply certain clearly identifiable criteria in making the decision to impose an individualized sentence and do so uniformly. Unfortunately, Nadin-Davis did not provide empirical support for this analysis, although a study by Brantingham (1984) suggests that the analysis does bear some resemblance to the manner in which sentencing decisions are actually made.

Researchers have used two major approaches to the issue of sentence disparity in Canada. The first approach focuses upon the background characteristics of the judges themselves and suggests that the roots of disparity may best be sought in the social and psychological factors that impact upon the judicial decision makers. The second approach casts the spotlight upon the background characteristics of the cases and the offenders, and lends support to the notion that these factors shape the outcome of the sentencing process.

The first approach is strongly represented by John Hogarth's classic work (1972) on sentencing in Canada. This researcher's basic premise was that sentencing must be regarded as a "human process" and is "subject to all the frailties of the human mind" (1972:356). Hogarth studied the sentencing behaviour of 71 Ontario magistrates. He examined the background characteristics of magistrates, their penal philosophies, judicial attitudes, and sociolegal constraints on sentencing. Hogarth found that judicial attitudes and judicial perceptions of the facts of the cases before them accounted for a considerable proportion of the disparity in sentencing. Indeed, Hogarth (1972:382) suggested that, while only about 9% of the variation in sentencing practice could be accounted for by "objectively defined facts," more than 50% of this variation could be explained by "knowing certain pieces of information about the judge himself." In characterizing sentencing as a very human process, Hogarth concluded that it is a:

> ...dynamic process in which the facts of the cases, the constraints arising out of the law and the social system, and other features of the external world are interpreted, assimilated, and made sense of in ways compatible with the attitudes of the magistrates concerned (1972:382).

Palys and Divorski (1984; 1986) also concluded that judicial attitudes and perceptions are related to disparity in sentencing. Unlike Hogarth, who examined actual cases, these researchers applied the "simulated cases" approach, which involves presenting a group of judges with hypothetical cases and asking them to indicate what sentence they would impose (Palys and Divorski, 1984:334). This approach permitted the researchers to employ a methodology in which the cases, upon which the judges were asked to make judgments, were held constant, thus permitting an "*unambiguous* demonstration of sentencing disparity" (Palys and Divorski, 1986:349). It was found that there was a considerable degree of disparity among the sentences handed down by the judges, although the degree of disparity did vary from case to case (Palys and Divorski, 1986:353). In the case with the most marked degree of disparity, sentences for a case of assault causing bodily harm (involving the loss of sight in one eye) ranged from a $500 fine plus 6 months' probation to 5 years in a penitentiary. The researchers suggested that a major source of sentencing disparity could be found in the judges' differential subscription to legal objectives (for example, rehabilitation, incapacitation, general deterrence), and the emphasis that they placed on different case facts. The researchers suggested (1986:358) that these two factors were closely related since "many, if not most judges perused case facts, chose salient ones, formulated legal objectives on this basis, and then proceeded to 'repackage' case facts in a manner which showed maximal harmony between legal objectives and case facts." This suggested to the researchers that the making of a sentencing decision and the justification of that decision are "two separate, sequential processes." In light of the finding by Hogarth and Palys and Divorski that the outcomes of sentencing decisions are strongly influenced by the particular sentencing philosophies of individual judges, the Canadian Sentencing Commission (1987:77) suggests that the "primary difficulty with sentencing as it exists at the moment is that there is no consensus on how sentencing should be approached."

The second approach to researching sentence disparity focuses upon the background characteristics of cases and offenders (Brantingham, 1984). Often, such research is concerned with the issue of whether courts discriminate against certain groups of individuals on the basis of socio-economic status, race, etc. (Debicki, 1985; Renner and Warner, 1981).

Brantingham (1984) conducted a sophisticated statistical analysis of a large number of criminal cases decided in two Canadian courts during

1979 and 1980.[7] Brantingham found that the overall pattern of sentencing was one of "more consistency than inconsistency" in judicial decision making. The most important factors affecting decisions both as to the type of sentence to be imposed and the length of prison terms imposed were "case facts" (including, for example, the existence of aggravating factors, such as the use of weapons, and mitigating factors, such as provocation by the victim) and the prior record of the defendant. While there was some inconsistency on the part of individual judges, factors relating to judges were relatively unimportant in explaining sentencing outcomes as compared with the case facts and the prior record of the accused. While the study indicates that there was a certain degree of disparity in sentencing, the general conclusion appears to be that, overall, judges applied legalistic criteria fairly consistently in arriving at their decisions. Nevertheless, the study did find that, even with the numerous variables that Brantingham took into account, some 35% of sentencing outcomes were unpredictable and that "some proportion of these cases" probably reflected inconsistent sentencing patterns from case to case *even for the same judge*.

It has been strongly argued that, while courts may apply legalistic criteria in a fairly consistent manner, the impact of their decisions, in fact, discriminates against certain disadvantaged groups within society. Mandel (1984) has noted that, even if legalistic criteria are applied by the court in a consistent manner, the end result will still be discriminatory because the legal rules themselves are biased against those of low socioeconomic status. For example, whether an offender is employed or unemployed may well affect the decision as to the appropriate disposition made by the sentencing court. Those who support such an approach may well argue that those who have steady employment have more to lose by being sentenced to imprisonment, while the fact of their employment demonstrates that they are a "better risk" to avoid re-offending. Furthermore, a court may feel that an unemployed person would not pay a fine and, therefore, impose a sentence of imprisonment immediately. Thus, although the courts have applied legalistic criteria consistently, the result of this policy is discrimination against the poor.[8] Two Canadian studies suggest that this is an appropriate perspective to apply to sentencing decisions in Canada.

Renner and Warner (1981) studied a number of cases heard by three magistrate courts and two county courts in Halifax. The researchers found that, even when the "legalistic" factors of nature of charge and prior record of the offender were controlled, unemployed persons were typically sentenced more severely than employed persons. Similarly, Debicki (1985) studied all 1,194 cases decided by the Winnipeg Provincial Court during a three-month period in 1983. He found evidence of differential sentencing on the basis of socioeconomic status:

> Whether income, social status or type of job is used as a measure, similar results emerge. Those of lower socio-economic status are treated more harshly. The best measure has proved to be employment status...The pattern is clear. Those who are employed pay for their crime with money, and those who are unemployed with a relatively short loss of freedom (1985:234).

The research is inconclusive as to whether there is a racial bias in Canadian sentencing practices. For example, Renner and Warner (1981) found that sentencing patterns were significantly associated with the defendant's race; for example, white defendants who were first offenders convicted of summary charges were given discharges in 23% of cases, whereas black first offenders, in exactly the same circumstances, never received a discharge. On the other hand, Debicki (1985) did not find that there was a relationship between sentencing severity and ethnicity, insofar as the treatment of Aboriginal Canadians was concerned.

In a recent review of the sentencing of Aboriginal peoples in Canada, LaPrairie (1992:135) notes that there is "considerable rhetoric about overt racism and unwarranted disparity in the conviction and sentencing of aboriginal people," and this author refers to two papers (Jackson, 1988; Morse and Lock, 1988) in which such claims are made. However, LaPrairie (1992:136) rejects these claims in light of the "limited methodologies and levels of analysis" manifested in these two papers. LaPrairie (1992:136) proceeds to examine Clark's (1989) review of the relevant sentencing literature and criminal justice research and states that this review "provides no conclusive evidence to support or reject the existence of unwarranted disparity or overt racial bias in the sentencing of aboriginal people." However, this lack of conclusive evidence does not necessarily mean that such disparity or bias does not, in fact, exist. Indeed, LaPrairie (1992:136) suggests that we cannot begin to answer this question until Canadian researchers develop a more solid base of empirical evidence. The existing research is just not adequate for the purpose of drawing any general conclusions about bias and sentencing disparity in relation to Aboriginal peoples in Canada. Overall, LaPrairie (1992:140) makes the point that "understanding the sentencing of aboriginal offenders is like trying to complete a jigsaw puzzle without all the pieces."

Nevertheless, the research literature does furnish some important information concerning the sentencing of Aboriginal peoples. LaPrairie (1992:138) notes that the existing data suggest that Aboriginal persons sentenced to imprisonment may receive shorter terms than non-Aboriginals (even when the type of offence is controlled in the studies concerned). However, LaPrairie (1992:141) also indicates that the existing research, despite all of its limitations, suggests that Aboriginal offenders may be disproportionately sentenced to imprisonment because there is an absence of alternative sentencing options, particularly in the more remote areas of Canada where many such offenders live.

Much greater attention has been paid to the issue of sentencing and racial bias in the United States, where a consensus appears to be emerging to the effect that racial discrimination in sentencing is an extremely difficult phenomenon to measure because bias against certain racial groups may be very subtle in nature (Archibald, 1989; Sweeney and Craig, 1992). For example, Zatz (1987:86) contends that the most recent research has "consistently unearthed subtle, if not overt, bias." While race/ethnicity is not "the major determinant of sanctioning," it is nevertheless "a determinant of sanctioning and a potent one at that." In her view:

> ...discrimination has not gone away. It has simply changed its form to become more acceptable. Increased formal rationality of the legal process has caused discrimination to undergo cosmetic surgery, with its new face deemed more appealing. The result is bias in a different form than it showed in the past. It is now subtle rather than overt. But, to borrow and twist an expression from Weber..., the "iron cage" still locks primarily minorities and lower class whites behind its bars.[9]

Another issue is the question of gender bias in sentencing (Chunn and Gavigan, 1991; Edwards, 1989; Mohr, 1990; Tjaden and Tjaden, 1981; Wickler, 1993). Graydon (1992:121) notes that "women have largely been ignored in the criminal justice system and in discussions of sentencing in Canada." Therefore, it is still too early to draw any firm conclusions as to the impact of gender bias on the sentencing process.

The U.S. literature suggests that two major models may be used to examine the impact of gender on sentencing practices. One theory is that courts impose *more lenient* sentences on female offenders because they have embraced a *chivalry* (or *paternalism*) model of sentencing in relation to women (Johnson and Scheuble, 1992). Alternatively, there is the theory that courts adopt a *more punitive* approach to female offenders because the latter have departed from the traditional female stereotype that dictates that they should be "dependent, gentle and compliant" (Johnson and Scheuble, 1991:678). This has been referred to as the "traditional sex role model" of sentencing (Edwards, 1989; Johnson and Scheuble, 1991:678).

According to Graydon (1992:123), although the state of the existing research in relation to the application of these two models is inconclusive, "most authors do agree that paternalistic attitudes and the reinforcement of female stereotypes are characteristic of the sentencing process." In this sense, it has been suggested that the chivalry model underlies many sentencing decisions and that females are generally less likely to receive severe punishments (Boyle *et al.*, 1985; Johnson and Scheuble, 1991).[10]

Ultimately, however, much depends on how the existing data are interpreted. For example, Chunn and Gavigan (1992:293) note that, although the absence of Canada-wide sentencing statistics makes it difficult to draw any definitive conclusions, the existing data tend to suggest that women are likely to receive more lenient sentences than men and are much more likely to be spared a term of imprisonment. On the other hand, the same authors (1991:298) suggest that this interpretation may be misleading. They note that the apparently more severe sentences meted out to men do not reflect a policy of lenience toward female offenders as much as they reflect the fact that men's offences are more serious and that men are more likely to have prior criminal records. In addition, as more women are sentenced for violent offences and have more extensive prior records, these authors detect a trend toward women being given longer prison sentences in Canada.

Of course, even if the courts treat men and women equally in meting out sentences, the impact of those sentences may be more severe on women than men (Mohr, 1990). As Graydon notes:

> Non-custodial penalties such as fines, probation and community service orders, although often seen as lenient sentencing alternatives, may have a disproportionately harsh impact on many female offenders as a result either of the offender's impecuniosity or inability to comply

with the Court's direction as a result competing child care duties (1992:128).

Similarly, Chunn and Gavigan (1991:300) point out that imprisonment is, in fact, a harsher sentence for women than men because there is a much smaller range of correctional programs and resources available to them in prison.

Finally, Graydon (1992:125) suggests that Aboriginal female offenders may suffer both gender and racial discrimination. Indeed, Chunn and Gavigan (1991:305) comment that Aboriginal women in Canada are much more likely to end up in prison than their non-Aboriginal counterparts because they are unable to pay the fines imposed on them.

Clearly, there is a great need for more systematic research into the impact of both race and gender on the sentence decision-making process in Canada. Such research is sorely needed if Canadian criminologists are to be placed in the position where they can make any definitive statements on the extent sentencing decisions discriminate against Aboriginal peoples and women.

REFORM OF THE SENTENCING PROCESS IN CANADA: NEW DIRECTIONS IN THE 1990s

At the time of writing, the Canadian criminal justice system stands on the threshold of a major overhaul of the sentencing process (Roberts, 1990a). The reports of the Canadian Sentencing Commission and the Daubney Committee have laid the groundwork for the present era of reform (Campbell, 1990:388-390).

The Report of the Canadian Sentencing Commission (1987)

In Chapter 8, we saw that the Canadian Sentencing Commission recommended that a major objective of sentencing reform should be to reduce reliance on imprisonment as a disposition and to encourage a much greater use of community-based sentences as alternatives to imprisonment in all but the most serious cases (Doob, 1990). This critical recommendation, however, constituted only one component of an ambitious blueprint for sentencing reform in Canada. This blueprint was contained in a report called *Sentencing Reform: A Canadian Approach,* published by the Canadian Sentencing Commission in 1987. The construction of this blueprint for sentencing reform addressed the following principles.

First, the Commission (1987:164) emphasized the need to bring clarity into the sentencing process: "To the greatest extent possible, this involves bridging the gap between the meaning of a sentence, as written in the law and as pronounced by the court, and its subsequent translation into practice." Second, the Commission (1987:165) stressed the need for restraint in the imposition of punishment, particularly since there is little evidence to suggest that sentencing decisions *per se* can have much of an impact upon reducing the level of crime in society. Third, the sentencing process should be seen as being both fair and equitable and, in order for this to be achieved, there must be some kind of structure that gives meaningful guidance to the courts as to the factors that should be taken into account in imposing a sentence (Canadian Sentencing Commission, 1987:167). Such a structure (in the form of sentencing guidelines) is deemed to be the most practical way to reduce the problems caused by sentencing disparity. Fourth, the Commission (1987:167) emphasized that sentencing reform should be specifically appropriate to the unique nature of the Canadian context, including Canada's geographic and cultural diversity and the broad scope of Parliament's criminal law jurisdiction that applies to the whole country.

It would be impossible to analyze the Commission's detailed proposals in any great depth here. However, the "highlights" of the proposals will be presented and, where appropriate, will be discussed. The Commission's own summary (1987:170) of these highlights was as follows.

a) Elimination of all mandatory minimum penalties (other than for murder and high treason).
b) Replacement of the current penalty structure for all offences other than murder and high treason with a structure of maximum penalties of 12 years, 9 years, 6 years, 3 years, 1 year, 6 months.
c) Elimination of full parole release for all sentences other than mandatory life sentences.
d) Provision for a reduction in time served for those inmates who display good behaviour while in prison.
e) Elimination of "automatic" imprisonment for fine default to reduce the likelihood that a person who cannot pay a fine will go to jail.
f) Establishment of presumptive guidelines that indicate whether a person convicted of a particular offence should normally be given

a custodial or a community sanction. In appropriate cases the judge could depart from these guidelines.

g) Establishment of a "presumptive range" for each offence normally requiring incarceration. Again, the judge could depart from the guidelines in appropriate cases.

h) Creation of a permanent sentencing commission to develop presumptive ranges for all offences, to collect and distribute information about current sentencing practice, and to review and, in appropriate cases, to recommend to Parliament the modification of the presumptive sentences in light of current practice or appellate decisions.

Perhaps the most striking aspect of the Commission's proposals was the extent to which they required that a prison sentence handed down in court bear a close resemblance to the sentence that is actually served (see Benzvy-Miller and Cole, 1990). Under the proposals, an offender would be able to earn a reduction of up to 25% of the custodial part of his or her sentence for "good behaviour" (remission). However, apart from this concession, the time that an offender would serve in prison would be the term actually imposed by the trial judge. This proposal would, of course, necessitate the abolition of parole, which at present is responsible for much of the uncertainty and unpredictability concerning the actual length of sentences served in prison (Brodeur, 1990). It would appear that the Commission's approach was strongly influenced by the just deserts philosophy, which advocates that sentence length should be determined by the seriousness of the offence and not by predictions as to the offender's future conduct (Gabor, 1990). In the words of the Commission:

> At the present time in Canada, sentences of imprisonment are both unclear and unpredictable. The absence of clarity and predictability can only have deleterious effects upon the administration of justice and perceptions of sentencing by offenders, the public and criminal justice professionals (1987:237).

It is interesting to note that the Commission also recommended (1987:259) that judges should have more say in determining the nature of the custody in which those sentenced to prison should serve their time. Where a court imposes a custodial sentence, the judge should be able to recommend that the sentence be served in open or closed custody. This recommendation is another reflection of the Commission's desire to shift discretionary power from the correctional authorities to the courts.

The Commission (1987:195ff.) recommended that there be a new structure of maximum penalties for offences other than murder and high treason; namely, 12 years, 9 years, 6 years, 3 years, 1 year, and 6 months. This represents a significant reduction in the length of maximum sentences that may currently be imposed under the *Criminal Code, Narcotic Control Act,* and *Food and Drugs Act.* However, it is important to bear in mind that, under the Commission's recommendations, an offender would serve a greater proportion of his or her prison sentence than is the case in the existing system (at least 75%).

The central feature of the Commission's blueprint was the recommendation that Canada adopt a system of sentencing guidelines made up of four components (1987:271).

The first component of the guidelines is a sentencing rationale and, to this end, the Commission recommended that a "Declaration of the Purpose and Principles of Sentencing" be adopted and enshrined in legislation. The Commission (1987:151) stated that "the fundamental purpose of sentencing is to preserve the authority of and promote respect for the law through the imposition of just sanctions." The Commission (1987:154-155) also articulated a number of sentencing principles, for example, that the sentence be proportionate to the gravity of the offence and the degree of responsibility of the offender.

The second component of the guidelines deals with guidance as to what the type of sentence should be imposed. This guidance is provided in the form of a presumptive disposition. The Commission (1987:309ff.) recommended that the guidelines should fix a presumptive sentence for each criminal offence. There would be four of these presumptive sentences:

- ▸ an unqualified presumption of custody;
- ▸ an unqualified presumption of non-custody;
- ▸ a qualified presumption of custody; and
- ▸ a qualified presumption of non-custody.

In the case of an *unqualified* presumption, the offender will be sentenced either to prison or a non-custodial disposition regardless of the particular circumstances of the individual case. On the other hand, in the case of a *qualified* presumption, the judge considers all the circumstances of the case in order to determine whether that presumption should prevail. For example, in the case of theft over $1,000, the Commission (1987:313) suggested that there should be a *qualified* presumption of non-custody. This means the usual sentence will be non-custodial in nature. However, in a case where the theft was very serious in nature (for example, $10,000 was stolen) and the offender has a long record of prior property offences, then the judge would be expected to send the offender to prison. In pursuit of its task of structuring judicial discretion, the Commission (1987:315) assigned a presumptive disposition to every offence in the *Criminal Code, Narcotic Control Act*, and *Food and Drugs Act.*

The third component of the proposed system of guidelines involves *numerical* guidance to judges imposing a term of imprisonment or day fines. For imprisonment, a custodial range of years or months would be assigned to each offence (for example, two to four years for certain kinds of robbery). The custodial ranges would be broad enough to permit the judge to take account of the particular circumstances of the case and would be proportionate to the seriousness of the offence. The Sentencing Commission (1987:316) notes that these custodial ranges would be developed by the permanent sentencing commission (whose establishment was also recommended in the Sentencing Commission's report). The Commission (1987:318) notes that the use of the guidelines should result in an overall decrease in the use of incarceration and an eventual reduction in the prison population. For day fines, the Commission recommended greater study.

The fourth component deals with "degree of constraint" — to what extent must judges apply the guidelines in a "slavish way"? The proposed guidelines permit a trial judge to depart from the indicated sentence in certain circumstances (Roberts, 1990b). However, if a judge wishes to impose a sentence that departs from the sentencing guidelines, then he or she must give written reasons (Canadian Sentencing Commission, 1987:303), and the departure would always be open to review by a Court of Appeal. The Commission (1987:320) prepared a list of aggravating and mitigating factors that would justify a judge in departing from the guidelines. For example, among the aggravating factors are the existence of a prior criminal record and the use of excessive cruelty in the commission of the offence, while mitigating factors include the absence of previous convictions and the existence of mental impairment on the part of the offender. In giving reasons for departing from the guidelines, the judge would be required to identify the aggravating or mitigating factors that would justify such a departure. The Commission (1987:305) recommended that either the Crown or the defence should be able to appeal a sentence, whether or not it departs from the guidelines.

The Sentencing Commission (1987:302) decided not to make the guidelines purely *advisory* in character, as was the case in those U.S. jurisdictions that have already adopted a system of guidelines. The evidence indicates that voluntary compliance with purely advisory guidelines was disappointingly low (Blumstein, 1982; Cohen and Tonry, 1983; Rich *et al.*, 1982). When guidelines have the force of law, however, it appears that there is a much greater degree of judicial compliance with them in the United States (Kramer and Lubitz, 1985). The Canadian Sentencing Commission (1987:305) rejected the notion that the sentencing guidelines should be enacted as legislation. It recommended (1987:308) instead that they should be submitted to Parliament and would come into effect within 90 days unless rejected by a negative resolution of the House of Commons. Although the proposed sentencing guidelines do not impose unbreakable fetters upon trial judges, they do require them to justify any departure from the indicated sentences and this requirement is likely to ensure a high degree of compliance in Canada.

The Commission also decided not to follow the model set by the earliest sentencing guideline systems established in the United States that merely codified existing sentencing practice (Wilkins *et al.*, 1978). Instead, the Commission looked to such states as Minnesota where the Minnesota Sentencing Guidelines Commission formulated its "own schedule of sentences based on normative principles" (Blumstein, 1982:322). The Canadian Sentencing Commission adopted this normative approach, as can been seen by its clearly articulated desire to change Canadian sentencing practice by reducing the use of the sanction of imprisonment and fostering a greater use of community sanctions.

An important element in the proposed system of sentencing guidelines was the creation of a permanent sentencing commission, the majority of whose members would be drawn from the judiciary. Among the commission's numerous functions would be the establishment and administration of a sentencing information system; the development and revision of the national guidelines for presumptive dispositions and the range of sentences; the making of recommendations to Parliament on matters such as the revision of maximum penalties for offences; and conducting research and providing information on sentencing. However, the Canadian Sentencing Commission (1987:328) wished to maintain a major policy-making role for the courts of appeal and recommended that they should be granted the power to set policy governing the actual application of sentencing guidelines and, most significantly, to amend the presumptive custodial ranges for "substantial and compelling reasons." In this sense, the various provincial courts of appeal would not be totally excluded by the national sentencing commission from policy making in sentencing matters. In a country as large and diverse as Canada, it clearly makes sense to encourage such a role for the provincial courts of appeal.

The proposal for a system for sentencing guidelines is not a revolutionary concept. Guidelines have been used for a number of years in many U.S. jurisdictions (Karle *et al.*, 1991; Heaney, 1991; Nagel, 1990), and other Canadian bodies, such as the Law Reform Commission of Canada, have recommended the establishment of a system of sentencing guidelines similar to that proposed by the Canadian Sentencing Commission (Ferguson and Jobson, 1987; Linden, 1986).

Of course, many criticisms have been made of the Sentencing Commission's proposals. Some critics of the sentencing guidelines' approach (for example, McIntyre, 1985:217) have voiced the concern that the establishment of a separate sentencing commission will add an unnecessary "new bureaucracy" to "our already cumbersome criminal process." Such critics would prefer to rely on a system in which the appellate courts took more responsibility for articulating sentencing principles. Vining and Dean (1980:147) suggest that an "extensive analysis of appellate sentencing decisions, in all provinces, will encourage the development of sentencing principles that are empirically grounded (that is, judges actually using such factors) and are normatively sound." This criticism may have some validity, but it is important to recognize that the Commission's proposals do include a major role for the provincial courts of appeal. Furthermore, it might be contended that a national sentencing commission is particularly necessary in a large country such as Canada in which one *Criminal Code* is applicable from west to east and north to south.

Palys (Palys and Divorski, 1986:360) suggests that guidelines *will* be of some benefit to judges because they will point out the "going rates" for particular offences and, hence, reduce one potential source of sentencing disparity (namely, misperceptions as to what sentencing standards are). However, he questions the assumption, implicit in the guidelines' approach, that it is the *amount of discretion per se* that causes sentencing disparity. In fact, the Palys and Divorski study found that the amount of discretion that the judges had in relation to sentencing an offender for any particular offence had no effect on the degree of sentencing disparity that was evident in the various hypothetical cases that the researchers presented to their sample of judges. In fact, where there was the greatest amount of discretion, the judges showed the least disparity! In Palys's view, it would be preferable to legislate *sentencing objectives* rather than to establish sentencing guidelines because the judges' differential subscription to legal objectives accounts for a considerable proportion of sentencing disparity. In addition, Palys rightly points out that a reduction in disparity does not necessarily equate with justice in any given case. As noted above, if the factors applied in the making of sentencing decisions are, in some way, biased against a particular group in society, the consistent application of those criteria will result in injustice even if there is no disparity (Griswold, 1985). However, in defence of the Canadian Sentencing Commission's proposals, it should be noted that the Commission's proposed list of aggravating and mitigating factors (1987:320) is strikingly free from the socioeconomic variables that are likely to discriminate against those of lower socioeconomic status.

It is always possible that any major reform, based on the adoption of a system of sentencing guidelines, could be frustrated by the exercise of discretion elsewhere in the criminal justice system (Griswold, 1989; MacMillan, 1984; Rothman, 1983). The possibility of the parole system defeating the purpose of the guidelines would be avoided if the parole were abolished, as recommended by the Commission. However, it is now clear that the federal government is not prepared to endorse the abolition of parole, and there is, therefore, the very real possibility that the clarity and equity sought in the guidelines would be counteracted by the inherent uncertainty generated by parole decisions that, unlike the original sentencing decisions, place considerably less emphasis upon the seriousness of the offence committed.

The reduction of the degree of discretion exercised by judges could well increase the power of other actors in the system such as the police or Crown counsel (Rothman, 1983). The major threat to any system of sentencing guidelines is that plea bargaining may defeat the underlying intent to bring about greater equity in the sentencing process (Verdun-Jones and Hatch, 1985). By controlling the charge that may be laid, the prosecutor, to some extent at least, controls the ultimate sentence that may be imposed. Furthermore, plea bargaining can possibly result in the case facts presented to the court being highly selective, thus defeating the purpose of the guidelines, which depend on the availability of full case facts in order to establish the appropriate sentence. The Canadian Sentencing Commission (1987:401ff.) clearly recognized this danger and recommended that there should be much greater regulation of the processes of plea bargaining in Canada. For example, it recommended (1987:428) that the relevant federal and provincial authorities should formulate and attempt to enforce ethical guidelines in relation to plea bargaining and that they should establish guidelines restricting the power of the Crown to reduce charges in those cases where it has the means to prove a more serious charge. In addition, it recommended that a prosecutor should be required to justify a plea bargain agreement in open court (or in chambers if the public interest so requires). The Commission's recommendations as to the control of plea bargaining are vital to the ultimate success of the sentencing guidelines; if these recommendations are not implemented, then the goals of the sentencing guidelines are highly likely to be frustrated or thwarted.

The Canadian Sentencing Commission's recommendations represented one of the most comprehensive attempts to overhaul the sentencing process in the history of Canada. The Commission's report has clearly had a significant impact on the evolution of sentencing policy by the federal government in recent years. More particularly, it has exercised a major influence on both the Daubney Report (1988) and a federal government white paper (Canada, 1990a; 1990b) that articulates many proposed reforms in the nature and structure of the sentencing process in Canada. The Daubney Report and the federal government's proposed package of reforms are discussed below.

The Daubney Report (1988)

One year after the Canadian Sentencing Commission released its report, the influential House of Commons Standing Committee on Justice and Solicitor General produced a report of its own following a thorough review of "Sentencing, Conditional Release and Related Aspects of Corrections." This report is generally known as the Daubney Report after its chair, David Daubney, M.P. The report emphasized the need for greater community involvement and understanding in relation to the sentencing process. In the Committee's view (1988:5), the sentencing courts should be held accountable to the community for "addressing the relevant needs and interests of victims, offenders and the community." In addition, the report suggested that reparation (redress of the victim's loss) and reconciliation with the community should be an important component of sentencing. Offenders should be required to "accept and demonstrate responsibility for their criminal behaviour and its consequences" (1988:6). Victims should be given an opportunity to participate more meaningfully in the sentencing process by being granted access to information about all stages of the criminal justice process insofar as it affects them and by being accorded the opportunity to provide input to sentence decision making (see Waller, 1990:465-466).

The Committee noted (1988:21) that the amendment of the *Criminal Code* by Bill C-89 in 1988 had met some of their concerns in relation to victims by introducing the concept of the victim impact statement to the sentencing process in Canada and by improving the provisions relating to restitution. However, it (1988:25) emphasized the ongoing need to provide more detailed and specific information to victims and their families about both the sentencing process and the correctional process.

The Daubney Committee followed the lead of the Canadian Sentencing Commission in calling for some structuring of sentencing discretion to prevent unwarranted disparity and in urging that imprisonment should be used with restraint; in its view, there should be a greater degree of reliance on community alternatives, where violence and or recidivism are not involved (1988:6). It stressed the need for public education in relation to all phases of the criminal justice system.

The Committee also agreed (1988:45) with the Canadian Sentencing Commission that the purposes and principles of sentencing should be enshrined in the *Criminal Code*. However, unlike the Commission, it felt that public protection should be considered the fundamental purpose of sentencing (1988:45).

With regard to imprisonment, the Committee (1988:49) noted that there will always be a need to incapacitate violent offenders where they continue to represent a risk to the safety of the community. However, it limited imprisonment to three situations: (1) where it is necessary to protect the public from violent crimes; (2) where there is no alternative sanction that will adequately express the condemnation of the community; or (3) where there is no other mechanism available for ensuring that the offender comply with the terms of any non-custodial sentence that has been imposed (1988:56).

On the other hand, "expensive prison resources should be reserved for the most serious cases" (1988:50). Like the Canadian Sentencing

Commission, the Daubney Committee felt that, wherever possible, sentencing courts should exhaust all possible alternatives before resorting to imprisonment. In making use of alternatives to imprisonment, the courts should concentrate on alternatives that require offenders to accept responsibility for their misdeeds and to make genuine efforts to restore their victims to the position they were in prior to their victimization and/or to provide victims with a "meaningful apology" (1988:50).

Rehabilitation should still be a goal of sentencing, where appropriate; the Committee rejected the belief that "nothing works." In the Committee's view, the sentencing process should — where necessary — continue to "provide offenders with opportunities which are likely to facilitate their habilitation or rehabilitation as productive and law-abiding members of society" (1988:52).

The Daubney Report also set out a number of principles to guide the exercise of sentencing discretion. Many of these principles were very similar to those previously articulated by the Sentencing Commission (1987:154-155). For example, the Report stated that the sentence imposed should be "proportionate to the gravity of the offence and the degree of responsibility of the offender" and should be "consistent with the sentences imposed on other offenders for similar offences committed in similar circumstances" (1988:55). However, unlike the Commission, it did not recommend introducing guidelines at the present time:

> The Committee has been persuaded of the value of offenders acknowledging responsibility for their criminal conduct and coming to terms with what has happened through positive steps designed to make reparations to the victim and/or community and to habilitate themselves. This strategy requires a more individualized approach to sentencing than that offered by sentencing guidelines, which are likely to be a more useful tool where the underlying goals are retributive and punitive, or perhaps where denunciation needs to be the primary consideration.

The Committee (1988:65) nevertheless recommended that *advisory guidelines* should be developed since the information they would generate would be of great use to the judiciary whether or not they are ever implemented. The Committee disagreed with the Canadian Sentencing Commission's recommendation that parole be abolished and contended that the sentencing guidelines can sit comfortably alongside a "well-structured conditional release system." The Committee (1988:65-66), like the Canadian Sentencing Commission, recommended that a permanent sentencing commission should be established to develop the guidelines as well as a list of aggravating and mitigating circumstances that might justify a departure from the guidelines.

The Committee contended (1988:62) that Canadian appellate courts have the power to review sentences and, thereby, to reduce the degree of unwarranted sentencing disparity. It was noted that, since March 1988, courts in the province of British Columbia have been able to access a "computerized information-storage system" developed by Professor John Hogarth that provides detailed information about sentencing principles applied by the B.C. Court of Appeal, as well as information about sentencing practices at both the trial and appellate levels. Such systems should be made available to other jurisdictions in Canada as a means of enabling appellate courts to minimize unwarranted sentencing disparity.

The major focus of the Daubney Report was on the need to place more reliance on sentencing alternatives and intermediate sanctions. In the Committee's view, sentencing alternatives include diversion, fines, discharges, probation, community service orders, fine option programs, restitution, and victim-offender reconciliation programs (1988:76). The Committee noted (1988:76) that the use of restitution and community service orders for non-violent offenders had met with considerable public approval. Intermediate sanctions are designed for those offenders who might otherwise be incarcerated. In terms of their impact on the offender, they fall somewhere between imprisonment and simple probation. They include intensive probation supervision, home confinement, and alternative sentence planning. Intensive probation supervision may involve one-to-one supervision combined with the provision of addiction counselling, treatment programs for assaultive spouses, etc., compulsory attendance at attendance centres, and supervised accommodation at hostels or halfway houses. Home confinement may be enforced with or without electronic monitoring. Alternative sentence planning involves the development of alternative sanctions that focus on making the offender acknowledge responsibility for his or her actions and provide restitution either to the specific victim(s) or to the community in general. Intensive supervision may be provided by community agencies, which may include offender-victim reconciliation. The Committee recommended that the federal government, in cooperation with the provincial/territorial governments, should provide more funding for the development of alternative sentences and intermediate sanctions (1988:252-253).

The Response of the Federal Government to the Reports of the Canadian Sentencing Commission and the Daubney Committee

In July, 1990, the federal government released a "consultation package" that drew extensively on the work of both the Canadian Sentencing Commission and the Daubney Committee. The package was called *Directions for Reform: Sentencing, Corrections and Conditional Releases* (see Canada, 1990a; 1990b).

In accordance with the recommendations of both the Canadian Sentencing Commission and the Daubney Committee, the federal government proposed the addition of a clear statement of the purpose and principles of sentencing in the *Criminal Code*. By clarifying the objectives of sentencing and providing guidance to judges on the principles they should take into account in determining the most appropriate sentence, the federal government hoped to eliminate confusion and reduce unwarranted disparity.

This statement was subsequently included in Bill C-90, which was introduced to Parliament in June 1992. The Bill proposes to amend the *Criminal Code* by adding the following articulation of the "purpose and principles of sentencing." The Bill states that:

> The fundamental purpose of sentencing is to contribute to the maintenance of a just, peaceful and safe society by imposing just sanctions that have one or more of the following objectives:
>
> (a) to denounce unlawful conduct;
> (b) to deter the offender and other persons committing offences;
> (c) to separate offenders from society;
> (d) to provide reparations for harm done to victims or to the community;
> (e) to promote a sense of responsibility in offenders, and acknowledgment of harm done to victims and to the community; and
> (f) to assist in rehabilitating offenders.[11]

As can readily be seen, the objectives stated in the Bill include reference to the goals of deterrence, incapacitation, rehabilitation, restitution, and denunciation. However, this statement of sentencing objectives must be read in light of the following "fundamental principle":

A sentence must be proportionate to the gravity of the offence and the degree of responsibility of the offender.[12]

This statement clearly reflects the influence of the "just deserts" principle discussed earlier in this chapter.

Bill C-90 also articulates a number of "other sentencing principles":

(a) a sentence may be increased or reduced to account for any relevant aggravating or mitigating circumstances relating to the offence or the offender;

(b) a sentence should be similar to sentences imposed on similar offenders for similar offences committed in similar circumstances;

(c) where consecutive sentences are imposed, the combined sentence should not be unduly long or harsh;

(d) an offender should not be deprived of liberty, if less restrictive alternatives may be appropriate in the circumstances; and

(e) all available alternatives to imprisonment that are reasonable in the circumstances should be considered, particularly in relation to aboriginal offenders.[13]

If this statement of the purpose and principles of sentencing is ultimately enacted, it will be interesting to see whether it will have the effect of reducing the degree of unwarranted sentencing disparity by clarifying the objectives of sentencing and providing guidance to judges as to how these objectives relate to the overall purpose of maintaining a "just, peaceful and safe society."

The federal government accepted the views of both the Sentencing Commission and the Daubney Committee that a permanent Sentencing Commission should be established to develop sentencing guidelines. However, the government sided with the Daubney Committee in rejecting the Sentencing Commission's call for the abolition of parole. Indeed, the government indicated the new commission would cover both sentencing and parole and would be responsible for harmonizing the sentencing and parole functions in the criminal justice system. The new commission would develop both sentencing and parole guidelines (Campbell, 1990:390-391).

The federal government asserted that the "Sentencing and Parole Commission will provide the mechanism by which both sentencing and parole can be considered within a consistent policy framework" (1990a:10). It will set guidelines for sentencing and give advice on parole decision-making policy. Apparently, the government has sided with the Canadian Sentencing Commission by laying the basis for the development of mandatory (rather than advisory) sentencing guidelines. The proposed sentencing and parole commission will also be charged with the task of examining the interaction between the proposed sentencing guidelines and other components of the justice system with a view to ensuring that structuring sentencing discretion does not have an adverse impact on other decision-making points in the criminal justice system. For example, the government white paper (1990b:19) states that "care must be taken not simply to shift discretion inadvertently from judges to the prosecution through enhanced plea bargaining conditions."

The federal government (Canada, 1990a) indicated agreement with the recommendations of the Canadian Sentencing Commission and the Daubney Committee that there should be less reliance on incarceration as a sentencing option. The government's statement of policy (Canada, 1990a:10) quotes the Nielsen Task Force Report on Government Programs (Canada, 1985:323) to the effect that "over-reliance on incarceration is a luxury which is quickly becoming difficult to afford." It notes that reliance on imprisonment is costly in both human and financial terms. While some 20% of all criminal justice expenditures (including those on the police and the courts) are currently directed toward prisons, less than 1% are directed toward community-based sentencing options. In order to reduce the dependency of the criminal justice system on prisons, the government recommends greater emphasis be placed on alternative sanctions (Canada, 1990a:10).

The federal government indicated that it was seeking to launch a program of consultation with the provinces with a view to increasing the use of intermediate sanctions (Canada, 1990b: 16-20; see also Campbell, 1990:392-394). In its consultation package, the government uses a much broader definition of intermediate sanctions than that used by the Daubney Committee. The government (Canada, 1990b:16-17) states that:

> We have chosen the term "intermediate sanctions" to reflect dispositions that involve both community programs and resources. Thus, the payment of a fine to the state, the return of goods through restitution, the financial payment to the victim for loss or damage, the performance of work for the community through either a fine option program or a community service order, are all examples of "intermediate sanctions." Other examples include compensation orders, and the following

group of sanctions in which an order of restitution or community service may or may not form part of the probation order: conditional discharge, suspended sentence and probation order. While fine option programs are not sentences *per se,* they nevertheless aim to restore community relationships disrupted by the commission of an offence; thus, they are considered here as intermediate sanctions.

One of the more important aspects of the federal government's approach is to attempt to improve the availability of intermediate sanctions programs in remote and northern communities, particularly Aboriginal communities (Canada, 1990b:18-19). The lack of sentencing alternatives in such communities may well result in the greater use of imprisonment for offenders at the present time.

The increasing reliance on intermediate sanctions as an alternative to incarceration will indubitably change the face of Canadian sentencing in a most significant manner. Hopefully, the federal, provincial, and territorial governments will have the collective political will to provide the funding necessary for the courts to take full advantage of these sentencing alternatives. In theory, it should be possible to re-direct funds saved from "down-sizing" the prisons to community-based sentencing alternatives. Whether this will actually occur remains to be seen.

The federal government also proposed the establishment of a new process for the imposition and collection of fines. In its package (Canada, 1990b:13-14), the federal government notes that there are two major problems with the current situation. First, many fines are never collected, resulting in a loss of respect for the criminal justice system as well as a loss of valuable revenue. Second, when an offender fails to pay his or her fine, the usual consequence is that he or she is automatically committed to prison. Under the proposed new procedures, there would be an inquiry into the ability of the offender to pay a fine before such a disposition is ordered. In addition, instead of resorting to imprisonment when offenders default on their fines, the courts will be given the power to use civil processes such as the seizure of assets and the garnishment of wages and salaries. Furthermore, when a court is contemplating imprisonment for non-payment of a fine, a further inquiry must first be made to ascertain the precise circumstances surrounding the default. Only where the offender fails to advance a reasonable excuse or wilfully refuses to pay will the court be permitted to resort to imprisonment. In the words of the federal government:

These measures will remove a socio-economic bias from the system of penalties and will assist the economically disadvantaged in society, including aboriginal people and women. The process should better ensure that the non-incarcerative intent of the judge in imposing a fine is, in fact, the sanction that the offender receives, rather than the much debilitating sanction of imprisonment (1990b:14).

These proposals were not included in Bill C-90, so it remains to be seen whether they will be included in future amendments to the *Code*.

The federal government's package also includes a proposal to include a code of sentencing procedure and evidence in the *Criminal Code* (Canada, 1990b:12-13). The new procedures would ensure that the offender has the right to speak prior to any sentence being imposed as well as require the judge to give explicit reasons justifying the sentence ultimately imposed:

By specifying the process by which evidence respecting sentencing is considered, by providing a specific right to the offender to speak to sentence, and by requiring the reasons for judgement to be set out, the proposed code should encourage greater sensitivity to the particular circumstances of different types of offenders.

Bill C-90 contains a number of provisions that will amend the *Criminal Code* with a view to enacting the government's proposals concerning a code of sentencing procedure and evidence.[14]

Finally, it may be noted that Parliament has already dealt with one concern expressed by the Canadian Sentencing Commission — namely, the disparity between the length of a prison term imposed by the sentencing court and the actual time served by the offender. In 1992, the *Criminal Code*[15] was amended so as to enable the judge to specify that the offender must serve at least half of his or her sentence (or 10 years, whichever is less) before being released on parole. This provision applies to prison sentences of two years or more and the court may take this step if it is "satisfied, having regard to the commission of the offences and the character and circumstances of the offender, that the expression of society's denunciation of the offences of the objective of specific or general deterrence so requires."

Clearly, the sentencing process in Canada is currently passing through an era of fundamental change. Some reforms have already been enacted, while numerous others have been included in Bill C-90, which is still being considered by Parliament. Other major reforms have been proposed, but the necessary legislation to implement them has not yet been prepared by the federal government. All of this reform activity has created a considerable degree of uncertainty as to exactly how the sentencing process in Canada will evolve during the 1990s. However, of one thing we can be reasonably certain: sentencing in the 1990s will be significantly different from sentencing as we have known it in the past.

NOTES

[1]Bill C-90, *An Act to Amend the Criminal Code (Sentencing) and other Acts in consequence thereof.* First reading, June 23, 1992.

[2]*Regina v. Clayton* (1983), 69 C.C.C. (2nd) 81, at 83, cited in Ruby, 1987:14.

[3]Another explanation for the discrepancy may be that the public and the judiciary have different sentencing goals. Roberts and Gebotys (1989) suggest that the Canadian public may place greater emphasis on the principle of just deserts than do the courts (which are also concerned with such goals as deterrence, incapacitation, and rehabilitation). In this sense, the public may attach much greater weight to the seriousness of the offence than to information about the specific offender.

[4]Ouimet and Coyle (1991) found that, based on a study of public attitudes in Montreal, citizens' fear of crime had no impact on the degree of punitiveness expressed in their attitudes, although court practitioners (judges, prosecutors, defence counsel, and probation officers) did seem to be affected by their perception of the level of public fear of crime in proposing sentences for less serious offences.

[5]*Per* Reid, P.C.J. in *Regina v. McLean et al.* (1980), 26 Nfld. P.E.I.R. 158 at 168, cited in Nadin-Davis (1982:8).

[6]Section 306 (1)(d).

[7]The sample of cases was limited to those in which legal aid had been granted to the defendant.

[8]U.S. research suggests that this process may well explain the high rate of imprisonment of black offenders south of the border (Chiricos and Bales, 1991). Myers (1987) suggests that socioeconomic bias in sentencing practices is a complicated phenomenon and that its precise nature may well vary according to the nature of different communities, particularly

the degree of economic inequality that may exist in any particular community.

[9]In one study, for example, Zatz (1984) found that the offender's prior record, which many criminal justice commentators would consider to be a legitimate factor to take into account in the sentencing process, was, in fact, relied upon *differentially*, depending on whether or not the defendant was white, black, or Chicano. This is a clear illustration of the subtle discrimination to which Zatz has referred. It has also been pointed out that, until very recently, most research had ignored the effect of the *race of the victim* on sentencing practices; in this respect, it has been suggested that, in the United States, harsher punishment appears to be imposed when the victim is white than is the case where the victim is black (Hawkins, 1987; Farrell and Swigert, 1986). This represents another example of "masked" discrimination in the sentencing process.

[10]However, it has been argued that, if the chivalry model does influence the sentencing of women, it is a twentieth-century phenomenon. Indeed, Boritch (1992) examined sentencing data in an Ontario jurisdiction in the period 1871-1920 and concluded that, in the late nineteenth century, women received *more severe* sentences than men, taking into account such variables as offence seriousness and prior record.

[11]Section 718

[12]Section 718.1.

[13]Section 718.2.

[14]Sections 720, 721, 722, 722.1, 723, 724, 725, 726, 726.1, and 726.2.

[15]Section 741.2.

REFERENCES

Akers, R.L. 1990. "Rational Choice, Deterrence, and Social Learning Theory: The Path not Taken." 81 *Journal of Criminal Law and Criminology*. 653-676.

American Friends Service Committee. 1971. *Struggle for Justice*. New York: Hill and Wang.

Andrews, D.A. 1990. "Some Criminological Sources of Anti-Rehabilitation Bias in the Report of the Canadian Sentencing Commission." 32 *Canadian Journal of Criminology*. 511-524.

Archibald, B.P. 1989. "Sentencing and Visible Minorities: Equality and Affirmative Action in the Criminal Justice System." 12 *Dalhousie Law Review*.

377-411.

Benzvy-Miller, S., and D.P. Cole. 1990. "Integrating sentencing and Parole." 32 *Canadian Journal of Criminology*. 493-502.

Blumstein, A. 1982. "Research on Sentencing." 7 *Justice System Journal*. 307-330.

Blumstein, A. 1983. "Selective Incapacitation as a Means of Crime Control." 27 *American Behavioral Scientist*. 87-108.

Blumstein, A. 1984. "Sentencing Reforms: Impacts and Implications." 68 *Judicature*. 129-139.

Boritch, H. 1992. "Gender and Criminal Court Outcomes: An Historical Analysis." 30 *Criminology*. 293-325.

Boyle, C. *et al.* 1985. *A Feminist Review of Criminal Law*. Ottawa: Minister of Supply & Services Canada.

Braithwaite, J. 1989. *Crime, Shame and Reintegration*. New York: Cambridge University Press.

Brantingham, P.L. 1985. "Sentencing Disparity: An Analysis of Judicial Consistency." 3 *Journal of Quantitative Criminology*. 281-305.

Bridges, G.S., and J.A. Stone. 1986. "Effects of Criminal Punishment on Perceived Threat of Punishment: Toward an Understanding of Specific Deterrence." 23 *Journal of Research in Crime and Delinquency*. 207-239.

Brodeur, J.-P. 1990. "The Attrition of Parole." 32 *Canadian Journal of Criminology*. 503-510.

Campbell, A.K. 1990. "Sentencing Reform in Canada." 32 *Canadian Journal of Criminology*. 387-395.

Canada. 1985. *The Nielsen Task Force Report on Government Programs*. Ottawa: Ministry of Supply and Services Canada.

_____. 1990a. *A Framework for Reform of Sentencing, Corrections and Conditional Release*. Ottawa: Minister of Supply and Services Canada.

_____. 1990b. *Directions for Reform in Sentencing*. Ottawa: Minister of Supply and Services Canada.

Canadian Sentencing Commission, Department of Justice. 1987. *Sentencing Reform: A Canadian Approach*. (Catalogue No. J2-67/1986E.) Ottawa: Minister of Supply and Services Canada.

Chambliss, W.J. 1967. "Types of Deviance and the Effectiveness of Legal Sanctions." 67 *Wisconsin Law Review*. 703-719.

Chiricos, T.G., and W.D. Bales. 1991. "Unemployment and Punishment: An Empirical Assessment." 29 *Criminology*. 701-724.

Chunn, D.E., and S.A.M. Gavigan. 1991. "Women and Crime in Canada." In M.A. Jackson, and C.T. Griffiths, eds. *Canadian Criminology: Perspectives on Crime and Criminality*. Toronto: Harcourt Brace Jovanovich Canada. 275-314.

Clark, S. 1989. *Sentencing Patterns and Sentencing Options Relating to*

Aboriginal Offenders. Ottawa: Department of Justice, Canada.

Cohen, J. 1983a. *Incapacitating Criminals: Recent Research Findings*. Washington, D.C.: National Institute of Justice.

Cohen, J. 1983b. "Incapacitation as a Strategy for Crime Control: Possibilities and Pitfalls." In M. Tonry and N. Morris, eds. *Crime and Justice: An Annual Review of Research*, vol. 5. Chicago: University of Chicago Press.

Cohen, J., and M.H. Tonry. 1983. "Sentencing Reforms and Their Impacts." In A. Blumstein *et al.,* eds. *Research on Sentencing: The Search for Reform*, vol. 1. Washington, D.C.: National Academy Press. 305-459.

Conklin, J.E. 1992. *Criminology*, 4th Ed. New York: Macmillan.

Daubney, D. (Chair). 1988. *Taking Responsibility: Report of the Standing Committee on Justice and Solicitor General on its Review of Sentencing, Conditional Release and Related Aspects of Corrections*. Ottawa: Queen's Printer.

Debicki, M. 1985. "Sentencing and Socio-Economic Status." In D. Gibson and J.K. Baldwin, eds. *Law in A Cynical Society: Opinion and Law in the 1980's*. Calgary: Carswell Legal Publications (Western Division).

Decker, S., Wright, R., and R. Logie. 1993. "Perceptual Deterrence Among Active Residential Burglars: A Research Note." 31 *Criminology*. 135-147.

Doob, A.N. 1990. "Community Sanctions and Imprisonment: Hoping for a Miracle but not Bothering even to Pray for it." 32 *Canadian Journal of Criminology*. 415-428.

Doob, A.N., and J.-P. Brodeur. 1989. "Rehabilitating the Debate on Rehabilitation." 31 *Canadian Journal of Criminology*. 179-192.

Doob, A.N., and J.V. Roberts. 1983. *Sentencing: an Analysis of the Public's View of Sentencing*. Ottawa: Department of Justice, Canada.

_____. 1984. "Social Psychology, Social Attitudes, and Attitudes toward Sentencing." 16 *Canadian Journal of Behavioural Science*. 269-280.

Durham, A.M. III. 1988. "Crime Seriousness and Punitive Severity: An Assessment of Social Attitudes." 5 *Justice Quarterly*, 131-153.

Edwards, A. 1989. "Sex/Gender, Sexism and Criminal Justice: Some Theoretical Considerations." 17 *International Journal of the Sociology of Law*. 165-184.

Farrell, R.A., and V.L. Swigert. 1986. "Adjudication in Homicide: An Interpretative Analysis of The Effects of Defendant and Victim Social Characteristics." 23 *Journal of Research in Crime and Delinquency*. 349-369.

Forst, M.L. 1982. "Sentencing Disparity: An Overview of Research and Issues." In M.L. Forst, ed. *Sentencing Reform: Experiments in Reducing Disparity*. Beverly Hills, California: Sage Publications. 9-34.

Friedland, N. 1990. "The Combined Effect of the Severity and the Certainty of Threatened Penalties." 20 *Journal of Applied Social Psychology*. 1358-1368.

Gabor, T. 1990. "Looking Back or Moving Forward: Retributivism and the Canadian sentencing Commission's Proposals." 32 *Canadian Journal of*

Criminology. 537-546.

Gendreau, P., and D.A. Andrews. 1990. "Tertiary Prevention: What the Meta-analyses of the Offender Treatment Literature Tell Us about 'What Works'." 32 *Canadian Journal of Criminology*. 173-184.

Gendreau, P., and R.R. Ross. 1979. "Effective Correctional Treatment: Bibliotherapy for Cynics." 25 *Crime and Delinquency*. 463-489.

Gendreau, P., and R.R. Ross. 1987. "Revivification of Rehabilitation: Evidence from the 1980's." 4 *Justice Quarterly*. 349-408.

Gibbons, D.C. 1992. *Society, Crime, and Criminal Behavior*, 6th ed. Englewood Cliffs, N.J.: Prentice-Hall, Inc.

Grasmick, H.G., and R.J. Bursik, Jr. 1990. "Conscience, Significant Others, and Rational Choice: Extending the Deterrence Model." 24 *Law & Society Review*. 837-861.

Grasmick, H.G., Bursik, R.J. Jr., and B.J. Arneklev. 1993. "Reduction in Drunk Driving as a Response to Increased Threats of Shame, Embarrassment, and Legal Sanctions." 31 *Criminology*. 41-68.

Graydon, C.F. 1992. "Habilitation: Sentencing of Female Offenders." 5 *Canadian Journal of Law and Jurisprudence*. 121-141.

Griswold, D.B. 1985. "Florida's Sentencing Guidelines: Progression or Regression?" 49 *Federal Probation*. 25-32.

Griswold, D.B. 1989. "Florida's Sentencing Guidelines: Six Years Later." 53 *Federal Probation*. 46-50.

Hagan, J., ed. 1982. *Deterrence Reconsidered: Methodological Innovations*. Beverly Hills, California: Sage Publications.

Hann, R.G. *et al.* 1983. *Sentencing Practices and Trends in Canada: A Summary of Statistical Information*. Ottawa: Department of Justice, Canada.

Hann, R.G., and F. Kopelman. 1986. *Custodial and Probation Sentences Project: Overview Report and Individual Offence Reports*. Ottawa: Department of Justice.

Hart, H.L.A. 1968. *Punishment and Responsibility*. Oxford: Oxford University Press.

Hawkins, D.F. 1987. "Beyond Anomalies: Rethinking the Conflict Perspective on Race and Criminal Punishment." 65 *Social Forces*. 719-745.

Heaney, G.W. 1991. "The Reality of Guidelines Sentencing: No End to Disparity." 28 *American Criminal Law Review*. 161-232.

Hogarth, J. 1971. *Sentencing as a Human Process*. Toronto: University of Toronto Press.

Horney, J., and I. Marshall. 1992. "Risk Perceptions Among Serious Offenders: The Role of Crime and Punishment." 30 *Criminology*. 575-594.

Howe, E.S., and Brandau, C.J. 1988. "Additive Effects of Certainty, Severity, and Celerity of Punishment on Judgments of Crime Deterrence Scale Value." 18 *Journal of Applied Social Psychology*. 796-812.

Jackson, M. 1988. *Locking Up Natives in Canada: A Report of the Special Committee of the Canadian Bar Association on Imprisonment*. Ottawa: Canadian Bar Association.

Jobson, K., and G. Ferguson. 1987. "Toward a Revised Sentencing Structure for Canada." 66 *Canadian Bar Review*. 1-48.

Johnson, D., and L.K. Scheuble. 1991. "Gender Bias in the Disposition of Juvenile Court Referrals: The Effects of Time and Location." 29 *Criminology*. 677-700.

Karle, T.E. *et al.* 1991. "Are the Federal Sentencing Guidelines Meeting Congressional Goals?" 40 *Emory Law Journal*. 393-444.

Kittrie, N.N. 1980. "The Dangers of the New Directions in American Sentencing." In B.A. Grosman ed. *New Directions in Sentencing*. Toronto: Butterworths. 32-50.

Kramer, J.H., and R.L. Lubitz. 1985. "Pennsylvania's Sentencing Reform: The Impact of Commission-Established Guidelines." 31 *Crime & Delinquency*. 481-500.

Lab, S.P., and J.T. Whitehead. 1988. "An Analysis of Juvenile Correctional Treatment." 34 *Crime & Delinquency*. 60-83.

LaPrairie, C. 1992. "The Role of Sentencing in the Over-representation of Aboriginal People in Correctional Institutions." In R.A. Silverman and M.O. Nielsen, eds. *Aboriginal Peoples and Canadian Criminal Justice*. Toronto: Butterworths. 133-144.

Law Reform Commission of Canada. 1974. *The Principles of Sentencing and Dispositions* (Working Paper 3). Ottawa: Information Canada.

_____. 1976. *A Report on Dispositions and Sentences in the Criminal Process: Guidelines*. Ottawa: Information Canada.

Linden, A.M. 1986. "A Fresh Approach to Sentencing in Canada." 48 *RCMP Gazette*. 1-7.

Lipton, D., R. Martinson, and J. Wilks. 1975. *The Effectiveness of Correctional Treatment: A Survey of Treatment Evaluation Studies*. New York: Praeger Publishers.

MacMillan, A.I. 1984. "Equitable Sentencing: Alternatives in Reducing Disparity." 42 *University of Toronto Faculty Law Review*. 184-193.

Mandel, M. 1984. "Democracy, Class and Canadian Sentencing Law." 21-22 *Crime and Social Justice*. 163-181.

Martinson, R. 1974. "What Works?: Questions and Answers about Prison Reform." 35 *Public Interest*. 22-54.

McIntyre, B.E. 1985. "Sentencing: The Need for Clear Standards." 27 *Criminal Law Quarterly*. 212-25.

Miller, J.L., and A.B. Anderson. 1986. "Updating the Deterrence Doctrine." 77 *Journal of Criminal Law & Criminology*. 418-438.

Minnesota Sentencing Guidelines Commission. 1981. *Minnesota Sentencing*

Guidelines and Commentary, rev. ed. St Paul, Minnesota: Minnesota Sentencing Guidelines Commission.

Mohr, R.M. 1990. "Sentencing as a Gendered Process: Results of a Consultation." 32 *Canadian Journal of Criminology*. 479-485.

Morris, N. 1974. *The Future of Imprisonment*. Chicago: University of Chicago Press.

Morse, B., and L. Lock. 1988. *Native Offenders' Perceptions of the Criminal Justice System*. Research Reports of the Canadian Sentencing Commission. Ottawa: Department of Justice Canada.

Murray, G.F., and P.G. Erickson. 1983. "Regional Variation in Criminal Justice System Practices: Cannabis Possession in Ontario." 26 *Criminal Law Quarterly*. 74-96.

Myers, M.A. 1987. "Economic Inequality and Discrimination in Sentencing." 65 *Social Forces*. 746-766.

Nadin-Davis, R.P. 1982. *Sentencing in Canada*. Toronto: Carswell.

Nagel, I.H. 1990. "Structuring Sentencing Discretion: The New Federal Sentencing Guidelines." 80 *Journal of Criminal Law & Criminology*. 883-943.

Nagin, D., and R. Paternoster. 1991. "The Preventive Effects of the Perceived Risk of Arrest: Testing an Expanded Conception of Deterrence." 29 *Criminology*. 561-587.

Ouimet, M., and E.J. Coyle. 1991. "Fear of Crime and Sentencing Punitiveness: Comparing the General Public and Court Practitioners." 33 *Canadian Journal of Criminology*. 149-162.

Palys, T.S., and S. Divorski. 1984. "Judicial Decision-Making: An Examination of Sentencing Disparity Among Canadian Provincial Court Judges." In D.J. Muller, D.E. Blackman, and A.J. Chapman, eds. *Psychology and Law*. New York: Wiley. 333-44.

Palys, T.S., and Divorski, S. 1986. "Explaining Sentence Disparity." 28 *Criminology*. 347-362.

Reid, S.T. 1991. *Crime and Criminology* (6th ed.). Fort Worth, Texas: Holt, Rinehart and Winston, Inc.

Renner, K.E., and A.H. Warner. 1981. "The Standard of Social Justice Applied to An Evaluation of Criminal Cases Appearing Before the Halifax Courts." 1 *Windsor Yearbook of Access to Justice*. 62-80.

Rich, W.D. *et al.* 1982. *Sentencing by Mathematics: An Evaluation of the Early Attempts to Develop and Implement Sentencing Guidelines*. Williamsburg: National Center for State Courts.

Roberts, J. 1988. *Sentencing in the Media: A Content Analysis of English-Language Newspapers in Canada*. Ottawa: Canadian Sentencing Commission.

Roberts, J.V. 1990a. "Sentencing in Canada: The Context for Reform." 32 *Canadian Journal of Criminology*. 381-386.

Roberts, J.V. 1990b. "Sentencing Reform: Last Words." 32 *Canadian Journal of Criminology*. 551-552.

Roberts, J.V., and A.N. Doob. 1989. "Sentencing and Public Opinion." 27 *Osgoode Hall Law Journal*. 491-515.

Roberts, J.V., and A.N. Doob. 1990. "News Media Influences on Public Views of Sentencing." 14 *Law and Human Behavior*. 451-468.

Roberts, J.V., and D. Edwards. 1989. "Contextual Effects in Judgments of Crimes, Criminals, and the Purposes of Sentencing." 19 *Journal of Applied Social Psychology*. 902-917.

Roberts, J.V., and R.J. Gebotys. 1989. "The Purposes of Sentencing: Public Support for Competing Aims." 7 *Behavioral Sciences & The Law*. 387-402.

Rothman, D.J. 1983. "Sentencing Reforms in Historical Perspective." 29 *Crime & Delinquency*. 631-647.

Ruby, C.C. 1987. *Sentencing* (3rd ed.). Toronto: Butterworths.

Siegel, L.J. 1983. *Criminology*. St. Paul, Minnesota: West Publishing Company.

Sweeney, L., and H. Craig. 1992. "The Influence of Race on Sentencing: A Meta-Analytic Review of Experimental Studies." 10 *Behavioral Sciences and the Law*. 179-195.

Tjaden, P., and C. Tjaden. 1981. "Differential Treatment of the Female Felon: Myth or Reality?" In M. Warren, ed. *Comparing Female and Male Offenders*. Beverly Hills, California: Sage.

Verdun-Jones, S.N., and A.J. Hatch. 1985. *Plea Bargaining and Sentencing Guidelines*. Ottawa: Canadian Sentencing Commission.

Vingilis, E. *et al.* 1988. "An Evaluation of the Deterrent Impact of Ontario's 12-Hour Licence Suspension Law." 20 *Accident Analysis and Prevention*. 9-17.

Vining, A.R., and Dean, C. 1980. "Towards Sentencing Uniformity: Integrating the Normative and the Empirical Orientation." In B.A. Grosman, ed. *New Directions in Sentencing*. Toronto: Butterworths. 117-154.

Von Hirsch, A. 1976. *Doing Justice: The Choice of Punishments*. New York: Hill and Wang.

Von Hirsch, A. 1984. "Selective Incapacitation: a Critique." 183 *NIJ Reports/SNI*. 5-8.

Von Hirsch, A. 1990. "The Politics of 'Just Deserts'." 32 *Canadian Journal of Criminology*. 397-413.

Waller, I. 1974. *Men Released from Prison*. Toronto: University of Toronto Press.

Waller, I. 1990. "Victims, Safer Communities and Sentencing." 32 *Canadian Journal of Criminology*. 461-469.

Watson, R.E.L. 1986. "Research Note: The Effectiveness of Increased Police Enforcement as a General Deterrent." 20 *Law & Society Review*. 293-299.

Webb, S.D. 1980. "Deterrence Theory: A Reconceptualization." 22 *Canadian Journal of Criminology*. 23-35.

Welch, S., J. Gruhl, and C. Spohn. 1984. "Sentencing: The Influence of Alternative Measures of Prior Record." 22 *Criminology*. 215-227.

Wikler, N.J. 1993. "Researching Gender Bias in the Courts: Problems and Prospects." In J. Brockman and D.E. Chunn, eds. *Investigating Gender Bias: Law, Courts and the Legal Profession*. Toronto: Thompson Educational Publishing, Inc. 46-61.

Wilkins, L.T. *et al*. 1978. *Sentencing Guidelines: Structuring Judicial Discretion — Report on the Feasibility Study*. Washington, D.C.: U.S. Department of Justice.

Williams, K.R., and R. Hawkins. 1986. "Perceptual Research on General Deterrence: A Critical Review." 20 *Law & Society Review*. 545-572.

Young, A. 1988. *The Role of an Appellate Court in Developing Sentencing Guidelines*. Ottawa: Department of Justice Canada.

Zatz, M.S. 1984. "Race, Ethnicity and Determinate Sentencing: A New Dimension to an Old Controversy." 22 *Criminology*. 147-171.

Zatz, M.S. 1987. "The Changing Forms of Racial/Ethnic Biases in Sentencing." 24 *Journal of Research in Crime and Delinquency*. 69-92.

10 THE STRUCTURE AND OPERATION OF CANADIAN CORRECTIONS

Any discussion of the structure and operation of corrections in Canada must consider the historical, social, and political context within which correctional systems developed. In the following discussion, we trace the historical response to crime and criminals in Canada and the emergence of the penitentiary as an instrument of punishment, control, and reform. We then examine the structure and operation of federal and provincial corrections today. Our discussion will reveal, among other things, that the use of prisons for punishment in Canada is a relatively recent development and that the term "corrections" is somewhat of a misnomer when applied to the ways in which Canadians have responded to criminal offenders throughout history and into contemporary times.[1]

CORRECTIONS IN EARLY CANADA

Historically, the response to criminal offenders in Canada from early times to the present has been influenced at various times by events in France, England, and the United States. However, Canada has its own unique correctional history, which has been affected by geography, the jurisdictional arrangements between the federal and provincial governments, as well as politics, economics, religion, and various philosophical movements. All of these influences are evident in the sanctions used to respond to offenders in early Canada and in the decision to construct the first penitentiary in 1835.

Punishment in Early Canada

The nature and severity of the response to criminal offenders in the seventeenth and early eighteenth centuries reflected the adoption of the English criminal law in English Canada and the influence of the French law in New France. The death penalty was inflicted on those offenders convicted of serious offences, while for less serious crimes, a wide variety of sanctions were used, including transportation, branding, fines, whipping, confiscation of property, and confinement in the stocks or pillory. In 1640, a 16-year-old girl convicted of theft became the first person to be put to death in Canada (Cooper, 1987).

Punishment was swift, severe, and progressive. There was little uniformity in sentencing practice: for a similar offence, one offender might be hanged, while the other would be given a sentence of servitude on a galley ship. Punishment was designed to shame and humiliate the offender, as well as to serve as a general deterrent for the community. The stocks and the pillory were particularly suited for these purposes:

> The pillory stood in the centre of every market place and the men who were brought to it for punishment had an ear clipped off and nailed to the pillory, in addition to being whipped publicly...When a prisoner was placed in the pillory, he faced the market where he was recipient of thrown eggs and rotten vegetables (Knafla and Chapman, 1983:258, 271).

Capital and corporal sanctions were often inflicted in public, and in many instances at the scene of the crime. The bodies of the hanged were often put on public display as a further deterrent to the citizenry. Bodies were then often donated to medical doctors for research purposes.

Early Canadians also used banishment and transportation to rid themselves of troublesome citizens. Banishment was first used in Upper Canada in 1802, a convicted offender being ordered to "depart the province at his or her own expense and peril" (Edmison, 1976:351). The use of transportation began in 1838, and until the practice was officially terminated in 1853, a large number of offenders were sent to England, Australia, and Bermuda.

The following historical accounts provide insights into punishment in early Canada.

- ▸ In Nova Scotia offenders convicted of theft were branded with the letter "T"; for a second offence, they were hanged (Coles, 1979).
- ▸ In St. John's, Newfoundland, one Patrick Knowlan was convicted of stealing a bedspread from a store. After receiving 20 lashes,...a halter was put around his neck and he was led to Mr. Prim's store where he received 20 lashes more on his bare back. Next, he was led to the Vice-Admiral's Beach and received another 20 lashes. In addition,

all his goods and chattels were to be forfeited, he was to pay the charges of the court, and to depart the Island by the first vessel never to return on pain of having the same punishment repeated every Monday morning (Fox, 1971:146).

▸ In 1692, an offender convicted of killing a merchant in Montreal was condemned by a judge to have his right hand cut off and his limbs broken before being placed on a rack to die, all in front of the house of his victim (Morel, 1963:28).

▸ In Halifax in 1795, 12 thieves, one of whom had stolen a bag of potatoes, were hanged (Anderson, 1982:9).

▸ In 1797, one David McLane, an American convicted of high treason in Canada for attempting to incite the French to join the United States, was sentenced to death by hanging, but with the unique provision that he be taken down before dying "and your bowels taken out and burned before your face; then your head must be severed from your body, which must be divided into four parts" (cited in Carrigan, 1991:311).

▸ In 1803, a 13-year-old boy was hanged in Montreal for stealing a cow, and in 1829, also in Montreal, three men were hanged for stealing an ox (Anderson, 1982:9).

Early Canadians had little patience with persons convicted of minor or major offences and little attempt was made by the courts to address the causes of criminal behaviour.

Jails in Early Canada

While Canadians used a wide variety of sanctions against offenders during the 1600s and 1700s, the use of incarceration as punishment for criminal offenders was not widespread. Municipal jails and lock-ups held individuals who were either awaiting trial or who had been convicted and were yet to be punished. A notable exception was in Nova Scotia, where a workhouse was constructed in 1754, patterned on the bridewell workhouses of England. Prisoners in the workhouses were employed at a variety of tasks, including cutting granite and laying road bed. Workhouses were extensively used in Nova Scotia until the mid-1800s, when their deteriorating physical condition made them unfit for habitation (Coles, 1979).

While legislation requiring the construction of houses of corrections was enacted in Upper and Lower Canada in the late 1700s, the historical record suggests that many municipalities did not construct such facilities (Baehre, 1977). Canadians at this time took a very lenient approach toward criminal behaviour, largely because it was so rare. In the more unpopulated areas of the country such as the Maritimes and Rupert's Land in the west, authorities sent offenders to England for trial and punishment.

The houses of correction that were built were woefully inadequate, and conditions soon approximated those of their English counterparts, as reflected in the following description of a bridewell that opened in Halifax in 1790:

> It was a general house of confinement for criminals, delinquents, debtors, and other social problem types...no systematic classification of offenders was attempted. The building was often cold, damp, and unhealthy. Prisoners slept on straw; the quality of clothing, blankets, and food depended upon the prisoner's ability to pay. The poorest were sustained on a diet of molasses and tea. The jail keeper supplemented his meagre income by selling liquor to the prisoners (Baehre, 1985:12).

The major problems afflicting the jails were the lack of classification, the failure to separate juvenile and adult offenders, corrupt and brutal administrators, and the lack of employment within the institutions. The lack of adequate classification is evident in the criticisms of the local jail by a grand jury in the York Assizes in 1850:

> The unthinking boy, and the young girl, as yet unhackneyed in the ways of vice, untainted by the germ of immorality, incarcerated for the first time and perhaps for some reckless, freak, or trifling offence...are associated with the old, the profligate, the abandoned offender (cited in Beattie, 1977:78-79).

Similar to their English counterparts, prisoners in these early Canadian jails were subjected to considerable exploitation by their keepers. In Nova Scotia, where responsibility for operating the jails had been turned over to the municipalities in the late 1870s, prisoners "had to pay for meals and liquor as well as rent for themselves and upon release further handed the jailkeeper a fee for this service. Failure to make this payment could result in longer detention, though more commonly, a prisoner was allowed to beg in the streets for his jail fees" (Coles, 1979:2). Despite various reform efforts, the poor conditions of confinement in municipal jails and provincial institutions were to continue throughout the 1800s and into the early twentieth century.[2]

The First Penitentiary in Canada: Kingston

One of the most significant developments in Canadian corrections was the building of the first penitentiary in Kingston, Ontario, in 1835. The decision by Canadians to construct a penitentiary was influenced by social, political, and economic changes that were occurring in Canadian society in the early 1800s, as well as by events in the United States.

The use of penitentiaries for the long-term confinement of offenders had first appeared in the United States in the period between 1790 and 1830. Until the late 1700s, Americans had viewed crime as a natural part of society and of no great threat to community stability. The colonists believed that the best defences against crime were strong community relations built around the family and the church. Detention facilities held individuals awaiting trial or punishment, and there was no attempt to create programs or institutions to rehabilitate offenders. As in Canada, punishment was progressive, and repeat offenders who did not respond to fines and corporal punishment were put to death.

Toward the end of the 1700s, however, increasing urbanization and industrialization precipitated a shift in the perceptions of and response to criminal behaviour. A rise in population and increased social mobility led to a breakdown in the effectiveness of community-based mechanisms of social control. Previously viewed as an individual phenomenon, crime came to be seen as a consequence of family disorganization and community corruption. There was a need to create an environment in which the offender could be separated from the influences of a corrupt community and be reformed. The penitentiary would provide the training and discipline the individual had not received from the family, church, or community. The penitentiary also satisfied the criticisms of the Enlightenment writers and of religious groups such as the Quakers who argued for the development of alternatives to capital and corporal punishments.[3]

Two types of penitentiary systems emerged in the United States during the 1800s: the Pennsylvania, or "separate and silent" system in which prisoners were isolated from each other at all times in small cells, and the Auburn, or "congregate," system, which allowed prisoners to work and eat together during the day and then segregated them in individual cells at night. The Auburn system was operated under a strict "silent system" that forbade prisoners from communicating or even gesturing to one another, and was the model upon which most prisons in the United States and Canada were patterned.

The building of the Kingston Penitentiary was also the result of a number of changes that occurred in Canadian society in the late 1700s and early 1800s, although the precise influence of the social, economic, and political factors on the decision to construct the prison is difficult to determine. It does appear that there was a shift in the perceptions of crime. While historians disagree as to whether there was an *actual* increase in the crime rate during the early 1800s (Beattie, 1977; Bellomo, 1972), it is evident that Canadians became increasingly concerned with criminality. Crime came to be viewed as the consequence of "immorality, intemperance, lack of religious practice, and idleness," and criminals comprised a "dangerous class" that was a threat to the moral and social fabric and stability of the emerging Canadian society (Bellomo, 1972:11). Immigrants (in particular the Irish) were singled out as the source of an increasingly troublesome crime rate.

There was also concern about the effectiveness of the capital and corporal punishments and the usefulness of the local jails, which were overcrowded and in disarray. In the view of politicians and other supporters involved in its design and construction, the penitentiary would not only provide an environment in which offenders could be educated and their ways corrected, but it would also serve as a model of order and stability for both offenders and society (see Taylor, 1979).

Smandych (1991), however, has challenged these traditional explanations. From an analysis of the political factors surrounding the decision to build the Kingston prison — what he terms the "politics of penal reform" — Smandych (1991:137-138) argues that Canadians of the time did not view crime as a serious problem and had no illusions about the ability of the new prison to prevent or deter crime. Also, many politicians were unimpressed by the performance of the newly constructed prisons in the United States and there was political opposition to building the prison. Smandych (1991:143) argues that the decision to build the

Kingston prison can be traced to the dominant conservative ideology of the time, to the "paternalist" mentality of Upper Canada's Tory government. This work suggests that a considerable amount of research remains to be done before we can present a complete and accurate account of this important event in Canadian correctional history.

Whatever the specific factors that influenced its creation, the Kingston Penitentiary opened in 1835. Unlike the local and district jails, the penitentiary provided for the separation of offenders on the basis of gender and offence, and prisoners were given bedding, clothing, and adequate food. The cornerstones of the Kingston penitentiary were hard labour, silence, and strict adherence to prison regulations, all of which were designed to punish the offender as well as to reform him (Curtis *et al.*, 1985). Prisoners were required to walk lock-step and were forbidden to "exchange looks, wink, laugh, nod, or gesticulate" (Splane, 1965:134). A similar regimen was imposed on the prisoners in the penitentiary in Halifax, completed in 1843:

> In passing to and from the cells, to and from the shops, and to and from their meals, the convicts must move in close single file with lock step, in perfect silence, and facing towards the officer in immediate charge of them... (Baehre, 1985:18).

By the early 1840s, however, concerns were being voiced about the excessive use of corporal punishments within Kingston and the effectiveness of the prison regimen in reforming offenders. In 1848, a Royal Commission of Inquiry (chaired by the editor of Toronto *Globe*, George Brown) was appointed to inquire into the operation of the Kingston Penitentiary and the activities of the warden, Henry Smith. In its first report, issued in 1848, the Commission condemned the use of corporal punishment within the penitentiary and recommended the removal of the warden. While the Commission criticized the manner in which Kingston had been operated, it did not question the effectiveness of the structure of the institution and the regimen imposed upon the prisoners.

In its second report a year later, the Commission proposed that the primary aim of the penitentiary should be the reformation of offenders. Although there is disagreement about the impact of the Brown Commission on correctional reform (Baehre, 1977; Bellomo, 1972), the reports of the Commission do appear to have significantly influenced subsequent legislation. The *Penitentiary Act* of 1851, for example, established specific guidelines for the use of corporal punishments within the institution, specified that mentally ill offenders be moved to a separate institution, and provided for the appointment of two inspectors who would oversee the operation of Kingston.[4]

At Confederation in 1867, the penitentiaries at Kingston, Halifax, and St. John, New Brunswick, came under the legislative authority of Parliament, and with the passage of the *Penitentiary Act* in 1868, the federal penitentiary system was created. Additional penitentiaries were constructed in Montreal, Quebec (1873), Stony Mountain, Manitoba (1876), New Westminster, British Columbia (1878), and Prince Albert, Saskatchewan (1911). These institutions, many of which are still in operation in the 1990s, were the foundation of the federal correctional system in Canada. Even with the expansion of federal and provincial systems of correction, it was not until the late 1930s that Canadian correctional policy incorporated the reformation and rehabilitation of the offender as an objective. And, even then, this model was to survive for only a relatively short period of time.

THE SHIFTING WINDS OF CORRECTIONAL PRACTICE

A detailed discussion of Canadian correctional practice is beyond the scope of this text; however, we can highlight some of the more important developments and shifts in correctional philosophy that occurred from the mid-1800s until more recent times. This will at least give some idea of the various models of correctional practice that have come in and out of vogue over the years.[5]

Punishment and penitence were the basis of correctional policy at the federal and provincial levels from the early 1700s until the late 1930s. It was not until the report of the Royal Commission on the Penal System of Canada (Archambault) issued in 1938 that the reformation of the offender was raised as an objective of the federal correctional system. However, the recommendations of this report did not result in any immediate changes to correctional practice.

In the years following World War II, vocational training and education programs, as well as a wide variety of therapeutic techniques, were introduced into federal and provincial institutions. These programs were accompanied by the involvement of psychologists and psychiatrists in developing and operating correctional treatment programs. The increased emphasis on the rehabilitation of offenders received additional support from a Committee of Inquiry chaired by Fauteux J. (1956). One of the more significant conclusions of the Committee was that individuals who violated the law had been somehow "damaged" in the process of growing up. This view of criminal offenders came to be known as the "medical model" and was a cornerstone of the myriad of correctional treatment programs that were developed during the late 1950s and throughout the 1960s.

By the late 1960s, however, there was increasing concern with the effectiveness of correctional treatment programs in rehabilitating criminal offenders. In 1969, the Canadian Committee on Corrections (Ouimet) concluded that the reformation of offenders was more effectively pursued in the community than within correctional institutions. Imprisonment, the Committee argued, should be used only as a last resort.

A report of the Law Reform Commission (1975) and the report of the Parliamentary Sub-committee on the Penitentiary System in Canada (MacGuigan, 1977) further concluded that penal institutions should not be used for rehabilitative purposes. These reports precipitated the expansion of probation, parole, and diversion programs and the development of community-based facilities and programs, particularly during the years 1970 to 1978, during what Ekstedt and Griffiths (1988) have labelled the "reintegration model" of correctional practice. Chapter 12 discusses these programs in more detail.

In 1977, a federal government task force proposed the adoption of the program opportunities model, whereby corrections would provide the programs for offenders, but it was the responsibility of the offender to take the initiative to participate in and benefit from them. No longer was criminal behaviour viewed as the symptom of some underlying disorder or sickness that required diagnosis and intervention. According to the Task Force (1977:31), the program opportunities model was based on the principle that "the offender is ultimately responsible for his behaviour...the offender is convicted and sentenced on the basis of his criminal behaviour, not on the basis of some underlying personality disorder or deprived socio-economic condition." In adopting the opportunities model, corrections shifted total responsibility for reformation onto the offender and discarded previous claims of expertise in diagnosing and treating offenders. The federal corrections system did, however, retain responsibility for making programs and services available for offenders, should they choose to participate.

Chapter 11 shows that while the responsibility for rehabilitation was shifted to offenders, often the Correctional Service of Canada did not provide the environment of positive support required. Rather, during the late 1970s and into the early 1980s, Canadian corrections returned to the punishment objective based on the concept of reparation (see Canadian Sentencing Commission, 1987; Ekstedt and Griffiths, 1988).

As we enter the 1990s, correctional practice at the federal level appears to be based on a mixture of the program opportunities model, with a strong emphasis on control of offenders, and perhaps a dash of what remains of the rehabilitation model of the 1960s. This is most succinctly illustrated by the mission statement of the federal Correctional Service of Canada (1990:4):

> The Correctional Service of Canada, as part of the criminal justice system, contributes to the protection of society by actively encouraging and assisting offenders to become law- abiding citizens, while exercising reasonable, safe, secure and humane control.

The mission statement provides the framework within which policies and programs are implemented and has five core values, each of which has attached to it a number of guiding principles and strategic objectives.[6]

The Correctional Service of Canada seeks to provide programs and opportunities to try to change criminal behaviour and reintegrate offenders with the community. These programs and opportunities try to maintain a balance between assistance and control: "Our aim is to assist and encourage to the extent that is possible and to control to the extent that is necessary" (Correctional Service of Canada, 1990:6).

The next three chapters will explore further the issues surrounding institutional corrections, the creation and expansion of community-based correctional programs, and several of the critical issues that confront correctional systems in Canada today.

CONTEMPORARY CANADIAN CORRECTIONS

In Canada, the responsibility for the provision of adult correctional services is shared between the federal, provincial, and municipal levels of government. The services and facilities can be divided into "custodial" and "non-custodial." Arrangements for the provision of correctional services for youths 18 years of age and under are quite different and will be discussed in Chapter 14.

Custodial facilities include RCMP/municipal lock-ups, provincial and federal institutions, and community-based facilities operated by the federal, provincial, and territorial governments. In addition, the John Howard Society, the Elizabeth Fry Society, and other private, non-profit organizations operate a variety of community-based facilities on a contract basis (see Figure 10.1). Within these facilities, a wide variety of programs and services are provided, including inmate employment and work programs and occupational/vocational training and counselling. Non-custodial programs and services include probation, parole, mandatory supervision, and a variety of other programs that attempt to assist the offender within the community (see Figure 10.2). The total expenditures for provincial/territorial and federal corrections during 1991-92 was $1.88 billion (Mihorean, 1993). Chapter 11 will explore further both custodial and non-custodial programs and services.

The basis for the split in correctional jurisdiction in Canada is the "two-year rule" that is embodied in section 731 of the *Criminal Code*. Those offenders who receive a sentence (or sentences) totalling two or more years fall under the jurisdiction of the federal corrections system, while those offenders receiving a sentence (or sentences) totalling less than two years are the responsibility of the provinces. The sole exception to this rule is in Newfoundland/Labrador, where the province maintains jurisdiction over federal offenders under an arrangement established when the province entered Confederation in 1949. Federal offenders in Newfoundland/Labrador can be transferred to federal facilities only with provincial consent.[7]

In 1991-92, the total average offender caseload for federal and provincial corrections (custodial and non-custodial) was approximately 136,000. The majority of these offenders are in provincial corrections systems and are under supervision in the community. Female offenders comprised approximately 7% of the total inmate population and over 95% of these were incarcerated in provincial/territorial facilities.

Although extreme caution must be exercised in making statistical comparisons between jurisdictions, note how the rates of incarceration in Canada compare with those of other countries. A recent analysis (Canadian Centre for Justice Statistics, 1992a) indicates that in 1990, Canada ranked third (92.1) in the number of adults incarcerated per 100,000 population, behind the United States (310.1) and Switzerland (133.8). The

FIGURE 10.1
CUSTODIAL SERVICES IN CANADA

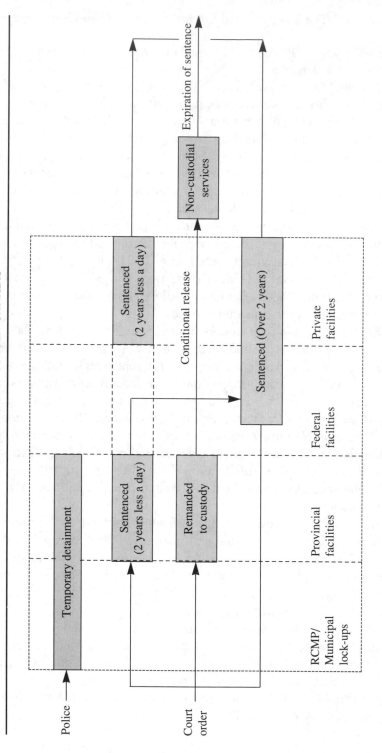

Source: Adapted from Canadian Centre for Justice Statistics. *Adult Correctional Services in Canada, 1991-92.* (Ottawa: Statistics Canada, 1993), p. 20. Catalogue no. 85-211. Reproduced with permission of the Minister of Industry, Science, and Technology, 1993.

FIGURE 10.2
NON-CUSTODIAL SERVICES IN CANADA

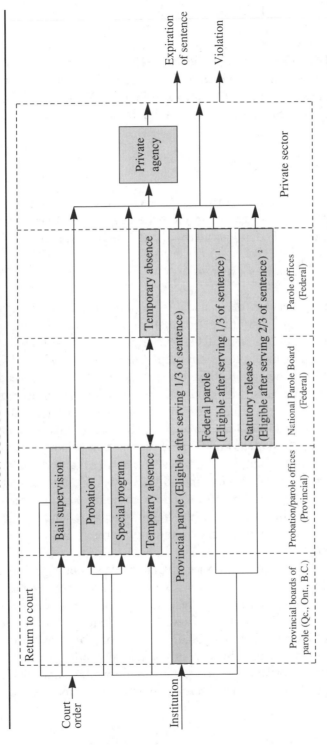

[1] First-time, non-violent offenders are eligible for an accelerated parole review before one-third of the sentence has been served. Also, the sentencing court may require that offenders convicted of serious drug offences and those convicted of violent crimes serve half of their sentence in prison prior to becoming eligible for parole consideration.

[2] Serious drug offenders and violent offenders may be required to serve their entire sentence in confinement and may not be released on statutory release.

Source: Adapted from Canadian Centre for Justice Statistics. *Adult Correctional Services in Canada, 1991-92* (Ottawa: Statistics Canada, 1993), p. 22. Catalogue no. 85-211. Reproduced with permission of the Minister of Industry, Science, and Technology, 1993.

incarceration rate in Canada remained relatively stable (+13.6%) during 1980-90, while it increased dramatically (+121%) in the United States. Other countries had similar increases in incarceration rates to Canada: Scotland (+18.5%), Australia (+19.7%), and England/Wales (11.4%). The United States remains quite distinct in its rate of incarceration (see Lowman and Menzies, 1986).

Federal Correctional Services

Two agencies provide federal correctional services for adult offenders: the Correctional Service of Canada and the National Parole Board, both of which are part of the Federal Ministry of the Solicitor General.

The Correctional Service of Canada

The Correctional Service of Canada is organized into three levels: national, regional, and institutional or district offices, and is under the direction of the Commissioner of Corrections who is appointed by the Governor-in-Council under provisions of the *Corrections and Conditional Release Act* (1992). The national headquarters is in Ottawa, and there are five regional headquarters: Moncton, New Brunswick (Atlantic region, including Newfoundland, Prince Edward Island, Nova Scotia, and New Brunswick), Laval, Quebec (Quebec region), Kingston, Ontario (Ontario region), Saskatoon, Saskatchewan (Prairie region, comprising Manitoba, Saskatchewan, Alberta, and the Northwest Territories), and Abbotsford, British Columbia (Pacific region, including British Columbia and the Yukon Territory) (see Figure 10.3). These regional headquarters are responsible for administering the maximum, medium, and minimum security institutions, as well as the community correctional centres and forest work camps.

In 1992, the Correctional Service of Canada was operating a total of 59 facilities: 2 high maximum security, 13 maximum security, 18 medium security, 13 minimum security facilities, and 13 community correctional centres (CCCs) (see Table 10.1). There are no federal institutions in Prince Edward Island, Newfoundland, the Yukon, or the Northwest Territories. The Correctional Service of Canada also operates 73 parole offices across the country and is responsible for the supervision of offenders on full parole, day parole, mandatory supervision, and temporary absences.

There are approximately 11,000 people employed in federal corrections, providing custodial services (79%), administration and staff training (12%), and in parole offices (9%). These personnel were responsible for supervising, in custodial and non-custodial settings, approximately 21,000 offenders. These figures suggest that corrections is highly labour-intensive, which is one of the primary reasons for the escalating costs of managing and supervising convicted offenders at the federal level. In contrast to the federal corrections system, a higher number of provincial offenders were in non-custodial settings.

In fiscal year 1991-92, the Correctional Service of Canada spent approximately $974 million on custody (74%), administration for the Correctional Service of Canada and the NPB (20%), and community supervision (7%). In 1991-92, it cost an average of $136 per day to house an inmate in a federal correctional facility. The per day costs are higher in maximum security institutions and lower in community-based facilities. Even higher average annual costs are associated with incarcerating federal female offenders in Kingston Prison for Women — up to $60,000 per annum. It is significant that, even though more federal offenders are in custodial settings than non-custodial facilities, only 7% of the expenditures were for community supervision.

During 1991-92, there were 11,783 inmates (average daily actual count) in federal correctional institutions, a 3% decrease from the previous year.[8] This includes approximately 130 females confined in the Kingston Prison for Women, the only federal institution for female offenders in Canada. Of the offenders admitted to federal facilities during 1991-92, 67% were serving sentences of less than four years, 7% of the admissions had been given sentences of ten years or more, and 4% had been sentenced to either an indefinite sentence or life imprisonment.

Of considerable concern has been the increase in the number of minority offenders in Canadian federal institutions. During the time period 1984-1989, there was nearly a 30% increase in Aboriginal admissions, a 16% increase in admissions of Métis offenders, and a 145.5% increase in Inuit admissions.

The National Parole Board

The National Parole Board (NPB) is an independent administrative agency in the Ministry of the Solicitor General. It has 36 full-time members, 18 of whom are distributed in five regional divisions, which are

FIGURE 10.3
ORGANIZATION OF THE CORRECTIONAL SERVICE OF CANADA

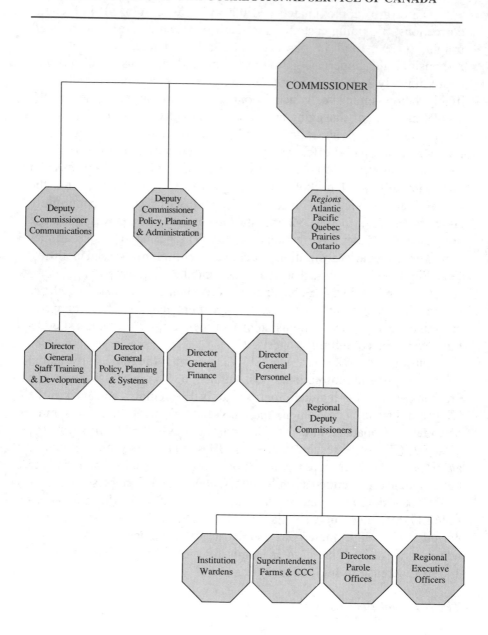

FIGURE 10.3
ORGANIZATION OF THE CORRECTIONAL SERVICE OF CANADA

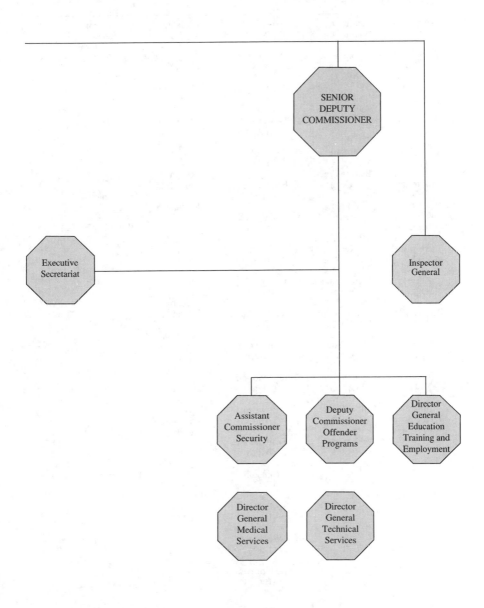

Source: Solicitor General of Canada. *Annual Report, 1986-87* (Ottawa: Supply and Services Canada, 1987), p. 50. Reproduced with permission of the Minister of Supply and Services Canada, 1993.

TABLE 10.1
FEDERAL CORRECTIONAL INSTITUTIONS
IN OPERATION, 1991-92; BY SECURITY LEVEL

Community Correctional Centre	Minimum	Medium	Maximum	High Maximum
Carlton (N.S.)	Westmorland Farm (N.B.)	Springhill (N.S.)	Atlantic (N.B.)	Regional Reception Centre (P.Q.)
Sand River (N.S.)	Montée-St. Francois (P.Q.)	Dorchester (N.B.)	Donnacona (P.Q.)	Sask. Pen. (Sask.)
Parrtown (N.B.)	Ste-Anne-des Plaines (P.Q.)	Archambault (P.Q.)	Port Cartier (P.Q.)	
Benoit XV (P.Q.)	Bath (Ont.)	Cowansville (P.Q.)	Regional Reception Centre (P.Q.)	
Laferrière (P.Q.)	Beaver Creek (Ont.)	Drummond (P.Q.)	Kingston Pen. (Ont.)	
Martineau (P.Q.)	Frontenac (Ont.)	Federal Tng. Centre (P.Q.)	Millhaven (Ont.)	
Ogilvy (P.Q.)	Pittsburgh (Ont.)	La Macaza (P.Q.)	Prison for Women (Ont.)	
Sherbrooke (P.Q.)	Prison for Women Annex (Ont.)	Leclerc (P.Q.)	Regional Treatment Centre (Ont.)	
Keele (Ont.)	Rockwood (Man.)	Collins Bay (Ont.)	Regional Psychiatric Centre (Sask.)	
Portsmouth (Ont.)	Sask. Farm (Sask.)	Joyceville (Ont.)	Sask. Pen. (Sask.)	
Osborne (Man.)	Bowden Annex (Alta.)	Warkworth (Ont.)	Edmonton (Alta.)	
Oskana (Sask.)	Elbow Lake (B.C.)	Stony Mountain (Man.)	Kent (B.C.)	
Sumas (B.C.)	Ferndale (B.C.)	Bowden (Alta.)	Regional Psychiatric Centre (B.C.)	
		Drumheller (Alta.)		
		Matsqui (B.C.)		
		Mission (B.C.)		
		Mountain (B.C.)		
		William Head (B.C.)		

Source: Canadian Centre for Justice Statistics. *Adult Correctional Services in Canada, 1991-92*. (Ottawa: Statistics Canada, 1993), p. 129. Catalogue no. 85-211. Reproduced with permission of the Minister of Industry, Science and Technology, 1993.

the same as most of those of the Correctional Service of Canada: Atlantic, Quebec, Ontario, Prairie, and Pacific. The remainder of the members are located at the NPB headquarters in Ottawa (see Figure 10.4). Each region also has community board members and temporary board members selected by the Solicitor General. During 1991-92, 36 community board members were involved in reviewing all cases of inmates either serving life sentences or serving indeterminate sentences as dangerous offenders. In addition, temporary board members, who numbered 77 in 1991-92, are often appointed for terms of up to one year to assist during periods of heavy caseloads. Parole board members are appointed by the Governor-in-Council on the recommendation of the Solicitor General of Canada. There are no formal qualifications for being a member of the NPB.

Under the *Parole Act*, the NPB has the authority to grant full and day parole to federal inmates and to provincial inmates who are confined in provinces where there is no provincial parole board; to grant temporary absences to federal inmates; and to terminate/revoke parole. The NPB also has authority to supervise and terminate/revoke statutory release and to review applications for pardons under the *Criminal Records Act*.

Historically, the NPB was not involved in the decision to release offenders on mandatory supervision (replaced in 1992 by statutory release) from institutions. Offenders who had served two-thirds of their sentence and who had not been granted a parole were released automatically by the Correctional Service of Canada. In response to public and political pressure and several highly publicized crimes involving offenders on mandatory supervision, the NPB was empowered to review and reject the applications for release on mandatory supervision (statutory release) of those offenders that it considers a clear danger to the community, forcing those offenders to serve their full sentence in confinement. In addition, under the provisions of the *Corrections and Conditional Release Act* (1992), offenders who are released on statutory release and are subsequently returned for a violation of conditions will not be eligible for a second release. While this legislation will result in many dangerous offenders serving longer periods of time in confinement, upon release they will receive no supervision whatsoever.

In 1991-92, there were 9,383 offenders supervised by the Correctional Service of Canada under full parole, day parole, or mandatory supervision. This figure includes provincial inmates in provinces that do not have

FIGURE 10.4
ORGANIZATION OF THE NATIONAL PAROLE BOARD

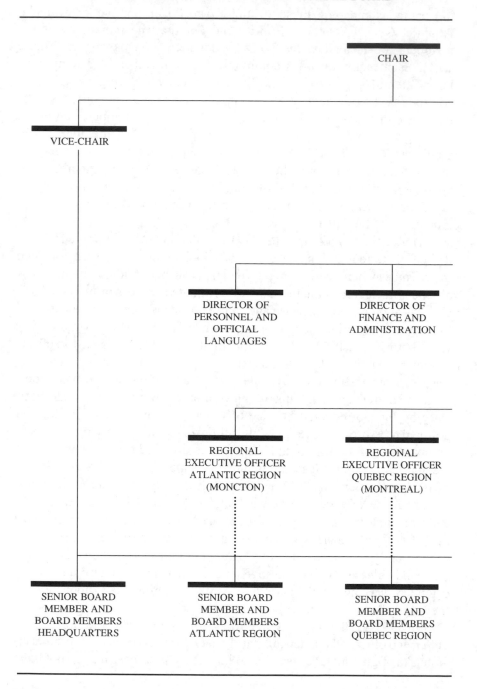

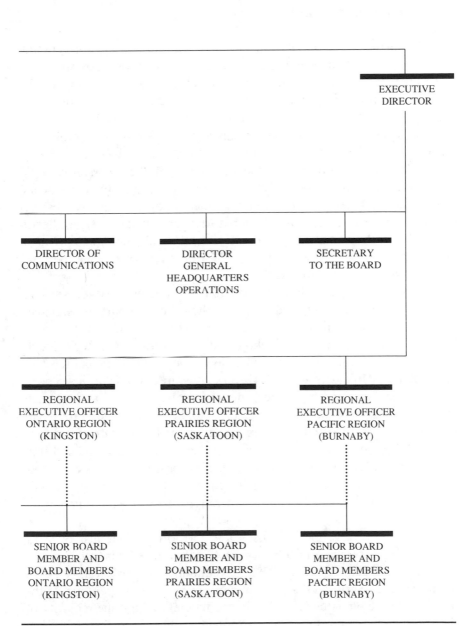

FIGURE 10.4
ORGANIZATION OF THE NATIONAL PAROLE BOARD

EXECUTIVE
DIRECTOR

DIRECTOR OF
COMMUNICATIONS

DIRECTOR
GENERAL
HEADQUARTERS
OPERATIONS

SECRETARY
TO THE BOARD

REGIONAL
EXECUTIVE OFFICER
ONTARIO REGION
(KINGSTON)

REGIONAL
EXECUTIVE OFFICER
PRAIRIES REGION
(SASKATOON)

REGIONAL
EXECUTIVE OFFICER
PACIFIC REGION
(BURNABY)

SENIOR BOARD
MEMBER AND
BOARD MEMBERS
ONTARIO REGION
(KINGSTON)

SENIOR BOARD
MEMBER AND
BOARD MEMBERS
PRAIRIES REGION
(SASKATOON)

SENIOR BOARD
MEMBER AND
BOARD MEMBERS
PACIFIC REGION
(BURNABY)

Source: Solicitor General of Canada. *Annual Report, 1986-1987* (Ottawa: Solicitor General of
Canada, 1987), p. 42. Reproduced with permission of the Minister of Supply and Services Canada, 1993.

their own parole board. We will consider the activities of the NPB in greater detail in Chapter 12.[9]

Provincial Correctional Services

The provincial governments are charged with providing correctional services for offenders receiving a sentence(s) totalling less than two years (see Table 10.2). However, there is considerable variability in the specific types of programs in provincial correctional facilities and in the non-custodial services provided for adult offenders (see Table 10.3).[10]

For example, while all the provinces/territories provide probation services, only British Columbia, Ontario, and Quebec have established provincial parole boards under the provisions of the *Corrections and Conditional Release Act* (1992). In these provinces, probation officers serve as parole supervisors for offenders released by the provincial parole board. In the remaining provinces/territories, provincial cases are heard by the NPB. Provincial probation officers across the country may also provide supervisory services for the NPB where no Correctional Service of Canada personnel are present.

Provinces may also have responsibility for temporary lock-ups in which offenders are detained prior to their initial court appearance, although in Newfoundland and Labrador, New Brunswick, Saskatchewan, Alberta, British Columbia, the Yukon, and the Northwest Territories, such facilities are maintained on a shared basis between the municipalities and the province. Offenders under lock-up status are those who have been detained for short periods of time under provincial statutes, have not been sentenced, and who are not considered to be on remand. Provincial institutions also hold offenders who are on remand. Under the provisions of the *Bail Reform Act*, the court may order an accused remanded into custody in order to ensure appearance in court or to protect the community. Also confined on remand status in provincial facilities are individuals who have been sentenced by the court but are awaiting the outcome of an appeal.[11]

During 1991-92, the provinces and territories spent just over $1 billion on the provision of adult correctional services, broken down as follows: custodial services (82%), community supervision (that is, probation and parole) (11%); administration (6%); and operation of the provincial parole boards (1%). As in the federal system, the majority of fiscal resources are consumed by custodial facilities. In contrast to federal

TABLE 10.2
PROVINCIAL/TERRITORIAL MINISTRIES AND DEPARTMENTS
RESPONSIBLE FOR ADULT CORRECTIONS

Government	Ministry/Department
Newfoundland and Labrador	Adult Correctional Division Department of Justice
Prince Edward Island	Community and Correctional Services Division, Department of Justice and Attorney-General
Nova Scotia	Correctional Services Division, Department of Solicitor General
New Brunswick	Correctional Services Division, Department of the Solicitor General
Quebec	Correctional Services Branch, Ministry of Public Security
Ontario	Ministry of Correctional Services
Manitoba	Corrections Division, Manitoba Justice
Saskatchewan	Corrections Division, Saskatchewan Justice
Alberta	Correctional Services Division, Alberta Solicitor General
British Columbia	Corrections Branch, Department of Justice
Yukon Territory	Corrections Branch, Department of Justice
Northwest Territories	Correctional Service Division, Department of Justice

Source: Canadian Centre for Justice Statistics. *Adult Correctional Services in Canada, 1991-92*. (Ottawa: Statistics Canada, 1993), p. 35. Catalogue no. 85-211. Reproduced with permission of the Minister of Industry, Science and Technology, 1993.

TABLE 10.3

COMMUNITY PROGRAMS FOR ADULTS PROVIDED BY PROVINCIAL/TERRITORIAL CORRECTIONAL AGENCIES[1]

Community Services	NFLD	PEI	NS	NB	PQ	ONT	MAN	SASK	ALTA	BC	YK	NWT
Probation	X	X	X	X	X	X	X	X	X	X	X	X
Provincial Parole				X[2]	X	X				X		
Community Service Orders	X	X	X	X	X	X	X	X	X	X	X	X
Temporary Absence Program	X	X	X	X	X	X	X	X	X	X	X	X
Drinking/Driving Program	X	X	X	X	X	X	X	X	X	X	X	X
Fine Option Program	X						X	X	X	X	X	
Victim-Offender Reconciliation	X		X	X	X	X	X	X	X		X	X
Victim-Witness Program		X		X	X	X						
Bail Verification Supervision						X	X	X	X	X	X	
Restitution Program				X	X	X	X	X	X	X		
Community/Based Halfway House Program	X	X		X		X	X	X	X	X		
Volunteer/Outside Agency Services	X	X	X	X	X	X	X	X	X	X	X	X

[1] In many jurisdictions, community services are operated by other criminal justice agencies. The Waterloo Region Victim Service Program, for example, is based in the Waterloo Regional Police Force.

[2] The New Brunswick Board of Parole has authority only over adults convicted of Provincial Statute violations and young offenders charged under the *Young Offenders Act*.

Source: Canadian Centre for Justice Statistics. *Adult Correctional Services in Canada, 1987–88.* (Ottawa: Statistics Canada, 1989), p. 35-52. Catalogue no. 85-211. Reproduced with permission of the Minister of Industry, Science and Technology, 1993.

corrections, however, the majority of provincial offenders are under some form of community supervision (generally probation).

In 1991-92, there were 126 "secure" institutions and 40 "open" facilities operated by the provinces/territories. The average offender count, sentenced and non-sentenced (lock-up and remand) in 1991-92 was 18,944. There were approximately 95,000 offenders on probation and parole during 1991-92.

The following were among the other more notable attributes of provincial/territorial corrections during 1991-92.

- ► Excluding New Brunswick and Ontario, 11% of all sentences at the provincial level were for intermittent sentences, which allow offenders to serve time on the weekends.
- ► The average provincial offender on probation is 28 years of age and is under supervision for 12 months.
- ► There has been a 22% increase in admissions to provincial/territorial institutions over the past decade.
- ► Aboriginal peoples accounted for 19% of all sentenced admissions to provincial/territorial facilities, although the figure is higher in the Prairie provinces and in the Yukon and Northwest Territories.

Of interest for our discussion of female offenders in Chapter 13 is the following information from 1989-90.

- ► The number of female offenders admitted to provincial/territorial institutions has increased 13% over the past five years.
- ► Nationwide, female offenders comprised 8% of all sentenced admissions to provincial/territorial institutions and 17% of persons on probation, although this varies from a low of 3% in Nova Scotia to a high of 11% in Saskatchewan and Alberta.
- ► The majority of female offenders sentenced to confinement spend one month or less in custody, although in Ontario, 58% of the women had previously been incarcerated.
- ► In 1989-90, Aboriginal women accounted for 29% of all female admissions to provincial/territorial institutions (Canadian Centre for Justice Statistics, 1991b; 1992b).

A Note on the Split in Correctional Jurisdiction

One of the longstanding (and unresolved) debates in Canadian corrections is the split in correctional jurisdiction. The delivery of correctional services by both federal and provincial governments has led to increasing concerns with duplication of administrative structures and program services. Both levels of government operate correctional facilities and community-based programs, as well as providing supervision for offenders in the community. In fact, the "two-year rule" has been surrounded by considerable debate since its inception in the 1840s, for reasons that are still unclear.

A report by a federal study team investigating the improvement of justice delivery (Task Force on Program Review, 1985:296) noted that the two-year rule was a "constitutional anomaly" and concluded that the current jurisdictional split impeded "effective service delivery and efficient administration."

While the Task Force on Program Review (1985:297) reported widespread interest among the provinces in assuming full responsibility for correctional services (provided that financial support was forthcoming from the federal government), the two-year rule remains, and it is uncertain when and if any modifications to it will be made. Recently, through increased use of exchange-of-service agreements, the federal and provincial governments have attempted to increase the sharing of correctional resources (see Task Force on Program Review, 1985:297).

The failure of the provincial and federal governments to resolve the long-standing issues surrounding the split in correctional jurisdiction appears to be due in large measure not to differences in correctional philosophy, but rather to financial considerations. Any alteration of existing arrangements, particularly if such changes involved provincial governments assuming a larger share of responsibility for correctional services, would require assurances of ongoing financial support from the federal government.[12]

THE FEDERAL CORRECTIONAL INVESTIGATOR AND PROVINCIAL OMBUDSPERSONS

Both the federal and provincial correctional systems, with the exception of Prince Edward Island, have established offices to investigate complaints by prison inmates and to inquire into various aspects of the operation of the correctional system. Such inquiries often address complaints by prison inmates about their treatment in correctional institutions and specific policies and procedures of the correctional system. At the federal level, these activities are carried out by the office of the correctional investigator, and in the provinces by the ombudsperson offices, which may be involved in investigating other areas as well.

The office of the correctional investigator was initially created under the *Inquiries Act,* largely as a result of complaints by inmates about their treatment in Canadian federal penitentiaries. In 1992, this office was formally established in statute with the enactment of the *Corrections and Conditional Release Act.* The correctional investigator acts as an ombudsperson for federal inmates in relation to all facets of the mandate of the Correctional Service of Canada. Investigations may be undertaken at the request of the federal Solicitor General, on the basis of complaints received from inmates, or on the initiative of the correctional investigator.

The annual report of the correctional investigator documents complaints received from inmates by category, institution, and month, as well as the institutional visits and interviews undertaken by the investigator and the disposition of complaints. The annual report also contains the recommendations of the correctional investigator to the Solicitor General of Canada, and recent reports have addressed such issues as the involuntary transfer of inmates due to overcrowding, the need for a review of the procedures for transferring inmates of special handling units, amendments to provisions relating to privileged correspondence for inmates, the practice of double-bunking inmates in segregation cells, and the failure of institutional personnel to adhere to inmate grievance and appeal response time frames. While the recommendations of the correctional investigator are not binding upon the Correctional Service of Canada or the federal Solicitor General, all reports must be tabled before Parliament. In each annual report the correctional investigator notes those areas where no action has been taken.[13]

THE ROLE OF CORRECTIONS IN CANADIAN SOCIETY

Chapter 9 examined the justifications for imposing a criminal sanction on offenders. These included the often conflicting objectives of rehabilitation, retribution, and deterrence (see Walker, 1991). As the primary mechanism through which the sanctions imposed by the court are carried out, corrections has encountered difficulties in defining goals and objectives. As a federal government study team report on the Canadian justice system noted:

> The debate over the objectives of corrections has raged for decades and is likely never to be resolved, principally because corrections is asked, and likely always will be asked, to serve multiple and even conflicting aims which are inherent in sentencing and other factors (Task Force on Program Review, 1985:287).

The *Corrections and Conditional Release Act* states that the purpose of federal corrections is "to contribute to the maintenance of a just, peaceful and safe society" by:

(a)   carrying out sentences imposed by the courts through the safe and humane custody and supervision of offenders; and

(b)   assisting the rehabilitation of offenders and their reintegration into the community as law-abiding citizens through the provision of programs in penitentiaries and in the community (1992:4).

The mission statement of the federal Correctional Service of Canada, discussed earlier in our consideration of Canadian correctional practice, embodies many of these principles. These are the most recent efforts to define the objectives for Canadian corrections, a task that has proved to be extremely elusive for the past 150 years.

As we saw in Chapter 9, two major purposes of punishment are "just desserts" and rehabilitation. Either offenders are viewed as deserving to suffer for the wrong they have committed or as needing rehabilitation to prevent further crime and to reintegrate them into society. Galvin *et al.* (1977:36) have illustrated the relation between the purpose of the sentence imposed by the presiding judge and the particular correctional option chosen (see Table 10.4).

One of the major difficulties surrounding these justifications for punishment is a lack of reliable information on the effectiveness of criminal sanctions. This is evident in the ongoing debate over specific and general deterrence, which Morris and Hawkins (1969:119) have characterized as a "boxing match between blind-folded contestants." Specific deterrence focuses on the relation between the sanction imposed and the subsequent behaviour of the offender, once released from an institution or other correctional program.

TABLE 10.4
EFFECT OF PURPOSE ON CHOICE OF SENTENCE OPTION

Purpose of Sentence	OPTION(S) LIKELY TO BE FAVORED				
	Incarceration	Restitution	Fine	Community Service	Probation
Punishment	X		X		
Incapacitation	X				X[1]
Reparation					
Victim-Oriented		X			
Community-Oriented			X	X	
Offender-Oriented		X[2]		X	
Rehabilitation				X[3]	X

[1] Probation with strict conditions and very close surveillance or some highly structured programs.

[2] Where more weight is placed on rehabilitative effects and the offender's ability to pay than full compensation for the victim.

[3] Some judges use community service as much as because of assumed rehabilitative value as for purposes of reparations.

Source: John J. Galvin et al., *Issues and Programs in Brief.* Volume 1 of *Instead of Jail: Pre and Post Alternatives to Jail Incarceration* (Washington, D.C.: U.S. Government Printing Office, 1977), p. 36 (L.E.A.A.).

It is extremely difficult, for example, to establish a direct relation between the sanction imposed and the subsequent behaviour of the offender. There are many reasons other than the specific sanction imposed that may contribute to an offender modifying his or her behaviour. It has proved equally difficult for social scientists to establish the extent to which sanctions imposed on individual offenders are successful in deterring members of the general population.

In corrections, as in policing, the "more is better" view of responding to offenders has prevailed. However, contrary to the belief of many legislators and members of the general public, increasing the severity of penalties for criminal offences may not deter specific offenders or the general public. Just as there is a point of diminishing returns in hiring more police officers and applying more technology in an attempt to prevent crime, so too are their limits to the effectiveness of criminal sanctions. The deterrent value of sanctions does appear to be strongly related to the certainty of punishment and the swiftness with which it is imposed. These relations were first noted by Beccaria in his *Essay on Crime and Punishment* (1764):

> The certainty of a punishment, even if it be moderate, will always make a stronger impression than the fear of another which is more terrible but combined with the hope of impunity...Promptness of punishments is more useful when the length of time that passes between the punishment and the misdeed is less, so much the stronger and more lasting in the human mind is the association of these two ideas, crime and punishment...(cited in Conklin, 1986:389, 392-93).

In the Canadian criminal justice system, however, there is often neither the certainty of punishment nor the prompt imposition of sanctions. Rather, there is a high rate of attrition of offenders, once detected, through the various stages of the criminal justice system from arrest to sentencing. Similarly, the legal provisions for offenders' rights and due process often act to slow the imposition of sanctions, even for those offenders convicted of offences. We will return to a consideration of the deterrent effect of sanctions in our discussion of capital punishment in Chapter 13.

Despite the varied objectives of the correctional system, research by Brillon, Louis-Guerin, and Lamarche (1984) suggests that the Canadian public has fairly specific ideas about the purpose of criminal sanctions.

The most commonly stated objective of sanctions imposed by the criminal justice system on offenders was deterrence — "to discourage people from committing crimes and to protect the citizens against any attempt on their person or property." Respondents in the survey rarely mentioned punishment, rehabilitation, reparation, or retribution as objectives of criminal justice. Rather, as the authors (1984:261) state, the focus is on victimization and the consequences of the criminal act: "...punishment should reduce the threat of crime rather than simply punish offenders or reform and rehabilitate them."

A further finding was that the public knew very little about alternative sanctions, often confusing programs such as probation and parole. You will recall from Chapter 2 that the stereotypical and oversimplified views of crime and criminals held by Canadians were also due to a lack of knowledge of, and experience with, the criminal justice system. In Chapters 11 and 12 we will consider further the role that the public plays in corrections, both in relation to correctional institutions and community-based initiatives. It becomes clear that this lack of knowledge has severely hindered the potentially positive role that the public could play in the correctional process.

NOTES

[1]For detailed discussions of the historical response to crime and criminals, see Eriksson (1976), Hay *et al.* (1975), Ignatieff (1978), Jacoby (1983), and Newman (1978). See Carrigan (1991), Ekstedt and Griffiths (1988), and Jackson (1983, c.2) for detailed discussions of the historical response to crime in Canada.

[2]There is an emerging body of material on the early institutions in the various regions of the country. See Baehre (1985; 1990) for an insightful analysis of the prison system in Atlantic Canada prior to 1880; see also Fingard (1984) and Price (1990). The report of the Langmuir Commission (1891) provides valuable insights into the conditions of institutions in Ontario in the late 1800s. Strange (1985) provides a historical account of the establishment of the first prison for women in Canada during the years 1874 to 1901, and Cooper (1987) provides a historical overview of the response to women offenders and evolution of the Kingston Prison for Women.

[3]For a discussion of the factors contributing to the emergence of the penitentiary in colonial America in the late 1700s, see Rothman (1990); Scull (1977); and Takagi (1975).

[4]Investigations were also conducted into the alleged mismanagement of other penitentiaries. In 1884, a Royal Commission inquiry chaired by Drake J. of the British Columbia Supreme Court heard allegations against the warden and deputy warden of the British Columbia Penitentiary, which included misappropriation of supplies, disregard for prison regulations, and failure to supervise the prison guards adequately (see Scott, 1984).

[5]Most historical analyses have focused on the federal correctional system and our discussion in this chapter and in Chapters 11 to 13 is largely limited to the federal level. Each provincial system of corrections has its own unique history and the models of correctional practice may not necessarily reflect that which is operative at the federal level at any one point in time. Two of the more valuable studies of provincial correctional history are Doherty and Ekstedt's (1991) study of British Columbia corrections and the examination of corrections in Saskatchewan compiled by Skinner *et al.* (1981).

[6]For an insightful view of the federal correctional philosophy and policy and the role of the mission statement in federal corrections, see *Our Story: Organizational Renewal in Federal Corrections,* edited by Jim Vantour (1991).

[7]Exchange-of-service agreements between the federal government and provincial governments have resulted in some flexibility in the two-year rule. Federal offenders are generally held in provincial institutions following sentencing for the 30-day appeal period prior to being sent to a federal facility. In addition, transfer agreements exist between the federal government and all provinces except Prince Edward Island and Ontario, under which federal offenders may be detained in provincial facilities and vice versa. Under an agreement reached between the federal government and the province of Quebec, all French-speaking female offenders whose sentence(s) place them under federal jurisdiction serve their sentence in Quebec.

[8]The average inmate count refers to the number of inmates actually present at the time the count is taken rather than on-register at the institution. The other measure that is used is the "average daily on-register" population, which includes those inmates actually in custody, those on day parole, temporary absence, hospitalized, and unlawfully at large. During 1990-91, for example, there were approximately 2,400 provincial and 1,600 federal inmates who were "on-register" but not in custody at the time of the count.

[9]For current materials on applied research related to policy, programs, and management issues in corrections, see the *FORUM on Corrections Research,* produced by the Correctional Service of Canada. The *FORUM* is available free of charge from Publishing and Editorial Services, Correctional Service of Canada, 340 Laurier Avenue West, Ottawa, Ontario K1A OP9.

[10]For a description of correctional services in the provinces/territories, see the annual report produced by the Canadian Centre for Justice Statistics entitled *Adult Correctional Services in Canada.*

[11]A survey of the use of custodial remand in Canada (Canadian Centre of Justice Statistics, 1986) found that approximately 7% of persons charged with offences are remanded into custody and that one-third of the admissions to provincial/territorial facilities are under remand status. Despite the large number of individuals on remand status, there was an information gap between the courts and correctional authorities regarding remanded persons, and the role of correctional authorities in the remand process was largely "passive and uninformed." Further, since there is no classification of inmates on remand status, most are housed in maximum-security quarters and are denied access to institutional programs and activities.

[12]Financial issues have also played a major role in federal-provincial discussions and arrangements in other areas of the criminal justice system, including the provision of "contract" policing services to the provinces by the RCMP and the sharing of costs associated with the provision of the justice services to youths under the *Young Offenders Act.*

[13]For detailed information on the activities of the federal correctional investigator, see the *Annual Report of the Correctional Investigator,* available from the Minister of Supply and Services.

REFERENCES

Anderson, F.W. 1982. *Hanging in Canada.* Surrey, British Columbia: Frontier Books.

Archambault, J. 1938. *Report of the Royal Commission to Investigate the Prison System of Canada.* Ottawa: King's Printer.

Baehre, R. 1977. "Origins of the Penitentiary System in Upper Canada." 69 *Ontario History,* 185-207.

_____. 1985. *The Prison System in Atlantic Canada before 1880.* Ottawa: Solicitor General of Canada.

_____. 1990. "From Bridewell to Federal Penitentiary: Prisons and Punishment in Nova Scotia Before 1880." In P. Girard and J. Phillips, eds. *Essays in the History of Canadian Law. vol. III, Nova Scotia.* Toronto: University of Toronto Press. 163-99.

Beattie, J.M. 1977. *Attitudes towards Crime and Punishment in Upper Canada, 1830-1850: A Documentary Study.* Toronto: University of Toronto, Centre of Criminology.

Bellomo, J.J. 1972. "Upper Canadians Attitudes towards Crime and Punishment, 1832-1851." 64 *Ontario History.* 11-26.

Brillon, Y., C. Louis-Guerin, and M.-C. Lamarche. 1984. *Attitudes of the Canadian Public toward Crime Policies.* Montreal: University of Montreal, International Centre for Comparative Criminology.

Canadian Centre for Justice Statistics. 1986. *Custodial Remand in Canada — A National Survey*. Ottawa: Supply and Services Canada.

_____. 1991a. *Adult Correctional Services in Canada. 1990-91*. Ottawa: Supply and Services Canada.

_____. 1991b. "Adult Female Offenders in the Provinical/Territorial Corrections Systems, 1989-1990." 11 *Juristat Service Bulletin*. Ottawa: Statistics Canada.

_____. 1992a. "International Incarceration Patterns, 1980-1990." 12 *Juristat Service Bulletin*. Ottawa: Statistics Canada.

_____. 1992b. "Trends in Custodial Counts and Admissions — Provinces and Territories." 12 *Juristat Service Bulletin*. Ottawa: Statistics Canada.

Canadian Sentencing Commission, Department of Justice. 1987. *Sentencing Reform: A Canadian Approach*. Ottawa: Supply and Services Canada.

Carrigan, D.O. 1991. *Crime and Punishment in Canada: A History*. Toronto: McClelland and Stewart.

Coles, D. 1979. *Nova Scotia Corrections — An Historical Perspective*. Halifax: Communications Project in Criminal Justice, Correctional Services Division.

Conklin, J.E. 1986. *Criminology*. 2nd ed. New York: Macmillan.

Cooper, S.D. 1987. "The Evolution of the Federal Women's Prison." In E. Adelberg and C. Currie, eds. *Too Few to Count: Canadian Women in Conflict with the Law*. 127-44. Vancouver: Press Gang Publishers.

Correctional Service of Canada. 1990. *Mission of the Correctional Service of Canada*. Ottawa: Minister of Supply and Services.

Curtis, D., A. Graham, L. Kelly, and A. Patterson, 1985. *Kingston Penitentiary: The First Hundred and Fifty Years, 1935-1985*. Ottawa: Supply and Services Canada.

Doherty, D., and J.W. Ekstedt. 1991. *Conflict, Care and Control — The History of the Corrections Branch in British Columbia*. Burnaby, British Columbia: Simon Fraser University, Institute for Studies in Criminal Justice Policy.

Edmison, J.A. 1976. "Some Aspects of Nineteenth-Century Canadian Prisons." In W.T. McGrath, ed. *Crime and Its Treatment in Canada*. 347-69. 2nd ed. Toronto: Macmillan.

Ekstedt, J.W., and C.T. Griffiths. 1988. *Corrections in Canada: Policy and Practice*. 2nd ed. Toronto: Butterworths.

Eriksson, T. 1976. *The Reformers: An Historical Survey of Pioneer Experiments on the Treatment of Criminals*. New York: Elsevier.

Fauteux, G. 1956. *Report of a Committee Appointed to Inquire into the Principles and Procedures Followed in the Remission Service of the Department of Justice of Canada*. Ottawa: Queen's Printer.

Fingard, J. 1984. "Jailbirds in Mid-Victorian Halifax." 18 *Dalhousie Law Journal*. 81-102.

Fox, A. 1971. *The Newfoundland Constabulary*. St. John's: Robinson Blackmore.

Galvin, J.J., *et al.* 1977. *Issues and Programs in Brief.* vol.1. *Instead of Jail: Pre- and Post Alternatives to Jail Incarceration.* Washington, D.C.: U.S. Government Printing Office.

Hay, D., P. Linebaugh, J.G. Rule, E.P. Thompson, and C. Winslow. 1975. *Albion's Fatal Tree.* New York: Pantheon.

Ignatieff, M. 1978. *A Just Measure of Pain: The Penitentiary in the Industrial Revolution 1705-1850.* New York: Pantheon.

Jackson, M. 1983. *Prisoners of Isolation: Solitary Confinement in Canada.* Toronto: University of Toronto Press.

Jacoby, S. 1983. *Wild Justice: The Evolution of Revenge.* New York: Harper and Row.

Knafla, L.A., and T.L. Chapman. 1983. "Criminal Justice in Canada: A Comparative Study of the Maritimes and Lower Canada 1760-1812." 21 *Osgoode Hall Journal.* 245-74.

Langmuir, J.W. 1891. *Report of the Commissioners Appointed to Enquire into the Prison and Reformatory System of the Province of Ontario.* Toronto: Warwick and Sons.

Law Reform Commission of Canada. 1975. *Working Paper no. 11: Imprisonment and Release.* Ottawa: Information Canada.

Lowman, J., and R.J. Menzies. 1986. "Out of the Fiscal Shadow: Carceral Trends in Canada and the United States." 26 *Crime and Social Justice.* 95-115.

MacGuigan, M. 1977. *Report to Parliament by the Sub- committee on the Penitentiary System in Canada.* Ottawa: Supply and Services Canada.

Mihorean, S. 1993. "Correctional Expenditures and Personnel in Canada." 12 *Juristat Service Bulletin.* Ottawa: Statistics Canada.

Morel, A. 1963. "La Justice Criminelle en Nouvelle-France." 14 *Cite Libre.* 26-36.

Morris, N., and G. Hawkins. 1969. *The Honest Politicians Guide to Crime Control.* Chicago: University of Chicago Press.

Newman, G. 1978. *The Punishment Response.* New York: Lippincott.

Ouimet, R. 1969. *Report of the Canadian Committee on Corrections — Toward Unity: Criminal Justice and Corrections.* Ottawa: Information Canada.

Price, B.J. 1990. "'Raised in Rockhead. Died in the Poor House': Female Petty Criminals in Halifax, 1864-1890." In P. Girard and J. Phillips, eds. *Essays in the History of Canadian Law. vol. III, Nova Scotia.* Toronto: University of Toronto Press. 200-31.

Rothman, D.J. 1990. *The Discovery of the Asylum.* 2nd Edition. Toronto: Little, Brown.

Scott, J.D. 1984. *Four Walls in the West — The Story of the British Columbia Penitentiary*. Vancouver: Retired Federal Prison Officer's Association of British Columbia.

Scull, A.T. 1977. *Decarceration: Community Treatment and the Deviant — A Radical View*. Englewood Cliffs, N.J.: Prentice-Hall.

Skinner, S., O. Dreidger, and B. Grainger. 1981. *Corrections: An Historical Perspective of the Saskatchewan Experience*. Regina: Canadian Plains Research Centre, University of Regina.

Smandych, R.C. 1991. "Beware the 'Evil American Monster': Upper Canadian Views on the Need for a Penitentiary, 1830-1834." 33 *Canadian Journal of Criminology*. 125-47.

Splane, R.B. 1965. *Social Welfare in Ontario, 1791-1893. A Study of Public Welfare Administration*. Toronto: University of Toronto Press.

Strange, C. 1985. "'The Criminal and Fallen of Their Sex': The Establishment of Canada's First Women's Prison, 1874-1901.' 1 *Canadian Journal of Women and the Law*. 79-92.

Takagi, P. 1975. "The Walnut Street Jail: A Penal Reform to Centralize the Powers of the State." 39 *Federal Probation*. 18-36.

Task Force on Program Review. 1985. *Study Team Report — Improved Program Delivery: The Justice System*. Ottawa: Supply and Services Canada.

Task Force on the Creation of an Integrated Canadian Corrections Service. 1977. *The Role of Federal Corrections in Canada*. Ottawa: Supply and Services Canada.

Taylor, C.J. 1979. "The Kingston, Ontario Penitentiary and Moral Architecture." 12 *Social History*. 385-408.

Vantour, J. 1991. *Our Story: Organizational Renewal in Federal Corrections*. Ottawa: Correctional Service of Canada.

Walker, N. 1991. *Why Punish?* New York: Oxford University Press.

11 CANADIAN CORRECTIONAL INSTITUTIONS

Two of the major components of the Canadian correctional system are institutions and community-based programs. In this chapter, we consider the major issues surrounding the operation of correctional facilities, while in Chapter 12, our focus shifts to community-based corrections programs for adult offenders.[1]

Most of the materials that have been produced on institutional corrections in Canada relate to federal correctional facilities. The largest number of offenders in Canada, however, are serving sentences of two years less a day and are confined in provincial institutions. While all of the provinces/territories operate a range of correctional facilities, there are differences in operational policies and in the specific programs that are available to incarcerated offenders across the country. Further, the relatively short period of time that provincial offenders are confined (in comparison with their federal counterparts) presents unique challenges to correctional policy makers and administrators in terms of developing education and training programs. Our discussion will focus primarily on the federal level, although we will note significant developments at the provincial level as well.

As stated in Chapter 10, there is a high rate of attrition of offenders throughout the various stages of the criminal justice process from detection and arrest to court. Only a very small proportion of offenders who are charged and found guilty of committing a criminal offence are ever sent to a correctional facility. However, since the time of the Brown Commission in 1848, correctional institutions have remained at the centre of controversy and have been the subject of numerous governmental and academic inquiries. As we consider the issues surrounding the operation of correctional facilities, we will experience considerable déjà vu, as many of the difficulties confronting Canadian correctional institutions today are strikingly similar to those that first appeared in the decades following the opening of the Kingston Penitentiary in 1835.

THE PRISON

Perhaps no one component of the correctional system has received more publicity or been the subject of more controversy than the prison (or penitentiary/correctional institution). Since the building of the first penitentiaries in Canada and the United States in the nineteenth century, a vast literature has developed documenting nearly every aspect of prison life from the perspectives of both keeper and kept. While an in-depth examination of all the critical issues surrounding the operation and management of correctional institutions is beyond the scope of this text, we will attempt to highlight some of the more important dimensions of the structure and operation of Canadian correctional institutions.

The Prison in Society

In Chapter 10, we discussed the emergence of prisons as a form of punishment in Canada and identified the various factors in Canadian society that influenced the decision to construct the Kingston Penitentiary. Canadian prisons continue to be affected by the social, political, and economic forces in society, and there are several readily identifiable sources of influence on their day-to-day operation.

Politicians and legislatures, ever responsive to the concerns of their constituents, may enact legislation that results in more offenders being sent to prisons for longer periods of time. One legislative change that has had a significant impact on correctional institutions, particularly administrators, is Bill C-84, passed in 1976. Under this law, offenders convicted of second-degree murder must serve 10-25 years before being eligible for parole, while offenders convicted of first-degree murder must serve a mandatory 25-year term before parole eligibility.[2]

This legislation has created an increasing number of "lifers" in the federal prison system: one in five federal offenders is a lifer (approximately 2,100 offenders) and a large number of them (700) are in the Ontario region. In 1991-92, lifers comprised 3.5% of the admissions to federal institutions, and it is anticipated that over the next ten years, two of every five federal offenders will be serving life terms. Bill C-36, the *Corrections and Conditional Release Act* (1992), also requires certain categories of offenders to serve more than the standard one-third of their sentence prior to being eligible for parole. This will result in many offenders spending longer periods of time in confinement. The issues surrounding the long-term offender are considered in Chapter 13.

The criminal courts have a direct impact on the operation of correctional institutions. The sentencing practices of the judiciary may result in overcrowding in correctional institutions, leading to increased violence and major disturbances. The courts may also be involved in issuing decisions against correctional institutions to reduce overcrowding. The courts have been particularly active in the United States, and many state institutions are currently under court-imposed deadlines to reduce the size of their inmate populations. The Supreme Court of the United States has held in several cases that being confined in an overcrowded prison is a violation of an inmate's constitutional rights.

The entrenchment of a constitutional *Charter of Rights and Freedoms* increases the likelihood that the Canadian judiciary will be more involved in issues related to inmate civil rights, due process, and discipline within correctional institutions (see Alderson, 1991). Canadian courts have abandoned their traditional "hands off" approach to corrections and there is increased emphasis on procedural due process, although it is less certain that the power and broad discretion of corrections officials has been curtailed (see Mandell and Mandell, 1985).[3] The mass media also play an important role in providing information about correctional institutions and are the primary source of information about corrections for most citizens. Unfortunately, the media often focus on the more dramatic (and negative) events of institutional life, such as disturbances, suicides, and escapes. The positive achievements of inmates while confined, innovative correctional programming, and the contributions of senior administrative staff, correctional officers, and program staff are rarely featured.

Once criminal offenders are sentenced by the court, for most of the general citizenry, they are "out of sight, out of mind." Throughout the history of corrections, the role of the public in the operation of prisons has been primarily reactive. It began in the mid-1700s with the opposition of labour groups to the employment of inmates in Nova Scotia workhouses and to teaching craft skills to the inmates of the Kingston Penitentiary in the 1850s. General community concern is raised when there are escapes and riots or when federal and provincial agencies announce plans to locate correctional institutions and facilities in neighbourhoods. Resistance to such initiatives may be organized by correctional interest groups who mobilize community opposition. There are few instances of community interest groups operating in support of correctional initiatives or offenders. Ironically, the recessionary downturn over the past several years has led many communities to *proactively compete* to have new correctional facilities sited in their locale, purely for the economic benefits that accrue to the community in terms of employment and provision of services to the facility!

The Citizen Advisory Committees (CACs) established by the Correctional Service of Canada are designed to increase citizen participation in the correctional enterprise. The objectives of the CACs, which are comprised of volunteers from the community, are: (1) to promote positive interaction between the local community and the Correctional Service of Canada; (2) to provide assistance to offenders; and (3) to participate in the development of community resources for the correctional service. CAC members have access to the administration, staff, and inmates in the institution, may be involved in institutional and community programs, and often function in a liaison role between the community and the institution.

To date, however, there have been no evaluations of the activities of CACs across Canada, the manner in which members are selected, and the impact that CACs have on the operation of correctional institutions. This precludes a determination as to whether CACs are effective mechanisms for securing meaningful community involvement and whether the activities of the CACs have any impact on the dynamics of life inside correctional institutions.

With the exception of the CACs and various volunteer groups that sponsor programs inside correctional institutions, the general public remains an underused resource, and there is a great more that could be done by both federal and correctional agencies (and the media) to provide citizens with accurate information and the opportunity to play a substantive role in the correctional enterprise. As the majority of offenders in confinement will be returning to society, it is in the interests of both the community and individual citizens to understand and have input into the operation of correctional institutions.

The Prison as a Total Institution

In his classic treatise *Asylums: Essays on the Social Situation of Mental Patients and Other Inmates,* Erving Goffman (1961) introduced the concept of the "total institution" to describe life inside hospitals, concentration camps, mental hospitals, and prisons. A total institution, according to Goffman (1961:6) is "a place of residence and work where a large number of like-situated individuals, cut off from the wider society for an appreciable period of time, together lead an enclosed, formally administered round of life."

Goffman outlined the structure of daily life in total institutions:

1) All aspects of life are conducted in the same place and under the same single authority.
2) Each phase of the member's daily activity is carried on in the immediate company of a large batch of others, all of whom are treated alike and required to do the same thing together.
3) All phases of the day's activities are tightly scheduled, with one activity leading at a prearranged time into the next, the whole sequence of activities being imposed from above by a system of explicit formal rulings and a body of officials.
4) The various enforced activities are brought together into a single rational plan purportedly designed to fulfil the official aims of the institutions (1961:6).

Another major characteristic identified by Goffman (1961:7) is the split between the staff (correctional officers) and the inmates, each group viewing the other in terms of stereotypes: correctional officers perceive the inmates as secretive and untrustworthy, while the inmates view correctional officers as condescending and mean.

There are a number of important differences, however, between the concept of total institutions and correctional institutions.

▸ *The relations between the correctional staff (the keepers) and inmates (the kept) are complex and not always characterized by mutual hostility and suspicion.*

As our discussion below will reveal, a considerable amount of positive interaction occurs between prison staff and the inmates. At the very least, the staff and the inmates develop accommodative relationships that serve their mutual interests.

▸ *While all prisons can be properly labelled "total institutions," they vary in such key attributes as the size of the inmate population, security level, and administration, all of which may significantly affect the patterns of interaction that occur within them.*

Not all prisons are the same: some are more "total" than others. To reflect these differences, individual prisons can be located along a rough continuum of correctional institutions, with institutions that are less "totalistic" at one end and those that are extremely "totalistic" at the other. While security level is a primary determinant of an institution's location on the continuum, the attitudes and actions of the staff and the administration also play a significant role in determining the dynamics that develop.

Research studies have indicated that the more "total" an institution is in terms of the control exercised over offenders, the higher the levels of violence and strained relations between the inmates and the correctional staff. However, this may be a consequence of the types of offenders who tend to be confined in maximum-security institutions which, in turn, require a more "totalistic" environment.

The attributes of the institution will affect behaviour of the staff and the inmates, as well as the contingencies that confront the senior administration. It would be expected, for example, that maximum-security institutions would evidence more severe conditions of confinement and patterns of interaction among the inmates and between the inmates and the staff than would occur at a minimum-security work camp. Similarly, the majority of inmates in Canada serve their time in provincial facilities and, given the relatively short period of time these offenders serve inside, it is unlikely that the dynamics of life inside these institutions is similar to their federal counterparts.

▸   *Much of the research literature on correctional institutions is based on studies conducted in the United States, and the findings may not reflect the dynamics that exist inside Canadian institutions.*

While it can be anticipated that correctional institutions in the United States and Canada, as total institutions, share many of the same attributes, there are key differences in the size and composition of prisons between the two countries that may affect the dynamics of institutional life. While it is unusual, for example, for a Canadian prison to have an inmate population of over 700, in the United States, many state prisons have over 2,000 inmates. In the United States there is also considerable ethnic diversity in prison populations, which often leads to rival inmate factions and prison violence.

▸   *How applicable is Goffman's notion of the total institution to the correctional institution of the 1990s?*

There is little doubt that prisons have many of the attributes of total institutions; for example, offenders are confined in a specific locale for 24 hours a day and are controlled by a myriad of regulations. However, correctional institutions at all security levels are much more "open" than their predecessors of even 20 years ago. Inmates have access to television, family visits, and a variety of educational and vocational programs.

The mission statement of the Correctional Service of Canada is specifically directed toward the reintegration of offenders. While not discounting the severe effects of incarceration on offenders, nor the violence and exploitation that often characterize relations within the institution (primarily between the inmates), nevertheless we must acknowledge that correctional institutions have changed over the years and do have more contact with the "outside" world than in earlier times (see Farrington, 1992).

The Goals of Prisons

When the Kingston Penitentiary was constructed in 1835, there was little doubt that the primary goal of the institution was to punish offenders and, as the historical record indicates, this task was carried out in earnest. It was not until after World War II that correctional institutions took on the task of reform, although control and punishment remained goals of incarceration as well. Thus began what has become known as the "split personality" of correctional institutions: that prisons are to confine and control, while at the same time reforming and rehabilitating the offender.

Despite an attempt to pursue the dual mandate of punishment and rehabilitation, there is little doubt that the primary purpose of the prison is the punishment of offenders. This is reflected in a report of the federal Solicitor General (1981:16):

> ...prisons are primarily places of punishment, though other activities may go on inside them. Punishment is an element in any decision to send an offender to a federal penitentiary, and punishment is what corrections does demonstrably best.

Our discussion of correctional treatment will show that the requirements of custody and control have hindered the potential effectiveness of many of the programs designed to rehabilitate and reform offenders.

The mission statement of the Correctional Service of Canada states that it will strive to protect society and assist offenders to become law-abiding citizens, while exercising reasonable and secure control over offenders. The role of the prison in this effort, however, has not been clearly defined. The research literature and the findings of commissions of inquiries beginning with the Brown Commission report in 1848-49 suggests that imprisonment has failed in its two primary objectives: (1) it does not provide long-term protection to society, and (2) it does not rehabilitate most offenders. There is no evidence that imprisonment serves as either a specific or general deterrent to criminal behaviour. Historically, prisons have been little more than warehouses to which convicted offenders are banished for a specified period of time.

In the following discussion, we identify several factors that have largely prevented prisons from achieving their more reform-oriented goals. There may be differing (and often conflicting) goals pursued by the inmates, treatment staff, security personnel, and administration. Differences between the treatment staff and the correctional officers reflect the inherent conflict and tensions between control and rehabilitation.

Further, while all inmates share the common goal of being released from the institution as soon as possible, their relations may be characterized by a considerable amount of violence and exploitation. In 1992, there was one murder inside a provincial correctional facility and four in federal institutions (Canadian Centre for Justice Statistics, 1993).

While the well-documented failure of prisons to reform offenders has led some to call for the total abolition of correctional institutions (Morris, 1989), other observers such as Johnson (1987) argue that prison environments can be created that have a positive impact on offenders:

> Prisoners must serve hard time. This is both just, since criminals deserve to suffer for the harms they have done to others, and inevitable, since prisons are inherently painful. But hard time can also be constructive time: prisoners can learn something worthwhile during their confinement. The most valuable lessons that prisoners can learn are those that enable them to cope maturely with the pains of imprisonment (1987:4).

DOING TIME: THE WORLD OF THE INMATE

Offenders who are sent to correctional institutions in Canada encounter a world unlike any other. According to Goffman (1961:18-20), individuals who enter total institutions undergo a process of "mortification" that transforms them from citizens of the outside community to residents of the institution. Through a series of "status degradation ceremonies," the offender is psychologically and materially stripped of possessions that identify him or her as a member of the "free" society (see Garfinkel, 1965). These are replaced by an identification number, prison issue clothing, and a list of institutional rules and regulations designed to control every aspect of the inmate's life inside the institution as well as contact with the outside world.[4]

In his classic work *The Prison Community*, Clemmer (1940) coined the term "prisonization" to describe the process by which new inmates are socialized into the norms, values, and culture of the prison. These include the adoption of antisocial attitudes and behaviours and opposition to the authority of the institution. New inmates also become familiar with accommodative relationships that exist with correctional officers and other staff members. The degree to which offenders become "prisonized," however, may depend upon their individual personality, their pre-prison experiences, and the nature of the primary group relations they establish with other inmates in the prison. For many individuals, particularly those who have been "raised" in youth homes and detention centres before "graduating" to adult facilities, institutional life is the only life they have ever known. The prison provides security, friends, and room and board, none of which is guaranteed to the offender in the outside world. Offenders who have long periods in confinement and who have lost touch with the outside world run the risk of becoming "institutionalized" and unable (or unwilling) to function in the outside world.

One of the major reasons why the prison may never be successful in deterring individuals from engaging in further criminal activity is that it is not possible to predict how the individual will respond to the incarceration experience and whether the prison experience will result in the development of pro-social or anti-social attitudes and behaviours during confinement and upon release.

The Inmate Social System

A universal characteristic of correctional institutions is the existence of a social system among the inmates. Despite administrative pronouncements to "do your own time," the conditions of confinement make it difficult for the inmate to remain isolated from and unaffected by the prison milieu. To survive the rigors of prison life, nearly all inmates have some affiliation with a group or clique. Such groups may be formed on the basis of sentence (for example, the lifers group); racial identity; participation in religious or self-help groups; or pre-prison affiliations and friendships.

Since Clemmer's work in the 1940s, there have been attempts to understand the origins and functions of the inmate social system. In 1958, Gresham Sykes published *Society of Captives*, which was based on an in-depth examination of the lives of inmates in a U.S. maximum-security prison. Sykes argued that incarcerated offenders experienced several pains of imprisonment, including the loss of liberty, individual autonomy, and personal security, as well as the lack of access to goods and services and heterosexual relations.[5]

The lack of privacy is a major source of stress for prison inmates:

> You can be sitting there, and you know you're not alone. Where I'm at, I've got twenty-five guys on the gallery I'm on. So I've got like guys laying there, guys defecating, guys coughing, and it's close quarters... (quoted in Toch, 1977:31).

Further difficulties are caused by the boredom of daily life inside and the lack of contact with family and friends. In what has become known as the "deprivation theory" of inmate subcultures, Sykes (1958) argued that the inmate social system functioned to mitigate these pains of imprisonment.

In 1961, John Irwin and Donald Cressey proposed an alternative explanation — the "importation theory" — for the formation of the inmate social system, arguing that the criminal attitudes and behaviours that characterized the inmate social system were brought with offenders from their criminal careers on the outside. Research studies have generally indicated that both the importation and the deprivation theories are useful in understanding the inmate social system.

The major components of the inmate social system include: (1) a code of behaviour; (2) a hierarchy of power among the inmates; (3) an "informal" economic system, which provides illicit goods and services; and (4) a variety of social or "argot" roles assumed by prisoners. The convict code is designed to increase inmate solidarity and implores prisoners not to exploit one another, to be strong in confronting the deprivations of confinement, and to assume an oppositional stance toward prison authorities. The social system is also characterized by differential status levels among the inmates. Some inmates hold high-status positions and wield considerable power, often on the basis of their criminal career or access to, and ability to control, illicit goods and services within the institution. Offenders confined for sexual offences, particularly against children, tend to have the lowest status and to be susceptible to attack by other inmates.

There also appears to be a variety of social roles among the inmates, based to a large extent on group membership, sentence length, current and previous offences, degree of adherence to the traditional convict code, and participation in illegal activities such as gambling and drug distribution/use inside the prison. While there has been little research on prison social roles in Canadian institutions, studies of inmate social systems in the United States have consistently found that the majority of inmates fall into one of the following four types.

1) *Square-John*: pro-social in attitudes and behaviour; not involved in inmate sub-culture; and positive toward staff and administration.
2) *Right guy*: anti-social; heavily involved in inmate social system and opposed to staff and administration.
3) *Politician*: pseudo-social; manipulates both staff and inmates.
4) *Outlaw*: asocial; uses violence to victimize both staff and inmates.[6]

There is among inmates considerable variability in their vulnerability to the pains of imprisonment and the strategies that they employ to cope with them. Of concern to corrections officials is the potential for suicide among offenders. In provincial institutions, suicide is the leading cause of inmate death (others being natural causes and murder). In 1992, there were 21 inmate suicides in provincial institutions and 16 in federal facilities (Canadian Centre for Justice Statistics, 1993).

In a study of coping behaviour among inmates in 10 federal institutions in the Ontario, Zamble and Porporino (1988) found that correctional programming did little to assist offenders in altering inappropriate coping strategies and resulted in depression, stress, anger, and feelings of alienation. Offenders became concerned with survival in the prison environment and adjusting to the prison routine, rather than with developing coping strategies that would allow them to address their problems and make positive decisions about their future.

In his analysis of doing time, Johnson (1987:55-73) argues that inmates can mitigate the pains of imprisonment in constructive ways and thereby increase their chances for reform and success upon release back into the community. This is done through *mature coping*, which has several components: (1) dealing with problems in a straightforward manner rather than engaging in denial and manipulation; (2) avoiding the use of deception and violence in addressing problems; and (3) making an effort to care for oneself and others, for example, being altruistic. Through mature coping, Johnson argues, inmates develop self-esteem and maturity, learn to manage failure, and use the incarceration experience for personal growth.

Johnson (1987) is one of the few correctional observers who provides an optimistic scenario about the potential value of confinement. It is clear, however, that the extent to which an individual offender can engage in mature coping depends not only on the offender, but also on the staff and administration of the institution.

The Inmate Subculture: Fact or Fiction?

The concept of the inmate subculture, like that of the prison as a total institution, has proved valuable in increasing our understanding of the dynamics of life inside correctional institutions. However, upon closer examination, there is some question as to the extent to which inmates in prison constitute an oppositional subculture. Research suggests that inmates exhibit considerable variability in the extent to which they participate in the social system and in the degree to which they adhere behaviourally to the tenets of the inmate code. Ramirez (1984:451) found in a survey of correctional officers and inmate attitudes toward the severity of prohibited acts that "some groups of inmates exhibited more agreement with some groups of staff than they did with other groups of inmates." Ramirez (1984) concluded that there may not always be an "us versus them" split between the inmates and the correctional staff.

Despite the existence of a code of conduct that includes among its basic tenets a pledge of solidarity and a prohibition against inmates exploiting one another, inmate relations are often characterized by psychological intimidation and physical force. A rule of thumb for all inmates is that if they are going to be beaten, sexually assaulted, or murdered, it will most likely be at the hands of another inmate. Canadian correctional institutions, while having smaller populations than their U.S.

counterparts, do experience violence. During 1991-92, there were 63 major assaults on inmates. Forty percent of these events occurred in four of the 43 federal institutions (Correctional Service of Canada, 1992).

While the convict code would place inmates in opposition to any initiatives sponsored by the institution, inmates participate extensively in available educational and vocational opportunities (and often voice complaints that there are *insufficient* program opportunities available).

There is little doubt that correctional institutions have changed appreciably since the 1940s and 1950s when Donald Clemmer, Gresham Sykes, and others first began to study the dynamics of prison life. While a social system will be present among inmates in all institutions, the "strength" and "form" of this system will vary depending upon the security level of the institution, the orientation of the prison administration, and the characteristics of the inmate population. The inmate social system will be more pronounced in institutions oriented toward custody and control and with a higher security level where the deprivations are greater than in facilities that are more treatment oriented and at a lower security level. Further, it is unlikely that inmate social systems become well established in provincial correctional institutions, given the relatively short period of time offenders are confined.

Rather than a monolithic oppositional bloc, however, inmates now separate themselves into small groups of friends in a pattern of ordered segmentation. These groups may find themselves in conflict with one another, often over control over the importation and distribution of illicit goods and services. Within the security offered by a group or clique of friends, however, it may be possible for inmates to "do their own time." Despite the difficulties of remaining free from involvement in illicit activities inside, it is apparent that many inmates are able to complete their period of confinement without additional difficulties. This is what Johnson (1987) would refer to as "mature coping." The challenge for correctional administrators and staff is to create prison environments where inmates can use their period of incarceration in a productive, rather than destructive, manner.

Life in Women's Prisons

The above discussion presents materials on the social systems in institutions for adult male offenders. There is, however, a lack of published research on life inside institutions for female offenders in

Canada, perhaps due to the relatively small number of women in provincial facilities and in the Kingston Prison for Women. Research conducted in the United States and England suggests that the patterns of interaction that develop among female inmates are considerably different from those of their male counterparts (see Carlen *et al.,* 1985; Dobash, Dobash, and Gutteridge, 1986).

While the inmate social system in female institutions may include identifiable social roles, such as "snitches" (rats or squealers), "squares" (the accidental criminals who are pro-administration), and "jive bitches" (troublemakers among the inmates), the different roles that males and females play in outside society appear to have a significant impact on the patterns of interaction that develop within the institution. Among the differences identified by the research are the following:

▸ patterns of interaction among female inmates are less violent and result in much lower rates of inmate victimization than do those that characterize male institutions;

▸ the "pains of imprisonment" for female inmates include the loss of close, supportive family relationships and contribute to the development of pseudo-families that include "parents" and "relatives";

▸ homosexual relationships, whether within a pseudo-family arrangement or involving two women, are entered into voluntarily and for emotional support rather than as an expression of physical dominance and aggression;

▸ institutions for female offenders are characterized by less overt conflict between the inmates and the staff and administration than are male institutions;

▸ the *sub rosa* economic system that provides illicit goods and services in male institutions is generally absent from female facilities, most likely due to the lack of pre-prison criminal career experiences among the women and the physical setting of female institutions, which is often less depriving than that of male facilities.

Wilson (1986:402) suggests that the differences in the social systems between male and female institutions may be due, at least in part, to "organizational rules, staff training and attitudes, and staff expectations of inmates." From a survey of male and female inmates in a mixed (co-educational) provincial facility in Alberta, Wilson (1986) found no differences between the two genders in their stated level of commitment on several measures of the inmate code, including group solidarity and distrust of staff. This finding led Wilson to conclude that "the prison environment plays a significant role in the degree of commitment to the inmate code held by its charges" (1986:405).

These attributes do not necessarily apply to female inmates in Canada. The short period of confinement of offenders in provincial institutions, for example, would seem to preclude the development of pseudo-families, while the confinement of all federal female offenders (except those who remain in provincial institutions under federal/provincial agreements) in the multi-level institution at Kingston (scheduled for closure in 1993) may result in patterns of interaction unique to the Canadian context. We will return to a consideration of the female offender in Canada in Chapter 13.[7]

THE CLASSIFICATION OF OFFENDERS

Classification is particularly important in any discussion of institutional programs. The initial classification decision following sentencing, and subsequent assessments by case management teams during the offender's term of confinement, will determine: (1) the level and type of institution the offender will be confined in, and (2) the program opportunities available to the offender. In Canada, the classification of offenders assumes a critical role in the correctional process, as convicted offenders are not sentenced to a specific institution by the court, but rather to a specific length of time in confinement.

Classification can be generally defined as "a continuous process through which diagnosis, treatment-planning and the execution of the treatment plan are coordinated to the end that the individual inmate may be rehabilitated" (Ouimet Committee, 1969:11). Federal classification policy is premised on two concepts: *direct penitentiary placement* and *cascading* (on the basis of assessments by an institutional case management team, conducted at least once a year, inmates are transferred to progressively lower levels of security as their time remaining to be served decreases). Following sentencing, those offenders whose sentence length (two years or more) places them under the jurisdiction of federal corrections are classified by a community case management officer, a parole officer of the Correctional Service of Canada, in the provincial institution to which they were remanded. The sole exception is in the province of Quebec, where the classification decision is made at a Regional Reception Centre. Classification decisions for offenders under provincial jurisdiction (a sentence or sentences totalling two years less a day) are made by classification units in each province.[8]

The community case management officer identifies the initial security level for the offender based on the security and programming needs of the offender, considering such factors as the nature and seriousness of the offence and criminal history and the length of sentence received. Under the Direct Penitentiary Placement scheme, the offender is then sent directly to a specific institution. The classification process continues throughout the offender's confinement through cascading.

A primary consideration in all classification decisions is the security risk of the offender. The Correctional Service of Canada uses three broad levels of security.

1) *Maximum security:* The inmate is likely to escape and, if successful, would be likely to cause serious harm in the community.
2) *Medium security:* the inmate is likely to escape if given the opportunity, but should not cause serious harm in the community should such an escape occur.
3) *Minimum security:* the inmate is not likely to escape and would not cause harm in the community if such an escape should occur.

Despite its pivotal role, the development and application of adequate classification systems has been an elusive goal. Historically, little concern was given to the age, gender, or criminal history of offenders, and in contemporary times, the Correctional Service of Canada has been criticized with "overclassifying" offenders — placing them at higher security levels than is warranted, often due to overcrowding and lack of adequate facilities.

Within the framework of the mission statement, however, federal corrections has given increased attention to the classification process. As part of the Corporate Operational Plan (COP), the Correctional Service of Canada has set out a correctional strategy designed to "ensure that offenders receive the most effective programs at the appropriate time in their sentences to allow them to serve the greatest proportion of their sentences in the community with the lowest risk of recidivism" (Delnef, 1992:6). A key component of the correctional strategy is a comprehensive assessment of the risk and needs of each offender upon their entry into the corrections system. And, in 1990-91, the Correctional Service of Canada initiated a custody rating system designed to ensure that the level of security to which the offender is assigned corresponds to the risk level of the offender.

INSTITUTIONAL PROGRAMS

The Correctional Service of Canada and the various provincial/territorial correctional agencies operate a wide variety of institutional programs for offenders. These include inmate employment and work programs; occupational and vocational training programs; educational programs; chaplaincy and religious services; athletic and recreational services; medical, dental, and psychiatric services; and programs and services provided by volunteer and outside agencies. These programs attempt to meet the needs of an offender population recently described as follows:

> ...40 percent are functionally illiterate; many have a drug or alcohol dependency; most have few marketable skills and a history of sporadic employment; many have learning disabilities, poor social skills, family problems, and low maturation. A few have severe mental disorders but cannot be accommodated by the mental health system (Government of Canada, 1986:287-88).

In 1938, the report of the Royal Commission on the Penal System of Canada, chaired by Justice Archambault, asserted that in addition to protecting the community, prisons should assume the task of reformation. In 1956, a Committee of Inquiry under the chairmanship of Justice Fauteux reaffirmed rehabilitation as the primary objective of corrections, and noted the failure of the correctional system to implement the recommendations of the Archambault Committee (1938) made nearly two decades earlier. Beginning in the late 1940s, a wide variety of educational, vocational training, and treatment programs were introduced in federal and provincial institutions, although the introduction of rehabilitative programs was slow and uneven.

A guiding principle of the rehabilitative approach was the "medical model," which viewed offenders as "sick" and criminal behaviour as symptomatic of some underlying disorder in the emotional makeup or psyche of the offender. Proper diagnosis of the "illness," followed by appropriate therapeutic intervention, would promote reformation. The strong clinical orientation of the medical model led to the increased involvement of psychologists and psychiatrists in designing and operating treatment programs. A wide variety of treatment modalities were introduced, including individual and group psychotherapy, reality therapy, transactional analysis, psychodrama, and behaviour modification.[9]

As noted in Chapter 10, the rehabilitation model was implemented with considerable optimism during the 1950s and 1960s, but fell out of favour in the mid-1970s, and correctional services underwent a period of retrenchment. With the mission statement, the Correctional Service of Canada appears to be moving, albeit cautiously, back toward a focus on reformation and reintegration of the offender. This has spawned a renewed emphasis on correctional programming, which includes education and vocational training initiatives, as well as various counselling and treatment programs.

The correctional strategy of the Correctional Service of Canada sets out the priorities for institutional programming. This includes core intervention programs, education programs, specialized intervention programs, programs for specific groups of offenders such as the female offender and Aboriginal offenders, and vocational training and industry programs. Below, we consider several of the more high-profile initiatives that have been undertaken and attempt to provide information on the extent to which these initiatives have been successful in achieving their objectives. We will consider programs for female offenders in Chapter 13 and initiatives designed to address the needs of Aboriginal offenders in Chapter 15.

Despite these initiatives, evidence suggests that the general public has very little information about the various rehabilitation programs offered in correctional institutions. Citizens in two surveys reported by Adams (1990) felt that rehabilitation should be one, but not the major, goal of confinement; that rehabilitating inmates is difficult because many are repeat offenders; and that some offenders cannot be rehabilitated. Support for the principle of rehabilitation has also been reported in surveys of the general public conducted in the United States:

> ...the public believes that rehabilitation should be a goal of correc-
> tions...citizens do not feel that time in prison should be wasted;

prisons should not be warehouses or places that inflict pain without clear purpose. Instead, most citizens take a more pragmatic stance: Inmates should be given education, training, employment experiences and...counselling that will enable them to become productive citizens (Cullen *et al.*, 1990:15-16).

Results from the Canadian studies indicate that citizens are much more familiar with community corrections programs, including halfway houses, most likely because of controversies where such facilities should be located. This finding suggests that the provincial and federal corrections services must do much more to solicit the general public's support for the rehabilitation and reintegration of offenders.

Core Intervention Programs

Core programs attempt to address the needs that a majority of offenders in prison have and include cognitive skills training, the personal and interpersonal development courses — Living Without Violence, Family Life/Parenting Skills, and Anger/Emotion Management — and various pre-release programs designed to prepare the offender for life on the outside. The life skills program is designed to teach offenders to think rationally and objectively and to take responsibility for their behaviour. An evaluation of the life skills training program at three federal institutions in Ontario (Marshall, 1989) found that the training produced the desired changes in the inmates participating in the program, changes that may be related to an increased likelihood of success upon release.

One component of life skills training is the cognitive skills program, which focuses on teaching inmates the basic principles of interpersonal relationships. The program:

> ...teaches offenders to identify problems, subject them to rational analysis, consider the alternatives and make objective and well-founded decisions. It also teaches them to prejudge their actions and to determine what the long-term consequences of those actions will mean to others and themselves (Andresen, 1990).

A preliminary assessment of two pilot projects (one in the Pacific region and one in the Atlantic region) using the cognitive skills training Program (Fabiano, Robinson, and Porporino, 1990:40) found that the two pilot programs were successful in impacting several key attitudinal and cognitive skills areas of the inmate participants:

> Offenders who received the program became more positive in their attitudes toward the law, courts and police, increased their social perspective-taking abilities, improved in critical reasoning skills, and showed more capacity for optional thinking.

Further research is needed to assess the impact of the cognitive skills program on participating offenders' behaviour once they are released from the institution. The results to date are encouraging, particularly in view of the fact that the inmates in the pilot program were considered to be "high need" in terms of treatment and "high risk" upon release.

A key attribute of all of these initiatives is the attempt to involve the inmate in a substantive way in the treatment process, a notable shift from the early days of the rehabilitation model when "experts" were presumed to possess the requisite skills to diagnose and treat.

Prison Education Programs

The regimen of strict discipline and hard labour in early Canadian institutions did not provide the opportunity for the development of education programs. The few literacy programs that were implemented in the 1800s were operated by prison chaplains and available to only a few selected inmates. Over the years, various reports and commissions of inquiry have criticized federal corrections for failing to make the education of inmates a high priority despite the fact that a large number of offenders have severe educational deficiencies. In 1991, for example, approximately 65% of inmates in federal correctional facilities (compared to 25% in the general population) had math and language skills below the level of grade eight.

Education appears to be receiving increased attention in federal corrections, although it is less certain whether provincial systems will follow suit. Through its education and training division, the Correctional Service of Canada offers courses in 26 institutions, including adult basic education (ABE) (to grade eight level), secondary education (high school), college and university-level courses, and vocational education. The highest percentage of inmates are enrolled in ABE courses.

The role of education in reducing subsequent criminal behaviour among inmates is unclear. A study by the Correctional Service of Canada found that inmates who complete the ABE program — a literacy and numerical skills program that, when completed, is equivalent to grade eight — had a readmission rate 12% lower than inmates who had withdrawn from the program (Porporino and Robinson, 1992). More specifically, those offenders who were classified as "high risk" — inmates who had previously served periods of confinement in federal correctional facilities, offenders who had received longer sentences, inmates convicted of violent offences, and younger offenders — benefitted more from ABE in terms of reduced readmission than did lower-risk offenders. Interviews with a sample of offenders provided evidence that the ABE program played a significant role in their reentry into the community.

There has also been an attempt to assess the effectiveness of university-level education offered within federal correctional facilities. Duguid (1981) found that only 15% of a group of 75 offenders who had participated in the university-level program operated by Simon Fraser University were reincarcerated during a three-year follow-up period, compared to a rate of 55% to 65% for those offenders who had not participated in the prison education program. However, Lockwood (1991) found no difference in serious criminal involvement upon release between those inmates who had participated in an university-level education program in a U.S. prison and those who had not. Much more research remains to be done on the potential role of education in reducing recidivism and ways to maximize the value of the educational experience for inmates.

Specialized Intervention Programs

In recent years, increased attention has been given to the specialized treatment needs of offenders. These include alcohol and drug abuse and the special needs of mentally disordered offenders.[10] Alcoholic Anonymous (AA) programs and Narcotics Anonymous (NA) programs operate in many institutions. In addition, attempts have been made to increase counselling and treatment programs for sex offenders. These initiatives have been precipitated by research that indicates that a high percentage of offenders have been involved in alcohol and substance abuse and that a large number of inmates have serious mental problems that require specialized intervention.

Among the more innovative initiatives is the ECHO (Experience,

Change and Orientation), which operates in facilities in the Quebec region of the Correctional Service of Canada and is directed toward substance abusers. The program is premised on a self-help philosophy and is designed to facilitate personal growth. At the Stony Mountain Institution in Manitoba, the Breaking Barriers program also focuses on self-awareness and personal growth and has been introduced in provincial facilities throughout the province as well. In the Ontario region, the Offender Substance Abuse Pre-Release Program assists offenders with alcohol and drug abuse problems to develop cognitive and behavioural learning skills to assist them in reentry.

The success of these various specialized treatment initiatives is difficult to determine. Again, any conclusive statements about the ability of these programs to reduce or eliminate criminal behaviour upon release are precluded by the lack of research evaluations.

Prison Industries and Vocational Training

Historically, correctional services have experienced difficulty in providing sufficient vocational training opportunities for inmates that would provide them with marketable skills upon release. Currently, occupational and vocational training are provided in a number of areas, including autobody repair, carpentry, and welding. The specific training provided is dependent upon the inmate's security classification and the programs available in the institution, although there is considerable variability between institutions in the types of vocational training opportunities available. These training initiatives are often integrated into prison industry programs and various programs operated by CORCAN, the federal prison industries corporation.

Historically, the primary obstacle to the expansion of prison industry programs was the *Penitentiary Act*, which specified that goods and services produced by federal inmates could be sold only to federal, provincial, and municipal governments or to charitable, religious, and non-profit organizations. This restriction reflected the legacy of the resistance by outside labour to allowing products produced in the prison to compete on the open market. However, among the provisions of the *Corrections and Conditional Release Act* (1992), which repealed the *Penitentiary Act*, is that CORCAN may enter into agreements with private sector companies to produce or supply goods and services and may dispose of inmate-produced goods in the private sector under competitive conditions. In addition, CORCAN is given the authority to enter into agreements with private firms to train and employ inmates in private ventures located within correctional institutions. It remains to be seen whether CORCAN's expanded mandate will result in the development of viable industries within federal correctional facilities that will serve to train inmates in marketable employment skills.

Evidence suggests that the anticipated resistance by the community and the business sector to expanded prison industries may have been overestimated. Research by MacDonald (1982) in Canada and Cullen and Travis (1984) in the United States found widespread support for paying inmates and allowing prison-produced goods to be sold on the open market, so long as such products were not subsidized or given any other unfair competitive advantage (see Gandy and Hurl, 1987).

THE EFFECTIVENESS OF TREATMENT PROGRAMS

The rehabilitative approach to criminal offenders came under attack in the late 1960s and early 1970s. However, federal and provincial corrections services appear to be returning to a focus on rehabilitation and reintegration of offenders. We have noted that the lack of evaluative research precludes an assessment of the effectiveness of various treatment initiatives. On a more general level, it is instructive to consider several of the issues that have been raised about the effectiveness of correctional programs, if only to avoid the mistakes of the past and increase the potential viability of current and future treatment initiatives.

Drawing the Battle Lines: "Nothing Works" vs. "Some Things Work"

"With few and isolated exceptions, the rehabilitative efforts that have been reported so far have had no appreciable effect on recidivism" (Martinson, 1974:25). This is the (in)famous "nothing works" conclusion of Robert Martinson who had examined over 200 evaluations of correctional treatment programs conducted between 1945 and 1967. This is also the widely reported finding that contributed to the decline of the rehabilitation model of correctional practice in U.S. and Canadian corrections in the late 1960s and early 1970s. It also sparked a debate over the effectiveness of correctional treatment that continues today (see Doob and Brodeur, 1989; Gendreau and Ross, 1987; Gendreau and Andrews, 1990; Lab and Whitehead, 1990). Unfortunately, the discussion of treatment effectiveness has often become bogged down in rhetoric and coloured by ideology. Gendreau and Ross (1979:464-65), two leading proponents of the "some things work" perspective of correctional treatment, note that in the effectiveness debate, "The antagonists seemed to be more intent on winning arguments than seeking the truth." Gendreau and Ross (1987) have been leading proponents of the "some things work" perspective of correctional treatment.

There are two critical ingredients to the treatment process: (1) the individual offender; and (2) how the treatment programs are delivered within the institution. Evidence suggests that some offenders are more amenable to treatment than others; that is, they have a higher level of motivation to change, have acknowledged responsibility for their criminal behaviour and view involvement in treatment as a way to facilitate change, rather than merely as a way to secure release through parole. Offenders, then, have a differential amenability to treatment that will play a significant role in determining treatment impact.

How treatment programs are delivered within the institution is also important and affects the potential success of interventions in reducing the level of criminal activity upon release (see Ekstedt and Griffiths, 1988). Every attempt must be made by the senior administration, the treatment staff, and the correctional officers to create an atmosphere in the institution that is conducive to offender reformation. The dynamics that develop in the total institutional world of the prison (including the strict rules and regulations that govern every aspect of inmate life), the violence and exploitation that often characterize relations between the inmates often compete with the objectives of treatment programs, which include developing self-confidence, accepting responsibility for one's actions, and behaving in a positive and productive manner. The following are among the more important questions that must be asked.

- ▸ Have the offenders been properly classified and their specific treatment needs identified?
- ▸ Are there adequate treatment resources in the institution to meet the identified needs of individual offenders?
- ▸ Have the senior administration, the treatment staff, and the correctional officers created an environment in the institution conducive to treatment and change?

The research evidence to date suggests that some treatment programs do work with some offenders. A critical factor is that of differential treatment effectiveness — recognizing that individual offenders must be "matched" with the appropriate treatment intervention. There must also be continuity of treatment from the institution to the community once the offender is released from the institution. This is particularly important for those people convicted of "high risk" offences, such as sexual assault against children. And the federal corrections service has now recognized that inmates serving life sentences require special handling and have different programming needs than inmates serving shorter sentences. The *Task Force Report on Long-Term Sentences*, produced by the Correctional Service of Canada (Perron, 1991), offered a number of recommendations relating to programming for lifers during their often lengthy periods of incarceration (see also Porporino, 1991).

In summary, despite Martinson's conclusion that nothing works, there is a growing body of research evidence that indicates that "appropriate correctional treatment — treatment that is delivered to higher risk cases, targets criminogenic need, and is matched with the learning styles of offenders — will be associated with reduced recidivism" (Andrews *et al.*, 1990:377).

Measuring the Success of Treatment Interventions

How is it determined that a specific treatment program is a "success"? Measuring the effectiveness of treatment programs continues to be a difficult task. The majority of evaluations use recidivism rates to assess the impact of treatment programs on the offender. This involves determining the "rate of return" of released offenders back to institutions, either due to a technical violation of their parole or mandatory supervision conditions or the commission of a new offence. To ascertain the effectiveness of a particular treatment program, the recidivism rate of offenders who have participated in a treatment program is compared with that of offenders who have not been involved in the program.

There is disagreement among correctional observers concerning the usefulness of recidivism rates as accurate indicators of treatment effectiveness. Critics argue that recidivism rates are poor indicators of the effectiveness of correctional treatment because:

> ► by focusing on the violation of the law as a measure of
> success, they obscure improvements in the individual, such

as an increased level of education or the acquisition of a vocational skill;

▸ the individual may have returned to criminal activity, but not have been detected by the criminal justice system;

▸ many factors, other than having participated in a program while confined, contribute to an individual's success upon release back into the community, including a supportive family, stable employment, and the process of maturation; and

▸ the fact that offenders who participated in a particular treatment program are returned to prison is not conclusive evidence that the program itself is ineffective.

In recent years, there has been an increasing recognition of the limitations of using recidivism rates to assess the effectiveness of correctional programs, although alternative measures have not yet been implemented.

Inmate Involvement in the Treatment Process

Correctional treatment during the 1950s and 1960s considered the inmate as a passive participant in the treatment process. Treatment "experts," for example, psychologists, psychiatrists, and social workers, were presumed to have the requisite skills to diagnose and prescribe a regimen of treatment. Offenders were rarely consulted as to their perceived treatment needs nor were they encouraged to become involved in activities related to the local community and the "outside" world.

There appears to be an increased emphasis, particularly by the federal Correctional Service of Canada, on involving inmates directly in the treatment process. One of the core values of the mission statement of the Correctional Service of Canada states: "We respect the dignity of individuals, the rights of all members of society, and the potential for human growth and development." Strategic objective 1.1 of this core value states: "To ensure that offenders are informed participants in the correctional process, we will establish and maintain mechanisms for discussion and cooperation."

Given that the "silent system" — which forbade inmates to speak with one another except with permission of the prison staff — was not abolished in federal correctional institutions until the early 1950s, the recognition of the offender as an active participant in the reformation process represents a significant step forward.

Another recognition of the offender as an active participant is reflected in the adoption of the opportunities model, whereby inmates are given the responsibility to take advantage of the various vocational, educational, and treatment programs that are made available in the institution and in various inmate-initiated programs that have appeared in many federal institutions.

Inmates across the country are also involved in a wide variety of community events, including·fundraising for charities, participating in various sporting events with outside teams and organizations, and volunteering. The following are a few of the more notable examples:

▸ Inmates from Springhill medium-security institution in Nova Scotia work with severely mentally and physically disabled residents of the Pugwash Sunset Residential and Rehabilitation Centre; inmates from the institution also participate in a River Enhancement Project, Barbs and Bars, where inmate and community volunteers work to enhance rivers and streams in the area.

▸ Inmates at William Head Institution, near Victoria, British Columbia, developed and operate a similar program for developmentally disabled persons from Glendale Lodge. Several times per week, the Glendale residents travel to the institution for one-on-one and group activities with the inmate group. Inmates also receive temporary absences to visit the residents at Glendale Lodge and several inmates on parole have been hired as staff at the lodge.

▸ Inmates at the Beaver Creek minimum-security facility in Ontario have been involved for the past 15 years with Camp Dorset, a special summer camp for kidney dialysis patients and their families.

There is little doubt that the pains of imprisonment first identified by Sykes in the 1950s are still very real for inmates in Canadian correctional institutions. The constant threat of violence, the loneliness and anxiety that accompany the loss of freedom, and the uncertainty of when one will be released all combine to make the prison, first and foremost, a place of punishment. Over the past decade, however, it does appear, as Farrington

(1992) has argued, that many correctional institutions have become less "total" and that there are developing, albeit very slowly, increasing contacts with the "outside" world.

CORRECTIONAL OFFICERS

While correctional officers occupy a critical position in the prison, the occupation has traditionally been characterized by low prestige, poor pay, inadequate training, and high turnover. Historically, the primary motivations for becoming a correctional officer were job stability and fringe benefits, rather than a keen interest in working with offenders (see Willett, 1983). Over the past decade, however, particularly at the federal level, there has been an increased focus on the role of correctional officers who heretofore have been an underutilized resource within correctional institutions. No longer are correctional officers viewed as merely "turnkeys" whose sole duty is custody and control; rather there has been an attempt to expand the role of correctional officers and make them active participants in the pursuit of various strategic objectives.

This shift is reflected in core value 3 of the Correctional Service of Canada's (1992) mission statement: "We believe that our strength and our major resource in achieving our objectives is our staff and that human relationships are the cornerstone of our endeavour." Among the guiding principles of core value 3 are the following.

> ▸ All staff are correctional staff and are responsible for being active, visible participants in the correctional process and in achieving the objectives of the Service.
> ▸ We will be sensitive to the staff members' individual needs, interests, capacities, values and aspirations in the workplace.
> ▸ We believe that staff have a lot to contribute and that they must be able to voice their ideas and concerns within the Service, without fear.

Federal institutions are structured on the Unit Management Program, which was introduced in 1986. Each unit has a unit manager, who is directly responsible to the deputy warden, correctional operations, for all of the unit's activities, including case management, security, programming, health and safety, as well as administrative concerns. The unit manager supervises the unit team, which consists of correctional supervisors, case management officers, and two levels of correctional officers. The objective of unit management is to decentralize authority and decision making to the individual unit level and to create an environment that facilitates close communication within the unit team and between team members and the inmates. Several provincial corrections systems have also adopted the unit management approach.

There are obstacles, however, to increasing correctional officer contact with inmates. The Correctional Service of Canada Committee on Staff/Inmate Interaction has found, for example, that the extent and quality of staff/inmate interaction has been reduced in recent years due to the "high tech" security systems in new correctional facilities and various security measures that have been implemented in an attempt to protect correctional staff.

Recruitment, Training, and Education of Correctional Officers

In an attempt to improve the overall quality of its correctional officers, the Correctional Service of Canada has strengthened its staff training and development program and now attempts to recruit only individuals who are graduates of universities or community colleges or of accredited correctional training programs. The Correctional Service of Canada operates a twelve-week Correctional Officer Training Program (COTP) and a one- to eight-week Correctional Staff Orientation Program (CSOP), which are designed to provide new correctional officers with the skills required to be effective in the institutional environment. Traditionally, there has been very little "carry-over" from training courses to the operational setting of the prison, and this has often hindered efforts to alter significantly the role of correctional officers.

A recent report (Price-Waterhouse, 1990) on the recruitment program of the Correctional Service of Canada provides interesting information on persons recruited for the service during the five-year period 1985-89. Sixty-three percent of the recruits were under the age of 30, 66% were male, and 50% of the recruits under the age of 21 had post-secondary education with a specialization in criminal justice. Over the five-year period of the study, 20% of the recruits left the Correctional Service of Canada. In 1992, nearly 33% of Correctional Service of Canada personnel were women, while visible minorities, Aboriginal peoples, and the disabled each comprised 2.1% of the total workforce.

There are no national standards for the selection and training of correctional officers at the provincial level, and there is considerable variability across the various jurisdictions in selection criteria and training programs. In British Columbia, correctional officers are trained at the Justice Institute, which serves as a training facility for municipal police as well. In other provinces, training programs for correctional officers are offered through college and university programs.

There are a number of disturbing findings from Price-Waterhouse (1990) relating to gender. Women were found to leave the Correctional Service of Canada at a rate twice that of men; men were promoted at a higher rate than women; and neither education nor prior experience was related to promotions.

In 1992, women represented 33% of Correctional Service of Canada personnel. However, while one-third of them are in administrative support positions, only 13% of senior management positions are filled by women. While 83% of the men surveyed felt that significant progress had been made in providing equal opportunities for women to advance, only 56% of the women surveyed held this view. Eighty-three percent of the men surveyed stated that senior management was committed to addressing the gender imbalance in employment opportunities, while only 37% of the women held this view. There was also concern among the men surveyed that affirmative action initiatives discriminated in favour of women, while women felt that, in order to advance within the organization, they were required to adapt to a male-dominated environment.

These facts raise some very serious questions about employment equity in the Correctional Service of Canada and suggest that there should be increased attention by senior management to gender issues. In 1992, the Correctional Service of Canada created the Career Correctional Management system, which sets objective job and performance standards against which all employees will be measured. This is the first step in what will be a long process to ensure employment equity in federal corrections. There are similar concerns regarding the recruitment and promotion opportunities for Aboriginal peoples, visible minorities, and the disabled. Such concerns exist in provincial corrections as well.

On the Line: The Occupation of Correctional Officer

Chapter 3 noted that police officers work within an occupational subculture that influences their attitudes and behaviour on the job. It has been suggested that a similar occupational subculture exists among correctional officers and, in recent years, studies have examined the various aspects of the correctional officer's position in the prison that may impact their perspective and behaviour.

Similar to their police recruit counterparts who must learn how to exercise discretion on the street, new correctional officers undergo a period of socialization into life inside the total institutional world of the prison. Through their actions, new officers must convince the other members of their workgroup that they are "solid," and there is often a period of "probation" until the neophyte proves that he or she can be trusted. It might be expected that, similar to the inmate social system, the patterns of interaction that develop among correctional officers will be in part determined by the "continuum of correctional institutions," that is by the security level, institutional "climate," and the administrative policies of the institution.

New officers must also learn the subtle non-verbal cues that help them to "read" individual inmates and to develop strategies to use in response to "being tested" by the inmates. This process is often called becoming "con-wise." The new officer must also become familiar with the intricacies of the inmate social system, the various "scams" that inmates become involved in, such as gambling and distribution of contraband, and how to interact with inmates to avoid being "taken in."

Many observers have argued that, similar to their police counterparts, the stigma attached to being a correctional officer by the community, the perceptions by officers that they cannot talk to "civilians" about their work, and the reliance of officers upon one another in an unpredictable, potentially dangerous environment contribute to solidarity among officers (see Philliber, 1987). Others, however, have argued that correctional officer solidarity and the extent to which officers constitute an occupational subculture have been overstated (see Klofas and Toch, 1982).

In his survey of correctional officers, Willett (1983) found that correctional officers did not tend to socialize with one another during off-hours, although officers did experience considerable stress associated with their occupation, which often adversely affected their family relationships. A more recent survey conducted by the Correctional Service of Canada (Robinson, Simourd, and Porporino, 1991) found that very few correctional officers were hesitant to reveal their occupation to people in the community, and the majority felt that they had made a good career choice in selecting to work in corrections.

A majority of the correctional officers in the sample expressed positive attitudes toward rehabilitation and a "middle" to "high" level of commitment to the organizational goals of the Correctional Service of Canada. Of particular significance is that those respondents who worked directly with offenders — the correctional officers and case managers — expressed the *lowest* levels of commitment to the organization, while the highest levels of commitment were expressed by administrative personnel. This is a somewhat ominous finding, given that the correctional officers and the case managers at the unit level in institutions are the ones who must carry out the policies and programs of senior administration and are the ones who have the most extensive contact with the inmates.

This same survey also attempted to identify the sources of stress experienced by correctional staff, including correctional officers. Interestingly, relations with inmates and with co-workers were identified as being equally stressful. The most commonly cited sources of stress were security issues in the institution, followed by poor communication in the organization and workload demands. For many officers, the stress associated with interacting with other officers is as great as that caused by staff-inmate relations.

While correctional officers play a major role in carrying out the policy directives of senior administration in the institution, relations between the two groups may be characterized by suspicion and distrust. Depending upon the particular "style" of senior management in the prison, administrators may be viewed as insensitive to the needs of officers, as far removed from the realities of daily life in the institution, and as having little understanding of inmates and the practical realities of implementing prison regulations and administrative directives.

Interviews with correctional officers conducted by Hughes (1990) found that inconsistent policy directives and a perceived lack of support from senior management were the greatest sources of stress for correctional staff. Relations with inmates and co-workers were the next most serious sources of stress. Respondents also indicated that stress from work caused serious family problems. These findings highlight the importance of the organizational environment in which correctional officers work and suggest that, similar to the inmate residents, correctional officers must develop coping strategies to work within the prison.

Patterns of Correctional Officer-Inmate Interaction

We have previously noted that, in practice, inmates do not often adhere behaviourally to the tenets of the inmate code. This is evident in the accommodative relations that develop between the inmates and correctional officers. While correctional officers may be referred to as "pigs," "the police," or "the man" by inmates, there are pressures on each group to accommodate the other — the inmates to reduce the pains of imprisonment and the correctional officers to ensure stability and order on a day-to-day basis.

The specific patterns of interaction that develop between the correctional officers and the inmates will depend upon a variety of factors, including the size of the inmate population, the security level of the institution, and the policies and management style of the senior administration. Similar to their police counterparts, correctional officers exercise considerable discretion in carrying out their tasks within the institution. Unlike police officers, however, much of the decision making of correctional officers is "invisible," and there is little danger of an abuse of power and authority (for example, the excessive use of force being videotaped by a bystander).[11]

As officers become familiar with the prison environment, stereotypical views of criminals are replaced by the realization that each inmate is an individual and that not all inmates are alike. Similar to police officers, correctional officers develop their own "style" of carrying out their tasks and of coping with the demands placed upon them by inmates and administration. New officers must become acquainted with the informal accommodative relations that exist between the inmates and the correctional officers. Should an officer fail to display flexibility in decision making, he or she may be the subject of criticism from both the inmates and fellow officers. Conversely, an officer must avoid being viewed as too "pro-inmate" by his or her colleagues, which will result in diminished status in the workgroup. It is indeed a fine line that correctional officers must walk in carrying out their duties day to day.

Correctional officers employ a considerable amount of discretion in the interpretation and enforcement of prison regulations. Most officers take a common-sense approach in applying regulations to specific situations, realizing that full enforcement of prison regulations would make life unbearable for both themselves and the inmates. To maintain control, officers may employ a variety of "informal" sanctions against inmates, such as ignoring inmate requests and delaying the movement of an inmate from one area of the prison to another.

A long-standing concern of correctional administrators is the corruption of correctional officers, which may take one of the following forms: (1) theft, including stealing from inmate cells; (2) bringing contraband, such as drugs, money, or weapons, into the prison; (3) misappropriating government property for private use; and (4) abusing authority for personal gain (see McCarthy, 1984). The extent of officer corruption in contemporary Canadian corrections is unknown, although incidents of malfeasance should be reduced with the increased training, education, and sense of professionalism of correctional officers. Increased education and training initiatives for correctional officers will produce positive results only if institutional environments are created in which officers can function as agents of change. There must also be increased attention to the impact of the various stressors that correctional officers experience and the impact of these on their attitudes and behaviours.

MANAGING CORRECTIONAL INSTITUTIONS

Despite the pivotal role of the warden in the operation of the prison, historically individuals occupying this position have often not been equal to the task. The focus of the Brown Commission inquiry in 1848 was the mismanagement of Kingston Penitentiary by its first warden, Henry Smith. Similar inquiries, such as the Royal Commission (Canada, 1895) inquiry into the activities of the warden of the British Columbia Penitentiary in 1894, also focused on allegations of misconduct. At the local level, the character and conduct of the individuals given responsibility for supervising jails were often indistinguishable from those of their inmate clients.

Prior to the 1940s, the management of prisons was based on a paramilitary model, under which wardens had total, dictatorial control. Within the walls, the warden's word was "law," and absolute power over both the guards and the inmates was maintained by strict regimentation and harsh responses to those who violated the rigid rules: "Wardens mixed terror, incentives, and favouritism to keep their subjects fearful but not desperate, hopeful but always uncertain" (Bartollas, 1981:266). Following World War II, correctional management systems were implemented and corrections became increasingly bureaucratized.

The prison warden of today is a highly educated professional manager who operates within an organizational structure that is becoming increasing "corporate." This is particularly true in the Correctional Service of Canada, where the mission statement provides a set of guiding principles for senior management and a number of strategic objectives that wardens are charged with pursuing. The mission statement requires wardens to create institutional environments in which all correctional staff are active participants in the management process. In a study conducted by Hale *et al.* (1992), two-thirds of a sample that included prison wardens and district parole directors ranked the ability to communicate as the most important prerequisite for successfully carrying out their role. Of the sample, 62% had obtained a master's degree, while 30% had a B.A. only, reflecting the increasing emphasis on education for senior managers.

The "Double-Bind" Management Style and the Bureaucratization of Leadership

Despite these developments, wardens are still charged with the almost impossible task of responding to demands from the general public and from the various groups within the institution. There are many "external" activities and decisions over which the wardens have no control, but which may have a significant impact on the operation of the institution, such as the sentencing patterns of the courts, the placement decisions of classification officers, decisions regarding when offenders will be released from the institution, and decisions about financial resources, which may result in overcrowding, staff shortages, and program cutbacks.

Within the institution, the warden is responsible for a wide range of administrative tasks, as well as for mediating the often conflicting interests of the inmates, security personnel, and treatment staff. The warden is also held accountable for disruptions such as riots, suicides, and escapes, all of which may be precipitated by overcrowding and inmate transfers or other decisions over which the warden has no control.

The warden, then, is often put in what Bowker (1982:208) has characterized as the "double-bind" — "no win" situations in which middle-ground decisions are "more likely to displease all groups than to satisfy any one of them." The decision to implement or expand a treatment program within the institution, for example, will have direct implications for the inmates, treatment staff, and correctional officers. The failure of the warden to balance the custody and control mandate of the prison with policies designed to create an environment conducive to inmate reformation may lead to disturbances among the inmates and low staff morale.

The management style of the warden will have a significant impact on the climate that develops in the institution. The institutional climate is an important determinant of the patterns of interaction that develop among the various groups within the institution, and institutions, even at the same security level, will have a distinctive "climate." However, the efforts of even the most enlightened warden may be severely hindered by overcrowding, a poor physical facility, and the resistance of correctional officers and/or security staff to specific programmatic initiatives.

One of the more serious difficulties confronting Canadian wardens is a consequence of the increasing bureaucratization of corrections noted earlier. A recent inquiry into the management of federal correctional institutions (Carson, 1984) identified the regional and national offices of the Correctional Service of Canada as a major source of difficulty for wardens. Wardens were found to have little actual authority to manage their institutions, but rather were being subjected to an increasing number of directives from regional and national headquarters. The Carson (1984) report also found that wardens tended to be assessed on the degree to which they complied with these directives, rather than on results obtained at the individual institutional level.

Recent organizational changes suggest that the Correctional Service of Canada is not heeding the recommendations of the Carson Committee (1984). Under the Unit Management program discussed earlier, wardens of institutions will be required to spend the majority of their time in a liaison role with regional headquarters, while deputy wardens will assume an increasing role in overseeing the operation of the institution on a daily basis. And, while the mission statement has been generally viewed as a step forward for corrections, it may accelerate the centralization of both institutional objectives and the assessment of the performance on individual wardens in achieving them. Because of this, it is likely that prison wardens will continue to find themselves at the centre of the conflicting demands of the public, the inmates, the correctional staff, and the Correctional Service of Canada.

NOTES

[1]For a detailed examination of correctional institutions and community-based corrections in Canada, see Ekstedt and Griffiths (1988).

[2]Section 745 of the *Criminal Code* provides that convicted murderers who have served at least 15 years of their 25-year minimum sentence may apply for

judicial review to have the minimum time to be served before parole eligibility reduced. Since 1988, 18 murderers have appeared before juries in an attempt to have their minimum sentence reduced. Eleven of the applicants (eight of whom were in Quebec) have had their minimum times reduced and several have been paroled.

[3]Increased attention is also being given to inmate grievance procedures, particularly at the federal level of corrections. The grievance procedure allows inmates who feel that they have been unjustly treated to file a complaint. The Inmate Complaints and Grievance Procedure encourages the solution of inmate complaints at the line level, between the inmate and the correctional staff. However, the inmate may file a formal complaint with the warden of the institution and then, if necessary, it will be considered at higher levels in the system by the deputy commissioner at regional headquarters and then to national headquarters by the commissioner of the Correctional Service of Canada.

[4]For insightful first-person accounts of life "inside," see Abbott (1983) and Caron (1978; 1985). In 1993, Roger Caron was convicted for a series of bank robberies in eastern Canada and returned to prison.

[5]While some sexual encounters between inmates occur as a result of coercion and intimidation, other sexual relations between inmates are consensual. Traditionally, sexual relations between inmates, when detected, often resulted in disciplinary measures being taken against the inmates involved in the activity. The increasing threat of AIDS has forced prison officials to acknowledge that sexual relations do occur between inmates. On New Year's Day, 1992, prison officials began distributing condoms, on request, to inmates in federal institutions. The potential for HIV infections and AIDS within correctional institutions is perhaps one of the greatest threats to prison inmates and presents an immense challenge to correctional administrators (see Paglairo and Pagliaro, 1992).

[6]Many inmates and correctional staff use the terms "convict" and "inmate" in describing the social role of confined offenders. Convicts are viewed as hard core inmates who are deeply committed to the criminal way of life and who live by the tenets of the convict code. Inmates, on the other hand, are seen as less committed to the criminal life and as concerned more about their own welfare than that of their fellow offenders. Convicts do not trust inmates to be "solid." As one offender, self-described as a convict, told a co-author of this text: "You can't trust an inmate. Their motto is 'Get high today and the hell with tomorrow.'" Convicts, who are often serving long-term sentences, often view inmates as a destabilizing force in the institution; inmates may, by their behaviour, disrupt the accommodative relationships that the convicts have carefully nurtured with correctional officers.

[7]Perhaps the most insightful examination of life inside the Kingston Penitentiary for Women is provided by the film *P4W*, available from Pan Canadian Films, 214 King St. West, Toronto, Ontario M5H 3S6. See also *C'est*

Pas Parce Que C'est un Chateau Qu'on est des Princesses (Castle/No Princess), a documentary film on female inmates at the Maison Gomin in Quebec, available from Video Femmes, 56 St.-Pierre, #203, Quebec, G1K 4A1.

[8]The Quebec Regional Reception Centre is all that remains of the network of federal regional reception centres that previously existed across Canada.

[9]For an in-depth consideration of issues surrounding the treatment of offenders, see Ekstedt and Griffiths (1988).

[10]There has been an increased concern with intellectually disabled and mentally disordered offenders. Endicott (1991) provides a review of the literature on intellectually disabled offenders, including the relationship between intellectual disability and criminal behaviour, the impact of incarceration, and the issues surrounding the development of treatment programs for this group of offenders. Motiuk and Porporino (1991) present data on the nature and extent of mental health problems among a sample of male inmates in federal correctional facilities.

[11]Increasing attention has been focused on the procedures for managing offenders in correctional institutions. See the federal *Corrections and Conditional Release Act* (1992) for provisions relating to the placement and transfer of inmates, administrative segregation, inmate discipline, and the guidelines to be followed in cases of search and seizure.

REFERENCES

Abbott, J.H. 1983. *In the Belly of the Beast — Letters from Prison*. New York: Random House.

Adams, M. 1990. "Canadian Attitudes Toward Crime and Justice." 2 *FORUM on Corrections Research*. 10-13.

Alderson, D.A. 1991. "The Charter, Fundamental Justice and Prison Administration: The Common Law's Doppelganger." 34 *Criminal Law Quarterly*. 12-54.

Andresen, M. 1990. "Clearer Thinking: New Cognitive Skills Program Offers Major Building Block to Offender Reintegration." *Let's Talk* (September): 4-6.

Andrews, D.A., I. Zinger, R.D. Hoge, J. Bonta, P. Gendreau, and F.T. Cullen. 1990. "Does Correction Treatment Work? A Clinically Relevant and Psychologically Informed Meta-analysis." 28 *Criminology*. 369-404.

Archambault, J. 1938. *Report of the Royal Commission to Investigate the Prison System of Canada*.   Ottawa: King's Printer.

Bartollas, C. 1981. *Introduction to Corrections*. New York: Harper and Row.

Bowker, L.H. 1982. *Corrections: The Science and the Art*. New York: Macmillan.

Canada. 1895. *Commission to Investigate the Administration and Affairs of New*

Westminster Penitentiary. Ottawa: Debates of the Senate.

Canadian Centre for Justice Statistics. 1993. *Adult Correctional Services in Canada, 1992-93.* Ottawa: Industry, Science and Technology Canada.

Carlen, P. J. Hicks, J. O'Dwyer, D. Christina, and C. Tchaikovsky. 1985. *Criminal Women.* Cambridge: Polity Press.

Caron, R. 1978. *Go-Boy: Memoirs of a Life Behind Bars.* Toronto: McGraw-Hill Ryerson.

____. 1985. *BINGO!* Toronto: Methuen.

Carson, J.J. 1984. *Report of the Advisory Committee to the Solicitor General of Canada and on the Management of Correctional Institutions.* Ottawa: Supply and Services Canada.

Clemmer, D. 1940. *The Prison Community.* Boston: Christopher Publishing Company.

Correctional Service of Canada. 1992. *Annual Report on Security Incidents, 1990-91.* Ottawa: Correctional Programs and Operations Sector, Correctional Service of Canada.

Cullen, F.T., and L.F. Travis. 1984. "Work as an Avenue of Prison Reform." 10 *New England Journal of Criminal and Civil Confinement.* 45-64.

Cullen F.T., S.E. Skovron, J.E. Scott, and V.S. Burton. 1990. "Public Support for Correctional Treatment: The Tenacity of Rehabilitative Ideology." 17 *Criminal Justice and Behavior.* 6-18.

Delnef, C. 1992. "Corporate Operation Plan." *Let's Talk* (January). 4-6.

Dobash, R.P., R.E. Dobash, and S. Gutteridge. 1986. *The Imprisonment of Women.* New York: Blackwell.

Doob, A.N., and J-P.Brodeur. 1989. "Rehabilitating the Debate On Rehabilitation." 31 *Canadian Journal of Criminology.* 170-92.

Duguid, S. 1981. "Moral Development, Justice and Democracy in the Prison." 23 *Canadian Journal of Criminology.* 147-62.

Ekstedt, J.W., and C.T. Griffiths. 1988. *Corrections in Canada: Policy and Practice.* 2nd ed. Toronto: Butterworths.

Fabiano, E., D. Robinson, and F. Porporino. 1990. *A Preliminary Assessment of the Cognitive Skills Training Program Pilot Project. Program Description, Research Findings and Implementation Strategy.* Ottawa: Research and Statistics Branch, Correctional Service of Canada.

Farrington, K. 1992. "The Modern Prison as a Total Institution: Public Perception Versus Objective Reality." 38 *Crime and Delinquency.* 6-26.

Fauteux, G. 1956. *Report of a Committee Appointed to Inquire into the Principles and Procedures Followed in the Remission Service of the Department of Justice of Canada.* Ottawa: Queen's Printer.

Gandy, J., and L. Hurl. 1987. "Private Sector Involvement in Prison Industries: Issues and Options." 29 *Canadian Journal of Criminology.* 185-204.

Garfinkel, H. 1965. "Conditions of Successful Status Degradation Ceremonies." 61 *American Journal of Sociology*. 420-24.

Gendreau, P., and B. Ross. 1979. "Effective Correctional Treatment: Bibliotherapy for Cynics." 25 *Crime and Delinquency*. 463-89.

Gendreau, P., and R.R. Ross. 1987. "Revivification of Rehabilitation: Evidence from the 1980s." 4 *Justice Quarterly*. 349-407.

Gendreau, P., and D.A. Andrews. 1990. "Tertiary Prevention: What the Meta-Analyses of the Offender Treatment Literature Tells Us about 'What Works.'" 32 *Canadian Journal of Criminology*. 173-84.

Goffman, E. 1961. *Asylums: Essays on the Social Condition of Mental Patients and Other Inmates*. Garden City, New York: Doubleday Books.

Government of Canada. 1986. *Study Team Report to the Task Force on Program Review. Improved Service Delivery: Justice System*. Ottawa: Supply and Services Canada.

Hale, M., C. Stuart, D. Carleton, and B. Fisher. 1992. "Studying Senior Managers' Career Paths." 4 *FORUM on Corrections Research*. 28-30.

Hughes, G. 1990. *Stress and Coping in Correctional Settings*. Ottawa: Correctional Service Canada.

Irwin, J., and D. Cressey. 1961. "Thieves, Convicts, and the Inmate Code." 10 *Social Problems*. 142-55.

Johnson, R. 1987. *Hard Time — Understanding and Reforming the Prison*. Pacific Grove, California: Brooks/Cole.

Klofas, J., and H. Toch. 1982. "The Guard Subculture Myth." 19 *Journal of Research in Crime and Delinquency*. 238-54.

Lab, S.P., and J.T. Whitehead. 1990. "From 'Nothing Works' to The 'Appropriate Works': The Latest Stop on the Search for the Holy Grail." 28 *Criminology*. 405-16.

Lockwood, D. 1991. "Prison Higher Education and Recidivism: A Program Evaluation." In S. Duguid, ed. *The Yearbook of Correctional Education, 1991*. S. Duguid, ed. Burnaby, British Columbia: Institute for the Humanities, Simon Fraser University. 187-201.

MacDonald, G. 1982. *Self-Sustaining Prison Industries*. Vancouver: Institute for Studies in Criminal Justice Policy, Simon Fraser University.

Mandell, C.C., and A.L. Mandell. 1985. "Accountability in Canadian Penitentiaries: Disciplinary Procedures and Judicial Review." In M. Maguire, J. Vagg, and R. Morgan, eds. *Accountability and Prisons: Opening Up a Closed World*, 245-63. London: Tavistock Publications Ltd.

Marshall, W.L. 1989. *Evaluation of Life Skills Training for Federal Penitentiary Inmates*. Ottawa: Corrections Branch, Ministry of the Solicitor General.

Martinson, R.M. 1974. "What Works? Questions and Answers About Prison Reform." 35 *The Public Interest*. 22-54.

McCarthy, B.J. 1984. "Keeping an Eye on the Keeper: Prison Corruption and Its

Control." 64 *The Prison Journal*. 113-25.

Morris, R. 1989. *Crumbling Walls...Why Prisons Fail*. Oakville, Ontario: Mosaic Press.

Motiuk, L.L., and F. J. Porporino. 1991. *The Prevalence, Nature and Severity of Mental Health Problems among Federal Male Inmates in Canadian Penitentiaries*. Ottawa: Correctional Service of Canada.

Ouimet, R. 1969. *Report of the Canadian Committee on Corrections — Toward Unity: Criminal Justice and Corrections*. Ottawa: Information Canada.

Pagliaro, L.A., and A.M. Pagliaro, 1992. "Sentenced to Death? HIV Infection and AIDS in Prisons — Current and Future Concerns." 34 *Canadian Journal of Criminology*. 201-214.

Perron, J.C. 1991. *Task Force Report on Long-Term Sentences*. Ottawa: Correctional Service of Canada.

Philliber, S. 1987. "Thy Brother's Keeper: A Review of the Literature on Correctional Officers." 4 *Criminal Justice Quarterly*. 9-37.

Porporino, F.J. 1991. *Differences in Response to Long-Term Imprisonment: Implications for the Management of Long-Term Offenders*. Ottawa: Correctional Service of Canada.

Porporino, F.J., and D. Robinson. 1992. *Can Educating Adult Offenders Counteract Recidivism?* Ottawa: Correctional Service of Canada.

Price-Waterhouse. 1990. *Final Report — Task One*. Ottawa: Correctional Service of Canada.

Ramirez, J.R. 1984. "Prisonization, Staff, and Inmates: Is It Really About Us Versus Them?" 11 *Criminal Justice and Behavior*. 423-60.

Robinson, D., L. Simourd, and F. Porporino. 1991. *Research on Staff Commitment: A Discussion Paper*. Ottawa: Research and Statistics Branch, Correctional Service of Canada.

Solicitor General of Canada. 1981. *Solicitor General's Study of Conditional Release — Report of the Working Group*. Ottawa: Supply and Services Canada.

Sykes, G.M. 1958. *Society of Captives — A Study of a Maximum Security Institution*. Princeton, New Jersey: Princeton University Press.

Toch, H. 1977. *Living in Prison: The Ecology of Survival*. New York: The Free Press.

Willett, T.C. 1983. "Prison Guards in Private." 25 *Canadian Journal of Criminology*. 1-17.

Wilson, T.W. 1986. "Gender Differences in the Inmate Code." 28 *Canadian Journal of Criminology*. 397-405.

Zamble, E., and F. Porporino. 1988. *Coping, Behavior and Adaptation in Prison Inmates*. New York: Springer-Verlag.

12 COMMUNITY-BASED CORRECTIONS PROGRAMS

While correctional institutions and inmates receive much of the attention of the media and the general public (and consume most of the fiscal resources), the majority of federal and provincial offenders are under some form of supervision in the community. These offenders have either been spared the pains of imprisonment or are being supervised on parole or statutory release following a period of incarceration. Community-based programs also provide a means for maintaining control and surveillance over offenders.

Community-based, non-custodial programs are operated by the Correctional Service of Canada and provincial/territorial correctional systems. Probation, diversion, fine-option, restitution, electronic monitoring, and community service orders are designed as alternatives to incarceration, although some may be used in conjunction with a sentence of incarceration. Parole and statutory release are post-release programs providing supervision to assist offenders in reentry and readjustment in the community. In addition, pre-release programs, such as temporary absence and day parole, provide the opportunity for inmates to participate in community-based programs.[1]

The Correctional Service of Canada and the National Parole Board (NPB) both have roles in granting and supervising offenders on temporary absences, parole, or statutory release. Inmates may take advantage of a variety of community-based residential facilities and programs while they are not incarcerated. Community correctional centres (CCCs) are residential programs operated by the federal government, while community residential centres (CRCs) are residences run by private agencies under contract. The provincial/territorial governments offer alternatives to incarceration as well as release programs. These are listed in Chapter 10, Table 10.3. In Canada, private, non-profit agencies, such as the John Howard Society and the Elizabeth Fry Society, play a major role in the provision of community corrections services under contract. Through non-profit agencies and community-based groups and organizations, volunteers are playing an increasingly larger role in Canadian corrections.

Community corrections programs in Canada are used to divert people entirely from the criminal justice system (diversion and probation); to provide temporary release from confinement (temporary absences and day paroles); and to supervise the reentry of offenders who have been incarcerated (parole and statutory release). Community corrections is premised on the philosophy that, for many offenders, the community provides a better milieu for reform and rehabilitation than correctional institutions. Over 90% of all offenders who are incarcerated will, at some future date, return to the community.

The increasing focus on alternatives to incarceration is reflected in the provisions of Bill C-90, proposed in 1992, but not passed as of June 1993. The legislation encourages the use of alternative measures whenever possible in lieu of a sentence of incarceration in a correctional facility. The discussion below reveals that there are already a wide range of community-based programs and services in place; however, this legislation is certain to give increased impetus to their use.

ALTERNATIVES TO INCARCERATION

Diversion

Diversion is a mechanism by which Crown counsel remove alleged offenders, usually charged with relatively minor offences and without a lengthy criminal record, from the formal criminal justice process and refer them to an appropriate program resource. Under most diversion schemes, the alleged offender is given the option of participating in a resource program or facing prosecution on the charge. Throughout the 1970s, a variety of diversion programs were established with the support of police and prosecutorial and correctional officials.

Probation

Probation is a disposition of the court that places the offender under supervision in the community. It falls under the jurisdiction of the provinces/territories and is the only community corrections program imposed by direct court order.

Probation began in 1889, with the passing of the *Act to Permit the Conditional Release of First Offenders in Certain Cases*. This legislation allowed judges to release offenders on "probation of good conduct" rather than impose a sentence. While this legislation was amalgamated into the *Criminal Code* in 1892, it was not until 1921 that an amendment to the

Act provided for supervision of probationers in the community (see Sheridan and Konrad, 1976). Between 1921 and 1967, the provinces/territories enacted legislation establishing probation services, which are now offered in all Canadian jurisdictions. A rapid, albeit uneven, expansion of probation services and offenders under supervision occurred during the 1960s.

During 1990-91, approximately 93,000 offenders were under probationary supervision in Canada, an increase of 12% from the previous year. Of this number, Ontario had the largest probation caseload (50% of the total), comprising just over 40,000 probationers. Quebec was a distant second with 12% of the total probationer caseload. The median probation-order length has remained fairly constant over the past 5 years at between 11 and 12 months, but the range was from 9 months in British Columbia to 24 months in Quebec (Canadian Centre for Justice Statistics, 1993:55).

An offender may be placed under probationary supervision for a period not to exceed three years. Probation orders may be accompanied by a conditional discharge, a suspended sentence, or a fine. They may also follow a provincial jail sentence. In addition to requiring the offender to report to a probation officer on a regular basis, general or specific conditions may be attached to the probation order by the court. General conditions require the probationer to be on good behaviour and obey the law, while specific conditions may require the offender to participate in a designated program, such as a community service order program or attendance centre program, or pay restitution to the victim of the crime. An offender's probation may be breached for either violating the conditions of the probation order or for committing a new offence.

The decision of the judge to place an offender on probation is strongly influenced by the pre-sentence report (PSR). The PSR is generally prepared by a probation officer after a conviction or a guilty plea and includes sociobiographical information on the offender, as well as details relating to the current offence and prior record. If appropriate, victim impact is also included. In many cases, the probation officer will conclude the PSR with a recommendation concerning the suitability of the offender for probation, as well as suggestions regarding general or specific conditions to be attached to the order, should one be issued.

Concerns have been expressed about the operation of probation, centering on the role of the PSR in determining the suitability of offenders for probation, the supervision of offenders, and the effectiveness of probation as a rehabilitative technique. The content of PSR may be influenced by the sociobiographical attributes of the offender (for example, age, gender, marital status, employment record, etc.), the organizational procedures of the probation office, and the personal orientation of the probation officer preparing the report. It is unclear as to how much the recommendations set forth by the probation officer in the PSR influence the decision making of judges. Some judges appear to rely heavily upon the recommendation of the probation officer, while others consider it only as one of many factors in reaching a decision.

Probationary supervision has also come under scrutiny. Part of the difficulty is the conflict between probation as a rehabilitative device and as a control mechanism and the uncertainty over whether probation officers should be *case managers,* functioning to make specialized community resources available to the probationer, or *case workers,* counselling probationers on a one-to-one basis (Hatt, 1985:302).

Jackson *et al.* (1982) reported that the decision to revoke probation in one Canadian jurisdiction was influenced by the personal style and orientation of the probation officer, as well as by the probationer's lifestyle. In nearly 50% of the cases studied, probation was listed as successfully completed despite non-adherence to the conditions of the probation order. Officers were generally reluctant to intervene in those cases where the probationer had a stable domestic life and employment. In an exhaustive study of the enforcement of probation conditions in British Columbia, Aasen (1985) found that under the provisions of the *Criminal Code*, it was virtually impossible to breach probationers for violating the conditions of probation and that it often took a long period of time to charge and convict an offender for breaching a probation order.

The proposed legislation, Bill C-90, has the following provisions concerning probation:

1) a requirement that the sentencing court set out a default sentence at the time the offender is placed on probation;
2) the delineation of two levels of probation: level 1 for less serious offenders and level 2 for more serious offenders (commission of a new offence while on probation by a level 1 offender would result in the automatic imposition of the default prison sentence; and for the more serious level 2 offenders, the default prison sentence would be imposed if the offender either violated the conditions of probation or committed a new offence);

3) probation officers would have authority to issue warrants for the arrest of probationers who violate their conditions; and
4) probation officers would be empowered to modify the conditions of probation, including increasing conditions and sanctions.

While these provisions are designed to address many of the difficulties that surround probation supervision, there is some concern that enforcement of these strictures will result in more offenders being sent to correctional institutions.

Conditions of Probation: Community Service Orders, Restitution, and Attendance Programs

Offenders placed on probation may be required to participate in one of several community-based programs operated at the provincial level. Among these are community service order (CSO), restitution, and attendance centre programs. In some jurisdictions, victim-offender reconciliation programs (discussed in Chapter 2) may be a condition of probation. CSOs, available in all jurisdictions except New Brunswick, are imposed as a condition of probation and require the offender to complete a specified number of hours of community service for non-profit agencies in the community in lieu of a period of confinement. Often, this work is performed for the victim of the offender's criminal behaviour. The philosophy behind the CSO programs is reparation — through the performance of services, the offender is "making amends" to the community and/or the victim of his or her offence — although several observers have noted that CSO programs satisfy a broad range of penal philosophies, including punishment, reformation, deterrence, and as an alternative to incarceration (see Menzies, 1986).[2]

CSO programs are administered by provincial probation services in all provinces/territories, with the exception of Ontario and British Columbia, where private agencies under contract are involved in operating most of the programs. In a survey of issues and attitudes surrounding the operation of CSO programs in Prince Edward Island, Ontario, and British Columbia, Ekstedt and Jackson (1986) found that criminal justice personnel, including judges and probation officers, held generally positive views toward CSOs, although there was a lack of consensus about the purpose of CSOs and in many instances judges were not using CSOs as an alternative to confinement. Additional difficulties that have surrounded the use of CSOs are the lack of an upper limit on the number of hours offenders may be required to perform and disparity between judges in the assignment of community service hours to various categories of offenders (Daubney, 1988).

Another condition of probation may require the offender to pay restitution to the victim of the crime, either in the form of a payment of compensation for harm done or through the performance of specified services for the victim. Restitution is premised on the philosophy of reparation, and programs are currently operating in five Canadian provinces and in the Yukon Territory. Other problems have included the enforcement of restitution orders and the difficulties in determining the categories of offender most suitable and amenable to a restitution order. Among the provisions of Bill C-89 (*An Act to Amend the Criminal Code* [*Victims of Crime,* S.C. 1988, c.30]) are a requirement that judges impose a penalty of restitution in appropriate cases and the expansion of restitution to include loss due to bodily injury and property damage.

The success of restitution programs across the country appears to be variable. Some jurisdictions have experienced a low payment rate of court-ordered restitution and, even in instances in which full payment has not been made, probation officers appear reluctant to breach the offender (see Zapf and Cole, 1985). Results of the restitution program in Saskatchewan have been positive, however. Special coordinators were hired to determine the offender's ability to pay, to supervise offenders in fulfilling restitution orders, and to maintain liaison with criminal justice agencies and officials and crime victims. Such an integrated program approach appears to have a higher likelihood of success. Success also appears to be higher with offenders convicted of minor property offences, with more serious offenders tending not to fulfill the conditions of restitution orders (Ekstedt and Jackson, 1986). An evaluation of the Rideau-Carleton Restitution Program in Ontario (Bonta *et al.,* 1983) found high levels of victim satisfaction with the program and concluded that even high-risk offenders in halfway houses might be suitable for participation in restitution programs.

Yet another condition of probation (or on the recommendation of a supervising probation officer) may require offenders to participate in an attendance centre program on a regular basis. Attendance centres may be residential or non-residential and may be used for offenders on temporary absences and parole, as well as probation. Among the attendance centre programs operated by provinces are impaired drivers courses, alcohol and drug treatment programs, counselling programs for shoplifters, and various therapy programs for specific categories of offenders, including assaultive males and sexual offenders.

Attendance centres may be operated under contract by non-profit agencies, such as the John Howard Society, the Elizabeth Fry Society, and church-sponsored groups. In Charlottetown, Prince Edward Island, the Protestant and Catholic Family Service Bureau co-sponsors a program for assaultive men; the Elizabeth Fry Society operates counselling programs for shoplifters in Calgary and Vancouver; and in New Brunswick, the John Howard Society sponsors a life skills program for probationers. In Manitoba, the Alcoholism Foundation operates a program for impaired drivers and in Saskatchewan, a similar program is offered by the Saskatchewan Alcoholism Commission.

PRE-RELEASE PROGRAMS: TEMPORARY ABSENCES AND DAY PAROLE

Temporary absences (TAs) and day paroles allow the temporary release of offenders from institutions in order to access programs and services available in the community. All provinces/territories operate TA programs, and TAs may be granted for educational, medical, humanitarian, employment, or family-related reasons, as well as for pre-parole planning. Offenders on TAs may reside either in the institution or in a residential facility situated in the community. TAs are granted for varying lengths of time, depending upon the situation of the individual offender, with the decision being made by an institutional TA committee.

TAs are either escorted (ETAs) or unescorted (UTAs). Typically, ETAs are not to be longer than five days and UTAs may run from 48 hours to 60 days. The Correctional Service of Canada has authority to issue ETAs, while the NPB has jurisdiction over UTAs, although, in practice, the Correctional Service of Canada has been given the authority to make UTA decisions for inmates serving sentences of less than five years and in cases where an offender is applying for a second or subsequent UTA. To be eligible for a UTA, an inmate must have served one-half the time before his or her parole eligibility date, or six months, whichever is longer. The two exceptions to this are those offenders who have been sentenced to life imprisonment, who are eligible for a UTA three years prior to their parole eligibility date, and offenders sentenced to detention for an indeterminate period of time, who must serve three years before becoming eligible for a UTA. As of 1992, offenders classified as maximum security are no longer eligible for UTAs.

Federal offenders who are eligible for UTAs may qualify to participate in work release programs outside of the correctional institution for a specified period of time. In addition, UTAs may be granted to allow offenders to participate in personal development programs or community service projects. UTAs are generally granted for a maximum period of 15 days, although if the UTA is for participation in a personal development program, it may be extended to 60 days, renewable.[3]

Day parole is a flexible form of release that provides an opportunity for correctional officials to employ gradual release, preparing the inmate for release on full parole and allowing the inmate the opportunity to participate in community-based programs and become readjusted to life outside the institution. Provincial inmates — those serving sentences of less than two years — are eligible for day parole after serving one-half of the time before their parole eligibility date.

Federal offenders, with the exception of those inmates in preventive detention or serving indeterminate sentences, are eligible for day parole six months prior to their parole eligibility date or after having served six months of their sentence, whichever is longer. Inmates in preventive detention must serve one year prior to applying for a day parole, while those serving indeterminate sentences must serve three years before being eligible. The majority of the inmates on day parole reside in community-based facilities operated by the provincial and federal corrections services or by private agencies.

The number of federal inmates and provincial inmates (in provinces with no provincial parole board) applying for and receiving day parole has remained fairly constant. In 1991-92, 66% of the requests for day parole were granted by the NPB. However, the revocation rate has risen over the past several years and in 1991-92 was 31% for federal inmates and 34% for provincial inmates.

POST-INCARCERATION RELEASE: FULL PAROLE

Full parole is a program of conditional release that allows inmates to serve a portion of their sentence in the community under supervision. Inmates are generally eligible for full parole after serving one-third of their sentence or seven years, whichever is shorter.[4] Under the *Corrections and Conditional Release Act* enacted in 1992, however, sentencing judges have the authority to set the parole eligibility for offenders convicted of violent and serious drug offences at one-half rather than one-third of the sentence. In such cases, the period until parole eligibility cannot exceed ten years. Federal inmates serving life sentences are eligible for parole consideration after seven years in confinement, dated from the day the offender was arrested and taken into custody. The exception to this are situations in which an offender is serving a life sentence with a mandatory minimum sentence. For example, first-degree murder conviction carries a mandatory 25 years confinement before parole eligibility.

Parole as a release mechanism was established in 1899 with the enactment of the *Act to Provide for the Conditional Liberation of Penitentiary Convicts*, which became known as the *Ticket of Leave Act*. In the early 1900s, a remission service was created in the Department of Justice, and the Salvation Army, the John Howard Society, and the Elizabeth Fry Society became increasingly involved in supervising offenders as well as in providing "after-care" services. In 1958, the *Parole Act* replaced the *Ticket of Leave Act*, the NPB was created, and the remission service became the National Parole Service.

The NPB reviews the cases of all inmates who are eligible for parole. Excluded from these cases are those offenders who are serving a specified minimum term of incarceration prior to being eligible for parole consideration and those offenders whose parole eligibility date was set by the sentencing judge at one-half. Eligible offenders must be reviewed for parole every year thereafter until parole is granted or until the offender is eligible for statutory release.

The *Corrections and Conditional Release Act* provides for an accelerated review process for full parole for non-violent, first-time offenders. Under this arrangement, two members of the parole board review the case without a regular parole board hearing, and parole will be granted if there is reasonable grounds to believe that the offender will not commit a violent offence prior to the end of his or her sentence.

The NPB also has the authority to deny the release of offenders eligible for statutory release if it believes that the release of the offender will threaten the safety and security of the community. These offenders may be required to serve the full term of their sentence in confinement.

The number of affirmative votes required for release on full parole varies by the length of the inmate's sentence. For example, while two affirmative votes are required for inmates serving single or aggregate terms of imprisonment of less than five years, five votes are required for inmates serving a single or aggregate term of ten years or more. In cases of tie votes, an additional vote is cast by either the chair of the NPB or by another parole board member.

An Internal Review Committee, comprised of three NPB members not familiar with the case under review, hears complaints filed by inmates who have been denied full parole or who have had their day parole, full parole, or statutory release revoked. Complaints generally include allegations that the reasons given by the NPB for its decision do not support the decision, not all the available evidence was heard, or the NPB committed an error in fact or in law in reaching its final decision.

Figures on the release decisions of the NPB indicate that full parole is difficult to obtain. In 1991-92, the NPB granted parole to only 33% of the federal offenders who appeared before it. Provincial inmates (in those provinces that do not have a provincial parole board) fared much better: the parole grant rate was 47%. The three provincial parole boards granted paroles in 37% (Quebec), 51% (Ontario), and 58% (British Columbia) of the cases brought before them.

STATUTORY RELEASE

Statutory release has its origins in an amendment to the *Parole Act* in 1970, which created a mechanism to provide assistance and control during the offender's readjustment to life in the community for inmates who had been denied parole. In contrast to parole, statutory release involves the release of offenders from the institution after serving two-thirds of their sentence, with the remaining one-third being served under supervision of the NPB in the community. In 1990-91, 26% of the federal offenders under community supervision were on mandatory supervision, the forerunner of statutory release.

The NPB can review statutory release and has the right to deny statutory release and detain an inmate. This is done if, in the opinion of the NPB, there is a likelihood that the inmate, if released, will commit another offence causing death or serious harm in the community prior to the expiry of the offender's sentence. The NPB also has the authority to attach additional conditions to a statutory release, such as the requirement that the offender reside in a community-based facility. Another condition that may be imposed on the release is called "one-chance" statutory release. Should the release be revoked, the offender is ineligible for early release prior to the expiration of their sentence.

In detention hearings to review the cases of federal offenders eligible to be released on mandatory supervision (the pre-1992 equivalent of statutory release), the NPB denied release in 72% of the cases; in 11% of the cases the offenders were directed to reside at a halfway house; and 9% of the cases were designated as "one-chance" mandatory supervision releases. In the rest of the cases, the board either granted the release or reserved judgment (Canadian Centre for Justice Statistics, 1993).

Inmates released under statutory release are supervised by parole officers and must abide by mandatory and any additional conditions set by the NPB. A violation of the conditions can result in suspension and revocation and return to the institution where the offender may have to serve the remainder of his or her sentence. Inmates who are detained by the NPB during the period of statutory release on the grounds that they would constitute a threat to the community if released may be required to serve the remainder of their sentence in the institution. Following completion of their sentence, however, these inmates are released into the community *without any supervision or assistance*. As a recent report of the Canadian Bar Association noted: "The new legislation clearly does not resolve the problem of threat to public safety, it simply postpones its impact" (1988:13).

PAROLE BOARD DECISION MAKING: DISCRETION AND DISPARITY

Perhaps no one point of decision making in the correctional process has been the subject of more controversy than the decision to grant or deny parole. Concerns with the decision-making activities of the parole board, as well as with the effectiveness of parole as a reintegrative technique, have resulted in its abolition in several states in the United States. The report of the Canadian Sentencing Commission (1987) recommended the elimination of full parole release for all offenders, with the exception of those serving sentences of life imprisonment. It is unlikely, however, that parole will be abolished in Canada in the foreseeable future.

Our discussion in this section will focus primarily on the activities of the NPB, as there are few published evaluations of the decision making of the provincial parole boards in British Columbia, Ontario, and

Quebec. It can be assumed, however, that many of the issues surrounding the decision making of the NPB apply to provincial parole boards as well.

Among the more significant issues that surround parole board decision making are the following.

▶   *The qualifications of parole board members.*

It appears that in recent years, political patronage has played a major role in the appointment of parole board members. Political interference in the appointment process has led observers to characterize the selection process as one in which parole board members were "anointed rather than appointed" (Daubney, 1988:168). There is the perception among many corrections observers that the overall calibre of appointments has declined, one indicator being the decrease in the number of parole board members with prior criminal justice experience, from 85% in 1977 to 52.1% in 1986.

To ensure that qualified persons, rather than political appointees, are placed on parole boards, it has been suggested that a screening committee be created composed of individuals from the public and private sectors.[5]

▶   *The failure of the NPB to establish clear decision-making criteria.*

This concern is reflected in the words of a corrections task force from two decades ago:

> Neither inmates nor members of the Board are able to articulate with any certainty or precision what positive or negative factors enter into the parole decision (Hugessen, 1973:32).

In the *Corrections and Conditional Release Act* (1992), the stated criteria for granting parole are: (a) the offender will not, by reoffending, present an undue risk to society before the expiration according to the law of the sentence the offender is serving; and (b) the release of the offender will contribute to the protection of society by facilitating the reintegration of the offender into society as a law-abiding citizen. Needless to say, all of these criteria are sufficiently vague to allow for wide latitude in the decision making of the parole board.

In addition, the *Policy and Procedures Manual* of the NPB includes as factors that may be considered by the board in its decision making the nature and gravity of the offence, prior history of criminal involvement, the inmate's total personality, efforts at self-improvement made by the inmate during imprisonment, release plans, and community reaction to the release. In 1988, the NPB adopted a pre-release policy that divides criminal offences into three categories for purposes of review for parole and standardizes a procedure for risk assessment.

▸   *The broad discretionary powers exercised by parole board members in making decisions.*

The powers of the NPB, in conjunction with the vagueness of the criteria for parole, combine to produce different philosophies and "styles" of decision making. This creates a situation in which "there are as many criteria as Board members" and decisions that are "highly unpredictable and inconsistent..." (Solicitor General of Canada, 1981:C-9). This also results in disparity in the parole-granting rates across the five regions of the Correctional Service of Canada.

As an administrative board, the NPB is not subject to the requirements of due process, and inmates historically were denied basic procedural rights. Parole boards, for example, were not required to grant hearings to inmates or to provide reasons for decisions. In recent years, however, the courts have become more involved in examining various aspects of parole board operations. Inmates now have the right to a parole hearing, to be represented at the parole hearing by legal counsel, and to have access to information being used by the parole board in its decision making. Parole boards must provide to the inmate, in writing, notification of whether parole has been granted and the reasons for the decision. It is likely that the *Canadian Charter of Rights and Freedoms* will result in further changes in the policies and procedures of the NPB.

▸   *The difficulties experienced by parole board members in priorizing information about the offender.*

In making the parole decision, NPB members have access to a large amount of information in the offender's case file and, similar to police officers and judges, exercise considerable autonomy and discretion in their decision making. Case files include information of a sociobiographical nature and documentation on the offender's prior criminal history and present offence, the results of diagnostic tests, institutional performance, and release plans, as well as reports by the inmate's institutional case management team and the recommendations of a parole officer after a community assessment. Any victim impact statements admitted by the Crown at the time of sentencing are also included in the parole file. In recent years, an attempt has been made to increase the reliability, clarity, and completeness of case file material.

Research indicates that the offence, prior criminal record, and the recommendation of the parole officer play a major role in most parole board release decisions. This is what we would expect. The influence of the sociobiographical attributes of the inmate (for example, age, marital status, employment record, ethnicity) on board decision making, however, is less clear. Evidence suggests that, all things being equal, younger and more highly educated offenders were more likely to be paroled than older offenders and those with lower levels of education (see Nuffield, 1982).

▸   *The difficulties in assessing risk and in predicting the future behaviour of the offender upon release.*

While the specific criteria used by parole board members in their decision making may vary widely between individual cases, the primary concern of most parole board members is whether the offender will reoffend upon release, either while on parole or at some future date after their period of supervision has expired. Parole hearings thus become an exercise in behavioural prediction and risk assessment. Questions asked of the prospective parolee will often centre on the circumstances of the most recent offence, efforts that the offender has made during the period of incarceration to address his or her particular problems, and the offender's parole plans.

The NPB uses the parole hearing to assess the offender's attitude and the extent to which the offender accepts responsibility for his or her criminal behaviour. While an attempt is made to balance the needs of the offender with the demands for protection of the community, the protection of the community is paramount. The parole board is sensitive to criticisms of past decisions that resulted in highly publicized crimes being committed by parolees and to the risks involved in granting parole to certain categories of offenders.

To assist it in assessing risk, the NPB has access to the "SIR Scale" — Statistical Information about Recidivism Scale — which involves examining information such as age at admission, current offence, age at first conviction, previous sentences, previous escapes, assaults, break and enter convictions, and previous violent sex offences. This information is used to generate a "score" that assists the board in assessing the likelihood that the offender will recommit an offence if released (see Nuffield, 1989).

▸ *The lack of feedback to parole board members about the outcomes of their decisions.*

One factor that hinders the assessment of risk by parole board members is the fact that members receive very little feedback on the "outcomes" of their decisions. Often, different members will be involved in hearing the applications of an inmate for a TA, a day parole, and full parole. There is no guarantee that the same board members will be present for each of these hearings. This makes it difficult for the same board members to have personal contact with the offender as the offender applies for the various types of release.

Parole board members may also have little knowledge about the "success" of the offender on release. Generally, members learn only about the failures, particularly when a parolee commits a particularly heinous crime. This lack of a "feedback loop" of information to board members as to the outcomes of their decisions is a critical gap in the parole decision-making process.

▸ *Inmate perceptions of the parole process.*

Recently, several attempts have been made to survey offenders as to their perceptions of the parole process and their views of the criminal justice system generally. This is a long-ignored but critical aspect of understanding the corrections process. Interviews with prison inmates conducted for the Canadian Sentencing Commission (Landreville *et al.,* 1988; Ekstedt and Jackson, 1986) revealed the following.

 ▸ *Inmates hold generally negative views of the media.* Offenders told Landreville *et al.* (1988:87) that the media used them to "sell a product" and that the media image of offenders is "incomplete, negative, and horrifying" and they feel "convicted before they are tried."

- ► *While offenders support the practice of parole, there are criticisms of its operation.* Concerns focused on the broad discretionary powers of the parole board members, the inconsistency of the criteria used in making release decisions, and the perception that those inmates who inform for the police are more likely to be granted release.
- ► *Offenders are nearly unanimous in the view that mandatory supervision should be abolished.* This is reflected in the statement of one inmate that "A guy who has served two-thirds of his time deserves to be left in peace" (Landreville, 1988:88) and "They [offenders] are told that they are being given time off their sentence, but they must still be supervised" (Ekstedt and Jackson, 1986:21).

THE PAINS OF REENTRY INTO SOCIETY

While there is an emerging body of material on the decision-making activities of the parole board and on the supervision of inmates in the community, the difficulties encountered by inmates applying for parole and on reentry into the community have received considerably less attention. In addition to the "pains of imprisonment" that offenders may experience during confinement are the "pains of reentry" associated with release from the institution. Offenders who have experienced the status degradation ceremonies and the process of mortification, as well as the stresses of adapting to and coping with the daily routine of prison life, may be unprepared for release.

While the Canadian criminal justice system has perfected the mechanisms for removing individuals from society and transforming them from citizens into inmates, techniques for reestablishing the status of citizen and reintegrating offenders back into the community are less well developed. As over 90% of all inmates will, at some future date, return to society, this long-neglected area of corrections assumes even greater significance.

Among the initial impacts on the parolee are the overpowering pace of life in the community compared to the predictable daily routine in the prison and the loss of what Irwin (1970:116) terms the "vast repertoire of taken-for-granted, automatic responses and actions" that civilians use to handle day-to-day encounters and situations. Parolees and offenders on statutory release may experience anxiety, isolation, and loneliness, and may feel self-conscious. For those offenders who have been confined for several years, the fast pace of society may be overwhelming.

Many offenders will have lost touch with their family and friends. They are confronted with a bewildering number of choices and decisions. Upon release the offender must find housing and employment, shop, and interact with a wide variety of people in diverse settings. Stable employment is the cornerstone for successful reentry. Federal offenders on parole told Battle (1990) that securing and maintaining employment was the key to a successful transition to the community. This finding emphasizes the importance of institutional vocational training programs designed to provide inmates with marketable employment skills.

Many offenders are unable to make the adjustment to the free community and often turn to alcohol or drugs to relieve stress and anxiety. They may reestablish contact with former criminal associates or other offenders whom they met while incarcerated, increasing the likelihood that their parole will be revoked or terminated. Offenders released under mandatory supervision may experience even greater pains of reentry and require more intensive supervision and assistance in order to make a successful transition back into the community.

There is some question as to whether parole officers alone can address all of the needs of parolees. Burdened by increasing paperwork and ever-expanding caseloads, most parole officers are able to provide only cursory supervision to the parolees on their caseload. Compounding this is the dual role — that of enforcer of the parole conditions and maintaining surveillance of offenders and that of a resource person and confidant — that the parole officer must play. Knowing that the parole officer may "violate" them for any breach of their parole conditions, many parolees are hesitant to establish close relations with their parole officer. The high rate of failures of offenders who are denied parole and receive statutory release suggests that such assistance may not be available or effective in addressing their needs. A federal Working Group on Conditional Release (Solicitor General of Canada, 1981:91-92) found evidence that this group of inmates was treated differentially (more harshly) by parole officers, who had little interest in their needs, and that these offenders were more likely to be revoked for technical violations rather than for reoffending.

An examination of reoffending patterns indicates the following.

▸   *There is a high rate of successful completion of parole by federal and provincial offenders.*

The rates of successful parole completion for federal offenders have remained fairly consistent around 70%. For offenders released by provincial parole boards in British Columbia, Quebec, and Ontario, the completion rate is higher, averaging around 84%. The success rates for offenders released on mandatory supervision, however, are quite low, generally around 50%.

▸   *The constant media focus on crimes committed by offenders under supervision in the community contributes to public perceptions that parolees and offenders on statutory release are responsible for larger numbers of heinous crimes.*

The research data indicate, however, that the offences committed by offenders on parole or mandatory supervision actually contribute very little to the overall Canadian crime rate.

▸   *There are identifiable factors related to parole success and failure.*

A study of female offenders released on parole conducted by Canfield (1989:58-60) found that 43% had committed new offences and were reconvicted within two years of being released on parole. Reconvictions were highest among those women who had committed their first criminal offence when they were less than 20 years old; had no record of employment; had most recently been admitted to a federal institution for having violated their prior release conditions by committing a new offence; and who had been released from custody on mandatory supervision. Women who were older at the time of their admission to prison and who had successfully completed a day parole had higher success rates.

It is important that offenders on release have friends and family members who provide support and who are law-abiding. Parolees who lack such support usually have higher rates of parole suspension.

SUPERVISION OF OFFENDERS IN THE COMMUNITY

Inmates granted a full parole are placed under the supervision of a parole officer employed by the Correctional Service of Canada and are required to adhere to the conditions of release imposed by the NPB. The standard general conditions for inmates released on full parole (as well as day parole and mandatory supervision) include the requirements that the inmate remain in designated areas and obtain the approval of, or inform, the supervising parole officer prior to changing address, incurring debts by borrowing money, or purchasing a weapon. The parolee is also obliged to obey the law and fulfill all legal and social responsibilities. Additional conditions may be attached to the release, such as a requirement to abstain from the use of alcohol and drugs and from associating with specific individuals in the community.

Failure to adhere to the conditions may result in the suspension and revocation of parole. Parole may by suspended where a breach of a parole condition has occurred, to prevent the breach of a parole condition, or in order to protect society. Following the decision to suspend parole, a "Warrant of Apprehension and Suspension" is issued and the parolee is taken into custody. The *Corrections and Conditional Release Act* (1992) sets out the procedures to be followed by the NPB in cases where parole or statutory release has been suspended. In conducting the post-suspension review, the NPB has several options:

- ▸ cancelling the suspension and reinstating the release;
- ▸ reprimanding the offender and reinstating the release;
- ▸ reinstating the release with additional conditions;
- ▸ detaining the offender for a period of up to 30 days in order to develop alternative release plans or as a disciplinary measure;
- ▸ terminating the parole release (the statutory release date remains as originally calculated); or
- ▸ revoking the parole, in which case the statutory release date is recalculated from the time remaining on the sentence at the time of revocation.

Court decisions based on the *Canadian Charter of Rights and Freedoms* have resulted in increased procedural safeguards for inmates during the suspension and revocation process, including the right to a hearing and the requirement that the inmate be provided with the reasons for the parole suspension. Considerable discretion, however, continues to be exercised by parole officers and NPB members in the suspension and revocation process.

A number of criticisms have been directed toward the supervision of offenders on parole. Parole conditions, it has been argued, are too vague, difficult to enforce, and may be too intrusive on the parolee's personal life. Concern has also been expressed about the broad discretionary powers exercised by parole officers in carrying out their supervisory tasks and in enforcing the conditions of parole. Individual parole officers may have different "styles" of supervision, with some officers being more "enforcement" and control-oriented, and others taking a more human service approach to their work. Needless to say, the style of the parole officer may play a significant role in the success or failure of the parolee. Remember, parolees can have their parole revoked or terminated for violating a general or specific condition of their parole. It is not required that a parolee be arrested and convicted of a new criminal offence in order for them to be sent back to the institution.

Non-Profit Organizations and Community Supervision

A unique attribute of Canadian corrections, particularly in comparison with its U.S. counterpart, is the extensive role played by non-profit organizations in the delivery of community corrections programs and services. Across the country, a variety of organizations are involved in providing programs and services to offenders on probation, parole, and mandatory supervision. These include the John Howard Society, the Elizabeth Fry Society, the St. Leonard's Society, Friendship Centres, and the Salvation Army. The Elizabeth Fry Society, for example, operates community residences, supervises women and men on federal parole, and supervises community service orders for offenders who have that as a condition of their probation order. Similar to the organizations noted above, Elizabeth Fry is a non-profit organization that contracts with the provincial and federal governments to provide services. A National Liaison Committee, a coalition of organizations that operate community corrections programs and services, provides a link between individual organizations and the Correctional Service of Canada, as well as a forum for the discussion of regional and national issues.

The increasing recognition of the needs of offenders who have been released from confinement has led to a number of unique initiatives by federal corrections. One such initiative is the Team Supervision Unit program. In an attempt to reduce the high failure rate of offenders released on mandatory supervision, a new program called the Team

Supervision Unit (TSU) has been developed in the Ontario and Pacific regions on a pilot basis. The program is designed for high-risk offenders who are released on "one-chance" mandatory supervision. Each parole officer is assigned a maximum of 12 offenders. Working as a team, parole officers attached to the TSU provide a range of activities, including biweekly meetings with the offender, attention to the offenders' family and friends, and the development of community resources for offenders. Intermediate sanctions, such as restricted curfew hours, increased parole officer-offender contact, and placement in a community residential facility are used. Offender performance is reviewed after six months and, if it is satisfactory, they are transferred to a normal supervision unit. We consider the issues surrounding the use of intermediate sanctions in greater detail in Chapter 13.

In 1990, the Correctional Service of Canada initiated a number of pilot projects for intensive supervision of high-risk/high-need federal offenders. These initiatives were undertaken in several Correctional Service of Canada regions across the country on the basis of recommendations from the Community Institutional Programs Task Force. The programs provide intensive parole supervision and parole officers' caseloads are limited to 12 parolees. Evaluations of the various pilot projects were being conducted during 1992.

In addition, a number of innovative programs are operated by non-profit organizations under contract with the Correctional Service of Canada and by provincial corrections services.

▶　*Cody Apartment Centre Program, London, Ontario*

Operated by an affiliate of the St. Leonard's Society of Canada, this apartment building contains a group home setting for offenders on day parole, and self-contained apartment units for offenders on full parole and mandatory supervision. Among the programs offered by the centre are alcohol and drug abuse education, programs design to prevent relapse, and life management skills (Kaye-Burge, 1991).

▶　*Prince George (B.C.) Activator Society*

The objective of the Society is to provide programs and services that will facilitate the successful reentry of federal and provincial offenders into the community. These programs include counselling, stress and anger management, and a program for sex offenders. The Society operates a hobby farm and woodshop that provides employment for ex-offenders, and a forestry camp for federal and provincial inmates. Offenders at the camp may complete a six-month certification course in forestry under the auspices of the local community college (Madhok, 1991).

▸   *Community Ministry with Ex-Offenders (C.M.E.O.)*

This program is an inter-denominational ministry in Winnipeg that provides a wide range of counselling and support services for ex-offenders and their families in an attempt to reduce family violence. These services are delivered within a holistic family-oriented approach that includes formal and informal counselling sessions, 24-hour telephone access to program staff, assistance with spiritual issues, and other crisis-intervention support. C.M.E.O. is funded by the federal Correctional Service of Canada (see Martens, 1992).

Readers are encouraged to become familiar with the community-based programs and services offered by provincial and federal corrections, as well as by non-profit organizations in their area.

THE CONTROVERSY OVER COMMUNITY CORRECTIONS

Much of the controversy surrounding community corrections in Canada has focused on two major issues: (1) the effectiveness of community corrections in achieving its objectives; and (2) the involvement (or lack thereof) of the "community" in community corrections initiatives.

Community Corrections: The Rhetoric and the Reality

Correctional observers disagree about the primary reason why corrections shifted its focus of attention to the development of community-based programs during the 1960s. Some explanations have focused on the perceived failure of institutional rehabilitation programs and increased humanitarian concerns with the negative consequences of confinement, although other observers contend that the move was economically motivated — an attempt to reduce the costs of incarcerating ever-increasing numbers of offenders.

A number of questions have surrounded the debate over the implementation of community corrections programs over the past two decades, including the following.

▶ *Have community corrections programs merely "expanded the net" of social control?*

A major justification for the development and implementation of community corrections programs, particularly diversion and probation, was that these initiatives would reduce the number of offenders involved in the criminal justice system and reduce institutional populations. However, there is considerable evidence that "net-widening" has occurred, resulting in more people being placed under some form of supervision or control. Chan and Ericson (1981:55) argue that "people are not diverted from, but into and within the system" (see Lowman and Menzies, 1986).

Since their inception, diversion programs have been surrounded by controversy, critics arguing that they have functioned to widen the net, placing under supervision first-time, minor offenders who would otherwise have been screened out of the criminal justice system. Further, concerns have been expressed about the coercive nature of diversion programs, the *alleged* offender being presented with the option of either participating in a diversion program or facing prosecution. Although diversion programs appear to provide a considerable cost-saving for the criminal justice system, there is no clear evidence of their effectiveness.

In many jurisdictions, increases in institutional populations have been accompanied by a growth in the numbers of persons being diverted and increases in the caseloads of probation offices. This was a finding of a major survey of alternative sentencing programs across the country undertaken by Ekstedt and Jackson (1986). Other findings of interest from the survey were that offenders who tend to be referred to diversion and probation programs are low-risk, minor offenders who would not generally be given a sentence of confinement. This raises the question as to whether such programs are operating as true alternatives to confinement. Conversely, in some jurisdictions, concern is being expressed that the number of serious offenders referred to alternative community-based programs has increased.

This has led critics to argue that diversion and probation have become supplements to, rather than substitutes for, incarceration. Supporters of community corrections counter by pointing out that the majority of federal and provincial offenders are under some form of community supervision. This despite the fact that institutional corrections consumes the large percentage of corrections resources, leaving around 10% of operating budgets for community corrections programs.

▸   *Are community corrections programs effective in assisting offenders in readjusting to society?*

Over the years, serious questions have been raised about the effectiveness of community-based corrections programs in assisting offenders to readjust successfully in the community. While many correctional observers have adopted the "nothing works" perspective, evidence suggests (as with institutional treatment programs) that "some things work." Preliminary insights as to the potential effectiveness of various programs can be gleaned from the following examples.

The limited release technique of TAs appears to be highly successful. Over 99% of ETAs and UTAs are successfully completed. Despite the difficulties that surround full parole noted above, 70% of federal offenders successfully complete their period of supervision in the community and the rate is higher for offenders granted full parole release by provincial parole boards. The provincial TA programs in Ontario appear to be successful in facilitating the payment of restitution to crime victims and assisting offenders to remain employed following discharge from supervision (Ekstedt and Jackson, 1986:91).

Holosko and Carlson (1986) reported that over two-thirds (67.4%) of a sample of offenders released from a community residential centre (CRC) had not been reconvicted of an offence during a two-year follow-up period. Kaill and Murphy (1985) found in a study of offenders released from a community correctional centre (CCC) in the Atlantic region that those offenders who had participated in the CCC program had lower re-arrest rates than those offenders who had been released directly from the institution. The highest reconviction rates were posted by offenders who had been convicted of property offences and younger offenders with lengthy criminal records. These findings suggest that older offenders with fewer prior convictions are the most likely to benefit from a CCC program.

Offenders released on statutory release fare the worst, with about one in every two failing to complete the required period of supervision. This high failure rate is not surprising, given that those offenders released on statutory release have not been granted parole and are generally the higher-risk offenders.

Many of the same factors may play a role in the potential effectiveness of community corrections programs as with their institutional counterparts. For example, it is important to match offender needs with the appropriate program and to impose the requisite amount of supervision and control required. This is the "risk principle," which holds that higher levels of service and supervision are required for higher-risk cases (see Andrews, 1989). Similarly, offenders must be provided with support services to assist them in coping with the "pains of reentry" and with employment and educational opportunities that give them a "stake" in becoming law-abiding citizens. These opportunities must be as attractive as those that would exist should the offender return to committing crimes.[6] Ekstedt and Jackson (1986) found that the success of alternative programs often depends upon the individuals involved in setting up and operating the programs and, as a consequence, personnel changes may result in a lack of continuity in service delivery.

Whither the "Community" in Community Corrections?

For community corrections programs to be not only "in" the community, but "of" the community, there must be substantive involvement on the part of the general public. Unfortunately, as we have already noted, there is very little actual participation in community-based corrections by Canadian citizens.

In recent years, an attempt has been made to gain a better understanding not only of the attitudes that citizens have toward community corrections, but also the factors that influence the opinions that the general public hold. Among the findings from two national surveys (Adams, 1990) and a survey conducted for the Canadian Sentencing Commission (Roberts, 1988) were the following.

▸ *The general public has little knowledge about early release and often confuse the various forms of release.*

Only one-third of the sample of citizens surveyed for the Canadian Sentencing Commission (1987) were able to correctly identify what full parole was, while 15% correctly identified mandatory supervision (the predecessor to statutory release). Many respondents confused the two.

This lack of knowledge extends to convicted offenders. In a survey of federal inmates in Quebec, Landreville *et al.* (1988) found that many offenders had little understanding of the operation of the criminal justice system generally, knew very little about how probation worked, and were confused about what minimum and maximum sentence terms meant.

▶   *The general public tends to overestimate both the leniency of the parole board and the numbers of offenders released on parole who reoffend.*

While the general public tends to view the parole board as becoming more lenient in its decision making in recent years, release figures indicate that the parole-granting rate has remained fairly stable at between 30% to 35%. Citizens also overestimate the percentage of released offenders who recommit property and violent crimes while under supervision in the community. For example, while only 2% of every 100 parolees commits a crime against the person prior to the expiry of their supervision period, 56% of citizens surveyed estimated that between 30% and 100% did so.

▶   *Many Canadians have serious reservations about the parole process.*

While the majority of citizens surveyed support the principle of early release and do not want to see the practice abolished, serious reservations were expressed about how parole was practiced nevertheless. More specifically, respondents felt that parole should be more difficult to obtain and that offenders should serve more than one-third of their sentence before being eligible for parole consideration. Citizens also felt that insufficient attention was given to the risks posed by the offender during the deliberations of the parole board (Adams, 1990).

▶   *Canadians are more supportive of rehabilitation in the community than in the prison, with some reservations.*

There appears to be support for the concept of halfway houses and other correctional services, such as counselling and community service, delivered in the community. However, there is a strong "NIMBY" (Not In My Backyard) factor at work as well. While the public generally recognizes the importance of halfway houses, there is concern about such facilities being located in their own neighbourhoods because of a concern over security and lack of supervision over the residents.

▸ *Citizens often have little information about community corrections programs, a knowledge gap that affects their perceptions and concerns.*

The failure of corrections to provide local residents with information about halfway house facilities and other community corrections programs and to solicit the active participation and support of residents prior to and after such programs are established exacerbates the fears and concerns of the citizenry. Too often, citizens learn about such plans and programs via the media. Also, it is from the media that the general public tends to hear about the failures of offenders under community supervision rather than about the successes, further contributing to their concerns.

While it is not uncommon for television and radio newscasters to note that individuals who have been charged with an offence are "on parole," rarely is attention given to those offenders who successfully complete their period of supervision in the community. Again, as we have so often noted, the corrections services have done very little to alter these perceptions by providing examples of successes and by disseminating information about parole board decision making and parole supervision. There is a need for the development of models for the delivery of community corrections services that involve the community in a significant way (see Byrne, 1989).

NOTES

[1]For an extensive discussion of community-based corrections in Canada, see Ekstedt and Griffiths (1988). See also the Working Group of the Correctional Law Review (Solicitor General of Canada, 1987) and the *Corrections and Conditional Release Act* (1992) for further details on the objectives and operation of conditional release.

[2]For discussions of the use of community service orders in various provincial jurisdictions across Canada, see Doyle and Gaudet (1984); Hackett (1980); Hermann and Carey (1985); Jackson (1982); and Polonski (1981).

[3]For an extensive review of the major issues surrounding the use of TAs or federal inmates, see Pepino (1992).

[4]*The Corrections and Conditional Release Act* (Bill C-36), enacted in 1992, eliminated remission. In the past, inmates had to earn their remission or "good time" through good conduct in the institution. Those inmates who committed disciplinary infractions could lose part of their good time. The use of earned remission to control inmate behaviour and to encourage inmate participation in correctional programs in the institution was widely criticized. Under the new scheme of statutory remission, all inmates not granted a parole will be released after having served two-thirds of their sentence unless they are subject to specific detention provisions. Remission can no longer be lost as a result of disciplinary charges, and "good time" no longer exists as an incentive for good conduct.

[5]Lisa Hobbs Birnie (1990) has written a first-person account of her experiences as a member of the NPB. *A Rock and a Hard Place* provides fascinating insights into the decision making of the NPB.

[6]One of the major issues confronting corrections officials is how to ensure continuity of treatment for offenders once their period of parole supervision or statutory release expires. This is particularly critical for certain categories of offenders, that is, sex offenders who may have long-term treatment needs. Generally, once offenders complete their period of parole or mandatory supervision, they are ineligible to participate further in programs operated or sponsored by provincial or federal corrections systems. We consider this issue in our discussion of sex offenders in Chapter 13.

REFERENCES

Adams, M. 1990. "Canadian Attitudes toward Crime and Justice." 2 *FORUM on Corrections Research.* 10-13.

Aasen, J.N. 1985. *Enforcement of Probation in British Columbia.* Master's thesis. Burnaby, British Columbia: Simon Fraser University, School of Criminology.

Andrews, D.A. 1989. "Recidivism is Predictable and Can Be Influenced: Using Risk Assessments to Reduce Recidivism." 1 *FORUM on Corrections Research.* 11-17.

Battle, J. 1990. *Reducing the Barriers — An Analysis of Employment Needs of Recently Released Federal Offenders, Edmonton Metropolitan Area.* Ottawa: Employment and Immigration Canada and Correctional Service of Canada.

Birnie, L.H. 1990. *A Rock and a Hard Place — Inside Canada's Parole Board.* Toronto: Macmillan.

Bonta, J., J. Boyle, L.L. Motiuk, and P. Sonnichsen. 1983. "Restitution in Correctional Halfway Houses: Victim Satisfaction, Attitudes, and Recidivism." 25 *Canadian Journal of Criminology.* 277-93.

Bryne, J.M. 1989. "Reintegrating the Concept of *Community* into Community-Based Corrections." 35 *Crime and Delinquency*. 471-99.

Canadian Bar Association. 1988. *Parole and Early Release*. Ottawa: Canadian Bar Association.

Canadian Centre for Justice Statistics. 1991. *Adult Correctional Services in Canada, 1990-91*. Ottawa Supply and Services Canada.

Canadian Sentencing Commission. 1987. *Sentencing Reform: A Canadian Approach*. Ottawa: Supply and Services Canada.

Canfield, C. 1989. *The Parole Process and Risk Upon Release for the Female Offender*. Ottawa: Solicitor General of Canada.

Chan, J.B.L., and R.V. Ericson. 1981. *Decarceration and the Economy of Penal Reform*. Toronto: University of Toronto, Centre of Criminology.

Daubney, D. 1988. *Taking Responsibility. Report of the Standing Committee on Justice and Solicitor General on Its Review of Sentencing, Conditional Release and Related Aspects of Corrections*. Ottawa: Solicitor General of Canada.

Doyle, P., and M. Gaudet. 1984. *Community Service Orders: Justice in the Community — The Prince Edward Island Experience*. Charlottetown: Department of Justice.

Ekstedt, J.W., and C.T. Griffiths. 1988. *Corrections in Canada:Policy and Practice*. 2nd ed. Toronto: Butterworths.

Ekstedt, J.W., and M.A. Jackson. 1986. *A Profile of Canadian Alternative Sentencing Programmes: A National Review of Policy Issues*. Burnaby, British Columbia: Simon Fraser University, School of Criminology.

Hackett, C. 1980. *The Community Service Order Program in Newfoundland*. St. John's: Adult Corrections Division, Department of Justice.

Hagan, J., J. Hewitt, and D. Alwin. 1979. "Ceremonial Justice: Crime and Punishment in a Loosely Coupled System." 58 *Social Forces*. 506-27.

Hatt, K. 1985. "Probation and Community Corrections in Neo-Correctional Era." 27 *Canadian Journal of Criminology*. 299-316.

Hermann, S., and C. Carey. 1985. *Alternative to Incarceration*.Toronto: Policy, Planning and Evaluation Branch, Ministry of Correctional Services.

Holosko, M.J., and T.M. Carlson. 1986. "Recidivism among Ex-offenders Residing at a CRC in St. John's, Newfoundland." 28 *Canadian Journal of Criminology*. 385-96.

Hugessen, J.K. 1973. *Task Force on Release of Inmates*. Ottawa: Information Canada.

Irwin, J. 1970. *The Felon*. Englewood Cliffs, New Jersey: Prentice-Hall.

Jackson, M.A. 1982. *Judicial Attitudes toward Community Sentencing Options*. Toronto: Ministry of Correctional Services.

Jackson, M.A., C.D. Webster, and J. Hagan. 1982. "Probation Outcome: Is It Necessary to Fulfil the Conditions?" 24 *Canadian Journal of Criminology*. 267-77.

Kaill, R.C., and D.A. Murphy. 1985. *Measuring Community Correctional Centre Effectiveness: An Empirical Evaluation*. Halifax: Atlantic Institute of Criminology, Department of Sociology and Social Anthropology.

Kaye-Burge, P. 1991. "Cody Centre Introduces New Program." *Let's Talk* (March). 12.

Landreville, P., M. Hamelin, and S. Gagnier. 1988. *Opinions of Quebec Inmates Regarding Questions Raised by the Mandate of the Canadian Sentencing Commission*. Ottawa: Department of Justice.

Madhok, I. 1991. "Prince George Activator Society: Helping Offenders Rebuild Their Lives." *Let's Talk* (July). 11.

Mandel, M. 1984-85. "Democracy, Class and the National Parole Board." 27 *Criminal Law Quarterly*. 159-81.

Martens, H.L. 1992. *An Eco-Systemic Approach to Family Violence and Related Recidivism*. Ottawa: Solicitor General of Canada.

Mayne, C., and G. Garrison. 1979. *Summary of the Study Report on Restitution*. Charlottetown: Probation and Family Court Services Division, Department of Justice.

Menzies, K. 1986. "The Rapid Spread of Community Service Orders in Ontario." 28 *Canadian Journal of Criminology*. 157-69.

Nasim, S.A., and R. Spellisay. 1985. *An Evaluation of the Saskatchewan Restitution Program*. Regina: Policy, Planning, and Evaluation Branch, Department of Justice.

Nicolas, M. 1976. *La Suspension de la Liberation Conditionelle: Processus et Decision*. Montreal: University of Montreal, Centre of Criminology.

Nuffield, J. 1981. "Parole Guidelines: Are They a Worthwhile Control on Discretion?" In *The National Parole Board Report on the Conference on Discretion in the Correctional System*. Ottawa: National Parole Board.

_____. 1982. *Parole Decision Making in Canada: Research toward Decision Guidelines*. Ottawa: Supply and Services Canada.

_____. 1989. "The 'SIR Scale': Some Reflections on Its Applications." 1 *FORUM on Corrections Research*. 19-22.

O'Connor, F.C. 1985. "The Impact of the Canadian Charter of Rights and Freedoms on Parole in Canada." 10 *Queen's Law Journal*. 336-91.

Ouimet, R. 1969. *Report of the Canadian Committee on Corrections — Toward Unity: Criminal Justice and Corrections*. Ottawa: Information Canada.

Pepino, N.J. 1992. *Report of the Panel Appointed to Review the Temporary Absence Program for Penitentiary Inmates*. Ottawa: Supply and Services Canada.

Polonski, M.L. 1981. *The Community Service Order Program in Ontario: Summary*. Toronto: Correctional Services Canada.

Roberts, J. 1988. "Early Release from Prison: What Do the Canadian Public Really Think?" 30 *Canadian Journal of Criminology*. 231-249.

Sheridan, A.K.B., and J. Konrad. 1976. "Probation." In W.T. McGrath, *Crime and Its Treatment in Canada*. 249-302. 2nd ed. Toronto: Macmillan.

Solicitor General of Canada. 1981. *Solicitor General's Study of Conditional Release. Report of the Working Group*. Ottawa: Supply and Services Canada.

_____. 1987. *Conditional Release. Correctional Law Review Working Paper No. 3*. Ottawa: Solicitor General of Canada.

Zapf, M.K. 1984. *Yukon Restitution Study*. Whitehorse: Department of Justice, Yukon Territory.

Zapf, M.K., and B. Cole. 1985. "Yukon Restitution Study." 27 *Canadian Journal of Criminology*. 477-89.

13 CRITICAL ISSUES IN CANADIAN CORRECTIONS

In our discussions of the history of the response to criminal offenders, we have seen that reform in institutional and community-based corrections has occurred at a glacial pace. Observers of corrections often experience déjà vu when reading the seemingly endless reports and recommendations of task forces and commissions of inquiry responding to the latest crisis.

The beginning of the 1990s, however, appears to have brought some "fresh winds" to corrections. Federal corrections, for the first time in its history, has a mission statement and a set of strategic objectives. The *Corrections and Conditional Release Act* (1992) contains a statement of principles for the National Parole Board (NPB), detailed provisions relating to prison disciplinary procedures, and a statutory basis for the Office of the Correctional Investigator. These measures have injected a measure of accountability — for offenders and for corrections personnel from the line level to senior management — that has been largely absent in previous eras. So too does there appear to be an emerging openness in the operation of the corrections system, a welcome change from the defensive, crisis-management orientation of past years. Research, long confined to the role of justifying policy decisions already taken, appears to be informing the formulation of policy and practice.

Corrections systems have changed because the society in which they operate has changed. Corrections systems have been forced to become more accountable, if only because of the massive operational costs (nearly $1 billion at the federal level), rising crime rates, and the changing legislative framework, for example, the *Canadian Charter of Rights and Freedoms,* within which corrections systems operate. While it is much too early to determine whether Canada is experiencing the dawn of a new, more humane and effective "era" in corrections, thus far it appears as if the 1990s hold the potential for substantive change.

In this chapter, we consider several of the critical issues confronting Canadian corrections: (1) the female offender; (2) sex offenders; (3) the continuing debate over the death penalty; (4) the long-term offender; and (5) intermediate sanctions and the use of electronic monitoring. While this list is by no means exhaustive, the selected topics do provide key insights into the changing landscape of corrections.

THE FEMALE OFFENDER

Historically, correctional systems have given little attention to female offenders. The treatment traditionally accorded to female offenders by the federal and provincial corrections system has been succinctly described as "a mixture of neglect, outright barbarism and well-meaning paternalism" (Berzins and Cooper, 1982:401). Until the construction of the Prison for Women (P4W) at Kingston, Ontario, in 1934, female federal offenders were often housed in temporary quarters in male prisons and had little or no access to programs and services. Such arrangements often gave rise to mistreatment. The Brown Commission noted in its reports in 1848-49 that women housed in the Kingston Penitentiary had been physically and sexually abused (Cooper, 1987). Historically, prison programs for female inmates reflected traditional role-model activities such as hair dressing and sewing. The relatively small number of female offenders was often used as an explanation by correctional agencies for the lack of program opportunities.

After decades of living in the shadows of their male counterparts, however, female offenders and the issues surrounding their involvement in provincial and federal corrections systems have surged to the forefront of political discussion and correctional policy. This change has been fueled by a number of factors, including the feminist movement, the increased pressure by Aboriginal peoples to assume greater control over justice issues, the enactment of the *Canadian Charter of Rights and Freedoms* and, in federal corrections, the Correctional Service of Canada's mission statement (see Adelberg and Currie, 1987; Axon, 1989a; Chunn and Gavigan, 1991).

Female Offenders in the Correctional System

In 1991, females accounted for approximately 10% of persons charged with violent crimes and 20% of those charged with property offences. The majority of *Criminal Code* offences committed by women involved theft or fraud, and a large number of these are theft under $1,000 (primarily shoplifting). In 1990-91, female offenders comprised 3% of all admissions to federal institutions and 8% of admissions to provincial facilities. At the provincial level, there is a disproportionate number of female offenders who are Aboriginal, as high as 90% in some facilities in the Prairie provinces.

In 1992, there were approximately 300 federally sentenced female offenders, with one-third on parole or mandatory supervision, one-third residing in provincial institutions under exchange-of-service agreements, and the remainder in the P4W in Kingston, Ontario.

The majority of female offenders have been described as "poor, uneducated members of minority groups who are lacking in marketable skills, dependent on welfare, alcohol and men, and are single parents who are solely responsible for child-care" (Ross and Fabiano, 1985:4). These attributes are evident in the profile of the female offenders admitted to the provincially operated Pine Grove Correctional Centre in Prince Albert, Saskatchewan, in 1985.

> ▸ 21% of the women were serving sentences for drinking and driving, 25% for property crimes, and 45% for non-payment of fines;
> ▸ 60% of the women were serving sentences of less than 30 days, consistent with data from other provinces that suggest that as many as 75% of women receive sentences of less than 30 days;
> ▸ 83% were Aboriginal;
> ▸ 75% were under age 30;
> ▸ 78% had more than two children;
> ▸ most had been unemployed prior to admission, and nearly three-fourths had a grade nine education or less; and
> ▸ 55% had been victims of sexual abuse, and nearly 80% admitted to serious drug or alcohol addiction problems (Daubney, 1988:221-22).

There is little evidence to suggest that the attributes of most female inmate populations at the provincial or federal levels have changed in the five years since these particular observations were recorded.

The primary catalyst for the current policy and program initiatives directed toward the federal female offender have been the *Report of the Task Force on Federally Sentenced Women* (Diamond and Phelps, 1990) and several companion reports (see Axon, 1989b; Evans, 1989; Heney, 1990; Shaw *et al.*, 1990; Shaw, 1989; Sugar and Fox, 1990). These documents examine in considerable detail the major issues surrounding the female offender in the federal corrections system, from sentencing and incarceration, to release and the expiry of sentence. Many of the reports and their recommendations are based on materials gathered in interviews with female offenders, including Aboriginal women.

The following were among the task force's more significant findings:

- ▸ The Kingston P4W was inadequate in terms of the physical environment, programmatic opportunities, its geographic distance from the offender's home communities and families, and its multi-level security rating, which resulted in most women being overclassified.
- ▸ There was a need for more community-based facilities for female offenders, situated close to their communities.
- ▸ 80% of federally sentenced women had experienced physical and/or sexual abuse during their lives; the rates were even higher for Aboriginal women.
- ▸ Many federally sentenced female offenders were involved in substance abuse, which contributed to their criminality.
- ▸ Two-thirds of the women interviewed were mothers who experienced severe hardship by being separated from their children.
- ▸ The majority of women interviewed lacked high-school-level education or training beyond high school.
- ▸ There was a critical need for programs in education to address alcohol and drug addiction, and to provide contact with families, children, and communities.
- ▸ Aboriginal offenders required culturally sensitive programs and facilities that would reduce their isolation from their culture and communities.

Facilities for the Federal Female Offender

There is perhaps no better illustration of the difficulties of reforming the correctional system to improve facilities and programs for female offenders than the saga of the Kingston P4W. With the exception of federal female offenders serving their time in provincial institutions under exchange-of-service agreements, all federal female offenders have served their time at P4W. Among the difficulties of P4W are the limitations, including cramped living quarters, imposed by the physical facility (built in 1934) and the distances that families of inmates have to travel for visitations. Further, the designation of P4W as a multi-level facility resulted in all levels of security being housed in the same institution, undermining "cascading," which is one of the major offender management techniques of the Correctional Service of Canada. As discussed in Chapter 11, cascading involves placing offenders in decreasing levels of security as they serve their term of confinement. The great distances between the inmate's home community and Kingston also hindered the development of release plans and the identification of community resources that might be used upon reentry.

Efforts to phase out the P4W and regionalize accommodation for women under federal jurisdiction can be traced back over 70 years. In 1914, a report of the Royal Commission on Penitentiaries (Canada, 1914) recommended that female offenders be transferred to provincial institutions to serve their federal sentences. Despite this, the P4W was opened in 1934, although only four years later, the Archambault Commission (1938) severely criticized the operation of the P4W and recommended the transfer of inmates to provincial facilities. Over the next 40 years, no fewer than nine correctional inquiries recommended that the P4W be closed and that services for female offenders be provided through provincial institutions. Now, finally, in 1993, it appears that the P4W will be closed permanently.

A number of alternatives were considered for housing federal female offenders in the post-P4W era, including housing them in provincial facilities under expanded exchange-of-service agreements and developing co-correctional facilities. However, following recommendations from the Task Force on Federally Sentenced Women (1990), the Correctional Service of Canada will build five small, regional, federally operated facilities across the country, to be completed in 1994. These facilities are to be situated to maximize the use of community mental health and education programs. In addition, a healing lodge is to be built in Saskatchewan that will provide a housing alternative for federally sentenced Aboriginal women should they choose not to be incarcerated in their home province or territory.

The Pains of Imprisonment

Chapter 11 noted that prison inmates experience "pains of imprisonment" as a consequence of their loss of freedom and confinement in the total institutional world of the prison. While both male and female offenders experience these "pains," an emerging body of evidence suggests that the stresses and anxieties associated with confinement may be much more severe for female offenders. This is due to a number of factors, including the often long distances between their home communities and the facilities in which they are incarcerated; the separation of inmate mothers from their children; and the impact of confinement upon women who have experienced physical and emotional abuse during their childhood.

One manifestation of the pains of imprisonment experienced by female offenders is self-injurious behaviour, which research findings suggest may be much more frequent among female inmates than their male counterparts. Interviews (Heney, 1990) with a sample of women at P4W revealed that self-injurious behaviour was a major coping strategy and that nearly 60% of the women interviewed had engaged in self-injurious behaviour during their confinement, including attempted suicide and self-mutilation. Seventy-three percent of these women had been the victims of childhood abuse.[1]

We have previously noted that female offenders in P4W were often hundreds and even thousands of miles from their homes. While the closing of P4W will alleviate some of the difficulties associated with distance, all of the proposed regional facilities for women will be situated in urban areas in the southern reaches of the provinces. Female inmates from northern and rural areas of the provinces will continue to be far removed from their communities, families, and children. And although the creation of a healing lodge for Aboriginal women can be considered a major step forward in addressing the unique needs of Aboriginal female offenders, it is likely that many of the women confined there will be hundreds of miles from their home reserve or community. In short, the relatively small numbers of female offenders makes difficult the development of facilities close to the offender's home communities. One remedy would be to create more community-based facilities such as halfway houses and to expand the use of intermediate sanctions, which would allow many female offenders to remain in their home communities.

Inmate mothers also suffer additional pains of imprisonment, although historically little attention has been given to the needs of inmate mothers and their children (see MacLeod, 1986). Unlike their counterparts in many foreign countries (for example, Mexico and Egypt), female inmates in Canada have only recently been allowed to keep their children in prison with them — and only until a very young age. Estimates are that between 50% to 70% of female offenders have children. There are substantial costs associated with incarcerating women who are mothers, not only in terms of the costs of providing alternative child-care arrangements, but also in terms of the social costs of separation for both the mother and the child(ren) (see Wine, 1992). Further, inmate mothers run the risk of being found "unfit" under provincial child welfare legislation and losing control of their children.

Across North America in recent years, a variety of innovative programs and services have been developed for inmate mothers and their children (see Cannings, 1990). In Canada, there have been isolated efforts by federal and provincial corrections officials to address the special needs of inmate mothers.

- ▸ For several years, women in P4W have recorded video-taped messages to their children and have had access to a Family Visiting Unit for periods up to 72 hours once every three months.
- ▸ Provincial facilities in Brandon, Manitoba, and in Guelph, Ontario, operate inmate-staffed child-care programs that provide supervision during visitation hours.
- ▸ At the Pine Grove Correctional Centre in Prince Albert, Saskatchewan, an annual camp retreat was initiated that allowed women and their children to spend weekends together at a local church camp.
- ▸ The Portage Correctional Centre in Portage la Prairie, Manitoba, has a "live in" program that allows newborn infants to remain with their mothers, in a private room with a crib, for up to ten months with the possibility of an extension if the mother is to be released within the following month or two.
- ▸ Maison Tanguay (Tanguay Prison) in Montreal, Quebec, operates a program entitled "Family Continuity After Imprisonment" designed to strengthen the bonds between inmate mothers and their children; there is an overnight visitation program, workshops on parenting skills, and assistance provided to released inmate mothers.
- ▸ Under the "mother-baby" program at the Burnaby Correctional Centre for Women in British Columbia, inmate mothers may keep their newborn children for up to two years.

It is at the community level that the greatest potential exists for programs for inmate mothers and their children. Across Canada, the Elizabeth Fry Society and the John Howard Society provide assistance to inmate mothers and their children by facilitating family contact and by locating short-term and long-term care for children. However, few community-based residential facilities allow children to live with their mothers. A great deal of research remains to be done on issues related to incarcerated female offenders who are also mothers. This research would focus on the impact of separation on the children and the mothers; strategies for increasing contact between inmate mothers and their offspring, particularly older children; and potential for developing community residential facilities for inmate mothers and their children, as well as community-based resources and services.

The Aboriginal Female Offender

Our discussion in Chapter 15 will reveal that Aboriginal peoples are overrepresented from arrest to incarceration in many Canadian jurisdictions. However, it is the Aboriginal female offender who is most disproportionately represented in provincial and federal female prison populations, while receiving the least attention from both researchers and correctional officials. This overrepresentation is particularly acute in the Prairie provinces, where Aboriginal women often comprise over 80% of institutional populations.

Interviews with a sample of Aboriginal women (Sugar and Fox, 1990) in the community revealed that:

- ▸ 70% had experienced sexual assault or sexual abuse during their childhood or had witnessed violence against members of their family;
- ▸ nearly all had experienced racism in their lives;
- ▸ nearly 90% had been the victims of spousal assault;
- ▸ 80% had abused alcohol and 70% considered themselves addicted to narcotics;
- ▸ many had attempted suicide or engaged in self-injurious behaviour; and
- ▸ two-thirds of the women who were mothers had severe difficulties in maintaining contact with their children and less than half had been reunited with them on release.

Incarcerated Aboriginal women have difficulty adjusting to white, urban culture, are often alienated from their home community and culture, and do not have access to specialized programs to address their spiritual, psychological, and vocational needs (Adelberg, 1985:17-18). Even less attention has been given to the development of community-based programs and services for Aboriginal female offenders in northern and rural areas of the country.

Among the recommendations of the task force (Diamond and Phelps, 1990) were that there be an increase in Aboriginal staff, the development of culturally sensitive programs for Aboriginal women, an increased involvement of Aboriginal communities and elders in the delivery of correctional programs in institutions and in the community, and the construction of a "healing lodge" where Aboriginal women could serve all or part of their sentence. The healing lodge would be staffed primarily by Aboriginal personnel and programming would be structured around Aboriginal culture and traditions.

Release and Community Corrections Programs

The Task Force (Diamond and Phelps, 1990) also reported that there were severe deficiencies in the facilities and programs available for female offenders reentering the community. From interviews with female offenders on conditional release, Shaw *et al.* (1991) identified a number of difficulties, including the lack of pre-release courses; serious financial hardship, particularly among those women who did not have work skills; an inability to locate low-cost housing; and continuing problems with substance abuse.

The findings from this study revealed considerable variability in terms of need among those interviewed. This led to the recommendation that a wide range of community release facilities be constructed that would address the needs of offender mothers, Aboriginal women, and those with special needs. Currently, there are a variety of non-profit organizations, including the Elizabeth Fry Society, the John Howard Society, St. Leonard's, and the Salvation Army, that are extensively involved in providing programs and services, under contract, for federal and provincial female offenders.

Unlike its many predecessors, it appears that the findings and recommendations of the Task Force on Federally Sentenced Women have had a significant impact on correctional policy, although it is too early to determine whether the momentum will continue in the coming years and whether there will be a similar impact on the design and delivery of correctional programs for female offenders.

SEX OFFENDERS

In recent years, sex offenders have become perhaps the most high-profile offender group in Canada. This has placed increased pressures on correctional systems to develop effective treatment programs that will reduce the risk of reoffending once sex offenders are released back into the community.

The following are some background facts about the sex offender population in Canada:

> ▸   sex offenders comprise an increasing percentage of the federal corrections caseload, accounting for 11.3% of the total offender population in 1991;
> ▸   14 of every 100 federal prison inmates are sex offenders;
> ▸   most sex offenders are under the jurisdiction of provincial corrections systems;
> ▸   less than one of four sex offenders during 1987-1989 who received a sentence of imprisonment were given two years or more; and
> ▸   eight of every 100 federal offenders on conditional release in 1991 were sex offenders (Correctional Service of Canada, 1991:3-4).

Treating Sex Offenders: What Works?

Sex offenders are widely regarded as presenting the greatest challenges to treatment personnel. Sex offenders, more than most categories of offenders, often deny committing the offence even after conviction, or minimize the significance of their behaviour by "blaming the victim." Most treatment experts do not speak in terms of "curing" sex offenders, but rather in terms of treatment strategies to "manage" the offender, over the long-term, in the community, following a period of incarceration. Relapse prevention is a primary objective of correctional system programming at the institutional and community levels.[2]

A wide range of treatment strategies have been employed with sex offenders, including physiological methods, for example, drug therapy and psychological approaches that centre on group and individual therapy (see Glackman, 1991). Sex offender treatment programs are also operated by the federal Regional Psychiatric Centres in the Pacific region, Prairie region, and Ontario region, as well as by the Philippe-Pinel Institute in Montreal. The Pacific region program is a two-year, in-residence program based on intensive group psychotherapy. The Regional Treatment Centre in Ontario employs both individual and group psychotherapy.

There are also treatment groups directed by the inmates themselves. At Mountain Institution near Vancouver, inmates convicted of sex offences formed the Phoenix Self-Help Group, a 12-month program patterned on Alcoholics Anonymous. The inmate-run program focuses on education, self-awareness, and encouraging offenders to confront and address their behavioural problems.

Research on the effectiveness of correctional treatment programs indicates the following:

> ▸ some categories of sex offenders remain high risks to reoffend even after participating in treatment programs;
> ▸ the recidivism rate for federal sex offenders is less than that of offenders generally;
> ▸ those federal sex offenders who reoffend are likely to do so by committing another sex offence; and,
> ▸ nearly 70% of federal sex offenders released from prison between 1985-87 had not reoffended during a three-year follow-up period (Correctional Service of Canada, 1991; Solicitor General of Canada, 1990).

Some evidence suggests that *some* sex offenders who receive specialized forms of treatment have a reduced chance of reoffending once released. An evaluation (Gordon *et al.*, 1991) of the Clearwater Program for sex offenders, operated by the Prairie Regional Psychiatric Centre since 1981, suggests that offenders experienced behavioural changes as a consequence of their participation in the program. Further, upon release, those offenders who had been in treatment had 37% fewer reconvictions than those sex offenders who had not been exposed to the program during their period of incarceration. Offenders who had initially enrolled in the Clearwater Program, but who had not completed treatment, were at a greater risk to reoffend when released. These findings provide preliminary, but encouraging, evidence that treatment can alter the behaviour of some sex offenders.

Some types of sex offenders, however, may be more difficult to treat than others. A long-term study (Hanson, Steffy, and Gauthier, 1992) of offenders convicted of molesting children found that, while incest offenders were reconvicted at a lower rate than homosexual pedophiles, the recidivism rates for those offenders who had been exposed to treatment was similar to the rates for offenders who had not participated in any treatment programs.

Continuity of treatment upon release is also important (see Marshall and Eccles, 1991). In British Columbia, sex offenders on conditional release are supervised by specially trained parole officers and may be required to attend the Community Sex Offender Program. A particularly problematic issue is access to treatment once an offender has completed parole or mandatory supervision. Currently, these offenders are no longer eligible to remain in treatment programs offered by the Correctional Service of Canada.

The current state of correctional intervention with respect to sex offenders is best summed up in the words of a federal working group:

> Despite a substantial and steadily growing level of knowledge in the field, there remains considerable speculation about what motivates these individuals to commit their offences, and considerable uncertainty about how best to treat or manage those who seem to pose the greatest risk (Solicitor General of Canada, 1990:9).

THE DEATH PENALTY: AN ENDLESS DEBATE

> The systematic and widespread application of the death penalty would preserve life. Its deterrent effect would be greater than that of any other punishment. By sparing the life of a murderer, we sacrifice the lives of the innocent (Lehtinen, 1977:251).

> The state has a duty to protect its citizens from crime. It should carry out this protective responsibility with a minimum of intervention in individual lives and the lowest net loss in human suffering. The use of the death penalty is inconsistent with the goal (Smith, 1977:259).

These quotations are illustrative of the centuries-old debate over the death penalty, a highly emotional controversy involving conflicting religious and political views, arguments over morality, and disagreements over statistical data and the methods used to obtain them.

The use of the death penalty for a wide range of offences in early Canada was documented in Chapter 10 (see Greenland, 1987). Concerns about the harshness of the criminal law and the ideas of the writers of the Enlightenment led to a search for alternative punishments, one of which was the increased use of incarceration. Dissatisfaction with the use of capital punishment was one of the primary reasons for the construction of the Kingston Penitentiary in 1835, although the death penalty continued to be used in Canada until 1976, when it was abolished by an amendment to the *Criminal Code*.

The last execution in Canada occurred in 1962, and all death sentences received from 1967 to 1976 were commuted. During the 1980s, there was increased political and community pressure on the federal government to reinstate the death penalty. In June 1987, a motion to reinstate capital punishment was defeated in Parliament, although this is not likely to resolve the issue.

The Arguments

There is an extensive body of literature in which the proponents and opponents of the death penalty argue their respective positions. Arguments in favour of the death penalty include the following assertions.

- ▸ The death penalty protects society and saves lives.
- ▸ There is no statistical evidence that the death penalty is not a deterrent to crime.
- ▸ The death penalty reinforces conformity to the law.
- ▸ Opinion polls consistently reveal that the majority of the general public support the death penalty.
- ▸ The failure to respond severely to persons who commit heinous crimes undermines community solidarity, heightens the fear of crime, and discredits the criminal justice system.
- ▸ The deterrent threat of punishment is reduced when there is less severe punishment than justice requires.
- ▸ There is no biblical prohibition against the use of the death penalty.

In response, the following arguments are generally offered in support of the position to abolish the death penalty.

- ▶ There is no statistical evidence to indicate that the death penalty deters crime.
- ▶ The deliberate taking of a human life is immoral and is harmful to the social order.
- ▶ The death penalty is administered in a discriminatory manner, with the poor and members of racial and ethnic minorities more likely to be subjected to it.
- ▶ Under the death penalty, innocent people have and will be executed for crimes they did not commit.
- ▶ The use of the death penalty does not increase respect for the law — it undermines it by placing a low value on human life.

Much of the controversy over the death penalty has focused on the concepts of deterrence and retribution. Research on the deterrent effect of the death penalty has involved statistical analysis that compares jurisdictions with and without the death penalty in terms of crime rates and homicide rates. Other studies have examined the homicide rates in jurisdictions before and after the abolition of the death penalty or prior to and following an execution.

At the present time, the research does not permit any substantive conclusions as to whether the death penalty serves as a general deterrent. Despite this, a majority of the Canadian public continues to support its reinstatement. Surveys in the United States have indicated that large numbers of people would continue to support the death penalty even if it were found to have no deterrent effect. This suggests that, for many members of the general public, the question as to whether the imposition of the death penalty serves as a general deterrent is less important than the offender receiving "just deserts" for the offence he or she has committed.

Canadian Attitudes toward the Death Penalty

Canadian public opinion polls have consistently revealed that the majority of Canadians favour reinstatement of the death penalty. From a survey of residents in Quebec, Ontario, and Manitoba, conducted as part of a larger study of Canadian attitudes toward crime policies, Brillon, Louis-Guerin, and Lamarche (1984:196) reported the following responses to questions about the death penalty:

> ▸ 15.8% were opposed to the death penalty under any circumstances;
> ▸ 29.9% were opposed to the death penalty except in a few cases where it may be appropriate;
> ▸ 31.4% were generally in favour of the death penalty except in cases where it may not be appropriate;
> ▸ 22.2% were strongly in favour of the death penalty as an appropriate measure; and
> ▸ 0.7% didn't know.

These figures and the results of numerous Gallup Polls indicate that the majority of Canadians favour the use of capital punishment, at least in certain specified situations. Similar results have been obtained in surveys and opinion polls in the States (see Ellsworth and Ross, 1983).

Brillon *et al.* (1984:199, 202) also attempted to determine the factors that influence attitudes toward the death penalty. The researchers found no relation between fear of crime and attitudes toward punishment and the use of the death penalty. Women, while more fearful of crime (and less victimized) than men, are not more punitive in their views of punishment, nor are persons who have been the victims of crime. Rather than the fear of crime, it is the image of criminal offenders, who have come to be seen as more violent and dangerous, that underlies support for the death penalty.

The decision of Parliament in 1987 not to reinstate the death penalty did not end the controversy; readers should become more acquainted with the materials on what is likely to remain a topic of great debate in Canadian criminal justice (see Bedau, 1982; Berns, 1979; 1980; 1972; Lempert, 1983; Seagrave, 1987; van den Haag, 1975; van den Haag and Conrad, 1983).

THE LONG-TERM OFFENDER

The abolition of the death penalty in Canada in 1976 led to an increase in the number of offenders serving long periods of time in prison. In the Canadian corrections system, "long-term offender" refers to those offenders who are serving life sentences, indeterminate sentences, or determinate sentences of at least ten years. In 1992, nearly 28% of the federal prison population had received a long-term sentence (at least ten years). Offenders serving life sentences have been convicted of offences such as first-degree/capital murder and attempted murder. Approximately one in five federal offenders is serving a sentence for first- or second-degree murder, and these individuals must complete a minimum of 25 years in confinement before being eligible for parole (although a judicial review of their sentence is possible after serving 15 years). Offenders serving life sentences now comprise nearly 4% of the inmate population in federal correctional facilities. During the decade 1981-1991, there was a significant increase (41.5%) in the number of long-term offenders in the federal correctional system (Weekes, 1992:4).

Indeterminate prison sentences may be imposed on those who have been designated as dangerous offenders, dangerous sex offenders, or habitual offenders, while determinate prison sentences of ten years or more may be imposed for a variety of offences, including aggravated sexual assault and robbery. Since the long-term offender population is defined by sentence length, a variety of offenders are included under this designation. Among the issues surrounding the long-term offender are the impact of long-term confinement on the individual, the development of programs for long-term offenders, and the reentry of long-term offenders into the community.

We have previously discussed the concerns that correctional observers have raised about the negative impacts of confinement in the total institutional world of the prison. There is an emerging debate over the effects of long-term imprisonment. On one side of the debate are those who argue that there are no permanent debilitating effects of long-term confinement. Research (see Zamble and Porporino, 1988; Zamble, 1992) on a sample of incarcerated long-term offenders found that the offenders did not become "social isolates," but maintained contact with the outside community and exhibited attributes of what Johnson (1987; see Chapter 11) has defined as "mature coping," that is, positive behavioural adaptation to prison life (see also Bonta and Gendreau, 1990; Zamble and Porporino, 1988). The sample of offenders interviewed, however, included only three offenders serving 25-year minimum sentences. The assertion that long-term incarceration does not cause permanent damage to an offender is limited by the data to offenders serving periods of confinement up to ten years.

Many scholars take strong exception to this position, including Roberts and Jackson (1991:558), who argue that "the available evidence does not permit one to draw a conclusion that flies in the face of centuries of human experience." Given the process of prisonization and the other attributes of the total institutional world of the prison, it remains to be conclusively established that confining offenders for long periods of time (up to 25 years in some cases) is *not* detrimental. It is not difficult to imagine the "pains of imprisonment" — the difficulties of maintaining ties with one's spouse, children, and family, as well as some sense of outside "reality" — that are experienced during a 25-year minimum sentence.

Since the legislation creating the 25-year minimum sentences was only enacted in 1976, it is not possible at this time to assess what impact these sentences will have upon offenders upon reentry into the community. It can be anticipated that the "pains of reentry" will be quite severe for individuals who have been in confinement for a quarter of a century. Studies of long-term offenders with lesser sentences indicate that 58% were successful on parole and, significantly, that only 15% of those offenders who had been convicted of murder were subsequently reconvicted of another criminal offence (Weekes, 1992).

Regardless of the outcome of the debate over the effects of imprisonment, it is now acknowledged that inmates serving long-term and life sentences have different programming needs than inmates serving shorter periods in confinement. In its report, the Correctional Service of Canada Task Force on Long-Term Sentences (Perron, 1991) offered a number of recommendations relating to institutional programming and increasing the participation of community-based agencies to facilitate the reentry and reintegration of long-term offenders back into the community.

One program that attempts to assist long-term offenders to prepare for release is the Life Line In-Reach program, which operates inside institutions in the Ontario region of Correctional Service of Canada. In-Reach workers supplement the activities of the Case Management Team, providing support for lifers in managing their sentence while incarcerated and in preparing a release plan (see French, 1992). There has also been an increased emphasis on the development of community-based facilities and programs to facilitate the reentry of long-term offenders back into the community. Lifeline House, operated by the St. Leonard's Society in Windsor, Ontario, is one such facility (Cunningham-Huston, 1991). This residence is designed to address the unique needs of offenders who have served long periods of confinement upon their reentry into the community. As more long-term offenders are released, the needs for community-based facilities and programs will increase as well.

INTERMEDIATE SANCTIONS AND THE RISE OF ELECTRONIC MONITORING

Over the past decade, correctional policy makers have given increased attention to limiting and reducing the numbers of offenders sent to correctional institutions. Unlike their U.S. counterparts, who are currently on a prison-building "binge," Canadian correctional administrators and legislators appear to be directing their efforts toward the development of alternatives to confinement. As noted earlier, it is expected that in 1993 the federal government will enact Bill C-90, which will result in an expansion of intermediate sanctions across the country.

Intermediate sanctions generally encompass those dispositions that fall between giving the offender an absolute discharge and imprisonment and that involve the use of community programs and resources. Among the more common intermediate sanctions are intensive probation supervision (IPS), home confinement, and intermittent sentences (generally served on weekends). In addition, electronic monitoring is often used in conjunction with intermediate sanctions.

The primary justification for the creation and expansion of intermediate sanctions is that there has been too extensive a reliance on the use of incarceration and that, given the questions about the effectiveness of confinement in protecting society and assisting the offender, it should only be used as a last resort. While most correctional observers applaud efforts to create alternatives to imprisonment, the legacy of community-based corrections initiatives over the past two decades requires some degree of caution. As we noted in Chapter 12, community corrections programs, ostensibly designed as alternatives to incarceration, often resulted in "widening the net," involving ever-increasing numbers of offenders in the criminal justice system.

The justifications offered by the proponents of intermediate sanctions have the faint ring of those used for developing and expanding community-based corrections programs — that intermediate sanctions are more humane, will be more effective than imprisonment, will reduce institutional populations, and will result in cost savings. While it is much too early to assess the validity of these arguments, suffice it to say that "caution" should be the watchword. Many correctional observers are also concerned about the ethical issues that may arise from the expanded use of intermediate sanctions (see von Hirsch, 1990).

Electronic Monitoring and Home Confinement

In the future, a unique and potentially controversial development in Canadian corrections may be the electronic monitoring (EM) of offenders. The use of EM emerged in the United States during the early 1980s, and subsequently, federal and provincial corrections systems in Canada have considered the viability of this technological innovation.

Currently, the most common application of EM is as a condition of probation in conjunction with home confinement (EMHC). Under EMHC, the offender is required to remain in his or her residence, except for approved absences for employment and other authorized activities. Participation in EM programs is generally restricted to offenders convicted of less serious, nonviolent offences and who have a stable residence and a telephone. Most EMHC programs require the offender to pay a fee to assist in offsetting the costs of equipment and monitoring, although this is generally waived in cases of financial hardship.

Offenders under home incarceration can be monitored in several ways. The most widely used system involves the offender wearing a transmitting device (usually a bracelet or anklet) that sends radio signals to a receiver attached to the offender's telephone, which, in turn, relays them to a central computer at the probation or parole office. Internal electronic safeguards inform the central computer if any attempt is made to tamper with the transmitter. Second-generation EM systems use cellular telephone systems and are capable of monitoring the offender's location on a continual basis. Recently, several jurisdictions in the United States have begun to use video-telephones (telephone connections that include a visual image on a screen) to monitor offenders at home.

At this point, the federal government has decided not to use EM; all existing EM programs are operated by provincial corrections systems. The province of British Columbia initiated the first Canadian pilot project in 1987, using EM for offenders convicted of impaired driving who would otherwise have been given intermittent sentences.

The rationale offered for the development of EMHC programs is similar to that used to justify the expansion of community-based corrections programs during the 1960s and 1970s; namely that EMHC is less costly than incarceration, provides a humane alternative to the negative impact of confinement, and, by allowing the offender to remain in the community and maintain family and employment ties, increases the likelihood that the offender will return to a law-abiding way of life. Further, it is argued, the widespread use of EMHC as an alternative to confinement would serve to lessen prison overcrowding and lower overall correctional expenditures.

The infancy of EM programs in Canada and the lack of controlled evaluations, however, precludes an assessment of the extent to which EMHC programs achieve these objectives. An evaluation of the British Columbia EMHC pilot project (Neville, 1989) found that the program had reduced the intermittent sentence population in the targeted group without any evidence of "net-widening." On the basis of these findings, the program was expanded to several regions of the province. A subsequent analysis of the original program by Mainprize (1988) found that while offenders and their families were able to adapt to the program and that EMHC was perceived by offenders to be a "just" alternative to prison, participation in EMHC had negative effects on offenders in the workplace in terms of the anklet they wore. Further, it is too early to determine whether the EMHC program in British Columbia will result in offenders actually being diverted from incarceration and also whether the antici-pated cost savings will be realized (see Mainprize, 1992).

In addition to concerns with widening the criminal justice "net," the controversies that arise over any intermediate sanction programs involving EM are likely to centre on the legal and ethical concerns surrounding the increased use of high technology for surveillance and the fear of "Big Brother." Critics argue that EM may violate individual rights under the *Canadian Charter of Rights and Freedoms*, although to date there have been no challenges or court decisions that would suggest it is. Decisions by state and federal courts in the United States have held that EM, if accompanied by legal safeguards such as informed consent on the part of the offender, does not violate citizens' rights under the U.S. Constitution. Interestingly, this position has also been adopted by the American Civil Liberties Union in many jurisdictions in the United States.

Given the escalating costs of delivering correctional services and the expense associated with incarcerating offenders in correctional institu-tions, it is likely that in the coming years EM will be an attractive alternative to incarceration. In the future, high technology will make possible even more accurate systems for monitoring the location of offenders outside the home and will have the capacity to control behaviour as well, either through implants or electronic signals. In the next century, it is likely that these developments will pose legal and ethical challenges not only for corrections, but also for Canadian society.[3]

Intensive Probation Supervision (IPS)

One of the major innovations in probation has been the development of Intensive Probation Supervision (IPS) programs by provincial corrections systems. IPS involves the close supervision of probationers who are perceived to constitute a higher risk while in the community. It often involves attaching special conditions to the probation order, such as requiring the probationer to receive counselling, to obtain employment, to abide by a curfew, and to provide restitution to the victim.

In 1990, Saskatchewan provincial corrections began a program of IPS in the city of Prince Albert that combines IPS with EM. The project targeted specific groups of offenders, including Aboriginal and female offenders, as well as offenders who receive a period of incarceration with probation to follow upon release. In British Columbia, an IPS program has been developed on a pilot basis as well. The proposed (but as of June 1993, not enacted) Bill C-90 is specifically directed toward the development of intermediate sanctions and provides for the expansion of intensive probation supervision and gives more powers to probation officers and to the courts to enforce probation orders.

While there is considerable variation in IPS programs across North America, a common element is an emphasis on control and surveillance of offenders, rather than treatment (see Byrne, 1989). While proponents contend that IPS programs assist in reducing prison overcrowding, save money, and reduce recidivism, there is insufficient research evidence to verify these claims (for example, see Clear and Hardyman, 1990; Latessa, 1987; Tonry, 1990).

The topics discussed in this chapter represent some of the more critical issues confronting Canadian corrections. However, they do provide us with insights into the complexities of corrections, as well as possible future objections that corrections will take in an attempt to address the challenges that seem to become more complex as we move toward the year 2000.

NOTES

[1]Perhaps the most insightful and moving account of a female offender has been written by Anne Kershaw and Mary Lawovich (1991). In *Rock-A-Bye Baby*, they document the life and death of Marlene Moore, who committed suicide in the Kingston P4W in 1988.

[2]For a discussion of all facets of the treatment of sex offenders, see Glackman, 1991.

[3]There is an extensive literature on the application of EM in corrections in the United States. See McCarthy, 1987; Lilly *et al.*, 1987; Lilly and Ball, 1990; Rogers and Jolin, 1989; see also Nellis (1991) for a discussion of the use of EM in England and Wales.

REFERENCES

Adelberg, E. 1985. *A Forgotten Minority — Women in Conflict with the Law.* Ottawa: Canadian Association of Elizabeth Fry Societies.

Adelberg, E., and C. Currie. 1987. *Too Few to Count: Canadian Women in Conflict with the Law.* Vancouver: Press Gang Publishers.

Archambault, J. (Chair). 1938. *Report of the Royal Commission to Investigate the Penal System of Canada.* Ottawa: King's Printer.

Axon, L. 1989a. *Criminal Justice and Women — An International Survey.* Ottawa: Solicitor General of Canada.

Axon, L. 1989b. *Model and Exemplary Programs for Female Inmates — An International Review.* Ottawa: Solicitor General of Canada.

Bedau, H.A. 1982. *The Death Penalty in America.* 3rd ed. New York: Oxford University Press.

Berns, W. 1979. *For Capital Punishment: Crime and the Morality of the Death Penalty.* New York: Basic Books.

_____. 1980. "Defending the Death Penalty." 26 *Crime and Delinquency.* 503-11.

Berzins, L., and S. Cooper. 1982. "The Political Economy of Correctional Planning for Women: The Case of the Bankrupt Bureaucracy." 24 *Canadian Journal of Criminology.* 399-416.

Blumstein, A., J. Cohen, and D. Nagin. 1978. *Deterrence and Incapacitation: Estimating the Effects of Criminal Sanctions on Crime Rates.* Washington, D.C.: National Academy of Sciences.

Bonta, J. and P. Gendreau. 1990. "Reexamining the Cruel and Unusual Punishment of Prison Life." 14 *Law and Human Behavior.* 347-72.

Brillon, Y., C. Louis-Guerin, and M.-C. Lamarche. 1984. *Attitudes of the*

Canadian Public toward Crime Policies. Montreal: Centre International de Criminologie Comparee, Universite de Montreal.

Byrne, J.M. 1989. "Reintegrating the Concept of Community into Community-Based Corrections." 35 *Crime and Delinquency*. 471-99.

Canada. 1914. *Report of the Royal Commission on Penitentiaries*. Ottawa: Government Printing Bureau.

Canadian Centre for Justice Statistics. 1992. *Adult Correctional Services in Canada, 1990-91*. Ottawa: Minister of Science, Industry and Technology.

Cannings, K.L. 1990. *Bridging the Gap: Programs and Services to Facilitate Contact Between Inmate Parents and Their Children*. Ottawa: Solicitor General of Canada.

Chunn, D.E., and S.A.M. Gavigan. 1991. "Women and Crime in Canada." In M.A. Jackson and C.T. Griffiths, eds. *Canadian Criminology — Perspectives on Crime and Criminality*. Toronto: Harcourt, Brace, Jovanovich. 275-314.

Clear, T.R., and P.L. Hardyman. 1990. "The New Intensive Supervision Movement." 36 *Crime and Delinquency*. 42-60.

Conklin, J.E. 1986. *Criminology*. 2nd ed. New York: Macmillan.

Cooper, S.D. 1987. "The Evolution of the Federal Women's Prison." In E. Adelberg and C. Currie, eds. *Too Few to Count: Canadian Women in Conflict with the Law*. Vancouver: Press Gang Publishers. 127-44.

Correctional Service of Canada. 1991. "Everything You Wanted to Know About Canadian Federal Sex Offenders and More." 3 *FORUM on Corrections Research*. 3-6.

Cunningham-Huston, C. 1991. "Life After Life: The Lifeline Project." *Let's Talk* (October). 4-6.

Daubney, D. 1988. *Taking Responsibility. Report of the Standing Committee on Justice and Solicitor General on Its Review of Sentencing, Conditional Release and Related Aspects of Corrections*. Ottawa: Supply and Services Canada.

Diamond, B., and J. Phelps. 1990. *Creating Choices — Report of the Task Force on Federally Sentenced Women*. Ottawa: Correctional Service of Canada.

Ellsworth, P., and L. Ross. 1983. "Public Opinion and Capital Punishment: A Close Examination of Views of Abolitionists and Retentionists." 29 *Crime and Delinquency*. 116-69.

Evans, M. 1989. *A Survey of Institutional Programs Available to Federally Sentenced Women*. Ottawa: Correctional Service of Canada.

French, T. 1992. "The Life Line In-Reach Program." 4 *FORUM on Corrections Research*. 36-38.

Glackman, W.G. 1991. "The Treatment of Sex Offenders." In M.A. Jackson and C.T. Griffiths, eds. *Canadian Criminology: Perspectives on Crime and*

Criminality. Toronto: Harcourt, Brace, Jovanovich. 239-55.

Gordon, A., R. Holden, and T. Leis. 1991. "Managing and Treating Sex Offenders: Matching Risk with Programming." 3 *FORUM on Corrections Research.* 7-11.

Greenland, Cyril. 1987. "The Last Public Execution in Canada: Eight Skeletons in the Closet of the Canadian Justice System." 29 *Criminal Law Quarterly.* 415-20.

Hanson, R.K., R.A. Steffy, and R. Gauthier. 1992. *Long-Term Followup of Child Molesters: Risk Predictors and Treatment Outcome.* Ottawa: Corrections Branch, Solicitor General of Canada.

Heney, J. 1990. *Report on Self-Injurious Behaviour in the Kingston Prison for Women.* Kingston: Ontario Regional Headquarters, Correctional Service of Canada.

Johnson, R. 1987. *Hard Time — Understanding and Reforming the Prison.* Belmont, California: Brooks/Cole.

Kershaw, A., and M. Lasovich. 1991. *Rock-A-Bye Baby — A Death Behind Bars.* Toronto: McClelland and Stewart.

Latessa E.J. 1987. "The Effectiveness of Intensive Supervision With High Risk Probationers." In B.R. McCarthy, ed. *Intermediate Punishments: Intensive Supervision, Home Confinement and Electronic Surveillance.* Monsey, New York: Criminal Justice Press. 95-115.

Lehtinen, M.W. 1977. "The Value of Life — An Argument for the Death Penalty." 23 *Crime and Delinquency.* 237-52.

Lempert, R.O. 1983. "Desert and Deterrence: An Assessment of the Moral Bases of the Case for Capital Punishment." 79 *Michigan Law Review.* 1177-1231.

Lilly, J.R., R.A. Ball, and J. Wright. 1987. "Home Incarceration with Electronic Monitoring in Kenton County, Kentucky: An Evaluation." In B.R. McCarthy, ed. *Intermediate Punishments: Intensive Supervision, Home Confinement and Electronic Surveillance.* Monsey, N.Y.: Criminal Justice Press. 189-203.

Lilly, R.J., and R.A. Ball. 1990. "Development of Home Confinement and Electronic Monitoring in the United States." In D.E. Duffee and E.F. McGarrell, eds. *Community Corrections: A Community Field Approach.* Cincinnati: Anderson Publishing Co. 73-92.

MacLeod, L. 1986. *Sentenced to Separation: An Exploration of the Needs and Problems of Mothers Who Are Offenders and Their Children.* Ottawa: Solicitor General of Canada.

Mainprize, S. 1992. "Electronic Monitoring in Corrections: Assessing Cost Effectiveness and the Potential for Widening the Net of Social Control." 34 *Canadian Journal of Criminology.* 161-80.

Mainprize, S. 1988. *Examination of Social, Psychological and Familial Impacts of the British Columbia Corrections Branch's Electronic Monitoring System*

Pilot Project Program on Participating Offenders. Victoria: Corrections Branch, Ministry of Solicitor General.

Marshall, W.L., and A. Eccles. 1991. "The Value of Community Treatment Programs for Released Sex Offenders." 3 *FORUM on Corrections Research*. 12-19.

McCarthy, B.R. 1987. *Intermediate Punishments: Home Confinement and Electronic Surveillance*. Monsey, New York: Criminal Justice Press.

Mohr, G.T. 1985. "The Long-Term Incarceration Issue: The Banality of Evil and the Pornography of Power." 27 *Canadian Journal of Criminology*. 103-12.

Nellis, M. 1991. "The Electronic Monitoring of Offenders in England and Wales." 31 *British Journal of Criminology*. 165-85.

Neville, L. 1989. *British Columbia Electronic Monitoring Pilot Project*. Victoria: Corrections Branch, Ministry of Solicitor General.

Perron, J-C. (Chairman). 1991. *Task Force Report on Long-Term Sentences*. Ottawa: Correctional Service of Canada.

Roberts, J.V., and M. Jackson. 1991. "Boats Against the Current: A Note on the Effects of Imprisonment." 15 *Law and Human Behavior*. 557-65.

Rogers, R., and A. Jolin. 1989. "Electronic Monitoring: A Review of the Empirical Literature." 5 *Journal of Contemporary Criminal Justice*. 141-52.

Ross, R.R., and E.A. Fabiano. 1985. *Correctional Afterthoughts: Programs for Female Offenders*. Ottawa: Solicitor General of Canada.

Seagrave, J. 1987. "The Death Penalty: Will Canada Restore This Punishment?" 29 *Canadian Journal of Criminology*. 405-19.

Shaw, M. 1989. *The Federal Female Offender — Report of a Preliminary Study*. Ottawa: Correctional Service of Canada.

Shaw, M., et al. 1991. *Survey of Federally Sentenced Women*. Ottawa: Correctional Service of Canada.

Smith, G.W. 1977. "The Value of Life — Arguments against the Death Penalty: A Reply to Professor Lehtinen." 23 *Crime and Delinquency*. 253-59.

Solicitor General of Canada. 1990. *The Management and Treatment of Sex Offenders — Report of the Working Group. Sex Offender Treatment Review*. Ottawa: Supply and Services Canada.

Sugar, F., and L. Fox. 1990. *Survey of Federally Sentenced Aboriginal Women in the Community*. Ottawa: Correctional Service of Canada.

Tonry, M. 1990. "Stated and Latent Functions of IPS." 36 *Crime and Delinquency*. 174-91.

van den Haag, E. 1975. *Punishing Criminals: Concerning a Very Old and Painful Question*. New York: Basic Books.

van den Haag, E., and J.P. Conrad. 1983. *The Death Penalty: A Debate*. New York: Plenum Press.

von Hirsch, A. 1990. "The Ethics of Community-Based Sanctions." 36 *Crime and Delinquency.* 162-73.

Vaughn, J.B. 1987. "Planning for Change: The Use of Electronic Monitoring as a Correctional Alternative." In B.R. McCarthy, ed. *Intermediate Punishments: Intensive Supervision, Home Confinement and Electronic Surveillance.* Monsey, N.Y.: Criminal Justice Press. 153-68.

Weekes, J.R. 1992. "Long-Term Offenders: Who Are They and Where Are They?" 4 *FORUM on Corrections Research.* 3-7.

Wine, S. 1992. *A Motherhood Issue — The Impact of Criminal Justice System Involvement on Women and Their Children.* Ottawa: Ministry of the Solicitor General.

Zamble, E. 1992. "Coping, Behavior and Adaptation in Long-Term Prison Inmates: Descriptive Longitudinal Results." Unpublished paper. Kingston, Ontario: Department of Psychology, Queen's University.

Zamble, E., and F.J. Porporino. 1988. *Coping, Behavior and Adaptation in Prison Inmates.* New York: Springer-Verlag.

14 THE CANADIAN YOUTH JUSTICE SYSTEM*

Thus far, we have focused primarily on the operation of the Canadian criminal justice system vis-à-vis adult offenders. In this chapter, we consider youth crime and justice in Canada, both in the historical and the contemporary context. While these materials could comprise an entire volume in themselves, it is possible, within the space limitations of this text, to consider the general patterns of youth crime, the history, current structure, and operation of youth justice, and the issues relating to the treatment of young offenders in institutional and community settings.

YOUTH CRIME IN CANADA

Official statistics on the nature and extent of youth crime in Canada must be viewed with caution because they are subject to the same influences as figures on adult criminality (see Chapter 2). As with official statistics on adult crime, there may be a "dark figure" of youth crime that remains undetected or unreported. Self-report studies consistently indicate that a large majority of youths engage in behaviour that could conceivably result in court processing. Those officially charged, therefore, represent only a fraction of all youths who are actually committing offences. And, as with the adult criminal justice system, the rate of youth offences may be as much a function of the attributes of the youth justice system in individual jurisdictions across the country, from the police to the Youth Court judge, as they are of actual youth misbehaviour.

These factors may have an even more pronounced effect upon youth crime statistics than they have upon those for adults, given the greater likelihood of youths being handled informally, for example, when crimes are discovered but no charges are laid. Factors that are unique to the youth justice system also affect the available crime data. For example, the province of Ontario did not participate in the national Youth Court Survey until January, 1991.

---

* This chapter was co-authored with Alison Hatch.

From published sources (Conway, 1992a; 1992b; Frank, 1991; Greenberg, 1992; Hatch and Griffiths, 1993; Hendrick and Lachance, 1991), it is possible to piece together a general picture of Youth Court caseloads in Canada:

- the overall rates of youth crime have steadily increased over the past 30 years;
- 82% of the cases in Youth Court involve males; 52% of the cases involve youths aged 16 and 17;
- over the past five years, the number of females charged by the police has increased twice as fast as the number for male youths; for nearly half of the cases involving females, the charge was theft under $1,000, most notably shoplifting;
- of all youths charged with offences against federal statutes, only about 10% were charged with committing a violent crime, and the vast majority of these were for non-sexual assault;
- the majority of youths (70%) were charged with property offences;
- theft under $1,000, which includes shoplifting, accounted for 42% of the property offences for which youth are charged, while break and enters amounted for 27% of the property offences;
- youths make up only a small percentage of those charged with drug offences; and
- the number of cases in Youth Courts involving violence increased 34% over the five-year period between 1986-87/1990-91; offences involving violence comprised the largest number of Youth Court cases in Quebec (22%) and the lowest in Saskatchewan (11%).

THE HISTORICAL RESPONSE TO YOUNG OFFENDERS

Separate justice systems for young persons are a relatively recent occurrence. Prior to the mid-1800s, children were treated in much the same manner as adult offenders. There was, however, recognition of the reduced capacity of children to make moral and legal judgments. Under the English common law, persons below the age of 7 years could not be convicted of committing an offence, as they were deemed incapable of forming the requisite criminal intent, or *mens rea*. Youths between the ages of 7 and 14 were subject to the doctrine of *doli incapax*, which involved a presumption of incapacity that could be contested by the Crown. Beginning at age 14, children were considered as responsible as adults for their behaviour and were subject to the same penalties.

In early nineteenth-century England, however, youths under the age of 14 were treated as adults and often received harsh sentences for relatively minor offences, as illustrated by the following cases from the records of Stafford Prison (cited in Stubbs, 1972:21).

- ▸ In 1834, George Saxon, aged 12 years, was sentenced to transportation for seven years for stealing a gold watch.
- ▸ In 1834, Thomas Tow, aged 10 years, was sentenced to transportation for seven years for stealing a donkey.
- ▸ In 1837, Matilda Seymour, aged 10 years, was sentenced to transportation for seven years for stealing one shawl and one petticoat.

(Transportation involved sending the youth out of the country, most often to the British colony of Australia.)

Knell (1965) has documented cases of 103 children sentenced to death in the Old Bailey in London between 1801 and 1836, almost all for the crime of theft (records indicate that one 13-year-old boy was hanged for murder in 1831). These sentences, however, were routinely commuted to a penalty of lesser severity.

During the early 1800s, English penal reformers began to voice concerns about the confinement of children with adult offenders and the failure of authorities to separate offenders on the basis of age and severity of offence. A number of philanthropic societies, first in Britain and later in the United States, began to lobby for the creation of facilities solely for child offenders. As a consequence of these efforts, houses of refuge, or reformatories, were opened to house delinquent, dependent, and neglected youths. The first U.S. reformatory was opened in New York in 1825, and by 1850, a large number of reformatories had been constructed. The facilities stressed education, vocational training, and religion, and were designed to provide to youths what had been denied to them by inadequate parents and poor home environments. The popularity of reformatories began to wane, however, when they came to be seen as little more than prisons for youths.

Young Offenders in Early Canada

In early Canada, child offenders were subjected to the same penalties as adults and, when sentenced to terms of incarceration, were confined in local jails (see Carrigan, 1991). Children were confined in the Bridewell, which opened in Halifax in 1790, and in 1864, 311 boys and girls under the age of 16 were admitted to the local jails in Upper Canada (Baehre, 1982; Hagarty, 1866). Children were also confined in the Kingston Penitentiary, following its completion in 1835, without regard for their age, prior record, or severity of their crimes (Shoom, 1972).

The reformatory movement was much slower in gaining widespread acceptance in Canada. As late as 1888, children were still being admitted to federal penitentiaries, as evidenced by the records from Dorchester Penitentiary in New Brunswick (cited in Sutherland, 1976:102-103):

- ▸ Herbert Smith, age 12: 5 years for breaking and entering;
- ▸ Enos Medley, age 13: 3 years for compound larceny;
- ▸ Edward Chambers, age 11: 2 years for burglary and larceny;
- ▸ Robert Welsh, age 14: 7 years for manslaughter.

In its investigation into the operation of the Kingston Penitentiary under Warden Henry Smith, the Brown Commission documented the excessive use of corporal punishment on child inmates. In the second of two reports issued in 1849, the Brown Commission criticized the practice of confining children in Kingston, noting:

> It is distressing to think that no distinction is now made between the child who has strayed for the first time from the path of honesty, or who perhaps has never been taught the meaning of sin, and the hardened offender of mature years. All are consigned together to the unutterable contamination of the common gaol; and by the lessons there learnt, soon become inmates of the Penitentiary.

Among the recommendations of the Brown Commission were that houses of refuge, for the "reformation" of youth, be constructed.

Additional factors led Canadians to construct reformatories, including influences from the United States and the general social climate of mid-nineteenth century Ontario, in which education and schooling were seen as the primary defences against social problems such as juvenile delinquency. During the mid-1800s, there was the widespread perception that juvenile crime was increasing, although Houston (1982) and others note that whether an actual increase in crime was occurring is unclear. What is evident is that illiteracy and immorality and the apparent rise in juvenile crime were viewed as causally related and as threats to the order and stability of Canadian society.

Prentice notes that Canadians of the time considered institutionalization a means of improving society by temporarily exposing children to an environment superior to that of their home:

> [They] sought solutions to the social ills of their times by institution-building, in the creation of controlled environments which would contain, suppress, or avoid what they found unacceptable in wider society (1977:46).

In 1857, two important pieces of legislation were enacted that responded to the concerns regarding the detention of children with adult offenders voiced by the Brown Commission nearly a decade earlier. The first, *An Act for the More Speedy Trial and Punishment of Juvenile Offenders,*[1] was primarily concerned with accelerating the processing of children's cases by granting bail to reduce the period of pre-trial detention for those under the age of 16. The second piece of legislation passed in 1857 was *An Act for Establishing Prisons for Young Offenders,*[2] which provided for the creation of two "reformatory prisons."

In 1859, two juvenile reformatories were opened — one on Isle aux Noix in Lower Canada and the other in Penetanguishene, Upper Canada — and the number of boys sentenced to these institutions steadily increased (see Shoom, 1972). Although these facilities were prisons, they responded to concerns for the classification and segregation of children from adults. Unlike their counterparts in the United States, initially at least, only children convicted of an offence could be sent to the juvenile reformatories.

As time passed, an increasingly larger group of children became subject to reformatory terms. Legislation enacted in 1875 allowed 16 year olds, who had previously been subjected to terms in adult penitentiaries, to be incarcerated in the reformatories. Reformatory terms were to be at least two years in length, but were not to exceed five years. If a term was to be greater than five years, the youth was sent to a penitentiary. Whenever possible, youths were to be placed in reformatories for pre-trial detention rather than in the local jail. In 1879, one section of the Mercer Reformatory in Ontario was designated for girls under 14 years of age.

Another example of the expansion of jurisdiction of the emerging juvenile justice system was the gradual inclusion of children who were thought to be destined for a future of criminal activity, so-called "pre-delinquents." Beginning in 1880, "incorrigible" children in Ontario could be sent to a reformatory for up to five years upon the complaint of their parents.[3] This was an early manifestation of what later came to be called "status" offences.

Industrial Schools and the Family Model

Disillusionment with the reformatories, first in the United States and then in Canada during the late 1800s, prompted the creation of industrial schools, which stressed academic and vocational education. These facilities were to approximate as closely as possible a family atmosphere, as the family was now seen as both the cause of, and potential cure for, child crime. It was thought that institutions, particularly those designed along the cottage plan, could replicate all the benefits of a supportive and loving family. One way to accomplish this was by greater participation of women in the administration and daily management of the industrial schools (see Morrison, 1976).

Initially, industrial schools were envisioned as facilities for neglected and dependent youth. Reformatories were still thought to be appropriate for delinquents. The Victoria Industrial School for Boys opened near Toronto in 1887, followed by the establishment of the Alexandria School, a similar institution for girls in 1891. From this time until the early 1900s, industrial schools were established in some provinces.

Industrial schools were viewed as residential schools rather than as prisons and were designed to "be supplementary to the family which lacked adequate control" (Leon, 1977:81). Parents could request that children be sent to an industrial school for an indeterminate period of time. These facilities soon replaced reformatories as the primary mechanism for controlling youth, except in those cases where a serious offence had been committed. Eventually in Ontario, youths under the age of 13 could be detained only in industrial schools.

In 1888, the *An Act for the Protection and Reformation of Neglected Children*[4] (also known as the *Child Protection Act*) was passed in Ontario, reaffirming the right of the government to place neglected children in industrial schools and creating the new option of children's homes. A notable feature of this legislation was that provision was made for the creation of magistrates' courts for the separate trial of those under the age of 16 charged with provincial offences. The *Act* allowed for the appointment of a special "commissioner" to hear cases of those under 16 years of age, and where "practicable," the cases of those under 21 were to be tried separately from adults. Although this idea was not immediately acted upon, the legislation was an important step toward the development of the juvenile court and further served to blur the distinction between the treatment of delinquent and dependent/neglected children.

An investigation of penal institutions for children and the response to juvenile delinquency was undertaken in 1890 by the Royal Commission on the Prison and Reformatory System in Ontario, chaired by J.W. Langmuir. Despite the provisions of the 1888 *Child Protection Act*, no separate courts for children had been established in Ontario, and in its final report, the Commission (Langmuir, 1891) was critical of the methods used to respond to child offenders, particularly the use of reformatories. The recommendations of the Langmuir Commission (1891) reflected a growing trend toward the deinstitutionalization of child care and the increased use of the child welfare system for delinquency-prone youths from poor home environments.

In 1890, the Children's Aid Society was founded in Toronto, largely as the result of the work of one J.J. Kelso, a young journalist-cum-reformer who had co-authored the *Child Protection Act* of 1888. Kelso was heavily influenced by the growing deinstitutionalization movement in the United States and viewed the Children's Aid Society as a way to "deal with all matters affecting the moral and physical welfare of children, especially those who from lack of parental care or other causes are in danger of growing up to swell the criminal classes" (quoted in Jones and Rutman, 1981:57). To accomplish this, it was necessary to enact legislation for neglected children and juvenile offenders, based on the motto: "It is wiser and less expensive to save children than to punish them" (Jones and Rutman, 1981:58).

SEPARATE JUSTICE FOR CHILDREN

The provisions of the 1888 *Child Protection Act*, which provided for separate trials for children, were put into effect in Toronto in 1890, although difficulties soon arose because the court was not empowered to hear cases involving contraventions of federal law. This was particularly problematic as a large number of youths at the time were charged with larceny, which was a federal offence. Reform at the federal level was required, and in 1892, provisions allowing for separate and private hearings for children under 16 years of age "where it appears expedient and practicable" were included in Canada's first *Criminal Code*.[5] This legislation was complemented by an 1893 Ontario statute that provided for separate detention and trials for provincial offenders.[6]

Although these statutes authorized the operation of juvenile courts in Ontario, the matter was left to the discretion of the judges, and with isolated exceptions, children's courts were not created. Substantive legislative change was finally achieved in 1894, when the separate trial of young offenders was made mandatory and a children's court was opened in Toronto. Montreal was the second city to provide separate trial facilities for children, and a few other Canadian cities responded by conducting hearings in the judge's chambers, or in regular courtrooms when adult court was not in session (see Sutherland, 1976).

In most parts of Canada, the law was a dead letter. Nevertheless, by the early 1900s, the idea of treating youths separately from adults was well entrenched. During this time, there was an increased emphasis on prevention with potential, as well as actual, offenders. Professionalization of what had previously been volunteer-based child welfare services increased, and the expanding network of children's aid societies had adopted delinquent youth as their responsibility, resulting in an overlap between the child welfare and juvenile justice systems (see Leon, 1977).

The move toward non-institutional, community-based responses to youthful misbehaviour included the use of foster home placements and the development of probation, first used in 1889.[7] Canadians were becoming disillusioned, as had their neighbours in the United States, with the reformatories, which were increasingly viewed as little more than prisons for children, embodying all the negative attributes that reformers had sought to avoid by removing children from adult prisons in the mid-1800s. In 1904, the Ontario Reformatory for Boys in Penetanguishene was closed, following several years of declining admissions (Jones, 1978). While plans were made to replace the reformatory, the industrial school was fast becoming the preferred option. Indeed, the seeds for the creation of the *Juvenile Delinquent Act* were all apparent by this time. What was needed was federal legislation that tied all these factors together and created statutory justification for current practice.

THE *JUVENILE DELINQUENTS ACT* (1908)

The *Juvenile Delinquents Act* (*JDA*) was principally drafted by W.L. Scott, president of the Children's Aid Society in Ottawa, and was passed by Parliament on July 8, 1908.[8] The provisions of the *Act* were modelled closely after the juvenile court statutes that were then in force in two dozen states in the United States. The underlying principles of the *Act*, as outlined by Scott (quoted in Kelso, 1907:109) were:

1. That children are children even when they break the law and should be treated as such and not as adult criminals. As a child cannot deal with its property, so it should be held incapable of committing a crime, strictly so called;
2. That juvenile delinquents can be reformed through probation officers; and
3. That adults should be held criminally liable for bringing about delinquency in children.

Provisions of the *JDA*

Earlier federal attempts to create separate courts for children had required federal/provincial coordination. Under the provisions of the *Constitution Act, 1867,* the provinces were restricted from creating laws for the prosecution of violators of federal statutes, such as the *Criminal Code*.[9] Under this same legislation, the federal government was prohibited from enacting legislation concerning those areas that fell under provincial purview, such as contraventions of provincial statutes or matters of child welfare. The *JDA* addressed this problem by creating the federal offence of being a "juvenile delinquent," described in section 2(c) as:

> ...any child who violates any provision of the Criminal Code, any (federal) or provincial statute, or of any by-law or ordinance of any municipality, for which violation punishment by a fine or imprisonment may be awarded; or, who is liable by reasons of any other act to be committed to an industrial school or juvenile reformatory under the provisions of any (federal) or provincial statute.[10]

The definition of juvenile delinquency under the *JDA* was extremely broad and included any child who broke an existing law or was declared in need of protection under provincial child welfare legislation. The legislation represented the blending of the juvenile justice and child welfare systems. Children could qualify as juvenile delinquents without having committed a criminal offence, and children who did violate a law could be inducted into the child welfare system upon adjudication.

In cases where the child was adjudicated as a juvenile delinquent, several dispositional options were available to the presiding judge. The *JDA* provided for the imposition of a fine (not to exceed $10), placement in a foster home, commitment to care of a children's aid society, or confinement in an industrial school.

The influence of anti-institutional forces was evident in the emphasis placed on probation as a dispositional option. Leon (1977:81) has argued that one of the primary objectives of the *JDA* was to expand the use of probation as an alternative to reformatories and industrial schools. Upon adjudication, the *JDA* allowed the judge to:

- ► commit the child to the care and custody of a probation officer;
- ► allow the child to remain at home, subject to the visitation of a probation officer, such child to report to the court or to the probation officer as often as may have been required; or
- ► cause the child to be placed in a foster home, subject to the friendly supervision of a probation officer.

In addition to creating separate court proceedings for juveniles, the *JDA* created further distinctions between juveniles and adults. Juveniles were not charged with specific crimes; rather, they were *accused* of delinquencies. They did not plead guilty or not guilty; they *admitted* or *denied* the allegation. More important, in contrast to the adversarial nature of the adult system of justice, section 31 of the *Act* adopted a paternal approach as the basis of the juvenile court:

> ...the care and custody and discipline of a juvenile delinquent shall approximate as nearly as may be that which would be given by its parents, and that as far as practicable every juvenile delinquent shall be treated, not as a criminal, but as a misdirected and misguided child, and one needing aid, encouragement, help and assistance.

Within the first few years of the passage of the *JDA*, juvenile courts were opened in some urban areas, including Vancouver (1910), Toronto (1912), and Calgary (1912) (see Hatch and Griffiths, 1991; MacGill, 1925). However, the provisions of the *JDA* were not widely adopted for many decades. Sutherland (1976:129) notes that due to the lack of facilities and resources in many jurisdictions, the proclamation of the *JDA* made little actual difference in the handling of juveniles.

Criticisms of the *JDA*

It soon became apparent that the juvenile court was not the panacea originally envisioned. The rate of youth crime appeared to grow in the first half of the century (Watts, 1932; Brannigan, 1987). However, only minor amendments were made to the *JDA* in the years following its passage.[11] It became increasingly popular among juvenile justice practitioners, and the jurisdiction of the court was expanded by a series of provincial amendments (Hatch and Griffiths, 1991).

The *JDA* remained substantially unchallenged until the 1960s, when critics began to voice a number of concerns, including:

- ▸ the financial penalties were not severe enough, being limited to a maximum fine of $25;
- ▸ there was no uniform upper age limit, the provinces and territories having adopted anywhere from 16 to 18 years old;
- ▸ the informality of court procedures had led to widespread diversity in practice across the country, including considerable disparity in sentencing;
- ▸ the language of the *Act* was stigmatizing;
- ▸ the *JDA* should have been in force nationwide; and
- ▸ the denial of due process rights for juvenile offenders was not warranted.

A major criticism of the *JDA* was its failure to provide a clear definition of delinquency. This lack of guidance left each province to devise its own policies and programs, resulting in inconsistent responses across the country. This situation, in conjunction with the variable upper age limit, led children committing the same crime in different provinces to be variously treated as juvenile delinquents, children in need of protection, or adult offenders. Further difficulties were caused by the wide range of behaviours being handled by the juvenile court, ranging from riding a bicycle on the sidewalk to murder. While some cited insufficient resources as the problem, by 1970 there was a widespread view that the *JDA*, as a strategy to reduce juvenile delinquency, had failed.

The decline of welfare-based juvenile courts was observed no more sharply than in the United States, where juvenile offenders were being granted due process rights with a series of Superior Court decisions. The United States Supreme Court observed that the due process rights of juvenile offenders had been taken away at the turn of the century for a promise that they would be assisted by juvenile authorities with the problems that had led to their appearance in court. In practice, over many decades, this assistance had not been provided. To the contrary, juvenile offenders were treated more punitively than adult offenders. Juvenile offenders often spent lengthy periods of confinement in institutions for minor transgressions. This was a major precipitating factor in the movement toward the elimination of welfare-based juvenile courts in favour of tribunals with increased levels of public scrutiny, accountability, and due process.

THE *YOUNG OFFENDERS ACT* (1984)

A series of proposed drafts for a new statute were advanced beginning in 1965, but it was not until April, 1984, that the new *Young Offenders Act (YOA)*[12] was proclaimed into force. The *YOA* begins with a section entitled "Declaration of Principle," which represents a sharp departure from the traditional view of youth crime under the *JDA* — a shift from the "social welfare" approach of the *JDA* to an "offence-oriented" approach. Young persons are held accountable for their behaviour while being provided with legal rights similar to those of adult accused.

However, statements in the "Declaration of Principle" also reflect a paternalistic orientation: "young persons should not in all instance be held accountable in the same manner or suffer the same consequences for their behaviour as adults" and that "because of their state of dependency and level of development and maturity, they have special needs and require guidance and assistance." This orientation is reflected in such features as an upper limit on the length of sentences, for example, five years maximum in confinement for murder. In addition, the *YOA* sets out a variety of dispositional alternatives designed to address the needs of individual offenders, and the use of community-based alternatives to confinement is encouraged (see Corrado and Markwart, 1992; LeBlanc and Beaumont, 1992). Needless to say, this "mixed message" of the *YOA* has had a significant impact on the youth justice system, particularly in the decision making of Youth Court judges.[13]

In addition to philosophical changes, the *YOA* introduced a number of other changes from the *JDA*: (1) it standardized the age of young offenders in all jurisdictions from 12 years to 17 years inclusive; (2) it defined criteria and procedures for diversion from court; (3) it mandated increased involvement of legal counsel; (4) it permitted the Youth Court to issue only determinate dispositions; and (5) it eliminated status offences (such as being ungovernable).

The operation of the youth courts and the development and operation of programs and services for young offenders falls under the jurisdiction of the provincial and territorial governments. As such, there is considerable variability in the specific programs and services that are available, as well as in the administrative arrangements for supervising young offenders (see Wilson, 1990).[14] In Ontario and Nova Scotia, for example, the responsibilities for young offenders are split between two departments: in Ontario, the Ministry of Community and Social Services handles 12 to 15 year olds, and the Ministry of Correctional Services handles 16 and 17 year olds; in Nova Scotia, the Department of Community Services supervises alternative measures programs for 12 to 15 year olds, while the Department of the Solicitor General handles 16 and 17 year olds.

Youth Court Jurisdiction

The *YOA* grants youth courts jurisdiction over young persons, aged 12 to 17 inclusive, who are suspected of violating any federal legislation, such as the *Criminal Code*, the *Food and Drugs Act*, and the *Narcotic Control Act*. Youth Courts may also hear the cases of young persons accused of provincial offences (for example, traffic violations) under the authority of provincial/territorial young offenders legislation and modifications of summary conviction acts.

Police Processing of Youths

The decisions that the police make upon the discovery of a young person suspected of committing an offence are very similar to those for adults described in Chapter 4. Under the *YOA*, all *Criminal Code* provisions governing arrest and bail apply to young persons. Youths must be informed of their rights by police officers when they are apprehended and/or arrested.

The options available to police officers include informal handling and formal measures.

Informal Handling

Given the minor nature of the majority of youth offences, the police are able to exert a great deal of discretion once they have identified a suspect. A large, yet unknown, number of cases are handled informally and no further action is taken by the officer. Young persons may be reprimanded, warned of the consequences of future offences, and/or returned to their parent(s). The frequency of this practice will vary with the personal discretion of the officer and the policies of the individual police force.

In several provinces, informal handling is the course of action specified by child welfare statutes for dealing with children under the age of 12 who are suspected of behaviour that would be criminal if committed by an adult or a young person. The police are also encouraged to identify children under 12 who, as indicated by their "criminal" behaviour, may be in need of protective services of the state (for example, in Alberta, the *Child Welfare Act*, S.A. 1984, c. C-81, ss. 4 and 5). In such cases, referral is made to the provincial child welfare authorities.

Formal Measures

If formal action is deemed necessary, the police will create a report recommending the laying of a charge. Who makes the final decision on the laying of an information varies across jurisdictions — in some areas, the police make this decision, while in others it is made by the Crown. In giving statements to the police, a young offender is entitled to be advised of the option of having a lawyer or a parent present. Those youths charged with an indictable offence may be photographed and fingerprinted.

In those cases in which there is cause to believe that a youth will not appear in court or presents a danger to him/herself or others, the youth may be detained, pending an appearance before a judge or a justice of the peace. Detainment is often used if the youth is apprehended after the issuance of a warrant. When this occurs, the parent(s) must be notified of the place of detention and the reason for arrest. While such detention should be in a place reserved exclusively for young persons, in many non-urban areas, such facilities do not exist.

The Role of Crown Counsel

As in the adult criminal justice process, the Crown counsel is responsible for reviewing the cases of youths referred by the police. After this review, the Crown may withdraw the charges, refer the youth to an alternative measures program (in some provinces), or proceed to Youth Court.

In those cases in which a court appearance is selected as the most appropriate option, the attendance of the accused is sought with a Notice to Appear, served on both the young person and a parent. Youths detained in custody are generally not considered candidates for alternative measures programs, and in such cases, charges are routinely laid. After a first appearance, the detained young person may be released into the care of a responsible adult who will ensure his or her attendance at the court hearing. Young offenders are entitled to release on bail under the same *Criminal Code* provisions as adults.

Court Appearances

Under the provisions of the *YOA*, appearances in Youth Court resemble those in adult court, one notable exception being that cases are heard by a judge alone, with no provision for a jury. In most jurisdictions, legal counsel is accessible and the procedures followed are formal. Arraignment occurs when a youth is told of the accusation against him or her, and usually a plea is entered. In cases where the offence is admitted, the matter may move to the dispositional stage.

In those instances in which a plea of not guilty is entered, the hearing is adjourned for trial at a later date. Legal counsel is often sought at this point, if not before. In certain cases, the Youth Court judge may order the preparation of a psychological or medical assessment to aid in the determination of such issues as fitness to stand trial and insanity.

The *YOA* also provides for cases to be transferred to adult court. The youth must be at least 14 years of age and be accused of having committed a serious indictable offence. Generally, Crown counsel makes application for the transfer, although the Youth Court judge must make the final determination based on a complete review of all the information surrounding the case. This decision must be made prior to a determination of guilt or innocence and may be appealed by the youth.

Youth Court Dispositions

For youths who are subsequently found guilty by the Youth Court, there are a number of dispositional options under the *YOA*:

- ▸ an absolute discharge;
- ▸ a fine of up to $1,000;
- ▸ a payment to the victim of the offence, in compensation for loss or damage to property, loss of income, or special damages that arose because of personal injury to the victim;
- ▸ an order of compensation in-kind or by way of personal service to the victim of the offence;
- ▸ a community service order, which would require the young offender to perform a specified amount of community work;
- ▸ detainment for treatment in a hospital or other facility (as long as the offender agrees), if deemed warranted by a medical or psychological report;
- ▸ probation;
- ▸ committal to intermittent or continuous custody for a specified period; or
- ▸ any conditions that the Youth Court judge considers in the best interests of the youth or the community (Solicitor General of Canada, 1986:11).

The Youth Court may be aided in this decision by a pre-disposition report, which includes an assessment of the youth's family life, prior record, and a variety of other types of information, such as the impact of the crime on the victim. The report is designed to identify the youth's particular needs, as well as provide information on programs and facilities that may be available to address these needs.

The Right to Appeal and Provisions for Review

Both the youth and Crown counsel have the right to appeal the decisions of the Youth Court. The youth can appeal either the court's finding of guilt or the disposition rendered upon such a finding. There are also provisions for the review of custodial and non-custodial sentences of the Youth Court, upon application by any of the parties involved in the case.

The sentences of youths placed in custody are automatically reviewed after 12 months. During these reviews, youths have the option of being represented by legal counsel. Reviews may result in confirmation or modification of the original disposition, although the severity of the sentence may not be increased without the consent of the youth.

Amendments to the *YOA*

Since 1984, there have been a number of important amendments to the *YOA*, including:

1) the suspension of the three-year maximum sentence in those instances in which a youth commits a subsequent offence while under sentence for a previous offence;
2) provision for the publication of the identities of young persons who constitute a danger to the community, so as to allow the police to enlist the public's assistance in apprehending offenders;
3) the inclusion of provisions to empower police to apprehend quickly youths who violate the conditions of their probation;
4) an increase, from three to five years, in the maximum term of confinement, for young offenders convicted of murder; and
5) provision for youths who are transferred to and sentenced in adult court to be eligible for parole in five years for second-degree murder (as opposed to 10 years for adults) and 10 years for first-degree murder (in contrast to the 25-year minimum imposed on adults).

There are concerns among many observers that these amendments, nearly all of which relate to increasing the enforcement provisions of the *YOA*, represent a shift toward a "crime control" model of youth justice (see Corrado and Markwart, 1992:159-163). Support for this perspective is provided by the dispositional patterns of Canadian youths courts, discussed below.

ALTERNATIVE MEASURES PROGRAMS FOR YOUNG OFFENDERS

Alternative measures (AM) programs provide an opportunity for a young person to avoid the formal Youth Court process, while facilitating victim/offender reconciliation and/or the payment of compensation through performance of general community service or specific tasks for the victim (see Pate and Peachey, 1988). Youths acknowledge responsibility for their offence and are able to "make amends" to the victim and the community for their behaviour. Prior to the *YOA*, AM programs were more commonly known as "diversion" programs. It has been estimated that up to one-third of young offenders are handled via AM programs across the country (Canadian Centre for Justice Statistics, 1990).

Each province/territory is given authority to determine how AM programs will operate and the arrangements for supervision. While referrals to AM programs generally occur prior to a charge being laid, several jurisdictions allow for referrals after the laying of a charge by the Crown. In Ontario, prior to being eligible for an AM program, the youth must be formally charged and appear in court.

In all jurisdictions there must be sufficient evidence to prosecute the young person for the offence and the youth must accept responsibility for the offence and be willing to participate in an AM program. Generally, youths must be first-time offenders who have committed either a summary conviction offence or a non-violent indictable offence that does not involve a great amount of damage or loss. However, individual jurisdictions may set the specific eligibility requirements and in some provinces, repeat offenders may be admitted to AM programs. The majority of youths referred to AM programs in Canada have been involved in shoplifting (Pate, 1990). When the youth successfully completes the AM program, the case file is closed and the charges against the youth are dismissed.

AM programs may be operated by police and probation agencies, as well as by private, non-profit groups such as the John Howard Society. All jurisdictions operate victim-offender reconciliation programs (VORPs) under which youths may be required to apologize to the victim, provide restitution, or perform specific tasks in the community. One example is the VORP operated by the John Howard Society in Calgary, which has the following objectives:

1) to operate the program in compliance with the principles and guidelines of the YOA;
2) to provide a means for young persons who so choose to account and take responsibility for their criminal offences by meeting directly with their victims;
3) to recognize and attempt to meet the needs of victims through the mediation process; and
4) to promote community awareness of and participation in the juvenile justice system (Pate, 1990:138).

Among the possible requirements of a VORP agreement is that the youth apologize to the victim, provide monetary restitution to the victim, perform a specified period of work for the victim, complete a number of community service hours, or participate in a counselling or treatment program (Pate, 1990:140).

In the Youth Alternative Society program in Halifax, volunteer mediators facilitate an agreement that address the youth's offence as well as the wishes of the victim (see Solicitor General of Canada, 1986). Also in Nova Scotia, community volunteers work in conjunction with youth justice personnel to provide community-based services for youth. In Nanaimo, British Columbia, the Neighbourhood Accountability Board, operated by the John Howard Society, and comprised of adults and high-school youth, receives referrals from the police and Crown counsel and identifies the needs of youths, arranges for restitution and refers youths to counselling. In Manitoba, youth justice committees provide a forum for the VORP. The objective of the VORP meeting is to secure an agreement between the youth and the victim. In Manitoba, youth justice committees have been established that facilitate community involvement in assisting youth in conflict with the law (Ryant and Heinrich, 1988).

As well as the programs designed specifically as alternative measures under section 4 of the *YOA*, there are programs that are preventative in nature and attempt to attract youths who may be "at risk" but who have not been accused of a specific offence. In the latter category are recreation, counselling, and education/life skills programs. The rationale of these initiatives is that early intervention is superior to the reactive nature of Youth Court processing. Examples of such programs include the Preventive Intervention at the Pre-court Level Program in Sault Ste. Marie, Ontario, and Project Intervention in Windsor, Ontario, in which volunteers participate in one-to-one counselling with youths.

The Youth Assisting Youth program in Scarborough, Ontario, operates on a Big Brother model, with senior youths aged 16 to 18 conducting peer counselling with youths aged 6 through 12. This program is directed to children still too young to be charged with offences. Rossbrook House, located in Winnipeg, is a drop-in centre that provides an alternative to youth involvement in street life and crime. The Harbour Boys' Club Youth Services in Thunder Bay, Ontario, the O'Lokal program in Ste.-Hyacinthe, Quebec, and the Drop-In Centre Youth Recreation Program in Charlottetown, Prince Edward Island, provide a variety of recreational activities for youth, and Project Rediscovery in the Queen Charlotte Islands is an education and culture awareness program for Aboriginal and non-Aboriginal youths conducted in the wilderness.

The Use and Effectiveness of AM Programs

While AM programs are a primary component of the *YOA*, numerous difficulties appear to be seriously undermining their potential effectiveness. These include the following.

▸   *The implementation of AM programs*

Under the provisions of the *YOA*, the development of AM programs, such as diversion, is the responsibility of the provincial/territorial governments. While one of the basic principles of the *YOA* is that it is sometimes appropriate to employ non-judicial intervention (section 3[1][d]), in actual practice there appears to be wide disparity among jurisdictions in the alternatives that have been developed and the extent they are used.

▸   *Community awareness of, and input into, AM programs*

In those jurisdictions with AM programs, the role that individual communities have played in the creation and implementation of such initiatives is unclear. Further, observers have noted that contrary to the original intent of diversion, many programs are created and staffed by members of the justice system (for example, Lemert, 1981). An evaluation by Morton and West (1983), for example, found that while the Frontenac Diversion Program in Kingston, Ontario, was widely known throughout the justice community in Canada, the local community had little knowledge of the program and was only minimally affected by it.

▶ *Organizational problems of AM programs*

An ongoing problem with many community-based initiatives, particularly those operated by non-profit groups and organizations, is securing sufficient resources. Increasingly, diversion programs rely on volunteers, and they have often been unable to secure long-term funding support. It is unclear whether the trend toward privatization of AM programs will resolve these and other organizational problems.

▶ *Widening the net*

Accompanying the expansion of diversion programs in the 1960s was the concern that such programs, rather than functioning to reduce the numbers of youths involved in the formal justice process, have served only to "widen the net," resulting in increased numbers of youths being placed under some form of supervision (see Austin and Krisberg, 1981). This factor also may serve to increase the costs of justice rather than reducing them, as had been originally anticipated.

▶ *Assessing the effectiveness of AM programs*

Among the more commonly cited objectives of AM programs are: (1) a reduction in the number of cases coming before the Youth Court; (2) a decrease in the costs of the youth justice system; (3) a positive change in the attitude of young offenders; (4) increased victim/community satisfaction with the response to youth crime; and (5) a lowering of the rate of youth crime and recidivism among youth participants.

Few evaluations, however, have been undertaken to assess whether AM programs achieve these objectives. Pate (1990) presents testimonial evidence from personnel involved in AM programs that *suggest* that the Calgary VORP has a recidivism rate of less than 4%. The lack of research also precludes an assessment of the impact of AM programs on the attitudes of young offenders or on the perceptions and levels of satisfaction among the victims of youth crime.

In one of the few Canadian attempts to measure the impact of diversion on the recidivism rates of young offenders and on the attitudes of youths and their parents who participated in a diversion program, Jaffe *et al.* (1985-86) compared matched samples of youths from London, Ontario, which had no diversion program, and youths who had participated in the diversion program in Windsor, Ontario. The results of the study revealed no significant differences between the two groups of youths in terms of their recidivism rates or in terms of the attitudes of the youths and their parents toward experiences with the court or the diversion process.

Similar findings were reported by Morton and West (1983) in a study of the Frontenac Diversion Program in Kingston, Ontario. The investigators found few differences between youths handled by the diversion committee and those sent to court, as measured by recidivism rates or the youths' sense of stigma as offenders. Somewhat more positive results, however, have been reported by Fischer and Jeune (1987) from a study of a diversion program in a western Canadian city. The diversion program did not function to widen the net, was delivered at a cost less than that of court processing, and was favourably viewed by the youths, their parents, and youth justice personnel.

These findings suggest that a wide variety of factors may influence the success of AM programs in many jurisdictions, including the structure and operation of the program, the eligibility criteria and the selection of youths for the program, and the actual requirements of the program. Given the continuing expansion of AM programs across the country, it is imperative that evaluations be conducted on the extent to which these initiatives are achieving their stated objectives.

It remains to be seen whether diversion programs developed within the framework of the *YOA* will be successful in avoiding the above-noted difficulties and achieve their stated objectives.

THE YOUTH COURT

Research conducted on the operation of youth courts across the country since the enactment of the *YOA* have produced some interesting results. A major change from pre-*YOA* days is the role of Crown counsel and defence counsel. Crown counsel have become more intimately involved in case screening and in the prosecution of cases involving young offenders, while defence counsel more often appear in court to insure that the rights of youths under the *YOA* are protected (see Corrado and Markwart, 1992; Milne *et al.*, 1992). Attention has also focused on Youth Court judges and the impact of the philosophical shift represented by the *YOA* on dispositions.

Youth Court Decision Making

Research in the United States has attempted to determine the factors that influence the operation and decision making of juvenile courts. The most valuable insights into the operation of youth courts have been provided by studies that have examined the court from an organizational perspective, considering not only the impact of the sociobiographical attributes of the youth (that is, age, sex, socioeconomic status, family life, and offence-related information such as prior record and seriousness of the present offence), but also the influence of community pressure on the court, the police, and the personal and professional perspectives of the judges and probation officers (see Bortner, 1982; Griffiths, 1982; Gabor *et al.*, 1986; Doob, 1989).

While the enactment of the *YOA* has produced some degree of uniformity in the youth justice system, for example, standardizing the upper age at under 18 years of age, the legislation does little to limit the discretion exercised by police officers, probation officers, or judges in responding to youth in conflict. Nor does the *YOA* provide any assistance to decision makers in determining the specific type of intervention that will most appropriately address the needs of the offenders, the victim, and the community.

A close reading of the *YOA* indicates that many of its provisions relate to the *procedures* to be followed in responding to youth, rather than to the way decisions are to be made. This critical distinction ensures that the variability in the response to young offenders by youth justice personnel will persist. Further, all of the traditional goals of sentencing, for example, punishment, rehabilitation, general deterrence, specific deterrence, and incapacitation are in the provisions of the *YOA*, further rendering the *Act* of little guidance to decision makers.

In a preliminary examination of the disparity in decision making among Youth Court judges, for example, Doob and Beaulieu (1992) found considerable variation among a sample of Youth Court judges both in the dispositions they assigned to two hypothetical cases and their stated goals in imposing the particular sentence. These authors (1992:49) attributed their findings to the failure of the *YOA* to provide clear guidelines for sentencing. This, in turn, results in individual judges using different approaches, with different decision outcomes, in identical cases.

In attempting to understand the decision making of the Youth Court, research scholars and practitioners would be well advised to bear in mind the primary conclusion of a major study conducted in the United States (Bortner, 1982:241-42):

> Court personnel...are charged with the awesome responsibility for evaluating a juvenile's entire life situation and offering a prognosis for the future. Court decisions are based on a multitude of considerations: the more identifiable factors such as alleged offense, a child's age, or number of referrals to court; decision-maker's evaluation of the juvenile's individual character and family situation; and the decision-maker's personal propensities and professional orientations...*Much of the research suggests that the more subjective considerations frequently outweigh the more objective factors* (emphasis added).

Youth Court personnel in Canada, operating under the provisions of the *YOA*, are no more restricted than those in the United States in their decision making involving youth in conflict with the law. Indeed, such variability may be required to ensure that the needs of individual young offenders and those of the community and victim are met through the decision making of the court.

Trends in Youth Court Decision Making

While the lack of evaluative studies of the Youth Court in Canada preclude definitive statements about how youth courts are operating, several trends appear to be emerging that should be the subject of further inquiry. Keeping in mind Doob's (1992) caveat that comparisons of Youth Court dispositions across time and jurisdictions are extremely difficult, it nevertheless appears that there have been some significant changes in the response to young offenders over the past decade. Among these are an increase in the number of trials and the length of time required for completion of cases (see Felstiner, 1985; Gabor *et al.,* 1986). These are due to the shift from the paternalistic, rehabilitative approach that was predominant under the *JDA* to a "justice-as-fairness" model under the *YOA* (see Caputo, 1987).

Many observers are concerned with what they perceive to be a shift in the punitiveness of the Youth Court. In many jurisdictions, there has been an increase in the numbers of youths being sentenced to closed and open custody facilities. However, 69% of these admissions were for periods of up to three months. As well, it appears that longer periods of probation are being imposed with the national average being ten months (Conway, 1992b). Since 1984, there have been significant increases in the use of custody in the provinces of British Columbia, Manitoba, and Ontario (Corrado and Markwart, 1988; Markwart, 1992; Markwart and Corrado, 1989; Leschied and Jaffe, 1987). These developments are taken by these authors as evidence that, under the *YOA*, there has been an increased emphasis on the control and punishment of youth at the expense of their treatment needs (see Leschied and Gendreau, 1986).

Within this general trend, however, there is variation in Youth Court decision making between the jurisdictions. For example, in British Columbia, 21% of cases result in custodial dispositions (Conway, 1992b). The figure for the Yukon is 47%, reflecting in part the widespread use of AM and other informal sanctions. Corrado and Markwart (1992:217) report, for example, that Ontario's per capita rate of custody for young offenders is double that of British Columbia. There is also evidence that, in some jurisdictions, judges have retained a treatment approach to youth crime, while in other jurisdictions, a more punitive approach is evident (see Gabor, Greene, and McCormick, 1986; Kopyto and Codina, 1986).

YOUTH CORRECTIONS

For those youths who admit guilt or who are found guilty in the Youth Court, there are a variety of sentencing alternatives available under the *YOA*. Thirty percent of cases result in custody dispositions; the majority of youths receive dispositions that can be categorized as community-based (see Figure 14.1). For those youths who are not directed into an AM program or granted an absolute discharge by the court, the dispositions may be categorized generally as either community-based or custodial.

Non-custodial Programs

The majority of young offenders receive non-custodial dispositions in Youth Court. The non-custodial dispositions available to the court include community service, a fine not to exceed $1000, the payment of compensation or restitution, compensation by personal service, and probation. Probation is the most frequently used disposition, being imposed in 42% of the cases in 1991/92 (Conway, 1992b). Probation is designed to provide supervision for the youth in the community, while at the same time allowing the court to attach specific conditions to the probationary

FIGURE 14.1
THE LEGAL PROCESS FOR YOUNG OFFENDERS
(This is a general framework only.)

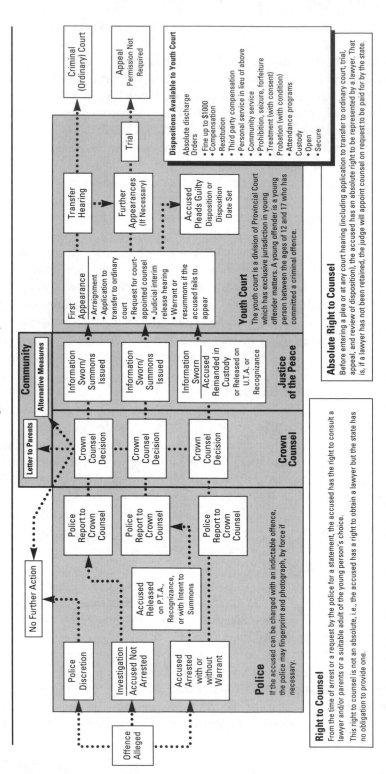

Source: *British Columbia's Legal System: A Guide to the Wall Charts* (Vancouver: Law Courts Education Society of British Columbia, 1992), p. 34. Reproduced with permission.

period. These conditions include completion of a specified number of community service hours, the payment of restitution to the victim, or participation in, and completion of, a specialized course such as a Wilderness Experience Program. The average length of probation terms in 1991-92 was 10.5 months.

Probation officers play a major role. They prepare social histories or pre-disposition reports for the Youth Court and provide supervision and counselling to youths placed on probation. To date in Canada there have been no published evaluations of youth probation, and the effectiveness of this particular Youth Court disposition in addressing the needs of the youth, the victim, and the community is unclear.

As in adult corrections, there is ongoing controversy over community-based programs for young offenders. Concerns have been raised regarding the extent of public involvement in such programs and whether community-based programs are more effective in reducing youthful misbehaviour than are institutionally based programs. Further concerns have been voiced about the "net-widening" tendencies of many community-based programs and about statistics indicating that more youths than ever are becoming involved in the Canadian youth justice system.

Youth in Custody

The Youth Court may sentence a young offender to a maximum period of two years' confinement, or to a maximum of five years if the youth has committed a crime for which an adult offender would be liable to life imprisonment or if the youth is being sentenced for two or more offences. In imposing a custody sentence, the Youth Court must specify whether it is to be served in an "open" or "closed" custody facility. Open custody facilities, which include group homes, wilderness camps, and community residential centres, may be operated by the provincial or territorial government or by private, for-profit and non-profit agencies under contract. Secure custody facilities, often called Youth Detention Centres, are operated by provincial/territorial governments (see Caputo and Bracken, 1988). There is wide variation across the country in the nature and types of facilities and the programs offered within them.

A custody disposition was given out in just over 20% of the cases heard in Canada in 1991-92 (Conway, 1992b). The majority (69%) of youths in custody are serving sentences of less than three months. Moreover, the proportion of youths serving terms of confinement of greater than three months has been steadily declining during the past six years, with a concurrent increase in shorter sentences (Conway, 1992b).

The increasing numbers of custodial sentences being given to young offenders raise concerns about not only the types of facilities within which youth are confined, but also the dynamics of life inside detention facilities and the effectiveness of institutional and treatment programs.

There are a number of "classic" studies of the social organization of institutions for young offenders, all of which were conducted in the United States.[15] While some of these studies are now over 20 years old, they provide insights into the world of confined youths and into the social systems and subcultures that develop in youth institutions (see Bartollas, Miller, and Dinitz, 1976; Feld, 1978; Giallombardo, 1974; Polsky, 1977; Propper, 1981).

By analyzing institutional policies, staff behaviour, and patterns of interaction among youth inmates, researchers have been able to identify the factors that contributed to or mitigated the amount of violence and victimization among the youth, as well as the conditions that led to the development of positive attitudes and behaviours. These investigations have also uncovered subcultures among male and female offenders in confinement and documented the patterns of exploitation and violence in these social systems (see Osgood *et al.*, 1985; Reichel, 1985).[16]

Generally, the research suggests that, similar to adult offenders, the dynamics of institutions for young offenders are strongly influenced by the "pains of imprisonment" experienced by incarcerated youth and by the orientation of the institutional staff and administration. As in adult institutions, the social system among young inmates may be the source of considerable violence and exploitation. For example, one youth facility was made up of cottages, some of which stressed goals of treatment, others of which goals of punishment. Feld (1978) found that in those cottages in which the goals of treatment were stressed, there were more positive attitudes and less violence among the youth than in cottages in which staff were more punishment oriented. Similarly, Sieverdes and Bartollas (1986), in a study of five co-educational youth institutions, found that group cohesion (the subculture) was more strongly developed in maximum security facilities (see also Leschied, Jaffe, and Stone, 1985).

As with inmate social systems among adult offenders, there appear to be differences in the patterns of interaction that develop in institutions for male and female youths. While little research has been conducted on Canadian youth facilities, findings from the United States suggest that institutions for females had fewer programs than their male counterparts, and the programs that did exist tended to reinforce sex role stereotypes. Also, studies conducted in female institutions reported the tendency of girls to form "make-believe" families (see Foster, 1975).[17]

Treatment Initiatives and Their Effectiveness

In Canada, there are few published evaluations of the effectiveness of these various correctional techniques. Many of the issues surround correctional treatment for adult offenders.

There is a large body of literature, primarily from the United States, on the various treatment approaches that have been taken with young offenders in confinement. As with adult corrections, the treatment of young offenders has been the subject of considerable debate. So has the "nothing works" argument been put forth in discussing the effectiveness of correctional intervention with young offenders (see Shamsie, 1981). However, as with adult correctional programs, there is emerging evidence that *some* treatment programs do have a significant impact on the attitudes and behaviour of *some* youths.

In rebuking the continued pessimism of the "anti-rehabilitation" criminologists, Leschied *et al.* argue:

> the *fact* is that every review of controlled studies of rehabilitation...has found that at least 40 percent and up to 80 percent of controlled studies of correctional services reported some evidence of positive effects of service in terms of reducing reoffending (1992:357-58).

The majority of treatment approaches applied to youths in custodial and community-based settings are psychological in orientation and include individual treatment methods, such as psychotherapy, reality therapy, vocational counselling, and behaviourial contracts, as well as group treatment methods, such as group counselling, group psycho-therapy, milieu therapy, and guided group interaction.[18] There is some question as to whether these treatment interventions adequately address the needs of Aboriginal youths, those youths from lower socioeconomic circumstances, youths from dysfunctional home situations that may have included physical or emotional abuse, or immigrant youths.

As in adult corrections, the primary method by which the effective-ness of youth treatment programs is measured is by the rate of reoffending, or recidivism. The most recent figures available (excluding Nova Scotia, Ontario, and the Northwest Territories), suggests that nearly 40% of youths appearing in Youth Court have prior convictions (Hendrick and Lachance, 1991). The majority of the recidivists were male and most were older. In court, recidivists were more likely than first-time offenders to receive either open or secure custody and less likely to receive probation.

In an 18-year follow-up of male youths who were admitted under the provisions of the *JDA* to Ontario training schools during the 1970s, Hundleby *et al.* (1992) found that 97% had some official contact with the criminal justice system after age 16. Nearly 80% of the youths were arrested five or more times after age 16, and just over one-half of the sample had been convicted of one or more serious crimes. The researchers (1992:45) caution against the findings of their study being used to fuel the "nothing works" debate, arguing that the lack of a control group precludes an assessment of the effectiveness of youth custody. This work does suggest, however, that youths who experienced conflict at a young age may have a higher likelihood of becoming involved in adult criminality and that treatment interventions should be directed toward youth in the age range 8 to 12 years:

> The best predictor of adult crime in our sample, both for seriousness and violence, is a history of anti-social, aggressive, and problem behaviour from at least late middle childhood to middle adolescence (Hundleby *et al.*, 1992:57).

Many of the same difficulties that have afflicted treatment programs for adult offenders, as discussed in Chapter 11, also have characterized youth correctional treatment: (1) the failure to consider the differential amenability of youths to treatment; (2) the need to "match" individual youths to specific treatment programs, commonly referred to as differential treatment effectiveness; and (3) the failure to examine how treatment programs are delivered in both institutional and community settings and how this affects the effectiveness of the programs.

The conclusion of Andrews *et al.* (1990:377) presented in our discussion of correctional treatment for adults in Chapter 11, bears repeating, since it appears to apply to young offenders as well: "...appropriate correctional treatment — treatment that is delivered to higher risk cases, targets criminogenic need, and is matched with the learning styles of offenders — will be associated with reduced recidivism."

It remains to be seen whether the "drift" toward an increased emphasis on the punishment of young offenders, which began in the 1970s, will continue throughout the 1990s, or whether the pendulum will swing back to a focus on the rehabilitation of youth in conflict with the law. In the long term, it must be acknowledged that there are distinct limitations to youth justice policies that focus only on punishment, even if procedures are followed to ensure that young offenders are provided with legal rights. The manner in which youth justice is administered throughout the country depends, to a great extent, on the philosophies of those who staff the system — the Youth Court judges, probation officers, and program personnel. As well, the policies of the provinces and territories, the availability of resources for addressing the needs of youth in conflict, and the nature and extent of public pressure that is placed on the youth justice system also play a significant role in the response to young offenders.

In the coming years, the *YOA* may come to be viewed as representing less of an enlightened approach to youth crime and young offenders and more of an impediment to addressing the needs of youths, victims, and the community. Canadian scholars must continue to explore the dynamics and outcomes of the youth justice system if we are to respond to young offenders in a just *and* effective manner.

NOTES

[1]S.C. 1857, 20 Vic., c.29.

[2]S.C. 1857, 20 Vic., c.28. In the next consolidation of federal statutes, this was renamed *An Act Respecting the Trial and Punishment of Juvenile Offenders*, Cons. S.C. 1859, c.106. It was eventually replaced by the *Juvenile Offenders Act*, S.C. 1869, 32 & 33 Vict., c.33, which was itself incorporated into the first *Criminal Code* of 1892.

[3]S.O. 1880, 43 Vic., c.34.

[4]S.O. 1888, 51 Vict., c.40.

[5]S.C. 1892, 55-56 Vict., c.29, s.550. Also incorporated into this statute were the provisions of the *Juvenile Offenders Act*, S.C. 1886, 49 Vict., c.177, a consolidation of what had been *An Act for the More Speedy Trial and Punishment of Juvenile Offenders*.

[6]*An Act for the Prevention of Cruelty to, and Better Protection of Children*, S.O. 1893, 56 Vict., c.45.

[7]*An Act to Permit the Conditional Release of First Offenders in Certain Cases*, S.C. 1889, 52 Vict., c.44. Two criteria to be considered by the court in imposing a sentence of probation were the age of the offender and the seriousness of the offence. Young offenders charged with minor offences were the primary recipients of probation until 1900, when an amendment to the *Criminal Code* expanded the scope of those who qualified for probation.

[8]*Juvenile Delinquents Act*, S.C. 1908, 7-8 Ed. VII, c.40.

[9]S.C. 1867, 30 & 31 Vict., c.3, ss.91 and 92.

[10]This definition of juvenile delinquency remained substantially unchanged until the repeal of the *JDA* in 1984, with the exception that, in 1924, "sexual immorality or any similar form of vice" was added as a criterion in *An Act to Amend the Juvenile Delinquents Act, 1908*, S.C. 1924, 14 & 15 Geo. V, c.53.

[11]In 1921, in *An Act to Amend the Juvenile Delinquents Act* (S.C. 1921, 11 & 12 Geo. V, c.37.), the upper age limit defining the court's jurisdiction was raised to 18 from 16. Each province/territory could choose the age it desired. In 1929, the *JDA* was reorganized and consolidated into the form that it took until its repeal in 1984.

[12]*Young Offenders Act*, S.C. 1980-81-82-83, c.110; now R.S.C. 1985, c.Y-1.

[13]For an extensive analysis of all facets of the *YOA* and its implementation across Canada, see Corrado *et al.*, 1992.

[14]The wide variability across provincial and territorial jurisdictions in the structure and operation of youth justice systems requires that considerable caution be used in comparing the structure and operation of youth justice systems. There are a myriad of factors, including police practices, case screening procedures, and program availability, that may significantly influence the numbers of youths who appear in Youth Court and the dispositions that they receive. There are also problems comparing data across jurisdictions. Until 1991, for example, the province of Ontario did not participate in the national Youth Court survey and information on youth justice was not included in national reports.

[15]For a historical analysis of the administration and operation of a boy's training school in Quebec, see Rains (1985).

[16]Valuable insights into the dynamics of institutional life are provided by Menzies *et al.* (1987) in their study of disruptive and self-destructive behaviour among youth in a Canadian youth detention facility.

[17]There is disagreement among observers over the extent to which "make-believe" families exist in institutions for girls, and it is unknown whether this phenomenon occurs in Canadian facilities. Many detention centres for youths in Canada are co-educational and house both boys and girls. The mixing of the sexes may have a significant impact on the social system that develops within the institutions.

[18]For a thorough look at the various individual and group treatment strategies used with young offenders, see Siegel and Senna (1991) and Whitehead

and Lab (1990). For an analysis of a Canadian program that attempts to address the needs of "hard to serve" youth, see Leschied and Thomas (1985).

REFERENCES

Andrews, D.A., I. Zinger, R.D. Hoge, J. Bonta, P. Gendreau, and F.T. Cullen. 1990. "Does Correction Treatment Work? A Clinically Relevant and Psychologically Informed Meta-Analysis." 28 *Criminology*. 369-404.

Austin, J., and B. Krisberg. 1981. "Wider, Stronger, and Different Nets: The Dialectics of Criminal Justice Reform." 18 *Journal of Research in Crime and Delinquency*. 165-96.

Baehre, R. 1982. *The Prison System in Atlantic Canada before 1880*. Ottawa: Solicitor General of Canada.

Bartollas, C., S.J. Miller, and S. Dinitz. 1976. *Juvenile Victimization: The Institutional Paradox*. New York: John Wiley and Sons.

Bortner, M.A. 1982. *Inside a Juvenile Court: The Tarnished Ideal of Individualized Justice*. New York: New York University Press.

Brannigan, A. 1987. "Mystification of the Innocents: Comics and Delinquency in Canada." 8 *Criminal Justice History*. 111-44.

Canadian Centre for Justice Statistics. 1990. "National Summary of Alternative Measures Services for Young Persons." 10 *Juristat Service Bulletin*. Ottawa: Statistics Canada.

Caputo, T.C. 1987. "The Young Offenders Act: Children's Rights, Children's Wrongs." 13 *Canadian Public Policy*. 125-43.

Caputo, T., and D.C. Bracken. 1988. "Custodial Dispositions and the Young Offenders Act." In J. Hudson, J.P. Hornick, and B.A. Burrows, eds. *Justice and the Young Offender in Canada*. Toronto: Wall and Thompson. 123-43.

Conway, J. 1992a. "Female Young Offenders, 1990-91." 12 *Juristat Service Bulletin*. Ottawa: Canadian Centre for Justice Statistics.

_____. 1992b. "Youth Court Statistics, 1991-92 Highlights." 12 *Juristat Service Bulletin*. Ottawa: Canadian Centre for Justice Statistics.

Corrado, R.R., and A. Markwart. 1988. "The Prices of Rights and Responsibilities: An Examination of the Impact of the *Young Offenders Act* in British Columbia." 7 *Canadian Journal of Family Law*. 93-115.

Corrado, R.R., and A. Markwart. 1992. "The Evolution and Implementation of a New Era of Juvenile Justice in Canada." In R.R. Corrado, N. Bala, R. Linden, and M. LeBlanc, eds. *Juvenile Justice in Canada: A Theoretical and Analytical Assessment*. Toronto: Butterworths. 137-227.

Corrado, R.R., N. Bala, R. Linden, and M. LeBlanc. 1992. *Juvenile Justice in Canada: A Theoretical and Analytical Assessment*. Toronto: Butterworths.

Doob, A. N. 1989. "Dispositions Under the Young Offenders Act: Issues

Without Answers?" In L.A. Beaulieu, ed. *Young Offender Dispositions: Perspectives on Principles and Practice.* Toronto: Wall and Thompson. 193-225.

———. 1992. "Trends in the Use of Custodial Dispositions for Young Offenders." 34 *Canadian Journal of Criminology.* 75-84.

Doob, A.N., and L.A. Beaulieu. 1992. "Variation in the Exercise of Judicial Discretion with Young Offenders." 34 *Canadian Journal of Criminology.* 35-50.

Feld, B.C. 1978. *Neutralizing Inmate Violence: Juvenile Offenders in Institutions.* Cambridge, Massachusetts: Ballinger.

Felstiner, J. 1985. "Some Observations of Practice and Procedure under the Young Offenders Act." *Ontario Association of Professional Social Workers Metro News* (Spring). 19-23.

Fischer, D.G., and R. Jeune. 1987. "Juvenile Diversion: A Process Analysis." 28 *Canadian Psychology.* 60-70.

Foster, T.W. 1975. "Make-believe Families: A Response of Women and Girls to the Deprivations of Imprisonment." 3 *International Journal of Criminology and Penology.* 71-78.

Frank, J. 1991. "Violent Offence Cases Heard in Youth Courts, 1990-91." 11 *Juristat Service Bulletin.* Ottawa: Statistics Canada.

Gabor, P., I. Greene, and P. McCormick. 1986. "The Young Offenders Act: The Alberta Youth Court Experience in the First Year." 5 *Canadian Journal of Family Law.* 301-19.

Giallombardo, R. 1974. *The Social World of Imprisoned Girls: A Comparative Study of Institutions for Juvenile Delinquents.* New York: John Wiley and Sons.

Greenberg, P. 1992. "Youth Property Crime in Canada." 12 *Juristat.* Ottawa: Canadian Centre for Justice Statistics.

Griffiths, C.T. 1982. "Law Enforcement-Juvenile Court Relations: The Impact on Decision Making." 6 *Criminal Justice Review,* 6-13.

Hagarty, J. 1866. "Vagrant Children in Our Cities." 19 *Upper Canada Journal of Education.* 4-5.

Hatch, A.J., and C.T. Griffiths. 1991. "Child Saving Postponed: The Impact of the *Juvenile Delinquents Act* on the Processing of Young Offenders in Vancouver." In R. Smandych, G. Dobbs and A. Esau, eds. *Dimensions of Childhood: Essays on the History of Children and Youth in Canada.* Winnipeg: Legal Research Institute, University of Manitoba. 233-66.

———. 1993. "Youth Crime in Canada: Observations for Cross-Cultural Analysis." 16 *Journal of Comparative and Applied Criminal Justice.* 165-83.

Hendrick, D., and M. Lachance. 1991. "A Profile of the Young Offender." 3 *FORUM on Corrections Research.* 17-21.

Houston, S.E. 1982. "The 'Waifs and Strays' of a Late Victorian City: Juvenile Delinquents in Toronto." In J. Parr, ed. *Childhood and Family in Canadian History.* Toronto: McClelland and Stewart. 129-42.

Hundleby, J.D., K.F. Scapinello, and G.A. Stasiak. 1992. *Thirteen to Thirty: A Follow-Up Study of Young Training School Boys.* Ottawa: Corrections Branch, Solicitor General of Canada.

Jaffe, P.G., and B.J. Kroeker, C. Hyatt, M. Miscevick, A. Telford, R. Chandler, C. Shanahan, and B. Sokoloff. 1985-86. "Diversion in the Canadian Juvenile Justice System: A Tale of Two Cities." 37 *Juvenile and Family Court Journal.* 59-66.

Jones, A. 1978. "Closing Penetanguishene Reformatory: An Attempt to Deinstitutionalize Treatment of Juvenile Offenders in Early Twentieth Century Ontario." 70 *Ontario History.* 227-44.

Jones, A., and L. Rutman. 1981. *In the Children's Aid: J.J. Kelso and Child Welfare in Ontario.* Toronto: University of Toronto Press.

Kelso, J.J. 1907. "Delinquent Children: Some Improved Methods Whereby They May Be Prevented From Following a Criminal Career." 6 *Canadian Law Review.* 106-10.

Knell, B.E.F. 1965. "Capital Punishment: Its Administration in Relation to Juvenile Offenders in the Nineteenth Century and Its Possible Administration in the Eighteenth." 5 *British Journal of Delinquency.* 198-207.

Kopyto, H., and A.M. Codina.1986. "Young Offenders Act Means More Frequent Custody Terms." 6 *Lawyers Weekly.* 8.

Langmuir, J.W. (Chair). 1891. *Commission Appointed to Enquire into the Prison and Reformatory System of Ontario. Report of the Commissioners.* Toronto: Warwick and Son.

LeBlanc, M., and H. Beaumont. 1992. "The Effectiveness of Juvenile Justice in Quebec: A Natural Experiment in Implementing Formal Diversion and a Justice Model." In R.R. Corrado, N. Bala, R. Linden, and M. LeBlanc, eds. *Juvenile Justice in Canada: A Theoretical and Analytical Assessment.* Toronto: Butterworths. 283-312.

Lemert, E. 1981. "Diversion in Juvenile Justice: What Hath Been Wrought." 18 *Journal of Research in Crime and Delinquency.* 35-46.

Leon, J. 1977. "The Development of Canadian Juvenile Justice: A Background for Reform." 15 *Osgoode Hall Law Journal.* 71-106.

Leschied, A.W., and P. Gendreau. 1986. "The Declining Role of Rehabilitation in Canadian Juvenile Justice: Implications of Underlying Theory in the Young Offender's Act." 28 *Canadian Journal of Criminology.* 315-22.

Leschied, A.W., and P.G. Jaffe. 1987. "Impact of the Young Offenders Act on Court Dispositions: A Comparative Analysis." 29 *Canadian Journal of Criminology.* 421-30.

Leschied, A.W., and K.E. Thomas. 1985. "Effective Residential Programming for

'Hard to Serve' Delinquent Youth: A Descrpition of the Craigwood Program." 27 *Canadian Journal of Criminology*. 161-77.

Leschied, A.W., P.G. Jaffe, and G.L. Stone. 1985. "Differential Response to Juvenile Offenders to Two Detention Environments as a Function of Conceptual Level." 27 *Canadian Journal of Criminology*. 161-76.

Leschied, A.W., P.G. Jaffe, D. Andrews, and P. Gendreau. 1992. "Treatment Issues and Young Offenders: An Empirically Derived Vision of Juvenile Justice Policy." In R.R. Corrado, N. Bala, R. Linden, and M. LeBlanc, eds. *Juvenile Justice in Canada: A Theoretical and Analytical Assessment.* Toronto: Butterworths. 347-66.

MacGill, H.G. 1925. *The Juvenile Court in Canada: Origins, Principles, Governing Legislation and Practice.* Ottawa: Canadian Council on Child Welfare.

Markwart, A. 1992. "Custodial Sanctions Under the *Young Offenders Act.*" In R.R. Corrado, N. Bala, R. Linden, and M. LeBlanc, eds. *Juvenile Justice in Canada: A Theoretical and Analytical Assessment.* Toronto: Butterworths. 229-81.

Markwart, A., and R.R. Corrado. 1989. "Is the *Young Offenders Act* More Punitive?" In L.A. Beaulieu, ed. *Young Offender Dispositions: Perspectives on Principles and Practice.* Toronto: Wall and Thompson. 7-26.

Menzies, R.J., R.R. Corrado, W. Glackman, and K. Ryan. 1987. *A Seven-Year Survey of Disruptive and Self-injurious Conduct among Residents of a Youth Detention Centre.* Ottawa: Solicitor General of Canada.

Milne, H.A., R. Linden, and R. Kueneman. 1992. "Advocate or Guardian: The Role of Defence Counsel in Youth Justice." In R.R. Corrado, N. Bala, R. Linden, and M. LeBlanc, eds. *Juvenile Justice in Canada: A Theoretical and Analytical Assessment.* Toronto: Butterworths. 313-45.

Morrison, T.R. 1976. "'Their Proper Sphere': Feminism, the Family, and Child-Centred Social Reform in Ontario, 1875-1900." 68 *Ontario History.* 45-64.

Morton, M.E., and W.G. West. 1983. "An Experiment in Diversion by a Citizen Committee." In R.R. Corrado, M.LeBlanc, and J. Trepanier, eds. *Current Issues in Juvenile Justice.* Toronto: Butterworths. 206-16.

Osgood, D.W., E. Gruber, M.A. Archer, and T.M. Newcomb. 1985. "Autonomy for Inmates: Counterculture or Cooptation?" 12 *Criminal Justice and Behavior.* 71-89.

Pate, K. 1990. "Victim-Young Offender Reconciliation as Alternative Measures Programs in Canada." In B. Galaway and J. Hudson, eds. *Criminal Justice, Restitution, and Reconciliation.* Monsey, N.Y: Criminal Justice Press. 135-44.

Pate, K.J., and D.E. Peachey. 1988. "Face-to-Face: Victim-Offender Mediation under the Young Offenders Act." In J. Hudson, J.P. Hornick, and B.A. Burrows, eds. *Justice and the Young Offender in Canada.* Toronto: Wall and Thompson. 105-21.

Polsky, H.W. 1977. *Cottage Six: The Social System of Delinquent Boys in Residential Treatment.* Huntington, New York: Krieger.

Prentice, A. 1977. *The School Promoters: Education and Social Class in Mid-Nineteenth Century Upper Canada.* Toronto: McClelland and Stewart.

Propper, A. 1981. *Prison Homosexuality: Myth and Reality.* Lexington, Massachusetts: D.C. Heath.

Rains, P. 1985. "La Justice des mineurs et the Boy's Farm: 1909-1968." 18 *Criminologie.* 103-27.

Reichel, P.L. 1985. "Getting to Know You: Decision Making is an Institution for Juveniles." 36 *Juvenile and Family Court Journal.* 5-15.

Ryant, J.C., and C. Heinrich. 1988. "Youth Court Committees in Manitoba." In J. Hudson, J.P. Hornick, and B.A. Burrows, eds. *Justice and the Young Offender in Canada.* Toronto: Wall and Thompson. 93-104.

Shamsie, S.J. 1981. "Antisocial Adolescents: All Treatments Do Not Work: Where do We Go From Here?" 26 *Canadian Journal of Psychiatry.* 357-64.

Shoom, S. 1972. "The Upper Canada Reformatory, Penetanguishene: The Dawn of Prison Reform in Canada." 14 *Canadian Journal of Criminology and Corrections.* 260-67.

Siegel, L.J., and J.J. Senna. 1991. *Juvenile Delinquency — Theory, Practice and Law.* St. Paul, Minnesota: West Publishing Company.

Sieverdes, C.M., and C. Bartollas. 1986. "Security Level and Adjustment Patterns in Juvenile Institutions." 14 *Journal of Criminal Justice.* 135-45.

Smandych, R., G. Dobbs, and A. Esau. 1991. *Dimensions of Childhood: Essays on the History of Children and Youth in Canada.* Winnipeg: Legal Research Institute, University of Manitoba.

Solicitor General of Canada. 1986. *The Young Offenders Act: Highlights.* Ottawa: Supply and Services Canada.

Stubbs, Roy. 1972. "The Young Offender." 5 *Manitoba Law Journal.* 19-39.

Sutherland, N. 1976. *Children in English-Canadian Society: Framing the Twentieth Century Consensus.* Toronto: University of Toronto Press.

Watts, R.E. 1932. "Trend of Crime in Canada." 39 *Queen's Quarterly.* 402-13.

Whitehead, J.T., and S.P. Lab. 1990. *Juvenile Justice.* Cincinnati: Anderson Publishing Company.

Wilson, L.C. 1990. "Changes to Federal Jurisdiction Over Young Offenders: The Provincial Response." 8 *Canadian Journal of Family Law.* 303-43.

15 ABORIGINAL PEOPLES AND THE CRIMINAL JUSTICE SYSTEM

This chapter explores the major issues surrounding Aboriginal peoples and the criminal justice system. We will consider the nature and extent of their contact with the law, as well as the policies and programs that have been developed by governmental agencies and by Aboriginal bands, communities, and organizations in an attempt to reduce Aboriginal conflict with the criminal justice system. The increased focus on Aboriginal justice issues in Canada is reflected in the growing number of research studies, task forces, and commissions of inquiry, and in the pronouncements of government and Aboriginal leaders (see Silverman and Nielsen, 1992). Self-government was one of the key issues of the proposed Charlottetown Accord in 1992; the Royal Commission on Aboriginal Peoples, co-chaired by Georges Erasmus, is expected to publish its results in 1994.[1]

THE ABORIGINAL PEOPLES OF CANADA

Approximately 3.6% of the total population of Canada is Aboriginal. This includes status and non-status Indians, Métis, and Inuit. Aboriginal peoples are, however, unevenly distributed across the country in terms of their percentage of territorial or provincial populations, ranging from 60% in the Northwest Territories and 20% in the Yukon, to 6% in Saskatchewan and Manitoba, and 3% in Alberta and British Columbia, 1.3% in Ontario, and 0.8% in Quebec. The highest absolute numbers of Aboriginal peoples are found in Ontario and British Columbia.

Aboriginal peoples in Canada are distinguished by their cultural and linguistic attributes, as well as their legal status. *Status Indians* are Aboriginal people who are registered under the *Indian Act*. *Non-status Indians* are those who identify themselves as Aboriginal but who are not registered under the *Indian Act*. Métis are of mixed Aboriginal and European ancestry, while the Inuit (Eskimo) are a distinct cultural group who reside in the Northwest Territories, Labrador, and Northern Quebec.

Census data, which should be taken as only a general indicator, suggest the following distribution of Aboriginal peoples in Canada: Status Indians (59.9%); Métis (20.0%); non-status Indians (15.3%); and Inuit

(5.2%). The population growth rates for status Indians and Inuit are higher than those for the general population. Throughout the chapter, the term "Aboriginal" is used to describe status and non-status Indians, Métis, and Inuit, although reference is made to specific groups where required.

There is considerable diversity among the 593 recognized Aboriginal bands in terms of their culture, social and political organization, and community resources. The majority of these bands, representing nearly 65% of the total registered Aboriginal population, are situated in either rural or remote northern areas, compared to 25% of the national population. As we will see later in our discussion, this remoteness has significant implications for the delivery of justice services.

Aboriginal Peoples in the Urban Setting

While the majority of Aboriginal peoples reside in rural areas, it is important to remember that there are also significant populations in the "southern," urban areas of the country. Nearly 60,000 Aboriginals reside in the city of Vancouver, representing a myriad of cultural and linguistic groups. Many urban residents experience difficulties in securing employment and in adapting to the urban environment, and, in many cities, there are high rates of Aboriginal involvement in the justice system. Data from Alberta (Cawsey, 1991) indicate that approximately 60% of the offenders in correctional institutions in that province are from urban areas. In an attempt to meet the needs of the urban Aboriginal population, an increasing number of counselling, education, vocational training, and housing programs have been developed.

It is uncertain whether Aboriginal peoples residing in urban areas will become involved in the movement toward the development of separate justice systems. There are a great number of obstacles to the creation of Aboriginal-controlled justice programs and services that do not exist at the reserve level or in smaller communities.

In many urban centres, however, Aboriginal peoples have established education centres, including high schools, as well as drug and alcohol counselling programs, housing cooperatives, and many other services designed to meet the needs of urban residents. There are also a variety of criminal justice initiatives directed specifically toward urban Aboriginals, including courtworker and legal service programs and various police-community relations initiatives.[2]

Aboriginal Peoples in Canada: The Legacy of Colonization

Any discussion of Aboriginal peoples and the criminal justice system must consider their political position and socioeconomic condition in Canadian society. Many observers argue that the subordinate political and economic position of Aboriginal peoples is a consequence of their colonization by Europeans and of Canadian government policies that have exerted control over virtually every aspect of Aboriginal life (Berger, 1991; Cole and Chaikin, 1990; Dickason, 1992; Dyck, 1991; Getty and Lussier, 1988; Miller, 1989; Morrison and Wilson, 1986; Titley, 1988).

Perhaps no one piece of federal legislation has had a more significant, and destructive, impact on Aboriginal culture and communities as the *Indian Act*, first passed in 1876. The provisions of the *Indian Act* reflected the long-term goal of assimilating Aboriginal peoples into Canadian society. The inherent rights of Aboriginal people to self-government and self-determination were rejected and the federal government and its agents assumed control over nearly all aspects of individual and community life. Through the *Indian Act*, the federal government revealed its intention to destroy Aboriginal culture and values by imposing new requirements relating to private property, religion, and lifestyle. Aboriginal women, in particular, suffered under the provisions of the *Indian Act*, and many lost their status and legal rights and became alienated from their communities and their culture.[3]

The impact of the policies of successive federal governments toward Aboriginal peoples can be seen in their marginalized position in Canadian society. This is reflected in pervasive poverty, high rates of unemployment and reliance upon public assistance, low levels of formal education, high death rates from accidents and violence, and increasing rates of family breakdown. Census data from Saskatchewan (Wolff, 1991), for example, reveal the following.

- ▸ One-half of the Aboriginal people residing on reserves had never been to high school and few had completed grade 12.
- ▸ Only 38% of reserve residents over the age of 15 were in the labour force.
- ▸ The average income of reserve residents was less than one-half that of persons living off the reserve.
- ▸ 25% of reserve families were headed by a single parent, compared to 11% of families off the reserve.

In his study of Aboriginal criminality, McCaskill (1985:24) found that the socioeconomic and offence profiles of a large sample of Aboriginal inmates and parolees were characterized by "serious social and personal disorganization, including family instability, alcohol abuse, and low levels of education and skill development."

While there have been some measurable improvements in the condition of the registered, or status, Aboriginal population (a decline in infant mortality rates, a rise in annual income, and an increase in life expectancy) Canada's Aboriginal peoples fall far short when compared with non-Aboriginals on nearly every quality of life indicator at the individual and community levels (Canada, 1989; Siggner, 1986). Particularly vulnerable are Aboriginal youth, aged 15 to 24, who are most susceptible to violent and accidental death, suicide, and alcohol and substance abuse (see Krotz, 1990; Shkilnyk, 1985; York, 1990.).[4]

As an illustration, information provided to the Indian Justice Review Committee (Linn, 1992a:6-8) in the province of Saskatchewan indicated the following:

- two-thirds of Aboriginal homes on reserves lacked central heating;
- over three-fifths lacked a bathroom;
- the unemployment rate among Aboriginal peoples was four times that of non-Aboriginals;
- three of four registered Aboriginals on the reserves received social assistance;
- the suicide rate on the reserves was three times that for the provincial population as a whole; and
- an estimated 30 to 40% of the Aboriginal population is involved in alcohol abuse, as compared to an estimated 6% of the general population in the province.

Materials presented to the Manitoba Aboriginal Justice Inquiry (cited in Hamilton and Sinclair, 1991a:481) indicated that the average annual income for Aboriginal women in Manitoba was less than 75% of that for non-Aboriginal women; the labour force participation rate was 40% less; and 72% of Aboriginal women in the province had not graduated from high school. In Winnipeg, 43% of the Aboriginal families were headed by a single woman, compared with only 10% of non-Aboriginal families. In recent years, however, Aboriginal women have assumed a major role in the revitalization of Aboriginal culture and communities, while at the same time providing challenges to both government and to the Aboriginal (male) political leadership.

In considering the "condition" of Aboriginal peoples across the country, we must keep in mind that there will be differences on these various measures between reserves and communities. Despite these differences, however, there is little doubt that many Aboriginal persons live in "Third World" conditions, often out of sight (and out of mind) of the majority of non-Aboriginal peoples, the majority of whom live in the southern, more urban areas of the country.

Over the past decade, Aboriginal peoples across Canada have become more aggressive in pursuing land claims and in exerting pressure on federal and provincial governments to transfer powers and control for administering Aboriginal lands and affairs to bands and communities. This has resulted in an escalation in the number and severity of confrontations between governmental authorities and Aboriginal groups. These conflicts include the standoff at Oka, Quebec, which was triggered by a decision to construct a golf course on sacred Aboriginal lands, and the blockades of logging roads in British Columbia in an attempt to halt clear-cutting on disputed lands. In Alberta, the Lubicon Cree have taken their claims against the federal government to the World Court in The Hague, Netherlands, and in Quebec, the Cree peoples have waged a legal and public relations battle against Hydro Quebec in an attempt to prevent the damming of rivers in northern Quebec for hydroelectric power. There is increasing concern that, should the federal and provincial governments move too slowly in addressing the land claims issue or attempt to hinder the movement of Aboriginal groups toward self-government, there could be increasing incidents of civil disobedience across the country.[5]

As the revitalization of Aboriginal culture and society continues, it is likely that there will be increasing pressures on the federal and provincial/territorial governments to negotiate, in good faith, with Aboriginal peoples, to resolve the outstanding land claims disputes as well as to transfer control for Aboriginal affairs to Aboriginal peoples.

ABORIGINAL CRIME AND CRIMINALITY

The marginal socioeconomic position of many Aboriginal people, as well as the consequences of losing their culture and communities through the process of colonization, likely contribute significantly to the conflict they experience with the law. However, a definitive discussion of patterns of crime and criminality among Aboriginal peoples is hindered by a lack of published research. Official criminal justice statistics, where they exist, generally include only status or registered Aboriginals. Few data exist on the involvement of Métis, Inuit, and non-status Aboriginals in the criminal justice system, and only recently has attention been given to the difficulties encountered by Aboriginal women and youth and to the reasons behind crime pattern variations between bands and communities.[6]

To date, much of the research has been descriptive and anecdotal, revealing little beyond the fact that Aboriginals are overrepresented in the criminal justice process in many jurisdictions. It must be remembered that Aboriginal crime is committed in a wide variety of settings, from urban areas such as Vancouver, Toronto, and Halifax, to reserve communities throughout the provinces, to the more isolated communities in the Canadian north. This will affect the patterns of criminality as well as the specific programs and services that must be developed for preventing and controlling criminal behaviour and to meet the needs of victims, offenders, and communities.

Among the *general* attributes of Aboriginal crime that can be gleaned from the research studies conducted to date are the following.

▸   *The rates of crime on Aboriginal reserves and in aboriginal communities, particularly in the northern regions of the country, are higher than the rates for the general population.*

The crime rate among Canada's registered Aboriginal peoples is nearly two times the national rate. In comparison with non-Aboriginals, Aboriginal peoples are more likely to commit violent offences and fewer property crimes (see Hyde and LaPrairie, 1987).

▸   *Many Aboriginal communities are afflicted by high rates of violence, particularly assaults.*

The violent crime rate for Aboriginal bands is three and one-half times the national rate. In many jurisdictions, Aboriginal peoples are charged with higher rates of violent crime than non-Aboriginals. In Saskatchewan, for example, violent crimes comprised 25% of all *Criminal Code* offences committed on the reserves, while the figure was less than 10% for other communities in the province (Wolff, 1991).

▸ *Alcohol is involved in a high percentage of Aboriginal crime.*

In many areas, alcohol is involved in over 95% of the offences. There are communities in which nearly 100% of the adult residents, and many of the youth, are involved in extensive alcohol abuse (see Shkilnyk, 1985; York, 1990).

▸ *In many Aboriginal communities, there are high rates of violence and abuse directed toward women and children.*

Materials presented to the Manitoba Aboriginal Justice Inquiry (Hamilton and Sinclair, 1991a) suggest that one in three Aboriginal women in that province were abused by their partners. In Ontario, nearly 80% of the Aboriginal women surveyed had been the victims of family violence. These findings led the commissioners (Hamilton and Sinclair, 1991a:481) to conclude that "Violence and abuse in Aboriginal communities has reached epidemic proportions."

▸ *There is considerable variation in the patterns of crime between Aboriginal reserves and communities.*

Even within the same jurisdiction, Aboriginal communities have different patterns of crime. This has been documented in studies conducted in Nishnawbe-Aski Nation communities in Ontario (Auger, Doob, Auger, and Driben, 1992), in northern Quebec (Laprairie and Diamond, 1992), and in the eastern Arctic (Wood, 1992). Among the factors that may be related to the crime rate are the enforcement practices of the police, the extent to which community residents and victims call the police, and the attributes of the individual communities, including their leadership, the persistence of culture and traditions, and the degree to which the community has assumed responsibility for addressing its problems (see LaPrairie, 1991).

ABORIGINAL PEOPLES IN THE CRIMINAL JUSTICE SYSTEM

One component of the colonization process was the imposition of "white" law upon Aboriginal peoples, beginning a pattern of conflict that continues to this day (see Moyles, 1989; Schuh, 1979). Little attempt was made to accommodate the laws and methods of social control that

Aboriginal peoples used to maintain order and prevent crime. Rather, the criminal justice system, as represented by the RCMP and later the courts and corrections services, became another way by which Aboriginals were brought under the control of the federal and provincial governments. Many of the difficulties that Aboriginals experienced with the criminal justice system can be traced to the conflict between the world view of Aboriginal peoples and that of Euro-Canadians (see Barkwell, 1991; Brodeur, LaPrairie, and McDonnell, 1991; Ross, 1992). In Euro-Canadian culture, for example, individuals are more important than the group and property, including land, can be owned by individuals. In Aboriginal culture, the group assumes primacy over individuals and all land and resources belong to the group. While Euro-Canadian law and justice focus on establishing blame or guilt, in Aboriginal culture, the focus is on solving the problem that created the trouble and on restoring order and harmony in the group. While remorse and forgiveness are not important factors in the Euro-Canadian justice system, they play a major role in Aboriginal culture.

In most jurisdictions, Aboriginal people are overrepresented in the criminal justice system from arrest to incarceration. Information gathered by the Manitoba Aboriginal Justice Inquiry (Hamilton and Sinclair, 1991a), for example, revealed that more than 50% of the inmates in correctional facilities in Manitoba were Aboriginal. Further, in comparison with non-Aboriginal accused, Aboriginal persons were more likely to be denied bail, were more likely to be held in pre-trial detention; more likely to be charged with multiple offences; spent less time with their lawyer; and were twice as likely to be incarcerated upon conviction. Similar findings have been reported by commissions of inquiry in Alberta (Cawsey, 1991) and Saskatchewan (Linn, 1992a; 1992b).

Evidence suggests that, in many jurisdictions, this overrepresentation is due to "a mixture of discrimination on the part of the justice system and actual criminal behaviour on the part of Aboriginal people" (Hamilton and Sinclair, 1991a:87). Within the past several years, a number of highly publicized cases have documented extensive negligence on the part of the criminal justice system in dealing with Aboriginals.

One of these involved Donald Marshall, a Mik'maq Indian, who served 11 years in prison for a crime he did not commit, before being released in 1982. A subsequent commission of inquiry (Hickman, 1989) concluded that "The criminal justice failed Donald Marshall, Jr., at virtually every turn from his arrest and wrongful conviction for murder in 1971 up to, and even beyond, his acquittal by the Court of Appeal in 1983." That such a wrongful conviction could occur and go undetected for so long a period of time was found to be due to a number of factors, including the incompetence of criminal justice officials and the racism that existed toward Aboriginal peoples in Nova Scotia.[7]

Aboriginal Peoples and the Police

A consistent finding of many commissions of inquiry and research studies is that the relations between the police and Aboriginals are often characterized by mutual hostility and distrust, increasing the likelihood of conflict and high arrest rates (Sunahara, 1992). The Manitoba Aboriginal Justice Inquiry (Hamilton and Sinclair, 1991a:610) characterized police-Aboriginal relations in that province as "seriously deficient," noting that "There are strong feelings of mistrust, if not hatred, directed towards RCMP members in some areas. Many officers are seen as being arbitrary and antagonistic toward Aboriginal people."[8]

Some police officers hold stereotypical and racist views of Aboriginal peoples. In its investigation into the circumstances surrounding the shooting death of J.J. Harper by a Winnipeg police officer and the subsequent mishandling of the investigation by the department, the Manitoba Aboriginal Justice Inquiry (Hamilton and Sinclair, 1991b:93) concluded that "racism played a part in the shooting of J.J. Harper and the events that followed."[9]

There are a number of reasons why police-Aboriginal relations have often been characterized by conflict.

▸ *Many police officers experience problems in policing Aboriginal peoples due to a lack of knowledge of Aboriginal culture, the community being policed, and its residents.*

Police officers often have only a limited knowledge about the communities and peoples they are policing. Too often, the knowledge that officers do have is acquired *after* they arrive in the community. Many of the difficulties that arise between police officers and Aboriginal peoples are due to a lack of communication and misperceptions that arise because of cultural differences between the officer and the Aboriginal person. One of the findings of an inquiry into policing the Blood Tribe in Alberta (Rolf, 1991) was that, while RCMP officers had not demonstrated any *conscious* bias in their interactions with band members, their behaviour was often perceived as insensitive and disrespectful. Such misunderstandings could be reduced by an increased focus on cultural awareness training for police officers.

▶   *Many Aboriginal people lack information about their legal rights as citizens and about the criminal justice process and the role of the police in it.*

Testimony provided to the Manitoba Aboriginal Justice Inquiry (Hamilton and Sinclair, 1991a:610) indicated that, because of difficulty with the English language, many Aboriginal accused do not understand their rights and often admit guilt so as to "get out and away from a frightening situation they do not understand."

▶   *In carrying out their duties, police officers often emphasize crime control at the expense of improving police-community relations through the strategy of community-based policing.*

A common complaint of many Aboriginal bands and communities is that police officers place too much emphasis on law enforcement and do not spend enough time on other activities that would better address community needs. Officers, in turn, complain that their performance is evaluated on crime control measures, such as the number of arrests made and the crime rate in the community. The extent to which police officers move beyond the traditional "crime control" model of policing and adopt a community policing model of service delivery is often directly related to the development of positive police-community relations (Depew, 1992). In addition, the transfer policy of the RCMP, which often results in officers spending only two or three years in a community, has been identified as a major obstacle to the development of positive police-community relations.

Increased training, greater awareness among officers as to the culture and community of the Aboriginal peoples they are policing, adoption of a community policing model of service delivery (see Chapter 5), and the use of alternative, non-crime control measures of assessing police officer performance are key ingredients to improving police-Aboriginal relations and creating a relationship based on mutual trust and respect.

Aboriginal Accused in the Criminal Courts

"Most of us don't know much about the legal system and aren't informed enough to tell whether or not we are given a fair judgement. We have no input or association with the Court system."[10] The overrepresentation of Aboriginal peoples in many provincial, territorial, and federal correctional institutions has led researchers to focus on the difficulties that Aboriginal accused experience during the criminal court process. Evidence suggests that, in many regions, Aboriginal accused often have little or no understanding of the legal proceedings and the language of the court, and may not have access to adequate legal services and representation. In addition, the geographic isolation of many Aboriginal communities hinders the effectiveness of existing urban-based programs, which are often staffed by non-Aboriginal lawyers and volunteers (see Cawsey, 1991; Linn, 1992a;1992b).

Aboriginal accused in many regions have a higher likelihood of being found guilty and receiving a sentence of custody than non-Aboriginals. Information presented to the Manitoba Aboriginal Justice Inquiry (Hamilton and Sinclair, 1991a) supports these assertions:

- ▸ Aboriginal persons plead guilty in 60% of cases, compared to a 50% guilty plea rate for non-Aboriginals;
- ▸ 25% of Aboriginal persons received sentences of incarceration, compared to 10% of non-Aboriginals;
- ▸ nearly 20% of Aboriginal female offenders between the ages of 18 and 35 received sentences involving confinement, compared to 4% of non-Aboriginal female offenders; and,
- ▸ the differences in guilty pleas and sentencing patterns between Aboriginal and non-Aboriginal accused were not explained by differences in the number of prior convictions.

A considerable amount of research remains to be done to explore and understand the issues dynamics that surround Aboriginal defendants in the criminal courts and the role that sentencing plays in their overrepresentation in correctional facilities (see LaPrairie, 1990).

Aboriginal Offenders in Corrections Systems

There has also been increasing pressure upon provincial and federal correctional systems to recognize and address the special needs and requirements of Aboriginal inmates. This has been prompted by the large numbers of Aboriginal offenders incarcerated in federal and, particularly, provincial, correctional facilities.

In 1990-91, Aboriginal peoples represented the following percentages of total inmate admissions to provincial institutions: Ontario, 8%; Manitoba, 49%; Saskatchewan, 68%; Alberta, 34%; British Columbia, 18%; the Yukon, 63%; and the Northwest Territories, 91%. These rates have remained fairly constant during the previous five-year period. Aboriginal persons represented 12% of sentenced admissions to federal correctional facilities (Canadian Centre for Justice Statistics, 1991:128).

Among the findings of a study of Aboriginal and non-Aboriginal admissions to federal, provincial, and territorial correctional institutions (Moyer *et al.*, 1985) were the following.

> ▸ Aboriginal peoples were heavily represented in admissions to custody in the Prairies and in the Yukon and Northwest Territories and constituted a higher proportion of institutional populations than would be expected by their representation in the general population in these jurisdictions.
>
> ▸ in most jurisdictions, Aboriginal and non-Aboriginal admissions for provincial offences and *Criminal Code* and non-*Criminal Code* federal violations were similar, with the notable exception of Ontario, where nearly one-half of the aboriginal admissions were for provincial offences relating to violations of provincial alcohol laws.
>
> ▸ Many of the Aboriginal admissions were for fine defaults, particularly in Saskatchewan.
>
> ▸ Aboriginal admissions to custody in Saskatchewan for non-payment of fines were twice that of non-Aboriginal admissions, despite efforts to reduce the use of imprisonment through fine option programs.
>
> ▸ In Ontario, 16% of all Aboriginal admissions were for non-payment of fines on provincial offenses.

Materials presented to an Alberta Task Force (Cawsey, 1991:6-8) revealed that Aboriginal offenders in Prairie provinces were less likely to receive day parole and full parole than their non-Aboriginal counterparts.

There have also been a number of inquiries that have made specific recommendations to address the deficiencies in institutional and community-based corrections for Aboriginal offenders (Cawsey, 1991; Solicitor General of Canada, 1989). These reports noted a lack of culturally relevant programming for Aboriginal inmates, recommended that more Aboriginal peoples be hired to work in the federal correctional system, and identified the need to develop new correctional programs such as wilderness camps and the need to address the problems encountered by Aboriginal offenders in applying for and returning to society under conditional release.

In the following discussion, we consider the attempts by the federal and provincial/territorial governments to reduce Aboriginal conflict with the law. Even with the development of Aboriginal-controlled justice systems, Aboriginal peoples will always have contact with non-Aboriginal criminal justice personnel. Equal attention, therefore, must be given to ways in which the existing criminal justice system can adapt to better meet the needs of Aboriginal victims, offenders, and communities. In fact, the basic premise should be that the criminal justice system has a great deal to learn from traditional Aboriginal justice strategies, which if implemented, would benefit non-Aboriginal peoples as well.

ADAPTING THE CRIMINAL JUSTICE SYSTEM TO MEET THE NEEDS OF ABORIGINAL PEOPLES

In an attempt to address the difficulties that Aboriginal persons experience with the criminal justice system, many jurisdictions have placed an increased emphasis on cultural awareness training for criminal justice personnel and on the development of programs, often in collaboration with Aboriginal bands and communities, designed specifically for Aboriginal offenders and victims of crime.

Sensitizing the System: Cultural Awareness for Justice Personnel

In Ontario, "Judges' Northern Education Circuits" are sponsored by the Office of the Chief Judge of the Provincial Court. Provincial Court judges travel to remote northern communities to meet face-to-face with Aboriginal peoples and to discuss justice-related issues. In Whitehorse, Yukon, the RCMP detachment offers a three-day orientation course to provide new members and their spouses with information on the communities they will be policing. The course was designed and is presented by Aboriginal community members. Both the Ontario Provincial Police and the Quebec Provincial Police offer cultural awareness seminars as part of recruit training, and most municipal departments across the country have a cultural awareness training component for in-service officers. Corrections personnel at both the federal and provincial levels also have access to an increasing number of workshops and conferences that address issues related to Aboriginal culture and criminal justice issues. In Alberta and most other jurisdictions, however, there is an almost complete lack of cross-cultural training programs for prosecutors, legal aid personnel, practicing lawyers, and members of the judiciary (Cawsey, 1991:8-39).

Where cultural awareness programs do exist, it is unclear whether they have had a significant impact on the rate of Aboriginal involvement in the criminal justice system. A number of factors may hinder their potential effectiveness, including:

- ▸ materials on aboriginal cultures and traditions are often included in more general courses on "multi-culturalism," resulting in a superficial consideration of Aboriginal culture and justice issues;
- ▸ cultural awareness programs are often relegated to one- or two-day seminars, rather than being integrated into all phases of recruit and in-service training;
- ▸ there is often no requirement that in-service justice personnel attend cultural awareness programs; and
- ▸ there are generally no mechanisms in place to assess the impact of cultural awareness training programs on the performance of criminal justice personnel or on the patterns of interaction between justice personnel and Aboriginals.

It is likely that, in the coming years, there will be increased pressures for cultural awareness training programs to be created and expanded.

Aboriginal Policing Programs

Despite an increase in the number of Aboriginal-controlled police forces, it is likely that the RCMP and the two provincial police forces will continue to be involved in policing Aboriginal peoples, even if such contact is restricted to off-reserve and urban areas.

In 1973, the RCMP established the Indian Special Constable program (ISC) to enhance the quality of police services provided to Aboriginal peoples. Indian Special Constables were recruited and trained by the RCMP, and deployed to detachments to assist in policing Aboriginal reserves and communities.

Until its termination in 1990, the ISC program experienced major operational difficulties, including (1) a lack of community input into the recruitment and deployment of ISCs; (2) the failure of the RCMP to identify the role of ISCs clearly, resulting in uncertainty among ISCs and wide discrepancies among individual detachments in how ISCs were used; (3) a reluctance on the part of many Aboriginal peoples to become, or remain, ISCs due to community hostility and the social isolation that many ISCs and their families experienced; and (4) less training and lower salaries than regular RCMP members (Griffiths and Yerbury, 1984).

In 1990, the ISC program was replaced by the Aboriginal Constable Development Program (ACDP), which is designed to increase the number of Aboriginals eligible to become regular RCMP members. More specifically, the ACDP provides an opportunity for Aboriginal individuals who do not meet all of the entrance requirements to become a constable. It is a two-year work/study program in which the recruits attend educational upgrading courses and receive on-the-job training from RCMP officers. Following successful completion of the program, the candidate enters recruit training.

In 1980, on the basis of an agreement between the Quebec Provincial Police and the representative of the Cree and Inuit peoples in Quebec, a program was developed for the provision of policing services to eight Cree reserves in the James Bay area and to 13 Inuit communities in northern Quebec. The agreement calls for the gradual transfer of management of the program from the Quebec Police Force to the band councils involved in the program. The Ontario Provincial Police have operated a First Nations constable program for policing on reserves. Under a self-government agreement signed in 1992, the program was transferred to Aboriginal control and will be expanded. (See Aboriginal Police Forces below.)

In cities such as Calgary, Regina, and Vancouver, municipal police departments have given increased attention to the special issues surrounding Aboriginal policing. The Native/Police Liaison Community Program of the Vancouver Police Department, for example, attempts to improve police-Aboriginal community relations through cultural awareness training, workshops, and seminars and to encourage Aboriginal peoples to consider a career in policing. Efforts have been made (with little success) by municipal departments across the country to hire Aboriginals.

The RCMP have established a national Aboriginal Advisory Committee, comprised of elders, which meets twice a year to discuss and provide the Force with input on policing issues. In addition, Community Advisory Committees have been set up in many of the communities policed by the RCMP in an attempt to open the lines of communication and understanding between officers and Aboriginal residents.

Addressing the Needs of Aboriginal Accused

Over the past two decades, a number of initiatives have been undertaken to improve the administration of justice for Aboriginal peoples in the criminal courts. These include the development of legal services, the creation of Native courtworker and justice of the peace programs, and public legal education programs.

Native Courtworker Programs

Native courtworkers provide Aboriginal defendants with information on their legal rights and responsibilities; explain court procedure; assist the accused in making application for legal aid; appear in court with the defendant; and provide assistance to the defendant's family. For the court, the courtworker may act as translator, provide information to increase cultural awareness among court officials, assist in the preparation of pre-sentence reports, and speak to sentence. At the general community level, courtworkers may be involved in public legal education, conducting workshops in the community and making school presentations.

Native courtworker programs have become an integral part of the criminal justice system and have generally received high marks from judges, lawyers, and other criminal justice personnel, as well as from Aboriginal clients. Evaluations of Native courtworker programs, however, have revealed several major areas of difficulty, many of which are similar to those that afflicted the now-defunct RCMP Indian Special Constable program. Courtworkers are often caught in the dual role of acting as an advocate for the defendant, while at the same time serving as an officer of the court. Other problems that have hindered the effectiveness of the courtworker programs are a lack of formal training and on-the-job supervision, low salaries, and high turnover rates among personnel. It has also been difficult to assess the impact of courtworker programs on either the conviction rates for Aboriginal offenders or on the rates of incarceration (see Hathaway, 1986).

Justice of the Peace Programs

Justice of the peace (JP) programs are designed to make justice services more accessible to Aboriginal communities, to serve as a buffer between Aboriginals and the police, to increase the sensitivity of the courts to the needs of Aboriginal defendants and communities, and to increase community awareness of, and responsibility for, crime-related problems. JPs hear less-serious matters, including violations of municipal or band by-laws, and provincial and *Criminal Code* offences. They also conduct bail hearings and issue arrest warrants, summonses, and licence suspensions.

The development of JP programs across Canada, however, has been uneven, and their effectiveness has been considerably impeded by the now-familiar problems of lack of training and supervision, pressures on the JP from the community, low salaries, high turnover, too few sentencing alternatives, and a lack of jurisdiction and authority.

Perhaps the most ambitious initiative is the Native JP program in Ontario. This program's mandate is to encourage Aboriginal individuals to assume a greater role in the administration of justice in their home communities by becoming JPs. Aboriginal JPs have the same powers as other JPs and receive extensive training by the Ontario Ministry of the Attorney-General. The program, which began in northwestern Ontario and is now being expanded, has produced encouraging results.

Sentencing

Provincial and territorial courts across the country are taking steps to strengthen ties with Aboriginal communities and to develop community-based dispositional alternatives for offenders. Many judges involve Aboriginal elders and other community residents in the resolution of cases and the imposition of sanctions. Case discussions proceed within a model of consensual decision making and are designed to consider the needs of the victim, offender, and community.

One of the more innovative approaches is "circle sentencing," which is being practiced by judges of the Territorial Court in the Yukon (see

Chapter 8). The significance of circle sentencing as practiced in the Yukon is that it involves all of the participants in a case — the judge, Crown counsel, defence lawyer, victim, offender, and community residents — sitting in a circular arrangement and discussing all facets of the case. The circle is designed to break down the traditional formality of the courtroom setting and to provide a forum for the disposition of cases that is premised on healing, consensus building, and on returning to communities the responsibility for resolving conflict.

In Manitoba, two systems for the hearing and disposition of cases involving Aboriginal offenders on reserves has been created under an Aboriginal Court model. The "guilty plea" model involves elders and a community-based judge who will reach a decision through consensus in cases in which the offender pleads guilty. The "guilty-not guilty" model is used in cases where the accused person pleads not guilty. A Provincial Court judge hears the case and the community determines the sentence if the person is found guilty. A requirement of the Aboriginal Court model is that all persons involved in making decisions in both types of systems must speak the language of the community in which the case is heard. The "guilty-not guilty" model will also involve community justice liaison workers who will liaise between the community and the court.

Corrections Programs for Aboriginal Offenders

Aboriginal communities and organizations have also become involved in developing alternatives to incarceration and in creating and staffing programs to assist Aboriginal offenders in institutional settings and upon release. Native prison liaison officers and Native correctional workers provide assistance to Aboriginal inmates and their families, and a number of wilderness camps for offenders are operated by Aboriginal organizations in collaboration with provincial correctional authorities. The Nishnawbe-Aski Wilderness Camp in Kenora, Ontario, for example, was established to treat Aboriginal offenders convicted of alcohol-related offences. In Nova Scotia, the Mik'maw Lodge is a facility for on the Eskasoni Reserve in Cape Breton for Mik'maq offenders.

In response to the recommendations of several task forces, the federal Correctional Service of Canada is creating all-Aboriginal institutions for male and female offenders. These facilities will emphasize culturally relevant education and treatment programs staffed by Aboriginal personnel. In federal correctional facilities, Aboriginal cultural and spiritual programs have been increased and are often led by Aboriginal elders. The *Corrections and Conditional Release Act* (Bill C-36) recognizes Aboriginal spirituality and Aboriginal elders as having "the same status as other religions and other religious leaders" and provides the basis for the development of Aboriginal-controlled parole programs and correctional institutions.

The experience of government-sponsored initiatives designed to reduce the conflict that Aboriginals experience with criminal justice system suggests a number of important points. First, the most successful initiatives are those that have been developed in collaboration with local communities and bands. Programs that are designed and delivered from the "outside" seem to have little long-term impact. Secondly, merely making administrative adjustments to the existing criminal justice system, including hiring more Aboriginal persons to staff the system, will not be sufficient to address the needs of Aboriginal peoples in conflict with the law. More fundamental structural changes are required, including the increased use of non-adversarial strategies such as reconciliation and restitution for resolving disputes.

Third, the traditional emphasis of Aboriginal communities on healing the victim, the offender, and, if required, the community, must be recognized and incorporated into future Aboriginal justice initiatives. In so doing, government agencies and ministries must recognize the uniqueness of each community, both in terms of crime problems and in the responses that will be most effective in preventing and responding to criminal behaviour. And, finally, we must recognize that there may be limits to the ability of the existing justice system to accommodate the needs of Aboriginal victims, offenders, and communities, due to the basic principles upon which the justice system operates. This, in turn, requires us to consider the potential for Aboriginal bands and communities to create and operate criminal justice programs and services.

ABORIGINAL-CONTROLLED JUSTICE PROGRAMS AND SERVICES

Recent years have witnessed the increased involvement of Aboriginal peoples in the creation and control of justice programs (Griffiths, 1989). Many communities have established local justice committees, which, in addition to serving as a liaison with the RCMP or provincial police, serve as mechanisms by which local justice initiatives are created and operated.

The impetus for the development of Aboriginal-controlled justice programs and services is the view held by Aboriginal peoples that they must assert ownership of problems in their communities and reserves.

There is also the widely held belief among Aboriginal peoples that the "white" justice system is unable (or, in some cases, unwilling) to address the needs of Aboriginal offenders, victims, and communities adequately and that the adversarial model of justice is inappropriate and ineffective in resolving conflicts. Cited as evidence is the continued overrepresentation of Aboriginal persons in the criminal justice system.

It is important to note that Aboriginal-controlled initiatives may be, but are not necessarily, premised on customary law. Most, however, do contain elements of traditional culture, involve community elders, and have a strong emphasis on healing, restitutive justice, and responding to offenders in a holistic fashion, which involves considering the needs of the victim, the offender, and the community.

The South Island Tribal Council on Vancouver Island has developed a justice program involving elders in the disposition of cases, a diversion program, and other community-based justice programs and services. The Gitksan and Wet'suwet'en people in northcentral British Columbia are developing a justice system premised on traditional cultural practices and centred around the clans and kinships networks. These and other justice initiatives, however, have occurred on reserve lands. Little attention has been given to the potential for developing autonomous, Aboriginal-controlled programs and services in off-reserve areas and urban settings.

The following are among the specific justice programs that have been developed.

Aboriginal Police Forces

It is in the area of policing that Aboriginal peoples have assumed the greatest control over the delivery of justice services. This is perhaps appropriate, given the conflicts that have occurred between the police and Aboriginal peoples historically and in contemporary times. Establishing an autonomous police force provides an opportunity for Aboriginal bands to assume control over one of the most significant components of the criminal justice process and to create the foundation for the development of autonomous criminal justice systems.

The two largest Aboriginal-controlled police forces are the Ontario First Nations Constable program in Ontario, with approximately 125 officers, and the Amerindian Police Program in Quebec, which, in 1993, had approximately 75 constables policing in 23 communities. These police forces are involved in policing reserves in the two provinces and the officers have full powers to enforce the *Criminal Code*, federal and provincial statutes, as well as band by-laws. There are smaller Aboriginal police forces in other areas of the country. For example, in Alberta, there are tribal police forces on the Louis Bull reserve as well as on the Hobemma, Saddle Lake, and Blood reserves. These forces generally have less than 20 officers who have limited enforcement powers on the reserve. Their activities are overseen by reserve-based police commissions or by the respective band councils.

There is some evidence that reserves policed by Aboriginal police forces have seen an improvement in police-citizen relations and, in some instances, a decrease in the rates of certain types of offences and a reduction in the numbers of arrests. However, Aboriginal police forces have also encountered difficulties. Many of the forces have experienced high turnover rates among officers who find the pressures of policing their home reserves too great. In addition, there have been instances of political interference by band leaders in the operation of the police forces.

There have also been discussions and disagreements with provincial and federal authorities over the powers and jurisdiction of Aboriginal police officers. While officers of many Aboriginal police forces have full enforcement powers under the provincial police acts, those in other forces have no *Criminal Code* powers and are relegated to band constable status with the authority to enforce only band by-laws and some provincial statutes. Despite these problems, it is likely that the trend toward the development of autonomous police forces on the reserves will continue. It is less clear whether this will, at some future date, extend to non-reserve communities as well.

Aboriginal Courts and Legal Services

Aboriginal communities have developed community-based programs to provide legal services to community residents. A model program is the Nishnawbe-Aski Legal Services Corporation established in 1990 in Ontario. The mandate of the corporation is to provide members of the Nishnawbe-Aski First Nations with better access to legal services, to develop and deliver legal education programs, cross-cultural training, and interpretation services. The Corporation also operates a Community Legal

Worker program that provides courtworker services to 48 communities, many of them in remote areas.

Although there are no autonomous Aboriginal courts operating in Canada, several communities have made proposals that may result in local courts with limited jurisdiction being created. The community of Povungnituk, Quebec, has proposed the creation of a local judiciary that would hear cases of a minor nature. The Saddle Lake Tribe in Alberta has outlined a two-level system of tribal justice, which includes the position of tribal peacemaker and a tribunal tribe of jurors that would be involved in mediating and resolving disputes on the reserve. And the Manitoba court model discussed previously may provide the basis for the development of a system of reserve-based courts.

There is little doubt that the potential for the development of courts and legal systems has increased with the move toward self-government by Aboriginal peoples. The experience to date, however, suggests that there is considerable variability across communities in their interest and/or ability to develop community-based justice programs and services. Initiatives appear to be most successful in those communities with strong leadership, a consensus among community residents regarding crime problems and the methods to address them, and the active involvement of community elders in decision making and program implementation.

Aboriginal Correctional Facilities and Community Programs

Aboriginal communities and organizations are also becoming more involved in the operation of correctional facilities and community-based programs. The federal *Corrections and Conditional Release Act* permits the Correctional Service of Canada to enter directly into agreements with Aboriginal communities for the provisions of correctional services. In Alberta, the Native Counselling Service of Alberta (NCSA) operates a number of adult institutional programs, including the Westcastle Minimum Security Forest Camp and the Grierson Community Correctional Centre. A majority of the staff at Grierson is Aboriginal. Programs include the spiritual and cultural teachings by elders, drug and alcohol counselling, a family life improvement program, and other services designed to prepare the Aboriginal offender for reentry. NCSA also provides supervision for offenders on probation and parole.

Given the rapid, yet uneven, development of Aboriginal justice initiatives across the country, it is impossible to predict the types of programs and services that will be created in the coming years. Neither is it clear how these initiatives will interface with the existing criminal justice system. It is evident, however, that the increasing movement of Aboriginal peoples toward self-government will provide the impetus as well as the framework for establishing criminal justice programs and even autonomous Aboriginal criminal justice systems. The following are questions that remain to be answered.

- ► Can the existing criminal justice system be adapted to better meet the needs of Aboriginal victims, offenders, and communities?
- ► Should parallel Aboriginal justice systems be developed? And, if so, what would be the form and structure of such systems? Would autonomous Aboriginal justice systems operate only on Aboriginal reserves, or in non-reserve areas, including urban centres, as well?
- ► What is the potential for revitalizing customary law as the basis for Aboriginal justice systems?
- ► What are the constitutional issues surrounding the development of autonomous, Aboriginal-controlled justice systems and to what extent would existing legislation, such as the *Canadian Charter of Rights and Freedoms*, the Canadian *Criminal Code*, and the *Young Offenders Act*, apply to reserve and non-reserve justice systems?

These and other questions are being discussed and debated (see Coyle, 1986; McDonnell, 1992; Nielsen, 1992; Schwartz, 1990). It is obviously much too early to determine the final outcome of the myriad of initiatives that are being undertaken.

BETWEEN TWO WORLDS: ABORIGINAL YOUTH IN CRISIS

The consequences of the marginal position of Aboriginal people in Canadian society are perhaps most evident in the plight of Aboriginal youth. In many jurisdictions, Aboriginal youth are extensively involved in the youth justice and child-care systems, evidence high rates of alcohol and solvent abuse and suicide, and experience considerable conflict in attempting to adapt to mainstream Canadian society while attempting to learn and retain their traditional culture.

The overrepresentation of Aboriginal youth in the justice system is often more pronounced than for Aboriginal adults and non-Aboriginal youth. Figures from Alberta (Cawsey, 1991:6-6), for example, indicate the following:

  ▸ there has been significant increases in the numbers of Aboriginal youths charged with offences;
  ▸ Aboriginal young offenders are less likely to be referred to alternative measures programs;
  ▸ all things being equal, Aboriginal youth are more likely to receive a disposition of confinement than their non-Aboriginal counterparts; and
  ▸ Aboriginal youth spend longer periods in custody than non-Aboriginal youth for the same offences.

There have also been concerns voiced about the use of the *Young Offenders Act (YOA)* to respond to Aboriginal youth in conflict. It has been argued that the *YOA* is more relevant to the administration of youth justice in urban areas of the country and that the *YOA*'s emphasis on procedural formalities may actually hinder the development of more informal, community-based mechanisms to address the needs of youth. Also, it has been noted that legal counsel are often not available in remote and rural areas and that in such regions it is difficult to maintain detainment facilities for youths separate from adults.

In response to these concerns, many Aboriginal communities have developed community-based programs and services to assist youth, including the following:

  ▸ *The Lennox Island Mik'maq Diversion Council*

The Mik'maq community of Lennox Island in Prince Edward Island has established a pre-charge diversion program for summary conviction and minor indictable offence cases. The Diversion Council meets with the accused and his or her parents, the victim, and the policing authority. Among the restitutive sanctions that can be imposed are the requirement that the offender apologize and/or pay restitution to the victim, or the offender may be required to perform a specified number of community service hours.

► *Youth Justice Committees (YJC), Northwest Territories*

The YJCs are composed of five to seven citizens from the communities who have an interest in assisting young persons in conflict with the law. Cases may be referred to the YJC at any time in the process by the police, Crown counsel, JPs, or Territorial Court judges. Cases are resolved by consensus in discussions involving the committee, the youth, and his or her parent or guardian. Among the dispositions available to the YJCs are: an apology to the victim; curfews or other restrictions on the youth; a period of community service; or removal of youth from home.

► *The Shubenacadie Band Diversion Program, Nova Scotia*

This program permits the diversion of offenders from the justice system. Diverted cases are sent to a justice panel comprised of three members of the band who are appointed by the chief and council. Meetings on cases are held in public, and representations are made by the offender, the police, Crown, victim, a provincial representative of the director of community corrections, and a representative of the Union of Nova Scotia Indians. Following this testimony, the justice panel determines an appropriate disposition, which may include restitution, community service work, participation in treatment or counselling programs, or temporary banishment from certain areas of the community.

► *The Youth Court System at St. Theresa Point, Manitoba*

This court illustrates the potential for creating alternatives to the youth justice system. Established in 1984, this reserve-controlled Youth Court system developed in response to the community desire to address youth crime in the community and to address the problems of youth with community standards and traditions. Referrals to the reserve Youth Court come from many sources, including the RCMP, school officials, and parents. Among the dispositions that may be imposed by the judge, who is selected from the community, are dismissal, probation with specified conditions, or placement of youth with an extended family member.

Programs for Aboriginal Youth

In recent years there has been a rapid expansion of programs for

Aboriginal youth in conflict with the law, many of them developed and controlled by aboriginal bands and communities. In several jurisdictions, youth courtworker programs have been developed, as well as community-based forums for the resolution of disputes involving youth.

The following are illustrative of the range of programmatic initiatives for Aboriginal youth.

▸   *Native Counselling Services of Alberta (NCSA) Young Offender Programs*

NCSA operates a variety of facilities for Aboriginal youths in conflict, including group homes, open custody facilities, and attendance centres, which offer programs such as life skills and recreational and cultural activities at the community level. NSCA is also involved in providing counselling and legal information to youth through a courtworker program for young offenders and also provides probation supervision under contract with the province.

▸   *Project Rediscovery, Queen Charlotte Islands*

This is a wilderness experience program in the Queen Charlotte Islands that teaches survival skills, self-confidence, and environmental awareness to Aboriginal and non-Aboriginal youths, many of whom have been in conflict with the law.

▸   *Northern Fly-In Sports Camps, Manitoba*

This program provides sports and recreation activities to remote communities. Developed in consultation with community leadership, the program develops leadership skills and provides opportunities for youths to become involved in structured activities. The program also relieves the boredom experienced by Aboriginal youth living in remote areas and, in turn, this has resulted in decreased rates of youth offences in many communities.

ABORIGINAL CHILD WELFARE PROGRAMS

Aboriginal youths are also overrepresented in child-care systems in many parts of the country, due in part to the deterioration of Aboriginal family life and the lack of alternative programs and resources at the community and band level. The delivery of child services to Aboriginal reserves and communities has traditionally been impeded by jurisdictional disputes between the federal and provincial governments over the responsibility for the provision of such services and by conflict between the Euro-Canadian approach to child welfare and Aboriginal values and traditions (Carasco, 1986). This conflict between values and traditions is evident in disputes between Aboriginal peoples and provincial authorities over the practice of traditional adoption (the practice of "giving" children to members of the extended family or community), which is currently recognized only in the Northwest Territories and Quebec. Aboriginal groups have also expressed concern with the placement of Aboriginal children with non-Aboriginal families and, in some jurisdictions, the past practice of placing Aboriginal youth in foster or adoptive homes in the United States.

These difficulties have provided the impetus for the development of Aboriginal-controlled child and family services, including the Dakota-Ojibway Child and Family Services, which serves eight reserves in southern Manitoba, the Tikinigan Child and Family Services in Sioux Lookout, Ontario, a child and family service program operated by the Champagne-Aishihik Indian Band in the Yukon, and a child welfare program operated by the Nishga'a Band in British Columbia.

VIOLENCE AND SEXUAL ABUSE IN ABORIGINAL COMMUNITIES

Aboriginal women have a high risk of becoming victims of crime, particularly of violent crimes such as spousal assault and sexual assault. Materials provided to the Manitoba Aboriginal Justice Inquiry (Hamilton and Sinclair, 1991a:482) revealed that one in three Aboriginal women in that province were abused by their partner. Among the findings of a study conducted by the Ontario Native Women's Association were:

- ▸ 85% of the women surveyed indicated that family violence occurred in their community;
- ▸ 80% of the women had personally experienced family violence, in comparison with the estimate of 10% in non-Aboriginal families;
- ▸ a high percentage of the women who were victims of

> violence sustained severe physical injury;
> ► alcoholism was identified by nearly 80% of the women as the main cause of family violence; and
> ► large numbers of women who are the victims of family violence do not seek assistance or make use of services for battered women (1989:18-21).

There are, in many areas of the country, inadequate services available to female victims of violence, including a lack of emergency shelter services and "safe" houses, services for children who have been the victims of and/or witnesses to family violence and abuse. Information provided to the Manitoba Aboriginal Justice Inquiry (Hamilton and Sinclair, 1991a), for example, revealed that there was only *one* Aboriginal women's shelter in the entire province — Ikwe Widdjiitiwin, located in Winnipeg. For Aboriginal women in Manitoba and in the other provinces/territories, the only alternative to continued victimization is to leave their home community, their family and, often, their children. For obvious reasons, this is not a viable alternative for most Aboriginal women. There is also a lack of community-based treatment programs for male batterers, although the departments of justice in the Yukon and Manitoba both operate programs for assaultive husbands.

Increasingly, Aboriginal bands and communities are addressing the causes and consequences of violence, spousal assault, and sexual abuse. Aboriginal-controlled programs for abusers and their victims, unlike the response of "outside" justice and social service agencies, centre on healing and restitution, rather than on punishment. It is important to note that many offenders were themselves the victims of sexual abuse, either while growing up in their home community or while students in the church-operated residential schools (see Haig-Brown, 1988).

► *The Hollow Water (Manitoba) Resource Group*

This program was initiated at the community level by several survivors of sexual abuse. An attempt is made to restore community, family, and individual peace and harmony. A healing contract is signed and offenders apologize publicly to the victims and to the community for the harm that has been done. The response, therefore, is one that considers the needs of all parties and is directed beyond merely punishing the offender.

▸ *The Canim Lake (British Columbia) Family Violence Program*

This community-based, band-controlled family violence program is designed for the management and treatment of adult and adolescent sex offenders, as well as for the victims of sexual abuse. It includes education and prevention programming, an "amnesty" period for undetected offenders to disclose their offences and receive treatment without being subjected to criminal charges, and specific treatment interventions that blend modern clinical techniques with traditional healing practices. The program addresses the needs of the offender and the victim within a family and community context, and blends modern clinical treatment intervention with traditional healing practices.

CRIME AND CRIMINAL JUSTICE IN THE CANADIAN NORTH

The areas of northern Canada, comprising the Yukon and Northwest Territories, as well as the northern portions of the provinces, are generally invisible to the majority of Canadians who reside in "southern" urban areas. Few Canadians have had the opportunity to travel north of the 60th parallel or even into the northern-most reaches of their own province, most of which are accessible only by air. These factors have tended to obscure the high rates of crime, particularly violent crime, that afflict many northern communities.

It is only in recent years that the delivery of justice services to Aboriginal peoples in the North has come under close scrutiny. Increasing concerns have been raised about the relevance of legislation, policies, and programs conceived and delivered by non-Aboriginal "southerners." Like their southern counterparts, Aboriginal peoples in the remote and northern regions of the country are becoming more involved in the design and delivery of community-based justice initiatives. This includes local justice and social service committees, the involvement of community elders in responding to conflict in the community, and collaboration with criminal justice agencies in creating localized corrections programs and services (see Griffiths, 1990; 1991; 1992).

Given the small size of communities in the North, the role of the police assumes even greater significance than in urban areas. The personal "style" of the police officer(s) in small detachments and the relations that exist between the police and the community will have a significant impact on the rates of arrest and charging, as well as on the success of any community-based initiatives designed to prevent or reduce crime. To be effective, police officers are required to adapt their role to fit the needs of the community in which they are policing.

While police officers are posted in northern communities, judicial services are provided via the circuit court (or "circuit circus," as it is called by many northerners), which has been the subject of increasing attention in recent years. Circuit court parties, comprised of the judge, court clerk, defence lawyer, and Crown counsel, travel to communities, generally by air, on a regular basis to hold court. While many communities are served monthly, others are visited every three months, or more infrequently if there are no cases to be heard or if weather or mechanical problems with the court airplane prevent a scheduled visit. The most extensive circuit court systems are in the Northwest Territories, northwestern Ontario, and northern Quebec, covering the James Bay and Ungava Bay regions of the province.

Recent years have seen increased concerns voiced about the circuit court system, including the problems of large court dockets that result from backlogs of cases; time constraints on the court party, which often preclude effective defence preparation and result in marathon court sessions, frequently lasting up to 12 hours; the lack of interpretative services for Aboriginal and Inuit defendants who speak and/or understand little English; and the general difficulties caused by the cultural differences of Canadian law and its practitioners and Aboriginal offenders, victims, and communities.[11]

More specifically, it has been argued that neither defendants nor community residents understand the function of the court, the role of the various members of the court party, or the court proceedings. Further, it is argued that the dispositions available under the *Criminal Code* do not address the unique needs of individual communities, offenders, and victims. A difficult decision that often confronts circuit court judges is whether to remove the offender from the community for a period of confinement or to use resources in the community, including the elders. In the Northwest Territories, offenders receiving sentences of incarceration are sent either to the Baffin Correctional Centre in Iqualit or to the Yellowknife Correctional Centre.

Evidence suggests that the judiciary in the North is becoming more sensitive to the need to tailor dispositions to the offender and to the community in which the offender resides. In the Northwest Territories, the *Jury Act* was amended to allow citizens who speak and understand only an Aboriginal language to serve as jurors. In addition, there has been a trend toward the development of community-based mechanisms for dispute resolution and alternatives to incarceration. Judges must also often balance the desires of the community to play a significant role in the disposition of cases while ensuring that the rights and safety of victims are protected. This is particularly true in cases involving women who have been the victims of spousal or sexual assault.

NOTES

[1]Given space limitations, we are only able to provide selected illustrations of government-sponsored and Aboriginal-controlled initiatives. Students and instructors are encouraged to explore the literature on Canada's Aboriginal peoples — their history, culture, and communities — in greater detail and to become familiar with the issues surrounding land claims and self-government, Aboriginal spirituality, and the various initiatives that are being undertaken by Aboriginal bands, communities, and organizations in the areas of education, economic and community development, self-government, and, of course, justice.

One of the most extensive library collections of Aboriginal justice-related materials is The Northern Justice Society Resource Centre, located in the School of Criminology at Simon Fraser University. This collection contains materials from across Canada, as well as from Alaska, the lower 48 states, Greenland, and Australia. The Centre also serves as a clearinghouse for justice-related materials and can be accessed by mail, c/o the School of Criminology, Simon Fraser University, Burnaby, B.C., V5A 1S6 or by telephone at (604) 291-4239. The Centre also disseminates the publications of The Northern Justice Society, one of which is a research bibliography listing the holdings in the collection.

[2]The unique difficulties encountered by some Aboriginal peoples in Canada's urban centres has been captured by Lynda Shorten in *Without Reserve — Stories from Urban Natives* (NeWest Press, 1991).

[3]For discussions of the impact of the *Indian Act* on Aboriginal women, and the political and spiritual resurgence of Aboriginal women, see Jeffries, 1991; Kirkness, 1987; Silman, 1988; Sugar and Fox, 1989-90.

[4]Consideration of the condition of Aboriginal peoples is hindered by the fact that the federal government gathers data only on registered, or status, Aboriginal peoples and on the Inuit. This excludes a large number of Aboriginal peoples, including status Aboriginals living off the reserve, the Métis, and non-status Aboriginals.

[5]For an insightful analysis of the Oka crisis, see York and Pindera (1991).

The struggle of the Lubicon Cree has been captured by Goddard (1992), and the ongoing conflict between the Cree peoples and the Quebec government and Hydro-Quebec over the expansion of hydroelectric dams in northern Quebec is documented in *Electric Rivers* by Sean McCutcheon (1991).

[6]The two volumes of the *Report of the Aboriginal Justice Inquiry of Manitoba* (Hamilton and Sinclair, 1991a; 1991b) contain a wealth of information related to Aboriginal justice issues, historically and in contemporary times, not only in Manitoba but across Canada as well. Also, see Corrigan and Barkwell (1991) for materials on Métis in Canadian society.

[7]The report of the Royal Commission on the Donald Marshall, Jr., Prosecution (Hickman, 1989) comprises several volumes. For a summary of the inquiry, see the volume *Digest of Findings and Recommendations*. For a more readable version of the events surrounding this case, see *Justice Denied: The Law versus Donald Marshall* (Harris, 1986). For a compendium of critiques of the Marshall Inquiry, see Mannette (1992).

[8]Caution must be exercised in generalizing the findings from research studies carried out in specific jurisdictions at any one point in time. High rates of arrest alone cannot be taken as conclusive evidence of discriminatory treatment by police officers. Further, Aboriginal-police relations vary appreciably within and between urban and rural settings, and the quality of these relations, even within the same community or neighbourhood, may change over time.

[9]Detailed materials on the death of J.J. Harper are presented in *Report of the Aboriginal Justice Inquiry of Manitoba. Volume 2. The Deaths of Helen Betty Osborne and John Joseph Harper* (Hamilton and Sinclair, 1991b). See *Conspiracy of Silence* (1990) by Lisa Priest for the story of Helen Betty Osborne, an Aboriginal woman murdered in The Pas, Manitoba, whose killers were protected by the town's silence for over a decade.

[10]Excerpt from brief prepared by the Federation of Métis Settlements, presented to the Task Force on the Criminal Justice System and Its Impact on the Indian and Métis People of Alberta (Cawsey, 1991:4-1).

[11]Many of the issues associated with the operation of the circuit court and the role of traditional, community-based mechanisms of social control are presented in the film *Arctic Bay: A Community and the Court*. This film documents a sentencing hearing in an Inuit community on Baffin Island in which the presiding judge must decide whether to remove a young adult convicted of sexual assault from the community or give over supervision of the offender to the council of elders in the community. The film is available from Magic Lantern Films, 136 Cross Avenue, Oakville, Ontario L6J 2W6. A documentary film has also been completed on the circuit court that services the Cree and Inuit communities in northern Quebec. The film is entitled *White Justice* and may be obtained from Parlimage Inc., 4398 boul. Saint-Laurent, Suite 103, Montreal, Quebec H2W 1Z5.

REFERENCES

Auger, D.J., A.N. Doob, R.P. Auger, and P. Driben. 1992. "Crime and Control in Three Nishnawbe-Aski Nation Communities: An Exploratory Investigation." 34 *Canadian Journal of Criminology.* 317-38.

Barkwell, L. 1991. "Early Law and Social Control Among the Métis." In S. Corrigan and L. Barkwell, eds. *The Struggle for Recognition: Canadian Justice and the Métis Nation.* Winnipeg: Pemmican Publications. 7-37.

Berger, T.R. 1991. *A Long and Terrible Shadow: White Values, Native Rights in the Americas, 1492-1992.* Vancouver: Douglas and McIntyre.

Brodeur, J.-P., C. LaPrairie, and R. McDonnell. 1991. *Justice for the Cree: Final Report.* James Bay, Quebec: Grand Council of the Crees.

Canada. 1989. *Basic Departmental Data.* Ottawa: Indian and Northern Affairs.

Canadian Centre for Justice Statistics. 1991. *Adult Correctional Services in Canada, 1990-91.* Ottawa: Industry, Science and Technology Canada.

Carasco, E.F. 1986. "Canadian Native Children: Have Child Welfare Laws Broken the Circle?" 5 *Canadian Journal of Family Law.* 111-38.

Cawsey, Mr. Justice R.A. (Chair). 1991. *Justice on Trial. Report of the Task Force on the Criminal Justice System and Its Impact on the Indian and Métis People of Alberta.* Vol. 1, Main Report. Edmonton: Attorney General and Solicitor General of Alberta.

Cole, D., and I. Chaikin. 1990. *An Iron Hand upon the People — The Law Against the Potlatch on the Northwest Coast.* Vancouver: Douglas and McIntyre.

Corrigan, S., and L. Barkwell. 1991. *The Struggle for Recognition: Canadian Justice and the Metis Nation.* Winnipeg: Pemmican Publications.

Coyle, M. 1986. "Traditional Indian Justice in Ontario: A Role for the Present?" 24 *Osgoode Hall Law Journal.* 605-33.

Depew, R. 1992. "Policing Native Communities: Some Principles and Issues in Organizational Theory." 34 *Canadian Journal of Criminology.* 461-78.

Dickason, O.P. 1992. *Canada's First Nations — A History of Founding Peoples from Earliest Times.* Toronto: McClelland and Stewart.

Dyck, N. 1991. *What's the Indian 'Problem'? Tutelage and Resistance in Canadian Indian Administration.* St. John's, Newfoundland: Institute for Social and Economic Research, Memorial University.

Getty, I.A.L., and A.S. Lussier. 1988. *As Long as the Sun Shines and the Water Flows: A Reader in Canadian Native Studies.* Vancouver: University of British Columbia Press.

Goddard, J. 1992. *Last Stand of the Lubicon Cree.* Vancouver: Douglas and McIntyre.

Griffiths, C.T., and J.C. Yerbury. 1984. "Natives and Criminal Justice Policy:

The Case of Native Policing." 26 *Canadian Journal of Criminology*. 147-60.

Griffiths, C.T. 1989. *The Community and Northern Justice* Burnaby: The Northern Justice Society, Simon Fraser University.

Griffiths, C.T. 1990. *Preventing and Responding to Northern Crime*. Burnaby: The Northern Justice Society, Simon Fraser University.

Griffiths, C.T. 1992. *Self-Sufficiency in Northern Justice Issues*. Burnaby: The Northern Justice Society, Simon Fraser University.

Haig-Brown, C. 1991. *Resistance and Renewal: Surviving the Residential School Experience*. Vancouver: Tillacum Library.

Hamilton, Associate Chief Justice A.C. and Associate Chief Judge C.M. Sinclair. 1991a. *Report of the Aboriginal Justice Inquiry of Manitoba. The Justice System and Aboriginal People*. Vol. 1 Winnipeg: Queen's Printer.

_____. 1991b. *Report of the Aboriginal Justice Inquiry of Manitoba. The Deaths of Helen Betty Osborne and John Joseph Harper*. Vol. 2. Winnipeg: Queen's Printer.

Harris, M. 1986. *Justice Denied: The Law versus Donald Marshall*. Toronto: Macmillan.

Hathaway, J.C. 1986. "Native Canadians and the Criminal Justice System: A Critical Examination of the Native Courtworker Program." 49 *Saskatchewan Law Review*. 201-37.

Hickman, T.A. (Chair). 1989. *Royal Commission on the Donald Marshall, Jr., Prosecution*. Halifax: Province of Nova Scotia.

Hyde, M., and C. LaPrairie. 1987. *Amerindian Crime Prevention*. Ottawa: Solicitor General of Canada.

Jeffries, T.M. 1991. "Sechelt Women and Self-Government." In D. Jensen and C. Brooks, eds. *In Celebration of Our Survival — The First Nations of British Columbia*. Vancouver: University of British Columbia Press. 81-86.

Kirkness, V. 1987. "Emerging Native Women." 2 *Canadian Journal of Women and the Law*. 408-15.

Krotz, L. 1990. *Indian Country — Inside Another Canada*. Toronto: McClelland and Stewart.

LaPrairie, C.. 1990. "The Role of Sentencing in the Over-representation of Aboriginal Offenders in Correctional Institutions." 32 *Canadian Journal of Criminology*. 429-40.

LaPrairie, C. 1991. *Justice for the Cree: Community, Crime, and Order*. James Bay, Quebec: Grand Council of the Crees.

LaPrairie, C. and E. Diamond. 1992. "Who Owns the Problem? Crime and Disorder in James Bay Cree Communities." 34 *Canadian Journal of Criminology*. 417-34.

Linn, Judge P. (Chair). 1992a. *Report of the Saskatchewan Indian Justice Review Committee*. Regina: Government of Saskatchewan.

Linn, Judge P. (Chair). 1992b. *Report of the Saskatchewan Metis Justice Review Committee.* Regina: Government of Saskatchewan.

Mannette, J. 1992. *Elusive Justice: Beyond the Marshall Inquiry.* Halifax: Fernwood Publishing.

McCaskill, D. 1985. *Patterns of Criminality and Correction among Native Offenders in Manitoba: A Longitudinal Analysis.* Saskatoon: Prairie Region, Correctional Service of Canada.

McCutcheon, S. 1991. *Electric Rivers — The Story of the James Bay Project.* Montreal: Black Rose Books.

McDonnell, R.F. 1992. "Contextualizing the Investigation of Customary Law in Contemporary Native Communities." 34 *Canadian Journal of Criminology.* 299-316.

Miller, J.R. 1989. *Skyscrapers Hide the Heavens: A History of Indian-White Relations in Canada.* Toronto: University of Toronto Press.

Morrison, R.B., and C.R. Wilson. 1986. *Native Peoples — The Canadian Experience.* Toronto: McClelland and Stewart.

Moyer, S., F. Kopelman, C. Laprairie, and B. Billingsley. 1985. *Native and Non-native Admissions to Provincial and Territorial Correctional Institutions.* Ottawa: Solicitor General of Canada.

Moyles, R.G. 1989. *British Law and Arctic Men.* Vancouver: The Northern Justice Society, Simon Fraser University.

Nielsen, M.O. 1992. "Criminal Justice and Native Self-Government." In R.A. Silverman and M.O. Nielsen, eds. *Aboriginal Peoples and Canadian Criminal Justice.* Toronto: Butterworths. 243-57.

Ontario Native Women's Association. 1989. *Breaking Free — A Proposal for Change to Aboriginal Family Violence.* Thunder Bay, Ontario: Ontario Native Women's Association.

Priest, L. 1990. *Conspiracy of Silence.* Toronto: McClelland and Stewart.

Rolf, Assistant Chief Judge C.H. (Commissioner). 1991. *Policing in Relation to the Blood Tribe. Report of a Public Inquiry.* Vol. 1. Findings and Recommendations. Edmonton: Lieutenant Governor in Council, Province of Alberta.

Ross, R. 1992. *Dancing With a Ghost - Exploring Indian Reality.* Toronto: Octopus Publishing Group.

Schuh, C. 1979. "Justice on the Northern Frontier: Early Murder Trials of Native Accused." 22 *Criminal Law Quarterly.* 74-111.

Schwartz, B. 1990. "A Separate Aboriginal Justice System?" 19 *Manitoba Law Journal.* 77-91.

Shkilnyk, A. 1985. *A Poison Stronger than Love.* New Haven: Yale University Press.

Shorten, L. 1991. *Without Reserve — Stories from Urban Natives.* Edmonton:

NeWest Press.

Siggner, A.J. 1986. "The Socio-Demographic Conditions of Registered Indians." *Canadian Social Trends* (Winter). 2-9.

Silman, J. 1988. *Enough is Enough! Aboriginal Women Speak Out.* Toronto: The Women's Press.

Silverman, R.A., and M.O. Nielsen. 1992. *Aboriginal Peoples and Canadian Criminal Justice.* Toronto: Butterworths.

Sissons, Judge J.B. 1968. *Judge of the Far North — The Memoirs of Jack Sissons.* Toronto: McClelland and Stewart.

Solicitor General of Canada. 1989. *Task Forcee on Aboriginal Peoples in Federal Corrections. Final Report.* Ottawa: Minster of Supply and Services Canada.

Sugar, F. and L. Fox. 1989-90. "Nistum Peyako Seht'wawin Iskwewak: Breaking Chains." 3 *Canadian Journal of Women and the Law.* 465-82.

Sunahara, D.F. 1992. "Public Inquiries into Policing." 16 *Canadian Police College Journal.* 135-56.

Titley, E.B. 1988. *A Narrow Vision — Duncan Scott Campbell and the Administration of Indian Affairs in Canada.* Vancouver: University of British Columbia Press.

Wolff, L. 1991. *Crime in Aboriginal Communities. Saskatchewan 1989.* Ottawa: Canadian Centre for Justice Statistics.

Wood, D.S. 1992. "Demographic Change, Relocation, and Patterns of Crime in the Baffin Region, Northwest Territories, Canada." Unpublished paper. Available from the Northern Justice Society Resource Centre, Simon Fraser University.

York, G. 1990. *The Dispossessed — Life and Death in Native Canada.* London: Vintage U.K.

York, G., and L. Pindera. 1991. *People of the Pines: The Warriors and the Legacy of Oka.* Toronto: Little, Brown, and Company.

INDEX

Readers wishing further information on data provided through the cooperation of Statistics Canada may obtain copies of related publications by mail from: Publications Sales, Statistics Canada, Ottawa, Ontario, Canada K1A OT6, by calling 1-613-951-7277 or toll-free 1-800-267-6677. Readers may also facsimile their order by dialling 1-613-951-1584.

READER REPLY CARD

We are interested in your reaction to *Canadian Criminal Justice, Second Edition,* by Curt T. Griffiths and Simon N. Verdun-Jones. You can help us to improve this book in future editions by completing the following questionnaire.

1. What was your reason for using this book?

☐ university course ☐ college course ☐ continuing
☐ professional development ☐ personal interest education course
☐ other . . . .

2. If you are a student, please identify your school and the course in which you used this book.

3. Which chapters or parts of this book did you use? Which did you omit?

4. What did you like best about this book? What did you like least?

5. Please identify any topics you think should be added to future editions.

6. Please add any comments or suggestions.

7. May we contact you for further information?

Name: . . . .

Address: . . . .

Phone: . . . .

(fold here and tape shut)

0116870399-M8Z4X6-BR01

Heather McWhinney
Publisher, College Division
HARCOURT BRACE & COMPANY, CANADA
55 HORNER AVENUE
TORONTO, ONTARIO
M8Z 9Z9